Lecture Notes in Computer Science   14345

Founding Editors

Gerhard Goos
Juris Hartmanis

The series Lecture Notes in Computer Science (LNCS), including its subseries Lecture Notes in Artificial Intelligence (LNAI) and Lecture Notes in Bioinformatics (LNBI), has established itself as a medium for the publication of new developments in computer science and information technology research, teaching, and education.

LNCS enjoys close cooperation with the computer science R & D community, the series counts many renowned academics among its volume editors and paper authors, and collaborates with prestigious societies. Its mission is to serve this international community by providing an invaluable service, mainly focused on the publication of conference and workshop proceedings and postproceedings. LNCS commenced publication in 1973.

Gene Tsudik · Mauro Conti · Kaitai Liang ·
Georgios Smaragdakis
Editors

Computer Security – ESORICS 2023

28th European Symposium
on Research in Computer Security
The Hague, The Netherlands, September 25–29, 2023
Proceedings, Part II

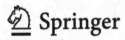

Springer

Editors
Gene Tsudik
University of California
Irvine, CA, USA

Mauro Conti ⓘ
University of Padua
Padua, Italy

Kaitai Liang ⓘ
Delft University of Technology
Delft, The Netherlands

Georgios Smaragdakis
Delft University of Technology
Delft, The Netherlands

ISSN 0302-9743   ISSN 1611-3349 (electronic)
Lecture Notes in Computer Science
ISBN 978-3-031-51475-3   ISBN 978-3-031-51476-0 (eBook)
https://doi.org/10.1007/978-3-031-51476-0

This Springer imprint is published by the registered company Springer Nature Switzerland AG
The registered company address is: Gewerbestrasse 11, 6330 Cham, Switzerland

Paper in this product is recyclable.

Preface

We are honoured and pleased to have served as PC Co-Chairs of ESORICS 2023. As one of the longest-running reputable conferences focused on security research, ESORICS 2023 attracted numerous high-quality submissions from all over the world, with authors affiliated with diverse academic, non-profit, governmental, and industrial entities.

After two rounds of submissions, each followed by an extensive reviewing period, we wound up with an excellent program, covering a broad range of timely and interesting topics. A total of 478 submissions were received: 150 in the first round and 328 in the second. 3–4 reviewers per submission in a single blind review driven by selfless and dedicated PC members (and external reviewers) who collectively did an amazing job providing thorough and insightful reviews. Some PC members even "went the extra mile" by reviewing more than their share. The end-result was 93 accepted submissions: 28 and 65, in the first and second rounds, respectively.

The 18-session ESORICS 2023 technical program included: (1) 93 talks corresponding to accepted papers, (2) a poster session, and (3) 3 impressive keynote talks by internationally prominent and active researchers: Virgil Gligor, Carmela Troncoso, and Mathias Payer. The program testifies to the level of excellence and stature of ESORICS.

We offer our deepest gratitude to:

- **Authors** of all submissions, whether accepted or not. We thank them for supporting ESORICS and for their trust in us and the PC to fairly evaluate their research results.
- **General Chairs:** Kaitai Liang and Georgios Smaragdakis, who dealt with (and addressed) numerous logistical and organisational issues. We very much appreciate it!
- **Submission Chairs:** Gabriele Costa and Letterio Galletta, for their super-human efforts and invaluable support during the submission and reviewing processes. We could not have done it without them!
- **Publication Chairs:** Florian Hahn and Giovanni Apruzzese, for handling the proceedings. We are especially grateful to them for handling numerous requests from the authors.
- **Web Chair:** Yury Zhauniarovich for creating and maintaining the conference website.
- **Poster Chair:** Bala Chandrasekaran, for taking care of the poster track.
- **All PC members** and their delegated reviewers, who were the main engine of success of ESORICS 2023 and whose hard work yielded an excellent program.

  – Special thanks to the recipients of the *Outstanding Reviewer Award*: Ferdinand Brasser and Brendan Saltaformaggio, for their exceptional reviewing quality.

In closing, though clearly biased, we believe that ESOIRCS 2023 was an overall success and we hope that all attendees enjoyed the conference.

September 2023   Mauro Conti
                                                                           Gene Tsudik

Organization

General Chairs

Kaitai Liang   Delft University of Technology, The Netherlands
Georgios Smaragdakis   Delft University of Technology, The Netherlands

Program Committee Chairs

Mauro Conti   University of Padua, Italy & Delft University of
    Technology, The Netherlands
Gene Tsudik   University of California, Irvine, USA

Submission Chairs

Gabriele Costa   IMT School for Advanced Studies Lucca, Italy
Letterio Galletta   IMT School for Advanced Studies Lucca, Italy

Workshops Chairs

Jérémie Decouchant   Delft University of Technology, The Netherlands
Stjepan Picek   Radboud University & Delft University of
    Technology, The Netherlands

Posters Chair

Bala Chandrasekaran   Vrije Universiteit Amsterdam, The Netherlands

Publication Chairs

Florian Hahn   University of Twente, The Netherlands
Giovanni Apruzzese   University of Liechtenstein, Liechtenstein

Publicity Chair

Savvas Zannettou   Delft University of Technology, The Netherlands

Sponsorship Chair

Giovane Moura   SIDN/Delft University of Technology,
                                    The Netherlands

Web Chair

Yury Zhauniarovich   Delft University of Technology, The Netherlands

Programme Committee

Gergely Acs	Budapest University of Technology and Economics, Hungary
Massimiliano Albanese	George Mason University, USA
Cristina Alcaraz (only Round 2)	University of Malaga, Spain
Alejandro Cabrera Aldaya	Tampere University of Technology, Finland
Mark Allman	International Computer Science Institute, USA
Elli Androulaki	IBM Zurich, Switzerland
Giovanni Apruzzese	University of Liechtenstein, Liechtenstein
Mikael Asplund	Linköping University, Sweden
Ahmad Atamli	Nvidia, UK
Vijay Atluri	Rutgers University, USA
Kiran Balagani	New York Institute of Technology, USA
Giampaolo Bella (only Round 2)	University of Catania, Italy
Antonio Bianchi	Purdue University, USA
Giuseppe Bianchi	Università di Roma Tor Vergata, Italy
Jorge Blasco	Royal Holloway, University of London, UK
Ferdinand Brasser	SANCTUARY Systems GmbH, Germany
Alessandro Brighente	University of Padua, Italy
Ileana Buhan	Radboud University, The Netherlands
Alvaro Cardenas	University of California Santa Cruz, USA
Xavier Carpent	University of Nottingham, UK
Anrin Chakraborti	Stony Brook University, USA
Sze Yiu Chau	Chinese University of Hong Kong, China
Liqun Chen	University of Surrey, UK

Paul Syverson (only Round 1)	Naval Research Laboratory, USA
Juan Tapiador	Universidad Carlos III de Madrid, Spain
Pietro Tedeschi (only Round 2)	Technology Innovation Institute, United Arab Emirates
Nils Ole Tippenhauer	CISPA, Germany
Mahesh Tripunitara	University of Waterloo, Canada
Fatih Turkmen (only Round 2)	University of Groningen, The Netherlands
Selcuk Uluagac	Florida International University, USA
Tobias Urban	Institute for Internet Security, Germany
Marloes Venema (only Round 2)	University of Wuppertal, Germany
Daniele Venturi	Sapienza University of Rome, Italy
Tran Viet Xuan Phuong	Old Dominion University, USA
Alexios Voulimeneas	KU Leuven, Belgium
Haining Wang	Virginia Tech, USA
Edgar Weippl	University of Vienna & SBA Research, Austria
Avishai Wool	Tel Aviv University, Israel
Stefano Zanero	Politecnico di Milano, Italy
Youqian Zhang (only Round 2)	Hong Kong Polytechnic University, China
Fengwei Zhang	Southern University of Science and Technology, China
Liang Zhao (only Round 2)	Sichuan University, China
Alf Zugenmaier	Munich University of Applied Sciences, Germany

Contents – Part II

Privacy

Remote

Network, Web and Internet

Time Will Tell: Exploiting Timing Leaks Using HTTP Response Headers

Vik Vanderlinden[✉], Tom Van Goethem, and Mathy Vanhoef

imec-DistriNet, KU Leuven, Leuven, Belgium
{vik.vanderlinden,tom.goethem,mathy.vanhoef}@kuleuven.be

Abstract. To execute timing attacks, an attacker has to collect a large number of samples to overcome network jitter. Methods to reduce such jitter, which is a source of noise, increase the signal-to-noise ratio and thereby improve the attack performance. In this paper, we propose an attack technique that uses timing information exposed in HTTP responses by backend servers or services to reduce the jitter included in an attacker's samples. By first synchronizing the attacker clock to the target, sources of low-accuracy timing data can still be used to exploit timing leaks. We collect real-world data on network latencies and use this data in millions of simulations of the synchronizations and attacks. Our simulations indicate that the synchronization can happen with less than 300 samples for accuracies of 1 ms and works down to an accuracy of under 13 μs. When comparing the performance of our novel synchronization-based timing attack to a classical timing attack which is simulated using the same dataset, our attack is able to reduce the exploitable difference in runtime by an order of magnitude to 1 μs. For equal difference in runtime our attack reduces the required samples up to a factor of 20.

Keywords: Timing Leaks · Side-channels · Network Security

1 Introduction

Timing leaks arise when the execution time of a program depends on private information. By measuring the execution time for a specific private input or state of the program, this input or state can be inferred solely based on the measured duration. Remote timing attacks do exactly the same, with the one difference that they exploit timing leaks over a network such as the Internet. It has been shown over the past twenty years that (remote) timing attacks are possible using a multitude of techniques, initially extracting cryptographic information (keys or coefficients) and later also personally identifiable information (PII) from web applications [4–6,10,15,31]. Due to browser mechanisms such as the Same-Origin Policy (SOP), multiple works have explored alternative mechanisms to time the round-trip as accurately as possible using JavaScript callbacks when triggering an error, or by constructing a highly accurate counter in the browser [13,18,29, 34]. The first timing attacks simply used the round-trip timings of requests, but

G. Tsudik et al. (Eds.): ESORICS 2023, LNCS 14345, pp. 3–22, 2024.
https://doi.org/10.1007/978-3-031-51476-0_1

more recently other sources of information and more complex attack scenarios are being used [12,35]. Defenses have been subsequently designed as a response to, or (in an attempt) to prevent these types of attacks [1–3,19].

In this paper, we introduce a novel technique that abuses timestamps in network responses to improve the performance of timing attacks. The abused timestamp can be coarse-grained and, for instance, might only increment ("tick") every second. We first synchronize the attacker and victim machines' clocks based on this timestamp by assuring that network requests arrive right before the timestamp is about to increment. After this synchronization process, the attack is executed by measuring how many responses are generated before or after the increment of the (coarse-grained) timestamp. We show that, for various timing differences, our attack technique improves the performance of timing attacks, requiring less samples than a classical timing attack that uses round-trip timings.

All combined, we make the following contributions:

- We introduce a novel timing attack that improves attack performance by utilizing timing information in a target's HTTP responses. We show that such timing information can leak the runtime of a server-side program, even if the accuracy of the exposed timestamp is low.
- We evaluate our clock synchronization method and analyze the performance of this synchronization process between two machines over a network, both in terms of the required number of network requests and the accuracy of the acquired synchronization. We also list the main difficulties of this process.
- We collect real-world network data to perform millions of attack simulations and compare our novel attack against a classical timing attack.

Responsible Disclosure: We have disclosed our findings to the developers of a number of web servers that are mentioned in this paper to warn them about the generation of the date-header after handling a request.

2   Background and Related Work

2.1   Timing Attacks

When timing attacks were introduced two and a half decades ago by Kocher in 1996, most of these attacks were aimed at exploiting cryptographic implementations to extract exponents or keys of specific operations [15]. By measuring the execution time of the cryptographic operations it was shown that these attacks were feasible. Not much later, in 2000, the first timing attack in a web browser was shown by Felten et al., who found a method to determine which pages were visited by a user, thus leaking their browsing history, steering more towards a privacy-related attack [10]. The attacks that are executed in these works always measure local runtimes in a browser or of smartcard-like devices and it was believed that timing attacks against general purpose web servers were infeasible due to the large amount of network noise that packets encounter when traveling over the network to the server [6].

To show that attacks over a network are in fact practical, Brumley and Boneh exploited cryptographic operations in OpenSSL running on a web server in a local network [6]. Two years later Bortz et al. defined the differences between direct timing attacks and cross-site timing attacks, and at the same time also showed that they could expose private information from a web application over a network [4]. These publications led to a multitude of attack vectors, such as the cross-site search attacks by Gelernter et al., which allow an attacker to test for the existence of search results on another site [11]. Other works explored different ways to more accurately time round-trip times or how to time cross-site requests while the necessary information is blocked by the browser [29,34]. Additionally, it was shown that arbitrary memory could be read over the network using a timing attack in a remote Spectre attack [30]. Over the last few years, other attack scenarios have been used to exploit timing leaks, by misusing the features of networking protocols to the advantage of the attacker [12]. Besides practical attacks, Crosby et al. tested multiple statistical methods to compare distributions of measurements and defined the box test to distinguish between roundtrip time distributions, which is now commonly used in timing attacks [8].

2.2 Clock Synchronizations

Every machine with an internal time source suffers from a concept known as clock drift [37]. Clock drift refers to the observation that a clock does not advance at the same rate as a reference clock, i.e., the speed at which a clock ticks differs from the reference clock. Some of the factors that make the clock tick at a different rate are: temperature, current CPU load, etc. Over time, the clock drift may shift the internal representation of time significantly, leading to confusion for the user or problems with the software running on the machine.

A solution is to regularly resynchronize the internal clock with a reference clock. The network time protocol (NTP) implements such a synchronization and is designed to sync the time of two machines over a network. It works with a hierarchy of devices where devices with a higher accuracy timestamp are located higher up in the hierarchy, as indicated by the lower so-called stratum number that is associated to them. A stratum number of zero is reserved for the reference clocks that hold the highest accuracy of time (atomic clocks and the like) [20]. This type of synchronization can be accurate down to the sub-millisecond level, but is very dependent on the network connection and conditions [22]. The threshold for a "synchronized" server is indicated by `MAXDIST` (distance threshold) with a value of 1 s [20]. Another protocol designed for the synchronization of clocks is the Precision Time Protocol (PTP). PTP is much more accurate than NTP but is usually only used on local area networks, and its accuracy is dependent on the latency and jitter of the network connections [23].

Additionally, the signals of a Global Navigation Satellite System (GNSS) such as GPS or Galileo could be used to synchronize multiple clocks over a large area. The signals received from a GNSS satellite can be used to triangulate a position, but also to derive the current time with high accuracy. A disadvantage is that all machines attempting to synchronize their clocks should have access to a physical receiver, which is usually not the case for on-premise servers or virtual instances in a (public) cloud [9,33].

These processes synchronize clocks from devices on a certain sized network to a specific accuracy depending on the network conditions, but the implementation or accuracy of the synchronization is not good enough for the purpose of using our technique to exploit timing leaks. NTP's accuracy is too low and PTP only works for small networks, both conditions that make our attack impossible. In addition, for NTP and PTP, client and server work together to synchronize their clocks, which would not be a feasible requirement for our attack. GNSSs on the other hand require no collaboration between multiple devices and are able to provide receivers with highly accurate timing information. Despite the advantages, synchronizations using these systems are not generally feasible due to the lack of hardware-support on most victim machines. As in every synchronization algorithm, clock drift may invalidate the correct synchronization requiring the process to be repeated regularly.

3   Threat Model and Attack Mechanism

In this section, we first discuss the threat model and outline the attack mechanism in detail, after which we introduce a formal model for timing attacks and use this model to illustrate the expected benefit of our synchronization-based timing attacks.

3.1   Threat Model

We assume the attacker is remote and will position themselves to have the most reliable upstream path possible. This is in contrast with typical timing attacks where the adversary locates themselves near the target to have both reliable upstream *and* downstream network characteristics. Since our attack eliminates downstream jitter, the goal is not necessarily to be as close to the target as possible, but to have the best possible network characteristics on the upstream path. Although being located near a target may help in achieving this goal, this may not necessarily be the closest position to the target because network characteristics can be different for up- and downstream paths [7,26]. Since only the upstream network characteristics matter, our threat model is more relaxed compared to typical classical attacks. An attacker can easily monitor multiple network connections and select the most advantageous one to use in the attack.

We assume the attacker can read responses that contain timing values and thus do not consider cross-origin attacks (which would require the SOP to be relaxed by the CORS header) [18,36].

In comparison with other attacks such as the Timeless Timing Attacks, this attack does not require the use of HTTP/2 [12]. In contrast, our attack is not limited to a specific HTTP version. We assume an attacker that can exploit timing leaks on endpoints that will leak data about the website state or about website users. In order to leak information, the timing values that are being

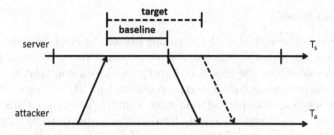

Fig. 1. Overview of the attack mechanism where T_s and T_a represent the server and attacker local time, respectively. The vertical bars in the server's timeline indicate a rollover of the observed timing value on the server.

returned have to be generated after a security-sensitive operation, otherwise private information can never be exposed by means of those timings. The attacker does this from a machine under their control in a direct attack.

3.2 Attack Mechanism

Our attack uses timing values in HTTP responses to gain knowledge about the relative runtimes of two endpoints on a server. By looking at the HTTP response and counting the number of times that the response has been sent by the server before or after a timing value rolls over to the next value, we can derive whether the execution time on the server took longer compared to another (default) page which will be referred to as the baseline page or request (see Fig. 1). The attack starts with a synchronization step in which we attempt to find an offset for the attacker to send baseline requests such that out of all respective responses 50% are sent before, and 50% after the server's clock rollover. By finding such an offset we are able to compare the baseline and a target endpoints. If the number of responses that were generated after the clock rollover for a specific target endpoint is significantly higher (say 90%) than in the baseline case (ideally 50%), it is clear that the request took longer to process.

We emphasize again that in order for this (and any) attack to work, the timing information used has to be generated after a security-sensitive operation has been executed. Otherwise there is no possibility that it leaks private data about that operation. This is inherently also depicted in Fig. 1. If in this figure a request's arrival time is reflected in the respective response, the value in both responses will be identical.

Also important is that this method of exploiting timing leaks does not facilitate the direct observation of the absolute difference in runtime between baseline and target endpoints, which will eliminate some attack variants that depend on the absolute runtime to estimate for instance sizes of server-side items [4]. Whether the difference in number of requests before and after the target clock rollover can be used to estimate an approximate difference in runtime is left for future work.

3.3   Formal Model

We first create a theoretical model of timing attacks to illustrate how our novel technique can improve the effectiveness of attacks. To ease comparison with related work, we follow the model of Crosby et al. [8], and split the response time R into the processing time T and propagation time B, leading to $R = T + B$. Both the processing and propagation time can be further split up into sub-operations, e.g., to account separately for decoding network packets, generating a response, the routing operations for every hop in the network path, etc. We can model this as the sum of all sub-operation $k \in \{1..K\}$ before the timestamp is generated, and the sum of all sub-operations $\ell \in \{1..L\}$ after the timestamp is generated. Without loss of generality, we assume the processing and propagation time can be split into the same number of sub-operations. Letting T_t denote the operation that generates the timestamp, we get:

$$R = \sum_{k=1}^{K} (T_k + B_k) + T_t + \sum_{\ell=1}^{L} (T_\ell + B_\ell) \tag{1}$$

In a typical timing attack, the jitter of all sub-operations before and after some security-sensitive operation T_s, where $1 \leq s \leq K$, reduce the performance of a timing attack.

In our attack, instead of using the round-trip response time, we use the timestamp in the response. Let T denote the received timestamp in a response, normalized to 0 or 1 to represent either before or after the clock tick. We use $\lceil \cdot \rceil$ to represent this normalization. This implies T is a random value depending on the propagation and processing time preceding the generation of the timestamp:

$$T(d) = \left\lceil d + \sum_{k=1}^{K} (T_k + B_k) + T_t \right\rceil \tag{2}$$

Parameter d represents when the attacker sends the request, i.e., the offset relative to the attacker's clock tick. The above formula highlights that the timestamp must be generated after the security-sensitive operation T_s, otherwise the value of T would not depend on T_s, meaning T would not leak sensitive info. Additionally, we can see that the result is independent of any latency that occurs after the generation of the timestamp. In the synchronization phase of our attack, we search for an offset d such that $E[T(d)] = 0.5$. In other words, we search for an offset d such that half of the requests arrive before the clock tick and the other half afterward. The value of d will be between zero and the precision (granularity) of the timestamp, e.g., if the timestamp is rounded down to seconds, then d lies between zero and one second. In practice, achieving exactly 0.5 is infeasible. Instead, in an attack, we determine whether a target request is processed faster or slower than a reference requests. That is, we are trying to answer whether:

$$E[T_{\text{baseline}}(d)] \overset{?}{=} E[T_{\text{attack}}(d)] \tag{3}$$

Here T_{baseline} is the (benign) request that we synchronize with, and the attacker's goal is to determine whether request T_{attack} takes a different amount of time to process. In practice, the adversary performs two requests *baseline1* and *baseline2* that have the same generation time T_s, and a *target* request with a different generation time T_s'. The attack succeeds when a classification method can be found that distinguishes *baseline1* from *target* while not distinguishing *baseline1* from *baseline2*. The remainder of the paper explores how to determine d in practice and how to distinguish requests with different processing times.

4 Clock Sync

In order to execute our attack, a vital step is to synchronize the attacker and victim clocks as accurately as possible. In this section, we introduce a novel method to perform such a synchronization by only relying on coarse-grained timestamps provided by the server.

4.1 Synchronization Mechanism

To synchronize the clock of the attacker to the victim clock, the same source of timing information as in the attack can be used. We will use the timestamp returned by a server, which is based on the server's internal clock and is usually truncated to a predefined accuracy (called the timestamp's granularity).

The goal of the clock synchronization is to find a local offset d for the attacker such that the server's responses are sent 50% of the time before and 50% of the time after the server's clock rollover. The method we use to find d is illustrated in Fig. 2. Initially, we know that $d \in [S_1, E_1]$, for instance, if the timestamp has a granularity of one second, then we start with $d \in [S_1 = 0, E_1 = 1]$. In each *sync iteration* we recursively decrease the size of this interval while assuring the resulting server's clock rollover remains inside the interval. To reduce the size of an interval, the attacker sends multiple requests at different offsets in this interval (see below for details). For instance, given the interval $[0, 1]$, multiple requests will be sent at offsets 0.0, 0.1, and so on up until 0.9. The requests that are sent at these different offsets are called *probes* and the number of probes sent at every offset is a parameter of our synchronization method. The adversary might then observe that the server's clock rolls over between, e.g., offset 0.3 and 0.4, and updates the interval to $[0.3, 0.4]$. In Fig. 2 this is illustrated by updating the interval $[S_i, E_i]$ to $[S_{i+1}, E_{i+1}]$. This process continues until a given number of sync iterations have been performed. In practice, each sync iteration reduces the interval by at most an order of magnitude and the attacker must at all times be able to send requests accurately at the offset d.

By repeatedly performing this process we can synchronize clocks as accurately as desired. Within an interval, the estimated location of the clock rollover can be found as follows: At each selected offset within the interval, a number of probes, i.e., network requests, are sent to the server. The number of probes to send is a parameter of the algorithm. Care must be taken when sending these probes: sending too many at once may congest the attacker's network, meaning a small waiting time must be enforced between sending consecutive probes.

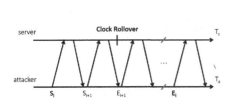

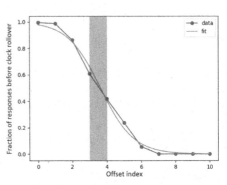

Fig. 2. Clock synchronization where the goal is to find an offset such that the server's response is sent right when its timestamp rolls over to the next value. This implies that 50% of responses will be sent before the server's rollover and 50% after.

Fig. 3. An example of the analyses of an interval using an inverse *tanh* fit on intervals with a width of 100 μs. The transition can now be defined as the point at which the *tanh* has a value of 0.5.

When all responses are received we can calculate, for each sampled offset, the percentage of responses with a timestamp before its rollover. When the size of the interval is large, meaning the sampled offsets are relatively far away from each other, there will be a clear instant transition from 100% to 0% and we can reduce the interval's size based on this. For higher accuracy synchronizations, e.g., when the interval is in the microsecond range, there will no longer be a clear transition. In that case, to determine the new smaller interval, we plot the percentage of responses containing a timestamp before the clock tick as a function of the sampled offset. An example of this is shown in Fig. 3. To now determine the new smaller interval, an inverse *tanh* function is fitted onto to the data due to the observed shape of the curve that approximates an inverse *tanh* and the computational ease of fitting this function. The estimated value of the clock tick is then the point where the fitted *tanh* function reaches 50%, and the new interval is where the *tanh* function is, for example, in the 40% to 60% range. Overall, the synchronization quickly reaches an accuracy of a millisecond and can go on into the microsecond range.

4.2   Influence of Clock Drift

The major difficulty when synchronizing two clocks is the clock drift. Any machine inherently has a specific amount of clock drift. This drift is often determined by external factors such as the temperature, processing load on the server (particularly important for a shared VM in the cloud) and other factors [21]. When two machines are used in the attack (one attacker, one victim), they experience a relative clock drift between the two machines. This has the implication that when their clocks are synchronized, the synchronization is not valid for an indefinite time, meaning clocks have to be resynchronized periodically.

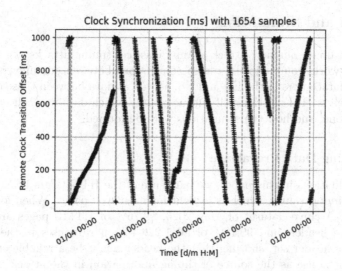

Fig. 4. Clock drift between a machine in our university network and an instance in a public cloud depicted over time.

Moreover, clock drift may impact the synchronization process itself, especially when performing many sync iterations. That is, when doing many sync iterations, more probes must be sent, and this significantly increases the duration of the synchronization process. Recall that we cannot send many requests simultaneously, as this would have complicated side-effects such as being blocked by firewalls or with very high amounts of traffic, self-induced network congestion, which decreases the synchronization and attack performances and should of course be avoided. Due to the long duration, the relative clock drift may in principle be so high that the synchronization is invalidated before it is found.

Fortunately, previous work, such as that of Zander and Murdoch [37], has shown that clock skew can be found and thus it can also be compensated for. To independently confirm this, we measured the drift of one machine on our university network and an instance in the public cloud, for over two months. Their clocks were synchronized every hour using our synchronization algorithm to an accuracy of a millisecond, with the resulting drift show in Fig. 4. The sudden jumps in the drift are either due to the data wrapping around to the other side of the interval or due to the client machine rebooting. The long, relatively straight tendencies in the drift confirm that compensating the drift is feasible. An attacker can monitor this drift and determine whether it is behaving linearly between some machines and the target and select a machine with optimal conditions to be able to compensate the drift as easily as possible for the attack.

Motivated by these observations, we will assume in the remainder of the paper that an adversary can measure and correct the influence of clock skew while performing our attack, meaning we do not explicitly have to model it in our experiments.

5 Data and Simulation

To fairly evaluate our new attack against classical timing attacks, we first collected real-world roundtrip data from connections between our university network and datacenters in the EU and US, as well as data between those datacenters themselves. This section will outline exactly which data was collected, how that was done, and how the simulations were performed.

5.1 Timing Data Prevalence

For all evaluations in this paper, we make use of the HTTP *date* header as the source of timing values, which is present for most web pages. When looking at the HTTP Archive dataset of May 2023, 99.76% of HTML pages are served with a date header, and 99.18% of all 1.226 billion responses in the dataset have a date header set, showing that the header might be a reliable choice for an attacker to use as the source of timing information in the attack [14]. It is important to mention that some date headers contain a fixed value, or a value that is updated less than once every second. These values would not be useable in our attack. Because the HTTP standard describes date formats to have a granularity of one second, it is expected that most servers update their date header about once a second [28]. Fixed values can never contain information related to security-sensitive operations on a server, and if the returned values have a too low granularity the attack becomes infeasible due to the amount of time it would take to synchronize the clocks and execute the attack. We crawled a number of pages of the Tranco top 10k domains[1] and evaluated the dynamic nature of the date headers [16]. To do so, each of the 24 928 pages was visited twice with a wait of 30 s in between, after which the detected timing values were matched between the two visits. If a timing value remains unchanged over the 30 s period, it was removed as an interesting value. We found that 92.36% of the crawled response documents were served with a dynamic date header, which makes it an ideal value to use in an attack. In some cases the date header is set to a fixed value, such as the Unix epoch. The results obtained in these experiments should be interpreted as absolute upper bounds on the number of pages that could be vulnerable, because many pages will return timestamps that do not include the duration of sensitive operations.

By using the date header, we also show that the used timestamp does not need to be very accurate, since this header is usually only accurate down to a second. It can be expected that more accurate timing information leads to even better results when using our attack, especially with regards to the synchronization process that becomes more obsolete with growing accuracy of timestamps, since the offset it attempts to find can be derived from the timestamp value up to a certain point.

It remains the case that the timing information has to be generated after a security-sensitive operation in order to be useful to leak private information.

---

[1] Available at https://tranco-list.eu/list/85NV.

We tested multiple popular servers such as nginx, litespeed, Apache httpd and the popular frameworks NodeJS Express and Python Flask [17,24,25,27,32]. Most of these platforms generate their date header values when a response is constructed on the server and thus after the execution of any backend script(s), hereby potentially allowing the leakage of private information depending on the backend operation(s). In fact, Apache's httpd was the only of these platforms that generated its date header values at the moment a request is received, and therefore a different timestamp would have to be used to attack a target that is running the Apache httpd server engine [32]. Such timestamp could for instance be set by the programming language or by a developer because the programming language may still have access to high accuracy clocks. It will, however, mean that the likelihood of finding such timing values decreases.

5.2   Collecting Roundtrip Times

We first collected real-world roundtrip data so we can accurately simulate both our new and classical timing attacks. For this, we set up servers in the west of the EU and the east of the US with Amazon AWS and in addition used servers from our university's internal network in Europe. Each of the 4 collection servers were located in one of two datacenter locations in the west of the EU and all of them collected information from two hosting servers, one of which was in another (nearby) datacenter in the west of the EU, the second one that was in the east of the US, gathering data over a transatlantic connection. There were no samples collected originating from the US with hosting servers in the EU.

Each of the collection servers collected over 15 million samples for EU-EU cases and over 5 million samples for EU-US cases. Obviously, the latency for packets traveling to the US is much higher resulting in a slower data-gathering process. In order to collect real-life data, we instruct the server to sleep for a number of milliseconds using PHP's builtin sleep function in order to simulate an actual time-consuming task on the server. For each request the roundtrip time was collected with nanosecond accuracy, as would be done in a classical timing attack.

The collected data shows that the roundtrip times at some times do not follow a perfect normal, or log-normal distribution, as can be expected when taking measurements on the Internet. In some cases, the actual distribution of the collected samples seems to be a collection of multiple (log-)normal distributions superimposed. The imperfections in the data are still used in the attack simulations in order to get the most accurate results possible rather than using some form of idealized, generated data. The main characteristic that is important and would be difficult to accurately generate or simulate is the network jitter. By using these real-world samples, the jitter is exactly the same as when an attacker would be performing the attack over these connections. Because the samples will be used in a sequential manner, possible short-term deviations or variations in the latency and jitter will also be mimicked in our simulations.

In our evaluation, we want to control the difference in the upstream and downstream network conditions, so we can evaluate the impact of asymmetric network paths on the performance of our attack. This difference is hard and arguably even impossible to fully control in real-world networks. Although an attacker would ideally like to be able to, they too cannot control the way the up- and downstream path behave, and will have to resort to monitoring multiple paths and selecting the best one. To nevertheless separately control the downstream and upstream parameters, while at the same time simulating real-world network jitter, we will simulate the server's date header based on the measured round-trip time. This allows us to easily simulate different conditions of the upstream network path, by using a varying fraction of the roundtrip time values.

A second reason to simulate the server's data header based on the round-trip time, is that it allows us to simulate or eliminate clock drift. In other words, real timestamps returned by the server are influenced by the server's clock drift, and this clock drift is practically impossible to afterwards eliminate or change.

During our simulations, we will also configure a random difference between the clock of the server and client. This timing difference, combined with the average upstream network latency, will be learned by our synchronization method. We will continue with a more detailed explanation of the simulations next.

5.3   Synchronization and Attack Simulations

The goal of the attack simulations is to be as similar to real-life attacks as possible. The simulation software was built in such a way that only the interaction with the server is mimicked and as such, only this interaction should be re-implemented to attack actual target servers.

For every simulation, a random offset between the client and server clocks is selected. It is the job of the synchronization process to find this offset, just as it would be required against an actual target server. Each simulation runs at a very high speed, which is the advantage compared to the real-life attacks. Without using simulations, new network requests would have to be made for every run of an experiment, making it much slower than a simulation. Another advantage of simulations is that each parameter can be evaluated independently if necessary. In order to correctly evaluate our synchronization-based attack against the classical timing attacks, the classical attacks were also simulation using the same data, to eliminate discrepancies between the used datasets. This also allows us to verify that the simulation is correct because the performance of the classical timing attack corresponds with the expected values of this type of attack.

After synchronization, to achieve a successful attack, the adversary should be able to detect that two baseline requests *baseline1* and *baseline2* are similar (baselines case), while being able to distinguish *baseline1* from *target* (baseline versus target case). Here *target* has a different execution time than the baseline. To perform classification, we calculate the following variables, where *attack* can equal either *baseline2* (baselines case) or *target* (baseline versus target case):

$$X_{attack} = \Pr[T_{\text{baseline1}}(d) = 0 \wedge T_{\text{attack}}(d) = 1] \tag{4}$$

$$Y_{attack} = \Pr[T_{\text{baseline1}}(d) = 1 \wedge T_{\text{attack}}(d) = 0] \tag{5}$$

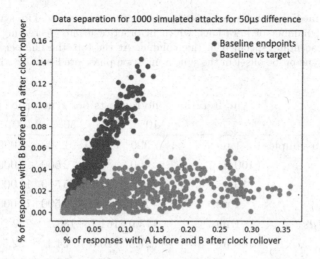

Fig. 5. Example simulation output, each dot is an attack.

Here X_* represents the percentage of times that the baseline response was sent before the clock tick and that the attack response was send after the clock tick (variable Y_* represent the opposite). The values for these variables are determined by sending a requests and calculating the percentage of times that the conditions in the above formulas hold.

Figure 5 shows the resulting data from 1 000 simulated attacks for both the baselines and baseline versus target cases, where the x-axis represents X_* and the y-axis represents Y_*. Each attack is plotted as a point and executing an attack boils down to finding a classification between the baselines and baseline versus target datasets that correctly classifies 95% or more of the attacks. In the baselines case, we see that $X_{\text{baseline2}} \approx Y_{\text{baseline2}}$ (blue dots in Fig. 5). This confirms that both baseline responses have the same probability of being generated after or before the clock tick. In the baseline versus target case, we see that $X_{\text{target}} \gtrsim Y_{\text{target}}$ (orange dots in Fig. 5). In other words, the attack response is more often generated after the clock tick compared to the baseline response, which is expected since the target response takes longer to generate.

To search for a classification, the regression lines of the two datasets were taken and 10 000 lines spanning the space in between these regressions were evaluated each time. If a line could be found that correctly distinguishes the datasets with the previously mentioned accuracy, the attack was considered successful.

6   Results

6.1   Clock Synchronization

The performance of the clock synchronization is important information for an attacker when they want to select the optimal synchronization parameters.

Table 1. The median of the accuracy and number of samples required for synchronizing for a specified number of iterations, which in practice means decreasing the tested offsets to the accuracy specified in this column. At the top, the number of requests sent for each sync probe offset in the synchronization phase are listed (recall Sect. 4.1).

Metric	Sync Iterations	nb requests per sync probe offset				
		10	20	50	100	200
Required nb samples	1 ms	300	600	1 500	3 000	6 000
	100 μs	400	800	2 500	5 000	10 000
	10 μs	800	2 000	5 500	12 000	24 000
	1 μs	4 200	11 000	32 500	70 000	144 000
Deviation (μs)	1 ms	173.9	161.7	188.1	242.2	348.2
	100 μs	27.5	26.5	24.1	22.5	21.2
	10 μs	38.9	29.6	19.3	14.9	12.9
	1 μs	40.3	29.3	19.9	16.2	14.7

Deciding if they want to synchronize for a number of iterations (which in practice means reducing the final offsets that are being tested to an accuracy of a microsecond or a millisecond) has a significant impact on the attack performance (as will be discussed later) but has the disadvantage that it requires a higher number of samples during the synchronization process, which will also take a longer time, thereby possibly counteracting the attack performance improvements. On top of that, for each number of sync iterations, the number of requests sent for each offset can be selected as a separate parameter.

To evaluate the performance of the clock synchronization, each simulation gathered metrics about its accompanying synchronization's performance. Specifically, the number of total requests that had to be made, the deviation from the correct clock rollover offset to be found, and the number of tries that were necessary to synchronize were gathered. From a total of over 2.5 million simulations, the median values for these metrics are shown in Table 1 (top). As expected, a synchronization with a lower number of iterations requires less samples. The increase in the number of samples required is not inversely linear in relation to the number of sync iterations. Due to the complexity of synchronizations with more iterations, the number of samples rises more than linear. The offsets used in the synchronization are now smaller than network jitter, which makes it increasingly difficult to continue synchronizing and adds uncertainty to the process. This means that instead of clearly finding a clock transition, the exact location is hidden by the network noise that cannot be removed. The implementation of the clock synchronization will thus not be able to locate the clock transition between two adjacent offsets and has to increase the search space for the next iteration. This also has an impact on synchronization time.

Table 2. The number of samples required to attack a server in the US, provided that clock synchronization has already been performed. In this table, the resulting samples sizes follow from the synchronization to 10 μs. A dash (−) is shown if the attack was unsuccessful or required more than 50 000 samples. Data showing the performance for other synchronization iterations can be found in Appendix A.

Attack	1 μs	2 μs	5 μs	10 μs	20 μs	50 μs	100 μs	200 μs	500 μs	1 ms
Classical	−	−	−	18 539	1 907	530	121	40	7	7
TWT (RTT/1.5)	−	45 329	6 104	1 830	468	136	96	36	34	33
TWT (RTT/2.0)	−	20 110	3 480	1 025	348	113	63	31	29	29
TWT (RTT/3.0)	48 126	9 204	1 741	519	202	104	46	43	40	40

For the deviation shown in Table 1 (bottom) the results show that the accuracy indeed increases when a higher number of synchronization iterations are performed. In the case of the 1 ms entry, the deviation increases with larger samples sizes for each tested probe offset, against intuition. This is because in the 1 ms entry, each iteration recurses on the interval for which the fraction of responses after the clock rollover is between 0% and 100%. For instance, if the current interval is $[0.02, 0.03]$, and only 10 requests per probe offset are used, the procedure may find that 100% of responses at offset 0.022 are sent before the clock rollover, and 0% at 0.023, meaning the new interval becomes $[0.022, 0.023]$. However, when using 200 requests per probe offset, 99.5% of responses at offset 0.022 may now arrive before the clock rollover, and 0.05% at offset 0.023, so the new interval, for instance, becomes $[0.021, 0.024]$ instead. This drives the number of samples required up and decreases the accuracy of the synchronization. In the sub-millisecond range, the *tanh* fit is used, which works better because even if there are a small number of samples returning on the other side of the clock rollover, this will not have a large impact on the fitted curve and thus the interval for the next recursion remains as small as when using fewer samples per probe.

6.2 Attack

Table 2 shows the attack performance after synchronization. That is, the number of requests used for synchronization are not accounted for in this table. Because a synchronization can be maintained against a specific server, an adversary can use one synchronization to perform multiple subsequent attacks, and we therefore evaluate the synchronization and attack separately. The clock synchronization iteration down to 10. μs was used to arrive at each of the sample sizes. In Appendix A, the full resulting data can be found, which shows the performance for each clock synchronization iteration.

The results show that the number of requests necessary to perform an attack are in most cases much lower than in the classic timing attack. Table 2 also shows the performance for three different upstream network conditions. For instance, the bottom row shows the attack performance when the jitter in the upstream path is 1/3rd of the round-trip time jitter that we collected empirically (and analogous for RTT/2.0 and RTT/1.5). We can observe that a better upstream connection, i.e., when the collected round-trip times are divided by a higher constant, less samples are needed to perform our novel attack. Results were similar when using the round-trip times that we collected between different servers and locations. All combined, we can successfully exploit a timing difference of 10, 5 and with a good upstream network path even down to 1µs, which is not possible using a classical timing attack.

6.3 Defenses

The main defense against this type of attack is to expose the time at which the request came into the server instead of the time at which the timing value is actually requested by the program. The compromise that is made is that the time that is communicated to the client may be out of sync for a couple of hundred milliseconds, but that can occur naturally due to high amounts of jitter as well.

Another defense is to decrease the accuracy of the timing information and instead of updating the header value for each second, round these values to five or ten seconds. This does not eliminate the vulnerability, but makes it even more difficult to exploit, due to the high waiting period between each clock tick.

7 Conclusion

While the exposure of timing information such as the current time on a server may be regarded as normal, we have shown that developers should be careful when exposing seemingly harmless information. Timing information that is exposed in HTTP responses can be used to exploit timing leaks by synchronizing the clocks of the attacker and the victim. We gathered real-world data on latencies between servers in the EU and the US, and used this data to run millions of simulations of our complete attack process. Our novel attack was shown to improve a classical timing attack by decreasing the necessary amount of requests and we could successfully exploit a smaller timing difference compared to the classical attack.

To finish we proposed two easy defenses. One defense suggests to always use the time at which a request arrives at the server in the responses. This defense always eliminates the timing leak. Another defense is to decrease the accuracy of the timing information. This is not as effective at the previously proposed defense.

Acknowledgements. This research is partially funded by the Research Fund KU Leuven, and by the Flemish Research Programme Cybersecurity.

Appendices

A   Complete Attack Data

Tables 3 and 4 show the full results that have been tested for a victim in the EU and US respectively. Each row lists the selected synchronization iteration and thereafter the required number of samples to differentiate a specific timing

difference. Based on this data, an attacker could select their preferred number
of synchronization iterations based on the requirements of their desired attack.
In both cases the results from the classical attack are shown in the first row
and perform significantly worse than the synchronization-based attack. From
these tables the importance of the synchronization is clear. When comparing
the performance of the 1 ms synchronization to the others, the most coarse synchronization clearly performs worse.

Table 3. The number of samples required to attack a server in the EU, provided that
clock synchronization has already been performed. Each row indicates what synchronization iteration was used to obtain the results in that row. A dash (–) is shown if the
attack was unsuccessful or required more than 50 000 samples.

Attack	Sync	1 μs	2 μs	5 μs	10 μs	20 μs	50 μs	100 μs	200 μs	500 μs	1 ms
Classical	/	–	–	–	–	2 249	436	151	44	8	7
TWT (RTT/1.5)	1 ms	–	–	–	–	–	37 444	9 035	2 285	391	62
TWT (RTT/1.5)	100 us	–	–	17 384	4 053	1 093	243	105	44	32	30
TWT (RTT/1.5)	10 us	–	–	14 400	3 481	996	221	94	41	28	28
TWT (RTT/1.5)	1 us	–	–	13 281	3 173	930	213	102	35	24	24
TWT (RTT/2.0)	1 ms	–	–	–	–	–	36 944	9 424	2 197	324	51
TWT (RTT/2.0)	100 us	–	–	9 054	2 399	691	198	92	36	29	27
TWT (RTT/2.0)	10 us	–	–	7 616	1 954	519	156	60	34	32	32
TWT (RTT/2.0)	1 us	–	–	7 418	1 882	556	146	63	30	29	29
TWT (RTT/3.0)	1 ms	–	–	–	–	–	27 734	5 001	1 265	394	70
TWT (RTT/3.0)	100 us	–	28 701	4 027	1 117	359	119	48	34	31	31
TWT (RTT/3.0)	10 us	–	24 798	2 990	878	255	101	40	25	25	25
TWT (RTT/3.0)	1 us	–	22 867	2 922	882	262	93	33	27	27	27

Table 4. The number of samples required to attack a server in the US, provided that
clock synchronization has already been performed. Each row indicates what synchronization iteration was used to obtain the results in that row. A dash (–) is shown if the
attack was unsuccessful or required more than 50 000 samples.

Attack	Sync	1 μs	2 μs	5 μs	10 μs	20 μs	50 μs	100 μs	200 μs	500 μs	1 ms
Classical	/	–	–	–	18 539	1 907	530	121	40	7	7
TWT (RTT/1.5)	1 ms	–	–	–	–	–	18 835	3 244	584	103	71
TWT (RTT/1.5)	100 us	–	48 944	7 844	2 101	625	178	120	49	42	41
TWT (RTT/1.5)	10 us	–	45 329	6 104	1 830	468	136	96	36	34	33
TWT (RTT/1.5)	1 us	–	37 300	6 447	1 736	476	133	91	45	37	37
TWT (RTT/2.0)	1 ms	–	–	–	–	–	22 605	3 909	940	84	84
TWT (RTT/2.0)	100 us	–	25 782	4 998	1 330	415	143	72	43	36	36
TWT (RTT/2.0)	10 us	–	20 110	3 480	1 025	348	113	63	31	29	29
TWT (RTT/2.0)	1 us	–	21 092	3 916	1 083	317	125	61	27	27	27
TWT (RTT/3.0)	1 ms	–	–	–	–	–	37 500	7 141	1 541	175	164
TWT (RTT/3.0)	100 us	–	13 668	2 524	671	262	112	53	42	43	43
TWT (RTT/3.0)	10 us	48 126	9 204	1 741	519	202	104	46	43	40	40
TWT (RTT/3.0)	1 us	43 816	9 521	1 821	466	190	91	40	35	35	35

References

1. Alex Christensen: Reduce resolution of performance.now. https://bugs.webkit.org/show_bug.cgi?id=146531 (2015)
2. Boris Zbarsky: Chromium: window.performance.now does not support submillisecond precision on windows. https://bugs.chromium.org/p/chromium/issues/detail?id=158234#c110 (2015)
3. Zbarsky, B.: Clamp the resolution of performance.now() calls to 5us because otherwise we allow various timing attacks that depend on high accuracy timers (2015). https://hg.mozilla.org/integration/mozilla-inbound/rev/48ae8b5e62ab
4. Bortz, A., Boneh, D., Nandy, P.: Exposing private information by timing web applications. In: 16th International World Wide Web Conference, WWW2007, pp. 621–628 (2007). https://doi.org/10.1145/1242572.1242656
5. Brumley, B.B., Tuveri, N.: Remote timing attacks are still practical. In: Atluri, V., Diaz, C. (eds.) ESORICS 2011. LNCS, vol. 6879, pp. 355–371. Springer, Heidelberg (2011). https://doi.org/10.1007/978-3-642-23822-2_20
6. Brumley, D., Boneh, D.: Remote timing attacks are practical. Comput. Networks 48(5), 701–716 (2005). https://doi.org/10.1016/j.comnet.2005.01.010, https://linkinghub.elsevier.com/retrieve/pii/S1389128605000125
7. Cox, B.: Splitting the ping (2022). https://blog.benjojo.co.uk/post/ping-with-loss-latency-split
8. Crosby, S.A., Wallach, D.S., Riedi, R.H.: Opportunities and limits of remote timing attacks. ACM Trans. Inf. Syst. Secur. 12(3), 1–29 (2009). https://doi.org/10.1145/1455526.1455530, https://dl.acm.org/doi/10.1145/1455526.1455530
9. EUSPA: European GNSS Service Centre. https://www.gsc-europa.eu/. Accessed 28 May 2023
10. Felten, E.W., Schneider, M.A.: Timing attacks on Web privacy. In: Proceedings of the 7th ACM Conference on Computer and Communications Security - CCS 2000, New York, New York, USA, pp. 25–32. ACM Press (2000). https://doi.org/10.1145/352600.352606, http://portal.acm.org/citation.cfm?doid=352600.352606
11. Gelernter, N., Herzberg, A.: Cross-Site Search Attacks. In: Proceedings of the 22nd ACM SIGSAC Conference on Computer and Communications Security. vol. 2015-October, New York, NY, USA, pp. 1394–1405. ACM (2015). https://doi.org/10.1145/2810103.2813688, https://dl.acm.org/doi/10.1145/2810103.2813688
12. van Goethem, T., Pöpper, C., Joosen, W., Vanhoef, M.: Timeless timing attacks: Exploiting concurrency to leak secrets over remote connections. In: Proceedings of the 29th USENIX Security Symposium, pp. 1985–2002 (2020)
13. van Goethem, T., Vanhoef, M., Piessens, F., Joosen, W.: Request and conquer: exposing cross-origin resource size. In: Proceedings of the 25th USENIX Security Symposium, pp. 447–462 (2016)
14. HTTP Archive Contributors: The HTTP Archive. https://httparchive.org/. Accessed 28 May 2023
15. Kocher, P.C.: Timing attacks on implementations of Diffie-Hellman, RSA, DSS, and other systems. In: Koblitz, N. (ed.) CRYPTO 1996. LNCS, vol. 1109, pp. 104–113. Springer, Heidelberg (1996). https://doi.org/10.1007/3-540-68697-5_9
16. Le Pochat, V., Van Goethem, T., Tajalizadehkhoob, S., Korczyński, M., Joosen, W.: Tranco: a research-oriented top sites ranking hardened against manipulation. In: Proceedings of the 26th Annual Network and Distributed System Security Symposium. NDSS 2019 (2019). https://doi.org/10.14722/ndss.2019.23386

17. LiteSpeed Technologies Inc.: LiteSpeed Web Server. https://www.litespeedtech. com/products/litespeed-web-server. Accessed 04 Jun 2023
18. MDN contributors: Same-origin policy (2023). https://developer.mozilla.org/en-US/docs/Web/Security/Same-origin_policy
19. Mehta, A., Alzayat, M., de Viti, R., Brandenburg, B.B., Druschel, P., Garg, D.: Pacer: network side-channel mitigation in the cloud (2019). http://arxiv.org/abs/ 1908.11568
20. Mills, D., Martin, B., Kasch: A Border Gateway Protocol 4 (BGP-4). RFC 5905, RFC Editor, June 2010. https://www.rfc-editor.org/rfc/rfc5905.txt
21. Murdoch, S.J.: Hot or not: revealing hidden services by their clock skew, pp. 27–36. ACM Press (2006). https://doi.org/10.1145/1180405.1180410, http://dl.acm.org/ citation.cfm?doid=1180405.1180410
22. Network Time Foundation: Clock discipline algorithm (2022). https://www.ntp. org/documentation/4.2.8-series/discipline/
23. Network Time Foundation: IEEE 1588 precision time protocol (PTP) (2022). https://www.ntp.org/reflib/ptp/. Accessed 28 May 2023
24. Nginx Contributors: Nginx. https://nginx.org/en/. Accessed 28 May 2023
25. OpenJS Foundation: Express - Node.js web application framework. https:// expressjs.com/. Accessed 04 Jun 2023
26. Pucha, H., Zhang, Y., Mao, Z.M., Hu, Y.C.: Understanding network delay changes caused by routing events. ACM SIGMETRICS Perform. Eval. Rev. **35**(1), 73–84 (2007). https://doi.org/10.1145/1269899.1254891, https://dl.acm.org/doi/10. 1145/1269899.1254891
27. Python Contributors: Welcome to Flask. https://flask.palletsprojects.com/en/2.3. x/. Accessed 04 Jun 2023
28. Fielding, R., Nottingham, M., Reschke, J.: Rfc 9110: Http semantics-date/time formats. https://www.rfc-editor.org/rfc/rfc9110#http.date
29. Schwarz, M., Maurice, C., Gruss, D., Mangard, S.: Fantastic timers and where to find them: high-resolution microarchitectural attacks in JavaScript. In: Kiayias, A. (ed.) FC 2017. LNCS, vol. 10322, pp. 247–267. Springer, Cham (2017). https:// doi.org/10.1007/978-3-319-70972-7_13
30. Schwarz, M., Schwarzl, M., Lipp, M., Masters, J., Gruss, D.: NetSpectre: read arbitrary memory over network. In: Sako, K., Schneider, S., Ryan, P.Y.A. (eds.) ESORICS 2019. LNCS, vol. 11735, pp. 279–299. Springer, Cham (2019). https:// doi.org/10.1007/978-3-030-29959-0_14
31. Smith, M., Disselkoen, C., Narayan, S., Brown, F., Stefan, D.: Browser history revisited. In: 12th USENIX Workshop on Offensive Technologies, WOOT 2018, co-located with USENIX Security 2018 (1) (2018)
32. The Apache Foundation: The Apache HTTP Server Project. https://httpd.apache. org/. Accessed 28 May 2023
33. United States Space Force: GPS: The Global Positioning System. https://www. gps.gov/. Accessed 28 May 2023
34. Van Goethem, T., Joosen, W., Nikiforakis, N.: The clock is still ticking: timing attacks in the modern web. In: Proceedings of the ACM Conference on Computer and Communications Security, vol. 2015-October, pp. 1382–1393 (2015). https:// doi.org/10.1145/2810103.2813632

35. Vanderlinden, V., Joosen, W., Vanhoef, M.: Can you tell me the time? Security implications of the server-timing header. In: Proceedings 2023 Workshop on Measurements, Attacks, and Defenses for the Web. No. March, Internet Society (2023). https://doi.org/10.14722/madweb.2023.23087, https://www.ndss-symposium.org/wp-content/uploads/2023/02/madweb2023-23087-paper.pdf
36. whatwg contributors: Fetch standard: Cors protocol (2023). https://fetch.spec.whatwg.org/#http-cors-protocol
37. Zander, S., Murdoch, S.: An improved clock-skew measurement technique for revealing hidden services (2008)

Peering into the Darkness: The Use of UTRS in Combating DDoS Attacks

Radu Anghel[1], Swaathi Vetrivel[1], Elsa Turcios Rodriguez[1],
Kaichi Sameshima[2], Daisuke Makita[2,3], Katsunari Yoshioka[2],
Carlos Gañán[1], and Yury Zhauniarovich[1(✉)]

[1] Delft University of Technology, Delft, Netherlands
{r.anghel,s.vetrivel,e.r.turciosrodriguez,c.hernandezganan,
y.zhauniarovich}@tudelft.nl
[2] Yokohama National University, Yokohama, Japan
{sameshima-kaichi-mx,yoshioka}@ynu.ac.jp
[3] National Institute of Information and Communications Technology, Tokyo, Japan
d.makita@nict.go.jp

Abstract. Remotely Triggered Black Hole (RTBH) is a common DDoS mitigation approach that has been in use for the last two decades. Usually, it is implemented close to the attack victim in networks sharing some type of physical connectivity. The Unwanted Traffic Removal Service (UTRS) project offers a free, global, and relatively low-effort-to-join and operate RTBH alternative by removing the requirement of physical connectivity. Given these unique value propositions of UTRS, this paper aims to understand to what extent UTRS is adopted and used to mitigate DDoS attacks. To reach this goal, we collected two DDoS datasets describing amplification and Internet-of-Things-botnet-driven attacks and correlated them with the information from the third dataset containing blackholing requests propagated to the members of UTRS. Our findings suggest that, currently, just a small portion of UTRS members (approximately 10%) trigger mitigation attempts: out of 1200+ UTRS members, only 124 triggered blackholing events during our study. Among those, with high probability, 25 Autonomous Systems (ASes) reacted on AmpPot attacks mitigating 0.025% of them globally or 1.03% targeting UTRS members; 2 countered IoT-botnet-driven attacks alleviating 0.001% of them globally or 0.06% targeting UTRS members. This suggests that UTRS can be a useful tool in mitigating DDoS attacks, but it is not widely used.

Keywords: UTRS · RTBH · DDoS attacks

1 Introduction

Distributed Denial-of-Service (DDoS) attacks are on the rise [10], and they are proving difficult to defend against. DDoS attacks aim to bring down a targeted server, service, or network by overwhelming the target system or its network infrastructure with traffic [22]. DDoS attacks have financial costs to victims,

G. Tsudik et al. (Eds.): ESORICS 2023, LNCS 14345, pp. 23–41, 2024.
https://doi.org/10.1007/978-3-031-51476-0_2

as they could lose thousands of dollars and possibly go out of business [10]. Attackers employ different techniques and tools to launch them. Lately, massive DDoS attacks are often fueled by embedded and IoT devices [4] and widely leverage reflectors to amplify the volume of traffic directed at victims [2].

To mitigate DDoS attacks, network operators and service providers have at their disposal various countermeasures and mitigation strategies. Among some of the most common countermeasures are clean pipe, content delivery network (CDN) attack dilution, antiDDoS proxy, and Remotely Triggered Black Hole (RTBH) service [9,14,20]. The latter has become popular and used by Internet Service Providers (ISPs) for about two decades [25]. RTBH leverages the Border Gateway Protocol (BGP) to reroute attack traffic to places that minimize harm, typically by dropping it [25].

There are two approaches to putting RTBH into practice. The first one relies on the direct connection between Autonomous Systems with customer-provider or peering relationships. The second approach employs an Internet Exchange Point (IXP), e.g., DE-CIX [8] or Equinix [11], that acts as a central point distributing blackholing requests to their participants. Regardless of the chosen approach, RTBH requires physical connectivity from all participants. Moreover, IXP-provided RTHB is typically a paid service [3].

For those network operators that do not have access to IXPs offering RTBH or the service is too expensive, there is at least one free alternative, namely joining an RTBH project. An example of such a project is the Unwanted Traffic Removal Service (UTRS) [17], a community project of Team Cymru. To the best of our knowledge, UTRS is currently the *only global free-to-participate RTBH initiative*. UTRS is essentially an RTBH operated by a trusted third party, similar to RTBHs operated by IXPs. In this case, instead of an IXP, UTRS acts as the central point that decides whether to accept and distribute the blackholing requests to its participants. Because it does not need the physical connectivity of participants, UTRS is not limited geographically.

UTRS is an initiative that any network can join with relatively low effort. As stated on the project webpage [23], UTRS is offered as a free service to owners of unique Autonomous System Numbers (ASNs). Joining the UTRS project is done by filling out an online form that is manually checked by Team Cymru to validate ownership/access of the AS. If the validation is successful, Team Cymru provides BGP configuration details and generic guides for various router types [24]. As of August 2021, 1200+ networks were participating in this initiative [7].

In contrast to an RTBH, UTRS helps to mitigate DDoS attacks *closer to their source* [23]. When implementing RTBH over direct connections such as with upstream ISPs, peering relationships or IXPs, the blackholing happens close to the attack destination, still causing congestion in networks transiting the attack. With UTRS, however, the participants could be all over the world, that, in theory, improves the chance of stopping an attack closer to its source. However, the likelihood that DDoS attacks are stopped near their source is diminished if the number of participants is low. Thus, it is important to incentivize ASes to join such initiatives to decrease transition junk traffic [26].

In this work, we focus on understanding to what extent UTRS is used globally among the ASes to mitigate attacks and which DDoS attacks trigger mitigation attempts via UTRS. To the best of our knowledge, we are *the first who study adoption and the effectiveness of this service in detail.* The closest work [13] has analyzed DDoS attacks and compared them to BGP blackholing events. The information provided in our work may be valuable for network operators who would like to asses joining UTRS as an alternative to the RTBHs offered through direct connectivity.

To reach our goal, we collect six months of blackholed prefixes from UTRS at five minutes intervals and compare them to two different data sources that provide information about DDoS targets. The first source is an IoT botnets Milker service designed to extract information about targets of IoT-driven DDoS attacks. It gathers IoT botnet malware samples, analyzes them, and then behaves as one of the bots, enabling us to gather DDoS attack commands from C&C servers. The second, AmpPot [16], tracks reflection and amplification attacks. We analyze the data collected from these sources to identify trends and patterns in using UTRS to mitigate DDoS attacks. We set up ourselves to answer the following research questions:

(RQ1): How many UTRS members use this service to mitigate attacks?

(RQ2): To what extent are DDoS attacks triggering mitigation attempts via UTRS?

(RQ3): To what extent can UTRS announcements be explained by amplification DDoS attacks?

(RQ4): To what extent can UTRS announcements be explained by IoT-botnet-driven DDoS attacks?

The contributions of this paper are the following:

- Our analysis provides valuable insights into the adoption of the UTRS service. It shows that only around 10% of all UTRS members actively use this service to mitigate attacks.
- We provide a comprehensive analysis of the usage of UTRS in mitigating DDoS attacks coming from IoT botnets and amplification attacks. Our results show that while UTRS is used to mitigate reflection attacks, it is barely triggered to handle IoT-botnet DDoS attacks.
- We identify trends and patterns in the use of UTRS to mitigate DDoS attacks.

2 Related Work

To combat DDoS attacks, various mitigation methods have been suggested, such as blackholing and rate limiting. In this section, we examine the current research on blackholing, a technique that discards traffic directed at a targeted IP address, preventing it from reaching the victim. We focus on recent studies investigating the effectiveness of blackholing, its limitations, and proposed enhancements to mitigate its drawbacks. We also discuss related work on detecting and analyzing blackholing events and their correlation with DDoS attacks.

In the closest work, Jonker et al. [13] correlate BGP blackholing events with the data from two attack datasets: "Randomly and Uniformly Spoofed Attacks" collected from CAIDA's telescope and AmpPot. The blackholing events are inferred by applying some heuristics to public BGP data collected by Route-Views and RIPE RIS. An attack is considered to be blackholed only if its target IP address is within the BGP announced network and happens no more than 24 h prior to the announcement. Their results show that only 456k of the 28.16M attacks (1.62%) from CAIDA/AmpPot datasets are blackholed, involving only 0.81% of all uniquely targeted IP addresses. Another finding shows that for attacks found in both CAIDA and AmpPot (447.6k attacks), 18.4k (4.12%) involving 5.7k (3.25%) unique IPs are blackholed, suggesting that more serious attacks are more likely to be blackholed.

In [26], the authors evaluated how much junk traffic is generated and transferred by ISPs due to amplification attacks. They proposed a method to filter this traffic out by using an AmpPot-like honeypot to obtain information about the victims and Software Defined Network (SDN) to block the traffic targeting those victims. Similarly, UTRS can be used instead of SDN.

Giotsas et al. [12] developed a methodology to detect BGP blackholing activity using datasets from RIPE RIS, RouteViews, PCH, and a "CDN." The findings reveal that 26 IXPs and 242 networks offer RTBH services to customers, peers, and members, and 96.64% of RTBH events are for IPv4, for the measurement period between August 2016 - March 2017.

Nawrocki et al. [21] analyze RTBH events at a large European IXP, and correlate the BGP data with IPFIX flows, which capture information about actual traffic passing through the IXP. The paper finds that more than 95% of traffic and more than 98% of RTBH events are for IPv4 addresses. The IXP had 830 member ASes on average during the measurement period (104 days), of which 78 member ASes announced 1107 IPs to be blackholed for 170 origin ASes (some customers of the 78 members). The events were repeated, indicating that the same IP was under different attacks at different times.

In [15], DDoS attack types at a major IXP from September 2019 to April 2020 are analyzed. The authors find that 89.9% of the attacks use known amplification protocols such as DNS and NTP and IP spoofing. The data is compared to a "commercial world-wide honeypot network," revealing a correlation with only 8% of the attacks observed at the IXP, covering only 33% of target IPs.

Finally, the authors in [9] introduced the "Advanced Blackholing" system that was tested at a major IXP. The system provides improved granularity and the authors claimed that it can successfully mitigate attacks without disrupting the service to the victim. The "Stellar Advanced Blackholing" combines the benefits of RTBH, FlowSpec, ACL filters, and Traffic Scrubbing, without requiring cooperation between networks participating in the IXP. The signaling in Stellar uses BGP, similar to RTBH, but the filters are deployed at the IXP level by utilizing OpenFlow, thus relying on the IXP for both the software and hardware implementation.

Table 1. Datasets description

Dataset	# entries	# targets	# unique target IPs	Duration (sec)		
				min	mean	max
UTRS	533,257	7,820	7,830	300.0	4,682.7	413,700.0
AmpPot	1,616,184	1,080,770	1,080,770	0.5	891.5	1,949,571.0
Milker	223,267	46,764	2,787,522	1.0	93.0	3,600.0

3 Data Collection and Datasets Descriptives

Our study aims to determine to what extent DDoS attacks lead to UTRS participants triggering mitigation attempts. To achieve this goal, from October 2022 to April 2023 (6 months), we gathered three datasets: UTRS, IoT Milker, and AmpPot. Table 1 describes the collected datasets. The number of entries per dataset presents the total number of observations per day in each data set aggregated for the whole period of observation. Next, the column number of targets presents the number of target networks in the case of UTRS and Milker, while for AmpPot the number displayed is the number of individual IPs targeted. The column number of unique targeted IPs is self-explanatory. Finally, the table shows the minimum (min), mean, and maximum (max) duration of attacks.

By combining these datasets, we aim to provide a comprehensive analysis of how amplification and IoT-botnet DDoS attacks influence UTRS participants to trigger UTRS mitigation attempts. In this section, we describe the methodology used to collect and analyze each of these datasets.

3.1 UTRS

To collect the UTRS data set, we registered our own AS and joined the UTRS project. This allowed us to receive the BGP announcements to black hole traffic to particular targets[1] from this service. We made snapshots of active BGP routes every 5 min. Then, we stitched the data using the following rule: if the same target appears in several consecutive snapshots, we assume that it was blocked during the whole period of time[2]. As a result, we get a dataset that consists of targets with start and end blackholing times with 5 min granularity.

Our UTRS dataset has 533,257 entries. Figure 1a shows entries distribution per day (hereafter, the UTRS dataset lines are colored orange). On average, we get 3,122 entries each day in the UTRS dataset, with the maximum reaching 9,427 entries.

In the dataset, there are 7,820 unique target networks (see Table 1) from 124 ASes that contain 7,830 individual IP addresses. The majority of UTRS

---

[1] UTRS members can announce up to a /25 of IPv4 addresses and up to /49 for IPv6 from their ASes as targets.

[2] If a target network is added and removed within a 5-minute interval, it will not appear in any dump and we will not record it.

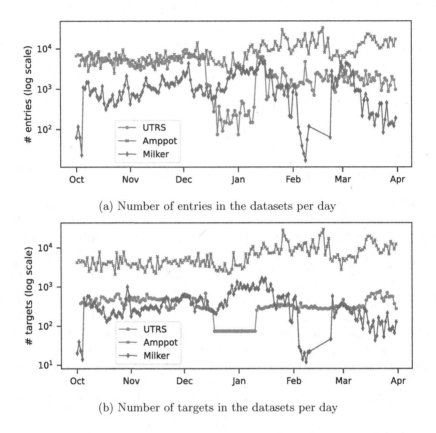

(a) Number of entries in the datasets per day

(b) Number of targets in the datasets per day

Fig. 1. Daily datasets characteristics

announcements target individual IP addresses (/32 prefix length). Only 2 entries within the 6-month observation period target the same /27 subnetwork on the same day. The number of targets in the UTRS dataset varies greatly from day to day (see Fig. 1b). The maximum number of observed IPs during one day was 776, and the minimum of 74. The mean is 357 IPs per day, with a standard deviation of 159.9. In terms of trends, there is no clear pattern in the data. At the same time, it is obvious that the number of targets in the months of 2022 seems to be consistently higher than in the ones of 2023.

There is a cluster of days between December 18th and January 11th where the number of targets is relatively low (74 unique targets). Interestingly, during the same period, the number of entries in the dataset varies from 74 to 654 (see Fig. 1a), but the same 74 targets are announced during these days. We suspect the service was not functioning properly because our test announcements were not propagated through the service during that period.

Figure 2 shows the empirical Cumulative Distribution Function (eCDF) and the corresponding Kernel Density Estimation (KDE) of durations. As we can see from this figure, the largest part of the UTRS announcements (around 21%) has a duration equal to 5 min, which is connected with the peculiarities of the UTRS dataset collection. This tells us that a huge portion of the UTRS announcements lasts less than 5-min, and we might miss them dumping BGP tables using this period. The longest duration of announcements in the UTRS dataset was 4 days, 18 h and 55 min (or 413, 700 s) happened at the end of October 2022, with the mean and the median of 4, 682.7 and 1, 798.0 s correspondingly.

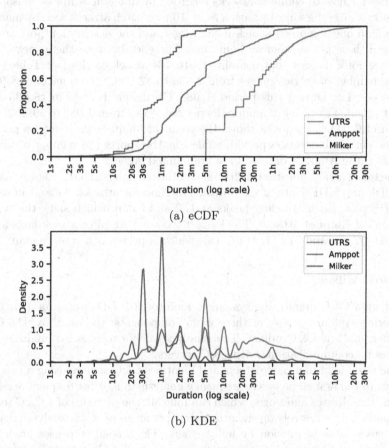

(a) eCDF

(b) KDE

Fig. 2. Events duration characteristics (axis x is in logarithmic scale)

3.2   AmpPot

As the second dataset, we gathered attack data provided by the AmpPot project[3], a reflection and amplification honeypot [16]. The AmpPot honeypot tracks reflection and amplification attacks by mimicking vulnerable protocols, such as DNS, NTP, and SSDP. This allows the honeypot to be discovered by

---

[3] https://sec.ynu.codes/dos.

attackers scanning for reflectors and subsequently used in their attacks. By logging the received requests, the AmpPot data allows for the inference of various information about an attack, including the victim's IP address and destination port, the start and end time of the attack, and the attack intensity.

We collected the amplification attack data from 19 AmpPot sensors (11 proxied and 8 agnostic, see [16] for details). As it was previously shown, e.g., in [18], AmpPot attacks recorded by different sensors are often related. There are several strategies for how to combine attacks recorded by different AmpPot sensors. In this work, we use the same approach as in [16]: we stitch attacks seen by multiple sensors into one combined attack if the target and the destination port are the same and there is less than an hour time difference between the attacks. As a result, we got a dataset that contains $1,616,184$ attack entries (see Table 1).

The number of entries ranges from $2,435$ to $32,908$, with a mean of $8,969.7$ attacks per day. During this period, $1,080,770$ unique IPs[4] from $15,825$ ASes were attacked. The count of unique IPs per day varies from $2,082$ to $29,402$, with a mean of $6,943.6$. Figure 1a shows the count of unique attack entries per day over the entire observation period, while Fig. 1b reports the number of targets (hereafter, the AmpPot dataset lines are painted green).

The mean attack duration is 891.5 s, and the median is 150.0 s. Figure 2 shows the eCDF and KDE plots of the duration of AmpPot attacks. As we can see on the KDE plot, there are clear peaks at 1, 2 and 5 min, which show the typical durations of AmpPot attacks. The longest recorded AmpPot attack lasts for 22 days 13 h 32 min and 51 s ($1,949,571$ s), which is probably a routine scan.

3.3   IoT Milker

We set up a C&C monitoring system to monitor IoT DDoS attacks. Our C&C monitoring system consists of three main components: the sandbox, the C&C identifier, and the C&C milker. The sandbox safely executes IoT malware and observes its communications with C&C servers.

The C&C identifier part detects and identifies C&C servers using a two-step process. In the first step, we use frequency analysis to look for frequent access to certain IP addresses and ports, which can indicate the presence of a C&C server. This method does not rely on signatures or other forms of static analysis, making it less susceptible to evasion by IoT botnets. The second step uses predefined rules, manually prepared by analysts, to identify the C&C protocol based on the first payload sent by the sandboxed malware. The initial set of rules is based on the Mirai source code, but new rules are added as needed. Each rule is associated with a corresponding milker script, which imitates the identified C&C protocol and allows the observation system to capture the real-time activities of the IoT botnet.

The Milker script is a manually created script that imitates the IoT bot behavior. Using the identified protocol, it connects to the combinations of IP

---

[4] For this dataset, the number of targets corresponds to the number of IPs because AmpPot records attacks to individual IPs rather networks.

addresses and ports of C&C servers detected with the frequency analysis and monitors the commands sent by the C&C servers. Thus, using the milker script, we are able to capture the real-time activities of IoT botnets, including the commands to DDoS particular victims. For this work, we collect the start time of a DDoS attack, the target IP and port, and its duration. Since we collect the commands sent by the C&C, we do not typically have other statistics on the attack, like the total number of packets and packets per second.

Over the entire collection period, we gathered a dataset containing $223,270$ entries. The majority of entries ($217,565$) attack individual IPs (have /32 prefix length). At the same time, there are several cases that attack large subnetworks: 1 attack targets /2, and 2 – /4. Such distributed attacks do not make sense; thus, we assumed that botnet owners initiated them due to mistyping. Most likely, in one /2 and one /4 cases, the prefix length was intended as /24 by the attacker. We decided to remove all these 3 entries from the dataset in order to not overcount potential unique IP addresses, that would also overlap with loopback ranges. As a result, we get a dataset that contains $223,267$ entries, targeting $46,764$ unique victim networks with $2,787,522$ unique IP addresses.

Figure 1a and Fig. 1b show the number of entries and targets per day (hereafter, the Milker dataset line has a blue color). On average, we observed $1,306.7$ entries per day targeting 399.2 networks, with the highest values being $5,396$ attacks and $1,648$ unique targets and the lowest 17 entries and 12 networks per day correspondingly. Note that we do not have Milker data for 11th–22nd February 2023, due to our infrastructure upgrade.

The duration of the Milker attacks, as observed by the value sent by the C&C to the bots, ranges from 1 second to a maximum of one hour (see Fig. 2). The upper limit of $3,600\,s$ is probably an artifact of the Mirai code[5] which raises an error if the duration is longer than an hour. As we can see in the figure, the majority of attacks in the Milker dataset have 30 s, 1 or 2 min durations.

4   Findings

The two collected DDoS datasets, AmpPot and Milker, are the sources of information about amplification and IoT-botnet DDoS attacks correspondingly. For each DDoS dataset, we compute two views representing the intersections with the UTRS dataset data. The first view (*Exact Interval (EI)*) contains data about exact time interval intersections between DDoS attacks and UTRS announcements, while the second (*Offset Interval (OI)*) represents the intersections of DDoS attack intervals with the UTRS announcement span extended by 12 h in both directions. The reason for computing the view with Offset Interval is the following. A sensor can record an attack that may be already over before it is blocked by UTRS. Similarly, some sensors can still continue registering attack packets even though the corresponding entry is removed from the UTRS table.

---

[5] https://github.com/jgamblin/Mirai-Source-Code/blob/master/mirai/cnc/attack. go.

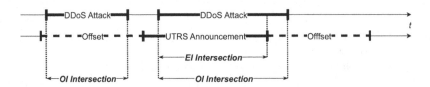

Fig. 3. Intersections views (EI - Exact Interval, OI - Offset Interval)

As we described in Sect. 3, both datasets, AmpPot and Milker, contain information about the victims (individual IPs in the case of AmpPot and prefixes for
the Milker dataset). To build the views described above, we first compute a map
relating DDoS attack victims with the UTRS announcement targets. Then, for
each UTRS target, we search for all intersections of UTRS announcement spans
with the time intervals of DDoS attacks targeting the same victim. In the case
of *Exact Interval (EI)*, we look for exact intersections of the time intervals. For
Offset Interval (OI), we, at first, expand the span of the UTRS announcement
in both directions by 12 h and then find the intersections of the attack's time
intervals with this expanded period. Figure 3 shows the relative position of these
intervals graphically and explains the concepts visually. As a result, we get four
views: two (EI and OI) for the UTRS-AmpPot datasets and another two for the
UTRS-Milker datasets.

4.1   General Overview

Table 2 reports the characteristics of the computed views. The first row, "# of
entries", contains the number of entries for the corresponding computed view.
As expected, the OI views contain considerably more entries. Interestingly, the
number of entries in the UTRS-Milker view is significantly lower than in UTRS-
AmpPot, although the number of target IPs in the former is higher than in
the latter (see Table 1). The reason is that the number of unique targets is
lower in the UTRS-Milker view. Additionally, the AmpPot attacks are longer
on average, which increases the probability of the intersection with a UTRS
announcement time interval. The row "# of unique UTRS targets" reports the
number of unique targets in the UTRS announcements. For UTRS-AmpPot,
the values in this row are equal to the ones in the "# of unique DDoS attack
targets" row, meaning that one AmpPot attack is typically covered by only
one UTRS announcement. At the same time, for UTRS-Milker, a Milker attack
may trigger several UTRS announcements because some Milker attacks target
networks rather than individual IPs. The values in the last row, "Mean entries
per UTRS announcement", show that one UTRS announcement covers more
than one attack. For instance, every UTRS announcement has an EI intersection
with about 1.55 AmpPot and 1.12 Milker attacks correspondingly.

Table 2. Views characteristics (EI - Exact Interval, OI - Offset Interval)

Parameter	UTRS-AmpPot		UTRS-Milker	
	EI	OI	EI	OI
# of entries	468	6,774	9	791
# of unique DDoS attack targets	249	1,268	2	143
# of unique UTRS targets	249	1,268	8	163
# of unique UTRS ASNs	25	43	2	6
Mean entries # per UTRS announcement	1.55	1.76	1.12	1.88

The "# of unique UTRS ASNs" row shows the number of ASes that launched the UTRS announcements in the corresponding views. With high probability, we can assume that only 25 and 2 ASes reacted to AmpPot and Milker attacks correspondingly by commencing UTRS announcements (EI intersections), while 43 and 6 of ASes are triggered by AmpPot and Milker attacks with lower probability (OI intersections).

Among those, there are 43 unique ASes. Table 3 (in appendix) lists the ASes (in the anonymized form) and what countries they belong to[6]. More than a quarter (11 out of 43) of all the ASes are from Brazil. While this may seem unexpected, a recent study [19] shows that Brazilian ISPs adopt anti-DDoS security best practices (e.g., source address validation) significantly faster than the providers in the rest of the world. Thus, it is highly likely that they have also employed the protection provided by UTRS. Other prominent countries where operators use UTRS to protect against DDoS attacks are the USA (21% or 9 ASes) and Argentina (16% or 7 instances).

Table 3 also reports the total number of AmpPot and Milker attacks and how many of those are mitigated with the help of UTRS per each AS individually. On average, only 1.03% of AmpPot and 0.06% of Milker attacks on the UTRS members trigger the announcements for EI, while for OI, those figures are equal to 8.86% and 6.88% correspondingly.

As for the absolute numbers, only 0.025% and 0.212% of all AmpPot attacks trigger UTRS announcements for EI and OI correspondingly. These numbers are considerably lower than the ones reported for AmpPot dataset in the work by Jonker et al. [13]. According to their measurements, 1.97% of all AmpPot attacks triggered BGP blackholing. There are two reasons for this difference. First, UTRS-based blackholing events represent only a tiny subset of all BGP blackholing events. Second, the authors use 24 h interval prior to a blackholing event to match the attacks, while we consider only 12 h. Moreover, the authors relied on the assumption that all BGP announcements targeting networks smaller or equal to /24 correspond to BGP blackholing events, that can be an optimistic overapproximation. In our work, we do not need to make such an assumption because we know exactly what BGP announcements are trig-

---

[6] The ASes' country codes are obtained using the Caida's AS Rank [6] dataset.

gered by UTRS. As for the Milker attacks, the numbers are even lower: only 0.001% and 0.147% of all attacks trigger UTRS announcements for EI and OI correspondingly.

4.2   Time Lags

Given the obtained views, we can analyze time lags between UTRS and DDoS attack events. Based on the timestamps in the UTRS-AmpPot and UTRS-Milker EI and OI views, we calculate time difference between the UTRS and the corresponding DDoS attack start and end events. Figure 4 shows the eCDFs of these time lags: a) for Exact Interval views, b) for Offset Interval views. The positive lag (values on the x axis) means that the UTRS event has happened later than the corresponding DDoS attack event.

For EI, as we can see in Fig. 4a, around 67% of all AmpPot attacks start before the UTRS announcement, which is expected. At the same time, around 32% of AmpPot attacks start after the corresponding UTRS announcement. One potential explanation is that attackers use different amplifiers, and our AmpPot sensors are exploited at later stages. Moreover, due to the peculiarities of our UTRS dataset collection, the reported time of a UTRS announcement is shifted into the future compared to the actual time. As expected, for a large portion of AmpPot attacks (around 79%), the corresponding target is removed from the UTRS BGP table after the attack is over. However, the peculiarities of the UTRS dataset collection may have a negative effect on such a high percentage. For 100% of all entries in the UTRS-Milker EI view, announcements happen $1 - 3\,h$ before the start of the corresponding attacks recorded by Milker. However, the size of the UTRS-Milker view is very small (only 9 entries), so the results may be nonrepresentative.

Considering OI views (see Fig. 4b), as expected, the majority of UTRS announcements (around 83%) and removals (roughly 83%) happen after the AmpPot attack start and end events correspondingly. At the same time, the same figures for the UTRS-Milker data constitute only 13% and 14% correspondingly. That indicates Milker attacks are highly unlikely caused by the corresponding UTRS announcement.

4.3   Characterization of Blackholed Attacks

To study the characteristics of the attacks that drive the UTRS requests, we examine the properties, namely duration, the total number of packets, and their intensity. Note that we can do this study only for the AmpPot attacks because the amplification honeypots collect the attack metrics, such as the number of packets and the duration of the attacks. Unfortunately, the Milker monitor does not have access to such metrics[7]. Additionally, we consider only the Exact Interval

---

[7] The Milker monitor registers attack durations, but those values are fixed by the IoT malware owners.

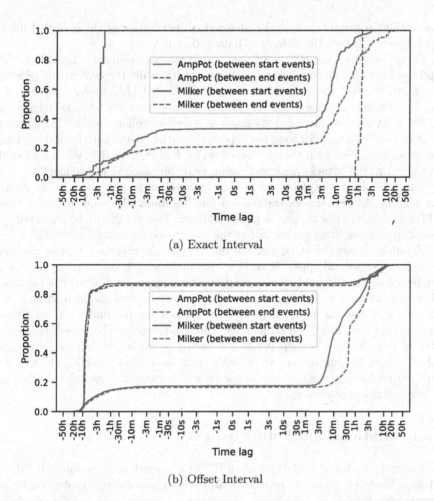

(a) Exact Interval

(b) Offset Interval

Fig. 4. Time lags between UTRS events and corresponding DDoS attack events (x axis has a symmetrical log scale)

intersections because the UTRS requests are more likely to be driven by the corresponding AmpPot attacks.

In this section, we compare the properties of the attacks that target only the ASes that trigger UTRS announcements (mitigated/blackholed by UTRS). To build the dataset for such analysis, we extracted all the attacks from the AmpPot dataset (see Sect. 3.2) that target 25 ASNs from the UTRS-AmpPot view (see Table 2). Then, we mark the attacks found in the UTRS-AmpPot view as *blackholed*. Thus, our dataset contains 38,251 entries overall, out of which 398 are marked as blackholed. Note that our dataset is highly unbalanced: only around 1% of all entries belong to the blackholed class, while the rest 99% are members of the non-blackholed class. Luckily, eCDFs, which we use in this section, accurately reflect the underlying distribution of the observed data, regardless of whether the dataset is balanced or not.

Figure 5a shows the eCDFs of the AmpPot attack duration. Hereafter, the solid line corresponds to all attack data (*Overall*), while the dashed one reflects the information of the attacks marked as blackholed (*Blackholed*). As we can see, the dashed line lies under the solid, showing that the attacks triggering UTRS generally last longer. This result is easy to explain because ISPs prefer to activate UTRS only for long-lasting attacks rather than short-lived ones. Our results also coincide with the ones reported by Jonker et al. [13], who also found that the AmpPot attacks mitigated using BGP blackholing last longer.

Figure 5b shows the eCDFs of the total number of packets recorded by Amp-Pot sensors. As we can see, the dashed line lies under the solid, meaning that UTRS-mitigated attacks have a higher volume. This result is also expected — indeed, it is more likely for an ISP to mitigate more volumetric attacks.

Figure 5c shows the eCDFs of the intensity of the attacks — mean number of packets per second (pps). Note that this parameter is obtained as the total number of packets divided by the duration of the corresponding stitched attack. Thus, this value correlates with the intensity of the attacks on a victim. As we can see, below the speed of 10 pps, the dashed line lies under the solid one, showing that the blackholed attacks are more intense below this speed. However, after 10 pps, the lines switch. While it is harder to explain, in our opinion, such behavior may be due to the victim ISPs (and their allies) starting to activate multiple protection mechanisms, some of which may also include filtering of attack packets to amplifiers.

5   Limitations and Future Work

In this study, we investigated the use of UTRS as a mechanism to mitigate DDoS attacks. However, there are certain limitations to our findings that need to be acknowledged.

Firstly, our study only captures data on the use of UTRS, and we do not have information on whether network operators used other mechanisms in conjunction with UTRS to mitigate DDoS attacks, or if the attack was successfully mitigated. This means that we cannot accurately quantify the effectiveness of UTRS as a standalone mechanism.

Secondly, our attack data only includes information from AmpPot and IoT Milker. Therefore, we may have missed attacks that were not detected by these sources. To address this limitation, we suggest future work to investigate the effectiveness of UTRS in conjunction with other DDoS attack data sources.

Thirdly, we collected the UTRS data as periodic snapshots every 5 min. We collected the data this way instead of logging all BGP updates due to the constant errors in the BGP sessions with the UTRS project that caused the recorded events to be mostly **announces** with few **withdraws**, thus making it impossible to track when a blackholing event stops. However, if an announcement happens within this interval, we will not be able to record it. This means we may miss

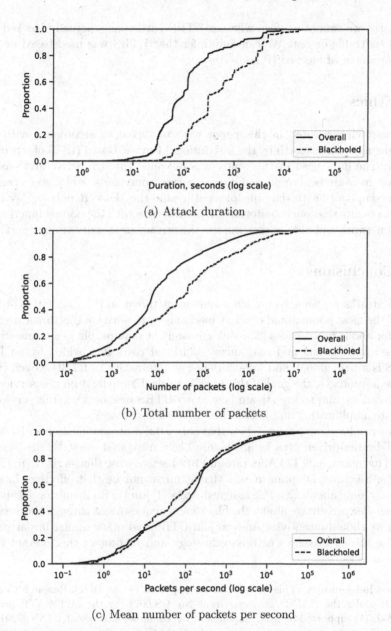

(a) Attack duration

(b) Total number of packets

(c) Mean number of packets per second

Fig. 5. Blackholed and non-blackholed attack characteristics eCDFs

some of the announcements, thus potentially underestimating the number of mitigated DDoS attacks and ASes making the announcements. Currently, we are exploring the feasibility of collecting data about the UTRS announcements as soon as they are propagated to the service members.

Lastly, we cannot confirm whether UTRS participants actually blocked the malicious traffic or not. We can only infer that UTRS was used based on the announcement of blocked IP addresses.

6   Ethics

The research presented in this paper was conducted in accordance with the ethical standards set forth by the Institutional Review Board (IRB) of our institution. The data used in this study was obtained through active and passive internet measurements and monitoring botnet commands, which were carried out in compliance with the principles outlined in the Menlo Report [5]. We took steps to ensure that our monitoring did not interfere with the normal functioning of any network and did not compromise the privacy or security of any operators.

7   Conclusions

DDoS attacks continue to remain a significant threat to the Internet. RTBH is one of the most popular and effective mechanisms to mitigate this threat used by ISPs for about two decades [25]. Unfortunately, it requires physical connectivity between participants and may incur additional costs if provided by an IXP. UTRS is a free, global, and low-effort-to-join alternative to RTBH. Given these unique advantages, the goal of this work is to shed more light on this service. In particular, we aim to investigate how many UTRS members use this service to mitigate amplification and IoT-botnet-driven DDoS attacks.

The results of our analysis show that only 0.025% of amplification and 0.001% of IoT-botnet-driven attacks are highly likely mitigated using UTRS. Among UTRS members, only 124 ASes (around 10%) actively use this service to mitigate attacks. Such low adoption means that it might not be that effective. Indeed, currently, only about 1% of all assigned ASNs [1] are UTRS members [7], and an even smaller percentage abides the blackholing requests sent through this service. Thus, we should incentivize ASes to join UTRS and other similar initiatives to increase the effectiveness of this technology and to protect the Internet from DDoS attacks.

Acknowledgements. This work is partly supported by the Dutch Research Council (NWO) under the RAPID project (Grant No. CS.007), by the MITIGATE project (JPJ000254) supported by MIC, Japan, and the commissioned research (No.05201) by NICT. This work was also supported by JSPS KAKENHI Grant Numbers 21H03444 and 21KK0178.

Appendix A: List of ASes Mitigating DDoS Attacks

Table 3. ASes mitigating DDoS attacks

AS	CC	AmpPot					Milker				
		Total attacks	EI mitigated #	EI mitigated %	OI mitigated #	OI mitigated %	Total attacks	EI mitigated #	EI mitigated %	OI mitigated #	OI mitigated %
UAO	AR	2	2	100.00	2	100.00	0	0	0.00	0	0.00
GNX	ES	1	1	100.00	1	100.00	0	0	0.00	0	0.00
VYC	DE	6	5	83.33	6	100.00	0	0	0.00	0	0.00
SMI	BY	5	3	60.00	4	80.00	0	0	0.00	0	0.00
H2W	AR	4	2	50.00	4	100.00	0	0	0.00	0	0.00
BME	AR	135	45	33.33	78	57.78	0	0	0.00	0	0.00
WO6	FR	99	30	30.30	30	30.30	0	0	0.00	0	0.00
WYU	AR	4	1	25.00	3	75.00	0	0	0.00	0	0.00
FAX	AR	15	3	20.00	3	20.00	0	0	0.00	0	0.00
MV3	TR	25	5	20.00	5	20.00	0	0	0.00	0	0.00
KIM	KH	15	2	13.33	6	40.00	0	0	0.00	0	0.00
44I	CA	24	2	8.33	7	29.17	1	0	0.00	0	0.00
FCF	BR	139	9	6.47	55	39.57	6	0	0.00	0	0.00
L7L	PL	173	9	5.20	66	38.15	38	0	0.00	1	2.63
IVB	AU	98	5	5.10	29	29.59	12	0	0.00	8	66.67
SHB	BR	315	11	3.49	20	6.35	0	0	0.00	0	0.00
QAM	US	124	4	3.23	33	26.61	46	0	0.00	22	47.83
73H	IE	38	1	2.63	7	18.42	3	0	0.00	0	0.00
564	US	6,140	141	2.30	743	12.10	819	2	0.24	116	14.16
QWW	BR	1,252	22	1.76	22	1.76	0	0	0.00	0	0.00
PZS	US	570	8	1.40	22	3.86	14	0	0.00	1	7.14
T7M	BR	1,391	8	0.58	9	0.65	0	0	0.00	0	0.00
JA4	US	21,615	77	0.36	2,229	10.31	3,835	1	0.03	182	4.75
ZNH	BR	308	1	0.32	1	0.32	0	0	0.00	0	0.00
RMF	IR	5,753	1	0.02	1	0.02	22	0	0.00	0	0.00
Z76	BR	2	0	0.00	2	100.00	0	0	0.00	0	0.00
4T2	PL	53	0	0.00	1	1.89	4	0	0.00	0	0.00
OVZ	US	2	0	0.00	1	50.00	0	0	0.00	0	0.00
RWB	GB	14	0	0.00	7	50.00	0	0	0.00	0	0.00
G6P	US	10	0	0.00	1	10.00	0	0	0.00	0	0.00
PXB	AR	32	0	0.00	1	3.12	0	0	0.00	0	0.00
63A	BR	7	0	0.00	4	57.14	0	0	0.00	0	0.00
6KY	AT	2	0	0.00	2	100.00	0	0	0.00	0	0.00
JUX	BR	3	0	0.00	1	33.33	0	0	0.00	0	0.00
XMN	AR	3	0	0.00	3	100.00	0	0	0.00	0	0.00
RQI	US	2	0	0.00	1	50.00	0	0	0.00	0	0.00
L4K	SG	3	0	0.00	2	66.67	0	0	0.00	0	0.00
3L4	PK	7	0	0.00	1	14.29	0	0	0.00	0	0.00
VJC	US	2	0	0.00	2	100.00	0	0	0.00	0	0.00
U75	BR	18	0	0.00	3	16.67	0	0	0.00	0	0.00
O2C	US	12	0	0.00	1	8.33	0	0	0.00	0	0.00
SHL	BR	3	0	0.00	3	100.00	0	0	0.00	0	0.00
QMK	BR	298	0	0.00	9	3.02	0	0	0.00	0	0.00

References

1. RIR Statistics. https://www.nro.net/about/rirs/statistics/
2. Alieyan, K., Kadhum, M.M., Anbar, M., Rehman, S.U., Alajmi, N.K.: An overview of DDoS attacks based on DNS. In: 2016 International Conference on Information and Communication Technology Convergence (ICTC), pp. 276–280. IEEE (2016)
3. AMSIX: Pricing — AMS-IX Amsterdam (2023). https://www.ams-ix.net/ams/pricing
4. Antonakakis, M., et al.: Understanding the Mirai botnet. In: 26th {USENIX} security symposium ({USENIX} Security 17), pp. 1093–1110 (2017)
5. Bailey, M., Dittrich, D., Kenneally, E., Maughan, D.: The Menlo report. IEEE Secur. Priv. **10**(2), 71–75 (2012)
6. CAIDA: AS Rank. https://asrank.caida.org/
7. Cymru, T.: network-security-templates/README.md at master · teamcymru/network-security-templates · GitHub (2022)
8. DE-CIX: Blackholing - Fight DDoS attacks effectively. https://de-cix.net/en/services/blackholing
9. Dietzel, C., Wichtlhuber, M., Smaragdakis, G., Feldmann, A.: Stellar: network attack mitigation using advanced blackholing. In: Proceedings of the 14th International Conference on Emerging Networking Experiments and Technologies. CoNEXT 2018, pp. 152–164, New York, NY, USA. Association for Computing Machinery (2018). https://doi.org/10.1145/3281411.3281413, https://doi.org/10.1145/3281411.3281413
10. Dnsfilter: Beyond Hackers in Hoodies: DNSFilter Mid-Year Cybersecurity Review (2022)
11. Equinix: Remotely Triggered Black Hole. https://docs.equinix.com/en-us/Content/Interconnection/IX/IX-rtbh-guide.htm
12. Giotsas, V., Smaragdakis, G., Dietzel, C., Richter, P., Feldmann, A., Berger, A.: Inferring BGP blackholing activity in the internet. In: Proceedings of the 2017 Internet Measurement Conference. IMC 2017, New York, NY, USA, pp. 1–14. Association for Computing Machinery (2017). https://doi.org/10.1145/3131365.3131379
13. Jonker, M., Pras, A., Dainotti, A., Sperotto, A.: A first joint look at DoS attacks and BGP blackholing in the wild. In: Proceedings of the Internet Measurement Conference 2018, pp. 457–463 (2018)
14. Jonker, M., Sperotto, A.: Measuring exposure in DDoS protection services. In: 2017 13th International Conference on Network and Service Management (CNSM), pp. 1–9. IEEE (2017)
15. Kopp, D., Dietzel, C., Hohlfeld, O.: DDoS never dies? An IXP perspective on DDoS amplification attacks. In: Hohlfeld, O., Lutu, A., Levin, D. (eds.) PAM 2021. LNCS, vol. 12671, pp. 284–301. Springer, Cham (2021). https://doi.org/10.1007/978-3-030-72582-2_17
16. Krämer, L., et al.: AmpPot: monitoring and defending against amplification DDoS attacks. In: Proceedings of the 18th International Symposium Research in Attacks, Intrusions, and Defenses, pp. 615–636 (2015)
17. Kristoff, J.: An Internet-wide BGP RTBH service. Technical report (June 2015). https://www.iab.org/wp-content/IAB-uploads/2015/04/CARIS_2015_submission_20.pdf
18. Krupp, J., Backes, M., Rossow, C.: Identifying the scan and attack infrastructures behind amplification DDoS attacks. In: Proceedings of the 2016 ACM SIGSAC Conference on Computer and Communications Security, pp. 1426–1437 (2016)

19. Lone, Q., Frik, A., Luckie, M., Korczynski, M., van Eeten, M., Gañán, C.: Deployment of source address validation by network operators: a randomized control trial. In: Proceedings of the 43rd IEEE Symposium on Security and Privacy (S&P 2022) (2022)
20. Mirkovic, J., Reiher, P.: A taxonomy of DDoS attack and DDoS defense mechanisms. ACM SIGCOMM Comput. Commun. Rev. **34**(2), 39–53 (2004)
21. Nawrocki, M., Blendin, J., Dietzel, C., Schmidt, T.C., Wählisch, M.: Down the black hole: dismantling operational practices of BGP blackholing at IXPs. In: Proceedings of the Internet Measurement Conference, pp. 435–448 (2019)
22. Srivastava, A., Gupta, B.B., Tyagi, A., Sharma, A., Mishra, A.: A recent survey on DDoS attacks and defense mechanisms. In: Nagamalai, D., Renault, E., Dhanuskodi, M. (eds.) PDCTA 2011. CCIS, vol. 203, pp. 570–580. Springer, Heidelberg (2011). https://doi.org/10.1007/978-3-642-24037-9_57
23. Team Cymru: Unwanted traffic removal service. https://www.team-cymru.com/ddos-mitigation-services
24. Team Cymru: UTRS Peering Guide. https://github.com/team-cymru/network-security-templates/blob/master/UTRS-Peering-Guide/README.md
25. Turk, D.: Configuring BGP to Block Denial-of-Service Attacks. RFC 3882 (2004). https://doi.org/10.17487/RFC3882, https://rfc-editor.org/rfc/rfc3882.txt
26. Zhauniarovich, Y., Dodia, P.: Sorting the garbage: filtering out DRDoS amplification traffic in ISP networks. In: Proceedings of the IEEE Conference on Network Softwarization, pp. 142–150 (2019)

Protocol Dialects as Formal Patterns

D. Galán[1], V. García[2], S. Escobar[2], C. Meadows[3(✉)], and J. Meseguer[4]

[1] ETH Zurich, Zürich, Switzerland
daniel.galan@inf.ethz.ch
[2] VRAIN, Universitat Politècnica de València, Valencia, Spain
{vicgarval,sescobar}@upv.es
[3] Naval Research Laboratory, Washington DC, USA
catherine.meadows@nrl.navy.mil
[4] University of Illinois at Urbana-Champaign, Champaign, USA
meseguer@illinois.edu

Abstract. A *protocol dialect* is a lightweight method to obfuscate the communication exchanges between legitimate protocol users to make it hard for malicious users to interact with legitimate ones. So far, dialects have been based on a single obfuscation transformation, which we call a *lingo*. In this work dialects are generalized to become *protocol and lingo generic*. In this way they can be *composed* with other dialects for greater security. We present a formal semantics of dialects as *formal patterns*, i.e., as protocol transformations formalized in rewriting logic. We also present several *attacker models* and explain how our generalized notion of dialect can be used to harden dialects against such attackers.

1 Introduction

Protocol dialects are modifications to existing protocols that provide lightweight security, especially against relatively easy attacks that could potentially be leveraged into more serious ones. The scenario is that of a network of mutually trusting principals, e.g. an enterprise network, that needs to defend itself from outside attackers. The most effective way is to prevent a potential attacker from even initiating a communication with group members, e.g. by requiring messages to be modified in some unpredictable way by means of a *dialect-based* modification of the protocol messages, that cannot be easily reproduced by the attacker.

A number of dialects have been proposed in the literature, for example [9, 10, 17, 20–22]. These dialects concentrate on protecting a group of principals by verifying group membership without authenticating individual members. All principals in the group possess a common parametric message transformation algorithm

S. Escobar and V. García have been partially supported by the grant PID2021-122830OB-C42 funded by MCIN/AEI/10.13039/501100011033 and ERDF A way of making Europe, by the grant CIPROM/2022/6 funded by Generalitat Valenciana, and by the grant PCI2020-120708-2 funded by MICIN/AEI/10.13039/501100011033 and by the European Union NextGenerationEU/PRTR. D. Galán, V. García, C. Meadows, and J. Meseguer have been partially supported by ONR Code 311. We also thank Eben Blaisdell and Carolyn Talcott for their comments.

G. Tsudik et al. (Eds.): ESORICS 2023, LNCS 14345, pp. 42–61, 2024.
https://doi.org/10.1007/978-3-031-51476-0_3

(that we call a *lingo*), whose parameters are updated in a synchronous fashion. Such a procedure is secure against a passive attacker that cannot block or alter traffic, and remains so even if the lingos are quite weak, as long as the attacker cannot predict what the next parameter will be, and as long as they are changed often enough so that the attacker cannot reconstruct it from observed traffic while it is still current. This has led to research on suitable lingos, surveyed in this paper.

However, there are a number of questions about dialects that remain open:

1. **Synchronization Methods** need to be lightweight, as for lingos; but they should not be predictable by an attacker. How can this be done?
2. **Protocol and Lingo Genericity**. This means that a dialect should be applicable to a large class of protocols and lingos without alteration of the protocol's code. Indeed, we can think of them as a virtual layer between levels 6 and 7 in the OSI model [5]. What is the best way of ensuring this?
3. **Attacker Models**. How do different attacker models affect the choice of dialects and synchronization methods?

To answer these questions, we need not only examples but a general framework supporting reasoning about classes of dialects. In this paper, we develop such a framework, that provides a formal basis for reasoning about dialects and their properties. Our framework is based on *formal patterns* [19], which allow us to generalize the notion of dialect so as to make it both protocol- and lingo-generic. This allows not only arbitrary classes of lingos, but even arbitrary combinations of lingos. This genericity has two important consequences: (1) dialects now become *composable*; and (2) composed dialects can be much harder to break than the simpler dialects they are composed out of.

We formally specify our framework in rewriting logic [18], supported by the Maude language [3]. This allows us to write formal executable dialect specifications for analysis and simulation. We then develop a class of attacker models that specify different types of attackers, using the attacker models of Ren et al. [20] as a starting point. We also show how our framework can be used to develop dialects that are secure against these different classes of attackers.

Our contributions: (i) a generalization of the notion of dialect, making dialects protocol- and lingo-generic, and enjoying new state- and time-based synchronization mechanisms for greater security; (ii) a formal semantics of lingos as formal executable patterns in rewriting logic; (iii) two new notions of *vertical* and *horizontal* dialect composition that can substantially increase dialect security and dialect diversity; (iv) hierarchies and *taxonomies* of lingos and dialects, including new, dynamic periodic and aperiodic dialects to substantially increase dialect security; (v) a family of protocol dialect attacker models; and (vi) use of our framework to derive dialects that are secure against different attacker models in the family. These are the outcome of extensive experimentation in Maude.

1.1 Related Work

Our approach is to develop message transformations (*lingos* in our terminology) that could be applied to a number of different protocols, and in which the underlying protocol may not use encryption. Work on these transformations includes the work of Gogineni, Garcia-Alfaro et al. [9,10,17], and Ren at al. [20]. Lingos use techniques such as packet transformations and modification of protocol flow, which can be applied to commonly existing protocol features. We discuss these techniques in more detail in Sect. 5. We note that [20] is of particular interest to us since it introduces concepts such as message transformations as functions and the composition of dialects, ideas that we further develop.

Less work has been done on the management and synchronization of transformations of lingos. In [15], Lukaszewski and Xie propose that protocol customizations of application protocols, including protocol dialects, be given its own layer. The proposed layer provides a logically centralized customization orchestrator that streamlines the process of deploying customized protocols, dealing with such issues as liveliness monitoring, rogue module detection, middlebox transversal, and modules that will assist in implementing customizations. Although we do not address such centralized customization, this work is still relevant to our approach because it provides insight into the types of guarantees needed in order for a dialect to work efficiently and correctly.

In terms of synchronization, Gogineni et al. use an AI system in [10] shared among all systems. It is used to choose dialect parameters and tasked with achieving unpredictability, minimizing cost, etc. Ren et al. [20] in turn propose a deterministic function that is used to update dialect parameters periodically.

1.2   Running Example: MQTT

Here we describe the MQTT protocol [12], which we will use as the basis for a running example in our paper. MQTT is a lightweight, publish-subscribe protocol that incorporates some message queuing services and is popular in devices with limited resources or network bandwidth. It requires a transport protocol such as TCP/IP that can provide ordered, lossless, bi-directional connections. MQTT provides no security itself, and, although it can be run over secure transport protocols such as TLS, it is known to be commonly misconfigured [11]. This makes it an attractive application for protocol dialects, see for example [10].

In MQTT, multiple clients publish and subscribe to reports via a broker. When any message is sent in MQTT, it is preceded by two control packets, the first sent by the message sender, and the second an acknowledgment sent by the receiver. The most important of these control packets from our point of view is the CONNECT packet sent by the client when it first contacts the broker. Sessions can last indefinitely, although this may require that the client send periodic ping messages to the broker. The CONNECT packet will play an important role in our development of MQTT dialects.

2   Preliminaries

Here we provide the background necessary to understand our formal framework. We use rewriting logic [18] and its natural way of modeling object-based distributed systems, and Maude [3,4], a high-level programming language and

```
rl  < Id : Client | broker : IdS, status : disc, Atts >
=> < Id : Client | broker : IdS, status : try, Atts > (to IdS from Id : conn(Id))

rl  < IdS : Broker | devices : Devices, Atts > (to IdS from Id : conn(Id))
=> < IdS : Broker | devices : (Devices, Id), Atts > (to Id from IdS : ack(Id))

rl  < Id : Client | broker : IdS, status : try, Atts > (to Id from IdS : ack(Id))
=> < Id : Client | broker : IdS, status : con, Atts >
```

Fig. 1. Some actor rules for MQTT

system implementing rewriting logic. Rewriting logic is a semantic framework
well suited for protocol dialects thanks to the following features (see [7] for further details): (i) support for concurrency and distributed objects; (ii) distributed
object reflection and adaptation; (iii) support for symbolic computation; and (iv)
formal verification methods and tools.

Actors [2] are a popular model for distributed systems, in which distributed
objects communicate through asynchronous message passing. When an actor
consumes a received message it can change its state, send new messages, and
create new actors. In [2], it is assumed that actor's actions are deterministic so
that *Generalized Actor Systems* (GASs) allow actors to perform internal actions
that exhibit no external behaviour but avoid infinite sequences of internal actions
without consuming received messages.

We formalize generalized actor systems as generalized actor rewrite theories
(GARwThs). These are object-oriented rewrite theories that (together with an
initial state) satisfy natural requirements. The distributed states of a GARwTh
(terms of sort `Configuration`) are multisets of objects (terms of sort `Object`)
and messages (terms of sort `Msg`). Multiset union is modeled by an associative
and commutative operator '`_ _`' (juxtaposition), where `null` is the empty multiset. The rewrite rules in a GARwTh have the form ('`[...]`' means optional)

$$\text{rl } [(\text{to } o \text{ [from } o'] : m)] \ < o : C \,|\, atts > \, => \, < o : C \,|\, atts' > msgs \, [\text{if } cond] \, .$$

where *msgs* is a (possibly the constant `null`) term of sort `Configuration` which,
applying the equations, reduces to a set of n messages ($n \geq 0$), each of which is a
term of sort `Msg`, of the form: $(\text{to } o_1 \text{ from } o\theta : mp_1) \cdots (\text{to } o_n \text{ from } o\theta : mp_n)$
where (i) θ is the matching substitution used when applying the rule; (ii) the
term mp_i is the message payload sent to the receiver o_i from the sender $o\theta$; and
(iii) messages cannot be sent to oneself, i.e., $o_1, \ldots, o_n$ are different from o.

Example 1. Consider the MQTT protocol. If we consider the initial step in which
a device wants to connect to the broker and the broker sends an acknowledgement
message back, described in Sect. 1.2, we can formalize it using the actor rules of
Fig. 1 (uppercase for variables and teletype font for constants).

The initial state `initconf` (of sort `Configuration`) of a generalized actor rewrite theory consists of a set of objects (with distinct names) and messages of the form:

$$< o_1 : C_1 \mid atts_1 > \cdots < o_n : C_n \mid atts_n >$$
$$(\text{to } o_{i_1}[\text{from } o_{l_1}] : mp_{i1}) \cdots (\text{to } o_{i_k}[\text{from } o_{l_k}] : mp_{i_k})$$

with $1 \leq i_1 < \cdots < i_k \leq n$, and $\{l_1, \ldots, l_k\} \subseteq \{1, \ldots, n\}$.

3   Dialects as Formal Patterns

In this section, we generalize the notion of *dialect*, which itself uses the notion of a *lingo*, i.e., an invertible message transformation. We make dialects *generic* on two dimensions: (i) *protocol generic*, so as to apply to a broad class of protocols *without changing the code of the original protocol*; and (ii) *lingo generic*, so that a dialect can, on the one hand, be instantiated with different lingos, and, on the other hand, may use *several lingos simultaneously* to achieve higher levels of obfuscation. This generic notion of dialect is an instance of the notion of a *formal pattern* [19], that is, a generic and formally specified solution to a computational problem that takes the form of a *transformation* of generalized actor rewrite theories (*GARwThs*). A dialect $\mathcal{D}$ is a theory transformation of the form: $\mathcal{P} \mapsto \mathcal{D}(\mathcal{P}, \vec{p})$ transforming the chosen protocol $\mathcal{P}$ into a new protocol $\mathcal{D}(\mathcal{P}, \vec{p})$ parametric on $\mathcal{P}$ and on additional parameters $\vec{p}$ (such as, e.g., the chosen lingos). $\mathcal{P}$ itself is not modified, rather, in the new protocol $\mathcal{D}(\mathcal{P}, \vec{p})$ each object of $\mathcal{P}$ is *wrapped* inside a corresponding *protocol meta-actor*, which obfuscates its communication with other objects of $\mathcal{P}$ without changing the original object's behavior.

Figure 2 describes our approach. It depicts two communicating objects of $\mathcal{P}$ (in purple) wrapped inside their dialect meta-objects (in blue). Messages are depicted as envelopes. The objects of $\mathcal{P}$ behave exactly as before: their meta-objects take care of obfuscating and de-obfuscating their messages. The lingo currently used takes the form of a pair of (parametric) functions (f, g), where f obfuscates messages and g puts them back in the format expected by participants in the original protocol $\mathcal{P}$. Our approach has two important advantages. First, it applies to unlimited classes of protocols without requiring any modifications in their code. Second, by using several lingos simultaneously, it can make the task of a malicious intruder much harder than if a single lingo were used.

3.1   Attacker Models

In this section we consider attacker models. One of the main applications of dialects is as a first line of defense. They are often proposed as low-cost means of preventing an attacker from even contacting its targets, so a target must be able to detect that the initial message from an attacker is not from a trusted party, and so refuse to respond. However, the authentication method used to protect that message does not have necessarily to be that strong, because the attacker itself may not yet be that strong. This is in contrast to the design of conventional

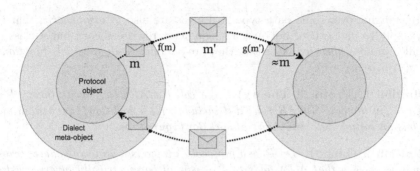

Fig. 2. Representation of dialects as meta-objects and their interactions.

cryptographic protocols, which use sophisticated encryption techniques, but do not always provide for protection of initial messages.

With this in mind, Ren et al. in [20] give two different attacker models. One is called the *off-path attacker*: an attacker that can send and receive traffic, but who has not seen any legitimate traffic between its targets. The other is called the *on-path attacker*. This attacker has all the capabilities of the off-path attacker, but is also able to observe legitimate traffic and may use its knowledge to try to break the dialect. This is the model most commonly used in work on protocol dialects, although it is usually assumed implicitly rather than stated outright. In addition, we propose a third, stronger attacker model, which we call the *active on-path attacker*, that is also able to block, redirect, and alter messages. However, it does not include attackers that compromise honest principals, since generally the goal of the dialect is to prevent the attacker from getting close enough to an honest principal to compromise it. In all three models, we assume that the goal of the attacker is to cause an honest principal to accept a message that was sent by the attacker: either a forged message, a replay, or (in the case in which timing is important) a delayed message. In addition, we assume that each attacker may have some information about the dialect, such as its design, and is able to recognize a well-formed packet from the original protocol.

We note, however, that these models may blur into each other. That is, an attacker may be able to see or interfere with some, but not all, traffic. This is especially important to take account of for lightweight security, where one needs to assure the maximum amount of security for a minimal amount of effort. We thus introduce the notion of an (m, n, t) attacker, that in time t can observe m messages and block n messages. A dialect is *secure against an (m, n, t) attacker* if the probability that it can send a forged, replayed, or delayed message that will be accepted by its intended recipient is low, where "low" is a design parameter.

3.2   Lingos

As described in Fig. 2, dialect wrappers use invertible *message transformations* called *lingos* (denoted f and g in the picture) to obfuscate a message m while in transit. These transformations are in fact *parametric*, with the parameter, say, a, ranging over some data type A. Lingos are also *theory-generic*, that is, they apply to and *extend* not just a single actor rewrite theory but a class of so-called *protocol theories*. Note that they are *parametrically inverse*[1] *functions*, i.e., $g(f(\vec{m}, a), a) = \vec{m}$.

Definition 1 (Protocol Theory).   *We call a GARwTh rewrite theory $\mathcal{P}$ a protocol (in the class PGARwTh) if it includes: (i) a sort* Configuration, *and (ii) has an initial state* initconf *of sort* Configuration.

Definition 2 (Lingo).   *Let $\mathcal{P}$ be a protocol. A lingo is a protocol-generic transformation Λ such that $\Lambda(\mathcal{P})$ adds to $\mathcal{P}$ a pair of parametrically inverse partial functions (f, g) using an extra parameter $a \in A$, $f : \mathrm{Msg}^n \times A \rightharpoonup \mathrm{Msg}^m$ and $g : \mathrm{Msg}^m \times A \rightharpoonup \mathrm{Msg}^n_\perp$ where the exact domain of definition of f (resp. g) is the set of pairs $(\vec{m}, a) \in \mathrm{Msg}^n \times A$ (resp. $(\vec{m'}, a) \in \mathrm{Msg}^m \times A)$ such that all messages in $\vec{m}$ (resp. in $\vec{m'}$) have the same sender and receiver, and results in a vector of m messages (resp. n messages) also agreeing on the same sender and the same receiver as those in $\vec{m}$ (resp. in $\vec{m'}$). We may also have $g(\vec{m'}, a) = \perp$ in some cases when the input $(\vec{m'}, a)$ can be detected to be illegal, that is, when there is no $(\vec{m}, a)$ such that $\vec{m'} = f(\vec{m}, a)$. A lingo Λ is protocol-generic, i.e., a theory transformation $\Lambda : \mathcal{P} \mapsto \Lambda(\mathcal{P})$ extending a protocol theory $\mathcal{P}$ into a richer protocol theory $\Lambda(\mathcal{P})$.*

Example 2. We consider three lingos. The first lingo is shuffle on bit strings: given a message m of a fixed length l, an initial position p, and an offset o such that $p + o \leq l$, the function $Sh_{p,o}$ exchanges bits p and $p + o$. For example, the lingo instance $Sh_{2,2}$ changes the bit string 10010 to 11000 with $p = 2$ and $o = 2$.

The second lingo is *exclusive-or* XOR on bit strings: given a message m of a fixed length l, and a key k of the same length, it performs $m \oplus k$. For example, $\oplus_{k_1}$ transforms 10010 into 11010 with $k_1 = 01000$. For both shuffling and exclusive-or, we use the same function to revert the change, because in both cases they are involutions, i.e., $Sh_{p,o}(Sh_{p,o}(m)) = m$ and $\oplus_k(\oplus_k(m)) = m$.

The third lingo is split: given a sequence of n messages $m_1, \dots, m_n$ of equal length, split them into m messages of equal length with $m > n$. For example, $Split_{2,4}$ receives 2 messages of 16 bits and returns 4 messages of 8 bits.

3.3   Dialects

Dialects are protocol transformations of the form $\mathcal{P} \mapsto \mathcal{D}(\mathcal{P}, \Lambda_1(\mathcal{P}), \dots, \Lambda_N(\mathcal{P}))$, where $\mathcal{D}(\mathcal{P}, \Lambda_1(\mathcal{P}), \dots, \Lambda_N(\mathcal{P}))$ endows $\mathcal{P}$ with N lingos, and wraps each protocol participant inside a *dialect meta-actor* that uses lingos $\Lambda_1(\mathcal{P}), \dots, \Lambda_{\bar{N}}(\mathcal{P})$ to obfuscate the communication between the honest protocol actors of $\mathcal{P}$.

Definition 3 (Protocol Dialect).   *Given a PGARwTh $\mathcal{P}$ and a sequence of lingos $\Lambda_1(\mathcal{P}), \dots, \Lambda_N(\mathcal{P})$, a protocol dialect $\mathcal{D}$ is a protocol transformation $\mathcal{D}$:*

---

[1] There are lingos that have an equivalence $g(f(\vec{m}, a), a) \equiv \vec{m}$ instead of equality. The generalization of lingos to allow for message equivalence will be developed elsewhere.

PGARwTh × Lingo^N ⇀ PGARwTh *of the form* $\mathcal{P} \mapsto \mathcal{D}(\mathcal{P}, \Lambda_1(\mathcal{P}), \dots, \Lambda_N(\mathcal{P}))$, *abbreviated to* $\mathcal{P} \mapsto \mathcal{D}_{\vec{\Lambda}}(\mathcal{P})$, *and such that: (i)* $\mathcal{D}_{\vec{\Lambda}}(\mathcal{P})$ *has a sort* `String` *with constant* `no-change`*; (ii)* $\mathcal{D}_{\vec{\Lambda}}(\mathcal{P})$ *has a family of* state view *functions* sv_i : Atts → A_i $1 \le i \le N$; *(iii)* $\mathcal{D}_{\vec{\Lambda}}(\mathcal{P})$ *has a tagging function* tag : Atts × Oid × Oid → String. $\mathcal{D}_{\vec{\Lambda}}(\mathcal{P})$ *adds a new actor class* DC *for each class* C *of the form*

class DC | *conf* : `Configuration`, *lingos* : `Map{String,` $[N]$ }

representing meta-objects *associated to each class* C *in the protocol theory* $\mathcal{P}$, *where each* CL ∈ `Map{String,` $[N]$ } *is a finite function mapping* tags *to* $[N] = \{1, \dots, N\}$. *In instances of this class, the object identifier of each protocol object will be reused by its meta-object, allowing a seamless and transparent integration.*

Furthermore, $\mathcal{D}_{\vec{\Lambda}}(\mathcal{P})$ *adds the new dialect meta-actor rules of Fig. 3 to the meta-object, where: (i) the rule labeled* out *processes messages produced by the wrapped protocol; (ii) the rule labeled* buff *collects incoming messages; (iii) the rule labeled* in *transforms some gathered incoming messages and gives them to the protocol; (iv) predicates* in *and* out *identify, respectively, received and sent messages; (v) predicate* classifyMs *identifies how many messages are necessary for each lingo; (vi) predicate* update *allows the possibility of changing a meta-object's attributes; and (vii) predicate* choice *allows the possibility of changing a meta-object's mapping for lingos. For static dialects (see Fig. 4),* choice *is the identity function. Also, let* $i(\mathcal{D})$ *and* $e(\mathcal{D})$ *be ingress and egress arities of the current lingo based on the direction of communication.*

Example 3. We first consider a dialect secure against an on-path, but passive, attacker, that uses the XOR lingo. Since the attacker is on-path, it can view the messages, and if multiple messages are exclusive-ored with the same string, the attacker may be able to figure out the string and forge a message. We introduce a deterministic synchronized way to update dialect parameters, which is described in Appendix B.

4 Dialects as Moving Targets

Every dialect should be a moving target. But some dialects move faster than others. A *static* dialect is one where the `lingos` attribute of the dialect meta-object never changes. It is still a moving target, because the *parameters* of the fixed lingo or lingos used are always changing. Faster moving targets can be achieved by means of what we call *dynamic* dialects, where the `lingos` attribute of the dialect meta-object changes dynamically. This frequent change of the communication format imposes a serious burden on intruders, because even if a specific lingo is successfully broken, the dialect will change this lingo after some time, forcing the intruder to start all over again its malicious efforts. As detailed further in Appendix B, one can obtain desirable security outcomes when lingos change faster than the time an intruder takes in correctly guessing and reverting each lingo transformation.

crl [out] : $< o_1 : DC \,|\, \text{conf} : (< o_1 : C \,|\, atts > M_{out} \, M_{in}), \text{lingos} : CL, \, atts' >$
   $\Rightarrow \; < o_1 : DC \,|\, \text{conf} : (< o_1 : C \,|\, atts > \, (M_{out} \setminus \text{to-multiset}(M_{selected})) \, M_{in}),$
          $\text{lingos} : \text{choice}(CL, atts'), \, \text{update}(atts') > f_i(M_{selected}, \text{sv}_i(atts'))$
   $\text{if } \text{in}(o_1, M_{in}) \text{ and } \text{out}(o_1, M_{out}) \wedge (M_{selected}, i) \cup S := \text{classifyMs}(M_{out}, CL) \, .$

rl [buff] : $< o_1 : DC \,|\, \text{in-buffer} : M_{in}, atts' > \, (\text{from } o_2 \text{ to } o_1 : m)$
   $\Rightarrow \; < o_1 : DC \,|\, \text{in-buffer} : (M_{in} \cup (\text{from } o_2 \text{ to } o_1 : m)), atts' > \, .$

crl [in] : $< o_1 : DC \,|\, \text{conf} : (< o_1 : C \,|\, atts >), \text{in-buffer} : M_{in}, \text{lingos} : CL, \, atts' >$
   $\Rightarrow \; < o_1 : DC \,|\, \text{conf} : (< o_1 : C \,|\, atts > \, (\text{if } g_i(M_{selected}, \text{sv}_i(atts')) \neq \bot$
                              $\text{then } g_i(M_{selected}, \text{sv}_i(atts')) \text{ else } \emptyset \text{ fi})),$
          $\text{in-buffer} : (M_{in} \setminus \text{to-multiset}(M_{selected})),$
          $\text{lingos} : \text{choice}(CL, atts'), \, \text{update}(atts') >$
   $\text{if } (M_{selected}, i) \cup S := \text{classifyMs}(M_{in}, CL) \, .$

Fig. 3. Dialect Meta-Actor Rules

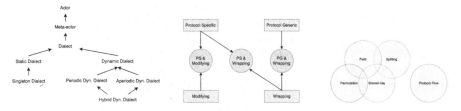

Fig. 4. Hierarchy of object classes   **Fig. 5.** Dialect taxonomy   **Fig. 6.** Lingo taxonomy

In Fig. 4 we present a subclass hierarchy of dialects as either static or dynamic. *Singleton dialects* are static dialects with a single lingo where the tagging function may return only two elements: change (apply the lingo) and no-change (leave message unchanged). To the best of our knowledge, all dialects proposed in the literature so far are singleton dialects. Dynamic dialects can be either *periodic*, when all dialect meta-objects simultaneously change their lingos attribute after a fixed time period, *aperiodic* if the lingos attribute is changed in a different manner, or *hybrid* if have periodic and aperiodic features.

Definition 4 (Dynamic Protocol Dialect). *A dynamic protocol dialect $\mathcal{D}$ is a protocol dialect such that $\mathcal{D}_{\vec{A}}(\mathcal{P})$ is as described in Definition 3 and includes the definition of a choice function capable of generating new mappings CL : $[String \rightarrow [N]]$, with typing choice : $[String \rightarrow [N]] \times \text{Atts} \rightarrow [String \rightarrow [N]]$ and such that it is not the identity (i.e., first projection) function. The transformation adds new actor subclasses of the form "*class DynDC $|$ previous-lingos : PL*" and "*subclass DynDC $<$ DC*" where the previous-lingos attribute holds the previous value of* lingos.

4.1   Periodic and Aperiodic Dialects

Each dialect defines an algorithm deciding *when* and *how* to choose a new mapping CL of current lingos. The choice function represents this algorithm: it uses contextual information about the current state to decide which lingos are to be considered current in the upcoming phase.

We distinguish two kinds of dialects according to the nature of this algorithm:

(i) **Periodic** dialects include a sort Time representing time and change their current lingos every time a predefined period T elapses, without taking into account the past message history. At the meta-object level, periodic dialects can be represented by adding a new subclass $PDynDC < DynDC$ with attributes **period:** T and **timer:** t such that t is the number of time units elapsed and a phase change occurs when $t \equiv 0 \mod T$:

$$\texttt{crl} < o_1 : DC \,|\, \texttt{timer}: t, \ \texttt{period}: T, \ \texttt{lingos}: CL, \ atts' >$$
$$\texttt{=>} < o_1 : DC \,|\, \texttt{timer}: 0, \ \texttt{period}: T, \ \texttt{lingos}: CL', \ atts' >$$
$$\texttt{if } t \geq T \ \wedge \ CL' \texttt{:=} \ \text{choice}(CL, atts') \ .$$

The choice function can then observe these attributes to determine phase changes. More complex periodic dialects can be defined, for instance, dialects where the period keeps changing as time phases advance.

(ii) **Aperiodic** dialects change their current lingos depending on the history of previous messages rather than depending on time. This is a new subclass $ADynDC < DynDC$ with an attribute **history:** $\tilde{M}$, which is then observed by the choice function.

This classification is not exclusive: our framework also supports *hybrid* dialects that take into account both the current time and the past history of messages to run more sophisticated lingo choice algorithms. Hybrid dialects belong to a subclass $HDynDC$ such that $HDynDC < PDynDC \ \wedge \ HDynDC < ADynDC$.

Periodic Dialects make an essential use of time. This raises a need for *time synchronization*. Protocol objects may run in different distributed devices, so that disagreements on a common view of time could lead to divergent and incompatible lingo transformations. We assume (but leave implicit) that in a periodic dialect all dialect meta-objects share a canonical view of time and perform actions in lockstep by synchronizing their local clocks (modulo a clock skew) before running the protocol, and remain synchronized during the entire duration of the communication process by means of well-known time synchronization protocols such as NTP [16] or its secure version NTS [8]. These assumptions ensure that all meta-objects will change their current lingos at approximately the same time when their timer for a phase expires using the rule above.

We can illustrate the behavior of a periodic dialect with the example in Fig. 7. The vertical axis represents time advancing from top to bottom. During a *time phase*, all participants of a particular modified protocol share the same set of *current lingos*. At *phase boundaries*, the phase changes, and then dialects use

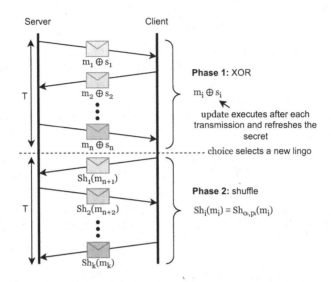

Fig. 7. Example sequence of two principals using a dynamic periodic dialect.

their choice function to agree on a new set of current lingos, as depicted by the dashed horizontal line. In the figure, during the first phase XOR is the current lingo, and shuffle becomes the current lingo during the second phase. Note that during each phase parameters $s_1, s_2, \ldots$ for XOR, resp. $\{o_1, p_1\}, \{o_2, p_2\}, \ldots$ for shuffle, change all the time in a synchronized fashion between server and clients.

The server and the client remain *synchronized* and change their current lingo sequence in lockstep because their dialect meta-objects: (i) share a common fixed period T, (ii) their local clocks are synchronized, and (iii) they both agree on the next lingo to use after XOR, namely shuffle. More generally, periodic dialect meta-objects must agree on their choice function and initial parameters, and, up to small skew, on time. Due to both clock skew and network delays, when a timer expires and all meta-objects choose the new current lingos there will still may be messages in transit transformed with the previous lingos. This means that *for a while*, the meta-objects must keep in their state both the current lingos and the previous ones, since both may be needed for different messages. To handle issues arising in phase boundaries and manage this state, dialects implement *phase change strategies*, as explained in more detail in Appendix A.

Aperiodic Dialects do not need a shared view of time or other time-related attributes. They instead rely on the history: $\vec{M}$ attribute, which is taken into account to change lingos with the choice function. In this way, meta-objects agree on a shared current lingo, not based on time, but on their message histories.

Example 4. We describe an aperiodic dialect for MQTT securing it against an active on-path attacker. During the connection phase, we protect the CON-NECT and CONNACK messages using some selection of meticulous, judiciously

selected lingos that do *not* modify the contained UUID. After this initial nego-
tiation is finished, we change the lingo configuration to protect future messages
with, for example, `shuffle` or `XOR`. We use the exchanged UUID as input to a
keyed pseudo-random function, where the key is shared among all principals, in
order to generate lingo parameters that are fresh yet identical on both sides.

5   Taxonomies of Dialects and Lingos

We propose an open-ended taxonomy of the dialects and a taxonomy of lingos
that have appeared in the literature. These taxonomies can help in understanding
and using various dialects and lingos, and are orthogonal to the class hierarchy
presented in Fig. 4.

5.1   A Taxonomy of Dialects

We set forth the different categories that dialects fall into and their relationships.
A general view of the characteristics and their relations is shown in Fig. 5.

- **Protocol Specific:** These are dialects that are designed and implemented
  to work for one, and only one, specific protocol.
- **Protocol Generic:** These dialects can be applied to classes of protocols
  meeting some requirements. That is, the PGARwTh given to $\mathcal{D}$ and to each
  Λ is not a fixed $\mathcal{P}$, but belongs to a class of protocols.
- **Protocol Modifying:** The dialect directly modifies the original protocol
  object, instead of exporting it to another layer. The modifications can be at
  the binary level, or changes can be made to the configuration.
- **Protocol Wrapping:** A dialect is characterized as wrapping when it acts as
  a layer for each original object, encapsulating it without modifying it.

We can think of protocol genericity as defining a partial order relation; e.g.
one dialect is more protocol generic than another if the first dialect applies to
more protocols. Our interest is in developing protocol wrapping dialects that are
as protocol generic as possible. Not only are such dialects easier to deploy, but
they make operations such as *dialect composition* possible (see Sect. 6).

5.2   A Taxonomy of Lingos

Since prior work on dialects has focused on *singleton* dialects using a single
lingo, this taxonomy summarizes prior work on dialects by grouping the various
example dialects in families of lingos. We classify lingos into five classes, but
combinations between them are possible as depicted in Fig. 6.

- **Permutation**: This lingo group originates in [17], where a *Shuffling* lingo is
  proposed. The basis of this transformation is to divide the message into several
  fragments and swap them to generate a new message. Using our framework,
  Shuffling, originally applied in a protocol modifying manner on FTP and

MQTT, is turned into a protocol generic lingo. The lingo is parametric over a seed, so a new permutation is obtained with each seed. In this family of lingos some instances defining the permutation are *involutions*, depending on the defined permutation. This means f and g are the same and the property $f(f(m)) = m = g(g(m))$ holds for any message m, a desirable property since it makes lingos easier to generate and parameterize. Another example of a shuffling lingo appears in [20], where the packet header fields are permuted.

- **Splitting**: The origin of this kind of lingos also comes from the work in [17], where the authors propose a *Splitting* packet lingo. The transformation of this kind of lingo is to split a message into several different messages, each containing a part of the original message. To recover the original messages one needs to gather the fragments and recompose them. The original *Splitting* can be lifted into a generic lingo to work over any protocol in which messages are coded as bit strings.
- **Protocol Flow**: This group of lingos emerges from [9], where the authors propose, among others, 15 lingos over FTP that modify the expected flow of the session by inserting custom messages. Custom messages will only be able to be processed by dialects that use the proper lingo. Whether this lingo can be made protocol generic may depend on how much knowledge of the underlying protocol is needed to create the custom messages.
- **Cryptographic**: These lingos involve the application of cryptographic functions to messages, e.g. a Hash Message Authentication Code (HMAC), as shown in [21], a keyed pseudo-random number generator, or *exclusive-or*ing with a pseudo-random string.
- **Unused and Random Fields**: This family comes from [21]. It works by using a field to store information the other end of the communication can verify. It is less protocol generic than lingos that transform an entire packet, but only the location and size of the field need to be specified.

6   Dialect Composition Operations

Our formal framework provides *dialect composition operations* to generate new, more sophisticated dialects out of simpler ones. If the simpler dialects are judiciously chosen, the resulting compositions may severely hamper the task of an intruder attempting to understand and reverse the actions performed by the ever-changing protocol mutations of the dialect composition.

Recall that a dialect applies one or more lingos $\Lambda_1, \ldots, \Lambda_n$, with each Λ_i representing a pair of (parametric) protocol transformation of arbitrary complexity, over a message sequence. There are two degrees of freedom enabling a dialect to become more complex: (i) increasing the complexity of the transformation functions further obfuscates the exact effects that each lingo Λ_i will exert on messages; and (ii) increasing the number of lingo choices available when processing sequences of messages are likely to hinder the potential prediction attempts of an intruder trying to determine which particular lingo Λ_i has been selected

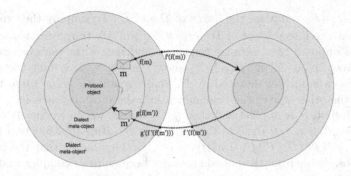

Fig. 8. Meta-object representation of the vertical composition of two dialects.

for a particular message sequence. We distinguish two kinds of dialect composition: (a) *vertical* composition increases both degrees of freedom (i)–(ii); and (b) *horizontal* composition increases degree of freedom (ii).

6.1 Vertical Composition

The vertical composition of two dialects combines the transformations expressed in their lingos in a function composition manner. From a meta-object point of view, vertical composition results in wrapping a second dialect meta-object on top of a first dialect meta-object that itself wraps an original protocol object, stacking them (see Fig. 8) and thus further modifying the protocol messages.

Let $\vec{\Lambda}$ abbreviate a sequence of lingos $\Lambda_1, \ldots, \Lambda_N$. Then, $\vec{\Lambda}(\mathcal{P})$ abbreviates the corresponding sequence of lingo instantiations $\Lambda_1(\mathcal{P}), \ldots, \Lambda_N(\mathcal{P})$. Likewise, $\mathcal{D}_{\vec{\Lambda}} : \mathrm{PGARwTh} \rightharpoonup \mathrm{PGARwTh}$ abbreviates the partial function applying $\mathcal{D}$ with chosen sequence $\vec{\Lambda}$ of lingos as input parameters, i.e., $\mathcal{D}_{\vec{\Lambda}}(\mathcal{P}) = \mathcal{D}(\mathcal{P}, \vec{\Lambda}(\mathcal{P}))$.

Definition 5. *Let $\mathcal{D}_{\vec{\Lambda}}$, resp. $\mathcal{D}'_{\vec{\Lambda}'}$, be two dialects with chosen lingo sequences $\vec{\Lambda}$, resp. $\vec{\Lambda}'$, and let $\mathcal{P}$ be a protocol. The vertical composition of $\mathcal{D}'_{\vec{\Lambda}'}$ over $\mathcal{D}_{\vec{\Lambda}}$, denoted $\mathcal{D}'_{\vec{\Lambda}'} \circ \mathcal{D}_{\vec{\Lambda}}$, is a PGARwTh transformation defined as $(\mathcal{D}'_{\vec{\Lambda}'} \circ \mathcal{D}_{\vec{\Lambda}})(\mathcal{P}) = \mathcal{D}'(\mathcal{D}(\mathcal{P}, \vec{\Lambda}(\mathcal{P})), \vec{\Lambda}'(\mathcal{D}(\mathcal{P}, \vec{\Lambda}(\mathcal{P}))))$, where for $1 \leq i \leq N$ the recursion $r_{i+1} = \frac{e(\mathcal{D}_i)}{i(\mathcal{D}_i)} r_i \in \mathbb{N}$, with $r_1 = 1$ and $i(\mathcal{D}_1) = 1$. This composition has an implicit notion of protocol compatibility, since it is defined if and only if $\mathcal{P} \in \mathcal{D}_{\vec{\Lambda}}^{-1}(\mathrm{dom}(\mathcal{D}'_{\vec{\Lambda}'}))$.*

Example 5. Consider the composition of the XOR and shuffle dialects. Neither of these is secure against an active on-path adversary: XOR because an attacker who has knowledge about the underlying message can alter it in a predictable way by flipping bits, and shuffle because the attacker can ultimately guess the parameters by observing enough traffic. In either case, the active attacker can then replace a message with an altered one. However, when the two are composed, the XOR lingo hides the results of shuffling, and because the attacker does not know how the packet is shuffled, it can no longer predict the results of flipping bits. For more details, see Appendix B.

$(\mathcal{D}'_{\vec{\Lambda}'} \circ \mathcal{D}_{\vec{\Lambda}})(\mathcal{P})$ *composes* the lingos of $\mathcal{D}$ and $\mathcal{D}'$. To simplify the exposition, assume that the lingos (f, g) of $\mathcal{D}$, resp. (f', g') of $\mathcal{D}'$, transform a single message m, as opposed to a message sequence, and ignore the parameters $a \in A$ of (f, g), resp. $a' \in A'$ of (f', g'). As shown in Fig. 8, m is first transformed by f and then is further mutated by f', finally sending $f'(f(m))$ into the network. On the other side of the communication, the *incoming* message $f'(f(m))$ is reversed: first, g' is applied and then g. Of course, we can vertically compose not just two, but $n \geq 2$ dialects this way, thus resulting in a function pipeline $g(g'(g''(\ldots g'^n(f'^n(\ldots (f''(f'(f(m)))) \ldots)) \ldots)))$. This means that the transformations observable from the outside network become more complex and harder to reverse. Furthermore, the number of possible transformations grows geometrically. Just for two single-lingo dialects $\mathcal{D}$, resp. $\mathcal{D}'$, with chosen lingo Λ, resp. Λ', having parameter set A, resp. A', we ideally get $|A| \cdot |A'|$ composed transformations. The dialects to compose must be chosen judiciously, as not all vertical compositions have the same properties; see Example 6.

Example 6. Recall the lingos `shuffle` and `split` from Example 2. Vertical composition may cause the sequential application of `split` and then `shuffle`, which illustrates how the union of certain security measures can result in unintended interactions that could become detrimental.

The obfuscation properties provided by `shuffle` are based on the notion that permuting the bits of a packet introduces entropy that must be actively detected and reversed by an intruder by, e.g., brute-forcing all possible permutations until a protocol-compliant message can be discerned. This entropy is a rapidly increasing function of message length: for a message of $n \in \mathbb{N}$ bits, the number of possible permutations is its factorial, $n!$. On the other hand, `split` divides a packet of n bits into k chunks of approximately n/k bits.

Consider the case where each packet is first split and then each one of its chunks of n/k bits is shuffled independently. As k grows, n/k approaches zero, and so does the number of available permutations $n!$. Thus, applying `split` *before* `shuffle` actively negates the security benefits provided by shuffling.

6.2 Horizontal Composition

Horizontal composition takes the lingos chosen by two dialects, merges them together, and uses a pseudo-random function to choose a lingo in one of the two dialects. This operation can be iterated to horizontally compose $n \geq 2$ dialects.

Definition 6. *Let $\mathcal{P}$ be a protocol. Let $\mathcal{D}_{\vec{\Lambda}}$, resp. $\mathcal{D}'_{\vec{\Lambda}'}$, be two dialects with chosen lingo sequences $\vec{\Lambda}$, resp. $\vec{\Lambda}'$. The horizontal composition of $\mathcal{D}_{\vec{\Lambda}}$ and $\mathcal{D}'_{\vec{\Lambda}'}$ with a bias $\sigma \in (0, 1)$, denoted $\mathcal{D}_{\vec{\Lambda}} +_\sigma \mathcal{D}'_{\vec{\Lambda}'}$, is defined as $(\mathcal{D}_{\vec{\Lambda}} +_\sigma \mathcal{D}'_{\vec{\Lambda}'})(\mathcal{P}) = \mathcal{D}''_{\vec{\Lambda},\vec{\Lambda}'}(\mathcal{P}, (\vec{\Lambda}, \vec{\Lambda}')(\mathcal{P}))$ where the tagging function tag'' of $\mathcal{D}''_{\vec{\Lambda},\vec{\Lambda}'}$ chooses either the tag (resulting from the tagging function) of $\mathcal{D}_{\vec{\Lambda}}$ or that of $\mathcal{D}'_{\vec{\Lambda}'}$ (appending, respectively, 0 or 1 at the end of the tag), with a bias σ, with $\mathrm{rand}(a, b)$ a pseudo-random function uniformly choosing a value in the interval (a, b):*

tag'' : Atts × Oid × Oid → String

tag'' : $(a, o_1, o_2) \mapsto$ **if** $rand(0, 1) \leq \sigma$ **then** $tag(a, o_1, o_2).0$ **else** $tag'(a, o_1, o_2).1$

where _._ *denotes string concatenation. Since all the meta-objects will use the same pseudo-random number generator with the same seed, they will all get the same toss of the σ-biased coin for choosing between tag or tag'. The choice function choice'' of $\mathcal{D}''_{\vec{\Lambda}, \vec{\Lambda}'}$ combines choice and choice' as follows (where n (resp. m) is the length of $\vec{\Lambda}$ (resp. $\vec{\Lambda}'$), so that $n + m$ is the length of $\vec{\Lambda}, \vec{\Lambda}'$):*

$$choice'' : Map\{String, [n + m]\} \times Atts \to Map\{String, [n + m]\}$$
$$choice'' : (CL, a) \mapsto \lambda l. \textbf{ if } last(l) = 0 \textbf{ then } choice(CL, a)(prior(l))$$
$$\textbf{else } choice'(CL, a)(prior(l)) + n$$

where the function $last(l)$ (resp. $prior(l)$) returns the last element of list l (resp. the prefix of l before the last element). That is, choice'' *acts as* choice *when the tag is indexed by 0, and as* choice' *increased by n (to choose a lingo in $\vec{\Lambda}'$) when the tag is indexed by 1.*

When horizontally composing two dialects $\mathcal{D}$ and $\mathcal{D}'$, dialect designers can favor $\mathcal{D}$ over $\mathcal{D}'$ (or vice versa) by using the bias σ in the pseudo-random tossing a σ-biased coin to choose between $\mathcal{D}$ and $\mathcal{D}'$ to determine the tag of each message.

7 Concluding Remarks

We have proposed modeling dialects as generic *formal patterns*, which transform protocols without changing their code. This is a vast generalization of the various dialects appeared so far in the literature that provides new methods to make dialects harder to break, e.g., by using *dynamic* dialects, and dialect *compositions*. We have also studied three classes of *attacker models* and how different dialects and dialect compositions can protect against them. We have also proposed lingo and dialect *taxonomies* to help in conceptually clarifying the various notions of dialect. These new notions are not just theoretical: all of them are the outcome of extensive experimentation with prior and new lingos and dialects in Maude.

This work advances or opens up several new research directions: (1) The new ideas on transactions and phase change synchronization led us to develop three new generic strategies (stalling, dual conformity and pairwise coordination). (2) Formal reasoning about dialects now becomes both possible (by having formal specifications), and easier to achieve by amortizing the verification effort thanks to protocol genericity. For example, preservation of protocol properties by their dialect extensions, and quantitative analysis of dialects by means of statistical model checking along the lines of [14] are two promising future topics. (3) The work on *dialect attacker models* has been substantially advanced, and if formalized further, could be used to help reason about quantitative aspects of security.

A   Handling Phase Boundaries

Under certain protocols and dialect combinations, changing the phase in the middle of some specific message sequences may cause the other end to not be able to successfully recover the semantics of the original protocol. This is illustrated in Example 7. In such cases, dialects must hold back and delay the next phase boundary until it is safe to change. We call such uninterruptible, change-sensitive message sequences *transactions*.

Example 7. Consider the lingos `shuffle` and `split` from Example 2. Let o and o' be two objects running the protocol $\mathcal{D}(\mathcal{P}, \texttt{shuffle}(\mathcal{P}), \texttt{split}(\mathcal{P}))$. At some moment, o sends a message m to o' using the lingo `split`, i.e., o sends $f_{\texttt{Split}}(m) = m_1, \ldots, m_k$. On the other side, o' receives the first fragment m_1. Because o and o' are synchronized, o' is aware that m_1 is a fragment of a bigger payload, and waits for $m_2, \ldots, m_k$.

Now, if o and o' change phase before m_2 can reach o', processing m_2 will fail as the context of `shuffle` has been lost. In this example, the phase has changed at an unfortunate time instant. We say $m_1, \ldots, m_k$ form a *transaction*. Both o and o' must wait until m_k has been transmitted before changing phase.

All dynamic dialects have the responsibility of correctly handling transactions using a *phase change strategy*. In aperiodic dialects, the choice function must consider a rich enough message history and determine transaction boundaries. In the periodic case, we propose a default strategy called *dual conformity* which considers transactions that are finite and have a static upper bound of n messages. Let $\tau \ll T$ be maximum trip time of one message. We define a *conflict time* $T_{\sharp}$ such that $T \gg T_{\sharp} > 2n\tau$. A *lax period* takes place during $T_{\sharp}$ before each phase change: participants assign $PL := CL$, choose new current lingos CL and use CL for new *outgoing* messages, but accept both CL and PL for *incoming* messages. When the phase finally changes, messages using PL will be rejected. This approach requires disambiguation of the lingo of incoming messages, which can be achieved by appending one bit to messages that is flipped every phase.

B   Dialects Secure Against Different Types of Attackers

We consider two classes of dialects.

Time-Synchronized Lingo Parameters. For the $(0, 0, t)$ attacker it is enough to apply a dialect to the CONNECT and CONNACK packets used to set up connections, since an attacker cannot hijack a connection once it is set up. Ren et al. [20] also point out that the same dialect parameters can be used in this case, i.e. in terms of our model, the update function can be constant. However, it is possible that dialect parameters may be leaked by some other means than direct observation, so it is unsafe to assume a *completely* off-path attacker. One defense against such potential leakage, suggested in [20], is to periodically change the lingo parameters.

State-Synchronized Lingo Parameters. For the $(m, 0, t)$ attacker, as the frequency with which lingo parameters need to be changed becomes higher, synchronization of updates becomes more difficult. This is particularly the case in which lingo parameters need to be changed more often, since all packets need to be protected in order to prevent connection hijacking. In that case one can update lingo parameters continually, relying on local state information for synchronization. A sender and a receiver will start out with some shared local state. Each time a sender sends or a receiver receives it will update its state and use it to produce the next lingo parameters. This requires a somewhat more complex infrastructure, since care must be taken so that the probability of any two pairs of communicating principals using the same lingo is low. Otherwise one runs the risk of doubling the amount of instances of a lingo an attacker could observe in a given amount of time.

We are left with one more problem to solve. The lingo parameters used for the connection message sent by the client are not necessarily bound to any particular time, and by definition cannot be bound to any previous parameters used by the client. Thus the dialect is subject to a replay attack in which, for example, the attacker sends an old CONNECT message which could be used for denial of service attacks, since it forces the broker to keep the connection open until it times out. One solution is to use a timestamp taken when the CONNECT message is constructed to build the parameters. MQTT does not itself use timestamps, so we use an unused header field in the CONNECT message, as might, e.g., be supplied by implementations such as Mosquitto [13].

We use a keyed pseudo-random function (prf) that can compute arbitrarily long output from arbitrarily long input. It should be possible to compute the prf incrementally, block by block, so its output does not need to be stored far in advance. Any lightweight cryptosystem with these properties would work, e.g. the prf in the Ascon family of lightweight cryptographic functions [6], recently chosen for standardization for NIST [1]. We require that all meta-objects share the key, the prf, a lingo, and a permutation function pm. We also assume for concreteness that the XOR lingo is used.

First, the client meta-object computes a unique UUID for itself, using its local timestamp and its MAC address, and stores it in an unused header field. The first ℓ bits of the prf are computed using the UIUD (concatenated with itself multiple times if necessary) as input, where ℓ is the number of bits in the CONNECT packet, minus the number of bits in the UUID. The CONNECT packet, *except for the UUID*, is exclusive-ored with the ℓ-bit string.

The broker meta-object receiving the CONNECT packet first checks that the UUID timestamp is current. If not, the packet is dropped. It then uses the UUID, prf, and key to compute the prf output, exclusive-ors it with the CONNECT packet (except for the UUID), and passes it to the broker, which returns a CON-NACK packet if it is well-formed. The broker meta-object then applies pm to the UUID, using the result as input to the prf. The first ℓ' bits produced are used to compute a string that is exclusive-ored with the CONNACK packet. Lingos are applied to the subsequent packets as well, using subsequent bits generated by the prf to choose lingos to the remaining packets. In this case we also extend the input length, e.g. by concatenating the UUID with itself as needed.

For the $(m, 0, t)$ attacker, this is enough. The attacker can't replay an old UUID, because it would fail the timestamp check. Nor could it create a new UUID that would be accepted by the meta-object.

It is not enough, however, for the (m, n, t) attacker. The shuffle lingo, especially if the number of the possible shuffles is small, is subject to an attack in which the attacker learns all possible shuffles through observation, intercepts a packet, figures out which shuffle was applied, and substitutes a new shuffled packet. The XOR lingo is malleable, so that an attacker that guesses any of the underlying plaintext can alter it as desired by flipping the appropriate bits and substituting the result for the original packet.

Instead, we use the vertical composition of shuffle and XOR. In this case, the attacker can no longer tell what shuffle is being used because it is hidden by XOR and, because it doesn't know what shuffle is being used, it no longer can predict the results of flipping bits.

References

1. Lightweight cryptography standardization process: NIST selects Ascon. NIST Computer Security Resource Center (2023). https://csrc.nist.gov/News/2023/lightweight-cryptography-nist-selects-ascon
2. Agha, G.: Actors: A Model of Concurrent Computation in Distributed Systems. MIT Press, Cambridge, MA, USA (1986)
3. Clavel, M., et al.: Maude manual (version 3.3.1). Tech. rep., SRI International (2023). http://maude.cs.illinois.edu
4. Clavel, M., et al.: All About Maude - A High-Performance Logical Framework. LNCS, vol. 4350. Springer, Heidelberg (2007). https://doi.org/10.1007/978-3-540-71999-1
5. Day, J., Zimmermann, H.: The OSI reference model. Proc. IEEE **71**(12), 1334–1340 (1983). https://doi.org/10.1109/PROC.1983.12775
6. Dobraunig, C., Eichlseder, M., Mendel, F., Schläffer, M.: Ascon PRF, MAC, and short-input MAC. Cryptol. ePrint Archive, Paper 2021/1574 (2021). https://eprint.iacr.org/2021/1574
7. Durán, F., et al.: Programming and symbolic computation in Maude. J. Log. Algebraic Methods Program. 110 (2020). https://doi.org/10.1016/j.jlamp.2019.100497
8. Franke, D.F., Sibold, D., Teichel, K., Dansarie, M., Sundblad, R.: Network Time Security for the Network Time Protocol. RFC 8915 (2020). https://doi.org/10.17487/RFC8915, https://www.rfc-editor.org/info/rfc8915
9. Gogineni, K., Mei, Y., Venkataramani, G., Lan, T.: Can you speak my dialect?: a framework for server authentication using communication protocol dialects (2022). https://arxiv.org/abs/2202.00500, publisher: arXiv Version Number: 1
10. Gogineni, K., Mei, Y., Venkataramani, G., Lan, T.: Verify-Pro: a framework for server authentication using communication protocol dialects. In: MILCOM 2022–2022 IEEE Military Communications Conference (MILCOM), pp. 450–457. IEEE (2022)
11. Hron, M.: Are smart homes vulnerable to hacking (2018). https://blog.avast.com/mqtt-vulnerabilities-hacking-smart-homes

12. Hunkeler, U., Truong, H.L., Stanford-Clark, A.J.: MQTT-S - a publish/subscribe protocol for wireless sensor networks. In: Choi, S., Kurose, J., Ramamritham, K. (eds.) COMSWARE, pp. 791–798. IEEE (2008). http://dblp.uni-trier.de/db/conf/comsware/comsware2008.html#HunkelerTS08

13. Light, R.A.: Mosquitto: server and client implementation of the MQTT protocol. J. Open Source Softw. **2**(13), 265 (2017)

14. Liu, S., Meseguer, J., Ölveczky, P.C., Zhang, M., Basin, D.A.: Bridging the semantic gap between qualitative and quantitative models of distributed systems. Proc. ACM Program. Lang. **6**(OOPSLA2), 315–344 (2022). https://doi.org/10.1145/3563299

15. Lukaszewski, D., Xie, G.G.: Towards software defined layer 4.5 customization. In: 2022 IEEE 8th International Conference on Network Softwarization (NetSoft), pp. 330–338. IEEE (2022)

16. Martin, J., Burbank, J., Kasch, W., Mills, P.D.L.: Network Time Protocol Version 4: protocol and algorithms specification. RFC 5905 (2010). https://doi.org/10.17487/RFC5905, https://www.rfc-editor.org/info/rfc5905

17. Mei, Y., Gogineni, K., Lan, T., Venkataramani, G.: MPD: moving target defense through communication protocol dialects. In: Garcia-Alfaro, J., Li, S., Poovendran, R., Debar, H., Yung, M.(eds.) Security and Privacy in Communication Networks, vol. 398, pp. 100–119. Springer International Publishing, Cham (2021). https://doi.org/10.1007/978-3-030-90019-9_6, series Title: Lecture Notes of the Institute for Computer Sciences, Social Informatics and Telecommunications Engineering

18. Meseguer, J.: Conditional rewriting logic as a united model of concurrency. Theor. Comput. Sci. **96**(1), 73–155 (1992). https://doi.org/10.1016/0304-3975(92)90182-F

19. Meseguer, J.: Taming distributed system complexity through formal patterns. Sci. Comput. Program. **83**, 3–34 (2014). https://doi.org/10.1016/j.scico.2013.07.004

20. Ren, T., Williams, R., Ganguly, S., De Carli, L., Lu, L.: Breaking embedded software homogeneity with protocol mutations. In: Security and Privacy in Communication Networks: 18th EAI International Conference, SecureComm 2022, Virtual Event, October 2022, Proceedings, pp. 770–790. Springer (2023). https://doi.org/10.1007/978-3-031-25538-0_40

21. Sjoholmsierchio, M.: Software-Defined Networks: protocol dialects. Master's thesis, Naval Postgraduate School, Monterey, California, USA (2019). http://hdl.handle.net/10945/64066

22. Sjoholmsierchio, M., Hale, B., Lukaszewski, D., Xie, G.: Strengthening SDN Security: protocol dialecting and downgrade attacks. In: 2021 IEEE 7th International Conference on Network Softwarization (NetSoft), pp. 321–329. IEEE, Tokyo, Japan (2021). https://doi.org/10.1109/NetSoft51509.2021.9492614, https://ieeexplore.ieee.org/document/9492614/

ResolFuzz: Differential Fuzzing of DNS Resolvers

Jonas Bushart[(✉)] and Christian Rossow[(✉)]

CISPA Helmholtz Center for Information Security, Saarbrücken, Germany
{jonas.bushart,rossow}@cispa.de

Abstract. This paper identifies and analyzes vulnerabilities in the DNS infrastructure, with particular focus on recursive DNS resolvers. We aim to identify semantic bugs that could lead to incorrect resolver responses, introducing risks to the internet's critical infrastructure. To achieve this, we introduce ResolFuzz, a mutation-based fuzzer to search for semantic differences across DNS resolver implementations. ResolFuzz combines differential analysis with a rule-based mechanism to distinguish between benign differences and potential threats. We evaluate our prototype on seven resolvers and uncover multiple security vulnerabilities, including inaccuracies in resolver responses and possible amplification issues in PowerDNS Recursor's handling of `DNAME` Resource Records (RRs). Moreover, we demonstrate the potential for self-sustaining DoS attacks in resolved and trust-dns, further underlining the necessity of comprehensive DNS security. Through these contributions, our research underscores the potential of differential fuzzing in uncovering DNS vulnerabilities.

1 Introduction

The Domain Name System (DNS) is often explained as the internet's phone book since it turns human readable names like esorics2023.org into an IP address. This analogy greatly simplifies the central role DNS plays on the internet besides just delivering IP addresses. In fact, DNS defines the singular namespace of the internet, provides cryptographic material for secure communications, and acts as a backbone for other services such as anti-spam measures or secure routing.

This makes DNS part of the critical infrastructure. Thus, risks and vulnerabilities in DNS are of the highest concern. Recursive resolvers are the centerpiece of DNS, as they resolve domains for clients, iteratively getting answers from authoritative name servers. By design, resolvers are public or at least semi-public, exposing them to various threats from malicious clients. Likewise, they interact with potentially malicious authoritative name servers. This complex setting also complicates the task of testing DNS resolvers, as it requires modeling both, clients and authoritative name servers. Combined with their central role, this means DNS servers are a highly prized target for malicious actors. Infiltration and manipulations of DNS allow far-reaching exploits like preparing for Denial-of-Service attacks, intercepting communication, or forging TLS certificates. Further security protocols like DNSSEC or full TLS encryption of services like email are not widespread enough to catch DNS manipulations.

G. Tsudik et al. (Eds.): ESORICS 2023, LNCS 14345, pp. 62–80, 2024.
https://doi.org/10.1007/978-3-031-51476-0_4

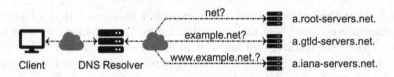

Fig. 1. Basic DNS resolution process. The client sends a query to the resolver, which then recursively resolves the query by interacting with multiple AuthNSes.

In this paper, our primary goal is to identify and analyze semantic bugs and gaps in the DNS resolver implementations. Such bugs could allow an attacker to get a resolver to return wrong answers. With this work, we want to support developers by highlighting problems earlier in the development process, as they hint at bugs or problems with the specification. To this end, we developed Resol-Fuzz, a fuzzer specifically designed for DNS and implementing differential testing mechanisms, allowing us to test thousands of scenarios. We build a rule-based mechanism to identify common and benign differences, such as random values, underspecified behavior, or feature differences.

In the course of our research, we have uncovered a multitude of critical issues. These range from cases where the DNS resolver returned incorrect values, to more complex problems like traffic looping bugs and potential amplification issues. These findings underscore the importance of our differential fuzzing approach in identifying and addressing vulnerabilities in the DNS infrastructure.

In summary, our paper presents the following contributions:

1. We create a fuzzer for recursive DNS resolvers to uncover vulnerabilities.
2. We build a differential analysis framework for investigating DNS outputs. This includes rules to separate common benign differences from other sources.
3. We have discovered multiple new bugs in popular open-source resolvers.

2 Methodology

In this section, we describe our methodology for finding semantic differences between DNS resolvers. Before we can dig into the technical details, we first need to provide a bit of background on the DNS protocol and the functionality of a DNS resolver. With that in mind, we can lay out our goals and the challenges we face. Lastly, we provide the technical details of ResolFuzz, the infrastructure choices we made, and describe the input generation and output analysis.

2.1 Threat Model

Recursive resolvers sit at a very precarious place on the internet, as shown in Fig. 1. They receive queries from client and answer them from their cache. If the information is missing, they traverse the DNS hierarchy to find the answer from an AuthNS (right). Many resolvers are exposed to the whole internet and have to talk to many untrusted AuthNSes, indicated by the blue clouds. This opens them up to attacks from clients, AuthNSes, or combined attacks.

For testing the behavior of resolvers, we need to assume that all network communication is potentially malicious. We assume an attacker can send arbitrary queries to the resolver and has control over one or more AuthNSes. While this assumption is trivially fulfilled for public resolvers, it even holds for private resolvers. Server-side requests in HTTP servers, like fetching link previews, or checking email authentication information in SMTP servers allow users to send queries to specific domains, although with less control over the query.

Creating different resolver states is trivial if the attacker is allowed to send different data to the resolvers. For a fair analysis, we must restrict the scenario such that all resolvers receive the same logical data. Some variation must be allowed, as DNS messages are not fully deterministic since they contain random values and have no canonical encoding.

2.2 Goals

We aim to develop a semi-automated approach for finding and evaluating semantic differences between DNS resolvers. We envision two use cases: i) Finding semantic bugs in DNS resolvers, which lead to differences, such that two DNS clients no longer agree on the same answer. In the worst case, this is a cache poisoning vulnerability, which can, e.g., lead to a Certificate Authority that wrongly issues a domain-validated certificate. ii) Our system can be used during the development of DNS resolvers, either to ensure a new resolver is compatible with the existing ecosystem or to check how a new RFC is implemented.

The system should be scalable to many resolvers and be easy to use, thus it should work with minimal domain-specific knowledge from the human user. This allows it to be run by developers and protocol designers to check their implementations. Integrating a resolver should be free of code modifications or complex adoption necessary by some fuzzing systems.

We do not aim for bugs in the network packet parsing code. Fuzzing on that level will not yield many interesting results in the DNS behavior, since most packets will be dropped early. Bugs in the parsers can be found better with fuzz harnesses for the parsers. Therefore, we only create syntactically valid DNS packets, i.e., following the size and allowed values of the fields.

2.3 Challenges

DNS is a complex protocol. Over 300 IETF RFCs [3,21] specify different aspects of it, and over 100 of them are relevant to resolver implementations [4,15]. This provides a lot of potential for implementation differences and bugs. Automatically exploring such semantic differences is challenging for several reasons.

State: A DNS resolver is inherently stateful. Resolvers cache answers, metadata about answers, and information about AuthNSes. Over time the same query can result in different answers. Even at the same time, the same query from different clients can result in different answers, since the client IP address can be part of the cache key with Extended DNS (EDNS) Client Subnet (RFC 7871 [5]).

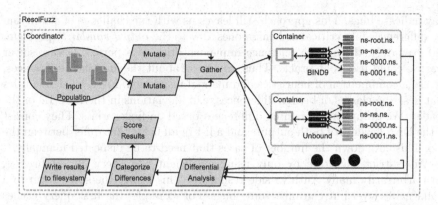

Fig. 2. Overview of our ResolFuzz fuzzer. The boxes indicate different components, where the main component is the Coordinator. The Helper (blue/yellow) runs inside each container and acts as client and servers. The arrows indicate the dataflow. From a pool of fuzzing inputs, some are selected and mutated. They are gathered into a larger set and sent to the resolvers. The yellow parts are controlled by the fuzzing input. The results are collected and compared. Inputs resulting in differences are written to the filesystem for later analysis. All new inputs are scored and added to the pool. (Color figure online)

Multiple Clients and Servers: The DNS resolvers sit in the middle between many clients and AuthNSes. Answering a single query can involve multiple servers, pointing the resolver to the next place to ask. The resolver only handles untrusted data. Clients can send queries for any domain name, even for attacker-controlled ones. Our system must be able to represent enough of this complex interaction to provide a large enough coverage but also to find bugs.

Feedback: A DNS resolver is for the most part a black box. It receives a query, does some processing, potentially triggering network requests, and returns an answer. On the protocol level, we only have input-output-based interaction, with multiple inputs and outputs. But this lacks information about what is happening inside the resolver, including its state (e.g., cache).

Output Similarity: The human language specification used in RFCs is often vague and leaves room for interpretation. Later RFCs might clarify or change the meaning of previous ones. This makes it hard to determine if a difference is a bug or a valid interpretation of the specification. For example, the wording around glue records in RFC 1034 [18] has been interpreted differently by different implementations, requiring further clarification [1].

2.4 Addressing the Challenges

We use differential fuzzing to tackle the aforementioned challenges. In differential fuzzing, the same fuzzing input is given to multiple implementations, here resolvers. The fuzzer then compares outputs to report on any differences, which may indicate bugs. This approach still leaves us with the challenge of classifying the differences into critical or benign ones, due to the *output similarity* problem. Unfortunately, there is no reference implementation of a perfect DNS resolver that we could use as an oracle. Thus, to reason about the identified differences, we use a combination of heuristics and manual inspection. First, we define rules that describe classes of benign differences, e.g., deviations in the DNS ID of the header. We group the remaining differences based on fingerprints. They consist of the DNS headers of both outputs and a list of all fields that differ between the two. This cuts down the number of cases that need to be inspected manually.

We restrict the *state* by only using one client-side query during fuzzing, with arbitrarily many AuthNS side responses. This brings the state down to a manageable level but can miss some bugs. For example, the first query caches the wrong AuthNS for a domain and the answer of the second query is based on that value. We do inspect the cache of the resolver, after the fuzzing. For this, we send cache probing queries, i.e., queries with the recursion desired (RD) bit set to 0. This forces the resolver to answer only from the cache. This cache snooping also allows us to obtain *feedback* for fuzzing. But only relying on cache state and DNS messages as output would be too coarse-grained for a fuzzer, which performs best if learning about incremental progress. We thus extend the definition of output and include edge coverage between basic blocks [31].

The fuzzer runs in a fully separated DNS environment with separate DNS root servers, as shown in the containers in Fig. 2. For the *multiple clients and servers* challenge we simulate all AuthNSes. The DNS environment is separated using a custom Root Hint [12] configuration for all resolvers and only pointing to AuthNSes on localhost, which is simulated by ResolFuzz.

2.5 Fuzzing Infrastructure

This section describes the architecture of ResolFuzz. A flowchart of our dataflow is shown in Fig. 2. ResolFuzz consists of multiple components. This is necessary to achieve scalability in the number of tested resolvers and to keep modifications on the resolvers minimal. The main component *Coordinator* is responsible for input generation, mutation, and output evaluation. A helper component *Helper* runs alongside each resolver and provides a simulated DNS ecosystem for the resolver and communicates with the Coordinator to get fuzzing inputs and deliver the outputs back. We describe how the Helper interacts with the resolver and afterward explain the interaction between the Coordinator and multiple Helpers.

Resolver Isolation: One of our goals is that adding a new resolver should require minimal adaptions. One way we achieve this is by running the resolver unmodified, with a normal network stack. However, this requires that we separate different resolvers from each other since all resolvers listen on the same port. For this, we use Linux namespaces in the form of containers. The Helper simulates a custom DNS ecosystem with separate roots and runs in each container.

The Helper also runs the fuzzing inputs against the resolver. Multiple fuzzing queries can be run sequentially, with separate AuthNSes on different IPs per query. This helps with the separation of state between multiple fuzzing inputs.

Lastly, the Helper gathers coverage information from the resolvers and communicates it to the Coordinator. Each resolver is instrumented with LLVMs Sanitizer Coverage [31] pass to gather edge coverage information and only include the edges between sending a query and receiving a response. All edges involved in startup and background tasks are excluded.

Container Startup: Spawning a resolver including the Helper in such a fashion is relatively expensive compared to individual DNS queries. For fast fuzzing iterations it is therefore necessary to limit the amount of time we wait for the resolvers to start. Generic network fuzzers like AFLNet [19] come with a fork-server to speed up the spawning of new processes, but that requires modifications to the program and is incompatible with threads. We pre-spawn the containers such that they are ready to receive fuzzing inputs and execute multiple fuzzing inputs sequentially, thus sharing the startup cost. Unfortunately, we cannot run them in parallel, as this would interfere with the coverage information gathering since coverage information is a global property of the resolver, and concurrent queries would interfere with each other.

Second, most of the resolver startup is independent of the concrete fuzzing input. We warm the resolver cache with unrelated DNS queries, such that all name servers will be cached before fuzzing. Testing the fuzzing inputs now only requires the Helper to read the inputs, configure the dynamic DNS server, and start sending the client queries.

Coordinator and Helper Interaction: The Coordinator is responsible for generating and mutating the fuzzing inputs and output evaluation, as well as, managing the containers with the Helper. We explain the steps of input generation and evaluations in more detail in Sects. 2.6 and 2.7, respectively. For now, it is sufficient to know, that input generation generates a batch of fuzzing inputs, each consisting of a DNS client query and a set of DNS responses.

After the batch is completed for all resolvers, the output results are collected. The output contains i) edge coverage information between basic blocks in the form of a hitmap, ii) all DNS queries sent to AuthNSes by the resolver, iii) the DNS responses provided to these queries, iv) the DNS response sent to the client, and v) information about the resolver cache state. From these outputs, we determine which inputs are "interesting", i.e., cover new code paths or uncover behavioral differences. More details are in Sects. 2.7 and 2.8.

2.6   Input Generation and Mutation

ResolFuzz uses mutation for input generation. By picking specific mutations, we can ensure that the mutated inputs stay syntactically valid DNS messages. Having a valid DNS message is important, such that we are fuzzing semantic bugs and not bugs in the DNS message parsers.

We have a population of inputs that we mutate and the ability to generate new inputs. In the beginning, our population is empty, and we start with only newly generated inputs. They are a single DNS query and response pair with randomized query names, labels, types, classes, and header flags. We always include some new random entries in a batch to ensure diversity in the population.

The top n inputs in our population with the highest score are mutated by adding, removing, or modifying the different fields and values of the DNS messages. The score is assigned before adding the input to the population and is decremented each time the input is used as a base for mutations. It covers information about the coverage increase, how many known differences, and unknown differences were found when the input was last used.

Mutation consists of modifying existing values and where possible adding or removing values. The typed in-memory representations of DNS messages allow us to walk over the structure and pick a mutation for each field. The DNS header has a fixed length, so the only mutations are changing the existing values to new ones. The different sections can have resource records added or removed. Each resource record has a domain, type, class, Time-to-Live (TTL), and data. These can be modified, but we always ensure that the data is still valid for the type.

Modifying domain names requires more care than random modifications to ensure enough "collisions" are created to trigger proper behavior in the resolvers. For example, the query name used in the DNS client query should also appear in one of the DNS responses, as otherwise the resolver likely ignores responses and we fail to test the core logic of a resolver. We use a small set of labels from which a domain name can be generated. The inputs use a fixed domain `test.fuzz.` during mutation, but the Helper will later replace the labels with unique ones to separate the inputs. We have two C-string specific mutations, by adding a zero-byte at the end of the last label, i.e., `test.fuzz\0.`, and adding the zero-byte but also duplicating the domain name, i.e., `test.fuzz\0.test.fuzz.`. Two labels can be merged into a new dot-containing label, i.e., `foo` and `bar` can be merged into `foo\.bar`. These mutations verify that the resolver treats domain names as a sequence of labels and not as a string.

Only a small set of RR type and Record Data (RDATA) is generated. While the RR type is a 16-bit value, most of the values are not assigned, and hence the creation of valid RDATA for them is impossible. Most RR types are for data storage, without interacting with the resolver, and only a few should be interpreted by the resolver. These include `A`/`AAAA` for the IP addresses of AuthNSes and `NS` for delegations between AuthNSes, `SOA` for caching, `CNAME`/`DNAME` for aliases/canonical names, and DNSSEC records when supported (`RRSIG`, `DNSKEY`, `DS`, `NSEC`, `NSEC3`, `NSEC3PARAM`). We only generate `A`, `AAAA`, `TXT`, `CNAME`, `NS`, `SRV`, `SOA` and the special query type (QTYPE) `*` often called `ANY`.

2.7 Fuzzing Output and Processing

We now explain the collected data for each input and how we use it to determine if an input is interesting. The coverage information we gather is edge coverage given from an instrumented resolver. We compile the resolver using LLVMs Sanitizer Coverage Instrumentation [31] and count how often each edge gets executed during the resolution for a single DNS client query.

For each input we capture the outgoing queries from the resolver, the responses sent to the DNS client, the cache state afterward, how the dynamic DNS servers answered, and the coverage information. This gives us all the information about what the resolver is doing.

We use all available data to determine if an input is interesting, i.e., produces new or different behavior, but the most important information is the client's response and the coverage information. The client responses reveal whether two resolvers behave significantly differently. If different responses are returned two clients might behave differently. The coverage information is important to allow for partial progress during fuzzing, by giving a means of identifying new behavior in a resolver, even if the client response remains unchanged. The cache state is important too, but harder to interpret, since a difference here does not necessarily mean a semantic difference. Lastly, the outgoing queries to the dynamic DNS server have a low value, since comparing them is hard and has many downfalls. For example, there are many ways in which a resolver can implement Query Name (QNAME) minimization, such as which query type is used and which labels are removed. For a conforming DNS server, this does not matter and in the end, the resolver will come up with the same answer in all cases. But these differences are a problem for automatic analysis since we have many semantically equivalent queries with different representations.

The collected data is cleaned and checked for known differences, like random DNS ID values, to only leave the unknown differences. DNS records in messages are unordered, but we normalize the representations by sorting them. We also have further known differences, for example, some resolvers already support extended DNS errors which will be added to the client response in some cases. We create rules for identifying these known differences and track them separately, see Sect. 3.2. The remaining differences are unknown and of the highest interest.

Unfortunately, the fuzzing is not fully deterministic, so we require a validation run for any found new differences. Randomness and unwanted interactions can come from many sources, such as choices the resolver makes, how we batch multiple inputs together, or the kernel via the network and scheduler. We detect non-deterministic differences by fuzzing the same input multiple times and only accepting those results that show the same class of differences each time.

Many differences have an identical root cause and we group them using a fingerprint to better model that. Our fingerprint consists of all the DNS header fields in the DNS client response and all the field names that differ between the two resolvers. For example, we describe the difference in the answer section of the client response using identifiers like `.fuzz_result.fuzzee_response.answers.0` which has the subfields `.name_labels`, `.dns_class`, `.rr_type`, `.ttl`, and `.rdata`. The `.0` refers to the first resource record in the answer section. We do not use the values here, only the field names, since the values often contain randomized data and thus would always lead to different fingerprints. The same problem does not exist for the header values since these are mostly booleans.

2.8 Finding Bugs

Table 1. Software versions used for the evaluation.

Software	Version	Language
BIND9	v9.18.0, v9.11.0	C
Deadwood	3.5.0032	C
Knot Resolver	5.5.3	C, Lua
PowerDNS Recursor	4.7.3	C++
resolved	463644c	Rust
trust-dns	0b6fefe	Rust
Unbound	1.15.0	C

Our main idea for finding semantic bugs is using differential fuzzing between many resolvers. DNS is a complex protocol with a lot of variability and edge cases. Defining valid behavior in the DNS is difficult as it requires a deep understanding of the standards and a lot of domain-specific knowledge. Instead, using differential testing, we can automatically leverage this knowledge as the resolvers are implemented by independent expert groups. Instead of deciding if every response we see is valid, we now can focus on a much smaller set of cases where multiple resolvers disagree. Each difference is a case for further manual analysis as they can indicate implementation or semantic bugs.

During the manual analysis, we also built further rules to describe known differences. For example, BIND9 has a strict DNS response validation and discards the whole message if a single value is invalid, while Unbound will only discard the single invalid resource record. This causes BIND9 to produce a SERVFAIL answer while Unbound responds with NOERROR or NODATA depending on the situation. We go into more detail about this in Table 2.

The effort for manual analysis and writing rules ranges from a couple of minutes to a few hours. Simple cases, like DNS ID randomization or optional features like extended DNS error, are easy to spot and describe and have no follow-on impacts. Other cases, like the BIND9 strict validation, are more complex and require more time to understand and describe, as the root cause can lead to non-obvious and large differences. Concretely, BIND9 might send more upstream queries than other resolvers.

ResolFuzz is guided by the score each input receives. The score is composed of the coverage results per resolver and the differences for each resolver pair, after validation. New differences score the highest, followed by differences we deem "interesting"; coverage is only a small contributing factor. New mutations partially inherit the score of their parent inputs. Finally, if the input population already contains many samples producing the same fingerprint, we apply a penalty to all samples in the population. This is to discourage further mutations based on those samples. This ensures that the input population is diverse and ResolFuzz will not get "stuck" mutating a group of similar inputs with high scores and thus drowning out other interesting inputs.

3 Evaluation

We evaluate our fuzzer on seven resolvers, as listed in Table 1. Where possible we disable features during compile time, to reduce the size of the binary and simplify fuzzing. These features do not affect our evaluation, as these relate to system integration, such as systemd, enhanced security with chroot and capabilities, extra logging like dnstap, or HTTPS support. Most of these features have no impact at all on the DNS protocol and HTTPS for DoH is not used by ResolFuzz as UDP is more efficient for us. Each resolver is compiled from scratch using LLVM with coverage instrumentation [31], which is available in clang and rustc, as both are LLVM-based compilers. The containers are a Fedora 37 image.

3.1 Case Studies

In this section, we highlight our findings in three case studies.

resolved fails with query and missing CNAME: resolved misbehaves for CNAME queries if no CNAME record exists. Instead of returning the expected NoErrror response code, resolved returns SERVFAIL. The CNAME record type redirects queries for a domain to another canonical domain. This means a resolver must follow the redirection, except here, because the original query is for the CNAME type. This means the first answer is the final one.

PowerDNS Recursor Self-loop: We discovered a bug in handling DNAME RRs, similar to a known issue for CNAMEs [6]. The problem occurs if the result after DNAME expansion matches the same DNAME again. DNAME and CNAME records both provide a way to specify a new canonical place where information is stored. In case of a CNAME RR like this.old.domain CNAME new.canonical.name, any query for this.old.domain should be redirected to new.canonical.name and the data from the new place should be used. A DNAME redirection is similar to CNAME. A CNAME only applies for a single specific domain, but a DNAME applies to a whole subtree. For example the DNAME RR old.domain DNAME new.name means that any query for *this*.old.domain redirects to *this*.new.name. The *italic* subdomain part is arbitrary and is preserved in the rewrite. The DNAME can point to itself, by having the re-written part match the pattern, for example, old.domain DNAME *extra*.old.domain, which will put *extra* many times in the domain. When PowerDNS Recursor encounters such a DNAME record, it applies the rewriting repeatedly. Consequently, in our setting, the resulting DNS answer will contain the same DNAME record 16 times. Further, each time the DNAME rewriting rule is applied, a synthetic CNAME record is created. Ultimately, the resolver gives up resolving this infinite loop and returns a SERVFAIL with 32 records. The effect is that PowerDNS Recursor spends time following the

Table 2. Higher level categories of the common differences we found between resolver outputs. Each category lists the number of rules that fall into it and gives an example.

Category	Size	Description	Example
Configuration	6	Configurable behavior	Limiting the maximal TTL values, EDNS buffer sizes
Error Handling	9	Behavioral differences in error messages (SERVFAIL, NOTIMP, FORMERR, REFUSED)	On receiving a query with TC bit set, SERVFAIL and FORMERR responses exist
Incomparable	3	Values that always differ	Random DNS ID
Metadata	3	Metadata about the captured results	Resolver Name, redundant Length Values
Missing Features	3	Optional missing features	EDNS Error Codes
Resolver Specific	10	Other uncategorized, but resolver specific behavior	EDNS buffer size (512B in PowerDNS vs. 1232B in others)
Upstream Queries	4	Behavior of the upstream queries	QNAME Minimization, re-transmissions

loop and creating ever-increasing answers, thus wasting resources. The answer becomes large, making it a target for reflective DDoS attacks [25].

Self-sustained DoS in Resolved and Trust-DNS: We found a vulnerability in resolved and trust-dns that enables a self-sustaining DoS attack. The vulnerability is caused by these resolvers answering DNS responses (QR bit=1). When receiving responses on their listening port (UDP/53), both resolved and trust-dns return a FORMERR error to indicate that the request was malformed.

Blindly responding to responses, even with error messages, can be abused for creating a traffic loop. If both resolvers are vulnerable, attackers can inject IP-spoofed responses to provoke the two resolvers to send responses to each other in an endless loop, causing a self-sustaining DoS attack. The traffic loop will not stop except when packet loss in the network causes the traffic to stop. Enough looping traffic will overwhelm the resolver or network and cause a DoS.

3.2   Result Statistics

The described case studies were found over multiple runs. We now describe how a *single* run of the fuzzer behaves and the kind of differences it finds.

The results of this section refer to a six-hour run of the fuzzer using all eight configurations listed in Table 1. During that time, 7140 inputs were generated or roughly 0.33/s. In total, the fuzzer made 198 240 comparisons, as each input takes part in 28 comparisons. This resulted in 1903 distinct fingerprints. The fingerprint count is larger than the number of root causes. For example, to trigger the resolved and trust-dns bug the only prerequisite is a query with QR=1 bit set, but a fingerprint includes all header fields.

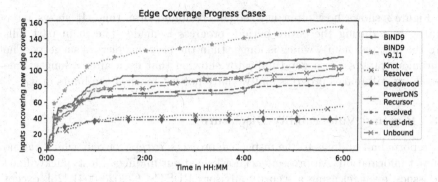

Fig. 3. The number of times new coverage edges are found over time.

We created 38 rules to describe benign differences, as shown in Table 2. The rules are grouped into seven categories. The nine *Error Handling* rules capture the variability of error messages (e.g., differences in error types). *Resolver-specific* behavior is similarly sized with ten rules, but the behavior covered here is more diverse. Two categories of differences will be found for any comparison of two outputs, *Metadata* and *Incomparable*. There are some fixed values about the captured results that are always different, such as the resolver names. In each comparison the DNS ID and edge coverage information are incomparable.

The 38 rules cover between 2017 to 6555 (28.2 % to 91.8 %) of the differences identified by the fuzzer, fluctuating based on the compared resolvers. Most similar is the pair of BIND9 (v9.18) and PowerDNS Recursor. Both are mature implementations and adhere to the DNS standard well. The worst pairing is Knot Resolver and trust-dns. The trust-dns recursor is quite new and not yet well developed. As such it still has many missing features and bugs, all resulting in differences. These numbers translate directly into differences not covered by our rules. The pairing of Knot Resolver and trust-dns leads with 5067 (71.0 %) uncovered differences, while BIND9 and PowerDNS Recursor have only 490 (6.9 %). The gap towards the total of 7140 is caused by inputs where the comparison was non-deterministic. We observed the highest rate here between both BIND9 configurations with 143 (2.0 %) non-deterministic comparisons.

Fuzzing Progress: We furthermore evaluate how much coverage our fuzzer achieves in the resolvers' code. This way we can understand when fuzzing saturates, i.e., no longer reveals new results. The coverage percentage increases sharply at the beginning, but then slows down but never stops. No resolver reaches a high edge coverage, with the highest being around 16 %. This can be explained by the fact that we only measure the coverage between sending a query and receiving a response. Any startup, background, or shutdown code is not included in the coverage. While we aimed to remove as many untested features as possible during compilation time, many features are still enabled but never activated by our fuzzer, such as DNSSEC, DNS forwarding or authoritative mode, and even complex features like Response Policy Zones (RPZs).

Figure 3 shows how often new edges are found over time. It shows more clearly, that during the entire period, progress is made. The main part falls into the first two hours, which is longer than the previous picture suggests. The continuous progress is a good indicator showing that even after a longer time ResolFuzz still makes progress and we have not yet reached the limits of it.

3.3   Bug and Vulnerability Disclosure

We reported all findings to the respective projects, except for one, which had no contact information. All projects acknowledged our findings. Most quickly fixed the issues, even releasing a security advisory RUSTSEC-2023-0041 [26], except for PowerDNS Recursor which deemed the risk as acceptable.

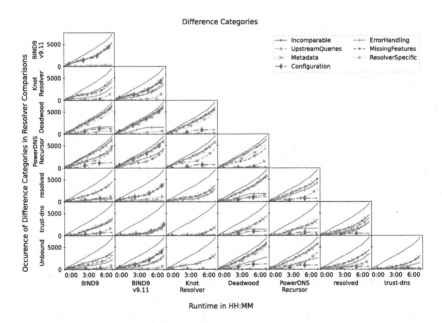

Fig. 4. The number of explainable differences between the resolver outputs. Only explainable differences are shown. The gray line shows the total number of fuzzing inputs tested. The gap between the gray line and the colored lines shows the number of unexplainable differences. The categories are explained in Table 2 (Color figure online).

4   Limitations

We now discuss limitations that arise out of the design decisions we took to address the complex challenges of fuzzing DNS resolvers.

First of all, our fuzzer has no notion of time. Indeed, faking time jumps requires knowledge of the resolver internals as these determine when time jumps can be inserted and which parts they affect—internals we wanted to abstract from. The Deckard [7] testing framework managed to solve some of the problems and could be an inspiration for future work.

We use cache snooping as a generic mechanism to learn about the resolver's cache state. In some cases this fails, e.g., for specific query classes or resolvers, such that we skip the records during diffing. Resolver-specific ways to retrieve the cache status (e.g., via CLI tools or log files) would require resolver adjustments.

Furthermore, we did not implement all DNS features, such as DNSSEC [10, 22–24,33]. Cryptographic operations are hard to fuzz, but may still represent interesting attack targets for malicious actors. Some part-way solutions are possible, like using a single validity bit and then dynamically signing the records, but we leave this for future work. Likewise, we ignored RPZ that can be used to block certain domains or IP addresses. They work by sending further queries and then changing or blocking the original request.

Table 3. Comparison of existing DNS testing tools, with a focus on fuzzing. The *Client* and *Server* columns indicate whether the project ships with a client or server component. *Search Strategy* indicates the strategy used for generating queries. Randomized means that all modifications are chosen by a random number generator, without any feedback. *Targets* indicates what the tool is looking for.

Project	Cli.	Srv.	Search Strategy	Targets
ResolFuzz	yes	yes	Evolutionary mutations guided by code coverage and differential testing	Crashes and differential testing
Deckard [7]	yes	yes	None. Scripted communication	Configurable checking. Comparison to fixed values
dns-fuzz-server [27]	yes	yes	Randomized	None
dns-fuzzer [17]	yes	no	Randomized	Crashes
honggfuzz [29]	yes	no	Evolutionary, Code coverage feedback	Crashes
IBDNS [32]	no	yes	Fixed, based on query	None. Not a full tool
nmap dns-fuzz [8]	yes	no	Randomized	Crashes
SCALE/Ferret [14]	yes	no	Statespace guided input generation	Diff. comparison between servers and formal model

We use a minimal configuration for each resolver, leaving most options as their upstream default. Configurations we changed include the IP address to listen, the root server hints, and the reduction of timeouts to speed up fuzzing. We deem this configuration realistic and modification necessary for fuzzing. We publish all our source code including configurations.

Recursive DNS resolution is the most complex part between clients, stub resolvers, and AuthNS. Stub resolvers could be tested similarly to the recursive resolvers, except they only forward the query to the recursive resolver.

5   Related Work

Automatic testing of network services has been subject to several other related works [2,8,11,14,16,17,19,20,27,29,32,34]. However, we are the first to create an advanced fuzzer for DNS resolvers. Indeed, DNS is a particularly challenging setting, as the resolver (i.e., the network service) acts as server and client at the same time—but most existing fuzzing frameworks test only single connections. Other projects solve DNS resolver fuzzing only partially. Related work can be grouped into two main categories: DNS testing and evaluation tools, and network fuzzers. We separately cover formal models for AuthNSes.

DNS Testing: Due to the complexities in DNS and the difficulty of covering a large input space, only few projects exist for testing or fuzzing DNS. Table 3 provides an overview of existing projects and their capabilities. Existing tools often only target crashes in the DNS resolver [8,17,29]. This makes them unsuitable for finding more complex failure conditions, which we can identify with the differential testing approach. Some projects use basic randomization for input generation. dns-fuzz-server [27] only creates random queries and responses, but has no target conditions, like crashes, it is looking for. ResolFuzz uses a more advanced evolutionary algorithm, which is better suited for complex inputs.

The Deckard [7] project is noteworthy in that it is a full testing framework for DNS resolvers. It has extensive customization options, for query generations, mocking AuthNSes, and checking the responses. This extensiveness is great for writing detailed tests, but they often rely on the resolver implementation and are not portable between different resolvers. Relying on scripted tests also means unknown behavior cannot be revealed.

The Intentionally Broken DNS Server (IBDNS) [32] is a new project by Afnic for testing DNS resolvers or DNS tools. It applies known defects to existing zone files and serves them to clients. Its goal is to test DNS tools and DNS resolvers. IBDNS is not public so we cannot describe it in detail.

Other DNS test frameworks are either old and unmaintained [28], only test against a reference implementation [9], or are commercial with no public information [30]. Testing against a reference output can be useful for limited features or regression testing, but is not viable for covering larger input spaces, because of a missing reference implementation.

Fuzzing Authoritative DNS Servers: Most relevant to ResolFuzz are the projects by Kakarla et al. [13,14]. They tackle the challenge of fuzzing AuthNSes in the two papers GRoot [13] and SCALE [14]. In GRoot they lay the foundations by creating a formal model for the semantics of authoritative DNS. The model creates equivalence classes (EC) for a given DNS zone file. Each EC captures distinct behavior, like the difference between two different existing labels, and combines variants like queries that match the same wildcard record. With this model, they can symbolically execute these ECs and find bugs in the zones, like lame delegations, if the sub-zone has no reachable nameserver, or rewriting loops when CNAME/DNAME records form a loop leading to unresolvable names. SCALE builds an executable version of the GRoot model, with the ability to create zone files and matching queries. Using symbolic execution they find a wide variety of behaviors and create matching test cases using a constraint solver. That is an expensive process, so the created zone files are limited to four records. The test cases are fed into various AuthNSes and the responses are checked for compliance with the RFCs. The AuthNSes only agree in 35 % on the same answer. The rest is grouped by fingerprints, to make investigations easier. Using SCALE they could identify 30 new bugs.

Network Service Fuzzing: Apart from DNS with its special requirements, there are other network fuzzing approaches, which come in many variants.

AFLnet [19] is a greybox fuzzer. It has a corpus of network exchanges, which it mutates and sends to the target. AFLnet is guided by code coverage and learns a state machine for the target server. Fuzzing uses a forkserver, which allows for fast restarts and parallelization. SnapFuzz [2] is an iteration of AFLnet with increased performance, achieved with new binary rewriting. The rewriting replaces file system accesses with a custom in-memory implementation, replaces the TCP and UDP socket calls with UNIX domain sockets, and optimizes the forkserver. Both AFLnet and SnapFuzz are designed to fuzz single client-server connections, which makes them unsuitable for DNS resolvers.

Lin et al. [16] use GANs to infer the protocol of a black box network service. The GAN learns how to generate attack packets for a protocol, not only the protocol syntax. They only tested their approach on stateless protocols so far, which makes it unsuitable for DNS.

Hoque et al. [11] use a model checker for finding temporal semantic bugs in protocols. From a protocol implementation, they extract a finite state machine describing it. The temporal properties are protocol specific and require expert knowledge, in contrast to ResolFuzz.

Differential fuzzing has been used successfully in contexts other than DNS. TCP-Fuzz [34] by Zou et al. uses differential checking as one bug detection method. They develop an input creation strategy that keeps track of dependencies between packets and system calls. The coverage metric is based on the state transitions of the TCP stack. DPIFuzz [20] by Reen and Rossow uses differential fuzzing for QUIC. It generates QUIC frames, and mutates them with shuffling, duplication, and deleting data. While both works are related due to their differential checking approach, they are not directly comparable. TCP and QUIC work point-to-point and on a well-defined sequence of packets. A DNS resolver has many point-to-point connections and there is no clear sequence of packets, as each point-to-point connection runs independently.

6   Conclusion

Our analyses encourages more research on securing DNS resolvers, a critical part of the internet infrastructure. With ResolFuzz, our differential fuzzer, we found multiple security-relevant bugs in both well-established and new resolver implementations. DNS' lack of a formal model makes semantic analysis hard, but we showed that differential fuzzing with specialized matching rules can be a powerful tool to find bugs. We publish ResolvFuzz as open-source in the hope that it will help to improve the security of DNS resolvers. This work provides a starting point for further research into the security of DNS resolvers and we hope to uncover more bugs through improved insights into resolver decisions and covering more complex deployment scenarios.

Acknowledgements. Our sincere thanks belongs to the anonymous reviewers for their valuable feedback and suggestions which helped to improve the paper Furthermore, we thank the Saarbrücken Graduate School of Computer Science for their support.

Data Availability Statement. To ease reproducibility, we have released i) the full source code of ResolFuzz, ii) the build scripts and configuration files for the resolvers, iii) the raw data of our evaluation, iv) a list of found differences, and v) scripts for further analysis. The code and data are available online at https://github.com/dns-differential-fuzzing/dns-differential-fuzzing.

References

1. Andrews, M.P., Huque, S., Wouters, P., Wessels, D.: DNS glue requirements in referral responses. Internet-Draft draft-ietf-dnsop-glue-is-not-optional-08, Internet Engineering Task Force (2023). https://datatracker.ietf.org/doc/draft-ietf-dnsop-glue-is-not-optional/08/, work in Progress
2. Andronidis, A., Cadar, C.: SnapFuzz: high-throughput fuzzing of network applications. In: ISSTA '22: 31st ACM SIGSOFT International Symposium on Software Testing and Analysis (2022). https://doi.org/10.1145/3533767.3534376
3. Cambus, F.: DNS related RFCs. https://www.statdns.com/rfc/
4. Consortium, I.S.: General DNS reference information, https://bind9.readthedocs.io/en/latest/general.html
5. Contavalli, C., van der Gaast, W., Lawrence, D.C., Kumari, W.A.: Client subnet in DNS queries. RFC 7871 (2016). https://doi.org/10.17487/RFC7871, https://www.rfc-editor.org/info/rfc7871
6. CVE-2022-48256. Available from MITRE, CVE-ID CVE-2022-48256 (2023). http://cve.mitre.org/cgi-bin/cvename.cgi?name=CVE-2022-48256
7. CZ.NIC: Deckard. https://gitlab.nic.cz/knot/deckard/
8. DNS-Fuzz in Nmap. https://nmap.org/nsedoc/scripts/dns-fuzz.html
9. Ereche, M.V.: DNS completitude and compliance testing (2020). https://github.com/mave007/dns_completitude_and_compliance/tree/2a18967d103d232e9072c4474e8c731dc3d79f7a
10. Hoffman, P.E.: DNS security extensions (DNSSEC). RFC 9364 (2023). https://doi.org/10.17487/RFC9364, https://www.rfc-editor.org/info/rfc9364
11. Hoque, M.E., Chowdhury, O., Chau, S.Y., Nita-Rotaru, C., Li, N.: Analyzing operational behavior of stateful protocol implementations for detecting semantic bugs. In: 47th Annual IEEE/IFIP International Conference on Dependable Systems and Networks (2017). https://doi.org/10.1109/DSN.2017.36
12. IANA: Root files. https://www.iana.org/domains/root/files

13. Kakarla, S.K.R., Beckett, R., Arzani, B., Millstein, T.D., Varghese, G.: GRooT: proactive verification of DNS configurations. In: SIGCOMM '20: Proceedings of the 2020 Annual conference of the ACM Special Interest Group on Data Communication on the applications (2020). https://doi.org/10.1145/3387514.3405871
14. Kakarla, S.K.R., Beckett, R., Millstein, T.D., Varghese, G.: SCALE: automatically finding RFC compliance bugs in DNS nameservers. In: 19th USENIX Symposium on Networked Systems Design and Implementation (2022)
15. Labs, N.: Unbound - RFC compliance. https://nlnetlabs.nl/projects/unbound/rfc-compliance/
16. Lin, Z., Moon, S., Zarate, C.M., Mulagalapalli, R., Kulandaivel, S., Fanti, G., Sekar, V.: Towards oblivious network analysis using generative adversarial networks. In: Proceedings of the 18th ACM Workshop on Hot Topics in Networks (2019). https://doi.org/10.1145/3365609.3365854D
17. Meinke, R.: DNS-Fuzzer (2019). https://github.com/guyinatuxedo/dns-fuzzer/tree/6487b0053d9ee227b515490b9e00289b15a1bbd5
18. Mockapetris, P.: Domain names - concepts and facilities. RFC 1034 (1987). https://doi.org/10.17487/RFC1034, https://www.rfc-editor.org/info/rfc1034
19. Pham, V., Böhme, M., Roychoudhury, A.: AFLNET: a greybox fuzzer for network protocols. In: 13th IEEE International Conference on Software Testing (2020). https://doi.org/10.1109/ICST46399.2020.00062
20. Reen, G.S., Rossow, C.: Dpifuzz: a differential fuzzing framework to detect DPI elusion strategies for QUIC. In: ACSAC '20: Annual Computer Security Applications Conference (2020). https://doi.org/10.1145/3427228.3427662
21. RFC editor search DNS. https://www.rfc-editor.org/search/rfc_search_detail.php?title=DNS&page=All
22. Rose, S., Larson, M., Massey, D., Austein, R., Arends, R.: DNS Security Introduction and Requirements. RFC 4033 (2005). https://doi.org/10.17487/RFC4033, https://www.rfc-editor.org/info/rfc4033
23. Rose, S., Larson, M., Massey, D., Austein, R., Arends, R.: Protocol modifications for the DNS security extensions. RFC 4035 (2005). https://doi.org/10.17487/RFC4035, https://www.rfc-editor.org/info/rfc4035
24. Rose, S., Larson, M., Massey, D., Austein, R., Arends, R.: Resource records for the DNS security extensions. RFC 4034 (2005). https://doi.org/10.17487/RFC4034, https://www.rfc-editor.org/info/rfc4034
25. Rossow, C.: Amplification Hell: revisiting network protocols for DDoS abuse. In: 21st Annual Network and Distributed System Security Symposium (2014)
26. Remote attackers can cause denial-of-service (packet loops) with crafted DNS packets. https://rustsec.org/advisories/RUSTSEC-2023-0041.html
27. Sakaguchi, T.: DNS-Fuzz-server (2019). https://github.com/sischkg/dns-fuzz-server/tree/6f45079014e745537c2f564fdad069974e727da1
28. Standcore: standcore DNS conformance. https://www.standcore.com/dnsconformance.tgz
29. Swiecki, R.: Honggfuzz bind-9 (2020). https://github.com/google/honggfuzz/tree/37e8e813c9daa94dff29654b262268481d8c53ee/examples/bind
30. Synopsys: DNS server test suite data sheet. https://www.synopsys.com/software-integrity/security-testing/fuzz-testing/defensics/protocols/dns-server.html
31. The Clang Team: Sanitizercoverage. https://clang.llvm.org/docs/SanitizerCoverage.html
32. van der Wal, M.: Introducing IBDNS: the intentionally broken DNS server (2022). https://indico.dns-oarc.net/event/44/contributions/949/

33. Weiler, S., Blacka, D.: Clarifications and Implementation Notes for DNS Security (DNSSEC). RFC 6840 (2013). https://doi.org/10.17487/RFC6840, https://www.rfc-editor.org/info/rfc6840

34. Zou, Y., Bai, J., Zhou, J., Tan, J., Qin, C., Hu, S.: TCP-Fuzz: detecting memory and semantic bugs in TCP stacks with fuzzing. In: 2021 USENIX Annual Technical Conference (2021)

Fingerprinting of Cellular Infrastructure Based on Broadcast Information

Anup Kiran Bhattacharjee[✉], Stefano Cecconello, Fernando Kuipers, and Georgios Smaragdakis

Delft University of Technology, Delft, The Netherlands
{A.K.Bhattacharjee,S.Cecconello,F.A.Kuipers,G.Smaragdakis}@tudelft.nl

Abstract. To avoid exploitation of known vulnerabilities, it is standard security practice to not disclose any model information regarding the antennas used in cellular infrastructure. However, in this work, we show that end-user devices receive enough information to infer, with high accuracy, the model-family of antennas. We demonstrate how low-cost hardware and software setups can fingerprint the cellular infrastructure of whole regions within a few minutes by only listening to cellular broadcast messages. To show the effectiveness and hence risk of such fingerprinting, we collected an extensive dataset of broadcast messages from three different countries. We then trained a machine-learning model to classify broadcast messages based on the model-family they belong to. Our results reveal a worryingly high average accuracy of 97% for model-family classification. We further discuss how inferring the model-family with such high accuracy can lead to a class of identification attacks on cellular infrastructure and we subsequently suggest countermeasures to mitigate the fingerprint effectiveness.

1 Introduction

Modern cellular networks, particularly 4G networks, provide extensive support for various applications, encompassing communications, manufacturing, logistics, smart homes, and more. In 2021, smartphone subscribers using 4G accounted for around 60% of the total number of subscribers worldwide and this percentage is predicted to be around 55% in 2025 [20], showing that 4G, and hence its security, is going to remain highly relevant in the coming years. Considering the crucial role of mobile networks in society, they run the risk of becoming prime targets for adversarial state actors [44,47,48]. Such adversaries have ample resources and often may go to great lengths to prepare and execute hacks and attacks. One type of security vulnerability is knowledge of the vendor and model of mobile network infrastructure equipment (e.g., antennas or radio units (RU)), which an adversary may leverage to increase the impact of a targeted attack. For example, attackers could exploit knowledge of the antenna model to create disturbances in mobile networks or to gain full authority over data and voice traffic [38]. O-RAN Work Group 11 (Security Group), for example, in their O-RAN Security Threat Modeling and Remediation Analysis [31]

G. Tsudik et al. (Eds.): ESORICS 2023, LNCS 14345, pp. 81–101, 2024.
https://doi.org/10.1007/978-3-031-51476-0_5

also highlights possible threats like T-O-RAN-04, T-RADIO-01, T-RADIO-02, which can aggravate if the attacker knows the model or model-family of the antenna. We use the term "model-family" to refer to a series of similar models offered by a specific vendor (see Sect. 6.3 for the full definition). While base stations do not directly broadcast such model information, *we demonstrate that with a combination of low-cost hardware and machine learning it is possible to accurately fingerprint and hence classify the antenna model-family in a mobile network.* In particular, our contributions can be summarized as follows:

– We show that broadcast messages from base stations can be utilized to fingerprint the model-family of an antenna.
– Our proof-of-concept fingerprint procedure has achieved an accuracy of 97% for model-family and vendor classification.
– Due to the sensitive nature of our data and measurements, we have decided to not release it as open data. Researchers with an interest in the data and/or a possible collaboration are invited to contact us.

2   Background

In this section, we start by introducing some terminology related to radio access networks. Subsequently, we discuss related work on device fingerprinting.

2.1   Terminology

In Fig. 1, we present a typical communication setup between user equipment and cellular towers (base stations) in a radio access network. *User Equipment* (UE) refers to devices that are able to communicate via telecommunication technologies, such as 4G and 5G. Unlike portions of the radio spectrum reserved internationally for industrial, scientific, and medical purposes, known as ISM bands, e.g., used in WiFi, in the telecommunications industry licensed spectrum is predominantly used. In the standards, the telecommunication operators that lease spectrum for mobile communication are called *Mobile Network Operators* (MNO). MNOs bid and lease, for a long period, spectrum through government-controlled auctions. In these auctions, the MNOs purchase the rights to transmit signals over specific frequencies in specific bands. These sets of frequencies are uniquely identified with the *E-UTRA Absolute Radio Frequency Channel Number* (EARFCN). EARFCN is registered following the *Evolved Universal Terrestrial Radio Access* (E-UTRA) standards. MNOs are also assigned unique identifiers, *Public Land Mobile Network* (PLMN), that are used in the cellular technologies provided by a specific network operator in a country.

MNOs install base stations, called *evolved Node Base Station* (eNB) in 4G. These base stations are the gateways of an MNO's Radio Access Network via which UEs connect to the mobile network. UEs can listen and search different licensed bands to get service or roam between operators. There are two directions in the communication between UE and eNB: (i) Downlink (DL) from eNB to

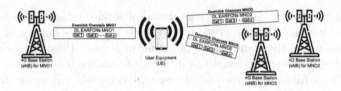

Fig. 1. Simplified overview of a Radio Access Network.

UE, and (ii) Uplink (UL) from UE to eNB. From a hardware perspective, an eNB deployment has multiple antennas that cover a specific area around the eNB. From a logical perspective, there are multiple cells of the MNO running on top of these antennas. A *Cell* is a combination of downlink and uplink MNO resources assigned to serve UEs in a particular area. The center frequency of a cell is called *Carrier Frequency*. Each Cell has a unique global identifier, the *E-UTRAN Cell Global Identifier* (ECGI), which is also a unique identifier within a PLMN.

The communication between UEs and eNBs utilizes the licensed spectrum used by a specific operator. In our study, we identify MNOs by listening to their corresponding PLMN ID that is received in the information contained in the downlink broadcast and control channels from the cell (uniquely identified by ECGI) of an eNB, as illustrated in Fig. 1.

3GPP has outlined different types of architectural splits for the Radio Access Network (RAN) in [7] for enabling various deployment scenarios. Among these, split 7.2x is often cited as a viable option for Open RAN. This split divides the base station into four main functional units: the antenna (which transmits and receives radio signals), the radio unit (which processes the signals), the distributed unit (which handles non-radio functions such as MAC layer operations), and the control unit (which manages radio resources).

2.2   Related Work

Device fingerprinting has been a popular research topic in various domains. Knowing the vendor or network equipment model could, for example, provide insights into the potential impact of exploiting known vulnerabilities in the identified equipment. We survey some generic active fingerprinting methods and zoom in on fingerprinting methods for radio access.

Active Fingerprinting. Active fingerprinting techniques send probe packets to trigger replies that can unveil the hardware vendor, hosted services, or operating system of network equipment [8,15,41]. These techniques are less successful in fingerprinting radio access network equipment that run proprietary protocols and require UE authentication. Moreover, active measurement methodologies are intrusive and thus can be detected by mobile network operators.

UE Passive Fingerprinting. Previous studies [18,27,39,49] show that it is possible to obtain UE information, e.g., the unique Subscriber Identity Module

(SIM) identifier, to launch attacks, e.g., denial-of-service attacks, impersonation, and location tracking. The proposed methods rely on passive fingerprinting techniques by analyzing the traffic traces of mobile operators. Passive remote fingerprinting using microscopic deviations in device hardware (clock skew), can also be applied [25]. Although these techniques can accurately fingerprint individual devices and the operating system, they do not fingerprint the hardware vendor. [40] demonstrates that hardware and software characteristics of UEs with cellular capabilities can be determined in LTE networks. This knowledge can be used to perform battery-draining attacks on IoTs cellular devices.

UE and eNB Localization. Fingerprinting has been used to localize UEs and eNBs [21,24,35,45,46,50]. These techniques utilize signal processing and machine-learning. Such localization information can be used to launch sophisticated attacks that target UEs or eNBs.

Cellular Infrastructure Data Fusion. Online information can be utilized to fingerprint cellular infrastructure. Crowd-sourcing projects collect information using mobile applications and other sources and maintain websites with maps of cellular infrastructure, e.g. with information about the location, bands, operator, etc. Examples of such projects are Cellmapper [12], OpenCellid [34], and Mozilla Location Services [29]. These websites may also utilize publicly available information about the exact location of the cellular antennas that is available in some countries. However, these websites do not offer information about the model-family and vendor of cellular infrastructure, e.g., antennas or Radio Units.

A few governments offer (public) documentation about the location of cellular antennas and sometimes even the vendor and model of the equipment. We, as part of the work for this paper, therefore investigated multiple countries to check whether vendor and model information was disclosed that could be used as ground truth for our work, but "luckily" this was found only for very few countries (or specific regions).

3   From Fingerprinting to Vulnerabilities

In this section, we present a fingerprinting methodology and possible vulnerabilities that can take advantage of knowing the model-family of the target antenna.

3.1   Fingerprinting

An adversary can receive and collect broadcast messages transmitted by base stations, for example by using a laptop equipped with a USB dongle. We assume that the UE of the adversary will never connect to the network, else a more detailed reconnaissance might be possible.

In this paper, we devise a proof-of-concept fingerprinting method that takes advantage of the information broadcasted by base stations. More precisely, since the base station's configuration directly affects the content of the broadcast information, if an MNO uses similar configurations or even the default vendor configuration on its devices, this will be visible from the broadcast message. The adversary can record such broadcast information and train a machine-learning model to predict the vendor or model-family of the device. This approach does require that the adversary collects – through visual inspection – the vendor or model-family ground truth necessary to train the machine-learning model.

While it is important to notice that, even if the visual inspection is providing information about the vendor/model-family, this procedure cannot be used to substitute our fingerprinting method. The main problems related to visual inspection are: (i) the antenna is rarely clearly visible, so visual inspection only occasionally leads to specific results; (ii) if the target antenna is inside a closed premise (like a restricted site) the ground truth collection is not possible without having access to the area; and (iii) to obtain ground truth, the bottom view of the antenna for the interface layout should be clearly visible, which is not often the case, as antennas are also placed on rooftops, especially in urban deployments.

3.2   Vulnerabilities

Given that cellular networks are of vital importance to society, they may be prime targets for adversary state actors [44,47,48]. The attackers can exploit the model's information to create disturbances in telecom networks or gain full authority over data and voice traffic [38]. Such adversaries have ample resources and often may go to great lengths to prepare and execute hacks and attacks. The precise threats from knowing the model-family of the equipment depend on the type of deployment, e.g.: (i) an antenna deployed separately from the radio unit (RU), distributed unit (DU), and control unit (CU); or (ii) antenna and RU deployed together [9,16,22,30], with DU and CU deployed separately. Via fingerprinting, for both deployments, knowing the model-family enables an attacker to infer information like antenna pattern, antenna transmission power and gain. With this information, the attacker can, for example, optimize smart jamming attacks [13,14,26,42]. The first attack that can be improved is the jamming of massive MIMO systems [42]: by knowing the antenna/antenna+RU model the attacker uses the information about the antenna to make better channel estimation techniques. This leads to increased vulnerability to jamming attacks that target their channel estimation process. Another attack that can be improved is the jamming of user equipment served by directional antennas by exploiting the main lobe and nulls [13] which helps to identify vulnerable areas where signal quality inside the coverage of the base station is low. By leveraging information such as antenna pattern, maximum transmitted power, and antenna gain, the attacker can more accurately calculate the link budget which allows the attacker to use way less power to make an attack on the uplink of UE in the vulnerable areas [23].

In the antenna and RU deployment, knowing the model of the hardware containing the RU deployment can reveal valuable information to attackers about the processing capabilities [19] of the base station's functional component. This can enable them to target those with lower processing power via a denial-of-service attack. Or, by making use of online databases such as MITRE [28] and

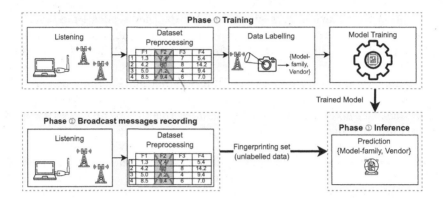

Fig. 2. Fingerprinting phases.

security company reports [43,51], specific identified CVEs related to base station models can be found. Such vulnerable base stations can then be scanned to exploit the CVEs for network attacks.

4 Methodology

Our proof-of-concept fingerprinting method consists of a preparatory phase in which a machine-learning (ML) model is trained. During this phase, the broadcast message emitted by the antennas and the corresponding ground truth, i.e., the model-family or vendor must be collected. The subsequent phases involve collecting the broadcast message from the target antennas and predicting their labels using the trained model. Figure 2 illustrates the three fingerprinting phases.

4.1 Fingerprinting Phases

Phase ① – Training. This phase aims to collect the labeled dataset needed for the ML training. The data collection is contained in the specific target country to provide better results. For the data collection one must first select the antennas for which both the broadcast message and the ground truth can be obtained. To find all available antennas, the data collector can rely on the support of numerous websites that provide information on the location of antennas in the target country. Even without such websites, the ground truth can be collected, but more deployment sites may have to be visited and checked by traveling around the country. For selected antennas, it may be possible to approach the deployment site and collect both the transmitted broadcast message and the ground truth. The message can be collected using a USB dongle connected to a laptop, while the ground truth can be collected through visual inspection, as explained in Sect. 5.4. Once the dataset is collected, a pre-processing step is

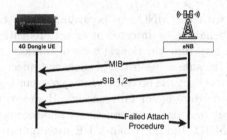

Fig. 3. Schema of the procedure to perform for collecting the messages.

applied to remove some features. After this step, the labeled dataset can be used to train an ML model. The trained model is the output of this phase.

Phase ② – Broadcast Message Recording. In this phase, the broadcast messages from the antennas are collected. This operation is performed only for antennas for which the ground truth is not available. Once the broadcast messages have been collected, the same data pre-processing as used in the training phase is applied to these data. The output of this phase is an unlabelled fingerprinting set of features from the target antennas.

Phase ③ – Model-Family Inference. The goal of this phase is to infer the model-family of the antennas collected in the fingerprinting set, relying only on their broadcast messages. To perform this task, the fingerprinting set is given as input to the trained model, thereby obtaining as output the predicted model-family for each antenna.

4.2 Listening

In this section, we describe the equipment that can be used to collect broadcast messages emitted by base station antennas. Connecting a UE to a network involves initiating a random access procedure. During this phase, the UE listens to the network's control and broadcast channels for the Master and System information blocks (i.e., MIB and SIB). The data received via these channels provides the UE with the information needed to send the initial message to begin communication with the network.

The data we collected only includes some of what is broadcasted in the access procedure. We decided to use only the SIB and not the MIB. The reason behind this decision is that the MIB is not always available through the use of the QCSuper [36] code that we used with the USB dongle. Therefore, to simplify the fingerprinting requirements, we decided to keep only the data contained in the SIBs. We also decided to restrict the data collection to only the first two SIBs (i.e., SIB 1 and SIB 2). These SIBs are indeed available in all the countries investigated, allowing us to make our results as generic as possible.

In Fig. 3, we illustrate the data collection procedure for the 4G Dongle UE. To perform the USB dongle attach procedure, we used a programmable SIM card from the Open Cells Project [32]. To ensure that the dongle minimizes the data exchanged with the MNO, we programmed the SIM card to fail to connect. To get this behavior, we inserted incorrect credentials in the SIM. The consequence is that every time the dongle tries to connect, the MNO rejects it since it is not part of the subscriber list. This does not affect our data collection, since our purpose is to collect the broadcast messages sent before the connection phase failure. This procedure is not fully passive. However, the generated data exchange is very short and does not constitute anomalous behavior from the point of view of an MNO. Indeed, when a UE attempts to authenticate itself in a country without a roaming connection, the failure of a connection due to invalid credentials is an expected occurrence, as the SIM card has not been provisioned for roaming.

It is worth mentioning that the data collection procedure can be rendered entirely passive by utilizing open-source UE solutions such as srsRAN and OpenAirInterface [33]. These projects provide the flexibility to modify the code, enabling a complete passive data collection approach.

5   Experimental Setting

To demonstrate the feasibility of the proof-of-concept fingerprinting methodology, we collected a large dataset of broadcast messages. We first describe the setup used to run the experiments along with our data collection procedure. We then discuss some ethical considerations about our work. Finally, a detailed procedure for the labeling phase, the pre-processing, and the considered ML models are presented.

5.1   Data Collection Setup

For our data collection, we used a machine equipped with Ubuntu 18.04 and Linux kernel 5.4.0-132-lowlatency. The data collection code has been implemented in Python version 3.6.9 using QCSuper commit 5c4e529 and Tshark version 2.6.10. As USB dongle, we used the Quectel EG25-G [37] with firmware version EG25GGBR07A07M2G. To collect the photos (i.e., visual inspection) of the antennas, we used a Samsung Galaxy A50 equipped with a 36× zoom lens [10].

5.2   Measurements

We performed three separate data collections in three different countries. To perform this data collection, we used a laptop equipped with a USB dongle. We collected the broadcast messages emitted by the antennas of 4G base stations (i.e., SIB 1 and SIB 2). To collect the data, we placed the laptop equipped with the dongle in proximity of the target antennas. Since the antennas do not spread their signal in close proximity, we kept a minimum horizontal distance between the dongle and the antennas of at least 15–20 m to avoid bad signal reception. We also kept a maximum distance of 200 m to maximize the likelihood of the dongle receiving multiple broadcast packets from the target antennas. For all

Table 1. Details about the data collection.

	Country 1	Country 2	Country 3
MNOs	3	3	3
Vendors	2	4	3
Vendors brand measured*	E, H	A, H, K, N	H, K, N
Model-families measured	4	17	18
Available bands	1, 3, 7, 8, 20, 28, 38	1, 3, 7, 8, 20, 28, 38	1, 3, 7, 20, 28
Municipalities measured	7	7	10
Physical cells measured	100	33	32
Collection period	August-December 2022	December 2022	December 2022

* A: Amphenol, E: Ericson, H: Huawei, K: Kathrein, N: Nokia-CommScope.

countries, we used public websites to collect information on available eNBs and their positions. We further tried to optimize the variety of the antennas included in our dataset, by collecting the data from an area as broad as possible. For the ground truth collection, we adopted two different strategies: (i) visual inspection, and (ii) public information. The details are provided in Sect. 5.4. In Table 1, we present an overview of our data.

In Table 2, we provide a detailed overview of all the measurements we performed. In total, we collected 112,806 measurements. The vast majority of measurements were collected in Country 1, which is the largest of the three countries in terms of population, mobile users, and number of cells. For Countries 2 and 3, we had access to detailed ground truth data to train our classifier. For Country 1 we had to perform visual inspections to create a labelled set. It is worth mentioning that collecting ground truth data for the model-family classifier was significantly more difficult than for the vendor classifier. Nevertheless, we could identify the ground truth at the model-family level for 73.75% of the total amount of antennas for which we found the vendor ground truth. In particular, 19,68% for Country 1 (visual inspection) and 97.81% and 99.07% in Countries 2 and 3, respectively. The received broadcast messages for a given antenna were identical during our measurements and at different times of the day.

5.3 Ethical Considerations

Although the 4G dongle UE we used initiates and sends a failed attach procedure with the eNB, it does not create any traffic load or harm to the mobile network infrastructure or other mobile users. We did not perform any authorized or unauthorized connection to any mobile networks during our experiments.

5.4 Labeling

This section describes the labeling process used for training.

Table 2. Statistics about our dataset.

Number of	Country 1	Country 2	Country 3
Measurement locations	62	29	13
Tower/pylon locations	10	17	10
Building deployment locations	52	12	3
Ground truth available	NO	YES*	YES
Manual inspection labeling	YES	NO	NO
eNodeBs measured (grouped by operator)	188	155	43
Vendor available	21	69	40
Vendor not available	167	86	3
Model identified	10	69	40
Model not identified	178	86	3
ECGI (grouped by operator)	2,036	992	807
Measurements	76,556	23,389	12,861
Measurements with ground truth for vendor	9,261	14,266	6,227
Measurements with ground truth for model-family	1,823	13,953	6,169
Unique measurements with ground truth for vendor before features removing	9,098	14,169	5,556
Unique measurements with ground truth for vendor after features removing	306	409	305
Unique measurements with ground truth for model-family before features removing	1,784	13,868	5,498
Unique measurements with ground truth for model-family after features removing	87	403	298

* The data was only available for a specific region in this country.

Public Sources. For Countries 2 and 3 the ground truth was already available online. Therefore, we did not need to perform a visual inspection for collecting the dataset labels. To match the broadcast messages collected to the corresponding antennas we exploited the ECGI and the TAC fields available in the broadcast message. These fields are also reported in the online website we used and they allowed us to match the broadcast messages with the corresponding ground truth. In particular, for one country the ground truth was provided for all available antennas, while in the other only a specific region was making this information publicly available. For the former, we collected data for the whole country, while for the latter, we collected data only for the region for which the data was available.

Visual Inspection. In Country 1, the ground truth was not provided by any public source. Therefore, we needed to collect the ground truth by visually inspecting the antennas. Since for most of the antennas, the ground truth can not be inferred through visual inspection, the first optimization was to define an antenna set for which it will probably be possible to extract the vendor/model-family. To perform this optimization, we took advantage of Google Street View [17]. Analyzing the images available on Street View, we did a preliminary screening. We excluded from the data collection those deployment sites where the antennas were not completely visible. For efficiency reasons, we performed the broadcast message collection and the ground truth collection at the same time.

Once the set of optimal antennas was defined, we started the ground truth collection task. We went close to the target deployment sites and took pictures of the antennas. To take the pictures, we used a zoom lens combined with a common smartphone camera. Sometimes, a basic picture analysis might be enough to collect the vendor identity, since the brand symbol might be directly visible on the collected pictures. However, since most of the time the brand was not present or not clearly visible, we compared the collected pictures with the pictures of the antennas provided by the vendors in their datasheet. In particular, we took advantage of two important peculiarities of the antennas: (i) their shapes usually differ from vendor to vendor, providing first immediate feedback on the vendor identity, and (ii) the connectors arrangement on these devices and the colors used to mark the connectors differ from vendor to vendor. Thanks to these peculiarities, we could retrieve the vendor ground truth for a relevant number of antennas for which we had collected data. The process to define the model-family is similar, however, the percentage of success is lower. Indeed, different models from the same vendor might look really similar, not allowing a clear definition of the exact model-family. In general, it is important to note that, for both classes, it is not always possible to gather ground truth for the reasons explained in Sect. 2.2 and Sect. 3.1.

5.5   Pre-processing

The data collected from the broadcast messages can be directly used as features for an ML algorithm. However, pre-processing is still required to remove some features (both for training and testing). The process we applied consisted in removing features from our dataset. In particular, we applied a three-step feature(s) removal. First, we removed features like the "tac", and "ecgi" which can identify the antennas. Second, we removed all the metadata introduced by Wireshark (e.g., timestamps), which might generate a bias for the classifier. Finally, we removed all the features that are not available in all countries. We applied this last step to generalize the results obtained through our experiments as much as possible. After this pre-processing, we obtained a final amount of 53 features. The remaining 53 features are all Information Elements collected from the SIB1 and SIB2 (of the broadcast information from the eNBs) and therefore 3GPP compliant. A full list of the features is provided in the Appendix.

5.6   Classification Methods

To identify the model-family of an antenna, we experimented with four well-known classifiers [11]: Logistic Regression (LR), Support Vector Classifier (SVC), k-Nearest Neighbors (KNN), and Random Forest (RF). We selected these classifiers since they are among the most popular and commonly used. We applied a nested cross-fold validation to evaluate the accuracy of our approach. In the outer loop, we performed a stratified 5-fold cross-validation. Since we made no preliminary assumption about the popularity of certain models, we applied an over-sampling on each training set of the outer loop (i.e., we duplicated random samples for the smaller classes). The over-sampling mitigates the over-fitting due to the imbalanced dataset, since the resulting set contains a balanced number of samples for each class. Since the number of samples available for some classes was limited, we preferred to perform an over-sampling instead of a down-sampling to avoid a strong reduction in the variety of samples for the bigger classes. In the inner loop, we performed another stratified 10-fold cross-validation to split the training set into a training set and a validation set. This inner split has been used to perform a grid search and find the best hyper-parameters on which to train the investigated model. In particular, LR was evaluated for ℓ_1 and ℓ_2 penalties, with C ranging from 10^{-4} to 10^4 (for a total of 20 steps). For SVC, we considered linear and RBF kernels, we varied C among $[10^{-2}, 10^{-1}, 10^0, 10^1]$ and (for the RBF) gamma among $[10^{-4}, 10^{-3}]$. For KNN, we varied the number of neighbors to among $[1, \ldots, 20]$. Finally, for RF we considered from 10 to 100 estimators (steps of 10 and extremes included) and a max depth from 6 to 31 (steps of 5 and extremes included).

The process applied for inferring the vendor was quite similar to the one just described for the model-family. The main difference is that we were able to apply a down-sampling instead of an over-sampling, since the number of samples per class were not so different.

6   Analysis

In this section, we evaluate the performance of our fingerprinting methodology for the scenarios described in Sect. 5.4. Section 6.1 describes how we assess the best classifier for our scenarios. In Sect. 6.2, we discuss the most important features of our fingerprinting methodology, while, in Sect. 6.3, we report the results. Finally, Sects. 6.4 and 6.5 investigate the robustness and limitations of our approach.

6.1   Classifier Evaluation

We evaluated the fingerprinting methodology in different scenarios and configurations. To select the best classifier, we compared the fingerprinting validation accuracy for all considered classifiers. For the model-family inference scenario, RF and KNN achieved an average accuracy of 0.95 with no statistical difference,

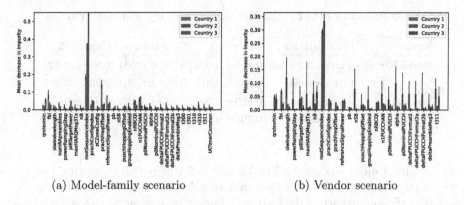

(a) Model-family scenario   (b) Vendor scenario

Fig. 4. Feature importance for the Random Forest model in our two inference scenarios. The variance reported refers to the results obtained over the different nested cross-fold runs.

while SVC and LR were both under 0.90. For this scenario, we decided to keep the RF classifier to take advantage of the feature importance function naturally provided by RF. Thanks to this score function, we have been able to determine which features are most important, and, consequently, suggest possible countermeasures. For the vendor fingerprinting scenario, RF outperformed the other classifiers with an average validation accuracy of 0.97. Among the other classifiers, KNN achieved an average accuracy of 0.88, while SVC and LR were 0.68 and 0.84, respectively.

6.2   Assessment of Feature Importance

As reported before, the Random Forest classifier provides an importance score for each feature given as input to the classifier. For each feature, the importance is computed as the mean of accumulation of the impurity decrease within each tree: the higher this value is, the more important the corresponding feature is. The variance reported in the Figs. 4a and 4b corresponds to the mean decrease in impurity variance among the five runs of the outer loop cross-validation. In Fig. 4a, we reported the importance of the features given as input to the Random Forest classifier for our main scenario (the model-family inference). As explained in Sect. 5.5, we kept only the features for which there were no missing values among all investigated countries. For readability, we only plot the features for which the importance was not zero. Analyzing the figure, we can see that rootSequenceIndex is in general the most important feature. Its importance, however, changes a lot between the different countries. In particular, in Country 1 the prachFreqOffset, and fbi had a higher impact compared to the other features, showing that in different countries the discriminating process between different model-families might focus on different information. The same insight is also visible between countries 2 and 3 based on qrxlevmin, pIRTargetPower, nRBCQI, and n1PUCCHAN. Indeed, for these three features the difference between the

Table 3. Results for the RF classifier in both scenarios and configurations.

Scenario	Configuration	Country 1	Country 2	Country 3
Model-Family	Three classifiers	0.967 ± 0.008	0.983 ± 0.004	0.985 ± 0.002
	One classifier	0.965 ± 0.010	0.989 ± 0.003	0.984 ± 0.002
Vendor	Three classifiers	0.999 ± 0.001	0.985 ± 0.005	0.941 ± 0.018
	One classifier	0.998 ± 0.001	0.965 ± 0.013	0.966 ± 0.020

feature importance for countries 2 and 3 were really high, still suggesting a difference in the factor that allows to discriminate between model-families. In Fig. 4b, we report the importance of the features for our vendor scenario. We can see that the results for countries 2 and 3 are more similar to each other than for the Country 1. The most relevant features for the Country 1 were siwindowlength, alpha, and p0NominalPUSCH, while for the other two countries the importance was more concentrated on the rootSequenceIndex features. This shows an entirely different pattern for the classification strategy adopted in Country 1. Another important difference is the higher variance of the mean decrease in impurity for Country 1. This higher variance indicates that the importance of the various features has undergone large changes between the different outer cross-validation runs. Therefore, the model has selected trees with varying features among the other runs.

6.3   Supervised Learning Results

We report the RF classifier accuracy on the collected datasets according to our validation results. For each scenario, we also evaluated the trained model in two distinct configurations. The first configuration consists in training three distinct classifiers (one for each country). Each classifier is tested only on data from the specific country it has been trained on. The second configuration consists in training only one classifier on data from all three countries. We evaluated the accuracy of the same classifier on the three subsets corresponding to our three countries. In Table 3, we show the performance of the RF model on our two scenarios (vendor and model) and for each of these on both configurations.

Model-Family Inference. This is our main scenario, where we evaluated the RF classifier's performance in identifying an antenna's model-family. Whenever possible, we do not try to identify the model directly, but the model-family. Indeed, knowing the specific model is not always necessary, since vulnerabilities are often related to groups of similar devices rather than a specific one.

Since the concept of "model-family" is not always explicitly defined, we manually define the vendors' families for this experiment. The starting point for defining a model-family is the model code reported in the data sheets made available online by the vendors. For different vendors, we applied different strategies. In particular, for Huawei's devices (which were present in all countries), we defined the family based on the semantics of the model name (which is composed of different parts that gradually become more specific): the identifier we used as the model-family consisted of the model code, from which we removed the last and most specific part. We do not individuate semantics in the model codes for the other vendors. Therefore, we only removed the version (that is frequently included in the model code).

For the results reported in Table 3, we can see that the results for both configurations are quite similar. Both accuracy and variance do not differ much. We can therefore assume that providing data from multiple countries does not provide an advantage to the classifier in terms of accuracy. Instead, we can see that the performance of Country 1 is slightly lower than those of the other two countries. This observation is important since the number of model-family classes for Country 1 is significantly lower compared to the number of classes for the other two countries. The average accuracy values were 97.8% and 97.9% for the first and the second configuration, respectively.

Vendor Inference. As in the previous scenario, we tested on two distinct configurations: three classifiers trained, each only on a single country, and one classifier trained on data from all countries. The classifiers were completely independent of the ones from the previous scenario.

The first configuration (three classifiers trained, one per country) reports good results with a minimum accuracy of 94.1% for Country 3. The performance for Country 1 reached values close to 100%. This result indicates that the collected samples are almost linearly separable. In Sect. 6.5, we further investigated the dataset from this country, trying to describe its differences from the other collected datasets. The second configuration (one classifier trained) shows similar results. The average accuracy values were 97.5% and 97.6% for the first and the second configuration, respectively.

6.4 Sensitivity Analysis

In this section, we propose an experiment that investigates the sensitivity of our classifier. In particular, this experiment analyzes the redundancy of information provided by our features for our specific classification problem. To perform this analysis, we implemented an iterative procedure to remove features from our datasets and evaluated the accuracy of our model. In particular, the cycle we implemented works like this: (i) we evaluate the accuracy of our RF classifier on the dataset and if the accuracy is lower than 85%, we exit the cycle, (ii) we calculate the importance of the features, and (iii) we remove the most important feature from the dataset and we restart the cycle. The result of this experiment for the model-family fingerprinting for Country 1 shows that the accuracy remains higher than 85% until 3 features have been removed. In the other two countries the results are slightly different: removing one feature for Country 2 the results drop down to 64.20%, while for the third the accuracy even dropped down to 56.15%. These results are important since they show that: (i) the performance of our algorithm might change from country to country, which demonstrates the big influence of configuration choices by the MNOs and vendors, and (ii) most of the information might be contained in few features, simplifying in part the task of providing a valid countermeasure.

6.5 Limitations

Our experiments demonstrate cellular infrastructure fingerprinting only based on broadcast information is possible. However, some limitations must be taken into account. Preliminary experiments testing the accuracy of a classifier trained on the dataset of one country on another country show that the model is not transferable between countries. As we collected data from three countries, we propose to extend the data collection from other countries. Another limiting factor for data collection is finding sites where only a single MNO is deployed. In fact, when there are antennas by several MNOs on a single deployment site, it is impossible to trace the collected broadcast message back to the antennas of the transmitting MNOs. Consequently, even if it is possible to collect the ground truth for all the MNOs that share the deployment site, it would not be possible to associate the labels with the corresponding collected broadcast message. If an attacker does not care about a specific MNO, and only wants to exploit antenna vulnerabilities in a specific region, then this limitation goes mute.

7 Countermeasures

The high accuracy that fingerprinting can achieve, together with the associated risks, call for countermeasures. Since the broadcast data are directly connected to the internal configuration of antennas, the natural countermeasure is to diversify the configuration of the different antennas of the same vendor. This countermeasure does have limitations though, as the configuration modification could have impact on the network's overall performance.

Our study also shows that in some countries (countries 2 and 3), it is easy for an adversary to have access to ground truth information that can be utilized to train classifiers. Details about the mobile network model-family and vendor are optional to be included in mobile network antenna installations, and we thus recommend leaving this information out from public sources.

8 Conclusion

Cellular networks play a critical role in communications and hence in the various applications that depend on secure communications. Society's (economic) dependence on cellular networks makes them prime targets for adversarial actors aiming to exploit vulnerabilities and disrupt communications, potentially thereby gaining control over data and voice traffic. To avoid exploitation of known vulnerabilities, it is good security practice to not disclose information regarding the model-family and vendor of the deployed cellular equipment. However, this work shows that it is nonetheless possible to accurately and swiftly identify the model-family of antennas. To our surprise, this is already possible with a low-cost hardware setup along with machine-learning techniques. Our results, based on extensive measurements collected in three countries, show that fingerprinting-based classification can achieve a staggering average accuracy of 97% for both model-family and vendor classification. Our future work will focus on developing countermeasures that modify the configurations of the base station to obfuscate information about the model-family while minimizing the impact on the network performance. We also plan to apply our method to mobile networks in other countries.

Acknowledgement. This research was made possible with support from the European Regional Development Fund and the Province of Zuid-Holland, the Netherlands, the Horizon Europe research and innovation programme of the European Union, under grant agreement no 101092912 (project MLSysOps), and from the European Research Council (ERC) under Starting Grant ResolutioNet (679158).

Appendix

We present the list of the 53 features used to train and test our ML model. Additionally, we provide descriptions of the key features (presented in Fig. 4a and 4b). Due to space issues, the names of the following features have been shortened in Figs. 4a and 4b: preambleInitialReceivedTargetPower → pIRTargetPower, zeroCorrelationZoneConfig → zCZoneConfig, timeAlignmentTimerCommon → tATimerCommon. For documentation on the specifications, we refer to 3GPP specifications [1–6]. **qrxlevmin**: The IE Q-RxLevMin is used to indicate for cell selection/re-selection the required minimum received RSRP level in the (E-UTRA) cell. Corresponds to parameter Qrxlevmin in TS 36.304 [5]. Actual value $Qrxlevmin = fieldvalue * 2[dBm]$.

fbi: The IE FreqBandIndicator indicates the E-UTRA operating band as defined in TS 36.101 [6].

siwindowlength: Common SI scheduling window for all SIs. Unit in milliseconds, where ms1 denotes 1 ms, ms2 denotes 2 ms and so on.

numRApreambles: Number of non-dedicated random access preambles in [1].

powerRampingStep: Power ramping factor in TS 36.321 [1]. Value in dB.

preambleInitialReceivedTargetPower: Initial preamble power in TS 36.321 [1]. Value in dBm.

maxHARQMsg3Tx: Maximum number of Msg3 HARQ transmissions in TS 36.321 [1], used for contention based random access. Value is an integer.

nB: nB is used as one of parameters to derive the Paging Frame and Paging Occasion according to TS 36.304 [5]. Value in multiples of 'T' as defined in TS 36.304 [5].

rootSequenceIndex: RACH_ROOT_SEQUENCE, see TS 36.211 [2, §5.7.1].

prachConfigIndex: prach-ConfigurationIndex, see TS 36.211 [2, §5.7.1].

zeroCorrelationZoneConfig: NCS configuration, see TS 36.211 [2, §5.7.2: Table 5.7.2-2] for preamble format 0-3 and TS 36.211 [2, §5.7.2: Table 5.7.2-3] for preamble format 4.

prachFreqOffset: prach-FrequencyOffset, see TS 36.211 [2, §5.7.1].

referenceSignalPower: Reference-signal power, which provides the downlink reference-signal EPRE, see TS 36.213 [3, §5.2]. The actual value in dBm.

Pb: P_B, see TS 36.213 [3, Table 5.2-1].

nSB: N_{sb} see TS 36.211 [2, §5.3.4].

puschHoppingOffset: see TS 36.211 [2, §5.3.4].

groupHoppingEnabled: Group-hopping-enabled, see TS 36.211 [2, §5.5.1.3].

nRBCQI: $N_{RB}^{(2)}$, see TS 36.211 [2, §5.4].

n1PUCCHAN: $N_{PUCCH}^{(1)}$, see TS 36.213 [3, §10.1].

p0NominalPUSCH: $P_{O\_NOMINAL\_PUSCH}$ See TS 36.213 [3, §5.1.1.1], unit dBm. This field is applicable for non-persistent scheduling only.

deltaFPUCCHFormatx: $\Delta_{F\_PUCCH}(F)$ for the PUCCH formats 1, 1b, 2, 2a, 2b, 3, 4, 5 and 1b with channel selection. See TS 36.213 [3, §5.1.2] where deltaF-2 corresponds to -2 dB, deltaF0 corresponds to 0 dB and so on.

alpha: α See TS 36.213 [3, §5.1.1.1].

T3xx: the T3xx timers(T300,T301,T310, and T311) are used to control various aspects of radio resource management and handover procedures. See TS 36.213 [3].

p0NominalPUCCH: $P_{O\_NOMINAL\_PUCCH}$ See TS 36.213 [3, §5.1.2.1] (unit dBm).

deltaPreambleMsg3: $\Delta_{PREAMBLE\_Msg3}$ see TS 36.213 [3, §5.1.1.1]. Actual value = field value * 2 [dB].

n310: Maximum number of consecutive "out-of-sync" or "early-out-of-sync" indications for the PCell received from lower layers.

TimeAlignmentTimerCommon: The IE TimeAlignmentTimer is used to control how long the UE considers the serving cells belonging to the associated TAG to be uplink time aligned. Corresponds to the Timer for time alignment in TS 36.321 [1]. Value in number of subframes.

Due to space limitations, the remaining features that do not appeared as model features, can be looked up in the 3GPP specifications [1–6]: cfou (**cellReservedForOperatorUse**), cbon (**cellBarred**), ifra (**intraFreqReselection**), **preambleTransMax, raResponseWindowSize,**

macContentionResolutionTimer, modificationPeriodicCoeff, default-
PagingCycle, highspeedFlag, hoppingMode, enable64QAM, groupAs-
signmentPUSCH, sequenceHoppingEnabled, cyclicShift, deltaPUC-
CHShift, nCSAN, n311, ulCyclicPrefixLength, additionalSpectrumE-
mission.

References

1. 3GPP: LTE; Evolved Universal Terrestrial Radio Access (E-UTRA); Medium
   Access Control (MAC) protocol specification (3GPP TS 36.321). 3GPP (2022).
   https://www.3gpp.org/dynareport/36321.htm
2. 3GPP: LTE; Evolved Universal Terrestrial Radio Access (E-UTRA); Physical channels and modulation (3GPP TS 36.211). 3GPP (2022). https://www.3gpp.org/
   dynareport/36211.htm
3. 3GPP: LTE; Evolved Universal Terrestrial Radio Access (E-UTRA); Physical layer
   procedures (3GPP TS 36.213). 3GPP (2022). https://www.3gpp.org/dynareport/
   36213.htm
4. 3GPP: LTE; Evolved Universal Terrestrial Radio Access (E-UTRA); Radio
   Resource Control (RRC); Protocol specification (3GPP TS 36.331). 3GPP (2022).
   https://www.3gpp.org/dynareport/36331.htm
5. 3GPP: LTE; Evolved Universal Terrestrial Radio Access (E-UTRA); User Equipment (UE) procedures in idle mode (3GPP TS 36.304). 3GPP (2022). https://
   www.3gpp.org/dynareport/36304.htm
6. 3GPP: LTE; Evolved Universal Terrestrial Radio Access (E-UTRA); User Equipment (UE) radio transmission and reception (3GPP TS 36.101). 3GPP (2022).
   https://www.3gpp.org/dynareport/36101.htm
7. 3GPP: Study on New Radio Access Technology: Radio Access Architecture and
   Interfaces (2023). https://www.3gpp.org/DynaReport/38801.htm
8. Albakour, T., Gasser, O., Beverly, R., Smaragdakis, G.: Third time's not a charm:
   exploiting SNMPv3 for router fingerprinting. In: ACM IMC (2021)
9. Amphenol: Amphenol small cells: Cell oDAS. https://amphenolwireless.com/
   small-cellodas/. Accessed 15 May 2023
10. Apexel: 36X Super Phone Camera Telephoto Lens for Mobile Phone. https://www.
    apexeloptic.com/product/36x-telescope-lens
11. Ben-David, S., Shalev-Shwartz, S.: Understanding Machine Learning: From Theory
    to Algorithms. Cambridge University Press, Cambridge (2014)
12. Cellmapper: Map (2022). https://www.o-ran.org/. https://www.cellmapper.net
13. CISCO: Antenna Patterns and Their Meaning. https://www.industrialnetworking.
    com/pdf/Antenna-Patterns.pdf
14. Clancy, T.C.: Efficient OFDM denial: pilot jamming and pilot nulling. In: 2011
    IEEE International Conference on Communications (2011)
15. Durumeric, Z., Wustrow, E., Halderman, J.A.: ZMap: fast internet-wide scanning
    and its security applications. In: USENIX Security Symposium (2013)
16. Ericsson: Small Cells: Radio Dots. https://www.ericsson.com/en/portfolio/
    networks/ericsson-radio-system/radio/small-cells/indoor/radio-dots
17. Google: Street View. https://www.google.com/streetview
18. Gorrepati, U., Zavarsky, P., Ruhl, R.: Privacy protection in LTE and 5G net-
    works. In: International Conference on Secure Cyber Computing and Communica-
    tion (2021)

19. Groen, J., DOro, S., Demir, U., Bonati, L., Polese, M., Melodia, T., Chowdhury, K.: Implementing and evaluating security in O-RAN: interfaces, intelligence, and platforms. arXiv preprint arXiv:2304.11125 (2023)

20. GSM Association: GSMA: The Mobile Economy 2022. GSMA (2022). https://www.gsma.com/mobileeconomy/wp-content/uploads/2022/02/280222-The-Mobile-Economy-2022.pdf

21. Gubiani, D., Gallo, P., Viel, A., Dalla Torre, A., Montanari, A.: A cellular network database for fingerprint positioning systems. In: Welzer, T., et al. (eds.) ADBIS 2019. CCIS, vol. 1064, pp. 111–119. Springer, Cham (2019). https://doi.org/10.1007/978-3-030-30278-8_14

22. Huawei: Huawei small cells: Lampsite. https://carrier.huawei.com/en/products/wireless-network-v3/Small-Cell/LampSite. Accessed 15 May 2023

23. Jover, R.P., Lackey, J., Raghavan, A.: Enhancing the security of LTE networks against jamming attacks. EURASIP J. Inf. Secur. **2014**(1), 1–14 (2014)

24. Joyce, R., Zhang, L.: Locating small cells using geo-located UE measurement reports & RF fingerprinting. In: 2015 IEEE International Conference on Communications (2015)

25. Kohno, T., Broido, A., Claffy, K.C.: Remote physical device fingerprinting. In: IEEE Symposium on Security and Privacy (2005)

26. Lichtman, M., Reed, J.H., Clancy, T.C., Norton, M.: Vulnerability of LTE to hostile interference. In: IEEE Global Conference on Signal and Information Processing (2013)

27. Meneghello, F., Rossi, M., Bui, N.: Smartphone identification via passive traffic fingerprinting: a sequence-to-sequence learning approach. IEEE Netw. **34**(2), 112–120 (2020)

28. MITRE: MITRE CVEs. https://cve.mitre.org/cgi-bin/cvekey.cgi?keyword=enodeb. Accessed 15 May 2023

29. Mozilla: Location Services (2022). https://location.services.mozilla.com/

30. Nokia: Nokia Small Cells: Airscale. https://www.nokia.com/networks/mobile-networks/airscale-radio-access/micro-rrh/. Accessed 15 May 2023

31. O-RAN: O-RAN Specifications. https://orandownloadsweb.azurewebsites.net/specifications. Accessed 22 May 2023

32. Open Cells: Open Cells Project. https://open-cells.com/

33. OpenAirInterface Software Alliance: penAirInterface. https://www.srslte.com/ and https://openairinterface.org/

34. OpenCellid: OpenCellid. OpenCellid (2022). https://opencellid.org/

35. del Peral-Rosado, J.A., Raulefs, R., López-Salcedo, J.A., Seco-Granados, G.: Survey of cellular mobile radio localization methods: from 1G to 5G. IEEE Commun. Surv. Tutor. **20**(2), 1124–1148 (2017)

36. QCSuper contributors: QCSuper toole. https://github.com/P1sec/QCSuper

37. Quectel: EG25-G. https://www.exvist.com/products/4g-lte-usb-dongle-wquectel-iot-eg25-g-mini-pcie-type-c

38. Security Week: Critical Baicells Device Vulnerability Can Expose Telecoms Networks to Snooping. https://www.securityweek.com/critical-baicells-device-vulnerability-can-expose-telecoms-networks-to-snooping/

39. Seyi, A.B., Jafaar, F., Ruhl, R.: Securing the authentication process of LTE base stations. In: IEEE International Conference on Electrical, Communication, and Computer Engineering (2020)

40. Shaik, A., Borgaonkar, R., Park, S., Seifert, J.P.: New vulnerabilities in 4G and 5G cellular access network protocols: exposing device capabilities. In: ACM WiSec (2019)

41. Shamsi, Z., Nandwani, A., Leonard, D., Loguinov, D.: Hershel: single-packet OS fingerprinting. In: ACM SIGMETRICS (2014)
42. Skokowski, P., et al.: Jamming and Jamming mitigation for selected 5G military scenarios. Procedia Comput. Sci. **205**, 258–267 (2022)
43. Synacktiv: Multiple Vulnerabilities in Nokia BTS AirScale. https://www.synacktiv.com/sites/default/files/2023-02/Synacktiv-Nokia-BTS-AirScale-Asika-Multiple-Vulnerabilities.pdf
44. The Times of Israel: 3 Israelis charged in Hamas plot to sabotage telecom networks used by IDF during war. https://www.timesofisrael.com/3-israelis-charged-in-hamas-plot-to-sabotage-telecom-networks-used-by-idf-during-war/
45. Timoteo, R.D., Cunha, D.C.: A scalable fingerprint-based angle-of-arrival machine learning approach for cellular mobile radio localization. Comput. Commun. **157**, 92–101 (2020)
46. Triki, M., Slock, D.T., Rigal, V., François, P.: Mobile terminal positioning via power delay profile fingerprinting: reproducible validation simulations. In: IEEE Vehicular Technology Conference, pp. 1–5 (2006)
47. VOANews: Somali Telecommunications Center, Tower Destroyed in Explosion. https://www.voanews.com/a/somali-telecommunications-center-tower-destroyed-in-explosion/6824753.html
48. Wired: The Last Cell Tower in Mariupol. https://www.wired.com/story/mariupol-ukraine-war/
49. Yu, L., Luo, B., Ma, J., Zhou, Z., Liu, Q.: You are what you broadcast: identification of mobile and IoT devices from (public) WiFi. In: USENIX Security Symposium (2020)
50. Zhang, Y., et al.: Transfer learning-based outdoor position recovery with cellular data. IEEE Trans. Mob. Comput. **20**(5), 2094–2110 (2020)
51. Zimperium: Analysis of multiple vulnerabilities in different open source BTS products. https://www.zimperium.com/blog/analysis-of-multiple-vulnerabilities-in-different-open-source-bts-products/

One IDS Is Not Enough! Exploring Ensemble Learning for Industrial Intrusion Detection

Konrad Wolsing[1,2]([✉]) [ID], Dominik Kus[2] [ID], Eric Wagner[1,2] [ID],
Jan Pennekamp[2] [ID], Klaus Wehrle[2] [ID], and Martin Henze[1,3] [ID]

[1] Cyber Analysis & Defense, Fraunhofer FKIE, Wachtberg, Germany
{konrad.wolsing,eric.wagner,martin.henze}@fkie.fraunhofer.de
[2] Communication and Distributed Systems, RWTH Aachen University, Aachen, Germany
{wolsing,kus,wagner,pennekamp,wehrle}@comsys.rwth-aachen.de
[3] Security and Privacy in Industrial Cooperation, RWTH Aachen University, Aachen, Germany
henze@cs.rwth-aachen.de

Abstract. Industrial Intrusion Detection Systems (IIDSs) play a critical role in safeguarding Industrial Control Systems (ICSs) against targeted cyberattacks. Unsupervised anomaly detectors, capable of learning the expected behavior of physical processes, have proven effective in detecting even novel cyberattacks. While offering decent attack detection, these systems, however, still suffer from too many False-Positive Alarms (FPAs) that operators need to investigate, eventually leading to alarm fatigue. To address this issue, in this paper, we challenge the notion of relying on a single IIDS and explore the benefits of combining multiple IIDSs. To this end, we examine the concept of ensemble learning, where a collection of classifiers (IIDSs in our case) are combined to optimize attack detection and reduce FPAs. While training ensembles for supervised classifiers is relatively straightforward, retaining the unsupervised nature of IIDSs proves challenging. In that regard, novel time-aware ensemble methods that incorporate temporal correlations between alerts and transfer-learning to best utilize the scarce training data constitute viable solutions. By combining diverse IIDSs, the detection performance can be improved beyond the individual approaches with close to no FPAs, resulting in a promising path for strengthening ICS cybersecurity.

Keywords: Intrusion Detection · Ensemble Learning · ICS

1 Introduction

Industrial Intrusion Detection Systems (IIDSs) represent a fundamental building block to defend Industrial Control Systems (ICSs) against constantly emerging and highly targeted cyberattacks [4]. Besides offering a cost-effective security upgrade and serving as a second line of defense once preventive measures have been breached, IIDSs are also suitable for deployment in legacy ICSs with poor

© The Author(s), under exclusive license to Springer Nature Switzerland AG 2024
G. Tsudik et al. (Eds.): ESORICS 2023, LNCS 14345, pp. 102–122, 2024.
https://doi.org/10.1007/978-3-031-51476-0_6

security where preventive measures, e.g., encryption and authentication, are hard to retrofit. To this end, research proposed a plethora of algorithms that automatically raise alerts for suspected malicious activities in ICSs [8,11,18,33,47,50].

Since ICS deployments are rather unique and adversaries in that domain are particularly sophisticated, ICSs often face zero-day attacks [4,33]. This threat significantly hampers the effectiveness of *supervised* detection approaches since their reliance on samples of (known) attacks for training runs the risk of detecting only these trained attacks or slight variants at best [2,24]. In contrast, *unsupervised* anomaly detectors [8], which can learn the expected behavior of repetitive physical processes by means of, e.g., machine learning, have proven successful across many scientific evaluations [5,14,22,29,46]. Their main benefit lies in training on benign-only data which can easily be recorded during regular operation of an ICS as well as their ability to detect novel cyberattacks.

Despite unsupervised IIDSs being capable of detecting even zero-day attacks, they come at the notorious risk of emitting False-Positive Alarms (FPAs) [2,41]. In practice, every alert has to undergo analysis by an operator to decide whether it is reasonable to interrupt operation in case of a suspected cyberattack. Consequently, as stated by Etalle et al. [13], FPAs significantly contribute to an IIDS's total cost of ownership. Moreover, since cyberattacks against ICSs' physical processes are still rare [4], minimizing the number of FPAs is equally as important as detecting attacks because they increase the risk of *alarm fatigue* where operators start ignoring the IIDS over time, such that actual attacks can slip through.

To meet these high detection standards, most scientific proposals aim to find yet another single-best, *monolithic* IIDS that outperforms existing work. But, studies of unsupervised IIDSs reveal that no approach currently detects all attacks contained in prominent datasets [46] or documented in literature [12]. Fortunately, real-world deployments are not restricted to integrating just the best-performing IIDS and may instead choose from the several available approaches to play off their advantages and disadvantages against each other. These observations raise the question whether one IIDS is enough to provide strong ICS security or if a combination of multiple IIDSs can join forces to optimize detection performance beyond what each individual approach can achieve.

The problem of combining a collection of classifiers (e.g., IIDSs) into a single system is generally known as ensemble learning [38,49,51]. However, while the training of an ensemble is relatively straightforward for supervised IIDSs, where simply another round of training suffices [16,25,27,34], retaining the unsupervised nature, i.e., requiring no attack knowledge during training, as is desirable for usage in ICSs, proves challenging. Consequently, we explore how *ensembles of unsupervised IIDSs* can be built and to which extent they are superior to monolithic deployments, e.g., by detecting more attacks in total or reducing FPA.

Contributions. To better understand the potential of ensemble learning for industrial intrusion detection, we make the following contributions:

- We uncover weaknesses in monolithic IIDS deployments and identify three challenges on the path to realize unsupervised IIDS ensembles (Sect. 3).

- Exploring the potential of IIDS ensembles, we reveal an enormous theoretical potential that, however, proves hard to transfer into practice (Sect. 4).
- Digging deeper, we find one reason inhibiting this potential in the ensembles' insufficiency to regard temporal information and prove that a novel class of time-aware ensembles can drastically improve this situation (Sect. 5).
- Lastly, we consider transfer-learning, i.e., training an ensemble in a different ICS under attack and transferring the model to the target ICS, as a promising method to tackle the lack of attack data during ensemble training (Sect. 6).

2　Industrial Intrusion Detection and Ensemble Learning

Before assessing whether the fusion of unsupervised IIDSs into an ensemble is feasible, we provide an introduction to intrusion detection methods in the ICS domain (Sect. 2.1), datasets, and metrics (Sect. 2.2) that we leverage in our evaluations. We then lay out the basic principles of ensemble learning (Sect. 2.3).

2.1　Unsupervised Industrial Intrusion Detection

The transition to Internet-connected ICSs establishes new paths for cyberattacks [4], where attackers can, e.g., manipulate sensors or actuators to cause harm [42,50]. Since ICSs are usually operated for decades without major downtime, retrofittable security measures are desirable [47]. To this end, IIDSs closely monitoring the physical behavior of an ICS can report even subtle deviations to an operator. As ICSs feature regular and repetitive patterns, IIDSs make great use of temporal coherences in this data for attack detection [5,22,29,46].

The methodologies followed in research to implement intrusion detection can broadly be classified into supervised and unsupervised IIDSs [2]. Supervised approaches rely on benign *and* malicious training data, which in return yields high detection rates [2]. However, not only is obtaining attack samples for the target ICS difficult [6], but supervised IIDSs are also prone to merely detecting those attacks presented to them during training [24] and thus fail to succeed on zero-day attacks. Unsupervised IIDSs, in contrast, require only benign training data and can thus indicate any deviation from the learned normality model [8]. Despite being prone to emit more FPAs, their promise to detect any attack violating normal behavior regardless of attack samples resembles a key feature for ICS.

Looking closer at how unsupervised IIDSs function, we present eight approaches from related work. The first approach (*Invariant*) [14] proposes a method to derive invariants that must be fulfilled by the ICS at all times, e.g., if the water level of a tank is rising, its inlet valve must be open. In contrast, *PASAD* [5] leverages a singular spectrum analysis to distinguish deterministic ICS behavior from non-determinism induced by attacks. *Seq2SeqNN* [22], which trains a neural network, and *TABOR* [29], based on timed automata, both alert deviations from the model's predicted ICS behavior. Lastly, Wolsing et al. [46] presented four lightweight approaches, i.e., minimum and maximum range checks

(*MinMax*), the detection of steep in- and declines (*Gradient*) as well as frozen physical values (*Steadytime*), and unnatural distributions of process data (*Histogram*). These eight IIDSs build the foundation for our subsequent analyses.

2.2 Evaluating Industrial Intrusion Detection Systems

In the ICS domain, researchers leverage specialized datasets [10,21] to prove their IIDSs' capabilities. The eight IIDSs considered in this publication have originally been designed for and evaluated on the SWaT [19] or WADI [1] datasets, which are predominantly used in the IIDS domain [10]. Those datasets are specifically suited to evaluate unsupervised IIDSs as they ship with a large training part of benign-only data and another testing part containing several cyberattacks. In total, SWaT, which models a water treatment plant, contains 36 cyberattacks, and WADI, which represents a water distribution testbed, contains 14 attacks.

Besides datasets, metrics play an important role in judging an IIDS's performance. However, since attacks against ICSs and their effects can last for a certain time, point-based metrics (e.g., accuracy, precision, recall, or F1 score) are heavily skewed in this case as they score more points to longer attacks than (several) shorter ones [17,20]. To cope with these issues, newer metrics implementing time-aware variants of precision, recall, and F1 score were recently proposed, with the enhanced time-aware (eTa) metrics [20] emerging as a promising idea.

For these reasons, we refer to the time-aware metrics $eTaP$ (precision), $eTaR$ (recall), and $eTaF1$ (F1) in our evaluations and, in addition, rely on the following two metrics from related work [29,46]: First, $FPAs$ counts the number of continuous alerts that do not overlap with any attack. Second, detected scenarios (*Scen.*) enumerates how many continuous attacks from the dataset are detected. Together, these metrics promise accurate insights into the IIDSs' performance.

2.3 Ensemble Learning

Instead of proposing and evaluating new IIDSs, leveraging multiple IIDSs side-by-side can be another path to more secure ICSs. In this regard, ensemble learning represents a subfield of machine learning concerned with the process of training multiple classifiers, i.e.,IIDSs, and fusing them into a single model to increase predictive performance [38,49,51] as proven successful in, e.g., the fields of computer vision [26] or biometric recognition [39]. The methods followed in the literature can be roughly divided into homogeneous and heterogeneous ensembles. Since homogeneous ensembles combine the same type of classifier, i.e., only Support Vector Machines (SVMs), they are rather suited to create monolithic IIDSs, as demonstrated before [9,23,30,31,35,48]. In contrast, heterogeneous ensembles combine diverging approaches. Considering the diversity of IIDSs proposed in the literature (cf. Sect. 2.1), our paper focuses on heterogeneous ensemble learning.

The general methodology for heterogeneous ensemble learning is visualized in Fig. 1. First, a set of *base-classifiers* is pre-trained on a training dataset. Then, their outputs are fed into a *combiner* which fuses them into a single classification. More precisely, the input of the combiner is a judgment of each IIDS,

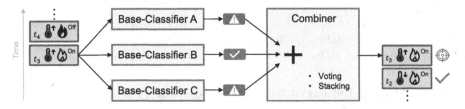

Fig. 1. With ensemble learning, a combiner joins the output of several base-classifiers into a single decision. In the case of learning-based ensembles, an additional training step on the outputs of the base-classifiers and the expected outcome may be necessary.

whether it has identified an alert (1) or classifies the situation as benign (0) for the current data point. For a set of n IIDSs, the algorithm receives an alert vector $v \in \{0,1\}^n$. Hereby, the combiner can either be learning-based, i.e., *stacking* machine-learning classifiers trained over a dataset, or rule-based, e.g., weighted *voting* to combine binary outputs [32,51]. According to best practices [37,52], a learning-based combiner must be trained on out-of-sample data for the base-classifiers, which can be achieved, e.g., by splitting the dataset into separate train sets for base-classifiers and combiner. When measuring the combiner performance, the evaluation must be conducted on a set of previously unseen data.

Lastly, although ensembles promise to improve detection performance, they can hinder interpretability [40] or accountability [13], i.e., they complicate reconstructing why an alarm is emitted, which is important for attack mitigation.

3   From Monolithic IIDSs to IIDS Ensembles

Given the tremendous efforts invested in designing IIDSs (cf. Sect. 2.1), ICS operators must decide which conceptual approach they adopt by weighing all proposals based on their capabilities. However, this decision can be difficult as prior work raised the suspicion that no optimal IIDS exists that detects sufficiently many attacks [12,46]. To confirm this claimed insufficiency, we analyze eight IIDSs in Sect. 3.1. We then examine to which extent related work on ensemble learning can provide a solution (Sect. 3.2) and identify three unique challenges for *unsupervised* ensemble learning that inhibit its immediate adoption (Sect. 3.3).

3.1   Insufficiency of Monolithic Detectors

To study the capabilities of the eight IIDSs (cf. Sect. 2.1), we leverage open-source implementations of them [47] and evaluate them on the SWaT dataset[1]. Given the results from Table 1, we can confirm the IIDSs' insufficiency, as no single approach detects all 36 cyberattacks (cf. Scen.), yet 33 would be detectable in combination. Moreover, across the five metrics introduced in Sect. 2.2, no monolithic IIDS performs best in more than one of the metrics (cf. grey

---

[1] The results for a second dataset (WADI) are compiled in Appendix A.

Table 1. These eight approaches from relevant literature to detect cyberattacks highlight that relying on a monolithic IIDS introduces risks, as none of them detects all attacks. Moreover, determining the "best" IIDS heavily depends on the chosen metric.

IIDS (Baseline)	eTaP	eTaR	eTaF1	Scen.	FPA
Invariant [14]	54.7	29.8	38.6	30	217
PASAD [5]	16.0	4.9	7.5	16	14
Seq2SeqNN [22]	42.8	47.2	44.9	26	37
MinMax [46]	67.8	47.1	55.6	23	9
Gradient [46]	20.5	6.0	9.2	25	64
Steadytime [46]	81.6	30.1	44.0	14	4
Histogram [46]	70.9	23.2	34.9	13	0
TABOR [29]	49.1	18.9	27.3	19	28

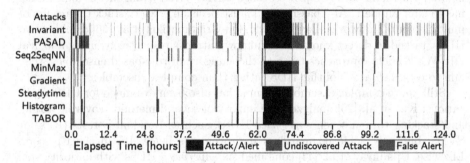

Fig. 2. The alerts emitted by IIDSs on the SWaT dataset exemplify the challenges operators face during investigations, as they each exhibit distinct alerting behavior.

cells in Table 1), indicating that certain compromises towards one or another metric have to be made by operators selecting an IIDS for their ICS. More precisely, while the Invariant IIDS excels in detected scenarios, thus likely unveiling most cyberattacks, it fares badly concerning FPAs (217). On the contrary, Histogram detects the fewest cyberattacks but also yields no FPAs, resulting in reliable indications that can counteract the risk of alarm fatigue. Both extremes seem undesirable for deployment, and a trivial combination, e.g., with a logical OR, would enable great detection yet add up all the FPAs from both approaches.

Aside from detection performance, the alerts should be accountable to ICS operators to initiate appropriate countermeasures [13,40]. Yet, when visually analyzing the alerts (cf. Fig. 2), we observe how differently these IIDSs indicate attacks. E.g., MinMax produces nine FPAs occurring near the actual attacks, which is in stark contrast to Invariant spreading alarms even across broad regions of benign behavior. This qualitative difference is not expressable with current metrics. Contrarily, PASAD, and Histogram exhibit a different phenomenon of "overhanging" alerts (red) after the attacks, which complicates determining the actual range of an attack. Given these distinct behaviors, truly understanding an IIDS's alerts requires expert knowledge of the underlying detection mechanism.

Takeaway. We observed that IIDSs have complementary strengths and opposing weaknesses. Thus, relying on a single IIDS can yields suboptimal ICS security. Furthermore, it increases the burden for operators, who must select an IIDS that best fits their deployment, as a trivial ensemble, where all alerts are simply ORed, would better detect attacks yet likely suffer from an excessive multitude of FPAs. This disappointing situation motivates looking for ensembles that cleverly combine the advantages of multiple IIDSs (cf. Sect. 2.3) to (i) improve the detection capabilities and (ii) make alarms generally more comprehensible.

3.2   IIDS Ensemble Learning in Related Work

In the past, the idea of ensemble learning has already been used to fuse (smaller) detection concepts into a final IIDS [3,22,29,36]. As an example, TABOR [29] fuses three detection methods together. Likewise, Seq2SeqNN [22] trains one neural network for each ICS process stage (six for SWaT), and only a single model has to emit an alert. Al-Abassi et al. [3] use decision trees to stack the results of multiple neural networks. Lastly, Radoglou-Grammatikis et al. [36] combine two IIDSs, tasked to detect known and unknown attacks respectively, using a logical OR. While such approaches fall into the category of rule-based ensembles, they aim to establish a monolithic IIDS rather than complex ensembles.

Still, more complex ensemble learning has also been examined for IIDS applications: Kus et al. [25] analyzed the impact of several methods covering voting and stacking to join seven *supervised* IIDSs, such as Random Forests (RFs) or SVMs, but only achieved marginal improvements below 1% in the F1 score. Likewise, Upadhyay et al. [44] combined six *supervised* IIDSs with majority voting achieving similar results. Gao et al. [16] combined two deep learning models using a stacked Multi-Layer Perceptron (MLP) with improvements in F1 score of only up to 0.41%. Nguyen et al. [34] combined three classifiers using stacking with an MLP. They achieved an increase of 0.14% in F1 score but had little room for improvement in the first place as the best base-classifier achieved an F1 score of 99.58%. Li et al. [27] combined three classifiers using majority voting to increase accuracy by up to 1.62%. Lastly, Balaji et al. [7], who experimented with Logistic Regression (LR) as ensemble method, conclude that they rather learned attack signatures and leave unsupervised learning to future work. However, to date, comparable research on unsupervised IIDS ensembles is still missing.

3.3   Challenges for Unsupervised IIDS Ensembles

In related work, ensemble learning managed to achieve only slight improvements (around +1% in F1 score) in the IIDS context, likely due to small margins within the used base-IIDSs. In our baseline results from Table 1, however, we observed grossly different behaviors and IIDSs distinctly detecting attacks, indicating much greater potential for ensembles to work with.

Notably, most related work from the IIDS domain considers *supervised* ensembles [16,25,27,34]. This severe limitation introduces the risk of only detecting the trained attacks [24], effectively transforming unsupervised base-IIDSs back into a supervised IIDS. Moreover, given their reliance on attack data during training which is scarce in the ICS domain [6,10], the standard methodology used to train (and evaluate) such supervised ensembles is incompatible with *unsupervised* training, which is imperative in the ICS domain. To this end, we explain the three challenges (**C1–C3**) pertaining to the current methodology.

C1—Benign Training Only. Unsupervised IIDSs train exclusively on benign data, eliminating the need for attacks in the training set. This property enables them to detect zero-day attacks [41] and simplifies their training, as benign data can be recorded during normal ICS operation and is, therefore, abundantly available, while attack data is rare and difficult to obtain [6]. While, in the ICS context, the ensemble's base-IIDSs could still be trained on benign data, ensemble learning usually remains dependent on observing the IIDSs under benign *and* attack conditions (cf. Sect. 3.2). This limitation effectively rules out the types of learning-based ensembles discussed in related work.

C2—Sequential Data Series. One property of IIDSs critical for their success is the ability to analyze dependencies in sequential data series (cf. Sect. 2.1). E.g., Seq2SeqNN accumulates the drift between predicted and observed behavior, detecting even subtle deviations [22]. Thus, the input data must be ordered chronologically, making the standard methodology from related work to randomly shuffle and split datasets into training and evaluation parts [16,25,27,34] infeasible for unsupervised IIDS ensembles as it alters a data series' order.

C3—Temporal Dependencies. Another temporal effect is that cyberattacks persist over a longer period, e.g., to thwart detection by inflicting the damage slowly [5]. Since the effects may not happen instantaneously, an IIDS may detect attacks with some delay. For example, one base-IIDS might detect the attack at an early stage while a second IIDS requires more time, such that their alerts do not overlap. This issue demands time-aware ensembles which are capable of correlating both alerts to one attack. Yet, current ensembles base their decisions on a single data point without considering recent history, and no methods that take advantage of such temporal dependencies are known to us.

Takeaway. Due to their individual inefficiencies, a single IIDS is not enough for strong ICS cybersecurity. However, ensemble learning promises to transfer precisely this diversity into an advantage, albeit existing ensemble methodologies turn out infeasible because of unsupervised IIDSs' unique requirements.

4 The Potential of Unsupervised Ensembles

As established learning-based ensemble methods are inapplicable to the *unsupervised* IIDSs predominantly used in ICSs (cf. Sect. 3.3), novel ways to fuse IIDSs into ensembles are required. First, we examine weight-based voting schemes and measure their maximal potential in Sect. 4.1 to establish a theoretical baseline. We then study to which extent this potential can actually be leveraged in Sect. 4.2.

4.1   Potential Analysis of Weight-Based Ensembles

Ensemble methods for unsupervised IIDSs have to fulfill a new set of criteria compared to related work relying on supervised training (cf. Sect. 3.3). For our first potential analysis, we consider voting mechanisms, an approach that is not dependent on attack data for training and retains the temporal order of the data.

Design. As the first step, we train every base-IIDS on benign data for the target ICS such that, when presented with new data, we obtain an alert vector v encoding the judgment of each IIDS. Next, the ensemble assigns an individual weight $w \in \mathbb{R}^n$ to each IIDS. Then, a combined alert is emitted if the weighted sum of IIDS outputs meets a threshold $t \in \mathbb{R}$, i.e., $v_1 \cdot w_1 + \cdots + v_n \cdot w_n \geq t$.

The crucial part is finding suitable weights w and a threshold t which can either be achieved manually to implement strategies such as majority votes, or derived from knowledge of previous deployments. Consequently, this ensemble method does not necessarily require training (**C1**). Moreover, it leaves the data series intact (**C2**) yet does not consider temporal dependencies (**C3**).

Selecting a Baseline. Before exploring this ensemble method's potential, we must define a baseline for comparison. However, as apparent from our previous study, an IIDS can be optimized for certain objectives, e.g., to perform well in a particular metric (cf. Sect. 3.1). This decision is also heavily influenced by how FPAs and the risk of missing an attack are weighted by researchers (or operators), which is why finding one suitable metric is difficult in general [20,22,29,46].

Consequently, we decided to compare our ensembles against two promising IIDSs from the baseline. Given the results from Table 1, we select the MinMax IIDS as our primary baseline since it features the best eTaF1 score, which is a tradeoff between good precision and recall. In addition, we compare the results against the Invariant IIDS as it exhibits the most detected scenarios but also the most FPAs to investigate how the ensembles cope with this input condition.

Results. To examine the *theoretical* potential achievable with this methodology in the first step, we leveraged an optimization algorithm to systematically search for optimized weights and thresholds (Opt. Weights). To this end, we leveraged Ray Tune [28] to optimize these parameters for the eTaF1 metric. Note that weights and the threshold were searched within the interval $[-1, +1]$ instead of the entire $\mathbb{R}$ w.l.o.g. (any weighted vote can simply be scaled such that all the parameters are within any arbitrary non-empty interval in $\mathbb{R}$). We now examine results on the SWaT dataset and detail the results on WADI in Appendix A.

A weight-based ensemble with optimized parameters manages to outperform any base-IIDS in eTaP, eTaR, and eTaF1 (cf. upper part of Table 2). Surprisingly, MinMax's eTaF1 score is exceeded by over $+11\%$ points, which is a major improvement, especially considering related work yielded improvements of only around $+1\%$ point (cf. Sect. 3.2). Aside from Invariant, this ensemble detects

Table 2. IIDS ensembles have the potential to yield better results than any monolithic approaches (cf. Opt. Weights). But, to find these weights via means of trivial strategies (lower part), a tradeoff between detected scenarios and FPAs has to be made.

SWaT	eTaP	eTaR	eTaF1	Scen.	FPA
MinMax [46]	67.8	47.1	55.6	23	9
Invariant [14]	54.7	29.8	38.6	30	217
Opt. Weights (eTaF1)	82.3	56.1	66.7	29	11
Any	21.1	35.3	26.4	33	160
≥2-Alerts	48.3	36.5	41.6	30	68
≥3-Alerts	61.6	35.3	44.9	26	60
Majority	82.4	34.4	48.5	17	34
≥5-Alerts	87.1	23.0	36.4	14	16
All	85.5	2.9	5.6	4	0

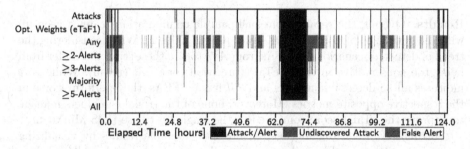

Fig. 3. Simple ensemble strategies drastically improve the understandability of alerts compared to the patterns shown in Fig. 2. Even though strategies like ≥2-Alerts measure 68 FPAs, these reside within the vicinity of attacks.

the most scenarios, namely 29 of the 33 attacks alerted by any base-IIDS. While this ensemble still exhibits 11 FPAs, they are confined to the vicinity of actual attacks (cf. upper part of Fig. 3). More importantly, the ensemble's alerts do not show any phenomena discussed in Sect. 3.1, i.e., overhanging or randomly distributed alerts are eliminated, drastically improving understandability.

When analyzing the optimized weights, it is unsurprising that MinMax, with the highest eTaF1 score among the base-IIDSs, received the highest weight with 0.99 and could already yield an alert on its own since $t = 0.99$. The ensemble can even make use of Invariant with a weight of 0.88 despite its FPAs. Interestingly, some IIDSs received negative weights (Gradient with -0.33 and PASAD with even -0.91). Since PASAD, in some cases, does not cover any attack at all (cf. Fig. 2), the ensemble seems to leverage this phenomenon to filter out FPAs.

4.2 Finding Parameters for Weight-Based Ensembles

Our theoretical results prove that weight-based ensembles are of practical use given a set of suitable weights and a threshold, but they do not provide ways to find such a configuration in a practical manner. Since performing such an optimization is infeasible in practice due to a lack of training data (**C1**), we now investigate six straightforward strategies to choose those parameters *manually*.

Manual Strategies. The most basic strategies we can implement with weights are *All* and *Any*, which emit an alert if all/any IIDSs emit an alert at the same time (corresponding to a logical AND or a logical OR). To realize them, setting all weights to 1 and the threshold to $t = 1$ (Any) or $t = n$ (All) is sufficient. Applications of these strategies can already be found in literature (cf. Sect. 3.2).

In between these extremes, further combinations are imaginable. For our evaluation, we consider just a subset of these combinations for the sake of simplicity: We define four more strategies that raise an alert when the *Majority* of IIDSs emit an alert or at least two, three, or five alerts are present. Note that these manual strategies can all be implemented with the proposed method, e.g., again setting all weights to 1 and $t = n/2$ corresponds to the Majority strategy.

Results. Overall, the results from such simple configurations cannot keep up with the optimized performance (cf. lower part of Table 2). When considering the trend of detected scenarios and FPAs from *Any* to *All*, these strategies suffer from being too conservative in either eTaP (precision) or eTaR (recall). While *Any* indicates all 33 detectable attacks and *All* has no FPAs, they perform worse in the respective opposite metrics. Moreover, none of the trivial combiners manage to improve the eTaF1 score compared to the single-best base-IIDS MinMax.

Fortunately, when digging deeper into the ensemble results by visualizing their alert patterns in Fig. 3 (lower part), all approaches, besides All and Any, score reasonably well on SWaT when evaluated qualitatively. Their alerts visually coincide with the attacks, and the FPAs are in close proximity to the actual attacks, notably eliminating Invariant's many randomly distributed FPAs. Compared to the original base-IIDSs' alerts from Fig. 2, even these straightforward ensemble strategies yield a usable result that can improve the perception for the ICS operator. However, this observation is not backed by current metrics.

Takeaway. Weight-based ensembles successfully increase the performance by up to +11% points in eTaF1 on the SWaT dataset. For the WADI dataset, we yield similar results (cf. Appendix A). Here, an ensemble with optimized weights can improve the eTaF1 score by nearly +12% points and even detects one more scenario than any base-IIDS. However, finding suitable parameters is non-trivial in the absence of training data because simple strategies, such as a Majority voting, leave a significant gap toward the optimum. Still, the advantages of weight-based ensembles lie in their simplicity, e.g., that parameters can be tuned manually throughout the operation, and their ability to reduce FPAs effectively.

5   Time-Aware Ensemble Learning

One property of IIDSs that could impair the success of actual unsupervised ensembles may be temporal effects (cf. **C3**). While recent metrics, such as eTaF1,

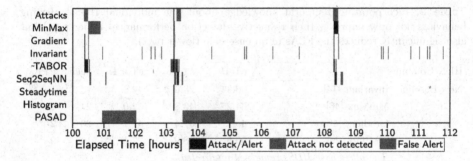

Fig. 4. This close-up reveals the individual alerting behavior of different IIDSs. However, by not considering temporal correlations, an ensemble cannot differentiate between, e.g., Invariant's short alarms that usually indicate FPAs and longer true alarms.

are already time-aware, i.e., they can deal with IIDSs that alert at different times during a longer attack, to the best of our knowledge, ensemble learning currently focuses solely on single instances without temporal dependence. To shed light on this issue, we first examine the alerting behavior of the IIDSs (cf. Sect. 5.1) and identify the potential for optimizing their alerts by taking temporal correlations into account (cf. Sect. 5.2). We then assess to which extent novel concepts of time-aware ensembles could improve the current situation (cf. Sect. 5.3).

5.1   Individual Alerting Behaviors Complicate Ensembling

Calculating optimal weights resulted in rather unexpected behavior (cf. Sect. 4.1): Gradient was given a negative score (-0.33), even though it visually performs nearly optimal (cf. Fig. 2). On the contrary, Invariant received a high score ($+0.88$), despite exhibiting 217 FPAs. To understand the roots of these outcomes, Fig. 4 provides a close-up of a few attacks and corresponding alerts.

Starting with MinMax, whose alerts are occasionally flagged as FPAs, these simply seem delayed such that a trained ensemble or an operator knowing this phenomenon could still use these indications for attack detection, especially if other IIDSs indicate attacks around the same time. Likewise, Gradient precisely indicates discontinuities at an attack's beginning and end. But, its second alert is often counted as FPA as the attack has ended at that time instance and is no longer labeled as malicious in the dataset [46]. Next, although hardly recognizable in Fig. 4, Invariant's FPAs, which occur randomly during benign regions, are usually short, i.e., lasting just a few seconds, compared to true alarms. Thus, Invariant can achieve a score of 0.81 in the point-based F1 score as these short alerts do not carry significant weight in that metric. The same effect can be observed for TABOR where FPAs are often just one second short.

Such effects pose issues to ensembles without temporal knowledge, as they can hardly distinguish different types of alarms. Yet, knowing such (often technically conditioned) effects provides unique opportunities for stronger ensembles.

Table 3. Incorporating temporal knowledge about the individual IIDSs' alerting behaviors not only improves their respective detection performance (upper part) but also significantly reduces the FPAs in an ensemble (lower part).

IIDS/Combiner		eTaP	eTaR	eTaF1	Scen.	FPAs
New Baseline	Invariant [14]	$90.3^{+35.6}$	$28.0^{-1.8}$	$42.8^{+4.2}$	13^{-17}	10^{-207}
	MinMax [46]	$64.2^{-3.7}$	$43.8^{-3.3}$	$52.0^{-3.5}$	24^{+1}	1^{-8}
	Gradient [46]	$45.7^{+25.2}$	$37.4^{+31.5}$	$41.1^{+31.9}$	26^{+1}	2^{-62}
	TABOR [29]	$50.5^{+1.4}$	$18.9^{+0.0}$	$27.5^{+0.2}$	19^{+0}	9^{-19}
	The other base-IIDSs remained unaffected.					
New Results	Opt. Weights (eTaF1)	$87.2^{+4.9}$	$57.0^{+0.9}$	$69.0^{+2.2}$	28^{-1}	6^{-5}
	Manually selected weights[a]	$72.7^{-9.6}$	$60.3^{+4.2}$	$65.9^{-0.8}$	29^{+0}	3^{-8}
	Any	$22.0^{+0.9}$	$33.6^{-1.7}$	$26.6^{+0.2}$	32^{-1}	40^{-120}
	$\geq$2-Alerts	$50.9^{+2.6}$	$42.3^{+5.8}$	$46.2^{+4.6}$	29^{-1}	15^{-53}
	$\geq$3-Alerts	$65.4^{+3.8}$	$41.9^{+6.5}$	$51.1^{+6.1}$	25^{-1}	7^{-53}
	Majority	$83.2^{+0.8}$	$34.7^{+0.3}$	$48.9^{+0.4}$	16^{-1}	6^{-28}
	$\geq$5-Alerts	$88.6^{+1.5}$	$28.2^{+5.2}$	$42.8^{+6.4}$	13^{-1}	5^{-11}
	All	$67.0^{-18.5}$	$3.9^{+1.0}$	$7.4^{+1.7}$	4^{+0}	0^{+0}

Superscript numbers show the difference between the prior baseline (Table 1) and results (Table 2).
[a] During experiments, we found an ensemble exceeding the eTaF1-optimized solution in Scen. and FPAs, indicating that eTaF1 does not fully coincide with subjective intuition.

5.2 Time-Aware Ensemble Learning on Normalized Alarms

Our initial attempt to leverage this time-aware information in ensembles is to introduce a postprocessing step per IIDS right after each IIDS has emitted its alerts. Thereby, we can implement simple strategies that "normalize" the alerts prior to forwarding them to the ensemble method for decision-making.

In our case study in Sect. 5.1, we identified four strategies for MinMax, Gradient, Invariant, and TABOR, which help to clean up their alerts. For MinMax and Gradient, we simply extend their alerts artificially by one minute such that scenarios are detected if the alert is just slightly off. For Invariant, which suffers from randomly placed short alerts, we only consider those alerts where an alarm is emitted for more than ten consecutive seconds. We chose a similar approach for TABOR, where we filter out every alert that lasts just one time instance.

Incorporating temporal information into ensembles may help obtain better models and ultimately reduce the number of FPAs due to "misinterpretation". In practice, IIDS authors can provide guidance to aid in developing such strategies.

5.3 Potential of Time-Aware Ensemble Learning

To assess the potential of time-aware ensembles, we applied these strategies in isolation for each of the four IIDSs: Invariant, MinMax, Gradient, and TABOR.

As shown in the upper part of Table 3 (New Baseline), this approach drastically improves their performance. Compared to the previous baseline, MinMax now correctly identifies one additional scenario and reduces the total number of FPAs by eight. The same observation holds for Gradient, which even reduces the FPAs by 62 and can increase its eTaF1 score by 31.9% points. These results indicate that most FPAs of MinMax and Gradient were in close proximity to actual attacks or triggered during the recovery of the ICS right after the attack. The strategies for Invariant and TABOR likewise yield a reduction in FPAs but also in the detected scenarios (in the case of Invariant). We assume that the reduction of detected scenarios for Invariant results from the filtered random alerts, which may have (falsely) contributed to the high number in the first place.

This improvement is not restricted to the base-IIDSs as it carries over to the ensembles, which now fare better using these "normalized" alerts (cf. New Results in Table 3). The optimized weight-based ensemble can slightly increase the eTaF1 score (+2.2) and reduce the FPAs by five. More importantly, the simple strategies with manually chosen weights now become usable as they feature a similar amount of FPAs compared to the optimized results, yet with slightly fewer detected scenarios. In that regard, the strategy ≥ 3-*Alerts* lacks behind the optimum, with just three fewer detected scenarios and one more FPA, significantly closing the gap between practically achieved and theoretical performance.

Takeaway. Temporal knowledge inside ensembles substantially improves their performances to a point where manual strategies become actually usable. Besides incorporating IIDS-specific information, future time-aware ensembles considering inter-IIDS alert dependencies may even exceed our initial results, but likely require sophisticated methods of finding (or training) an adequate model.

6 A Chance for Learning-Based Ensembles

Until now, we evaluated the potential of IIDS ensembles on a single dataset. But one advantage of unsupervised IIDSs is that they can operate in different environments, i.e., generalize to new industrial domains after another training phase [47]. E.g., MinMax, Gradient, Steadytime, and Histogram have been designed, trained on, and evaluated for three datasets originating from different domains [46]. Given that the set of base-IIDSs remains fixed, training a learning-based ensemble on one dataset (or in the lab) under attack conditions and then transferring the *ensemble's model* to a different deployment/dataset without known attacks might be feasible. While it remains necessary to retrain the base-IIDSs on the new scenario, it hopefully suffices to keep the ensemble's model, i.e., the way in which the detection results are aggregated. This transfer-learning [43] is still in line with **C1** as only the unsupervised IIDSs would require retraining on benign-only data, while the pre-trained ensemble model is simply reused.

Transfer-learning promises a new level of flexibility for ensembles and may circumvent the issue of finding appropriate weights identified in Sect. 4.2. Also, it enables leveraging methods from related work such as ensemble stacking (cf. Sect. 3.2). To examine the feasibility of ensemble transfer-learning, we explain our new methodology in Sect. 6.1 and subsequently present the results in Sect. 6.2.

Table 4. Transfer-learning proves helpful in training unsupervised IIDS ensembles. E.g., if trained on the dataset SWaT and applied to WADI, most ensembles outperform the manual strategies (cf. Majority) in eTaF1 and come close to the Opt. Weights.

Transfer-learning		eTaP	eTaR	eTaF1	Scen.	FPAs
WADI → SWaT	Opt. Weights (Table 3)	87.2	57.0	69.0	28	6
	≥3-Alerts (Table 3)	65.4	41.9	51.1	25	7
	WADI's Opt. Weights (eTaF1)	75.1	33.8	46.6	18	11
	SVM [25]	76.6	43.1	55.2	21	12
	MLP [16,34]	75.9	55.5	64.1	27	18
	LR [25]	80.5	49.2	61.0	25	13
	Heuristic [25]	68.3	38.5	49.2	20	17
SWaT → WADI	Opt. Weights (Table 7)	86.9	62.2	72.5	11	2
	Majority (Table 7)	79.8	42.1	55.1	7	2
	SWaT's Opt. Weights (eTaF1)	76.6	50.4	60.8	10	2
	SVM [25]	71.3	63.5	67.2	11	9
	MLP [16,34]	80.2	63.5	70.9	11	3
	LR [25]	88.0	42.6	57.4	9	1
	Heuristic [25]	76.7	60.2	67.4	11	6

6.1 A New Methodology for Learning-Based Ensembles

Learning-based ensembles require training on a dataset of exemplary attacks and expected labels of the outcome. Therefore, the methodology leveraged across related work usually bases on a *single* dataset artificially split into training and evaluation parts. Since we target an unsupervised scenario, we cannot assume to observe the ensemble's IIDSs under attack conditions in the target ICS (**C1**).

However, assuming that the same set of base-IIDSs behaves similarly in a different ICS, operators may have a strong interest in reusing a well-performing, pre-trained ensemble model. On the one hand, this approach enables assessing how well weights optimized for one scenario transfer to another ICS and, thus, helps to find these weights. On the other hand, supervised learning-based ensembles, which we neglected so far, may generalize too, such that approaches from related work can be leveraged even in the context of unsupervised IIDSs.

6.2 Putting Transfer-Learning to the Test

To test the idea of transfer-learning, we leverage the SWaT and WADI datasets to which all eight base-IIDSs are applicable [47] and use one of the two datasets exclusively for training and evaluate the obtained ensemble model on the respective other dataset. Note that we use the "normalized" alerts according to Sect. 5 in this experiment to provide cleaner input data. As the first approach, we consider transferring the parameters of our weight-based ensembles. Furthermore, we analyze four learning-based variants from previous work. First, as leveraged in two publications [16,34], an MLP resembles a neural network classifier. Further classifiers include SVM [25] and LR [7,25]. Besides these, Kus et al. [25] proposed a heuristic that maps each possible alert vector to its most frequent output (benign or malicious), thereby optimizing the number of correct classifications.

Under the right conditions, transfer-learning can be an alternative to manual strategies (cf. Table 4). Yet, starting with ensembles trained on WADI and applied to SWaT (WADI → SWaT), all ensembles emit more FPAs than ≥ 3-Alerts. Nonetheless, MLP and LR outperform every base-IIDS and all manual strategies in eTaF1 (cf. Sect. 4.2), falling behind Opt. Weights by just 4.9% points. MLP even detects two more scenarios than ≥3-Alerts. Unfortunately, transferring the weights optimized on WADI to SWaT yields the worst ensemble.

The reverse direction (SWaT → WADI) is more promising. Here, the weight-based ensemble detects ten scenarios with two FPAs, close to the optimum (cf. Opt. Weights). Also, learning-based ensembles perform better. Here, LR features just one FPA and nine detected scenarios, a great improvement over Majority. Again, MLP optimizes eTaF1 among all ensembles and exceeds the best base-IIDS by 12.8% points, with only three FPAs. To validate whether this success stems from the larger training data (SWaT contains 36 attacks and WADI 14), we repeated this experiment by restricting the training data to the first 14 attacks of SWaT, making it similar to WADI. But, we could not verify this assumption as the outcomes were similar and differed on average by only 1.05% points.

Takeaway. Given suitable training data, transfer-learning can be successful. Yet there is still room for improvement, i.e., by leveraging multiple datasets for training in the future. Most importantly, transfer-learning can outperform simple strategies (SWaT → WADI), thus providing an alternative to manually finding performant ensembles for actual ICS deployments with nearly no FPAs.

7   Conclusion

Enhancing ICSs' cybersecurity by augmenting them with an unsupervised IIDS promises to detect even zero-day attacks for which no training data exists. Despite a large research community inventing strong algorithms for IIDSs, we have outlined that relying on a single detector is insufficient given their individual weaknesses. Thus, we propose to leverage ensemble learning, as, e.g., used in computer vision, to combine a set of IIDSs and their strengths into one detector.

Surprisingly, we identify significant unused potential to improve not only the *combined* detection performance beyond what individual approaches can achieve but also their alerts' understandability for ICS operators. Incorporating temporal correlations into the ensemble's decisions reduces the number of FPAs further. Lastly, to ease the process of finding effective ensembles, we consider *transfer-learning*, i.e., training ensembles on attacks from a different ICS, to circumvent the difficulty of accessing training data for a target ICS under attack conditions.

In conclusion, ensemble learning poses an exciting direction for future work to strengthen ICSs' cybersecurity by tightly integrating strong methods for intrusion detection into an effective solution. To bootstrap ICS-specific research, we publish the ensembles' implementations [15], as well as the base-IIDSs' alerts and configuration files underlying our evaluations [45] as a dataset.

Acknowledgments. This work is part of the project MUM2 and was funded by the German Federal Ministry of Economic Affairs and Climate Action (BMWK) with contract number 03SX543B managed by the Project Management Jülich (PTJ). Funded by the German Federal Office for Information Security (BSI) under project funding reference number 01MO23016D (5G-Sierra) and by the Deutsche Forschungsgemeinschaft (DFG, German Research Foundation) under Germany's Excellence Strategy – EXC-2023 Internet of Production – 390621612. The responsibility for the content of this publication lies with the authors.

Availability Statement. We open-source the ensembles' implementations [15] and publish the base-IIDSs' alerts and experiments as public artifacts [45].

A   WADI Results

In addition to the results of our experiments from Sect. 3, and Sect. 4, based on the SWaT dataset, we repeated the same analyses for the WADI dataset.

Table 5. No IIDS detects all attacks on WADI, and there is no single best detector that excels in all metrics. Also, the best IIDS for each metric differs from SWaT.

IIDS (Baseline)	eTaP	eTaR	eTaF1	Scen.	FPA
Invariant [14]	92.3	32.6	48.1	6	3
PASAD [5]	5.4	4.3	4.8	5	3
Seq2SeqNN [22]	45.4	31.3	37.1	9	7
MinMax [46]	74.8	47.4	58.1	7	4
Gradient [46]	69.6	18.1	28.8	7	12
Steadytime [46]	87.0	38.7	53.5	6	2
Histogram [46]	63.7	43.2	51.5	7	6
TABOR [29]	14.9	13.0	13.9	8	4

In the baseline results, we observe a similar insufficiency for WADI (cf. Table 5) as previously discussed for SWaT in Sect. 3.1. No single IIDS is capable of detecting all 14 cyberattacks, and there is no single best IIDS for all metrics. MinMax achieves the highest score in two metrics, but Seq2SeqNN detects two more scenarios. In total 13 of WADI's 14 attacks would be detectable in combination.

Table 6. Weight-based ensembles yield similar results on WADI as on SWaT (cf. Table 2) and can outperform each base-IIDS in eTaF1. While they have the potential to improve upon the base-IIDS, finding suitable weights is again non-trivial.

WADI	eTaP	eTaR	eTaF1	Scen.	FPA
MinMax [46]	74.8	47.4	58.1	7	4
Seq2SeqNN [22]	45.4	31.3	37.1	9	7
Opt. Weights (eTaF1)	88.9	57.7	70.0	10	4
Any	25.5	47.0	33.1	13	14
$\geq$2-Alerts	36.2	42.6	39.2	13	4
$\geq$3-Alerts	61.2	50.0	55.0	8	10
Majority	85.8	36.4	51.1	7	2
$\geq$5-Alerts	89.0	21.4	34.5	5	4
All	0.0	0.0	0.0	1	0

Table 7. As for SWaT (cf. Table 3), temporal knowledge improves the individual IIDSs' alerting behavior (upper part) and the ensembles' performance (lower part).

Transfer-learning		eTaP	eTaR	eTaF1	Scen.	FPAs
New Baseline	Invariant [14]	$96.6^{+4.3}$	$32.2^{-0.4}$	$48.3^{+0.1}$	6^{+0}	0^{-3}
	MinMax [46]	$65.9^{-8.9}$	$41.4^{-6.0}$	$50.9^{-7.2}$	8^{+1}	1^{-3}
	Gradient [46]	$57.6^{-12.0}$	$31.6^{+13.5}$	$40.8^{+12.1}$	7^{+0}	3^{-9}
	TABOR [29]	$14.1^{-0.8}$	$13.0^{+0.0}$	$13.5^{-0.4}$	8^{+0}	1^{-3}
	The other base-IIDSs remained unaffected.					
New Results	Opt. Weights (eTaF1)	$86.9^{-2.0}$	$62.2^{+4.6}$	$72.5^{+2.5}$	11^{+1}	2^{-2}
	Any	$23.0^{-2.5}$	$43.4^{-3.6}$	$30.1^{-3.0}$	13^{+0}	8^{-6}
	$\geq$2-Alerts	$34.6^{-1.6}$	$40.3^{-2.4}$	$37.2^{-1.9}$	13^{+0}	2^{-2}
	$\geq$3-Alerts	$56.7^{-4.4}$	$43.7^{-6.3}$	$49.4^{-5.6}$	8^{+0}	8^{-2}
	Majority	$79.8^{-6.0}$	$42.1^{+5.7}$	$55.1^{+4.0}$	7^{+0}	2^{+0}
	$\geq$5-Alerts	$79.0^{-10.0}$	$27.1^{+5.7}$	$40.3^{+5.8}$	5^{+0}	2^{-2}
	All	$100.0^{+100.0}$	$4.1^{+4.1}$	$8.0^{+8.0}$	1^{+0}	0^{+0}

Superscript numbers show the difference between the prior baseline (Table 5) and results (Table 6).

We again assess the theoretical and practical potential for an ensemble on WADI as described in Sect. 4.1. Hereby, the eTaF1-optimized ensemble outperforms the best base-IIDS by +11.9% points in the eTaF1 score, detects more cyberattacks than any IIDS, and keeps the FPAs comparatively low (cf. upper part of Table 6). The manual voting strategies, however, fall short of this theoretical potential (cf. lower part of Table 6) with the best strategy lacking −25% points behind in the eTaF1 score. Nonetheless, the $\geq$2-Alerts ensemble indicates *all* 13 cyberattacks detected by any base-IIDS while maintaining only four FPAs.

Incorporating temporal knowledge (cf. Sect. 5) enhances the optimum by +2.5% points in eTaF1 and improves the manual strategies, especially in FPAs (cf. Table 7). We see a substantial improvement in the eTaF1 score of the best manual vote (+5.8% points for ≥5-Alerts), and the ≥2-Alerts strategy still detects 13 cyberattacks, now with just 2 FPAs, matching the number of FPAs achieved by Opt. Weights. Unfortunately, this great result is not expressed by eTaF1.

These results support the previous conclusion that weight-based ensembles are useful given suitable weights and thresholds, yet finding them remains non-trivial. Lastly, adding time-awareness yielded a significant performance boost.

References

1. Ahmed, C., Palleti, V.R., Mathur, A.P.: WADI: a water distribution testbed for research in the design of secure cyber physical systems. In: CySWATER (2017)
2. Ahmed, C.M., Raman, M.R.G., Mathur, A.P.: Challenges in machine learning based approaches for real-time anomaly detection in industrial control systems. In: ACM CPSS (2020)
3. Al-Abassi, A., et al.: An ensemble deep learning-based cyber-attack detection in industrial control system. IEEE Access **8**, 83965–83973 (2020)
4. Alladi, T., Chamola, V., Zeadally, S.: Industrial control systems: cyberattack trends and countermeasures. Comput. Commun. **155**, 1–8 (2020)
5. Aoudi, W., Iturbe, M., Almgren, M.: Truth will out: departure-based process-level detection of stealthy attacks on control systems. In: ACM CCS (2018)
6. Bader, L., et al.: Comprehensively analyzing the impact of cyberattacks on power grids. In: IEEE EuroS&P (2023)
7. Balaji, M., et al.: Super detector: an ensemble approach for anomaly detection in industrial control systems. In: Percia David, D., Mermoud, A., Maillart, T. (eds.) CRITIS. LNCS, vol. 13139, pp. 24–43. Springer, Cham (2021). https://doi.org/10.1007/978-3-030-93200-8_2
8. Chandola, V., Banerjee, A., Kumar, V.: Anomaly detection: a survey. ACM Comput. Surv. **41**(3), 1–58 (2009)
9. Chen, X., et al.: Ensemble learning methods for power system cyber-attack detection. In: IEEE ICCCBDA (2018)
10. Conti, M., Donadel, D., Turrin, F.: A survey on industrial control system testbeds and datasets for security research. IEEE Commun. Surv. Tutor. **23**(4), 2248–2294 (2021)
11. Ding, D., et al.: A survey on security control and attack detection for industrial cyber-physical systems. Neurocomputing **275**, 1674–1683 (2018)
12. Erba, A., Tippenhauer, N.O.: Assessing model-free anomaly detection in industrial control systems against generic concealment attacks. In: ACSAC (2022)
13. Etalle, S.: From intrusion detection to software design. In: ESORICS, vol. 10492 (2017)
14. Feng, C., et al.: A systematic framework to generate invariants for anomaly detection in industrial control systems. In: NDSS (2019)
15. Fraunhofer FKIE-CAD: IPAL - Industrial Intrusion Detection Framework. https://github.com/fkie-cad/ipal_ids_framework (2021)
16. Gao, J., et al.: Omni SCADA intrusion detection using deep learning algorithms. IEEE Internet Things J. **8**(2), 951–961 (2021)

17. Gensler, A., Sick, B.: Novel criteria to measure performance of time series segmentation techniques. In: KDML (2014)
18. Giraldo, J., et al.: A survey of physics-based attack detection in cyber-physical systems. ACM Comput. Surv. **51**(4), 1–36 (2018)
19. Goh, J., et al.: A dataset to support research in the design of secure water treatment systems. In: CRITIS (2016)
20. Hwang, W.S., et al.: Do you know existing accuracy metrics overrate time-series anomaly detections?. In: ACM SAC (2022)
21. Kavallieratos, G., Katsikas, S.K., Gkioulos, V.: Towards a cyber-physical range. In: CPSS (2019)
22. Kim, J., Yun, J.H., Kim, H.C.: Anomaly detection for industrial control systems using sequence-to-sequence neural networks. In: CyberICPS (2020)
23. Kumar, A., Saxena, N., Choi, B.J.: Machine learning algorithm for detection of false data injection attack in power system. In: ICOIN (2021)
24. Kus, D., et al.: A false sense of security? revisiting the state of machine learning-based industrial intrusion detection. In: ACM CPSS (2022)
25. Kus, D., et al.: Poster: ensemble learning for industrial intrusion detection. Technical report, RWTH-2022-10809, RWTH Aachen University (2022)
26. Lee, J.J., et al.: AdaBoost for text detection in natural scene. In: ICDAR (2011)
27. Li, Y., et al.: Intrusion detection of cyber physical energy system based on multivariate ensemble classification. Energy **218**, 119505 (2021)
28. Liaw, R., et al.: Tune: a research platform for distributed model selection and training. arXiv:1807.05118 (2018)
29. Lin, Q., et al.: TABOR: a graphical model-based approach for anomaly detection in industrial control systems. In: ACM ASIACCS (2018)
30. Louk, M.H.L., Tama, B.A.: Exploring ensemble-based class imbalance learners for intrusion detection in industrial control networks. Big Data Cogn. Comput. **5**(4), 72 (2021)
31. Maglaras, L.A., Jiang, J., Cruz, T.J.: Combining ensemble methods and social network metrics for improving accuracy of OCSVM on intrusion detection in SCADA systems. J. Inf. Secur. **30**, 15–26 (2016)
32. Mendes-Moreira, J., et al.: Ensemble approaches for regression: a survey. ACM Comput. Surv. **45**(1), 1–40 (2012)
33. Mitchell, R., Chen, I.R.: A survey of intrusion detection techniques for cyber-physical systems. ACM Comput. Surv. **46**(4), 1–29 (2014)
34. Nguyen, D.D., Le, M.T., Cung, T.L.: Improving intrusion detection in SCADA systems using stacking ensemble of tree-based models. Bull. Electr. Eng. Inform. **11**(1), 119–127 (2022)
35. Ponomarev, S., Atkison, T.: Industrial control system network intrusion detection by telemetry analysis. IEEE Trans. Dependable Secure Comput. **13**(2), 252–260 (2015)
36. Radoglou-Grammatikis, P., et al.: DIDEROT: an intrusion detection and prevention system for DNP3-based SCADA systems. In: ARES (2020)
37. Rokach, L.: Ensemble-based classifiers. Artif. Intell. Rev. **33**(1–2), 1–39 (2010)
38. Sagi, O., Rokach, L.: Ensemble learning: a survey. WIREs Data Min. Knowl. Discov. **8**(4), e1249 (2018)
39. Singh, M., Singh, R., Ross, A.: A comprehensive overview of biometric fusion. Inf. Fusion **52**, 187–205 (2019)
40. Sommer, R., Paxson, V.: Outside the closed world: on using machine learning for network intrusion detection. In: IEEE SP (2010)

41. Stallings, W., Brown, L.: Computer Security: Principles and Practice, 4th edn. Pearson (2021)

42. Teixeira, A., et al.: Attack models and scenarios for networked control systems. In: HiCoNS (2012)

43. Torrey, L., Shavlik, J.: Transfer Learning, chap. 11. IGI Global (2010)

44. Upadhyay, D., et al.: Intrusion detection in SCADA based power grids: recursive feature elimination model with majority vote ensemble algorithm. IEEE Trans. Netw. Sci. Eng. **8**(3), 2559–2574 (2021)

45. Wolsing, K., et al.: Artifact: One IDS is not Enough! Exploring Ensemble Learning for Industrial Intrusion Detection. Zenodo (2023)

46. Wolsing, K., et al.: Can industrial intrusion detection be SIMPLE? In: ESORICS (2022)

47. Wolsing, K., et al.: IPAL: breaking up silos of protocol-dependent and domain-specific industrial intrusion detection systems. In: RAID (2022)

48. Yazdinejad, A., et al.: An ensemble deep learning model for cyber threat hunting in industrial internet of things. Digit. Commun. Netw. **9**(1), 101–110 (2023)

49. Zhang, C., Ma, Y.: Ensemble Machine Learning: Methods and Applications, 1st edn. Springer, Cham (2012)

50. Zhang, D., et al.: A survey on attack detection, estimation and control of industrial cyber-physical systems. ISA Trans. **116**, 1–16 (2021)

51. Zhou, Z.H.: Ensemble Methods: Foundations and Algorithms, 1st edn. CRC Press, Boca Raton (2012)

52. Zhou, Z.H.: Machine Learning, 1st edn. Springer, Cham (2021)

Evaluating the Security Posture of 5G Networks by Combining State Auditing and Event Monitoring

Md Nazmul Hoq[1(✉)], Jia Wei Yao[1], Suryadipta Majumdar[1], Luis Suárez[2], Lingyu Wang[1], Amine Boukhtouta[2], Makan Pourzandi[2], and Mourad Debbabi[1]

[1] Concordia University, Montreal, Canada
{mdnazmul.hoq,jiawei.yao,suryadipta.majumdar,lingyu.wang,
mourad.debbabi}@concordia.ca
[2] Ericsson, Montreal, Canada
{luis.suarez,amine.boukhtouta,makan.pourzandi}@ericsson.com

Abstract. 5G network technology is being rapidly adopted in various critical infrastructures, mainly due to its unique benefits (e.g., higher throughput, lower latency, and better scalability). This wide-spread and fast adoption necessitates securing those critical services deployed over 5G technology. However, evaluating the security posture of a 5G network is challenging due to the heterogeneous and large-scale nature of 5G networks coupled with new security threats. Moreover, existing 5G security approaches fall short as their results are typically binary and difficult to be translated into the overall security posture of a 5G network. In this paper, we propose a novel solution for evaluating the security posture of 5G networks by combining the results of existing security solutions for state auditing and event monitoring. To that end, our main idea is to first build a novel *event-state model* that captures both events and states in a 5G network, and then extend this model to evaluate the overall security posture and how such security posture may evolve over time due to persistent threats. We integrate this approach with free5GC (a popular 5G open-source project) and evaluate its effectiveness.

1 Introduction

Characterized by its higher throughput, lower latency, and better scalability, 5G technology has become a popular choice for telecommunication networks. By 2025, more than two-fifths of the global population will be under the coverage of 5G networks, and 5G connections will make up about a quarter of all mobile connections [1]. Therefore, the security of 5G networks becomes essential to its wide-range of users and applications. To that end, evaluating the security posture of a 5G network deployment can provide a direct measurement of the current security status as well as the potential impact of specific future plans (e.g., deploying a security appliance). However, evaluating the security posture of a 5G network renders unique challenges, such as understanding its heterogeneous

G. Tsudik et al. (Eds.): ESORICS 2023, LNCS 14345, pp. 123–144, 2024.
https://doi.org/10.1007/978-3-031-51476-0_7

components across multiple aspects and how those components interact, and attacker's capabilities in exploiting those unique system dependencies to cause an evolving impact on the system.

Most existing works (e.g., [2,3]) for measuring 5G security fall short to overcome those challenges, as they are limited to a particular aspect (e.g., user, network, or infrastructure) of a 5G network and do not evaluate the system's overall security posture. On the other hand, the majority of existing works (e.g., [4–6]) for non-5G environments do not consider the 5G-specific threats that may exploit a 5G network across different aspects and cause sustained impact. Moreover, existing security tools (e.g., Kubescape [7] and Falco [8]) for 5G networks are mostly designed to find a specific security breach or incident, respectively, and it would be highly challenging for security admins to interpret and correlate the results of those different tools into an overall security posture of a 5G network. We further highlight these limitations and motivate towards our work using the following example.

Motivating Example. The left side of Fig. 1 shows an attack scenario (based on a well-known advanced persistent threat (APT) to telecommunications networks, LightBasin [9]) to illustrate an attacker's capability to exploit a 5G network from multiple aspects (e.g., user, network, and infrastructure) by following *Steps 1– 6* and cause an evolving impact (from user aspect to infrastructure aspect). The right side of the figure first shows the limitations of existing works towards evaluating the security posture of a 5G network during the APT attack, and then illustrates our idea to overcome those limitations, as detailed in the following.

- While working with existing security solutions (e.g., auditing and monitoring tools [7,8]) and relevant security controls (e.g., [10–12]), a 5G admin observes both compliant (T) and non-compliant (F) states of a system as the attack progresses over time (t_1-t_4). However, the admin faces challenges about how to interpret those binary results from auditing individual security controls, and how to aggregate them towards evaluating the overall security posture of the 5G network.
- To address this limitation, our key idea is to combine the results of existing security tools (e.g., auditing and monitoring) to build a probabilistic model (Bayesian network) that correlates the different aspects of a 5G network and captures the evolving nature of an APT attack over time. As a result, an admin can obtain security posture values for a given goal node (G_1 and G_2) from observed breaches or events (E_1 and E_2) to have a better understanding about the security status of the system.

More specifically, we propose a 5G Security Posture Evaluator (namely, *5GSPE*) based on the results of state auditing and event monitoring. First, we build a *state model* from auditing results that capture breaches of organization-specific security controls based on 5G network states at different times, and an *event model* from monitoring results that capture the attacker's activities performed in-between breaches. Second, we combine these two models to build an *event-state model* as a Bayesian network that captures the evolving nature of 5G

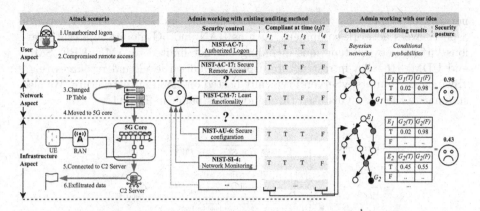

Fig. 1. A motivating example based on the LightBasin attack

attacks. Finally, we leverage this probabilistic *event-state model* to evaluate the security posture of a 5G network through Bayesian inference of the model. We implement *5GSPE* based on free5GC [13] (a popular project for deploying 5G core) with Kubernetes [14] (a major container orchestrator), and demonstrate its effectiveness through extensive experiments. The main contributions of this paper are as follows.

- As per our knowledge, we are the first to propose a solution for evaluating the security posture of 5G networks that can cover persistent threats involving multiple aspects in the 5G technology stack and threat evolution over time.
- To achieve this, we study security controls from multiple system aspects; we propose a novel *event-state model* by combining results of state auditing and event monitoring; we design a custom algorithm to combine those results and quantify the overall security posture of a 5G network.
- We integrate our solution with free5GC [15] and Kubernetes [14] and conduct experiments to show its effectiveness in reflecting the effects of attack progress, network scalability, and security appliances, among others on the overall security posture.

The rest of the paper is organized as follows. Section 2 provides preliminaries. Section 3 describes our methodology. Section 4 details its implementation. Section 5 presents experimental results. Section 6 reviews the literature. Section 7 concludes the work.

2 Preliminaries

This section provides the necessary preliminaries.

2.1 Background on 5G Network

Figure 2 shows an overview of 5G network that contains components from three major aspects: A user aspect is concerned with the administration of the 5G core network including UE, which can be both mobile and IoT devices. A network aspect covers network equipment, such as RAN and 5G mobile core (with various virtual network functions including but not limited to AMF, UPF, SMF, and UDM) [16]. An infrastructure aspect includes the virtual resources (e.g., vSwitches, vRouters, vServers) typically hosted on cloud infrastructure. We also summarize the acronyms used throughout this paper in Table 1.

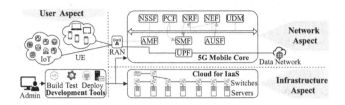

Fig. 2. An overview of the 5G network

Table 1. Acronyms used in this paper

Term	Description	Term	Description	Term	Description
3GPP	3rd Generation Partnership Project	5GC	5G Core	AMF	5G Access and Mobility Management Function
AUSF	5G Authentication Server Function	BN	Bayesian Network	CN	Core Network
EM	Event Model	ESM	Event-State Model	LTE	Long-Term Evolution
NEF	5G Network Exposure Function	NF	Network Functions	NRF	5G Network Repository Function
NSSF	5G Network Slice Selection Function	PB	Policy Breach	PCF	5G Policy Control Function
RAN	Radio Access Network	SM	State Model	SMF	5G Session Management Function
UDM	5G Unified Data Management	UE	User Equipments	UPF	5G User Plane Function

2.2 Security Posture Evaluation in 5G and Its Challenges

In the following, we define security posture in the context of 5G and outline the challenges involved in its evaluation.

Definition of Security Posture in 5G. Based on 3GPP [17], a major project to develop 5G standards, the security posture of a 5G network is defined from two main factors: (i) by checking how well security practices and guidelines are followed in a 5G deployment and its operation (as captured in our state model); and (ii) by monitoring network elements, infrastructure, and communication (as captured in our event model).

Challenges. The main challenges of evaluating security posture in 5G are:

- **Complexity of the composition of a 5G network.** Unlike pre-5G networks (e.g., LTE and 4G), which are typically deployed on an operator-managed infrastructure, 5G network components (i.e., CN, RAN, UE, etc.) are distributed across multiple aspects (user, network, and infrastructure [18]) which can be deployed and instantiated across third party clouds and systems. The interactions between network functions, virtualized environment and infrastructure owners further complicate the nature of a 5G network. Due to such added complexity, evaluating the security posture of a 5G network requires a thorough understanding of this system.
- **Capturing attack progress with existing security solutions.** Attacker capabilities (skills, tools, and resources) for exploiting a 5G network vary based on the attacker's motivation, sophistication, and objectives [19]. While different attackers can advance differently across various aspects of 5G depending on their capabilities, the current security solutions are insufficient to understand the relationship between various breaches and to capture the attacker's progress for assessing the system's overall security posture.
- **Interpreting and aggregating the results of existing security solutions.** There are a few 5G security solutions for auditing (e.g., [20]), monitoring (e.g., [7]), and alert reporting (e.g., [8]). Different (sometimes inconsistent) security controls, formats of results, and operational mechanisms, across those solutions, may impede correlation among them to evaluate the system's overall security posture. It is also challenging to interpret the binary results to evaluate the security posture of a 5G network.

These challenges will be addressed in Sect. 3.

2.3 Threat Model

The *in-scope threats* of this work include the attacks whose impact on the security controls of a 5G network can be identified using existing auditing/monitoring techniques (e.g., [7,8]). We assume the 5G network and infrastructure management systems (e.g., Kubernetes) may be trusted for the integrity of the API calls, event notifications, logs, and database records. The system may have implementation flaws, misconfigurations, and vulnerabilities that can be potentially exploited by malicious attackers to violate security controls. We assume that admins are interested in the security posture with respect to given attack goals (i.e., targeting critical assets). For identifying privilege escalation nodes, we rely on expert's intervention with the help of the MITRE FiGHT [21], a 5G-specific knowledgebase of attacker strategies, which extends the generic MITRE ATT&CK [22].

The *out-of-scope threats* include the attacks that do not violate the specified security controls, that are not captured by existing security solutions, and that may remove or tamper their own logged events. We also assume loose synchronization of events across different aspects such that their order are correctly reflected in Kubernetes logs and Systems logs. Even though this work can evaluate the effects of attacks on a system, its main objective is not to detect any specific attack or exploit, but to evaluate security postures for admins.

3   Methodology

This section presents our methodology of *5GSPE*.

3.1   Overview

Figure 3 shows an overview of our methodology, which contains three major steps. First, we build a state model from auditing results of 5G network states to capture the compliance breaches by an attacker and an event model from monitoring results of 5G network events to capture an attacker's activities (as detailed in Sect. 3.2). Second, we fuse these two models and build an *event-state* model (which is formally defined in Appendix A) using both *horizontal fusing*, which correlates the results of auditing and monitoring, and *vertical fusing*, which links different aspects (e.g., user and infrastructure) of a 5G network (as detailed in Sect. 3.3). Finally, we evaluate the security posture of a 5G network by converting our event-state model to a probabilistic model as a Bayesian network (as detailed in Sect. 3.4).

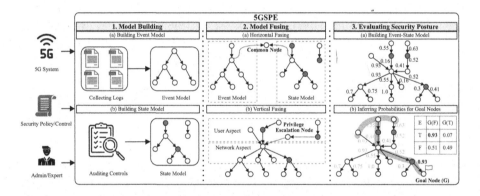

Fig. 3. Overview of our methodology

3.2   Building Event and State Models

To capture an attacker's activities and their impacts, we build the *state model* using auditing results and the *event model* using monitoring results, as follows.

Building State Model. A major angle of the attacker's activities would involve the execution of malicious operations that could result in non-compliant system states. Therefore, to capture this aspect of the attacker's activities, we build the state model. First, we obtain auditing results (e.g., compliant/non-compliant) over a period of time by applying existing security auditing tools (e.g., KubeScape [7]) and security controls (e.g., NIST [10]) covering different aspects of a 5G network. Then, we measure the frequency of both compliant and non-compliant results for each security control to calculate the probability of a non-compliant result. Next, we determine the pre-condition (cause of the breach) and the post-condition (impact of the breach) for each non-compliant result using the description of the control, and MITRE FiGHT [21] and ATT&CK framework [22]. Afterward, for each non-compliant control, we add its pre-condition and post-condition as parent and child, respectively, allowing us to correlate attackers non-compliant state related activities with 5G related activities. Finally, we combine all non-compliant controls, and their pre-conditions and post-conditions to build a *state model* using model fusing (described in Sect. 3.3).

Example 1. We utilize the same attack scenario as in our motivating example to illustrate how attackers compromise system states. Figure 4 explained how to build the state model. Initially, an attacker performs an unauthorized logon that violates the `AC-7: Authorized LogOn` control from NIST in the user aspect and enables the attacker to escalate to the network aspect. Afterwards, s/he violates two additional security controls (i.e., `SI-4` and `CM-7`) through further malicious activities. To capture the effects of these malicious activities, a state model is built as follows. (i) We collect auditing results from three tools, KubeScape [7], Falco [8], and a custom tool based on formal verification [23]. (ii) We count the number of compliance (3) and non-compliance (2) for `AC-7` and calculate the probability of non-compliance (0.40). (iii) We check `AC-7` description (*"consecutive invalid logon attempts should be limited"*) and its corresponding MITRE tactics `Credential Access (MITRE TA0006)` and with the help of an expert, we find MITRE sub-technique `Password Spraying` as a pre-condition (cause of the breach), and `Bypass User Account Control` as a post-condition (a potential result of the breach). Afterwards, we connect the pre-condition as a parent and the post-condition as a child of the breach node of `AC-7` control. Following these same steps for other controls, we build the entire state model.

Fig. 4. Example of building a state model

Building Event Model. Another angle of the attacker's activities would involve performing activities supported by 5G network. Therefore, to capture such activities, we build the event model. First, as a source of events, we collect the monitoring results (e.g., event logs) from multiple sources of a 5G network to cover its different aspects: system logs for users, auditing logs for infrastructure, and 5G core logs for networking. Then, to extract the event-related information (e.g., timestamps and details of relevant events [24]), we filter out any extraneous logs and trim the log data. Subsequently, we combine all the logs from different sources based on their timestamp, resulting in a single processed log. We also identify similar events (e.g., performing the same operations) that are named differently in different logs, and uniquely categorize them as a single event type in our model. Then, to capture attacker activities (represented as a BN), we generate event sequences where each sequence ends as soon as any event is repeated to avoid cycles in our model (mainly because a BN is acyclic). Finally, we construct our *event model* (as further illustrated using the following example).

Example 2. After gaining unauthorized access as an admin, an attacker may: `access to server` at the Kubernetes [14] level to alter the IP table to avoid detection, and `query to SMF` at the 5G level to get subscriber information from UDM. Figure 5 shows the steps to build the event model. (1) We collect and parse raw logs from Kubernetes and free5GC. (2) We eliminate the entries with the message `set report call: false`, and the `Log Level`, `Component`, and `Module` columns, as they do not provide event-related information. (3) We combine both logs, and sort them based on the *Timestamp*. (4) We rename both `Created container UPF` and `Started container UPF` messages as `connect to UPF` event, and identify the repetition of `Query to SMF` events for sequence generation without a cycle. (5) We obtain three event sequences. (6) We construct an event model, where nodes `access server` and `Query to SMF` and their transition probability (0.7) are learned from the sequences. Thus, the event model shows the activities of the attacker.

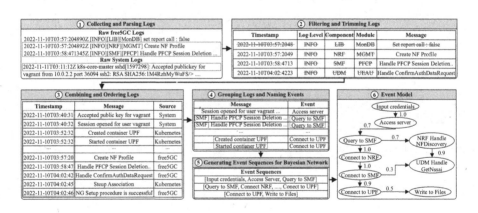

Fig. 5. Example of building an event model

3.3   Model Fusing

To capture the overall impacts of the attacker's activities on the system, both models are fused in this step by performing two major steps as follows.

Horizontal Fusing. This step is to show the combined effects of the attacker's activities causing non-compliance system states from the state model (SM) and in-between breach activities supported by the 5G network from the event model (EM). First, we identify all the common nodes between *EM* and *SM* caused by the impact of a privilege escalation resulting from a non-compliant system state. Second, for each common node, we record and merge their parents and children from both models with their respective transition probabilities. This merged list represents the steps an attacker might perform, whether by mimicking legitimate users or causing a breach, and it captures the transition between these two. Third, we create a new model by adding each common node to their parents and children. Finally, the remaining nodes (which have not been added yet) from both EM and SM are added to this new model.

Example 3. In Fig. 6a, we fuse the event model (on left) and state model (on right) using their common node, `Access Server`; which combines two different activities, `Password-based Authentication` representing attacker mimicking a legitimate user, and `Bypass User Account Control` representing a post-condition of a breach. Prior to this step, we also use the same procedure within the state model in combining two breach-related activities `LogOn Policy Breach (PB)` and `Remote Access PB`, leading to a common privilege escalation `Bypass User Account Control`. We use dashed lines to indicate the model's instance before fusing and solid lines to indicate its instance after fusing.

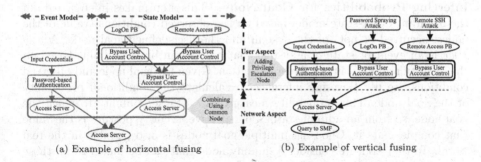

(a) Example of horizontal fusing   (b) Example of vertical fusing

Fig. 6. Examples of fusing event model with state model into event-state model

Vertical Fusing. This step is to show the impacts of a breach among different aspects (e.g., user, network) of a 5G network. First, we identify the privilege escalation (post-condition) that occurs as a result of a breach (explained in Sect. 3.2). Then, using the MITRE FiGHT [21] and ATT&CK [22] framework, we identify the impact of this privilege escalation. This impact could be a legitimate event from the EM or another breach of the system state from the SM. Moreover, an expert verifies the decision using his/her understanding of attack and mitigation. Finally, we connect the impacted node with the privilege escalation node to show the attacker's progress in different aspects.

Example 4. As shown in Fig. 6b, vertical fusing connects the user aspect and network aspect of the system where an attacker uses two breaches `LogOn PB`

and `Remote Access PB` to gain the same privilege of `Bypass User Account Control`. Using expert assistance and MITRE framework, we determine that `Bypass User Account Control` can be used for both `Credential Access (MITRE TA0006)` and `Lateral Movement (MITRE TA0008)` which impact is the `Access Server` in EM. Therefore, we connect `Bypass User Account Control` from the user aspect of the state model (on top), to `Access Server` from the network aspect of the event model (on bottom) by adding an edge between these two nodes. This shows the attack progress from the user aspect to the network aspect and allows attackers to execute the `Query to SMF` operation.

3.4 Evaluating Security Posture

Evaluating security posture is performed using the following two steps.

Building Event-State Model. First, we use the fused model from the previous step to build the structure of Bayesian Network (BN). Then we use the historical log data from both monitoring events and auditing states of a 5G network to learn its parameters. Each incoming edge to a node in the resultant BN model indicates the probability of an activity and each node is represented as follows: (i) white nodes represent normal events, (ii) red nodes represent a breach state, and (iii) rectangular nodes represent privilege escalation, as depicted in Fig. 7.

Inferring Probabilities for Goal Nodes. This step makes inferences from the resultant event-state model based on the observed conditions (value of the nodes: occurred or not) of the system and the user-defined goal node. A *goal node* is an event or state of a system that are chosen by the admins based on the security requirements of the organization. Given the goal node and observed conditions, we use Bayesian inference to calculate the conditional probability of the goal node. This probability measures an attacker's ability to reach the goal node, so from an administrator's perspective, security posture is the value that complements it. Choosing multiple goal nodes is also possible in the real world. To that end, we consider a dummy node that can be linked to all those goal nodes. Then, we re-build the model so that it adds the dummy node and re-calculates the conditional probability for each node based on this change. Using the same approach, we can infer the value for this combined node which represents the combined security posture for all those goal nodes.

Example 5. Figure 7 shows an excerpt of our event-state model where we evaluate the security posture for the user-defined goal: `Exfiltrate Data`. Admin set the value of `Access Server`, `Deploy Malware`, and `Configuration PB` as occurred as observed conditions. Then Bayesian inference method on the event-state model yields a conditional probability of 0.07 and taking the complement, we get the security posture value of 0.93 for `Exfiltrate Data`. Moreover, to facilitate multiple goal nodes, a new node is created and labeled as `Combined Goal` which connects three different goal nodes (`Token Impersonation`, `Launch Agent`, and `Exfiltrate Data`). After rebuilding the model using the same

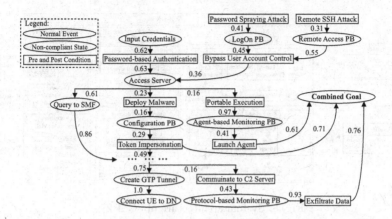

Fig. 7. Evaluating security posture based on the event-state model

observed conditions, the new security posture value is 0.76 because there are now more paths to the combined goal, thereby decreasing the security posture value.

4 Implementation

This section discusses the implementation and integration details of 5GSPE.

4.1 5G Testbed Implementation

For our 5G testbed, we use Towards5GS-helm [15] to automate the deployment of Free5GC [13] (version 3.2.1) on top of Kubernetes [14] (version 1.22). The simulation of RAN is ensured in conjunction with UERANSIM[1] for testing 5G core functionalities. We also use existing auditing tools, KubeScape [7], Falco [8], and a custom tool based on Sugar [23], to monitor and audit the security of a 5G network. We use KubeScape (v2.0.183) [7], to scan for potential vulnerabilities and misconfigurations in a Kubernetes cluster. However, since KubeScape does not focus on runtime detection, we use Falco (v0.33.1) [8] for detecting potential run-time security breaches in Kubernetes. As, Falco does not audit any activities in 5G network functions, we use custom detection rules, and a first-order logic-based tool called Sugar [23] to detect breaches in 5G network functions. Table 2 shows a few example rules for those tools. **Challenges:** We face a memory limit issue in Kubescape, and reconfigure the `kube-apiserver.yaml` file and set `--audit-webhook-mode` to `blocking` so that the Kubernetes API server does not send a response for each event. We also use `journactl` to dynamically retrieve all Falco alerts to address the issue of varying time precision among tools.

---

[1] https://github.com/aligungr/UERANSIM.

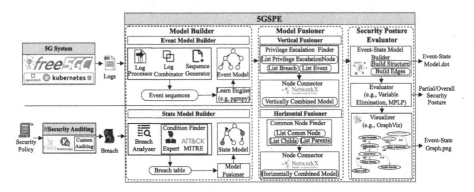

Fig. 8. System architecture of 5GSPE

4.2 5GSPE Implementation and Integration to Free5GC

Figure 8 depicts the system architecture of 5GSPE. The *model builder* module is responsible for building both the event and state model. 5GSPE first automatically collects logs from different components, e.g., Kubernetes, Falco, KubeScape, etc., and pre-processes them to identify event sequences from the logs. These event sequences are converted to the input (in .text) to PGMPY [25] (v0.1.19), a Python library used for building models and learning with a Bayesian network. Next, to build the state model, we first deploy a breach analyzer to analyze the security breach and construct a breach table. The model fuser module is implemented based on a customized algorithm (Algorithm 1 in Appendix B). We use networkX [26] to implement various graph operations, such as add_node, find_cycle. Lastly, the security posture evaluator module uses different classes (e.g., Max-Product Linear Programming (MPLP) and variable elimination) from PGMPY to evaluate the security posture. We also use graphviz [27] to visualize the models. **Challenges:** Identifying relevant security controls from thousands of existing controls is a laborious and time-consuming process. To summarize and extract keywords from the controls, we use NLP tools (e.g., BERT [28], NER [29]). We also use them to determine the pre- and post-conditions of a security control breach from the MITRE framework. Graphviz's default layouts limit the user's ability to analyze, and arrange nodes and edges aesthetically; therefore, we employ pydotplus [30] coupled with Graphviz to solve this issue.

Table 2. Example of detection rules for security tools

Security Tool	Detection Rules	Auditing Source
Falco	Detect any attempt to attach/exec into a Pod	Kubernetes audit log
Falco	Detect any inbound connection from a source outside of an allowed set of IPs, networks, or domain names	Systemcalls
KubeScape	Check for delete or deletecollection RBAC permissions on workloads	RoleBindings
Custom scripts	Detect any unexpected HTTP requests to UDM	free5GC UDM logs

5   Experiments

This section describes the experimental setup and results.

5.1   Experimental Setup

Our testbed is deployed on an OpenStack [31] environment with one master node, and two worker nodes on a server running with Ubuntu 20.04. In addition to our testbed data, we generate synthetic data in a simulated environment that creates 25,000 event sequences including 25 unique event types including breaches of specific security controls from NIST [10] (AC-7: Logon Policy Breach (PB), AC-17: Remote access PB, AC-8: System use notification PB, CM-7: Configuration PB, SI-4 (2): Agent-based monitoring PB, SI-4 (7): Rule-based monitoring PB). To generate event sequences synthetically, we follow the dependency among event types captured from our testbed and assign different event types to attackers in a random but realistic manner. We first define the *attacker capability*, which is the number of events (both regular and attack events) in a sequence that an attacker is capable of completing. Then, we generate attackers with different capabilities using an exponential distribution (where the majority of attackers possess an initial capability and comparatively fewer attackers with higher capabilities) and assign generated events accordingly. We also divide each event sequence into three attack stages based on the MITRE ATT&CK framework, with each stage showing the attacker's attack progression (in Table 3). We conduct each experiment 1,000 times and calculate the average value.

Table 3. Statistics of our dataset

Attack Stage	MITRE Tactics	No. of Seq.		Attacker Level	Sequence Length	No. of Seq.
1	Reconnaissance to Initial Access stages	9,290		1	1 to 2	17,242
2	Execution to Credential Access stages	5,938		2	3 to 4	5,518
3	Discovery to Exfiltration stages	10,556		3	5 to 6	1,737
	Total	25,784		4	more than 6	1,287

5.2   Experimental Results

In the following, we present our experimental results.

Effects of Attack Progress. The purpose of our first set of experiments is to accurately determine the overall security posture as the attack progresses. Experiment parameters include the different attack stages and goal nodes. To better interpret the security posture values derived from our solution, we also measure the attacker success ratio (ASR), which is the proportion of successful attackers reaching to the goal node during an attack stage. Figures 9a, 9b, 9c, and 9d show the relationship between the attack stages and the overall security posture value for different goal nodes: combined goal (considering all the following goal nodes), exfiltrate data, launch agent, and token impersonation, respectively. We observe that the security posture values and the attacker success ratio are roughly inversely proportional. This is expected because a higher security posture value indicates a better-secured system, and vice versa. On the other hand, as an attack advances from one stage to the next, the value of the whole security posture declines as shown in Fig. 9. Moreover, the average security posture value reduces more when the goal node is closer to the attacker (e.g., for token impersonation as the goal node, the average posture value decreases by 29% (0.93 to 0.66 in Fig. 9d) whereas, for exfiltrate data as target node, it decreases by just 1% (0.99 to 0.98 in Fig. 9b) from attack Stage 1 to attack Stage 2. Therefore, we can conclude that, in addition to the goal node, the attack stage also plays a critical role in affecting the overall security posture.

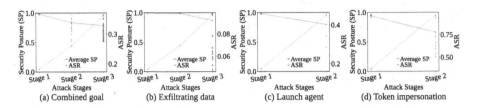

Fig. 9. Effects of attack progress for different goal; ASR: Attacker Success Ratio

Effects of Scaling Network Size (of 5G Core Network). This second set of experiments examines how network size affects security posture. We generate different 5G core networks by varying the number of NFs (e.g., UPF and AMF) between 1 and 20 [32]. Then, for each network, we generate random event sequences (as described in Sect. 5.1). Finally, we calculate the average security posture value, model size (total number of nodes and edges), time to build the model and time to evaluate it for different network sizes. Figure 10a depicts the linear increase in model size due to network scaling which remains reasonably small compared to the size of other related graphs (e.g., attack graph [33], which can exceed 10,000 nodes). Here, NF1 represents a user plane function, and NF2 represents a control plane function. Figure 10b shows that both model building time and prediction time grow linearly with the scaling of the network. However, up to 15 NFs, the time needed to build the model is less than two seconds, showing that our model is efficient up to a certain level of network scaling. We also notice a significant increase in the build time for 20 NFs, which may be brought on by the interconnection of several NEFs with other NFs, leading to an increase in the number of edges. Note that if the network size remains constant, we do not need to rebuild the model with each increase in data, and updating the model with new data takes very little time. Figure 10c shows that the security posture value does not change much with network size because network size does not necessarily increase security control breaches. The red line in the figure illustrates a magnified version of NF2_EXfiltrate using the right y-axis with a different scale. It is evident that the difference in security posture is minuscule (i.e., 0.02 while increasing the number of NFs from 1 to 20).

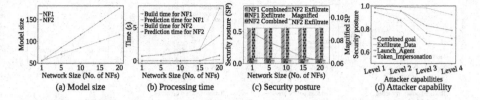

Fig. 10. Effects of scaling network size and Effects of attacker capabilities

Effects of Attacker Capabilities. The third set of experiments illustrates how the capabilities of an attacker affect the values of the overall security posture. Figure 10d demonstrates that, as the attacker's capability grows, the security posture value declines. The average security posture value for an attacker with capability *Level 1* (the lowest, defined in Table 3) is 0.98, whereas, for an attacker with capability *Level 4* (the highest), it is 0.78 for the combined goal node (a dummy node, as described in Sect. 3.4). Additionally, as most attackers with initial capability level (e.g., 1) can reach the goal node closer to the attacker (e.g., `Token Impersonation`) more easily, the security posture value is lower for that goal node than for the far-end goal node (e.g., *Exfiltrate data*). However, since the combined goal node additionally considers all other goal nodes, its security posture value falls between those of the other goal nodes.

Effects of Reducing Policy Breach by Implementing Security Solutions. The final set of experiments investigates how our solution can find the overall effect on security posture after implementing security solutions in a system. To do so, first, we calculate the security posture value using the attack example in Fig. 1, which has six policy breaches, without reducing its breaches. Then, we reduce individual security policy breaches (as a potential impact of implemented security solutions) and recompute the security posture value. Figure 11a indicates that as the number of security policy breaches is reduced, the size of the model reduces, with the greatest reduction occurring when there are more than two policy breaches. Both build time and prediction time also decrease, but we do not observe a significant change as the model is not large enough and, therefore, the compute time is not much affected (in Fig. 11b). Figure 11c illustrates that the security posture value is minimum when no policy breach is addressed (without reduction), and it increases as security policy breaches are solved. The red line illustrates a magnified version of `EXfiltrate Data` using the right y-axis with a different scale which shows an increase in security posture value. Figure 11d corroborates this trend with data from two distinct attacks deployed on our testbed: LightBasin (blue line) and a custom APT attack (orange line), both of which breach three security policies described in Table 4. In both attacks, with all three policy breaches, the security posture is minimal, and it increases as the number of policy breaches reduces. The average security posture value increases for the custom APT attack from 0.62 with all three breaches (EIP, TSCF, and ACR) to 0.99 with no breaches.

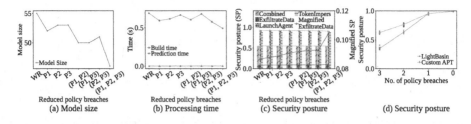

Fig. 11. Effects of reducing security policy breaches where WR: Without Reduction, P1: Reducing System Use Notification Policy Breach (PB), P2: Reducing Remote Access PB, P3: Reducing LogOn PB

Table 4. Implemented attacks description

Attack	Attack Steps	Purpose	Breached Security Policy
Light Basin	Unexpected Inbound Connections (UIC)	To gain access to the system	AC-3 (Access Enforcement)
	Creating NodePort Services (CNS)	To expose containerized 5G Network Functions(NFs) to the Internet	CM-6 (Configuration Settings)
	Unexpected HTTP Requests to UDM (UHRU)	To exfiltrate subscribers' data from the UDM	SC-7 (Boundary Protection)
Custom APT	Exec Into Pods (EIP)	To execute malicious codes in pods	AC-3 (Access Enforcement)
	Tampering Shell Configuration Files (TSCF)	To weaken the system security	SI-7 (Software, Firmware, and Information Integrity)
	Attaching Cluster-admin Role (ACR)	To impersonate network admin	AC-6 (Least Privilege)

6   Related Works

This section reviews the related literature.

5G Security and its Requirements. Existing works (e.g., [2,34]) in 5G use an attack graph-based approach to propose a 5G-specific metric using cross-layer information shared among 5G network stakeholders and focusing more on its user aspect. Whereas, other works (e.g., [35]) measure the security of commercial 5G deployment while considering the user aspects (e.g., subscriber protection, user plane protection). However, all of them are limited to a particular aspect (e.g., user, network, or infrastructure) of a 5G network. There are a few works (e.g., [36]) that quantify other aspects of 5G, but they do not evaluate its security posture. Ericsson researchers recommend continuous monitoring, logging, least privilege principles, data encryption, threat detection and response, etc. to evaluate security posture and identify areas for improvement [37]. 5G network vulnerabilities include hardware, firmware, and software weaknesses, as well as issues with signaling and control plane protocols, containers, and Kubernetes. This is a call to a comprehensive, multi-layered approach required to assess network security and address all service aspects and internal components [38].

Security Posture of Non-5G network. Several works (e.g., [4,5]) involve attack-graph analysis, where the likelihood and potential impact of a specific threat is evaluated using probabilistic models. Specifically, Frigault et al. [4] incorporate temporal factors using dynamic Bayesian networks. Whereas Wang et al. [5] focus on causal relationships between vulnerabilities encoded in attack graphs. Other works (e.g., [39,40]) evaluate security metrics either from the vulnerabilities or from the behavior of network devices. However, none of them address 5G-specific challenges to capture the persistent threats with evolving impacts on multiple aspects of a 5G network. Additionally, there are several risk assessment frameworks, such as the NIST Cybersecurity Framework [10] and the ISO 27001 [24], for organizations to assess risks. However, they usually provide a more generic assessment, whereas our objective is to evaluate the overall security posture for a particular 5G network deployment.

Standalone Security Solutions. There are a few built-in tools (e.g., Kubescape [7] and Falco [8]) that support auditing and monitoring for 5G environments on Kubernetes. Moreover, different auditing techniques are for specific applications, such as auditing in the cloud [41] and IoT [42]. Other solutions in 5G (e.g., [43–47]) focus on various security objectives (e.g., attack and interference detection, log management, etc.) However, none of those works focus on security posture evaluation. Also, the European Telecommunications Standards Institute (ETSI) proposes a security framework [48] to manage virtualized networks securely, while 3GPP proposes a data analytic architecture for 5G networks [49,50]. These efforts demonstrate the significance of considering security as a crucial factor for the stability and availability of services deployed using 5G networks. However, none provides an overall security posture of a 5G network.

In summary, 5GSPE differentiates from other works by addressing 5G-specific challenges (e.g., covering its multiple aspects, capturing evolving impact of persistent threats) in evaluating the overall security posture of a 5G network.

7   Conclusion

In this paper, we proposed 5GSPE, a new approach for evaluating the security posture of 5G networks while considering the 5G-specific security threats (e.g., persistent threats with evolving impacts from multiple aspects of a 5G network). Specifically, we first built an event model using monitoring results and a state model using auditing results. We then combined these two models as a Bayesian network by leveraging their common nodes along with privilege escalation nodes. Finally, we evaluated the security posture of a 5G network through Bayesian inference of the model. We implemented and integrated our solution for free5GC and Kubernetes, and demonstrate its effectiveness through extensive experiments.

There are a few limitations of this work. Our work presently focuses on measuring the current security posture of the system and does not predict future security posture. In the future, we intend to extend our work to support predictive capabilities based on historical data analysis. We currently rely on the knowledge of security experts to identify the pre- and post-conditions of a security breach. Our future work will focus on reducing this reliance. Also, we plan to apply our work to other systems (e.g., clouds, IoT).

Acknowledgments. The authors thank the anonymous reviewers for their valuable comments. This work is mainly supported by Ericsson Canada and the first author was partially supported by the Natural Sciences and Engineering Research Council of Canada under the Discovery Grants RGPIN-2021-04106.

Appendix

A   Definition of Event-State Model

To evaluate security postures in 5G, we build a model, namely, *event-state model* (a combination of the event model and state model). The *state model* captures the results of auditing system states, and the *event model* captures the results of monitoring system events. We define these models more formally as follows.

Event Model (EM). Given a list of event types *event-types* and the log of historical events *hist*, the event model is defined as a Bayesian network $EM = (G_e, E_e)$, where G_e is a directed acyclic graph (DAG) in which each node represents an event type in *event-types*, and each directed edge between two nodes indicates the first node would immediately precede the other in some event sequences in *hist* whose probability is part of the list of parameters E_e.

State Model (SM). Given a list of breaches of different security control from different security standards, B and the pre-, and post-conditions of individual breach, P, and the auditing logs of the system over time *auHist*, the state model is defined as a dependency graph [51] $SM = (G_s, E_s)$, where G_s is a set of DAGs in which each node corresponds to the breach of security control and their pre-or post-condition from B and P, and each directed edge between two nodes indicates the transition probability derived from *auHist* and it is part of the list of parameters E_s.

Event-State Model (ESM). Event-State Model is a Bayesian network $ESM = (G_c, E_c)$, where $G_c = \{G_e \cup G_s\}$ (i.e., all the nodes in both the event and state models) and $E_c = \{E_e \cup E_s \cup E_p\}$, where E_p is the set of edges that connects the privilege escalation vertices (responsible for lateral movement caused by a breach) to the resulted vertices (either from *EM* or *SM*) and the edge values are coming from *hist* and *auHist* as a probability which is part of the list of parameters E_c.

B   Algorithm for Building Event-State Model

Algorithm 1 is used to construct an event-state model from the event model, and the state model. We define two distinct functions: `vertical_fusing` (Lines 3 to 16), and `horizontal_fusing` (Lines 17 to 28) to combine the model vertically and horizontally. For vertical fusing, in Line 6, we first list all the privilege escalation nodes manually by taking help from an expert. Then, for each privilege escalation node, we attach the breach node and the event node to the privilege escalation node in Lines 9–13. In Lines 29–36, we define one utility function named `findCommonNode` to list all the common nodes between two models for horizontal fusing. Line 18 of the `horizontal_fusing` function utilizes this utility function. Line 23 and 24 adds the parent and child subgraphs from both the event model and the state model to the common node.

Algorithm 1: Building event-state Model

```
Input:
        stateModel ← state model;
        eventModel ← event model;
Output:
        combinedModel ← CombinedModel
 1  combinedModel ← vertical_fusing(stateModel, eventModel);
 2  combinedModel ← horizontal_fusing(stateModel, eventModel);
 3  Function vertical_fusing(stateModel, eventModel):
 4  │    combinedModel ← [];
 5  │    foreach breachState in stateModel do
 6  │    │    privilegeEscalationNode ← breachState.privilegeEscalation;
 7  │    │    normalEvent ← eventModel.breachState;
 8  │    │    if privilegeEscalationNode ∉ combinedModel then
 9  │    │    │    combinedModel.add_node(privilegeEscalationNode) ;
10  │    │    │    combinedModel.add_node(breachState) ;
11  │    │    │    combinedModel.add_node(normalEvent) ;
12  │    │    │    combinedModel.add_edge(node1, newNode) ;
13  │    │    │    combinedModel.add_edge(newNode, node2)
14  │    │    end
15  │    end
16  │    return combinedModel;
17  Function horizontal_combination(stateModel, eventModel):
18  │    commonNodeList ← findCommonNode(stateModel, eventModel);
19  │    foreach cnode in commonNodeList do
20  │    │    if cnode ∉ combinedModel then
21  │    │    │    if isCreateCylce(cnode, combinedModel) == False then
22  │    │    │    │    combinedModel ← add_node(cnode);
23  │    │    │    │    combinedModel ← add_subgraph(cnode.parent);
24  │    │    │    │    combinedModel ← add_subgraph(cnode.child);
25  │    │    │    end
26  │    │    end
27  │    end
28  │    return combinedModel;
29  Function findCommonNode(stateModel, eventModel):
30  │    listOfCommonNodes ← ∅;
31  │    foreach node ∈ stateModel do
32  │    │    if node ∈ eventModel then
33  │    │    │    listOfCommonNodes ← listOfCommonNodes ∪ {node};
34  │    │    else
35  │    end
36  │    return listOfCommonNodes;
37  return combinedModel;
```

References

1. GSMA. The Mobile Economy 2022 (2022). https://www.gsma.com/mobil eeconomy/wp-content/uploads/2022/02/280222-The-Mobile-Economy-2022.pdf. Accessed 24 May 2023
2. Zhao, L., Oshman, M.S., Zhang, M., Moghaddam, F.F., Chander, S., Pourzandi, M.: Towards 5G-ready security metrics. In: ICC 2021-IEEE International Conference on Communications, pp. 1–6. IEEE (2021)
3. Yocam, E., Gawanmeh, A., Alomari, A., Mansoor, W.: 5G mobile networks: reviewing security control correctness for mischievous activity. SN Appl. Sci. 4(11), 1–17 (2022)
4. Frigault, M., Wang, L., Singhal, A., Jajodia, S.: Measuring network security using dynamic Bayesian network. In: Proceedings of the 4th ACM workshop on Quality of protection, pp. 23–30 (2008)
5. Wang, L., Singhal, A., Jajodia, S.: Measuring the overall security of network configurations using attack graphs. In: Barker, S., Ahn, G.-J. (eds.) DBSec 2007. LNCS, vol. 4602, pp. 98–112. Springer, Heidelberg (2007). https://doi.org/10.1007/978-3-540-73538-0_9
6. Zhang, M., Wang, L., Jajodia, S., Singhal, A., Albanese, M.: Network diversity: a security metric for evaluating the resilience of networks against zero-day attacks. IEEE Trans. Inf. Forensics Secur. 11(5), 1071–1086 (2016)
7. Github: Kubescape (2022). https://github.com/kubescape/kubescape
8. Falco. Falco (2022). https://github.com/falcosecurity/falco
9. LightBasin: a roaming threat to telecommunications companies (2022). https://www.crowdstrike.com/blog/an-analysis-of-lightbasin-telecommunications-attacks/
10. NIST. SP 800–53 Rev. 5, Security and Privacy Controls for Information Systems and Organizations (2022). https://csrc.nist.gov/publications/detail/sp/800-53/rev-5/final. Accessed 14 May 2023
11. CSA. CSA Cloud Controls Matrix (CCM). https://cloudsecurityalliance.org/research/cloud-controls-matrix/. Accessed 14 May 2023
12. 5G Security Controls Matrix-ENISA. https://www.enisa.europa.eu/publications/5g-security-controls-matrix/
13. free5GC. https://www.free5gc.org/. Accessed 14 May 2023
14. K8s. Kubernetes. https://kubernetes.io/. Accessed 14 May 2023
15. Towards5GS-helm (2022). https://github.com/Orange-OpenSource/towards5gs-helm. Accessed 16 May 2023
16. Ericsson. 5G Core (5GC) network: Get to the core of 5G (2022). https://www.ericsson.com/en/core-network/5g-core. Accessed 24 May 2023
17. 3GPP. TR 33.894 Study on zero-trust security principles in mobile networks (2022)
18. Yang, M., et al.: Cross-layer software-defined 5G network. Mob. Netw. Appl. 20, 400–409 (2015)
19. Taxonomy of attacker capabilities (2023). https://cloud.google.com/blog/produ cts/identity-security/identifying-and-protecting-against-the-largest-ddos-attacks. Accessed 16 May 2023
20. Nadir, I., et al.: a1-an auditing framework for vulnerability analysis of IoT system. In: 2019 IEEE European Symposium on Security and Privacy Workshops (EuroS&PW), pp. 39–47. IEEE (2019)
21. Mitre. MITRE FiGHT. https://fight.mitre.org/. Accessed 24 June 2023
22. Mitre. MITRE ATT&CK (2022). https://attack.mitre.org/

23. Tamura, N.: Sugar: a SAT-based constraint solver (2022). https://cspsat.gitlab.io/sugar/. Accessed 14 May 2023
24. ISO/IEC 27002:2022 Information security, cybersecurity and privacy protection-Information security controls (2022). https://www.iso.org/standard/75652.html. Accessed 14 May 2023
25. pgmpy. pgmpy 0.1.19 documentation (2022). https://pgmpy.org/
26. NetworkX (2023). https://networkx.org/. Accessed 16 May 2023
27. graphviz. Graphviz (2023). https://graphviz.org/
28. Devlin, J., Chang, M.-W., Lee, K., Toutanova, K.: BERT: pre-training of deep bidirectional transformers for language understanding (2019)
29. BERT-base-NER (2023). https://huggingface.co/dslim/bert-base-NER
30. PyDotPlus Homepage (2023). https://pydotplus.readthedocs.io/
31. Open Source Cloud Computing Infrastructure - OpenStack (2023). https://www.openstack.org/. Accessed 16 May 2023
32. 3GPPspace. Inside TS 23.501: AMF Load Balancing (2021)
33. Ou, X., Govindavajhala, S., Appel, A.W., et al.: Mulval: a logic-based network security analyzer. In: USENIX security symposium, Baltimore, MD, vol. 8, pp. 113–128 (2005)
34. Shafayat Oshman, M.: Assessing security in the multi-stakeholder premise of 5G: a survey and an adapted security metrics approach. Ph.D. thesis, Carleton University (2022)
35. Nie, S., Zhang, Y., Wan, T., Duan, H., Li, S.: Measuring the deployment of 5G security enhancement. In: Proceedings of the 15th ACM Conference on Security and Privacy in Wireless and Mobile Networks (2022)
36. Bartoletti, S., et al.: Uncertainty quantification of 5G positioning as a location data analytics function. In: 2022 Joint European Conference on Networks and Communications & 6G Summit (EuCNC/6G Summit), pp. 255–260. IEEE (2022)
37. Ericsson. 5G security for public and hybrid cloud deployments (2022). https://www.ericsson.com/en/reports-and-papers/further-insights/5g-security-for-hybrid-cloud
38. Spirent. Keeping Pace with the Requirements of 5G Security (2022). https://www.spirent.com/assets/white-paper-keeping-pace-with-the-requirements-of-5g-security
39. Pendleton, M., Garcia-Lebron, R., Cho, J.-H., Xu, S.: A survey on systems security metrics. ACM Comput. Surv. (CSUR) 49, 1–35 (2016)
40. Xie, M., May, R.A.: Network security framework based scoring metric generation and sharing. US Patent 10,791,146 (2020)
41. Majumdar, S., et al.: ProSAS: proactive security auditing system for clouds. IEEE Trans. Dependable Secure Comput. 19, 2517–2534 (2021)
42. Huang, K., et al.: EVA: efficient versatile auditing scheme for IoT-based datamarket in jointcloud. IEEE Internet Things J. 7(2), 882–892 (2019)
43. Apruzzese, G., Vladimirov, R., Tastemirova, A., Laskov, P.: Wild networks: exposure of 5G network infrastructures to adversarial examples. IEEE Trans. Netw. Serv. Manage. 19, 5312–5332 (2022)
44. Boeira, F., Asplund, M., Barcellos, M.: Provable non-frameability for 5G lawful interception. In: ACM WiSec (2023)
45. Orsós, M., Kecskés, M., Kail, E., Bánáti, A.: Log collection and SIEM for 5G SOC. In: 2022 IEEE 20th Jubilee World Symposium on Applied Machine Intelligence and Informatics (SAMI), pp. 000147–000152. IEEE (2022)

46. Brighente, A., Mohammadi, J., Baracca, P., Mandelli, S., Tomasin, S.: Interference prediction for low-complexity link adaptation in beyond 5G ultra-reliable low-latency communications. IEEE Trans. Wireless Commun. **21**(10), 8403–8415 (2022)

47. Mitchell, C.J.: The impact of quantum computing on real-world security: a 5G case study. Comput. Secur. **93**, 101825 (2020)

48. ETSI. Network Functions Virtualisation (NFV) Release 4 Security; Security Management Specification (2021)

49. 3GPP. TS 23.288 architecture enhancements for 5G System (5GS) to support network data analytics services v17.4.0 (2022-03) (2022)

50. Prasad, A.R., Arumugam, S., Sheeba, B., Zugenmaier, A.: 3GPP 5G security. J. ICT Stand. **6**(1–2), 137–158 (2018)

51. Hamlet, J.R., Lamb, C.C.: Dependency graph analysis and moving target defense selection. In: Proceedings of the 2016 ACM Workshop on Moving Target Defense, pp. 105–116 (2016)

PrivMail: A Privacy-Preserving Framework for Secure Emails

Gowri R. Chandran[1]([✉]), Raine Nieminen[1], Thomas Schneider[1], and Ajith Suresh[2]

[1] ENCRYPTO, Technical University of Darmstadt, Darmstadt, Germany
chandran@encrypto.cs.tu-darmstadt.de
[2] Cryptography Research Centre, Technology Innovation Institute, Abu Dhabi, UAE

Abstract. Emails have improved our workplace efficiency and communication. However, they are often processed unencrypted by mail servers, leaving them open to data breaches on a single service provider. Public-key based solutions for end-to-end secured email, such as Pretty Good Privacy (PGP) and Secure/Multipurpose Internet Mail Extensions (S/MIME), are available but are not widely adopted due to usability obstacles and also hinder processing of encrypted emails.

We propose PrivMail, a novel approach to secure emails using secret sharing methods. Our framework utilizes Secure Multi-Party Computation techniques to relay emails through multiple service providers, thereby preventing any of them from accessing the content in plaintext. Additionally, PrivMail supports private server-side email processing similar to IMAP SEARCH, and eliminates the need for cryptographic certificates, resulting in better usability than public-key based solutions. An important aspect of our framework is its capability to enable third-party searches on user emails while maintaining the privacy of both the email and the query used to conduct the search.

To evaluate our solution, we benchmarked transfer and search operations using the Enron Email Dataset and demonstrate that PrivMail is an effective solution for enhancing email security.

Keywords: Private Email · Secret Sharing · Private Keyword Search · Secure Two-party Computation · Private Information Retrieval

1 Introduction

Despite the widespread use of social media, text messages, and online messaging services such as WhatsApp, Signal, and Telegram, electronic mail (email) is still a popular method of communication, and it has a growing user base. In 2020, there were roughly 4 billion users of email; by 2024, it is predicted that there would be nearly 4.5 billion users, with an annual growth rate of 3% [21,23]. The majority of email users are corporate companies and small businesses. For instance, 81% of small businesses rely on email as their primary customer acquisition channel, and 80% for retention [17].

G. Tsudik et al. (Eds.): ESORICS 2023, LNCS 14345, pp. 145–165, 2024.
https://doi.org/10.1007/978-3-031-51476-0_8

As the use of emails has grown in popularity, it has also caught the attention of attackers who endanger security and privacy. One significant issue is related to data breaches, in which email servers are frequently targeted [45]. Attackers may publicly release the breached data or attempt to profit by selling or negotiating with the email service provider [19,43]. For example, the 'Collection #1' breach revealed 2.7 billion identification records with 773 million emails and made the data available for sale online [55]. Data breaches also threaten the economy significantly, with the average cost of a breach increasing by 15% from 2020 to 4.45 million USD in 2023 [28]. Another concern is the privacy of email content from the Service Provider (SP). Often, emails are processed without encryption by mail servers or are encrypted by the SP, requiring users to trust them completely. However, with the growing concern for individual privacy and the implementation of privacy laws like the EU General Data Protection Regulation (GDPR) and California Consumer Privacy Act (CCPA) [53], many users hesitate to use email for communicating sensitive information.

The aforementioned concerns led to the emergence of service providers such as ProtonMail [56] and Tutanota [58], who developed solutions for private emails using End-to-End Encryption (E2EE) techniques. These techniques addressed privacy issues regarding the SP, while also allowing the users to perform search on emails. However, they pose other limitations, for example, only the user can perform the search [38,59]. Furthermore, solutions such as E2EE, which keep the email content hidden from the SP, may not be enough in some situations and require other options. To better illustrate these concerns, we will use a company's email system as an example and provide more information below.

Example Use Case—Company Email System. Consider PrivCorp, a company that wants to establish an email infrastructure for its employees while upholding individual data privacy. PrivCorp is concerned about the potential impact of data breaches, which have recently hit a number of enterprises. Furthermore, unlike some companies that monitor employee emails with or without their consent based on legal jurisdiction, PrivCorp is committed to implementing email monitoring in a privacy-preserving manner. In summary, PrivCorp's email infrastructure development goals include:

1. *Privacy from SP:* The email content[1] should be hidden from the SP. To achieve the desired goal, the company is willing to use multiple SPs, if needed.
2. *Data breach protection:* The email should remain private even if all but one of the SPs are compromised.
3. *Spam filtering:* The company should be able to analyse external emails and perform spam filtering in a privacy-preserving manner to respect the privacy of the email content.
4. *Unintended data leakage prevention:* The company should be able to monitor emails from its employees to the outside world in a privacy-preserving manner for accidental data leaks or other content that violates company policies such as defamation against the company, character assaults, and abusive content.

---

[1] Mostly the subject and content fields but not other meta data.

To address goals (1) and (2) above, a simple approach is to use E2EE methods, like PGP [5] and S/MIME [50], in which emails are encrypted and signed by the sender using public-key cryptography and decrypted and verified by the receiver. However, the strong privacy guarantees of E2EE make achieving goals (3) and (4) extremely difficult, as both require some sort of processing over the encrypted email content by an external entity.

While techniques like Searchable Symmetric Encryption (SSE) [54] enable encrypted data search, their utility is limited due to: 1) the need for email sender and receiver to manage keys for search, restricting search access to these parties, and 2) practical SSE methods having limitations in terms of information leakage, which can compromise the privacy of the encrypted data [24,31,42]. Additionally, SSE doesn't align with our use-case as it lacks support for external agent search, a requirement for goal (4).

To achieve the aforementioned goals simultaneously and efficiently, we combine Secure Multi-Party Computation (MPC) [7,22] and Private Information Retrieval (PIR) [12,16] techniques.

Overview of Our Solution. At a high level, the idea behind PrivMail is to use multiple email Service Providers (SPs) and secret sharing techniques to ensure that no individual SP sees the email content in the clear. Our idea was inspired by the observation that most people already have multiple email accounts for varied purposes such as personal and professional correspondence, with the average user having 1.75 email accounts [23,60].

In our approach, rather than encrypting emails with cryptographic keys, we secret share them (both subject and content) between multiple SPs using MPC techniques. For example, if PrivCorp uses two SPs, say `gmail.com` and `outlook.com`, then each employee with id `empid` is assigned two email addresses, e.g., `empid@gmail.com` and `empid@outlook.com`. The sender splits the email content into secret shares, sending each via regular email to one of two addresses. The employee retrieves and locally combines these shares to access the content. We provide additional optimizations ensuring that the total communication is the same as a single unencrypted email. With this approach, the users are only required to exchange email addresses except some simple splitting and reconstruction operations (cf. Sect. 3). In contrast to exchanging cryptographic keys or certificates needed with PGP and S/MIME [23,60], such email addresses can be easily shared by the users (e.g., by writing on business cards or websites).

Besides providing privacy from the SP through secret sharing, our approach allows private server-side processing/search using MPC. However, we cannot guarantee privacy in case of a government agency forcing access to all servers. In this scenario, the best solution is to select the servers that are from different jurisdictions such that at least one of the servers is very hard to compromize.

Our Contributions. We propose PrivMail, a privacy-preserving system for emails. PrivMail provides a secure way to transfer and store emails without requiring to use keys or certificates. Our main idea is to secret share emails between multiple (non-colluding) mail servers (e.g., Gmail, Outlook, etc.), thereby keeping the data on each server private. Our approach has the advantage that privately sending and receiving emails can directly run on the existing email infrastructure *without server-side modifications*. PrivMail offers resilience against data breaches since the attacker must breach all of the email service providers involved in order to obtain any useful information. Furthermore, it reduces the usability issues that have been observed for schemes such as PGP and S/MIME [23,60].

A key feature of PrivMail is its support for privacy-preserving server-side processing on secret shared emails. We propose privacy-preserving drop-in replacements for the standard Internet Message Access Protocol (IMAP) SEARCH and FETCH commands, allowing a search agent to securely and efficiently search for keyword(s) over secret shared emails and retrieve the results. Our scheme combines techniques from Secure Multi-Party Computation (MPC) and Private Information Retrieval (PIR) while avoiding leakages and the key management required by schemes like Searchable Symmetric Encryption (SSE) [24,31,42].

We also simulate Simple Mail Transfer Protocol (SMTP) servers and run extensive benchmarks on private keyword search over the Enron Email Dataset [34]. We are able to demonstrate practical performance, which can encourage real-world email service providers to incorporate PrivMail's private search functionalities into their existing feature set. To summarize:

1. We propose PrivMail, a privacy-preserving framework for emails that enhances usability and data breach resilience without needing keys or certificates.
2. PrivMail offers privacy-preserving server-side processing on secret shared emails, facilitating private searches and retrieval while avoiding key management issues and leakages. We also propose multiple efficient keyword search techniques, utilizing specific properties of email text and language.
3. We published an open-source prototype implementation of PrivMail[2] and demonstrate its practicality via benchmarks on private keyword searches on the Enron Email Dataset [34].

2   Preliminaries

The generic design of PrivMail allows to seamlessly use any MPC protocol for secure computation. However, in this work, we focus on the well-explored setting with two servers ($n = 2$), and the scheme is explained using this setting in the majority of the sections. PrivMail comprises of four entities: the sender ($\mathcal{S}$) and receiver ($\mathcal{R}$) of an email, a collection of MPC servers, and a search agent ($\mathcal{A}$).

Threat Model. All entities in PrivMail are considered to be *semi-honest*. The two MPC servers are assumed to be *non-colluding*. This is justifiable given that the MPC servers in our case are well-established email service providers such as Gmail and Outlook. Because their reputation is at stake, these service providers have strong incentives to follow the protocol and not conspire with other service providers to leak their information. They could even operate in different countries

---

[2]. https://encrypto.de/code/PrivMail.

with different legislations. Such setup of non-colluding servers have already been deployed in the real-world for services such as Firefox telemetry [8], privacy-preserving machine learning [29], cryptocurrency wallets [18,52], and COVID-19 exposure notification analytics [4]. The search agent $\mathcal{A}$ will be either the email sender or receiver, or a pre-consented third party (for instance, in the use-case mentioned in Sect. 1, the company PrivCorp's email filtering service) and is expected to semi-honestly follow the protocol specifications.

Notations. We use the following logical gates: XOR ($\oplus$), AND ($\wedge$), OR ($\vee$), and NOT ($\neg$). Since XOR and NOT gates can be evaluated locally in Secret Sharing (SS)-based MPC, an OR gate can be realised at the cost (communication) of an AND gate as $a \vee b = \neg(\neg a \wedge \neg b)$. Given a set of m bits $b_1, \ldots, b_m$, $\bigwedge_{i=1}^{m} b_i = b_1 \wedge b_2 \wedge \cdots \wedge b_m$ represents the cumulative AND and the other logic operators follow similarly. When performing boolean operations with a single bit b and a binary string $v \in \{0,1\}^{\ell}$, we assume that the same bit b is used to perform the operation with each bit in the string v.

The values in PrivMail are secret shared between the two MPC servers via *boolean sharing* [22]: For a secret x, the i-th server, for $i \in \{1,2\}$, holds the share $\langle x \rangle_i$ such that $x = \langle x \rangle_1 \oplus \langle x \rangle_2$. We sometimes abbreviate the notation and use x_i instead of $\langle x \rangle_i$ for the sake of brevity.

Existing Email Architecture. In a standard email communication, the sender $\mathcal{S}$ sends a message to the receiver $\mathcal{R}$ via a Mail User Agent (MUA) such as Thunderbird as follows. First, the MUA converts the message to email format and sends it to a Mail Transfer Agent (MTA). Upon receiving the email, the MTA transmits it to the receiver's Mail Delivery Agent (MDA) via the Simple Mail Transfer Protocol (SMTP). Finally, the MDA delivers the mail to $\mathcal{R}$'s mailbox. We leave out low-level details such as domain validation and refer to [33] for specifics.

On the receiver's side, $\mathcal{R}$ uses the Internet Message Access Protocol (IMAP) [13] to retrieve the email from the receiving server.[3] In more detail, the two functionalities IMAP *SEARCH* [13, §6.4.4] and *FETCH* [13, §6.4.5] are used to accomplish this. SEARCH provides a comprehensive search interface similar to the Structured Query Language (SQL). FETCH retrieves all the emails from the mail server returned by the SEARCH functionality.

3   PrivMail Architecture

In this section, we specify the architecture of PrivMail. In PrivMail, the sender and the receiver can choose their own independent set of Service Providers (SPs) whom they trust to not collude. W.l.o.g., we first explain our architecture assuming that both the sender and the receiver are registered with two distinct SPs

---

[3] The older Post Office Protocol (POP) downloads the email from the server and optionally deletes it from the server, but in contrast to IMAP provides no server-side search.

each. In concrete terms, each SP owns an email path that connects the sender's Mail Transfer Agent (MTA) to the receiver's Mail Delivery Agent (MDA).

At a high level, the sender S splits the original mail (Subject, Body) into two shares and sends them to receiver R via the two SPs, denoted by Priv-Mail Servers (PMS). The SPs are not required to perform any additional work to support our email transfer because the email shares are simply treated as *regular emails*, thus standard SMTP servers are sufficient for this. The email is retrieved by the receiver R by locally reconstructing the shares received from the SPs. Unlike an end-to-end encrypted email system (like PGP or S/MIME), this approach does not require either the sender or the receiver to handle any cryptographic keys or certificates. This also eliminates the challenges associated with implementing PGP or S/MIME in practice, where the users have to setup, manage and exchange keys and certificates [48–50].

Security Guarantees: PrivMail guarantees confidentiality, integrity and correctness. Confidentiality and correctness of PrivMail are ensured by the security of the underlying MPC protocols, while its integrity is assured as the users and the MPC servers are assumed to be semi-honest. To provide integrity of email transfer even with malicious servers, an honest sender can simply append a salted SHA256 hash of the email content together with the salt to each shared email. When the email is reconstructed, the receiver can verify that it matches both hashes/salts. This is secure as long as one of the servers is not corrupted and the sender is honest. In the case of search with malicious servers (which we leave as future work), the underlying MPC protocol is responsible for providing integrity, which is typically achieved using authentication tags for protocols in the dishonest-majority setting.

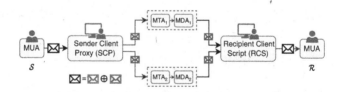

Fig. 1. PrivMail Communication: 2 Server Case.

Two Server Case: Now, we explain the communication phase for the two server case in more detail. As illustrated in Fig. 1, the first step is to split the email $E = $ (Subject, Body) into secret shares as per the underlying MPC protocol. The secret sharing can be done either at S's Mail User Agent (MUA) using a custom plug-in for mail clients like Thunderbird or Outlook, or using a Sender Client Proxy (SCP) service between S's MUA and MTAs. In this work, we use the latter method as it is independent of the specific MUA. The email is shared as boolean shares, i.e., $E = E_1 \oplus E_2$ with $E_1 \in_R \{0,1\}^{|E|}$.[4] Each of the email

---

[4] Later in Sect. 3.2 we describe an optimization to send a seed for a Pseudo Random Function (PRF) instead of the whole share E_1.

shares are now treated as *independent emails* and are sent using the sender's respective mail accounts using the regular email procedure. Similar to the SCP, we use a Recipient Client Script (RCS) at the receiver's end to reconstruct the original email from the shares.

3.1 Integration with the Existing Email Infrastructure

So far, we have assumed that each user sends and receives emails through a fixed set of distinct SPs. This assumption, however, may take some time to be adopted in practice, so we will now discuss how our scheme can be integrated with the existing email infrastructure.

The basic goal is to provide a private alternative on top of the existing email system such that the users can choose to communicate their emails either via PrivMail or via the existing email system. Let the sender S be registered to N_S SPs and let PMS^S be the set of these outgoing mail servers. Similarly, PMS^R denotes the set of incoming email servers of receiver R of size N_R. Furthermore, we assume that both S and R have chosen their respective PMS servers in such a way that not all of the servers in their respective set will collude.

Naïve Approach: The naïve approach for integrating PrivMail to the existing email infrastructure is by splitting the mail at the sender's end into $n = N_S \cdot N_R$ shares using an n-out-of-n secret sharing scheme. Then each outgoing server PMS^S_i will receive N_R shares, one for each of the receiver's N_R servers. These shares can then be sent to the corresponding receiver's servers as *regular mails*. This setting corresponds to having a path between each pair of PMS^S_i and PMS^R_j.

Before looking deeper into the security of this approach, we define the term *secure path* in the context of email servers at the sender's and recipient's ends.

Definition 1. *A path connecting outgoing mail server $PMS^S_i \in PMS^S$ and incoming mail server $PMS^R_j \in PMS^R$ is said to be "secure" if neither PMS^S_i nor PMS^R_j colludes with the other servers in the set $PMS^S \cup PMS^R$. Here, $N_S, N_R \geq 2$, where $N_S = |PMS^S|$ and $N_R = |PMS^R|$.*

Privacy: Let $N_{min} = min(N_S, N_R)$. Considering the entire set of servers, i.e., $PMS^S \cup PMS^R$, the approach is secure as long as the adversary compromises no more than $N_{min} - 1$ servers. This is due to the fact that in this case, there will be at least one secure path (cf. Definition 1) from PMS^S to PMS^R, and one share out of the $N_S \cdot N_R$ shares will be communicated via this path. Because the adversary has no knowledge of this share, the email content's privacy is guaranteed due to the privacy guarantee of the underlying n-out-of-n secret sharing scheme.

We observe that it is preferable to consider security at S's and R's ends separately rather than combining them, since in real-world scenarios, the servers in PMS^S and PMS^R may be from different legal jurisdictions. In such cases, the number of servers at the clients side does not ensure additional security. As a result of treating the servers separately, the scheme's security is preserved at the S's (or R's) end as long as not all servers in PMS^S (or PMS^R) are compromised.

Note that the naïve approach requires a communication of $N_S \cdot N_R$ email shares. We now present an optimized approach that reduces the communication between PMS^S and PMS^R to $\max(N_S, N_R)$ email shares.

Optimized Approach. In this method (Fig. 2), the sender splits the email into $N_{max} = \max(N_S, N_R)$ shares as per the underlying MPC protocol. Without loss of generality, consider the case where $N_S < N_R$ and the other case follows similarly. Once the email shares are generated, SCP at S's end will compute a mapping from the servers in PMS^S to PMS^R.

If there are common servers, i.e., $PMS^S \cap$ $PMS^R \neq \emptyset$, then a mapping is formed between the corresponding servers for each server in the intersection (e.g., in Fig. 2 Gmail server PMS_1^S is mapped to Gmail server PMS_1^R). The remaining servers are then assigned a random mapping so that each of the servers in PMS^R receives exactly one email share. When $N_S \geq N_R$, the mapping is s.t. each server in PMS^S is assigned exactly one email share, whereas servers at the receiver's end may receive multiple shares. More details on applying our email sharing in practice are provided in the full version [10, §4.1].

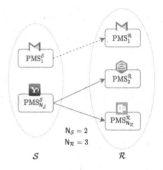

Fig. 2. Optimized Approach

Privacy: Similar to the naïve approach, the privacy of the optimized approach is ensured as long as there is at least one secure path between the servers at the S's and R's ends, i.e., as long as an adversary corrupts a maximum of $N_{min} - 1$ servers, this approach is secure.

3.2   Sharing Optimization Using PRF Keys

In the two approaches mentioned in Sect. 3.1, each share is of the same size as the original mail. Therefore, the total communication required for sending a mail of size $|E|$ would be $\max(N_S, N_R) \cdot |E|$ for the optimized approach.

To further optimize the communication and storage, we can adopt techniques similar to those used in multi-server PIR schemes [12,15,16], that also use n-out-of-n secret sharing to split the PIR query. In these works, the query is partitioned into several *chunks*. In line with this technique, we divide each mail E into n chunks of size $|E|/n$ each. Each chunk is then shared among the servers PMS_i using boolean sharing such that $chunk_j = flip_j \oplus_{i=n,i\neq j}^{n} rnd_i^j$, where flip is a boolean share and $rnd_i^j = PRG(key_i)[j]$, where key_i is a 128-bit symmetric key. Server i then receives the tuple $(flip_i, key_i)$ as its share of the mail which has size $|E|/n + 128$ *bits*. The mail can thus be reconstructed by concatenating all the chunks together, i.e., $chunk_1 \| chunk_2 \| \cdots \| chunk_n$. For the correctness of this sharing, we set the number of chunks $n = \max(N_S, N_R)$. This reduces the total communication of the optimized approach to $|E| + \max(N_S, N_R) \cdot 128$ *bits*, which is about the size of the original email.

4 Private Queries Using MPC

The main advantage of PrivMail is that private server-side processing of the mails is easily possible because the emails are secret shared among the servers. This allows commonly used functions like keyword search to be implemented using various MPC techniques. Furthermore, keyword searches can be utilised for other functionalities, such as checking for data leakage in outgoing emails or detecting spam in incoming emails. Given the ubiquituous usage of keyword search in the existing email infrastructure, we present multiple private keyword search techniques and discuss optimizations and extensions. Note that the search agent $\mathcal{A}$ can be either of the email users, i.e., $\mathcal{S}$ or $\mathcal{R}$, or a third party with prior consent, e.g., a company mail service.

The discussion that follows assumes that the communication phase (cf. Sect. 3) has been completed and that the email content has been secret shared among the PrivMail servers (PMSs). Consider a mailbox containing p emails that are secret shared among n non-colluding servers. Given a keyword K, the private query phase proceeds using two sub-protocols: i) Private Search ($\mathcal{F}_{\mathsf{Search}}$) emulating IMAP SEARCH and ii) Private Fetch ($\mathcal{F}_{\mathsf{Fetch}}$) emulating IMAP FETCH, which are executed in the order detailed next.

1. The search agent $\mathcal{A}$ secret shares the keyword K among the n servers in accordance with the underlying MPC protocol.
2. Upon receiving the shares of K, the servers initiate the $\mathcal{F}_{\mathsf{Search}}$ functionality that enables $\mathcal{A}$ to obtain a list of indices that corresponds to emails containing the keyword. Concretely, $\mathcal{A}$ obtains a p-bit vector $\mathbf{H} \in \{0,1\}^p$ with $H[i] = 1$ if the ith email contains K and 0 otherwise. We instantiate $\mathcal{F}_{\mathsf{Search}}$ using different techniques in Sect. 4.2.
3. $\mathcal{A}$ and the n servers jointly execute $\mathcal{F}_{\mathsf{Fetch}}$ (cf. Sect. 4.3) to privately fetch each email from the mailbox. We efficiently instantiate $\mathcal{F}_{\mathsf{Fetch}}$ using an extension of 2-server PIR to a secret shared database (cf. Sect. 4.3).

To summarize, $\mathcal{F}_{\mathsf{Search}}$ and $\mathcal{F}_{\mathsf{Fetch}}$ provide a privacy-preserving drop-in replacement for the standard Internet Message Access Protocol (IMAP) [13] functionalities SEARCH and FETCH respectively. Similar to IMAP SEARCH, PrivMail also supports combining multiple keyword searches for comprehensive filtering of the emails by privately applying boolean operations on the output vectors $\mathbf{H}$. In the following we concentrate on single keyword searches.

4.1 Private Search $\mathcal{F}_{\mathsf{Search}}$

Recall from Sect. 3 that our basic approach secret shares the email's subject and body fields in their original form. One disadvantage of this strategy is that the private search becomes case-sensitive. Working over the actual shares with MPC incurs additional computation and communication to provide a solution similar to the standard IMAP SEARCH, which is case-insensitive. A simple way to avoid this overhead is to let the sender $\mathcal{S}$ secret share a lowercase version of the email as well which doubles the size of the email. The $\mathcal{F}_{\text{Search}}$ function will then be performed over these shares, and the actual shares will be used to reconstruct the original email (in $\mathcal{F}_{\text{Fetch}}$). The search's efficiency can be further improved by employing a special encoding described next.

Special Encoding: We define our own special 6-bit character encoding without losing much information for standard emails in English text that use 7-bit ASCII character encoding, similar to the SixBit ASCII code by AIS [47]. The encoding space is sufficient for all the lowercase alphabets and numbers (0–9) along with 28 special characters.For this, we omit all ASCII control characters as well as a small set of special characters that are uncommon for a keyword. We call this 6-bit encoded email a *compact email* from now on. As shown later in Sect. 4.2, the bit length reduction due to this encoding also helps to improve the performance of the $\mathcal{F}_{\text{Search}}$ protocols.

Computing Servers (CSs): Now that $\mathcal{F}_{\text{Search}}$ operates over shares of the compact email and these operations are computationally intensive (as will be evident from the subsequent sections), the PMS servers can use powerful dedicated servers for this task. Henceforth, we refer to the servers for $\mathcal{F}_{\text{Search}}$ as Computing Servers (CSs). Note that the PMS servers can be used as the CSs as well.

$\mathcal{F}_{\text{Search}}$ *for the 2-Server Case:* As before, we resort to a simple setting of two servers and use a Secure Two-Party Computation (STPC) protocol for our computations, where the CSs enact the role of MPC servers for the private query phase. The functionality $\mathcal{F}_{\text{Search}}$ takes the shares of the search keyword and the emails as input and returns the shares of the p-bit binary vector **H**. Looking ahead, in the protocol, the shares of the keyword are generated by the search agent $\mathcal{A}$ and sent to the corresponding servers (the PRF optimization from Sect. 3.2 can be used here as well for long keywords). Furthermore, both shares of the result of $\mathcal{F}_{\text{Search}}$ are given to $\mathcal{A}$, who reconstructs the result locally.

Remarks: When the search agent $\mathcal{A}$ is the email user ($\mathcal{S}$ or $\mathcal{R}$), it may be preferable to download the entire mailbox and perform keyword search locally over the cleartext. Though this naïve solution appears to be much cheaper for the CSs,, it may not always be an ideal solution from the perspective of the email user due to factors such as limited (mobile) bandwidth, local storage, battery usage, or cross-device accessibility.

4.2   Instantiating $\mathcal{F}_{\text{Search}}$

In this section, we look at concrete instantiations of the $\mathcal{F}_{\text{Search}}$ functionality. First, we discuss a generic instantiation, called Circuit-Based search, applicable to keywords of varying lengths and frequencies. Then, we present two optimizations: i) Bucketing-Based, and ii) Indexing-Based searches. The former is more efficient for single word keywords, while the latter is more efficient for keywords with higher frequency of appearance in the text. While primarily discussed within a two-server framework, these approaches can be generalized to multiple servers.

Circuit-Based Search. In this approach, the email is treated as a continuous string of characters and the keyword is then matched at each position of this string using an equality test circuit. To be precise, consider a text $W = w_1 \| \cdots \| w_t$ of length t and a keyword $K = k_1 \| \cdots \| k_s$ of length s, with $s \leq t$. Let b denote the bit-length of characters (e.g., $b = 7$ for ASCII characters and $b = 6$ for compact emails, cf. Sect. 4.1). At a high level, the strategy is as follows: beginning with the i-th character position of W, a block of s characters denoted by $\widetilde{W}_i$ is derived and compared to the keyword K. We use an equality test functionality $\mathcal{F}_{\mathsf{EQ}}$ over ℓ-bit inputs to compare K and $\widetilde{W}_i$, defined as $\mathcal{F}_{\mathsf{EQ}}^\ell(x, y) = 1$ if $x = y$, and 0 otherwise. We use the EQ circuit of [35,36,51] to instantiate $\mathcal{F}_{\mathsf{EQ}}$ which is defined as follows:

$$\mathsf{EQ}^\ell(x, y) = \bigwedge_{i=1}^{\ell} \neg(x_i \oplus y_i). \tag{1}$$

There are $t - s + 1$ blocks ($\widetilde{W}_i$) with one EQ protocol executed per block. All of these executions are independent and can be carried-out in parallel. Once the results have been evaluated, a cumulative OR of the results can be used to find at least one matching block. To summarize, the search circuit SC is defined as

$$\underset{\text{(Keyword, Text)}}{\underbrace{\mathsf{SC}(\; \overset{\text{\# blocks}}{\mathsf{K}, W}\;)}} = \bigvee_{i=1}^{t-s+1} \mathsf{EQ}^{\underset{\text{bit length}}{sb}}(\mathsf{K}, \widetilde{W}_i). \tag{2}$$

Complexity: An instance of EQ over ℓ bit inputs require a total of $\ell - 1$ AND gates (cf. Eq. (1)) and has a multiplicative depth of $\lceil \log_2 \ell \rceil$ when evaluated as a tree. The SC consists of $t - s + 1$ such EQ circuits and additionally $t - s$ AND gates (as OR can be implemented via AND). Moreover, another $\lceil \log_2(t - s + 1) \rceil$ rounds are required to compute the final result. Hence, for $\ell = sb$ in our case, the SC circuit has a total of $(t + 1)sb - s^2b - 1$ ($\approx tsb$, when $t \gg s, b$) AND gates and a depth of $\lceil \log_2 sb \rceil + \lceil \log_2(t - s + 1) \rceil$. Note that the depth of the circuit can be further reduced at the expense of increased communication using multi-input AND gates [37,44].

The method described above assumes that the lengths of the text and the keyword are known to all Computing Servers (CSs). In our case, because the subject and body of an email are the text, hiding its length during computation is impractical for efficiency reasons. However, we can hide the length of the s-length keyword by padding it to a fixed length, which results in the following modifications to the above approach.

Length-Hiding Keyword Search. Given two $\ell_{\max}$-bit values x, y, let the functionality $\mathcal{F}_{\mathsf{LEQ}}$ be defined as $\mathcal{F}_{\mathsf{LEQ}}^{\ell_{\max}, \ell}(x, y) = 1$ if $x[i] = y[i]$ for $i \leq \ell$ and 0 otherwise. For a given $\ell \leq \ell_{\max}$, $\mathcal{F}_{\mathsf{LEQ}}$ returns 1 if the first ℓ-bits of x match with y and 0 otherwise. To hide the length $\ell = sb$ bits of keyword K, we use an additional

$\ell_{\max}$-bit *length mask*[5] of the form $\mathrm{M}_x = m_1 \| \cdots \| m_{\ell_{\max}} = \{1\}^\ell \| \{0\}^{\ell_{\max} - \ell}$. Given these values, we instantiate $\mathcal{F}_{\mathsf{LEQ}}$ by using a length hiding equality test circuit LEQ, which is defined as

$$\mathsf{LEQ}^{\ell_{\max}}(x, y, \mathrm{M}_x) = \bigwedge_{i=1}^{\ell} \neg((x_i \oplus y_i) \wedge m_i). \tag{3}$$

The logic of the LEQ circuit is similar to that of EQ (Eq. (1)) in that the bits of x, y are compared, but the result for the padded bits (last $\ell_{\max} - \ell$ bits) is discarded by ANDing them with the zero bits of the M_x value. This only adds a layer of parallel AND gates to the EQ circuit.

Optimizations to the Circuit-Based Search: We further optimize the Circuit-Based search using different properties of the mail text and keywords. If the keyword contains no spaces, i.e., is a single word, it is beneficial to "jump" over *spaces* in the target text to avoid unnecessary comparisons. However, checking for spaces in the Circuit-Based Search is difficult as the entire email is treated as a single string. Including the logic to check for spaces within the search circuit SC (cf. Eq. (2)) is costly. Therefore, for our optimizations, each mail is considered as a collection of distinct words rather than a continuous string of characters. This also gives us advantages when the mail contains repeated words, since now we can omit the duplicates from the search.

Bucketing-Based Search. To search on distinct words, we let the sender $\mathcal{S}$ secret share each *distinct* word in the email text individually in a randomized order. The words can also be padded to a fixed length to hide the original lengths.

Padding for length obfuscation should be done with caution, as it is a trade-off between efficiency and privacy. Padding every word to a large fixed length would yield maximum privacy. However, the efficiency may now be even worse than that of the Circuit-Based Search. On the other hand, the padding can be removed completely to maximize efficiency. As a compromise, we propose a *bucketing* technique that allows users to tailor the trade-off between efficiency and privacy to their specific needs.

A naïve way of instantiating a search given a list of secret shared words and a keyword would be to use a circuit-based Private Set Intersection (PSI) protocol [27,39,46]. However, linear complexity PSI protocols do exact but not sub-string matches, and thus cannot be used easily to add padding to the words for increased privacy. Therefore, we use our Circuit-Based Approach to search through the list of words in the email.

The idea behind bucketing is to select buckets for different ranges of character length and do the padding accordingly. For example, if we define a bucket for words with lengths ranging from 1 to 4 characters, each word of that range in the bucket is padded to 4 characters. Furthermore, the search keyword must be padded in accordance with the bucketing scheme. To facilitate substring matches,

---

[5] The agent $\mathcal{A}$ generates the shares of the mask and sends them with the keyword shares.

the search must be performed over the bucket defined for the keyword length as well as the buckets for longer words. As a result, the bucketing technique is more efficient for longer keywords as the shorter buckets can be ignored. In order to hide the actual length of the keyword, we must use the LEQ circuit, see Eq. (3) for the equality tests.

Indexing-Based Search. All search approaches described before were primarily concerned with searching over each email individually. Multiple emails in a mailbox, on the other hand, are likely to have many words in common. With this observation, we further optimize the Bucketing-Based Search for single-word search and build a *search index* for *all* emails in a mailbox.

Consider a mailbox containing p emails $\{E_1, \ldots, E_p\}$ and let d be the number of distinct words in those emails. In the index table, each distinct word, denoted as $\mathcal{W}_i$, forms one row of the table and is associated with a p-bit string. The vector is referred to as *occurrence bit-string* and has the following format: $\mathbf{B}^{\mathcal{W}_i} = B_1^{\mathcal{W}_i} \| \cdots \| B_p^{\mathcal{W}_i}$. Here, $B_j^{\mathcal{W}_i} = 1$ denotes the presence of word $\mathcal{W}_i$ in the email E_j and 0 denotes its absence. The index table is then secret shared among the Computing Servers (CSs).

In contrast to the previous approaches where a bit value was returned for each email, in the indexing-based approach, a keyword is first searched against all the distinct words in the table and a d-bit string $\mathbf{u} = u_1 \| \cdots \| u_d$ is generated, where d is the number of distinct words. The final search result is nothing but a cumulative OR of all the occurrence bit-strings corresponding to the matched rows. Formally, the p-bit result of the search is

$$\text{Search Result} = \bigvee_{i=1}^{d} u_i \cdot \mathbf{B}^{\mathcal{W}_i}, \tag{4}$$

where the OR operations over a bit vector are simply the operator applied to each bit position.

Given the secret shares of $\mathbf{u}$ among the CSs, one method for completing the above task is to involve the search agent $\mathcal{A}$. The vector $\mathbf{u}$ is reconstructed by $\mathcal{A}$ and the corresponding occurrence bit strings are obtained securely using $\mathcal{F}_{\text{Fetch}}$ (as will be explained later in Sect. 4.3). The agent can then perform the OR operation locally to obtain the final result. Another method that avoids agent intervention is to let the CSs compute the expression in Eq. (4) using the underlying MPC protocol.

The index-based approach makes the search complexity *independent* of the number of mails, as the search depends only on the number of distinct words, except for final computation in Eq. (4), enhancing efficiency for large mail boxes.

Comparison: Each of the search techniques discussed above, i.e., Circuit-Based, Bucketing-Based and Indexing-Based, have their own pros and cons, depending on the search keyword length, number of mails in the mailbox and distinct keyword occurring. We compare the different methods in Table 2 in Sect. A.

4.3 Private Fetch $\mathcal{F}_{\mathsf{Fetch}}$

The $\mathcal{F}_{\mathsf{Fetch}}$ functionality, enables the search agent $\mathcal{A}$ to privately retrieve emails from the Computing Servers. $\mathcal{F}_{\mathsf{Fetch}}$, takes the p-bit string as input and returns the mails corresponding to the bit positions with value 1. Although the standard IMAP FETCH [13, §6.4.5] command can be used to retrieve the desired email shares from each server, in the long run, frequency analysis can reveal details of the search queries to the servers, particularly the keywords used [31]. To avoid this, we adapt multi-server Private Information Retrieval (PIR) to instantiate $\mathcal{F}_{\mathsf{Fetch}}$.

Consider a database $\mathfrak{D}$ containing p documents with the server CS_i holding the share $\mathfrak{D}_i = \{\langle D_1 \rangle_i, \ldots, \langle D_p \rangle_i\}$, where each $\langle D \rangle_i = (\mathsf{flip}_i \| \mathsf{key}_i)$ for $i \in \{1, 2\}$ (cf. Sect. 3.2). First, the client $\mathcal{A}$ samples two symmetric keys sk_1, sk_2 for a symmetric-key encryption scheme $\mathsf{Enc}()$ and sends key sk_i to server CSi. The next step, on a high level, is that each CSi will encrypt its share (corresponding to each document) with sk_i and send this to the other server. Let $\widetilde{\mathfrak{D}}_i$ denote the encrypted database share of CSi. The encrypted database is now defined as $\widetilde{\mathfrak{D}} = \widetilde{\mathfrak{D}}_1 \| \widetilde{\mathfrak{D}}_2$. Then the client $\mathcal{A}$ sends the shares of the selection bit vector $\mathbf{b}$ to each server and the servers compute $\mathbf{b}_i \cdot \widetilde{\mathfrak{D}}$ and send the result to $\mathcal{A}$. The client $\mathcal{A}$ then combines these results by XORing them and decrypts the result using the encryption keys to obtain the queried email.

5   Implementation and Benchmarks

This section describes our implementation of PrivMail and evaluate the performance of reconstruction and keyword search over secret shared emails. A detailed discussion and more benchmarks are provided in the full version [10].

5.1   Email Transfer

The implementation of PrivMail consists of several parts, which were discussed in Sect. 3. Our implementation of the Sender Client Proxy (SCP) runs in a Docker container [1] and works with any Mail User Agent (MUA) that allows the user to manually specify the outgoing SMTP server (i.e., basically any email client). We also implemented a simple Recipient Client Script (RCS) for email reconstruction at the receiver's end and use it for performance evaluation. We use the YAML data-serialization language [3] to store the emails in the filesystem.

Reconstruction Performance. The reconstruction of the shares consists of three steps: fetching of the email shares from the (IMAP) servers, pairing, and finally combining the shares. For our Recipient Client Script (RCS), the retrieval is handled using the `imaplib` module [2] and after each fetch, the email is stored in a dictionary, where the email's Unique Identifier (UID) is the key and the share is the value. In the second step, the dictionaries are combined together. Since the dictionaries are hash maps in Python and the keys are random looking identifiers, the lookup for each email is a constant time operation. The runtime to pair and combine 500 emails from two servers takes only around 0.235 seconds, giving us a throughput of 2,127 emails per second on a regular laptop using Intel Core i7-8565U. The runtime of the fetching step depends on the IMAP server capacity, geographic location, and network setup, but is likely to be dominant (throughput was only 20 emails per second in our experiments). Thus the overhead introduced by PrivMail compared to fetching and viewing regular emails is negligible.

5.2 Email Search

We implement the private queries described in Sect. 4 using the mixed-protocol Secure Multi-Party Computation (MPC) framework MOTION [9]. We use the boolean GMW protocol [14, 22] between two parties for our performance evaluation, but our implementation can also be used in the N-party setting with full threshold. Our code is publicly available under the MIT License[6].

Benchmark Settings for Search. We tested all three approaches from Sect. 4.2 for private search (Circuit-Based, Bucketing-Based, and Index-Based) on a real-world dataset with varying parameters, using our special encoding from Sect. 4.1. For the Bucketing-Based approach, we chose to create four buckets, each of size 5 characters, i.e., buckets for words with (1–5, 6–10, 11–15, 16–20) characters. All words that are more than 20 characters long are ignored. We instantiate the MPC protocols with computational security parameter 128 and statistical security parameter 40.

We run experiments against subsets of the publicly available Enron Email Dataset [34], which contains over 500,000 emails, with each email containing on average 1,607 characters and 237 words. On examining the distribution of distinct words in this database, we conclude that the bucket size distribution for our chosen buckets are (18.8%, 50.6%, 21.7%, 8.9%). This implies that, on average, more than half of the words are between 6 and 10 characters long. Our benchmark subsets are drawn from Kenneth Lay's inbox.

The benchmarks are run on two dedicated simulation machines, each with an Intel Core i9–7960X (16 physical cores @ 2.8 GHz) processor and 8×16 GB DDR4 RAM. We simulate a Wide Area Network (WAN) setting with bandwidth limited to 100 Mbit/s, and Round-Trip Time (RTT) of 100 ms. To ensure consistency, we iterate each simulation 5 times and compute the mean for the final result.

Search Performance. We implement and compare our three search methods from Sect. 4.2. Since the Bucketing and Indexing-Based approaches already provide keyword length hiding, we use the Circuit-Based search's length hiding variant for a fair comparison. The Circuit-Based approach thus requires an additional layer of AND gates over the keyword length non-hiding variant.

Table 1 compares the performance of our three search methods in the online phase across various keyword lengths. Except for keyword length $s = 3$, we find that the Indexing-Based Approach outperforms the other two approaches in all cases. This is justified because the search domain for both the bucketing

---

[6] https://encrypto.de/code/PrivMail.

Table 1. Evaluation of online phase of keyword length-hiding search methods: circuit, bucketing and indexing. Best results are in bold.

Keyword Length s	Method	# Emails = 100		# Emails = 200	
		Time (s)	Comm. (MiB)	Time (s)	Comm. (MiB)
3	Circuit	9.63	**2.61**	18.19	**5.80**
	Bucketing	9.15	16.28	14.07	35.76
	Indexing	**3.57**	6.41	**6.58**	11.22
8	Circuit	13.68	4.62	25.96	10.41
	Bucketing	7.51	7.09	12.98	15.91
	Indexing	**3.19**	**3.73**	**5.22**	**6.97**
13	Circuit	13.78	6.59	23.73	14.93
	Bucketing	4.59	1.27	10.09	2.91
	Indexing	**2.48**	**0.63**	**4.26**	**1.48**
18	Circuit	15.38	8.58	27.51	19.47
	Bucketing	4.19	0.16	8.97	0.45
	Indexing	**2.68**	**0.06**	**3.96**	**0.25**

and Indexing-Based Approaches shrinks for long keywords due to the omission of buckets for short keywords. We also see that the Indexing-Based Approach improves by $\approx 2\times$ over the Bucketing-Based Approach in terms of both runtime and communication. Furthermore, the Indexing-Based method is expected to be more and more efficient compared to the other methods for a larger number of emails, since it eliminates duplicate words across the entire email set. We remark that in settings where the number of target documents is large and the document format is more regular, our indexing-based search can be orders of magnitude more efficient than bucketing-based search.

A detailed benchmark of the search approaches from Sect. 4.2, along with the details of the Thunderbird plugin, is provided in the full version [10, §6.2].

6   Related Work

A line of work that is very closely related to the secure keyword search in Sect. 4 is Secure Pattern Matching (SPM). SPM [25,57,61,62] entails a server with text $x \in \Sigma^n$ (over some alphabet Σ) and a receiver with pattern $p \in \Sigma^m$ with $m \leq n$. Without revealing additional information, the receiver learns where the pattern occurs as a substring of the server's text. SPM is a highly researched field with applications in various areas such as database search [11,20], network security [40], and DNA analysis [41]. Circuit-based approaches for pattern matching techniques have been proposed in [30,32]. These circuits are designed primarily for genomic computing and DNA matching, thus they aren't directly applicable in our context of keyword search (cf. Sect. 4.2). Later works such as [6,26,62] presented techniques based on homomorphic encryption. However, in these works, one of the parties involved owns the keyword while another (or a group of parties) owns the database, so they are not directly applicable to our case. In Sect. 4.2, we create custom circuits for our use cases in PrivMail.

We give a detailed discussion of related works on topics such as E2EE, SSE, MPC, PSI and PIR in the full version [10, §2].

Acknowledgements. This project received funding from the European Research Council (ERC) under the European Union's Horizon 2020 research and innovation program (grant agreement No. 850990 PSOTI). It was co-funded by the Deutsche Forschungsgemeinschaft (DFG) within SFB 1119 CROSSING/236615297 and GRK 2050 Privacy & Trust/251805230.

A Comparison of the Different Search Techniques

Each of the search techniques discussed in Sect. 4, i.e., circuit-based, bucketing-based, and indexing-based, have their own pros and cons depending on the keywords being searched. The user or the email client can therefore choose the most beneficial technique according to their requirements. In Table 2, we give a comparison between the different techniques for various use-cases, highlighting the most efficient techniques for each use-case.

Table 2. Efficiency comparison of the different search techniques for different types of keywords. The most efficient technique is marked in bold.

	Circuit	Bucket	Index
Longer Keywords	More efficient for longer keywords than for smaller	**Significantly more efficient as smaller buckets will be completely skipped**	Efficient only if the keyword is frequent in the text
Higher Frequency Keywords	Efficiency remains the same as for any keyword	Efficient if the keyword is of longer length	**Very efficient for frequent words in the text**
Partial Matches	**Very efficient as the text is considered as a continuous string of characters**	Would incur higher cost to implement	Would incur higher cost to implement
Special Words	**Efficient, as all words are treated with same priority**	**Efficient if the word is of medium to long length**	Not very efficient as the word won't be frequent in the text

Performance of Circuit-Based Search. Table 3 summarizes our benchmarks for search across four different keyword lengths, $s \in \{3, 8, 13, 18\}$ (corresponding to the average of our bucket sizes), on email sets of sizes 100 and 200. The total computation and communication overheads grow proportionally to the keyword length and number of emails in the sets as the search circuit size grows.

Table 3. Evaluation of circuit-based search (Sect. 4.2). Runtime (Time) is in seconds and communication (Comm.) between the servers in mebibytes (MiB).

Keyword Length s	Phase	# Emails = 100		# Emails = 200	
		Time (s)	Comm. (MiB)	Time (s)	Comm. (MiB)
3	Online	4.80	1.22	11.67	2.72
	Total	12.19	63.42	33.45	145.28
8	Online	5.20	3.12	10.15	7.03
	Total	20.96	174.25	48.65	399.61
13	Online	5.12	5.03	11.35	11.33
	Total	25.33	284.15	60.43	652.05
18	Online	4.31	6.89	9.40	15.52
	Total	32.47	393.07	73.74	902.54

We parallelize each equality test circuit (see Eq. (1)) with Single Instruction, Multiple Data (SIMD) operations, which results in an almost linear total runtime with respect to the keyword length. The minor difference in online runtime is caused by runtime fluctuations in our WAN simulation and can be evened out with additional iterations. The remaining cumulative OR in Eq. (2) dominates the online runtime, giving a nearly constant runtime.

References

1. Docker Container. https://www.docker.com
2. imaplib. https://docs.python.org/3/library/imaplib.html#imaplib.IMAP4.fetch
3. YAML Data Serialization Language. https://yaml.org
4. Apple and Google: Exposure Notification Privacy-Preserving Analytics (ENPA) white paper (2021)
5. Atkins, D., Stallings, W., Zimmermann, P.: PGP Message Exchange Formats. RFC 1991 (1996). https://www.rfc-editor.org/rfc/rfc1991.txt
6. Baron, J., Defrawy, K.E., Minkovich, K., Ostrovsky, R., Tressler, E.: 5PM: secure pattern matching. In: SCN (2012)
7. Ben-Or, M., Goldwasser, S., Wigderson, A.: Completeness theorems for non-cryptographic fault-tolerant distributed computation (extended abstract). In: STOC (1988)
8. Blog, M.S.: Next steps in privacy-preserving Telemetry with Prio (2019). https://blog.mozilla.org/security/2019/06/06/next-steps-in-privacy-preserving-telemetry-with-prio/

9. Braun, L., Demmler, D., Schneider, T., Tkachenko, O.: MOTION - a framework for mixed-protocol multi-party computation. ACM TOPS **25**(2), 1–35 (2021)

10. Chandran, G.R., Nieminen, R., Schneider, T., Suresh, A.: PrivMail: a privacy-preserving framework for secure emails (full version). ePrint Archive, Paper 2023/1294 (2023). https://encrypto.de/code/PrivMail

11. Chase, M., Shen, E.: Substring-searchable symmetric encryption. PoPETs (2015)

12. Chor, B., Goldreich, O., Kushilevitz, E., Sudan, M.: Private information retrieval. In: FOCS (1995)

13. Crispin, M.: Internet Message Access Protocol - Version 4rev1. RFC 3501 (2003). https://rfc-editor.org/rfc/rfc3501.txt

14. Demmler, D., Schneider, T., Zohner, M.: ABY – a framework for efficient mixed-protocol secure two-party computation. In: NDSS (2015)

15. Demmler, D., Herzberg, A., Schneider, T.: RAID-PIR: practical multi-server PIR. In: CCSW (2014)

16. Demmler, D., Holz, M., Schneider, T.: OnionPIR: effective protection of sensitive metadata in online communication networks. In: Gollmann, D., Miyaji, A., Kikuchi, H. (eds.) ACNS 2017. LNCS, vol. 10355, pp. 599–619. Springer, Cham (2017). https://doi.org/10.1007/978-3-319-61204-1_30

17. ETail Emarsys WBR SMB Report: Adapting to the pace of omnichannel commerce (2016). https://emarsys.com/learn/white-papers/adapting-to-the-pace-of-omnichannel-commerce/

18. Fireblocks: MPC Wallet as a Service Technology (2022). https://www.fireblocks.com/platforms/mpc-wallet/

19. Franceschi-Bicchierai, L.: T-Mobile says hacker accessed personal data of 37 million customers (2023). https://techcrunch.com/2023/01/19/t-mobile-data-breach/

20. Gennaro, R., Hazay, C., Sorensen, J.S.: Text search protocols with simulation based security. In: Nguyen, P.Q., Pointcheval, D. (eds.) PKC 2010. LNCS, vol. 6056, pp. 332–350. Springer, Heidelberg (2010). https://doi.org/10.1007/978-3-642-13013-7_20

21. Gilbert, N.: Number of Email Users Worldwide 2022/2023: Demographics & Predictions (2022). https://financesonline.com/number-of-email-users/

22. Goldreich, O., Micali, S., Wigderson, A.: How to play any mental game: a completeness theorem for protocols with honest majority. In: STOC (1987)

23. The Radicati Group, Inc.: Email Statistics Report, 2019–2023 (2018). https://www.radicati.com/wp/wp-content/uploads/2018/12/Email-Statistics-Report-2019-2023-Executive-Summary.pdf

24. Gui, Z., Paterson, K.G., Patranabis, S.: Rethinking searchable symmetric encryption. In: S&P (2023)

25. Hazay, C., Lindell, Y.: Efficient protocols for set intersection and pattern matching with security against malicious and covert adversaries. J. Cryptol. **23**, 422–456 (2010). https://doi.org/10.1007/s00145-008-9034-x

26. Hazay, C., Toft, T.: Computationally secure pattern matching in the presence of malicious adversaries. J. Cryptol. **27**, 358–395 (2014). https://doi.org/10.1007/s00145-013-9147-8

27. Huang, Y., Evans, D., Katz, J.: Private set intersection: are garbled circuits better than custom protocols? In: NDSS (2012)

28. IBM Security: Cost of a Data Breach Report 2023 (2023). https://www.ibm.com/reports/data-breach

29. Inpher: XOR Secret Computing Engine (2022). https://inpher.io/xor-secret-computing/

30. Jha, S., Kruger, L., Shmatikov, V.: Towards practical privacy for genomic computation. In: S&P(2008)
31. Kamara, S., Kati, A., Moataz, T., Schneider, T., Treiber, A., Yonli, M.: SoK: cryptanalysis of encrypted search with LEAKER - a framework for LEakage AttacK Evaluation on Real-world data. In: EuroS&P (2022)
32. Katz, J., Malka, L.: Secure text processing with applications to private DNA matching. In: CCS(2010)
33. Klensin, D.J.C.: Simple Mail Transfer Protocol. RFC 5321 (2008). https://rfc-editor.org/rfc/rfc5321.txt
34. Klimt, B., Yang, Y.: The enron corpus: a new dataset for email classification research. In: Boulicaut, J.-F., Esposito, F., Giannotti, F., Pedreschi, D. (eds.) ECML 2004. LNCS (LNAI), vol. 3201, pp. 217–226. Springer, Heidelberg (2004). https://doi.org/10.1007/978-3-540-30115-8_22. https://www.cs.cmu.edu/~./enron/
35. Kolesnikov, V., Sadeghi, A.-R., Schneider, T.: Improved garbled circuit building blocks and applications to auctions and computing minima. In: Garay, J.A., Miyaji, A., Otsuka, A. (eds.) CANS 2009. LNCS, vol. 5888, pp. 1–20. Springer, Heidelberg (2009). https://doi.org/10.1007/978-3-642-10433-6_1
36. Kolesnikov, V., Schneider, T.: Improved garbled circuit: free XOR gates and applications. In: Aceto, L., Damgård, I., Goldberg, L.A., Halldórsson, M.M., Ingólfsdóttir, A., Walukiewicz, I. (eds.) ICALP 2008. LNCS, vol. 5126, pp. 486–498. Springer, Heidelberg (2008). https://doi.org/10.1007/978-3-540-70583-3_40
37. Koti, N., Patra, A., Rachuri, R., Suresh, A.: Tetrad: actively secure 4PC for secure training and inference. In: NDSS (2022)
38. Martinoli, M.: Behind the scenes of ProtonMail's message content search (2022). https://proton.me/blog/engineering-message-content-search
39. Mohassel, P., Rindal, P., Rosulek, M.: Fast database joins and PSI for secret shared data. In: CCS (2020)
40. Namjoshi, K.S., Narlikar, G.J.: Robust and fast pattern matching for intrusion detection. In: INFOCOM (2010)
41. Osadchy, M., Pinkas, B., Jarrous, A., Moskovich, B.: SCiFI - a system for secure face identification. In: S&P(2010)
42. Oya, S., Kerschbaum, F.: Hiding the access pattern is not enough: exploiting search pattern leakage in searchable encryption. In: USENIX Security (2021)
43. Page, C., Whittaker, Z.: It's All in the (Lack of) Details: 2022's badly handled data breaches (2022). https://techcrunch.com/2022/12/27/badly-handled-data-breaches-2022/
44. Patra, A., Schneider, T., Suresh, A., Yalame, H.: ABY2.0: improved mixed-protocol secure two-party computation. In: USENIX Security (2021)
45. Perlroth, N.: Yahoo Says Hackers Stole Data on 500 Million Users in 2014 (2016). https://www.nytimes.com/2016/09/23/technology/yahoo-hackers.html
46. Pinkas, B., Schneider, T., Tkachenko, O., Yanai, A.: Efficient circuit-based PSI with linear communication. In: Ishai, Y., Rijmen, V. (eds.) EUROCRYPT 2019. LNCS, vol. 11478, pp. 122–153. Springer, Cham (2019). https://doi.org/10.1007/978-3-030-17659-4_5
47. Raymond, E.S.: AIS Payload Data Types (2017). https://gpsd.gitlab.io/gpsd/AIVDM.html
48. Ruoti, S., et al.: A usability study of four secure email tools using paired participants. ACM TOPS **22**(2), 1–33 (2019)
49. Ruoti, S., Andersen, J., Zappala, D., Seamons, K.E.: Why Johnny still, still can't encrypt: evaluating the usability of a modern PGP client. CoRR 1510.08555 (2015)

50. Schaad, J., Ramsdell, B.C., Turner, S.: Secure/Multipurpose Internet Mail Extensions (S/MIME) Version 4.0 Message Specification. RFC 8551 (2019). https://rfc-editor.org/rfc/rfc8551.txt
51. Schneider, T., Zohner, M.: GMW vs. Yao? Efficient secure two-party computation with low depth circuits. In: Sadeghi, A.-R. (ed.) FC 2013. LNCS, vol. 7859, pp. 275–292. Springer, Heidelberg (2013). https://doi.org/10.1007/978-3-642-39884-1_23
52. Sepior: Advanced MPC Wallet^{TM} (2022). https://sepior.com/products/advanced-mpc-wallet/
53. Simmons, D.: 17 Countries with GDPR-Like Data Privacy Laws (2022). https://insights.comforte.com/countries-with-gdpr-like-data-privacy-laws
54. Song, D.X., Wagner, D.A., Perrig, A.: Practical techniques for searches on encrypted data. In: S&P (2000)
55. Song, V.: Mother of All Breaches Exposes 773 Million Emails, 21 Million Passwords (2019). https://gizmodo.com/mother-of-all-breaches-exposes-773-million-emails-21-m-1831833456
56. Proton Technologies: ProtonMail Security Features and Infrastructure (2016). https://protonmail.com/docs/business-whitepaper.pdf
57. Troncoso-Pastoriza, J.R., Katzenbeisser, S., Celik, M.U.: Privacy preserving error resilient DNA searching through oblivious automata. In: CCS (2007)
58. Tutanota: Secure email made for you. https://tutanota.com/security
59. Tutanota: Searching encrypted data is now possible with Tutanota's innovative feature (2017). https://tutanota.com/blog/posts/first-search-encrypted-data
60. Watson, T.: The number of email addresses people use [survey data] (2019). https://www.zettasphere.com/how-many-email-addresses-people-typically-use
61. Wei, X., Zhao, M., Xu, Q.: Efficient and secure outsourced approximate pattern matching protocol. Soft. Comput. **22**, 1175–1187 (2018). https://doi.org/10.1007/s00500-017-2560-4
62. Yasuda, M., Shimoyama, T., Kogure, J., Yokoyama, K., Koshiba, T.: Privacy-preserving wildcards pattern matching using symmetric somewhat homomorphic encryption. In: Susilo, W., Mu, Y. (eds.) ACISP 2014. LNCS, vol. 8544, pp. 338–353. Springer, Cham (2014). https://doi.org/10.1007/978-3-319-08344-5_22

Towards Efficient Privacy-Preserving Deep Packet Inspection

Weicheng Wang[1], Hyunwoo Lee[2], Yan Huang[3], Elisa Bertino[1], and Ninghui Li[1(✉)]

[1] Purdue University, West Lafayette, IN 47907, USA
{wang3623,bertino,ninghui}@purdue.edu
[2] KENTECH, Naju-si, Jeonnam 58330, Republic of Korea
hwlee@kentech.ac.kr
[3] Indiana University, Bloomington, IN 47405, USA
yh33@indiana.edu

Abstract. Secure Keyword-based Deep Packet Inspection (KDPI) allows a middlebox and a network sender (or receiver) to collaborate in fighting spams, viruses, and intrusions without fully trusting each other on the secret keyword list and encrypted traffic. Existing KDPI proposals have a heavy-weighted initialization phase, but also require dramatic changes to existing encryption methods used to the original network traffic during the inspection phase. In this work, we propose novel KDPI schemes CE-DPI and MT-DPI, which offer highly competitive performance in initialization and guarantee keyword integrity against malicious middlebox. Moreover, our methods work readily with AES-based encryption schemes that are already widely deployed and well-supported by AES-NI. We show that our KDPI schemes can be integrated with TLS, adding marginal overhead.

Keywords: MPC · DPI · BlindBox · Garbled Circuit · Oblivious Transfer

1 Introduction

Deep packet inspection (DPI) is a widely used security technique for detecting intrusions, scanning for malware, and preventing data exfiltration [9,57]. DPI relies on a middlebox that sits between two communication endpoints to examine the payloads of network traffic to improve security [12,42]. Many DPI solutions, e.g., OpenDPI [29] and nDPI [14], have been adopted by enterprises. The global DPI market size is projected to reach 16.6 billion USD by 2026, up from 4.6 billion USD in 2020, at a yearly growth rate of 25.0% during 2021–2026 [54].

Since Transport Layer Security (TLS) [16] was introduced to secure Internet communications, its usage has been growing [20,43]. At the time of writing, more than 90% of HTTP traffic from Google products is encrypted with TLS, according to Google Transparency Report [22]. However, the end-to-end security

© The Author(s), under exclusive license to Springer Nature Switzerland AG 2024
G. Tsudik et al. (Eds.): ESORICS 2023, LNCS 14345, pp. 166–192, 2024.
https://doi.org/10.1007/978-3-031-51476-0_9

provided by TLS makes it challenging for a middlebox to perform DPI. Some proposals such as SplitTLS [28] used a TLS interception scheme to allow a middlebox to access plaintext traffic, which, unfortunately, turns out introducing vulnerabilities [11,17,50,60], and compromise the privacy of TLS [40,59]. This situation prompted the research community to consider alternative solutions [44].

In 2015, Sherry et al. [56] proposed BlindBox, a keyword-based DPI protocol, which enables the middlebox to detect occurrences of preset keywords in the encrypted traffic, while assuring that the middlebox does not learn other information about the encrypted traffic and that the communicating endpoints do not learn the keywords. The initialization phase of their protocol heavily relied on the garbled circuit protocol to securely generate tokens for each keyword. Their approach, however, has three serious limitations: (1) It only considered semi-honest middleboxes and did not offer integrity of the keywords against malicious middleboxes. Hence, although legitimate keywords (also known as rules) should only be decided by a third party called Rule Generator (RG), BlindBox did not prevent a corrupted middlebox from replacing legitimate keywords with any keywords of an adversary's choice to compromise traffic privacy. (2) As their experiments showed, BlindBox's initialization phase is rather heavy-weighted, requiring gigabytes of communication overhead [56], even without guaranteeing keyword integrity. (3) Their traffic inspection phase is very expensive, since it requires invoking the AES cipher a large number of times each with a different AES key, making it hard to leverage efficient pipelining of AES-NI instructions.

Therefore, we asked, "Can we have KDPI protocols that require minimal modification to the already wide-deployed symmetric-key encryption schemes while offering keyword integrity and performing significantly better than Blind-Box?" In this regard, we study new constructions of KDPI and provide positive answers to the question above.

Contributions. Aiming at resolving those limitations of BlindBox, we propose three efficient keyword-based DPI protocols, MT-DPI, CE-DPI, and BH-DPI. All three protocols offer keyword integrity and can be integrated with an AES-based underlying encrypted channel with minimal change, while significantly outperforming BlindBox in both initialization and traffic inspection phases.

Our first approach, MT-DPI, is based on binary multiplicative triples that we can efficiently generate using Ferret OT [63]. The resulting protocol is an order of magnitude more efficient than BlindBox in communication cost and runs a few times faster in realistic network environments where middleboxes are deployed. A major challenge in the design of MT-DPI is keyword integrity, because the traditional secret share and multiplicative triple-based protocol cannot withstand active attacks. To address this challenge, we developed a novel use of the cut-and-choose technique for secret-share-based two-party computation protocols, which may be of independent interest. We proved our protocol is secure against actively corrupted middleboxes. Our second approach, CE-DPI, extends BlindBox with a more efficient keyword verification method using Oblivious Commitment-Based Envelope (OCBE) [37]. Compared with the keyword verification suggested by BlindBox, CE-DPI is proven secure against semi-honest middlebox but uses only 1/10 the bandwidth of BlindBox. The third approach, BH-DPI, improves BlindBox with a batched hashing verification, and uses 1/6 the bandwidth of BlindBox.

2 Background

2.1 Keyword-Based DPI

We consider the problem of enabling Deep Packet Inspection (DPI) under end-to-end encryption, e.g., when TLS is used. The following parties are involved.

Sender (S) and Receiver (R). DPI is performed by a third party when the communication between S and R is encrypted. The content being sent is a sequence of packets.

Middlebox (MB). Given a set of inspection rules, MB inspects the traffic between S and R, to find out whether a packet matches any of the rules.

Rule Generator (RG). This party defines the inspection rules. An RG is trusted and specializes in creating effective rules that are useful for various DPI tasks. However, they are not trusted to inspect network traffic. In fact, they will not participate in running DPI protocols. Instead, an MB subscribes to an RG in order to obtain the rules and offer the inspection service. The role of RGs can be played by major security vendors (e.g., Symantec).

Keyword-Based DPI Systems. One class of DPI systems uses rules that are fixed-length **keywords**. That is, the RG creates a list of ℓ-byte keywords (where ℓ is a fixed parameter), and the goal of DPI is to determine whether a packet contains any keyword in the list.

To realize keyword-based DPI, a sender S will compute a **token** for every ℓ-byte substring (**word**) in the traffic, and send them to the MB. MB checks the token to learn whether any of them matches that of a keyword. Note each pair of neighboring ℓ-byte words has $\ell - 1$-byte overlap. So in an N-byte packet, the total number of ℓ-byte words is $N - \ell + 1$.

In KDPI, ℓ, the length of keywords, and K, the number of such keywords, are public information. Figure 1 depicts a keyword-based DPI System. A KDPI protocol has the following sub-protocols.

1. **Rule delivery.** MB and RG run a protocol so that MB obtains information about the keywords. Note that this does not necessarily mean that MB learns the actual keywords which can be RG's private business asset. Rule delivery happens infrequently, only when initializing MB's subscription or when rules need to be updated.
2. **Session initialization.** Before S establishes its connection with R, S runs an initialization protocol with MB to prepare MB to allow it to later inspect the traffic between S and R. The initialization protocol only needs to be executed once per new pair of connecting peers.
3. **Traffic inspection.** Before S sends a packet, S extracts all ℓ-byte words in the packet, and computes a token for each word (which we call *token computation*) and sends them to MB. MB inspects the tokens to determine whether each token is generated from a keyword (which we call *token inspection*).

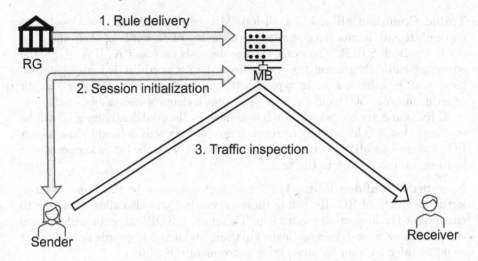

Fig. 1. A Keyword-based DPI System.

Table 1. Notation used in the paper

Symbol	Description	Symbol	Description	Symbol	Description
ℓ	length of a keyword (or a word)	ω	a word (ℓ-byte)	w	a keyword (ℓ-byte)
W	a list of keywords	K	the number of keywords in W	$\eta(\omega)$	a handle of ω
$T(\omega)$	a token computed from ω	k	the secret key of S (or R)	ctr_ω	a counter for ω

Notations. We summarized our notations in Table 1. Here we emphasize two abstractions.

- **Handle**: For each **word** ω, there is a corresponding handle $\eta(\omega)$. Possession of $\eta(\omega)$ enables a party to identify all occurrences of ω in the traffic. During session initialization, MB, with help from S, learns the handle $\eta(w)$ for each **keyword** $w \in W$, where W denotes the list of all keywords determined by RG.
- **Tokens**: For each appearance of ω in the traffic, S computes a token $T(\omega)$, and sends $T(\omega)$ to MB. It is necessary to ensure that different occurrences of the same word result in unlinkable tokens except to a party who knows the handle $\eta(\omega)$. One way is to use per-word counters, and set all such counters to 0 at the beginning of the session, and increment the counter for ω by 1 each time ω appears in the traffic. Then, S computes tokens on both a word and its corresponding counter value not to repeat the same tokens on the same word.

Traffic Confidentiality. If a malicious MB colludes with RG, our goal is to ensure MB only learns the occurrences of the set of K words of their choice in the traffic from S to R. The exact leakage depends on ℓ and K. If $K \geq 2^{8\ell}$, the adversary can fully recover the traffic since the keyword list is long enough to include all possible words. In typical settings, however, $K \ll 2^{8\ell}$ (e.g., in our experiments $K = 3000$ and $\ell = 5$ or 8) so that leakage is reasonably small.

If RG and S are honest while MB is malicious, the confidentiality goal will be to ensure that MB learns only the occurrences of keywords defined by the honest RG. A malicious MB should not be able to tamper with the list of keywords and learn extra information in the traffic.

Keywords Confidentiality. The list of keywords may be the valuable intellectual property of RG. Revealing these keywords could also allow attackers to circumvent the inspection mechanism. Therefore, a KDPI system should ensure that malicious S (or R) do not learn anything about the keywords beyond what could be inferred from the observable outcome of the system.

2.2   BlindBox

Sherry et al. [56] proposed BlindBox, which became a benchmark for KDPI systems.

Using AES for Handles and Tokens. In BlindBox, the handle for each word ω is $\eta(\omega) = \mathsf{AES}_k(\omega)$, where the key k is known to S and R, but not to MB. MB learns the handles for keywords with help from S, but cannot compute the handles for other words. The token for an occurrence of a word ω is the AES encryption using $\eta(\omega)$ as key, and the counter for ω as plaintext. Because of counters, the tokens computed from different occurrences of $\omega' \notin W$ are unlinkable by MB.

Using Table Lookup for Inspection. At the beginning of each session, MB computes $T = \{\mathsf{AES}_{\eta(w)}(0) \mid w \in W\}$ and maintains the tokens generated from keywords in a table. (In [56], it is suggested to implement the table using a balanced binary tree.)

When MB receives a token t, it checks whether $t \in T$. That is, the check takes the form of a table lookup. When $t \in T$, this means that t is computed from a keyword w, MB can identify the keyword, update the corresponding counter, and update T by replacing $\mathsf{AES}_{\eta(w)}(0)$ with $\mathsf{AES}_{\eta(w)}(1)$. This way, MB can maintain counters for $w \in W$ in synchronization with S, so long as it processes all the tokens in order.

Token Computation Overhead. For S to compute a token, it needs to find the counter corresponding to the word, and perform 2 AES operations using two different keys.

Token Transmission Overhead. In order to match keywords that appear in arbitrary positions of the payload, S needs to use a sliding window to extract words to compute tokens. The number of tokens is thus about the same as the length of the payload in bytes. That is, for every byte in the payload, S needs to send a token to MB. If each transmitted token is 16 bytes (i.e., 128 bits), then the extra communication overhead is 16x the payload.

This overhead can be reduced by using truncated tokens. For example, one can only use the first 5-bytes of the AES encryption to make a 5-byte token. This results in reducing the communication overhead from 16x to 5x. See 3.4 for more details.

Using Garbled Circuits to Hide Rules. To ensure that MB does not learn the handles for words not in W, and S does not learn W, BlindBox uses a secure two-party computation protocol. RG generates a signature for each $w \in W$ using its own public key. MB and S run Yao's Garbled Circuit protocol where MB provides w and RG's signature over w, and S provides k.

Here the garbled circuit first verifies that the signature on w is valid, and if so, gives the handle $\eta(w) = \text{AES}_k(w)$ to MB. The usage of garbled circuits introduces significant overhead in terms of both time and bandwidth. This overhead is especially large if signature verification needs to be part of the circuit.

Drawbacks of BlindBox. As we discussed in the previous sections, Blind-Box is less efficient in the token initialization phases due to the high bandwidth requirements for the garbled circuit. The initialization phase requires roughly 4.3GB bandwidth between S and MB which makes the BlindBox hard to be practical. Another drawback for BlindBox is the lacking of keyword verification. The threat model of BlindBox assumes that MB is semi-honest but in practice MB may replace the keywords to other sets of words without being detected. Though the paper suggests using a hash to verify each keyword before initialization, it did not clearly describe the steps.

2.3 Secure Two-Party Computation Protocols

Given a Boolean circuit, cryptographically secure computation protocols allow two mutually-distrustful parties to compute the circuit over their secret inputs. *Garbled Circuit* and *Additive Secret-Sharing based* protocols represent two approaches to cryptographic secure computation. The garbled circuit approach features a small constant round of interaction but requires a large amount of network bandwidth, typically at least 32 bytes per binary AND gate. In contrast, additive secret-sharing based protocols cost a linear number of rounds in the depth of the circuit but little bandwidth, about 2 bits per binary AND gate. We refer the readers to the literature [18,39,64] for the garbled circuit technique, but describe Beaver's protocol [5] as a representative secret-sharing based approach since it is used in our main protocol.

Beaver's Circuit Randomization Protocol. Let C be a binary circuit consisting of XOR and AND gates. Two parties P_1 with input x and P_2 with input y want to compute $C(x, y)$ without leaking extra information about x, y. Beaver's protocol process the circuit in a topological order:

- For every initial input associated with secret bit v owned by P_i: P_i divides v into two uniform random bits v_1, v_2 where $v_1 \oplus v_2 = v$ and distribute the shares such that P_i holds v_i.
- For every binary gate with secret input bits u, v: let the secret shares of u be u_1, u_2 and that of v be v_1, v_2 where P_1 holds u_1, v_1 while P_2 holds u_2, v_2.
  - If it is an XOR gate, to derive the shares of the secret output bit $z = u \oplus v$, P_1 sets $z_1 := u_1 \oplus v_1$ and P_2 sets $z_2 := u_2 \oplus v_2$.
  - If it is an AND gate, to derive the shares of the secret output bit $z = u \cdot v$,
    1. P_1 and P_2 generate a multiplicative triple (see Sect. 2.3 for the triple generation protocol) so that P_1 obtains random bits a_1, b_1, c_1 while P_2 obtains random bits a_2, b_2, c_2 such that

    $$(a_1 \oplus a_2) \cdot (b_1 \oplus b_2) = c_1 \oplus c_2.$$

    2. P_1 and P_2 compute u', v' where $u' = u \oplus a$ and $v' = v \oplus b$, by revealing $u_1 \oplus a_1$, $u_2 \oplus a_2$, $v_1 \oplus b_1$, $v_2 \oplus b_2$.
    3. P_1 sets $z_1 := u' \cdot v' \oplus u' \cdot b_1 \oplus v' \cdot a_1 \oplus c_1$. P_2 sets $z_2 := u' \cdot b_2 \oplus v' \cdot a_2 \oplus c_2$.
- To reveal the secret value v on an output wire of the whole circuit, P_1 and P_2 simply exchange their respective secret shares of v and each party locally xor the shares.

For correctness, it is easy to verify that $z_1 \oplus z_2 = u' \cdot v' \oplus u' \cdot (b_1 \oplus b_2) \oplus v' \cdot (a_1 \oplus a_2) \oplus (c_1 \oplus c_2) = u' \cdot v' \oplus u' \cdot b \oplus v' \cdot a \oplus a \cdot b = (u' \oplus a) \cdot (v' \oplus b) = u \cdot v$. For confidentiality, we note that all exchanged bits are uniform random and independent of each party's secrets.

Generating Multiplicative Triples. Multiplicative triples used above for securely computing the ANDs are typically computed in batches using Random Oblivious Transfers (ROT). ROT is a two-party cryptographic functionality that, once invoked, will generate two uniform random strings x_1, x_2 and one uniform random bit b, then sends (x_1, x_2) to one party while sending (b, x_b) to the other. The seminal work of Ferret [63] provides an efficient implementation of ROT. Using ROT, P_1 and P_2 can securely generate multiplicative triples as follows:

1. P_1 and P_2 invoke $ROT()$ twice (with flipped roles) so that after the first call P_1 obtains (x_0, x_1) and P_2 obtains (b, x_b), whereas after the second call P_1 obtains $(b', x'_{b'})$ and P_2 obtains (x'_0, x'_1).
2. Let H be a random oracle with 1-bit output. P_1 computes and outputs

$$a_1 := H(x_0) \oplus H(x_1); \quad b_1 := b';$$
$$c_1 := a_1 \cdot b_1 \oplus H(x_0) \oplus H(x'_{b'}).$$

P_2 computes and outputs

$$a_2 := H(x'_0) \oplus H(x'_1); \quad b_2 := b;$$
$$c_2 := a_2 \cdot b_2 \oplus H(x'_0) \oplus H(x_b).$$

It is easy to check that for all $b \in \{0, 1\}$, $a_1 \cdot b_2 = H(x_0) \oplus H(x_b)$, and that for all $b' \in \{0, 1\}$, $a_2 \cdot b_1 = H(x'_0) \oplus H(x'_{b'})$. Therefore, we have $(a_1 \oplus a_2) \cdot (b_1 \oplus b_2) = (c_1 \oplus c_2)$. The unpredictability of H's output, together with the security of ROT guarantees that P_1 (resp. P_2) learns nothing about (a_2, b_2, c_2) (resp. (a_1, b_1, c_1)).

3   Proposed Protocols

In this section, we elaborate on new different KDPI schemes, MT-DPI, CE-DPI, and BH-DPI, which have different initialization protocols but share the same AES-based traffic inspection scheme.

Public Input: $\{cert_i\}_{i \in [K]}$ where $cert_i = cert(w_i, r_i) = H(w_i, r_i)$.
MB's Input: The keywords $\{w_i\}_{i \in [K]}$, certificate randomness $\{r_i\}_{i \in [K]}$.
S's Input: Handle generation key k.
Output: MB obtains $\{\eta_i\}_{i \in [K]}$ where $\eta_i = \eta(w_i) = H(k \oplus w_i)$.
Protocol:

1. For every $i \in [K]$,
   (a) Repeat the following s times where s is a statistical security parameter. In the j-th repetition:
       i. MB picks 128-bit uniform string r'_i and securely compute with S the function f

   $$f(\{w, r', r\}; \{k, b\}) = H(\text{mux}(b, k \oplus w, (w, r))) \oplus \text{mux}(b, r', 0)$$

   where MB's secret input is w_i, r'_i, r_i and S's secret inputs are k and b_j.
   (b) For every $b_{i,j} = 1$, S learns $\dot{H}(w_i, r_i)$, which is compared against the $cert_i$ signed by RG (if they are not equal, S aborts immediately, reporting that MB was cheating).
   For every $b_{i,j} = 0$, S learns a value $H(k \oplus w_i) \oplus r'_i$. S verifies that the result is identical across all iterations with $j \in \{j \mid b_{i,j} = 0\}$ (otherwise, S aborts, reporting that MB was cheating).
   (c) S chooses any j such that $b_{i,j} = 0$ and sends the corresponding output $H(k \oplus w_i) \oplus r'_i$ to MB. MB then recovers η_i by XOR-ing the received value with r'_i.

Fig. 2. MT-DPI: Secure generation of handles for certified keywords (with malicious MB and semi-honest S)

3.1   Session Initialization in MT-DPI

Rule Delivery. For each keyword w_i, RG randomly generates a 128-bit r_i, and computes

$$cert_i = cert(w_i, r_i) = H(w_i, r_i).$$

where H is modeled as a random oracle, hence evaluating H leaks no information on how H behaves on other input values. We instantiate H based on AES using the Davies-Meyer construction [61]:

$$H(x) = \text{AES}_{\hat{k}}(x) \oplus x.$$

where $\hat{k}$ is a key picked by RG and known to both S and MB. When AES is modeled as an ideal block cipher, even if $\hat{k}$ is not secret, H is still *collision-resistant* thanks to the security of Davies-Meyer.

RG then sends a signed message $\{(w_i, r_i, cert_i)\}_{i \in [K]}$ to MB and a signed message $\{cert_i\}_{i \in [K]}$ to S, where messages are signed with a standard digital signature scheme. Because H is collision-resistant and S does not know r_i, $cert_i$

does not leak anything about w. In addition, we note that a malicious MB cannot forge a certificate for a word of his/her choice because S knows $H(w, r)$ and H is collision-resistant (MB cannot find a $(w', r') \neq (w, r)$ such that $H(w', r') = H(w, r)$).

Handle Generation. We define a handle of a keyword w as

$$\eta_w = H(k \oplus w)$$

where H is the same random oracle as described above and the key k is S's secret and w is MB's secret. MB and S will launch a secure two-party computation protocol to allow MB to obliviously learn the handle. However, without additional treatment, a malicious MB can obtain handles for any word $\omega \neq w$ of his/her choice and monitor the occurrence of ω in S's traffic. Next, we show how we prevent this attack using a cut-and-choose mechanism. Our full protocol is shown in Fig. 2.

To obtain the handle of a keyword w, MB holding w, r', r and S holding k, b would jointly compute:

$$f(\{w, r', r\}; \{k, b\}) = H(\mathsf{mux}(b, k \oplus w, (w, r)) \oplus \mathsf{mux}(b, r', 0)$$

where $\mathsf{mux}(b, x, y)$ denotes evaluating a multiplexer on an input bit b and two same-length inputs x, y, which returns x if $b = 0$ and y if $b = 1$. That is,

$$f(\{w, r', r\}; \{k, b\}) = \begin{cases} H(k \oplus w) \oplus r' & \text{if } b = 0. \\ H(w, r) & \text{if } b = 1. \end{cases}$$

Since b is S's input, S controls whether the result will be a (masked) handle (by setting $b = 0$) or the certificate (by setting $b = 1$). For each w, the circuit will be evaluated s times, each with a freshly sampled b. S can then verify that for all $b = 1$, the outputs are all equal to $cert(w, r)$; and for all $b = 0$, the results all equal to an identical value $H(k \oplus w) \oplus r'$ where r' is the mask picked by MB. (Without the mask r', S will learn $H(k \oplus w)$ thus can launch selective probes to learn w.) Note that MB does not know b. So if MB used some $\omega \neq w$ in any of the s iterations, it will either fail to produce the correct certificate or output some inconsistent masked handles.

The cut-and-choose procedure above will be repeated s times. This statistical security parameter s directly impacts both overhead and security. The protocol cost is linear in s, and a malicious MB who tries to learn the token for a word different from a certified keyword will be caught with probability $1 - 2^{-s}$. It is standard to set $s = 40$, but in some settings it could be justified to use a smaller s. When MB cheats without being detected, it only gains the ability to scan for the presence of one word not in the keyword list. On the other hand, when MB is detected, the sender S learns that MB is trying to cheat, and can take action accordingly, such as not cooperating in traffic inspection, informing other parties, etc.

Security. The handle generation protocol given in Fig. 2 is essentially a secure two-party computation protocol. Its security can be established follow-

---

Public Input: Commitment of each bit of the keyword $\{c_j\}_{j \in [\ell]}$ where $c_j = g^{b_j} h^{y_j}$. Group elements g, h for computing the commitments.

MB's Input: The bit of keywords $\{b_j\}_{j \in [\ell]}$, commitment randomness $\{y_j\}_{j \in [\ell]}$,

S's Input: GC input labels $\{(X_j^0, X_j^1)\}_{j \in \ell}$ each corresponding to an input wire in the circuit

Output: MB obtains X_j^b, which can be used to evaluate the circuit

Protocol:

For every $j \in [\ell]$,

1. S chooses a random value r_j, and computes $e_j := h^{r_j}$, $\sigma_j^0 := H(c_j^{r_j})$, and $\sigma_j^1 := H(c_j^{r_j} \cdot g^{-r_j})$.
2. S computes two envelopes: $E_j^0 = \mathsf{AES}_{\sigma_j^0}(X_j^0)$, and $E_j^1 = \mathsf{AES}_{\sigma_j^1}(X_j^1)$.
3. S sends E_j^0, E_j^1, e_j to MB.
4. MB computes $\sigma_j^b = H(e_j^{y_j})$. MB can decrypt $X_j^b = \mathsf{AES}_{\sigma_b}^{-1}(E_j^b)$.

Fig. 3. CE-DPI: Keyword verification methods for one keyword (with malicious MB and semi-honest S)

ing the real-world/ideal-world paradigm. Consider a malicious MB and semi-honest S that interact in an ideal-world execution where a trusted third-party $\mathcal{F}_{\text{handle-gen}}$ exists:

1. $\mathcal{F}_{\text{handle-gen}}$ accepts a key k from S, and accepts (w_i, r_i) for all $i \in [K]$ from MB.
2. $\mathcal{F}_{\text{handle-gen}}$, with cert_i from RG, checks if $H(w_i, r_i) = \text{cert}_i$ for all $i \in [K]$. If the check passes, $\mathcal{F}_{\text{handle-gen}}$ sends $H(k \oplus w_i)$ to MB, and sends $\perp$ to S; otherwise, $\mathcal{F}_{\text{handle-gen}}$ sends "MB Cheats" to both MB and S.
3. If MB is honest, it outputs what was received from $\mathcal{F}_{\text{handle-gen}}$; otherwise, it can output anything. S always outputs what was received from $\mathcal{F}_{\text{handle-gen}}$.

A real-world protocol Π, where MB and S are the two interacting parties, is defined to be secure if for all $\text{cert}_i, (w_i, r_i), k$, the joint distribution of the outputs of MB and S is indistinguishable from that of the ideal-world execution.

If MB is honest while the sender S is compromised (but still semi-honest), we note that S cannot gain more information than every single run of the s repetitions of step (1a) because all s must be over exactly the same inputs (since S cannot deviate from the protocol to use different inputs across different runs of the circuit randomization sub-protocol). In this case, the whole protocol of Fig. 2 simply reduces to a single run of Beaver's circuit randomization protocol and the security of our protocol can be derived directly from Beaver's protocol. Hence we have:

Theorem 1. *The handle generation protocol described in Fig. 2 is a two-party computation protocol secure against a semi-honest S.*

If S is honest while MB is fully compromised, it is easy to see that the protocol is secure if MB does not deviate from the protocol. In case MB deviates from our protocol, its cheating behavior will be caught by step (1b) except for 2^{-s} probability, thus S outputting MB Cheats like in the ideal world.

Theorem 2. *The handle generation protocol described in Fig. 2 is a two-party computation protocol secure against a malicious MB.*

Proof. For a malicious MB and honest S, we can construct a simulator $\mathcal{S}$ that is connected to the ideal-world $\mathcal{F}_{\text{handle-gen}}$ and interacts with MB as follows:

1. $\mathcal{S}$ runs the Fig. 2 protocol as S to interact with MB.
2. If $\mathcal{S}$ aborts in step (1b), it generates random values and sends them to $\mathcal{F}_{\text{handle-gen}}$ as (w_i, r_i) (so these values cannot pass $\mathcal{F}_{\text{handle-gen}}$'s check of $H(w, r_i) = \text{cert}_i$).

   If $\mathcal{S}$ does not abort in step (1b), it extracts MB's effective input (w_i, r_i) through Beaver's circuit randomization protocol (note that Beaver's protocol offers input ex-tractability from an adversary) and sends them to $\mathcal{F}_{\text{handle-gen}}$.
3. $\mathcal{S}$ outputs whatever MB outputs.

A real-world execution (consisting of MB and S) will produce an indistinguishable output distribution from that of an ideal-world execution (consisting of the simulator $\mathcal{S}$ defined above, the sender S, and $\mathcal{F}_{\text{handle-gen}}$), because a deviating MB only gets to flip the values of any wires (including the input wires) in the Beaver's protocol to compute the handle, which will only result in one of the following consequences:

1. The value of $f(\{w, r', r\}; \{k, b\})$ is unaffected. In this case, MB's cheating behavior has no effect on the output distribution.
2. The value of $f(\{w, r', r\}; \{k, b\})$ is changed. In this case, however, for MB to successfully evade S's checks in step (1b), the results must be consistently changed for all $\{b_{i,j}\}_{j \in [s]}$, which happens only if MB guessed all s bits of b_j correctly, that is, with probability 2^{-s}.

Overall, the difference between the two output distributions are 2^{-s} at most.

Security Against Malicious S. It is easy to make our protocol also secure against a malicious sender by simply adding the following (rather symmetric) check in step (1b):

> For every $b_j = 1$, S sends all of $H(k \oplus w_i) \oplus r'_i$ back to MB, so that MB can verify that all these values are identical (otherwise, MB aborts and reports that S was cheating) before recovering $H(k \oplus w_i)$.

The security proof is also based on cut-and-choose, similar to what has been shown earlier against malicious MB. We did not include this treatment in our main protocol because in the context of KDPI, even if the handle generation protocol can handle malicious S, because a deviating S can easily sabotage other parts of the DPI system (such as the token computation step during the traffic inspection phase).

3.2 CE-DPI

CE-DPI (Commitment Envelope-DPI) combines garbled circuit protocol with Oblivious Commitment-Based Envelope (OCBE) [37] to ensure keyword integrity. Recall that in the DPI initialization phase, S constructed the garbled circuit and sends to MB. In the circuit, each bit of a keyword corresponds to an input wire of the circuit and has two associated secret values (one for 0 and one for 1). The protocol enables MB to learn the wire value corresponding to correct keyword bit, without S learning anything about the keyword.

In CE-DPI, RG stores cryptographic commitments for each bit of a keyword in a digitally signed certificate. For each keyword bit, S constructs two envelopes (encrypted messages) so that one can be decrypted when the committed value is 0, and the other when the committed value is 1.

More specifically CE-DPI uses the Pedersen commitment scheme [51]. To commit to a secret bit b, the committer generates a random value r, and publishes a commitment $c_i = g^b h^r$, where g, h are two generators of a group in which discrete logarithm is hard. The verifier receiving c_i cannot learn the secret b without knowing the random value r.

CE-DPI uses an OCBE where the opening condition is that the committed bit equals to a pre-determined bit value. See [37] on how such an OCBE protocol works.

In CE-DPI, for each keyword w, RG computes a commitment for every bit of w:

1. RG computes $\{c_j\} = \{g^{b_j} h^{y_j}\}$ for all $j \in [\ell]$, where b_j is the j-th bit of w, and y_j is a fresh random value.
2. RG reveals $\{y_j\}_{j \in [\ell]}$ to MB and published a digitally signed $\{c_j\}_{j \in [\ell]}$.

S will verify the signed $\{c_j\}_{j \in [\ell]}$, and then construct two envelopes to deliver wire labels representing those bits to MB (Fig. 3).

Since S sees only the commitments of the keywords, and the Petersen commitment scheme used in CE-DPI is information-theoretically hiding, S learns nothing about the keywords. It has been proven in [37] that ability to open the envelope not corresponding to the committed bit value implies the ability to compute the discrete log of $\log_g h$. Thus MB can obtain only the wire values corresponding to the keywords. Finally, note that S receives nothing from MB, it is easy to prove CE-DPI is secure against malicious MB and semi-honest S in the OT-hybrid model.

Public Parameter: sliding window size ℓ. H modeled as a random oracle.
MB's Input: The list of keywords $\{w_i\}_{i \in [K]}$ and their handles $\{\eta_i\}_{i \in [K]}$.
S's Input: Handle generation key k and a stream of packets.
Output: MB learns every occurrence of w_i in the packet stream for all $i \in [K]$.
Protocol:

1. Initialize Counters and MB's token set:
   - S initializes a map M_S from ℓ-byte words to their counters (initialized to 0).
   - MB initializes a map M_{MB} from his list of keywords to their counters (initialized to 0).
   - MB computes the token set $TS := \{T_i\}_{i \in [K]}$ where $T_i = H(\eta_i \oplus M_{MB}[w_i])$.
2. For $j \in [N - \ell + 1]$, S moves its fixed-size sliding window to start at the j-th byte. Then,
   (a) Compute Tokens:
       - S computes $\eta := H(k \oplus \omega)$, $\mathsf{ctr}_\omega := M_S[\omega]$, $T := H(\eta \oplus \mathsf{ctr}_\omega)$ where ω is a word in current sliding window.
   (b) Match Tokens:
       - S sends T to MB.
       - If $T \in TS$ with $T = T_{i^*}$, MB learns w_{i^*} occurred at the jth byte in the packet stream; otherwise, MB learns no keywords appeared at this location of the packet stream.
   (c) Update Counters and MB's token set:
       - S sets $M_S[\omega] := M_S[\omega] + 1$.
       - If it was a match of keyword w_{i^*}, MB sets $M_{MB}[w_{i^*}] := M_{MB}[w_{i^*}] + 1$ and $T_{i^*} := H(\eta_{i^*} \oplus M_{MB}[w_{i^*}])$; otherwise, MB do nothing.

Fig. 4. The traffic inspection protocol for MT-DPI, CE-DPI and BH-DPI

3.3 BH-DPI

For keyword integrity, BlindBox initially suggested RG to digitally sign each keyword, then use garbled circuits (or other 2PC protocols) to verify the signature without revealing the keywords. However, for any public-key signature scheme, implementing its verification function in garbled circuits is challenging and very expensive. At the time of writing this paper, we are not aware of any open-source code for garbled circuits support public-key signature verification.

Alternatively, one can use a cryptographic $\underline{B}$atched $\underline{H}$ash BH-DPI: (1) RG samples a secret random nonce, computes $h = H(w\|\mathsf{nonce})$, signs h using a signature scheme, and sends nonce, h and the signature to MB. (2) MB sends S the value h with RG's signature. Later, S can verify h is indeed signed by RG, and use a garbled circuit to ensure that $h = H(w_1\|w_2\|...\|w_n\|\mathsf{nonce})$ (where H is modeled a random oracle and MB provides w_i and nonce) while the same w_i's are used for handle generation.

Table 2. Initialization costs in various network settings.

	Time cost (s)											B/W (MB)
	50 Mbps	100 Mbps	200 Mbps	300 Mbps	400 Mbps	500 Mbps	600 Mbps	700 Mbps	800 Mbps	900 Mbps	1 Gbps	
MT-DPI	135.6	109.2	95.2	91.2	90.4	89.2	67.2	66	65.2	64.3	64.3	425
BH-DPI	210.7	174.4	132.4	110.0	94.7	92.5	89.4	85.1	82.5	81.9	81.6	769
CE-DPI	181.1	122.5	112.4	100.8	96.7	93.6	91.5	89	88.2	87.8	87.6	530
BlindBox	817.9	455.6	273.4	212.0	180.4	163.7	151.7	142.3	137.0	132.2	132	4300

RTT for all network settings: 20ms. All timings include keyword verification. Bandwidth unit is MB.

3.4 Traffic Inspection

The traffic inspection protocol for both MT-DPI and CE-DPI is described in Fig. 4, enhancing BlindBox's in several respects.

More Effective Use of AES-NI. In BlindBox, the tokens for ω are computed as $T(\omega) = \text{AES}_{\eta(\omega)}(\text{ctr}_\omega)$. The security property this achieves is that any adversary who knows multiple tuples in the form $(\omega, \text{ctr}_\omega, T(\omega))$ but does not know η_ω cannot monitor ω in the traffic. However, Their design fails to fully take full advantage of AES-NI [27] capabilities, since the tokens for different words are computed using AES with different keys. This means a key needs to be freshly scheduled per token, to introduce data-dependent stalls in the pipeline of AES-NI instructions.

To avoid such data-dependent stalls when running AES-NI instructions, we observe that the same security property desired for tokens can also be achieved by defining
$$T(\omega) = H(\eta(\omega) \oplus \text{ctr}_\omega)$$
where H is also modeled as a random oracle, defined the same as that used in MT-DPI's session initialization (Sect. 3.1), except that a different public fixed-key would be used to instantiate this random oracle.

Refreshing the Counters. S will have to maintain a table of words that it has encountered so far and associate a counter with each word. The size of S's table is linear in the number of unique length-ℓ words in the traffic. As our experiments in Sect. 4 show, this table grows quickly. For example, over a 700 MB traffic stream, we observed 7 million unique ℓ-byte words. It would be infeasible for S to efficiently maintain this large table of counters. Hence, S will periodically reset its counter table after inspecting a fixed amount (e.g., 100 KB–1 MB) of traffic. Note that MB also needs to maintain a list of counters, one for each keyword. Thus, when S resets its table of counters, MB will do the same to stay synchronized on the keyword handles.

Comparing Tokens. Using 16-byte tokens can be a waste of bandwidth. Instead, S could just send the first t bytes of the tokens to MB for comparison. The benefit is substantial bandwidth savings, which can be more than 50% if $t \leq 8$. The downside is that it will require an extra communication round between S and MB to avoid matching packets that contain the substring but not the actual keyword. It may also come with a potential information leakage of the keyword that MB learns extra information in the form of each occurrence of portions of the keywords. Hence, it is a trade-off between performance and efficiency.

4 Evaluation

In this section, we present a comparative evaluation of BH-DPI, CE-DPI, MT-DPI with existing protocols. We released our source-code at https://github.com/mt-dpi.

Table 3. Initialization cost in various RTT setting

	RTT = 1 ms	RTT = 10 ms	RTT = 20 ms	RTT = 200 ms
MT-DPI	60.2	61.2	62.4	164
BH-DPI	13.8	48.2	81.6	665.5
CE-DPI	24.3	43.2	87.5	634.7
BlindBox	61.4	132	197.8	1341.7

The unit of time used to report the numbers is a second (s). The network speed is set to 1 Gbps.

4.1 Experiment Setup

Testbed. Our testbed consists of two machines (each has 8-core i7-3770 and 16 GB memory) connected by a router, which supports 1 Gbps Ethernet. We run S and MB on the two machines. The round-trip time (RTT) between the machines is selected from 1 ms, 10 ms, 20 ms, and 200 ms. Those RTTs simulate local network, enhanced regional network [58], regional network with CDN [58] and different continents connections [35]. As MB usually processes multiple connections, we experiment on several bandwidth capacities, ranging from 50 Mbps to 1 Gbps. We use Throttle [26] to configure both bandwidth capacities and RTTs.

Parameters. We assume that all the words and keywords are represented by 8-byte sequences, and set the length of a truncated token to 5 bytes.

In the traffic inspection phase, the counters (of tokens) are refreshed every 1M tokens. For instance, after i million tokens are sent from S to MB, S and MB set all of their word/keyword counters to i million.

We instantiate AES with AES-128 and implement it with OpenSSL-1.1.11 that supports AES-NI for fast token computation. We set $s = 40$ for 40-bit statistical security to run experiments for MT-DPI.

4.2 Initialization Phase

MT-DPI. The cost of MT-DPI is mainly due to multiplicative triple generation and circuit evaluation. Since there is no data dependency across different invocations of AES circuits, the entire circuits of $K \cdot s$ AES instances can be finished in 40 rounds (where K is the total number of keywords).

Thanks to the efficiency of Ferret OT [63] (about 0.5 bits and 4 μs per random OT), the majority of the triple generation cost is due to constructing multiplicative triples from random OTs. The time cost of triple generation does not vary much across different network settings. However, the cost of triple generation exhibits a linear growth in terms of the statistical security parameter s, which determines the number of AES circuits to be securely evaluated.

Compared with CE-DPI and BH-DPI (see Table 2 and Table 3), MT-DPI uses less bandwidth, and we believe it is more suitable for network environments where real-world middle-boxes are deployed (RTT $\geq$ 20 ms). Only when the network condition is ideal (very high bandwidth with at the same time very low round-trip latency), CE-DPI and BH-DPI could have some performance advantages.

BH-DPI and CE-DPI. We measure the initialization cost of BH-DPI and CE-DPI. These include (1) secure handle generation for the keywords, and (2) verification of the keywords. The time and bandwidth costs of representative DPI variants are given in Table 2.

Table 2 shows that CE-DPI costs about 31.1% less bandwidth comparing to BH-DPI. Because of SHA3-256, 38,400 garbled AND gates must be computed per 15 keywords (960 bits); hence, 81.9K bytes of traffic is required per keyword. On the other hand, in CE-DPI, each keyword requires computing 1 group exponentiation and 2 additions, and sending one group element and two 16-byte envelopes. Thus, roughly 4.2 KB bandwidth is used.

We also note that CE-DPI spends much time computing the envelopes whereas BH-DPI requires much time to transmit the garbled circuit. We find that as the connection speed increases, BH-DPI outperforms CE-DPI for connections over 350 Mbps (see Table 3).

Comparison with Existing Protocols. Compared with BlindBox, we find that the three new protocols are always better. That is because (1) BlindBox requires each word to be verified by one hash, while the verification parts are optimized in the new protocols; (2) the new protocols allow better utilization of AES-NI instructions.

Compared with other ECC-based protocols, AES-based protocols do not have much benefits. However, the heavy cost in traffic inspection makes ECC-based protocols much less attractive and almost unpractical. More details are in Table 4.

4.3 Traffic Inspection Phase

Comparison with BlindBox. We experimentally studied the benefit of AES-NI (used by MT-DPI, BH-DPI, and CE-DPI) for traffic inspection. Since MT-DPI, BH-DPI, and CE-DPI run identical traffic inspection algorithm, we use MT-DPI as a representative. The per-token costs (averaged over 1M tokens) are 67.78 ns for MT-DPI and 241.04 ns for BlindBox. That is, MT-DPI's traffic inspection runs 3.6x faster than BlindBox. BlindBox does not fully benefit from AES-NI because it uses a handle as an AES key, which not only requires running the more expensive key schedule frequently but also introduces data dependency that prevents the AES-NI instructions from leveraging a fully pipelined execution.

Table 4. Cost of computing one million tokens.

	MT-DPI	BlindBox	PrivDPI	P2DPI	PEDPI
Time (s)	0.07	0.24	57.9	15.2	720
Methods	AES-based		ECC-based		

Comparison with PrivDPI, P2DPI and PE-DPI. We compare the AES-based protocols (MT-DPI, BlindBox) with ECC-based protocols (PrivDPI,

P2DPI and PE-DPI) in Table 4. For each token, ECC-based protocols require S to compute at least one group multiplication, which is far more expensive than AES operation. Therefore, the cost for ECC-based protocols is at least 100x more expensive for traffic inspection phase than AES-based ones. This makes the ECC-based protocols impractical even if they allow leaner initialization.

4.4   Integration with TLS

Table 5. Performance Evaluation of MT-DPI Integrated with TLS.

	RTT (S– MB, <1 ms)			RTT (S– MB, 20 ms)			RTT (S– MB, 200 ms)		
	SplitTLS	BlindBox	MT-DPI	SplitTLS	BlindBox	MT-DPI	SplitTLS	BlindBox	MT-DPI
Elapsed Time to Retrieve Data (in ms)									
One Packet (1K)	0.68	3.35	2.87	40.88	42.77	42.42	400.79	403.28	402.72
One TLS Record (16K)	0.78	12.64	4.24	41.18	51.53	44.02	401.07	412.37	404.11
CPU Processing Overhead of S (in ms)									
One Packet (1K)	0.02	1.16	0.51	0.10	1.46	0.84	0.08	1.60	0.87
One TLS Record (16K)	0.10	9.11	1.97	0.13	9.46	2.14	0.10	9.31	2.22

Since TLS is the most widely deployed end-to-end protocol and is used with many application protocols such as HTTP, we integrate MT-DPI into the TLS protocol by leveraging the TLS extension mechanism [16]. Our main focus in designing the TLS extension is to make MT-DPI run within the TLS protocol so that it can be *easily and immediately deployed* without requiring any changes to the applications.

We extended the TLS handshake protocol so that for S and R: (1) each has a copy of the key used to generate tokens, and (2) each establishes a separate TLS session with MB after authenticating the agreed MB between S and R. In addition, we instrument the TLS record protocol with the MT-DPI traffic inspection phase. Our implementation is based on OpenSSL-1.1.1l. We have verified, by running our TLS extension with curl [13] and two open-source web servers (Nginx [46] and Apache [13]), that no modifications are needed to these applications.

We evaluate the overhead incurred due to the integration of the TLS protocol with MT-DPI during the traffic inspection phase. We build our testbed on the Ubuntu 20.04 machine with i7 CPU @ 3.60 GHz and 16 GB memory. The machine runs two virtual machines each of which has one i7 core and 1 GB memory. One is used as S and the other is used as R. MB runs over the host machine so that MB can capture all the packets from or to the virtual machines. We use the Linux tc command to set the RTT between S and MB, and between R and MB. For the former RTT, we set it to 20 ms and 200 ms, and we set the latter RTT to less than 1 ms. We measure the elapsed time from when R sends an HTTP request message to S to when R receives the data after the token inspection by MB. Also, we measure the CPU overhead of S as the overhead should be marginal to support multiple simultaneous connections [44].

We compare MT-DPI with SplitTLS [28] and BlindBox [56]. We choose Split-TLS in our comparison because it is widely deployed in practice. We want to see if the overhead of MT-DPI is marginal compared to SplitTLS; otherwise, MT-DPI would not be deployable. In SplitTLS, two different TLS sessions are separately established between S and MB, and between MB and R. S encrypts the data with the established session key between S and MB and sends the encrypted data to MB. Then, MB decrypts the data, performs its functionality (e.g., intrusion detection, compression, or others), and encrypts the data with the key between MB and R. Finally, R receives the data. In our experiment, we do not define any functionality of MB. MB simply forwards the packets that it receives. Therefore, the experimental results of this MB show the lower bound of the overhead that it can incur related to the protocols. For the size of the data that S sends, we select 1.5K and 16K as the former is one packet size (i.e., the maximum transmission unit) of the Internet and the latter is the maximum length of the TLS message called the TLS record. The experiment results are shown in Table 5.

Elapsed Time to Retrieve Data. To confirm our token computation and inspection approach does not inflate data exchange within the TLS protocol, we measure the elapsed time from the time when R requests a content from S to the time when R finally receives the content after the inspection by MB. The experimental results show that MT-DPI is faster than BlindBox in all the scenarios. With MT-DPI, the best scenario is that R receives a data from S for one TLS record in the 20ms RTT case. MT-DPI is 14.57% faster than BlindBox.

Interestingly, MT-DPI does not inflate the elapsed time for data retrieval compared with SplitTLS. It incurs only 3.77% of overhead for one packet and 6.90% for one TLS record that R receives from S with 20ms RTT. Note that in our experiment, MB in SplitTLS does not perform any functionality and the MB can see the plaintexts.

CPU Processing Overhead. Since MT-DPI requires S to compute lots of tokens, it may incur high CPU processing overhead. To quantify the overhead, we evaluate CPU processing time while S gets a request message and sends a response message with the corresponding tokens. Our numerical results show that though MT-DPI requires relatively high processing overhead compared with SplitTLS, it reduces the overhead of BlindBox. The main reason is that our approach fully benefits from AES-NI, which makes the AES operation instantly completed. Finally, the processing time decreased.

5   Related Work

In this section, we analyze three more existing KDPI approaches that uses different strategies and identify their security and performance weaknesses. More specifically, we describe PE-DPI [36], PrivDPI [48], and P2DPI [30]. PE-DPI uses elliptic curve public key encryption; and PrivDPI and P2DPI combine elliptic curves with AES. We illustrate the tradeoffs among these approaches, with an emphasis on their security vulnerabilities and performance weaknesses.

Table 6. Existing KDPI approaches

	BlindBox	PE-DPI	PrivDPI	P2DPI
Handle:	$\eta(\omega) = \text{AES}_k(\omega)$	$\eta(\omega) = g^{n-\omega}h^{s_1}$	$\eta(\omega) = g^{\alpha k\omega}g^{k^2}$	$\eta(w) = g^{H_1(w)k}$
Token:	$T(\omega) = \text{AES}_{\eta(\omega)}(\text{ctr}_\omega)$	$T(\omega) = g^\omega h^{s_2}$	$T(\omega) = \text{H}(\text{ctr}_\omega \| \eta(\omega))$	$T(\omega) = \text{H}_2(\text{ctr}_\omega \| \eta(\omega))$
Inspection:	whether $T(\omega) \in$ $\{T(w) \mid w \in W\}$	Whether $\exists w \in$ W s.t. $(\eta(w) \cdot T(\omega))^p = 1$	whether $T(\omega) \in \{T(w) \mid w \in W\}$	whether $\exists w \in W$ s.t. $T(\omega) = \text{H}_2(\text{ctr}_\omega \| \eta(\omega))$
where		g, u are generators of a cyclic group of order $n = pq$; $n, g, u, h = u^q$ are public; p and q are secret of RG; s_1 and s_2 are secret values sampled per word by MB and S, resp.	α is a secret of RG, H is a cryptographic hash.	H_1 and H_2 are secure hash functions

Different protocols use different methods for computing handles, computing tokens, and performing traffic inspection, which we summarize in Table 6.

Later, we discuss some other related works.

5.1 PE-DPI

Motivated by the apparent high overhead of BlindBox's session initialization step, Li et al. [36] proposed PE-DPI, which uses asymmetric cryptography to compute both handles and tokens. At the high level, one can view each token computed from a word ω as a randomized encryption of ω, and the handle for ω is the key to enable decryption.

Token Computation Overhead. To compute the token $T(\omega) = g^\omega h^{s_2}$, S needs to perform two exponentiations and one multiplication in Boneh-Goh-Nissim cryptosystem (BGN) [7]. This overhead is significantly higher than that of BlindBox.

Token Transmission Overhead. In PE-DPI, each token is an element in the group. Since the inspection step requires computation using the token as input, S has to transmit the full token, and cannot use truncation to reduce this overhead. The size of the token depends on the size for elements in the group. While the detail of the group is not provided in [36], the group size needs to be large. The group needs to be of order $n = pq$, where p, q are primes and the factorization of n needs to be secret. This means that the size of the group should be at least 2048 bits (i.e., 256 bytes). Thus PE-DPI has very high token transmission overhead.

Token Inspection Overhead. PE-DPI assumes that the functionality of MB is split into two non-colluding parties, with MB_1 knowing the handles and receiving the tokens and MB_2 knowing p. One can roughly view MB_2 as an online presence of the RG, since it knows p and q, which were chosen by RG.

For each token τ, MB_1 computes $\Sigma_\tau = \{\tau \cdot \delta \mid \delta \in \Delta\}$, where Δ is the set of all keyword handles, and sends Σ_τ to MB_2. MB_2 computes $\Sigma_\tau^p = \{\sigma^p \mid \sigma \in \Sigma_\tau\}$, and checks whether $1 \in \Sigma_\tau^p$. This is expensive since the inspection for one token requires K exponentiations.

Rather than lookup protocols (such as BlindBox and MT-DPI), PE-DPI requires MB to conduct computation on the tokens received from S for inspection. S cannot use truncated tokens to save the bandwidth, and has to send the full tokens.

Vulnerability to Frequency Analysis. A token for a word ω takes the form $g^{\omega}h^{s_2}$, where s_2 is a random number, and h^{s_2} hides ω. This ensures that MB_1 cannot tell whether two tokens are generated from the same word. However, because $h^p = u^{pq} = u^n = 1$, the randomized hiding effect of h^{s_2} is completely gone after being raised to the p-th power. Thus, MB_2, after receiving $\Sigma(\tau)$, can raise all elements in it to the p-th power, and store the results. When the same word appears again, after raising all elements in $\Sigma(\tau)$ to the p-th power, the set will be exactly the same as that from the previous occurrence of the same word. MB_2 can thus conduct frequency analysis on the traffic. To the best of our knowledge, this vulnerability has not been documented in the literature, and the author has confirmed it in our email communication.

5.2 PrivDPI

Ning et al. [48] proposed PrivDPI, which uses Elliptic Curve Cryptography (ECC) for computing the handles to avoid garbled circuits. To maintain low inspection overhead, it uses cryptographic hash functions to compute tokens from handles.

Token Computation Overhead. For S to compute the token of a word ω, it needs to first compute the handle $\eta(\omega) = g^{\alpha k \omega}g^{k^2}$, and then it needs to compute the hash. Even with precomputation for $g^{\alpha k}$ and g^{k^2}, this requires one exponentiation and one multiplication for each token.

Token Transmission Overhead. In PrivDPI, each token is a hash of an ECC point on the curve. However, since inspection is by lookup, one can use truncated tokens to reduce the token transmission overhead to around 5x, similar to PrivDPI.

Vulnerability in Traffic Confidentiality. As also pointed out in [47], PrivDPI has a critical vulnerability that totally compromises traffic confidentiality. In the handle $\eta(w) = g^{\alpha k w}g^{k^2}$, the term g^{k^2} is intended to help hide the term $g^{\alpha k w}$, from which one can compute $g^{\alpha k \omega}$ for any word ω by raising $g^{\alpha k w}$ to the power of $\frac{\omega}{w}$. Unfortunately, this design fails because knowing two handles $\eta(w_1)$ and $\eta(w_2)$ for $w_1, w_2 \in W$, one can cancel out the g^{k^2} term: simply dividing $\eta(w_1)$ by $\eta(w_2)$ then solving for $g^{\alpha k}$ from w_2, w_1 and $\eta(w_1)/\eta(w_2)$. With $g^{\alpha k}$, MB can easily obtain $g^{k^2} = \eta(w_1)/g^{\alpha k w_1}$, and further obtain the handle for any keyword of its choice.

This means that MB can scan for arbitrary words in the traffic, violating traffic confidentiality.

5.3   P2DPI

Kim et al. [30] considered a slightly different adversary model in which they assume that the RG may be able to eavesdrop on the communication between S and MB, and proposed P2DPI to counter this threat. We first observe that this threat can be countered by using standard secure communication techniques (such as TLS) between S and MB, instead of a new KDPI protocol. Furthermore, like PrivDPI P2DPI has a serious vulnerability in traffic confidentiality.

Discussion in Traffic Confidentiality. Given the handle for one keyword w_1, $\eta(w_1) = g^{\mathsf{H}_1(w_1)k}$, MB can compute the handle for arbitrary word w_2 as follows:

$$\eta(w_2) = \eta(w_1)^{\mathsf{H}_1(w_2)/\mathsf{H}_1(w_1)}$$

This means that MB can use the handle for arbitrary words to match a received token.

After informing the authors of [30], we learned that the authors have already updated the scheme in a preprint [31]. In the new version of P2DPI, each handle has the form $\eta(w) = g^{H_1(w)k}h^k$. The added term h^k aims to make $g^{H_1(w)k}$ more difficult to extract, similar to the usage of g^{k^2} in PrivDPI.

5.4   Other Related Work

Several TLS extensions, including mcTLS [45], maTLS [34], and others [38, 41,49], have been proposed for enabling middleboxes to perform DPI within TLS sessions. With these protocols, endpoints can authenticate middleboxes and grant them permission to read (or write) all (or part) of the packets. Such access control relies on encryption keys (or MAC keys) established between endpoints and the middleboxes. Middleboxes are then able to read all the plaintext that can be decrypted with the keys. Unlike these TLS extensions, our scheme does not allow middleboxes to learn the plaintext.

Systems such as mbTLS [44], SGXBox [25], and others [24,52], relied on trusted hardware like Intel SGX [1]. The basic idea is to let either one of the endpoints perform remote attestation to verify the middleboxes' integrity and sends cryptographic keys to the enclave (a protected execution context). The middlebox decrypts the ciphertext and performs DPI within the enclave. In comparison, our scheme does not require special trusted hardware.

The work of Pine [47] identified the traffic leakage of PrivDPI to MB and tried to fix it by introducing an extra party called Gateway (GW) as well as requiring RG to participate in every session initialization. In their protocol, knowledge about keywords is secret-shared among S, MB, and GW. However, if any two parties collude, the keywords will still be leaked. In practice, finding extra non-colluding protocol participants can be cumbersome, and requiring RG to establish every session can easily raise scalability concerns.

Embark [33] supports keyword match and prefix match. Embark does not include RGs. A gateway generates a set of rules and encrypts (AES) them with a secret key k_{GS} known by the gateway and S, and sends the encrypted rules to the MB (service provider). The missing of the trusted RG may lead to cheating of gateway without being detected.

EV-DPI [53] splits a traditional MB into two parties: TFS (token filtering server) and RFS (rule matching server), and assumes that they cannot exchange information. That is not practical in practice since they have motivation to do so and their collusion cannot be detected by any other entities.

SEPM [8] uses cyclic group exponent computation for encryption and test. The time cost of such operations is hundreds times more than AES, which makes the protocol inefficient during the inspection phase.

Lai et al. [32] proposes a solution assuming the GW (it is very close to the sender in our paper) to be a trustworthy party, and the sender encrypts the rules. There is motivation that GW to cheat during the rule generation step by replacing the real rules to random patterns, and such actions cannot be detected by any entities.

The more recent work ZKMB by Grubbs et al. [23] combines zero knowledge and TLS to provide inspection. Their basic protocol does not hide rules against the sender, which is not acceptable in our threat model. They discussed enhancement on leveraging asymmetric cryptography over cyclic groups to keep the rules private. However, those group operations can be orders of magnitude slower than AES-NI instructions that our protocols use.

There are other related approaches, such as Yuan et al. [65], BlindIDS [10], EndBox [21], SEST [15], PEDPI [36], P2DPI [30], SplitBox [4], SPABox [19] and some machine learning approaches [2,3,6,62] that try to analyze the encrypted contents to find some features. However, they either have a weaker threat assumption, e.g., MB cannot be actively malicious, or have efficiency shortcomings, e.g., using curves to generate tokens or using a public key to verify handles.

6   Conclusion

We studied efficient privacy-preserving keyword deep packet inspection protocols for network middleboxes. Through a close-up analysis of BlindBox [56], we proposed three new protocols MT-DPI, CE-DPI and BH-DPI that reduce the overhead and address vulnerabilities of lacking keyword verification. We implement and evaluate these protocols and compare them with BlindBox. Our experiment results show that they can outperform all prior protocols.

Acknowledgement. This work was supported by the KENTECH Research Grant (KRG202200048A).

A   Integration with TLS

Since the TLS protocol is the most widely used security protocol in practice, we integrate MT-DPI into TLS. We extend the TLS protocol following the extension mechanism described in [16]. In the TLS protocol, two endpoints exchange their supporting extensions with corresponding extension messages during the first round-trip of the TLS handshake protocol. Our TLS extension is based on TLS 1.3 [55] where the extension messages from the TLS server are encrypted.

TLS Extension for the DPI Protocols. As TLS is a two-party protocol, it is challenging to introduce MB in the TLS session. To address such a challenge, our TLS extension should provide 1) a way to make an agreement between S and R to use a particular MB and 2) a way to negotiate parameters for MT-DPI with MB. To this end, we make S and R execute the two different TLS extensions – one with each other and the other with MB– and use the TLS extension messages to negotiate necessary parameters, resulting in two TLS sessions per each entity. We design the TLS handshake for the latter session to be executed within the TLS handshake for the former session; thus, we refer to the former TLS extension as the *master TLS extension* and the latter as the *slave TLS extension*. We also consider how to bind two resulting TLS sessions while designing the two extensions.

Master TLS Extension. The main objective of the master TLS extension protocol is to agree on what MB to use in DPI and share secrets between S and R. Although both S and R can be either of a TLS client or a TLS server in the master TLS extension, we refer to a TLS server as S and a TLS client as R for ease of presentation. During the master handshake, R includes its list of preferred MBs in its extension message. Then, S selects which MB to be used, and responds with the name of the MB and the DPI key in its extension message. We also let S send a nonce to bind the master and the slave. Note that the extension message from the TLS server is encrypted in TLS 1.3; thus, the DPI key and the nonce are secret. If there is no DPI key usable with MB, S should perform the initialization protocol with MB before sending its extension message. Then, S and R respectively execute the slave TLS extension protocol with MB.

Slave TLS Extension. The slave TLS extension protocol aims to authenticate MB, negotiate parameters for MT-DPI between endpoints and MB, and bind master and slave sessions. In the slave TLS extension protocol, S and R are the TLS clients and MB is the TLS server. S and R can authenticate MB with the name negotiated in the master extension and the certificate provided by MB according to the TLS handshake protocol. With the extension messages, S and R respectively exchange parameters with MB, such as the token size or the initial counter value, to be used for the token computation and the token inspection. All the parameters are finally decided by MB and the values are sent to S and R via the MB's extension message.

Binding the Master and the Slave Extensions. To bind the master and the slave sessions, the endpoint can include the nonce from the master TLS extension in its extension message of the slave TLS extension. However, the extension message from the TLS client is not encrypted; thus, the nonce should not be sent as it is. If only the nonce is sent by one party (say, S), a network adversary can know the nonce and argue to be the other endpoint (say, R) to MB. To address this issue, we leverage the random values exchanged between the TLS server and the TLS client in the master TLS protocol. Before the extension messages, in the first round-trip of the TLS protocol, the endpoints exchange two random values in the plaintext – a server random and a client random, generated by the TLS server and the TLS client. We let S and R send a hash of the nonce and its random value of the master TLS extension to MB respectively in the slave TLS extension. Then, MB forwards the hash from S (or R) to R (or S). Then, R (or S) verifies the hash and aborts the connections with S (or R) and MB if the hash is not verified. Otherwise, S begins with sending the actual data to R in the master TLS session while performing the DPI protocol with MB in the slave TLS session.

Implementation. To show feasibility of the TLS extensions with the DPI protocols, we implement the master and the slave TLS extensions in the OpenSSL-1.1.1l library, which we will release at the public repository. We also design our implementation so that it does not require any revision to the off-the-shelf applications. That is, all the applications can use our protocol immediately by replacing their OpenSSL shared object with our shared object. We show that the protocol is immediately deployable in our testbed where cURL [13] is used as a TLS client and open-source web servers (Nginx [46] and Apache [13]) are used as TLS servers in the master TLS extension.

References

1. Anati, I., Gueron, S., Johnson, S., Scarlata, V.: Innovative technology for CPU based attestation and sealing. In: International Workshop on Hardware and Architectural Support for Security and Privacy (2013)
2. Anderson, B., McGrew, D.: Identifying encrypted malware traffic with contextual flow data. In: ACM Workshop on Artificial Intelligence and Security (2016)
3. Anderson, B., Paul, S., McGrew, D.: Deciphering malware's use of TLS (without decryption). J. Comput. Virol. Hacking Tech. (2018)
4. Asghar, H.J., Melis, L., Soldani, C., De Cristofaro, E., Kaafar, M.A., Mathy, L.: SplitBox: toward efficient private network function virtualization. In: Workshop on Hot Topics in Middleboxes and Network Function Virtualization (2016)
5. Beaver, D.: Efficient multiparty protocols using circuit randomization. In: Annual International Cryptology Conference (1992)
6. Blake, A., David, M.: Machine learning for encrypted malware traffic classification: accounting for noisy labels and non-stationarity. In: ACM International Conference on Knowledge Discovery and Data Mining (2017)
7. Boneh, D., Goh, E.-J., Nissim, K.: Evaluating 2-DNF formulas on ciphertexts. In: Kilian, J. (ed.) TCC 2005. LNCS, vol. 3378, pp. 325–341. Springer, Heidelberg (2005). https://doi.org/10.1007/978-3-540-30576-7_18
8. Bouscatié, É., Castagnos, G., Sanders, O.: Public key encryption with flexible pattern matching. In: Tibouchi, M., Wang, H. (eds.) ASIACRYPT 2021. LNCS, vol. 13093, pp. 342–370. Springer, Cham (2021). https://doi.org/10.1007/978-3-030-92068-5_12

9. Bujlow, T., Carela-Español, V., Barlet-Ros, P.: Independent comparison of popular DPI tools for traffic classification. Comput. Netw. (2015)
10. Canard, S., Diop, A., Kheir, N., Paindavoine, M., Sabt, M.: BlindiDS: market-compliant and privacy-friendly intrusion detection system over encrypted traffic. In: AsiaCCS (2017)
11. de Carné de Carnavalet, X., Mannan, M.: Killed by proxy: analyzing client-end TLS interception software. In: Network and Distributed System Security Symposium (2016)
12. de Carné de Carnavalet, X., van Oorschot, P.C.: A survey and analysis of TLS interception mechanisms and motivations. arXiv e-prints (2020)
13. cURL: cURL: command line tool and library for transferring data with URLs (1998). https://curl.se/
14. Deri, L., Martinelli, M., Bujlow, T., Cardigliano, A.: NDPI: open-source high-speed deep packet inspection. In: International Wireless Communications and Mobile Computing Conference (2014)
15. Desmoulins, N., Fouque, P.A., Onete, C., Sanders, O.: Pattern matching on encrypted streams. In: International Conference on the Theory and Application of Cryptology and Information Security (2018)
16. Dierks, T.: The TLS protocol version 1.2 (2008)
17. Durumeric, Z., et al.: The security impact of HTTPS interception. In: Network and Distributed Systems Symposium (2017)
18. Evans, D., Kolesnikov, V., Rosulek, M., et al.: A Pragmatic Introduction to Secure Multi-Party Computation. Now Publishers Inc. (2018)
19. Fan, J., Guan, C., Ren, K., Cui, Y., Qiao, C.: SPABox: safeguarding privacy during deep packet inspection at a middlebox. IEEE/ACM Trans. Network. (2017)
20. Felt, A., Barnes, R., King, A., Palmer, C., Bentzel, C., Tabriz, P.: Measuring HTTPS adoption on the web. In: USENIX Security (2017)
21. Goltzsche, D., et al.: EndBox: scalable middlebox functions using client-side trusted execution. In: IEEE/IFIP International Conference on Dependable Systems and Networks (2018)
22. Google: HTTPS encryption on the web. https://transparencyreport.google.com/https/overview. Accessed 27 June 2021
23. Grubbs, P., Arun, A., Zhang, Y., Bonneau, J., Walfish, M.: Zero-Knowledge middleboxes. In: USENIX Security (2022)
24. Han, J., Kim, S., Cho, D., Choi, B., Ha, J., Han, D.: A secure middlebox framework for enabling visibility over multiple encryption protocols. IEEE/ACM Trans. Network. (2020)
25. Han, J., Kim, S., Ha, J., Han, D.: SGX-Box: enabling visibility on encrypted traffic using a secure middlebox module. In: Asia-Pacific Workshop on Networking (2017)
26. Hedenskog, P.: Simulate slow network connections on Linux and MAC OS X (2021). https://github.com/sitespeedio/throttle
27. Hofemeier, G., Chesebrough, R.: Introduction to intel AES-NI and intel secure key instructions. Intel, White Paper (2012)
28. Jarmoc, J.: SSL/TLS interception proxies and transitive trust. In: Black Hat Europe (2012)
29. Khalife, J., Hajjar, A., Díaz-Verdejo, J.: Performance of openDPI in identifying sampled network traffic. J. Netw. (2013)
30. Kim, J., Camtepe, S., Baek, J., Susilo, W., Pieprzyk, J., Nepal, S.: P2DPI: practical and privacy-preserving deep packet inspection. In: AsiaCCS (2021)
31. Kim, J., Camtepe, S., Baek, J., Susilo, W., Pieprzyk, J., Nepal, S.: P2DPI: practical and privacy-preserving deep packet inspection. IACR Cryptol. ePrint Arch. (2021)

32. Lai, S., et al.: Practical encrypted network traffic pattern matching for secure middleboxes. IEEE Trans. Dependable Secure Comput. (2021)
33. Lan, C., Sherry, J., Popa, R.A., Ratnasamy, S., Liu, Z.: Embark: securely outsourcing middleboxes to the cloud. In: NSDI (2016)
34. Lee, H., et al.: maTLS: how to make TLS middlebox-aware? In: NDSS (2019)
35. Lee, J., Lee, H., Jeong, J., Kim, D., Kwon, T.: Analyzing spatial differences in the TLS security of delegated web services. In: AsiaCCS (2021)
36. Li, H., Ren, H., Liu, D., Shen, X.S.: Privacy-enhanced deep packet inspection at outsourced middlebox. In: International Conference on Wireless Communications and Signal Processing (2018)
37. Li, J., Li, N.: OACerts: oblivious attribute certificates. In: The Conference on Applied Cryptography and Network Security (2005)
38. Li, J., Chen, R., Su, J., Huang, X., Wang, X.: ME-TLS: middlebox-enhanced TLS for internet-of-things devices. IEEE Internet Things J. (2019)
39. Lindell, Y., Pinkas, B.: A proof of security of Yao's protocol for two-party computation. J. Cryptol. (2009)
40. Marquis-Boire, M., et al.: Planet blue coat: mapping global censorship and surveillance tools (2013)
41. McGrew, D., Wing, D., Nir, Y., Gladstone, P.: TLS proxy server extension. https://tools.ietf.org/html/draft-mcgrew-tls-proxy-server-01
42. Moriarty, K., Morton, A.: Effects of pervasive encryption on operators. Technical report, RFC (2018)
43. Naylor, D., et al.: The cost of the "s" in HTTPS. In: ACM International Conference on Emerging Networking Experiments and Technologies (2014)
44. Naylor, D., Li, R., Gkantsidis, C., Karagiannis, T., Steenkiste, P.: And then there were more: secure communication for more than two parties. In: The International Conference on Emerging Networking EXperiments and Technologies (2017)
45. Naylor, D., et al.: Multi-context TLS (mcTLS): enabling secure in-network functionality in TLS. In: ACM SIGCOMM Computer Communication Review (2015)
46. Nginx: Nginx (2022). https://www.nginx.com/
47. Ning, J., et al.: Pine: enabling privacy-preserving deep packet inspection on TLS with rule-hiding and fast connection establishment. In: Chen, L., Li, N., Liang, K., Schneider, S. (eds.) ESORICS 2020. LNCS, vol. 12308, pp. 3–22. Springer, Cham (2020). https://doi.org/10.1007/978-3-030-58951-6_1
48. Ning, J., Poh, G., Loh, J.C., Chia, J., Chang, E.C.: PrivDPI: privacy-preserving encrypted traffic inspection with reusable obfuscated rules. In: ACM Conference on Computer and Communications Security (2019)
49. Nir, Y.: A method for sharing record protocol keys with a middlebox in TLS (2012). https://tools.ietf.org/id/draft-nir-tls-keyshare-02.html
50. O'Neill, M., Ruoti, S., Seamons, K., Zappala, D.: TLS proxies: friend or foe? In: The Internet Measurement Conference (2016)
51. Pedersen, T.: Non-interactive and information-theoretic secure verifiable secret sharing. In: Annual International Cryptology Conference (1991)
52. Poddar, R., Lan, C., Popa, R.A., Ratnasamy, S.: SafeBricks: shielding network functions in the cloud. In: USENIX Security (2018)
53. Ren, H., Li, H., Liu, D., Xu, G., Cheng, N., Shen, X.S.: Privacy-preserving efficient verifiable deep packet inspection for cloud-assisted middlebox. IEEE Trans. Cloud Comput. (2020)
54. Reports, V.: Deep packet inspection market size to reach USD 16620 million by 2026 at a CAGR of 25.0 percent valuates reports (2021). https://tinyurl.com/438yktzs

55. Rescorla, E.: The TLS protocol version 1.3 (2018)
56. Sherry, J., Lan, C., Popa, R.A., Ratnasamy, S.: BlindBox: deep packet inspection over encrypted traffic. In: The ACM Conference on Special Interest Group on Data Communication (2015)
57. Silowash, G.J., Lewellen, T., Costa, D.L., Lewellen, T.B.: Detecting and preventing data exfiltration through encrypted web sessions via traffic inspection (2013)
58. Singh, R., Dunna, A., Gill, P.: Characterizing the deployment and performance of multi-CDNs. In: Internet Measurement Conference (2018)
59. Soghoian, C., Stamm, S.: Certified lies: detecting and defeating government interception attacks against SSL. In: ACM Symposium on Operating Systems Principles (2010)
60. Waked, L., Mannan, M., Youssef, A.: To intercept or not to intercept: analyzing TLS interception in network appliances. In: AsiaCCS (2018)
61. Winternitz, R.: A secure one-way hash function built from des. In: IEEE Symposium on Security and Privacy (1984)
62. Yamada, A., Miyake, Y., Takemori, K., Studer, A., Perrig, A.: Intrusion detection for encrypted web accesses. In: International Conference on Advanced Information Networking and Applications Workshops (2007)
63. Yang, K., Weng, C., Lan, X., Zhang, J., Wang, X.: Ferret: fast extension for correlated OT with small communication. In: the ACM Conference on Computer and Communications Security (2020)
64. Yao, A.C.C.: How to generate and exchange secrets. In: Annual Symposium on Foundations of Computer Science (1986)
65. Yuan, X., Wang, X., Lin, J., Wang, C.: Privacy-preserving deep packet inspection in outsourced middleboxes. In: IEEE INFOCOM (2016)

PANINI — Anonymous Anycast and an Instantiation

Christoph Coijanovic[1]([✉]), Christiane Weis[2], and Thorsten Strufe[1]

[1] Karlsruhe Institute of Technology, Karlsruhe, Germany
{christoph.coijanovic,thorsten.strufe}@kit.edu
[2] NEC Laboratories Europe, Heidelberg, Germany
christiane.weis@neclab.eu

Abstract. Anycast messaging (i.e., sending a message to an unspecified receiver) has long been neglected by the anonymous communication community. An *anonymous* anycast prevents senders from learning who the receiver of their message is, allowing for greater privacy in areas such as political activism and whistleblowing. To design protocols with provable guarantees for anonymous anycast, a formal consideration of the problem is necessary, but missing in current work. We use a game-based approach to provide formal definitions of anycast functionality and privacy. Our work also introduces PANINI, the first anonymous anycast protocol that requires only existing infrastructure.

We show that PANINI allows the actual receiver of the anycast message to remain anonymous, even in the presence of an honest but curious sender. In an empirical evaluation, we find that PANINI adds only minimal overhead over regular unicast: Sending a message anonymously to one of eight possible receivers results in an end-to-end latency of 0.76 s.

1 Introduction

In an *anycast*, messages are received by any one of a group of eligible receivers. Anycast is widely used in domain name resolution and content delivery networks [8]. Because the actual receivers are not predetermined, anycast also lends itself naturally to anonymous communication: Consider a group of political activists who fear retribution from the opposing regime. The activists want to implement *dead man's switches* among themselves, i.e., if someone is caught, someone else will be notified and can leak sensitive documents or take over their duties. If an arrested activist played a prominent role in the opposition, the regime will be particularly interested in her replacement. We can derive two main requirements from sending the dead man's notification via anonymous anycast:

First, no one (including the anycast sender) should be able to identify the receiver. This way, the captured activist cannot be forced to reveal her successor. To hide this information, the receiver must chosen non-deterministically.

Second, the set of possible receivers should be constrainable by the sender. This ensures that one of the activist's trusted allies becomes her successor.

G. Tsudik et al. (Eds.): ESORICS 2023, LNCS 14345, pp. 193–211, 2024.
https://doi.org/10.1007/978-3-031-51476-0_10

A third non-functional requirement is that sending an anonymous anycast should be as easy to set up as possible. Any obstacles, such as the need to set up a server infrastructure, will limit adoption.

Of course, anonymous anycast is not limited to political activism. Anonymous anycast is preferable to the much more common anonymous *unicast* [12,14,20] in any setting where receiver information is not relevant to, or should be hidden from the sender.

While not receiving the same amount of attention as anonymous unicast and multicast, there is some literature that addresses related issues. Mislove et al. mention that their AP3 protocol can be extended to support anycasts [26]. A recent line of research [4,6,16] focuses on anonymously selecting committee members to receive messages. We see one major shortcoming in these contributions:

Related work considers anonymous anycast from a protocol perspective, rather than a formal viewpoint. Without a formal understanding of the properties of anonymous anycast, it is difficult to compare current and future protocols. Each may define its own 'flavor' and requirements. Thus, our goal is to provide a concrete definition of the anonymous anycast problem and to formally define the main privacy goals of an anonymous anycast system.

Based on the desired functionality, we identify Message Confidentiality, Fairness, and Receiver Anonymity as the main goals of anonymous anycast. We formalize these goals using a game-based approach as it is common in cryptography (e.g., IND-CPA [3]) and already well established in anonymous unicast communication [21]. Our game-based privacy goals are unambiguously defined and allow for rigorous analysis of anycast protocols.

In this paper, we also propose PANINI, an anonymous anycast protocol, to show that our defined privacy goals are achievable by efficient protocols. PANINI relies on an anonymous unicast channel (e.g., Nym[1]) over which randomness is sent from possible receivers to the anycast sender. From this randomness, the sender can derive the key of an unknown receiver. This key is then used to encrypt a broadcast message. In summary, we make the following contributions:

- The formalization of functionality and privacy goals in anonymous anycast
- The proposal of PANINI, the first protocol that allows anonymous anycast over readily available infrastructure
- A security analysis of PANINI, showing that it achieves our previously defined privacy goals.
- In-depth empirical evaluation of PANINI including long-term latency measurements of Nym.

The rest of this paper is organized as follows: Sect. 2 introduces the related work in greater detail. Sect. 3 presents the necessary background on provable privacy, linkable ring signatures, and Nym. Sect. 4 contains our formal treatment of the anonymous anycast problem including definitions of the privacy goals. Sect. 5 describes the PANINI protocol. Sect. 6 contains PANINI's empirical evaluation. Finally, Sect. 7 concludes the paper.

---

[1] https://nymtech.net — Accessed 08/24/2023

2   Related Work

Recall our requirements for anonymous anycast: (1) no entity expect the receiver (including the anycast sender) should learn who is receiving the anycast message, (2) the set of possible receivers should be constrainable, and (3) the anycast should be as easy to set up as possible. In this section, we will present anonymous anycast-related work and discuss whether it meets these requirements.

Target-Anonymous Channels. A recent line of work considers *target-anonymous channels* [4,16]. Benhamouda et al. informally define a target-anonymous channel as one that allows "anyone to post a message to an unknown receiver" [4]. In both papers, one protocol participant is chosen to select the receiver of the channel. The participant then provides all other participants with a way to contact the receiver without revealing the receiver's identity to them. Since the selecting participant inherently learns who the receiver will be in future uses of this target-anonymous channel, our first requirement is not met.

AP3. AP3 [26] is a mix network that implements the publish/subscribe communication pattern. Publishers and subscribers are both connected through the mix network to a common root node. The root node receives messages from the publishers and forwards them to the subscribers. Mislove et al. do not discuss in detail how AP3 can be extended to provide anycast functionality. We assume, based on the available information, that the root node randomly selects a subset of subscribers as actual receivers, rather than forwarding to all.

In AP3, the anycast sender must trust the root node to perform the anycast correctly (e.g., not send the message to all users). AP3's authors do not mention that the ability to subscribe to a publisher is limited. Thus, there seems to be no way for the anycast sender to define the set of possible receivers. So our second requirement is not satisfied.

Encryption to the Future. Encryption to the Future (EtF) [6,7,13] is a cryptographic primitive where messages can be encrypted for a given *role*, rather than for a specific receiver. Later, a lottery is held to determine who gets to hold the role and thus be able to decrypt the ciphertext. To the best of our knowledge, suitable lottery primitives are all based on proof-of-stake blockchains [2,15].

Even assuming the general availability of a suitable blockchain, the requirement that users acquire a cryptocurrency stake in order to receive an anycast message is a significant barrier to adoption. Thus, our third requirement is not met.

3   Background

This section gives background on provable privacy (Sect. 3.1), linkable ring signatures (Sect. 3.2), and the Nym anonymous communication protocol (Sect. 3.3).

3.1   Provable Privacy

When designing protocols for sensitive information, privacy and security are critical. Concrete proof that a protocol protects sensitive information is desirable, but it requires unambiguous definitions of what information must be protected. In cryptography, formal definitions of security have been established since the 1980s using indistinguishability games such as IND-CPA [17].

In privacy, there is a much wider variety of possible goals than in classical security: Some protocols may focus on protecting the privacy of the sender, while others may consider the receiver, or both. Indeed, many provable privacy frameworks have been proposed [1,19,21,28]. We base our formalized anycast privacy on the work of Kuhn et al. [21], as their framework can express all the previous goals and bases them on a common indistinguishability game.

Kuhn et al.'s game is played between a challenger and an adversary. The adversary gets to choose two sets of communications, denoted as scenarios. The challenger chooses a scenario at random and simulates the protocol execution of the enclosed communications. The adversary receives any protocol output it could observe in the real world and has to decide which of its sets was selected.

Different privacy goals are expressed by restrictions on how communication may differ between scenarios: Any information that the protocol does not aim to hide must be identical between the sets. These restrictions ensure that the adversary cannot gain an unfair advantage.

A common goal of anonymous communication protocols is to unlink senders from their messages [10,14,22,31]. Kuhn et al. formalize this goal in the privacy notion of Sender-Message Pair Unlinkability $(SM)\overline{L}$. Intuitively, a protocol that achieves $(SM)\overline{L}$ can reveal which senders are active and even which messages are being sent, but not who is sending which message.

3.2   Linkable Ring Signatures

Linkable ring signature (LRS) schemes [24] allow verification against a set of multiple verification keys. Linkability allows a verifier to determine whether two signatures were created using the same key. LRS schemes provide unforgeability (i.e., verification succeeds only if the signature was created with one of the corresponding secret keys) and signer anonymity (i.e., it cannot be determined which secret key was used to sign). For a more formal definition of LRS, see Liu et al.'s model of a linkable ring signature system [23]. An LRS scheme consists of the following algorithms [5]:

- SIG.SETUP(1^λ) → pp: On input of security parameter 1^λ, return public parameters pp.
- SIG.KEYGEN(pp) → (vk, sk): On input of public parameters pp, returns a pair of public and secret key (vk, sk).
- SIG.SIGN(sk, m, R) → σ: On input of a secret key sk, a message m, and a ring $R = \{vk_0, \dots, vk_\ell\}$, output a signature σ.

- SIG.VERIFY$(\sigma, m, R) \rightarrow \{0, 1\}$: On input of a signature σ, a message m, and a ring $R = \{vk_0, \ldots, vk_\ell\}$, output 1 (accept), iff σ was generated by executing SIGN(sk, m, R), where sk corresponds to some $vk \in R$ and 0 (reject) else.
- SIG.LINK$(\sigma, \sigma') \rightarrow \{0, 1\}$: On input of two signatures σ and σ' output 1, iff σ and σ' were created using the same secret key and 0 otherwise.

3.3   Nym

Most proposed anonymous communication networks exist only on paper, and do not provide a public instance for people to use. A recent exception is Nym [11], which provides both client software to download and servers to connect to[2].

While Nym has not yet been subjected to much scientific scrutiny, it adopts the communication architecture of the well-established Loopix mix network design [29]. In Nym, messages are onion-encrypted and sent through a series of mix nodes, each of which removes an encryption layer and adds a random delay to the messages. Nym also uses cover traffic from both clients and servers to 1) hide communication patterns, 2) detect denial of service attacks, and 3) ensure that mix nodes have a sufficient amount of alternative traffic in which to hide messages. As a result, Nym unlinks senders from their messages, as long as at least one mix node is honest.

Nym differentiates itself from Loopix by introducing an optional blockchain-based reward system. The reward system is independent of the actual communication infrastructure, not relevant to our use of the system, and therefore not considered in the remainder of this paper.

4   Problem Definition

In this section, we consider the anonymous anycast problem from a formal perspective. Sect. 4.1 defines which functionality an anycast protocol has to provide to be considered *correct*. Sect. 4.2 introduces our assumed adversary model. Sect. 4.3 contains game-based formalizations of anycast privacy goals.

In the following, we use $X \subset_i Y$ to express that set X is a strict subset of set Y consisting of i elements. $X \subseteq_i Y$ is used analogously. Further, $|X|$ expresses the number of elements in X. We use U to denote the set of all protocol participants.

4.1   Functionality

An anonymous anycast is a protocol between $q = |U|$ users. The anycast's *sender* selects a set of $l \leq q$ *possible receivers* U_p, of which $n \leq l$ shall receive the anycast message. The anycast functionality then selects n *actual receivers* U_a out of the set of possible receivers at random and forwards the message to them. This functionality can be trivially provided by a trusted third party $\mathcal{F}$. Definition 1 describes $\mathcal{F}$'s behavior and bases anycast correctness on equivalence to it.

---

[2] https://nymtech.net — Accessed 08/24/2023

Definition 1 (Anonymous Anycast Correctness). *The anonymous any-cast functionality $\mathcal{F}$ interacts with a set of q users $U = \{u_1, \ldots, u_q\}$. It behaves as follows:*

1. *$\mathcal{F}$ waits for input of the form (m, n, U_p) from sender $u_s \in U$. The symbol m denotes the message, $U_p \subseteq_l U$ the set of possible receivers and $n \in \{1, \ldots, l\}$ the requested number of actual receivers.*
2. *$\mathcal{F}$ locally selects $U_a \subset_n U_p$ uniformly at random.*
3. *$\forall u \in U_a$: $\mathcal{F}$ sends m to u.*

An anonymous anycast protocol is correct if it provides $\mathcal{F}$'s functionality.

Following Definition 1, we consider a multicast (i.e., $n = l$/all possible receivers are selected as actual ones) a special form of anycast.

4.2 Adversary Assumptions

We assume an adversary $\mathcal{A}$ who can globally observe any network link, as well as actively interfere (i.e., drop, delay, modify, insert, and replay) with arbitrary packets. We further assume that $\mathcal{A}$ can corrupt the sender as well as a fraction of possible receivers. We assume that corrupted users are honest but curious and share all their knowledge with $\mathcal{A}$. We exclude arbitrarily malicious users, since they can trivially bypass any protocol's protection mechanism and send the anycast message directly to a receiver of their choice.

4.3 Privacy and Security Goals

In general, we must assume that both senders and receivers of an anycast are of interest to an adversary. However, to express sender-related privacy goals, existing notions of privacy for unicast communication can be used [21]. Thus, when considering the privacy and security goals of anonymous anycast, we focus on the receiver side. Based on the anonymous anycast functionality, we propose the following three main goals for our anycast setting:

1. **Message Confidentiality** (MC). Outside of the sender and actual receivers, nobody shall learn information about the content of the anycast message.
2. **Receiver Anonymity** (RA). Any adversary shall only learn trivial information about the *actual* receivers. Trivial information includes, for example, that a user learns that she is an actual receiver.
3. **Fairness** (F). Any possible receiver shall be chosen as the actual receiver with the same probability, except for negligible deviations. In a protocol without fairness, an adversary learns that some users are more likely to receive the anycast message, even without observation.

While these informal descriptions of our goals give a good intuition of the information that should be protected, stating them informally is not sufficient to prove that a protocol achieves them. Thus, we use a game-based approach to formalize our privacy goals next.

Our games have a common structure: They are played between a challenger C and an adversary A. The challenger internally simulates the anycast protocol Π. A can provide input (a "challenge") to the protocol and receives its output from C. Based on the output, A must determine some information about the protocol execution.

Formalizing Message Confidentiality. To formalize message confidentiality, we build on Kuhn et al.'s privacy game (see Sect. 3.1). We need to make the following modifications to adapt to the anycast setting:

1. While unicast communications are defined by a sender, a message, and a single receiver, an anycast message is defined by the sender, the message, the number of intended receivers, and the set of possible receivers. Thus, communications are expressed as tuples (s, m, n, U_p).
2. We assume that A is able to corrupt both the sender and a fraction of the receivers. Note that the anycast sender trivially learns the content of the message. Possible receivers also learn the message content if they are selected as actual receivers. To give the protocol a fair chance of achieving message confidentiality, C only provides protocol output to A if the sender and the actual receivers are not corrupted.

The resulting game $\mathcal{G}_{MC}$ for anycast protocol Π proceeds as follows:

1. C selects a challenge bit $b \in \{0, 1\}$ uniformly at random
2. A submits a challenge $Ch = (s, \{m_0, m_1\}, n, U_p)$
3. C simulates the anycast protocol Π's execution of (s, m_b, n, U_p) and saves the set of actual receivers U_a as well as Π's output $\Pi(s, m_b, n, U_p)$
4. If $\forall u \in U_a \cup \{s\} : u$ is *not* corrupted, C forwards $\Pi(s, m_b, n, U_p)$ to A
5. A submits her guess $b' \in \{0, 1\}$ to C. A wins if $b = b'$ and looses otherwise.

Analogous to Kuhn et al.'s game, steps (2–4) can be repeated an arbitrary number of times (with different challenges) to allow A to adapt its strategy based on its observations.

We say that a protocol Π achieves message confidentiality if there is no probabilistic polynomial-time algorithm A that can win $\mathcal{G}_{MC}$ with a non-negligible advantage over random guessing. Since there are two possible values for b, random guessing has a probability of success of $1/2$.

Receiver Anonymity. One could define a receiver anonymity game analogous to the message confidentiality game: A submits two possible sets of actual receivers and must decide which one was chosen by the challenger. However, since actual receivers are supposed to be chosen non-deterministically, they cannot be set by the challenger. We adapt the game model so that the adversary has to make a guess for an actual receiver instead of making a binary decision.

Note that, as with message confidentiality, user corruption may allow A to trivially determine an actual receiver. If one of the users corrupted by A receives the anycast message, $\mathcal{A}$ unambiguously learns that this user was chosen as the actual receiver. If $\mathcal{A}$ has corrupted all but n users, and none of them receives the anycast message, then all remaining users must be actual receivers. Thus, the challenger must check if one of these conditions is true after the actual receivers have been selected, and stop the game accordingly.

The complete $\mathcal{G}_{RA}$ game proceeds as follows:

1. $\mathcal{A}$ submits a challenge $Ch = (s, m, n, U_p)$
2. $\mathcal{C}$ simulates the protocol Π's execution of Ch and saves the chosen actual receivers U_a. $\mathcal{C}$ checks if $\mathcal{A}$ can trivially win due to user corruption. This is the case if there is a corrupted $u \in U_a$, or if *all* $u \in U_p \setminus U_a$ are corrupted. In case of a trivial win, $\mathcal{C}$ discards Π's output $\Pi(s, m, n, U_p)$. Otherwise, $\Pi(s, m, n, U_p)$ is forwarded to $\mathcal{A}$.
3. $\mathcal{A}$ can either choose to (a) unveil the challenge or (b) submit her guess $u^* \in U$
   (a) If $\mathcal{A}$ requested to unveil the challenge, $\mathcal{C}$ forwards U_a to $\mathcal{A}$
   (b) If $\mathcal{A}$ submitted her guess, $\mathcal{C}$ checks if $u^* \in U_a$. If so, $\mathcal{A}$ wins.

To allow $\mathcal{A}$ to adapt her strategy, steps (1-3) can be repeated a polynomial number of times as long as $\mathcal{A}$ chooses to unveil the challenge. Once $\mathcal{A}$ has submitted her guess, the game ends.

Analogous to message confidentiality, Π achieves receiver anonymity if there is no probabilistic polynomial-time algorithm $\mathcal{A}$ that can win $\mathcal{G}_{RA}$ with a non-negligible advantage over random guessing. Note that random guessing gives a probability of success of $n/|U_p|$, not $1/2$.

Formalizing Fairness. Fairness is closely related to receiver anonymity: If the protocol is not fair and favors some receivers over others, this information can be used by $\mathcal{A}$ to gain an advantage in $\mathcal{G}_{RA}$. However, a protocol could be perfectly fair but fail to achieve receiver anonymity; Consider a toy protocol that chooses the actual receivers uniformly at random, but then announces them publicly.

If the protocol is not fair, $\mathcal{A}$ should have an advantage in guessing the actual receivers without relying on the protocol output. Thus, $\mathcal{G}_F$ differs from $\mathcal{G}_{RA}$ only in that $\mathcal{A}$ must submit her guess with the challenge, *prior* to receiving the protocol output. The resulting game is similar to the EUF-CMA game used to test the unforgeability of digital signatures [18].

User Corruption Within Games. As described in Sect. 4.2, the adversary has the ability to corrupt the anycast sender as well as a fraction of the possible receivers. This ability is implemented in the games via a special challenge: Instead of sending a challenge Ch, $\mathcal{A}$ can send a *corruption query* specifying which users to corrupt in future runs. In response, $\mathcal{C}$ returns the internal state of the specified users. The protocol output $\Pi(Ch)$ may also change in future runs.

5   Protocol

Next, we propose PANINI, a possible instantiation of anonymous anycast, to demonstrate that our defined notions of privacy are readily achievable. PANINI relies on a unicast channel that unlinks senders from their messages (i.e., the receiver or any outside observer does not learn which message was sent by whom). This channel is used to provide the anycast sender with randomness, which is used to determine the actual receiver.

Prerequisites. Sending an anonymous anycast via PANINI requires:

1. An authenticated and confidential bidirectional unicast communication channel between the anycast sender and each possible receiver. We denote s sending a message m to r over this channel as $Ch_{sec}(s, m, r)$. Candidates for Ch_{sec} include the Signal messaging application[3], or email with S/MIME [30].
2. A unidirectional unicast communication channel that achieves Sender-Message Pair Unlinkability $(SM)\overline{L}$ and end-to-end confidentiality from every possible receiver to the sender. We denote s sending message m to r over this channel as $Ch_{anon}(s, m, r)$. Candidates for Ch_{anon} include Nym (see Sect. 3.3).

We first present a base version of PANINI secure against passive adversaries in Sect. 5.1, then extend it to protect against active adversaries in Sect. 5.2. Appendix A presents a pseudocode description of the full PANINI protocol. Finally, we analyze PANINI's security against our privacy notions in Sect. 5.3.

5.1 Basic PANINI

The PANINI protocol works in three distinct phases: In phase P_0 (Init), the sender uses Ch_{sec} to send a KEYREQ message to all possible receivers, notifying them of the pending anycast. The KEYREQ message contains instructions for the receivers to contact the sender via Ch_{anon}.

During the second phase P_1 (Key Submit), each possible receiver u generates a random symmetric key k_u and sends it to the sender using Ch_{anon}. We cannot expect all receivers to send their keys at exactly the same time, especially if the adversary has the ability to selectively delay packets. Therefore, we assume that Ch_{anon} has the ability to compensate for delays up to some threshold T[4]. If the keys are delayed within this threshold, Ch_{anon} will still unlink them from their sender. If the threshold is exceeded and the anycast sender has not received all the keys, it terminates the protocol run.

The third phase P_2 (distribution) begins once the sender has received a key from each possible receiver. First, the sender verifies that all keys are unique. Then, the sender chooses a random key from the received keys and uses it to encrypt the message m to be anycast along with a publicly known *tag* which is used to check for correctness after decryption. The resulting ciphertext is then distributed to all possible receivers using Ch_{sec}. Each receiver decrypts the ciphertext with their k_u and checks if the revealed *tag* matches the correct one. If so, the receiver knows that she has been selected as the actual receiver and

---

[3] https://signal.org — Accessed 08/24/2023
[4] The exact value for T depends on the protocol used to initialize Ch_{anon}.

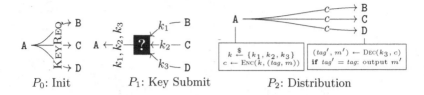

P_0: Init P_1: Key Submit P_2: Distribution

Fig. 1. Simplified PANINI protocol run. ? unlinks senders from their messages. We use $x \xleftarrow{\$} X$ to denote that x is chosen uniformly at random from set X.

saves the message. The *tag* does not serve any privacy or security purpose, it is only used to determine if the message was correctly decrypted in cases where it is not obvious from the revealed plaintext. So it can be a fixed byte that is hard-coded into the protocol. Figure 1 visualizes a simplified run of PANINI.

If the sender wants to anycast to more than one possible receiver, P_2 can be repeated n times, discarding previously selected keys. To send subsequent messages to the same actual receiver, the sender can use the same encryption key as for the initial message and multicast the resulting ciphertext again.

5.2   Defending Against Active Adversaries

The basic PANINI protocol described in the previous section protects against passive adversaries: Ch_{anon} ensures that the adversary cannot link keys to receivers, while the encrypted broadcast in phase P_2 ensures that the adversary cannot identify the actual receiver from the message sent to her. Basic PANINI, however, cannot achieve confidentiality against *active* attacks:

During phase P_1, $\mathcal{A}$ discards some fraction or even all of the temporary keys submitted to the sender and replaces them with self-chosen ones. Then, during phase P_2, $\mathcal{A}$ intercepts the ciphertext. If the sender (unknowingly) chose one of $\mathcal{A}$'s keys, then she can decrypt it and break confidentiality.

If possible receivers add a digital signature to their temporary keys, then $\mathcal{A}$ is no longer able to exchange them for their own keys without the sender noticing. In our setting, the signature should only reveal that the communication partner is part of the set of possible receivers, not her concrete identity. To do this, we can use a linkable ring signature scheme [5,25,27]. See Sect. 3.2 for background on linkable ring signatures.

To protect against *external* active adversaries, phases P_0 and P_1 are updated as follows: In P_0, the anycast sender runs SIG.SETUP and distributes the public parameters pp as part of the KEYREQ message. After receiving pp, each possible receiver u executes SIG.KEYGEN to generate its own signing key pair (vk_u, sk_u). sk_u is stored for future use and vk_u is sent to the anycast sender using Ch_{sec}. After receiving a verification key from each possible receiver, the anycast sender assembles $R \leftarrow \{vk_1, \ldots, vk_l\}$ and sends it to each possible receiver using Ch_{sec}. Each receiver checks if R contains its verification key and, if so, saves R for later use. If it does not, the sender is assumed to be malicious and the receiver is dropped from the anycast.

In P_1, each possible receiver u generates a signature σ_u for its tempo-rary key k_u by executing Sig.Sign(sk_u, k_u, R). The receiver u then sends (k_u, σ_u) to the anycast sender using Ch_{anon}. Finally, the anycast sender exe-cutes Sig.Verify(σ_u, k_u, R) on each received key to ensure that all keys were generated by someone within the set of possible receivers (and not an external adversary).

While the steps described above prevent an external adversary from inserting keys, a corrupted possible receiver could expose their private signature key to the adversary. Using this key, the adversary can still generate (and validly sign) multiple keys on behalf of the malicious receiver without the sender noticing (assuming the same number of keys from other receivers are dropped by the adversary). To ensure that each possible receiver can only submit one key, we can use the *linkability* property of the signature: The anycast sender executes Sig.Link($\sigma_u, \sigma_{u'}$) for each pair of signatures received. If Sig.Link returns '1' for at least one pair of signatures, the sender detects that *some* malicious possible receiver has sent multiple keys to increase their chance of being selected. In response, the sender terminates the protocol run. If Sig.Link returns '0' in all cases, the sender proceeds as described above.

Receiver Impersonation. We do not limit validity of the submitted keys to sup-port (very) asynchronous communication. This comes with some security draw-backs: For example, an actively malicious possible receiver who was previously a sender within this group of receivers could replace all submitted keys with known keys from the previous protocol run to ensure that she can decrypt the anycast. As we assume that senders are honest-but-curious, such attacks are out of scope in this work. However, to handle active attacks, one can add a signed timestamp to each submitted key and let the sender discard received keys with too out-of-date timestamps.

5.3   Security Analysis

Finally, we want to show that Panini achieves our privacy notions of message confidentiality, receiver anonymity, and fairness.

We start by proving that Panini achieves message confidentiality. This is intuitively the case, as messages are encrypted such that only the actual receiver can unveil the plaintext. The use of linkable ring signatures further ensures that an adversary cannot insert their own keys.

Theorem 1. Panini *achieves message confidentiality against the adversary* $\mathcal{A}$.

Refer to the extended version of this paper [9] for proof of Theorem 1.

Theorem 2. Panini *achieves receiver anonymity against the adversary* $\mathcal{A}$.

Argument. Our goal is to show that there is no efficient $\mathcal{A}$ who has an advantage over random guessing in winning the $\mathcal{G}_{RA}$ game. To do so, we iterate through all of $\mathcal{A}$'s abilities as listed in Sect. 4.2 and argue that none of them helps her to gain an advantage.

Passive Observation. Passive observation allows $\mathcal{A}$ to analyze incoming and outgoing packets anywhere in the network. During phase P_0, the sender sends an identical KEYREQ package to every possible receiver. As all packages are identical, they cannot contain information about any actual receiver. We can analogously argue for phase P_2, where the sender sends an identical ciphertext to all possible receivers. In phase P_1, each possible receiver sends a unique key to the sender. If $\mathcal{A}$ were able to track who sends which key, she could identify the actual receiver based on their key and the ciphertext from phase P_2. However, if this were the case, $\mathcal{A}$ would also be able to break $(SM)\overline{L}$ for Ch_{anon}.

Timing. $\mathcal{A}$ can time sending behavior of any user. In phases P_0 and P_2, packets are sent simultaneously by the sender to the receivers. In P_2, the sender selects a random key from the received ones and encrypts using the selected key prior to sending. As all keys are randomly chosen and of equal length, we can assume that this selection and encryption do not vary in the time it takes based on which key is selected. If $\mathcal{A}$ were able to utilize timing in P_1 to identify actual receivers, she could also break $(SM)\overline{L}$ for Ch_{anon}.

Active Interference. $\mathcal{A}$ can actively interfere (i.e., drop, delay, modify, insert, and replay) with arbitrary packets. Active interference in phase P_1 would break $(SM)\overline{L}$ of Ch_{anon}.

Drop. If $\mathcal{A}$ drops KEYREQ messages, the receiving clients are not informed about being possible receivers and will not participate further in the protocol. As the sender will only choose actual receivers if she has received the expected number of keys, the anycast will not be executed. The same behavior occurs if $\mathcal{A}$ drops keys in P_1. If $\mathcal{A}$ drops ciphertexts in P_2, the actual receivers may not receive the message. However, as we assume that receivers show no outward reaction to received (or not received) data, this does not reveal any information about the identity of possible receivers to $\mathcal{A}$.

Delay. Delays of packets other than the receivers' keys have no effect other than prolonging the protocol execution, as users wait for all expected packets to arrive before continuing with the execution. Delays of receivers' keys within the threshold T disclose no additional information as we assume that Ch_{anon} can compensate for these delays. Delays in excess of T cause the anycast sender to terminate the run prior to selecting the actual receiver and thus cannot reveal any information about the actual receiver to $\mathcal{A}$.

Modify. Due to the use of MACs, KEYREQs cannot be modified without detection. If keys in P_1 or ciphertexts in P_2 are modified, actual receivers might not be able to successfully decrypt the message. However, as we assume no reaction from receivers, this does not reveal any information to $\mathcal{A}$.

Insert. In phase P_0, $\mathcal{A}$ cannot insert further valid KEYREQs due to the use of MACs. In phase P_1, $\mathcal{A}$ cannot insert further keys, as the sender only proceeds with the anycast if the expected number of keys arrives. If $\mathcal{A}$ drops keys to insert its own ones, it is not able to do so without detection due to the use of linkable ring signatures for the key messages. In phase P_2, $\mathcal{A}$ may insert new ciphertexts, but the receiving clients will not show any outward reaction.

Replay. Replaying KeyReqs in phase P_0 will only lead to the receiving clients discarding any extra ones. Replaying keys in P_1 will result in the sender receiving more keys than expected and not executing the anycast as a result. Replaying ciphertexts in P_2 elicits no reaction from receivers by assumption.

User Corruption. $\mathcal{A}$ can corrupt the sender as well as a fraction of possible receivers. Recall that $\mathcal{A}$ only receives protocol output (and therefore has a chance to not randomly guess) in $\mathcal{G}_{RA}$ if no actual receiver is corrupted and there exists at least one other possible receiver who is not corrupted.

By corrupting a receiver, $\mathcal{A}$ gains access to their internal state, including all key material. However, as the anycast message is only encrypted with the keys of actual receivers (who are not corrupted) and there remain honest possible receivers, $\mathcal{A}$ cannot use the gained information to determine which honest clients are actual receivers versus non-chosen possible receivers.

Ch_{anon}'s achievement of Sender-Message Pair unlinkability ensures that a corrupted anycast sender cannot link received keys to their owner. The ring signature scheme's signer anonymity property ensures that the corrupted anycast sender cannot link based on the key's ring signature. Thus, we have argued that none of $\mathcal{A}$'s abilities help her in winning $\mathcal{G}_{RA}$.

As fairness is implied by receiver anonymity (see extended version [9]), Theorem 2 also implies that PANINI achieves fairness.

6   Evaluation

We evaluate the performance of PANINI concerning two metrics: 1) Computational overhead for senders and receivers (Sect. 6.1) and 2) end-to-end latency between sender and actual receiver (Sect. 6.2). We suspect that PANINI's latency largely depends on that of the underlying anonymous channel and hence benefits from improvements in this active field of research. To get a more robust view of latency, the extended version [9] provides long-term latency measurements of Nym.

6.1   Computational Overhead

We want to determine how the computational overhead of PANINI for sender and receivers scales with the number of possible receivers. A PANINI protocol run can be divided into several distinct steps. Each step consists of different cryptographic operations and might scale differently with the number of receivers. Thus, we construct a series of microbenchmarks to measure each step separately.

We have split protocol execution between sender and receivers into six distinct steps to gain insight into the contribution to the overhead of different components:

- KG is executed by each receiver in phase P_0 and entails the generation of one linkable ring signature key pair.
- SIG is executed by each receiver in phase P_1 and entails the generation of a 32-byte AES key and the signing of it.

- VER is executed by the anycast sender in phase P_1 and entails the ring signature verification.
- LINK is executed by the anycast sender in phase P_1 and entails the linkability test of each signature.
- S&E is executed by the anycast sender in phase P_2 and entails the selection of receiver key(s) as well as the encryption of the message.
- D&C is executed by each receiver in phase P_2 and entails the decryption of the received ciphertext as well as the check of the tag.

We have implemented a prototype in go, which can be found on GitHub[5]. For all our measurements, we use a virtual machine running Ubuntu 22.04.1 on a server with an AMD EPYC 7502 Processor, 2 assigned cores, and 4GB of RAM. We use `lirisi`[6] as our linkable ring signature, which implements a signature scheme proposed by Liu et al. [24]. For symmetric encryption, go's standard `crypto/aes` package is used. To determine the impact of the number of possible receivers on the computational overhead, we execute each step for 10, 20, and 40 possible receivers and one actual receiver. In all experiments, a 1024-byte message of random content is used.

We expect steps VER and LINK to account for most of the computational overhead and to scale quadratically in the number of possible receivers: For VER, one signature needs to be verified for every receiver and each verification requires computations dependent on every public key. For LINK, every signature has to be compared to every other signature. We expect steps SIG and S&E to scale linearly in the number of possible receivers as the required computations depend on every receiver. Finally, we expect steps KG and D&C to be independent of the number of possible receivers.

We provide mean values as well as standard deviation of 100 individual measurements for each step in Table 1. One can see that the ring signature verification has by far the biggest impact on the computational overhead for the sender. For receivers, the largest contributor to computational overhead is also the linkable ring signature scheme, which is used to sign the keys.

Results for steps KG, SIG, VER, and D&C are as expected. However, LINK shows superlinear, not quadratic growth. We suspect compiler optimizations to cause this discrepancy. Step S&E takes constant rather than the expected linear growth. Note the high standard deviation on our measurements. We suspect CPU scheduling to be the cause of the high deviation and to hide the linear growth.

As we suspected, signature generation and verification are responsible for the largest part of computational overhead by far. Verification further scales quadratically in the number of receivers, which limits scalability. On the bright side, we have seen that PANINI's other computational steps are very lightweight. Future—more efficient—linkable ring signature schemes, therefore, have the potential to also make PANINI equally more efficient.

Note that we have evaluated anycast to a *single* actual receiver. For n actual receivers, the computational overhead for steps S&E and D&C increases by a

---

[5] https://github.com/coijanovic/anycast-bench — Accessed 08/24/2023
[6] https://github.com/zbohm/lirisi — Accessed 08/24/2023

factor of n, as it has to be repeated for every actual receiver. The overhead for the other steps is independent of the number of actual receivers.

Table 1. PANINI microbenchmarks. Results are mean of 100 runs ± std. dev.

# Pos. Rec.	10	20	40
KG	$15.79\,\mu s \pm 0.95$	$15.96\,\mu s \pm 1.02$	$15.88\,\mu s \pm 1.17$
SIG	$2.70\,ms \pm 0.12$	$5.45\,ms \pm 0.19$	$10.85\,ms \pm 0.22$
VER	$28.07\,ms \pm 1.12$	$109.78\,ms \pm 2.84$	$432.18\,ms \pm 5.76$
LINK	$0.80\,\mu s \pm 0.175$	$2.67\,\mu s \pm 0.45$	$8.62\,\mu s \pm 0.95$
S&E	$1.82\,\mu s \pm 0.59$	$1.69\,\mu s \pm 0.39$	$1.63\,\mu s \pm 0.38$
D&C	$0.85\,\mu s \pm 0.27$	$0.75\,\mu s \pm 0.14$	$0.74\,\mu s \pm 0.12$

6.2   End-To-End Latency

In Sect. 1, we suggested that political activists can use anonymous anycast to implement a dead man's switch. We expect the dead man's notification to be similar in size and expected latency to instant messaging (IM). ITU Recommendation G.1010[7] states that "delays of several seconds are acceptable" for IM. We thus want to determine how latency in PANINI scales with the number of receivers and size of the message and if it meets G.1010.

We define the end-to-end latency as the time difference between the start of the sending client and the plaintext output of the actual receiver. To determine the impact of the number of receivers on the end-to-end latency, we will run an experiment with a fixed message size of 512 Byte and vary the number of receivers between 4 and 16. To determine the impact of the message size on the end-to-end latency, we will run an experiment with a fixed number of receivers of 8 and vary the message size between 512 Byte and 2 KB. To enable these experiments, we implemented a prototype of PANINI in go[8]. Ch_{sec} was instantiated with aes-encrypted and ecdsa-signed messages sent over TCP. Ch_{anon} was instantiated with Nym (WebSocket client v1.1.1). All clients ran on an AMD Ryzen 5 5600G with 32 GB of RAM. We repeat each measurement 16 times and present the median of the observed latencies ± standard deviation.

We expect PANINI's latency to be largely independent of both the number of receivers as well as the message size. As we have shown in Sect. 6.1, computational times for senders and receivers are well below 0.5 s. Message size only impacts phase P_2, where the message is sent via Ch_{sec}. However, for IM-size messages, we expect Ch_{sec} to not be a bottleneck. The more receivers participate, the more connection over Ch_{anon} have to be made. While receivers can send their data in parallel, the sender has to wait for the slowest receiver before continuing the execution. If there is variance in the latency of Ch_{anon}, we can expect PANINI's end-to-end latency to increase with the number of receivers.

---

[7] https://www.itu.int/rec/T-REC-G.1010-200111-I — Accessed 08/24/2023
[8] https://github.com/coijanovic/panini — Accessed 08/24/2023

We measured a median end-to-end latency of $0.71s \pm 0.64$ for 4 receivers, $0.76s \pm 0.34$ for 8 receivers, and $0.82s \pm 2.13$ for 16 receivers. For the message size experiments, we measured $0.65s \pm 0.62$ end-to-end latency for 256 B message, $0.76s \pm 0.34$ for 512 B, $0.84s \pm 0.83$ for 1024 B, and $0.75s \pm 0.54$ for 2048 B.

As we expected, latency increases with the number of possible receives. For the message size experiments, we suspect that Nym's latency variance is to blame for the unexpected results: As sending 2048 B messages leads to lower latency than sending 1024 B messages, it seems unlikely that the message size itself is to blame. Nym's latency fluctuates over time, depending e.g., on network utilization. If the measurements for 2048 B messages were made during a period of lower utilization than the measurements for 1024 B messages, our results can be explained. Finally, the high standard deviation we observed in our measurements can also be explained by Nym's latency variation.

In summary, we have shown that—for up to 16 receivers and 2 KB messages— PANINI achieves sub-second end-to-end latency and is therefore suitable for IM according to the ITU's recommendation. For use cases with larger payloads, we expect the ciphertext distribution in phase P_2 to dominate latency, but leave concrete evaluation to future work. While we have only evaluated PANINI with Nym, we want to note that the two protocols are not inherently linked to each other. If a future anonymous communication network that achieves sender-message pair unlinkability with lower latency is proposed, PANINI can utilize it, lowering its end-to-end latency in turn.

7   Conclusion

In this paper, we considered anycast from the perspective of anonymous communication. As necessary privacy goals, we identified message confidentiality, receiver anonymity, and fairness, which we also formalized in the style of indistinguishability games. Based on our formal definitions, it is now possible to analyze anonymous anycast protocols and provide rigorous proofs of privacy. We have also introduced PANINI, the first protocol that allows anonymous anycast over readily available infrastructure. We have provided proof that PANINI satisfies all of our previously defined privacy goals. Our empirical evaluation shows that PANINI introduces only minimal computational overhead for anycast senders and receivers, and achieves end-to-end latency suitable for instant messaging.

Acknowledgements. This work has been funded by the Helmholtz Association through the KASTEL Security Research Labs (HGF Topic 46.23), and by funding of the German Research Foundation (DFG, Deutsche Forschungsgemeinschaft) as part of Germany's Excellence Strategy – EXC 2050/1 – Project ID 390696704 – Cluster of Excellence "Centre for Tactile Internet with Human-in-the-Loop" (CeTI) of Technische Universität Dresden.

A   PANINI Pseudocode

Refer to Algorithm 1 for a pseudocode description of PANINI.

Algorithm 1 Sender and receiver behavior for PANINI. $\text{SEND}(s, m, n, U_p)$ is executed by user s who wants to send message m to n users out of the set of possible receivers U_p. $\text{RECEIVE}(u)$ is executed by receiver u to receive possible anycast messages. λ and tag are fixed protocol parameters known to all users. During the execution of SEND, three lists are assembled: R contains the possible receivers' signature public keys, K contains the possible receivers' ephemeral keys, and Σ contains their signatures.

---

procedure $\text{SEND}(s, m, n, U_p)$
  $pp \leftarrow \text{SIG.SETUP}(1^\lambda)$
  $\text{KEYREQ} \leftarrow (hello, pp)$
  for $u \in U_p$ **do**
    $Ch_{\text{sec}}(s, \text{KEYREQ}, u)$
  $R \leftarrow \{\}$
  while $|R| < |U_p|$ **do**
    on vk **from** u **do**
      $R \leftarrow R \cup \{vk\}$

  for $u \in U_p$ **do**
    $Ch_{\text{sec}}(s, R, u)$
  $t \leftarrow \text{TIMER.start}()$
  $K \leftarrow \{\}$
  $\Sigma \leftarrow \{\}$
  while $|K| < |U_p|$ **do**
    if $t \geq T$ **then**
      return
    on (k, σ) **from** $\perp$ **do** $\triangleright$ Ch_{anon} does not disclose sender.
      if $\text{SIG.VERIFY}(\sigma, k, R) \neq 1$ **or** $k \in K$ **then**
        return
      $K \leftarrow K \cup \{k\}$
      $\Sigma \leftarrow \Sigma \cup \{\sigma\}$

  for $\sigma \in \Sigma$ **do**
    for $\sigma' \in \Sigma$ **do**
      if $\sigma \neq \sigma' \wedge \text{SIG.LINK}(\sigma, \sigma') \neq 0$ **then**
        return
  for $i \in \{1, \dots, n\}$ **do**
    $k^* \xleftarrow{\$} K$
    $K \leftarrow K \setminus \{k^*\}$
    $c \leftarrow \text{CIPHER.ENC}((tag, m), k^*)$
    for $u \in U_p$ **do**
      $Ch_{\text{sec}}(s, c, u)$
procedure $\text{RECEIVE}(u)$
  on KEYREQ **from** s **do**
    $(sk, vk) \leftarrow \text{SIG.KEYGEN}(pp)$
    $Ch_{\text{sec}}(u, vk, s)$

  on R **from** s **do**
    if $vk \notin R$ **then**
      return
    $k \leftarrow \text{CIPHER.KEYGEN}(1^\lambda)$
    $\sigma \leftarrow \text{SIG.SIGN}(sk, k, R)$
    $Ch_{\text{anon}}(u, (k, \sigma), s)$

  on c **from** s **do**
    $(tag', m') \leftarrow \text{CIPHER.DEC}(c, k)$
    if $tag' = tag$ **then**
      return m'

References

1. Backes, M., et al.: AnoA: a framework for analyzing anonymous communication protocols. In: IEEE CSF (2013)
2. Baldimtsi, F., et al.: Anonymous lottery in the proof-of-stake setting. In: IEEE CSF (2020)
3. Bellare, M., Desai, A., Pointcheval, D., Rogaway, P.: Relations among notions of security for public-key encryption schemes. In: IACR Cryptol. ePrint Arch. (1998)
4. Benhamouda, F., et al.: Can a public blockchain keep a secret? In: TCC (2020)
5. Beullens, W., et al.: Calamari and Falafl: logarithmic (linkable) ring signatures from isogenies and lattices. In: IACR Cryptol. ePrint Arch. (2020)
6. Campanelli, M., et al.: Encryption to the future: a paradigm for sending secret messages to future (anonymous) committees. IACR Cryptol. ePrint Arch. (2021)
7. Cascudo, I., et al.: YOLO YOSO: fast and simple encryption and secret sharing in the YOSO model. In: IACR Cryptology ePrint Archive (2022)
8. Cicalese, D., Rossi, D.: A longitudinal study of IP Anycast. Comput. Commun. Rev. 48, 10–18 (2018)
9. Coijanovic, C., et al.: Panini: Anonymous AnyCast and an instantiation (extended version). ArXiv (2023)
10. Das, D., et al.: Organ: organizational anonymity with low latency. PoPETs (2022)
11. Díaz, C., et al.: The NYM network the next generation of privacy infrastructure (2021)
12. Dingledine, R., et al.: Tor: The second-generation onion router. In: USENIX Security (2004)
13. Döttling, N., et al.: McFly: verifiable encryption to the future made practical. IACR Cryptol. ePrint Arch. (2022)
14. Eskandarian, S., et al.: Express: lowering the cost of metadata-hiding communication with cryptographic privacy. In: USENIX Security (2021)
15. Ganesh, C., et al.: Proof-of-stake protocols for privacy-aware blockchains. IACR Cryptol. ePrint Arch. (2018)
16. Gentry, C., et al.: Random-index PIR with applications to large-scale secure MPC. IACR Cryptol. ePrint Arch. (2020)
17. Goldwasser, S., Micali, S.: Probabilistic encryption. J. Comput. Syst, Sci (1984)
18. Goldwasser, S., et al.: A digital signature scheme secure against adaptive chosen-message attacks. SIAM J. Comput. 17, 281–308 (1988)
19. Hevia, A.G., Micciancio, D.: An indistinguishability-based characterization of anonymous channels. In: PETS (2008)
20. van den Hooff, J., et al.: Vuvuzela: scalable private messaging resistant to traffic analysis. In: SOSP (2015)
21. Kuhn, C., et al.: On privacy notions in anonymous communication. PoPets (2019)
22. Langowski, S., et al.: Trellis: Robust and scalable metadata-private anonymous broadcast (2022)
23. Liu, J.K., Wong, D.S.: Linkable ring signatures: Security models and new schemes. In: ICCSA (2005)
24. Liu, J.K., et al.: Linkable spontaneous anonymous group signature for ad hoc groups (extended abstract). IACR Cryptol. ePrint Arch. (2004)
25. Lu, X., et al.: Raptor: a practical lattice-based (linkable) ring signature. IACR Cryptol. ePrint Arch. (2018)
26. Mislove, A., et al.: Ap3: cooperative, decentralized anonymous communication. In: EW 11 (2004)

27. Nassurdine, M., et al.: Identity based linkable ring signature with logarithmic size. In: Inscrypt (2021)
28. Pfitzmann, A., Hansen, M.: A terminology for talking about privacy by data minimization: anonymity, unlinkability, undetectability, unobservability, pseudonymity, and identity management (2010)
29. Piotrowska, A.M., et al.: The loopix anonymity system. ArXiv (2017)
30. Schaad, J., Cellars, A., et al.: Secure/Multipurpose Internet Mail Extensions (S/MIME) Version 4.0. RFC 8551, RFC Editor, April 2019
31. Vadapalli, A., et al.: Sabre: Sender-anonymous messaging with fast audits. In: IEEE SP (2022)

Curveball+: Exploring Curveball-Like Vulnerabilities of Implicit Certificate Validation

Yajun Teng[1,2], Wei Wang[1(✉)], Jun Shao[3], Huiqing Wan[1,2], Heqing Huang[1], Yong Liu[4], and Jingqiang Lin[5]

[1] State Key Laboratory of Information Security, Institute of Information Engineering, CAS, Beijing 100085, China
wangwei@iie.ac.cn
[2] School of Cyber Security, University of Chinese Academy of Sciences, Beijing 100049, China
[3] School of Cyber Security, Zhejiang Gongshang University, Hangzhou 310018, Zhejiang, China
[4] Qi An Xin Technology Group Inc, Beijing 100012, China
[5] School of Cyber Security, University of Science and Technology of China, Hefei 230027, Anhui, China

Abstract. The Curveball vulnerability exploits defective ECC public-key comparisons without matching domain parameters on X.509 certificates in MS Windows. Attackers can forge certificate chains that have the same public key value as a Windows-trusted certificate to establish fake HTTPS websites or sign malware binaries, which will be successfully verified without any alerts. This paper expands the Curveball attack to Elliptic-curve Qu-Vanstone implicit certificates, which are ECC-specific and have reduced certificate size and computation cost of certificate validation. We present two versions of the Curveball+ attack that target the implicit certificate validation where the verifiers are prone to the Curveball vulnerability. We discuss different types of certificate chains, implicit and hybrid, and various certificate trust list entry structures and certificate formats. We prove that verifiers that compare the final public key of implicit certificates are secure against Curveball+ version 1 attacks, but Curveball+ version 2 attacks will succeed certificates in M2M format due to the assailable standard description. Our work has preventive values for developers to avoid some of the potential implementation pitfalls.

Keywords: Curveball vulnerability · Implicit certificate · ECC

1 Introduction

The *Curveball* vulnerability was discovered and first publicized by National Security Agency (NSA) [19] in January 2020, numbered CVE-2020-0601. It is a spoofing flaw in validating X.509 certificate chains on Windows 10 and Windows

This work was supported by the National Key R&D Program of China (Award No.2020YFB1005800). Wei Wang is the corresponding author.

Server 2016/2019 [20]. When inspecting the ECC public keys during matching certificate trust list (CTL) entries, the deficient MS Windows ignores the comparison of ECC domain parameters, particularly the generator. By exploiting this defect, an attacker can produce a certificate with an arbitrary subject without knowing the private key for a legitimate certificate and enable the vulnerable MS Windows to validate this certificate successfully. As a result, the vulnerability might cause severe consequences with no warning, such as letting Windows accept any malicious code with a suspect code signature or entering a fake HTTPS website with the Edge browser [25,26,28].

Elliptic-Curve Qu-Vanston scheme (ECQV) [7] implicit certificates (referred to as *impCerts*) offer performance advantages in size and validation computation, compared to conventional explicit X.509 certificates (referred to as *expCerts*). ECQV certificates use the EC-Schnorr signature technique [27] in key pair generation, ensuring integrity and authenticity without a signature field. Validation combines the public key reconstruction and the further signature verification of a signed message, improving performance by eliminating a scalar multiplication step. Despite the lack of the signature field, attackers cannot forge valid implicit certificates. Several fundamental applications attempt to use ECQV implicit certificates, such as the Internet of Vehicles [24,30], ZigBee [4], NFC [12], and TLS/DTLS [21].

ECC-based *expCerts* are vulnerable to Curveball attacks when domain parameters are improperly processed; *impCerts* are also ECC-based (ECC-specific, actually). Each certificate in the *explicit* certificate chain might employ a different ECC algorithm, where the generator should be used to confirm the signature of the lower-level certificate; in contrast, the process of public key reconstruction under the *implicit* certificate chain does not involve generators since both upper- and lower-level certificates utilize the same ECC domain parameters. In light of the investigation above, a question is raised below. *Does the deficient validation of impCerts suffer from some Curveball-like attacks?*

It is not easy to directly answer this question for the following reasons.

1. The provable security of the ECQV scheme [7] is inapplicable to answer the above question directly. Predetermined domain parameters are premised on ECQV's security model. This is unsuitable for Curveball-like attacks that involve different generators.
2. A variety of implicit certificate scenarios requires additional and intricate analysis. Concretely, the public key infrastructures (PKIs) supporting implicit certificates can be built hierarchically with implicit certificates only or in a hybrid way (i.e., with both explicit and implicit certificates).
3. Specific implicit certificate formats may also affect the success of attacks. Various formats such as X.509-compliant [9], MES [9], M2M [11], IEEE 1609.2 [14], and ETSI [10], designed for multiple applications before the disclosure of Curveball. Further analyses are necessary to answer this question.

In this paper, we re-examine the original Curveball attack to various spoofing attacks, which we call *Curveball+*. This is a much larger family of Curveball attacks against verifiers validating implicit or hybrid certificate chains (i.e., implicit or hybrid verifiers) with similar Curveball vulnerabilities and influences to MS Windows. Our contributions and conclusions are described as follows.

1. We propose two independent versions of Curveball+ attacks targeting positions where the implicit verifiers are likely to ignore the domain parameter comparisons: matching the CTL entry (version 1) and reconstructing the final public key (version 2). We prove that if they store and check the final public key rather than the reconstruction value of the certificate, the Curveball+ v1 attacker will fail due to the impossibility of generating its forged root impCert.
2. We also cover the cross-type Curveball+ v1 attacks against hybrid verifiers. We find that ignoring the certificate type when matching the CTL entry is sufficient, but attacks occur if the verifiers also have improper processes of domain parameters.
3. Moreover, we analyze the existing five certificate formats supporting impCerts. We conclude that MES, IEEE 1609.2, and ETSI are safe against Curveball+ attacks with their restrictive designs, while M2M, with an inherent flaw in its design, allows for successful Curveball+ v2 attacks.

2   Background

2.1   ECC Domain Parameters in X.509 Certificates

Elliptic curve domain parameters $\mathbb{E}(G)$ over $\mathbb{F}_p$ are a sextuple: (p, a, b, G, n, h), where the first triple (p, a, b) is EC parameters for point additions and scalar multiplications. The generator G, its order n and its cofactor h are mainly used in ECC algorithms, such as ECDSA [15], EC-Schnorr [27], and SM2 [3].

Domain parameters have been embedded in X.509 certificates as the parameters of a subject's public key. Two alternative formats are supported [23]: ① an object identifier (OID) to specify the pre-defined sextuple; and ② all sextuple explicitly included and encoded (i.e., support customized domain parameters).

2.2   ECQV Implicit Certificates

Elliptic Curve Qu-Vanston(ECQV) scheme [9] is the most prominent impCert issuing scheme. As shown in Fig. 1, the EC Point P in an impCert is called *the reconstruction value*, and *the final public key value* $Q \neq P$ of the certificate holder needs to be reconstructed, whereas $Q = P$ for an expCert.

Issuance. Given the domain parameter $\mathbb{E}(G)$ and a collision-resistant hash function Hash, the process of a user U applying for an ECQV impCert $\mathsf{ICert}_U[P_U, \mathbb{E}(G)]$ from a CA holding a key pair (d_{CA}, Q_{CA}) can be described as follows.

1. The user selects $k_U \in [1, n)$ and sends $\{U, R_U := k_U \cdot G\}$ to the CA.

2. The CA selects another $k \in [1, n)$, computes the reconstruction value $P_U := R_U + k \cdot G$, and generates the impCert $\mathsf{ICert}_U[P_U, \mathbb{E}(G)]$.
3. The CA computes $r := e \cdot k + d_{CA} \bmod n$, where $e := \mathsf{Hash}(\mathsf{ICert}_U)$.
4. After receiving $\{\mathsf{ICert}_U[P, \mathbb{E}(G)], r\}$, the user calculates its private key $d_U := e \cdot k_U + r \bmod n$ and *reconstructs* the public key $Q_U := e \cdot P + Q_{CA}$.

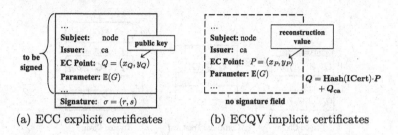

(a) ECC explicit certificates   (b) ECQV implicit certificates

Fig. 1. An overview of ECQV implicit certificates and ECC explicit certificates.

Validation. When verifying signed data under an impCert, the verifier first reconstructs the final public key and then uses it to verify the data signature. Compared to verifying an ECDSA signature, the reconstruction saves one scalar multiplication operation, which speeds up the certificate validation.

The generator G is *common* of two key pairs: ① the CA's key pair, i.e., $Q_{CA} = d_{CA} \cdot G$; and ② the user's key pair, i.e., $Q_U = d_U \cdot G$. Thus, the identical G is also required for the user to sign messages, denoted as $\mathsf{Sign}(m, d_U)|_{\mathbb{E}(G)}$.

Implicit Chains. Implicit certificates compose a chain when CAs cooperate hierarchically, where a CA applies for its impCert from its upper-level CA. The root CA of an implicit certificate chain works as follows [9]. It generates a random integer $k_R \in [1, n)$, computes $P_R := k_R \cdot G$ as the public key reconstruction value, and publishes its "self-signed" certificate $\mathsf{ICert}^R[P_R, \mathbb{E}(G)]$. Its private key is $d_R = e_R \cdot k_R \bmod n$ where $e_R = \mathsf{Hash}(\mathsf{ICert}^R)$, and the public key $Q_R := e_R \cdot P_R$. Given an implicit certificate chain $\{\mathsf{ICert}_i, \mathsf{ICert}_{i-1}, \ldots, \mathsf{ICert}_0^R\}$, the end entity i's public key is computed by $Q_i := \sum_{k=0}^{i} \mathsf{Hash}(\mathsf{ICert}_k) \cdot P_k$. Note that the generators of all impCerts in the chain need to be consistent.

3 Curveball Vulnerability on MS Windows

This section explains the Curveball vulnerability in matching certificate trust list (CTL) entries on MS Windows.

CTL is a local list of all root/intermediate CA certificates trusted by Windows. During the certificate chain validation, the verifier matches the top-level certificate with CTL entries and verifies the CAs' signatures of lower-level certificates. In MS Windows, CTL is referred to as a "certificate cache" in the memory, expediting the validation process.

3.1   Attack Overview

A Curveball attacker can exploit the Curveball vulnerability to create a *forged certificate* that matches $Q^\star$ in some CTL entries while binding another key pair $(d', Q^\star)$ without breaking any ECC signature algorithms.

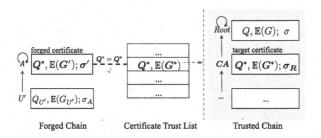

Fig. 2. Overview of the Curveball attack in explicit certificates.

The Curveball attack against a vulnerable explicit verifier is outlined in Fig. 2. The attacker begins by selecting an ECC expCert (the *target certificate*) trusted by the verifier. First, it generates a private key d' and the forged generator G' using a special key generation process. Next, it creates the forged expCert $\mathsf{ECert}_A^R[Q^\star, \mathbb{E}(G'); \sigma']$, where the signature $\sigma' := \mathrm{Sign}([Q^\star, \mathbb{E}(G')], d')\big|_{\mathbb{E}(\mathbb{G})}$. Then, it signs another expCert $\mathsf{ECert}_{U'}[Q_{U'}, \mathbb{E}(G_{U'}); \sigma_A]$ to bind any key pair $(d_{U'}, Q_{U'})$ of U' where $\sigma_A := \mathrm{Sign}([Q_{U'}, \mathbb{E}(G_{U'})], d')\big|_{\mathbb{E}(G')}$. Finally, it outputs a certificate chain $\{\mathsf{ECert}_{U'}, \mathsf{ECert}_A^R\}$ with the private key $d_{U'}$. A *successful Curveball attack*[1] is that the attacker ① constructs a key pair whose public key is accepted by the verifier's validation algorithm, and ② should not require the participation of the private key corresponding to the CTL entry.

3.2   Attack Details

The key generation process is the core of the original Curveball attack. By executing Algorithm 1, the attacker can get a key pair $(d', Q^\star)$ on $\mathbb{E}(G')$, where the public key consists of *identical* (x, y)-coordinates and curves to the CTL entry $[Q^\star, \mathbb{E}(G^\star)]$ but on *different* generators $G' \neq G^\star$. Since $\mathbb{E}$ is a finite field, and the multiplicative group of EC points except $\mathcal{O}$ is cyclic, other tuples (e.g., the order and the cofactor) will *not* change. The remaining fields of the forged certificate, such as the subject and extension fields, are arbitrary.

---

[1] The definition is also suitable for our Curveball+ v1/v2 attacks.

Algorithm 1. Key Generation of an original Curveball Attack

Require: CTL entry $[Q^\star, \mathbb{E}(G^\star)]$
1: randomly select $d' \in [1, n)$
2: $t := d'^{-1} \bmod n$
3: $G' := t \cdot Q^\star$
4: **return** d', G'

When validating the received certificate chain, the vulnerable verifier will accept and use the public key value $Q_{U'}$ with its domain parameters $\mathbb{E}(G')$. $(Q_{U'}, \mathbb{E}(G'))$ are under the attacker's complete control, with the corresponding private key $d_{U'}$, but not certified by any CA in the verifier's CTL, resulting in a *successful* Curveball attack.

3.3 Vulnerability Discussions

A complete chain validation on Windows without Curveball vulnerability is described in Algorithm 2[2] where the verifier accepts and outputs the end entity's public key $(Q_i, \mathbb{E}(G_i))$ for future use. It is feasible whether the top-level certificate ECert_0 is self-signed or not.

Matching the CTL entry is described in Lines 1 ∼ 3, where MS Windows compares the fingerprint of public keys, i.e., the digest, not the complete certificate (e.g., in OpenSSL). This approach draws on the idea of the Certificate Key Matcher (CKM) for checking whether a private key matches a certificate. For example, a matcher in SSLShopper [2] compares the digests of public keys between the private key and the certificate.

However, the deficient Windows only compares the (x, y)-coordinates of two public keys. In Line 1, it returns false only if $(Q_0 \neq Q^\star)$. After matching the public key of ECert_0 with a CTL entry, the deficient verifier directly uses Q_0 and $\mathbb{E}(G_0)$ to verify other expCerts with independent generators.

Algorithm 2. Validation of an explicit certificate chain

Require: An explicit certificate chain $\{\mathsf{ECert}_i, \mathsf{ECert}_{i-1}, \ldots, \mathsf{ECert}_0^{(R)}\}$ where ECert_k
  contains $[Q_k, \mathbb{E}(G_k); \sigma_{k-1}]$
Ensure: CTL entry$[Q^\star, \mathbb{E}(G^\star)]$ of $\mathsf{ECert}^{(R)}$
1: **if** $Q_0 \neq Q^\star$ **or** $\mathbb{E}(G_0) \neq \mathbb{E}(G^\star)$ **then**
2:     **return** not-valid
3: **end if**
4: **for** $k := 1$ **to** i **do**
5:     **if** $\mathsf{Verify}(\mathsf{ECert}_k, Q_{k-1}, \sigma_{k-1})|_{\mathbb{E}(G_{k-1})} = $ **false then**
6:         **return** not-valid
7:     **end if**
8: **end for**
9: **return** $Q_i, \mathbb{E}(G_i)$

---

[2] For simplicity, the algorithm only displays one CTL entry but the full CTL list is used. In addition, several crucial checks are omitted, but they are irrelevant to our analysis and can be easily modified by a Curveball attacker.

Why Does MS Windows only Match Public Keys? McAfee [16] offers its insight: It takes into account changes in the subject field due to the company's renaming or acquisition. The CKM method matches the new certificate received with the old certificate locally, which is more convenient for offline verifiers.

Why Does Curveball Attack only Exist in ECC Certificates? The ECC public key format in X.509 certificates differs from the previous RSA format. Big integers N in RSA are stored in *the key value* because each user holds a different value; however, generators G in ECC are almost the same under a selected elliptic curve, and it exists in *the key parameters*. The CKM matching method did not consider ECC public keys, resulting in the Curveball vulnerability.

Two CTL Entry Designs. TrendMicro [28] and Qi'anXin [25] conducted details of Windows' Curveball vulnerability. The vulnerability in CryptoAPI, the built-in closed-source cryptographic library in Windows, has two main entrances. The first is the normal method `CertGetCertificateChain`, which caches the full certificate content of each CTL entry but only compares the MD5 digest of public keys. The second is `CertVerifyCertificateChainPolicy`, used to check the special validity of the certificate chain [1]. It only caches and compares the SHA256 digest of the public keys in each CTL entry. We refer to the former CTL entry design as *full-size* and the latter as *limited-size*. The subsequent analysis of implicit and hybrid chains will be based on these two CTL entry designs.

4   Curveball+ v1 Attacks Against Implicit Chains

This section extends the original Curveball attack to an impersonation against pure implicit certificate chains described in SEC4 [9].

We consider the *implicit verifiers* that match their CTL entries with the same idea as the CKM. They have the same flaw that ignores matching public-key parameters as explicit verifiers. The Curveball attacks against these implicit verifiers are referred to as *Curveball+ version 1*. Note that the implicit certificates mentioned in Sects. 4, 5, 6 allow custom domain parameters, such as the X.509-compliant format described in SEC4 [9].

4.1   Overview of Curveball+ v1 Attacks

When matching a CTL entry for an impCert, the negligence in matching the ECC domain parameters allows the attackers to deceive the verifier by creating different domain parameters, making Curveball+ v1 attacks feasible.

In the Curveball+ v1 attack, the attacker selects a target impCert $\mathsf{ICert}^{\mathrm{R}}[P^\star, \mathbb{E}(G^\star)]$, generates a forged root impCert $\mathsf{ICert}^{\mathrm{R}}_A[P', \mathbb{E}(G')]$ and a private key d' using specific key generation algorithms, where the forged generator $G' \neq G^\star$. The remaining fields of the forged certificate are also arbitrary. Next, the attacker signs an impCert $\mathsf{ICert}_{U'}[P_{U'}, \mathbb{E}(G')]$ with the same forged ECC parameter $\mathbb{E}(G')$

through the ECQV procedure using d'. The corresponding private key is $d_{U'}$. Finally, the attacker signs a malicious message with $d_{U'}$, and outputs the certificate chain $\{\mathsf{ICert}_{U'}, \mathsf{ICert}_A^R\}$.

If the attacker has a "key generation algorithm" that allows the vulnerable verifier to match the target CTL entry, the verifier will successfully verify the signature with $Q_{U'}$ and $\mathbb{E}(G')$ due to the same reconstruction, thus accepting the malicious message and the output implicit chain.

4.2 Attack Details

Next, we explain whether and how the attacker completes its key generation algorithm with the given CTL entry.

Possible v1 Attack against Implicit Verifier $\mathcal{V}_P$. If the implicit verifier stores and compares the content of the `PublicKey` field, i.e., the public-key reconstruction value P in the CTL entry, the Curveball+ v1 attack will succeed. We name this implicit verifier $\mathcal{V}_P$. Specifically, it performs Algorithm 3 to generate its forged key pair, where the forged root impCert ICert_A^R is generated during the algorithm before calculating the final private key d'. The algorithm ensures equivalence of reconstruction values $P' = P^\star$ but contains different final public keys $Q' \neq Q^\star$. The user's final public key is $Q_{U'} := \mathrm{Hash}(\mathsf{ICert}_{U'}) \cdot P_{U'} + Q'$ satisfying $Q_{U'} = d_{U'} \cdot G'$.

After building the certificate chain, the implicit verifier $\mathcal{V}_P$ validates whether the root certificate matches one of its local CTL entries. The matching method is shown in Fig. 3(a), where $P_0 := P' = P^\star$ and $\mathbb{E}(G_0) := \mathbb{E}(G') \neq \mathbb{E}(G^\star)$. It only compares the (x, y)-coordinates of the reconstruction value. The verifier will accept the forged root certificate ICert_A^R and reconstruct the final public key $Q_0 := Q'$, thus using $(Q_{U'}, \mathbb{E}(G'))$ for subsequent signature verification. Therefore, when $\mathcal{V}_P$ is deficient in matching CTL entries, such a Curveball+ v1 attack will succeed.

Algorithm 3. Key Generation of Curveball+ v1 Attack against the implicit verifier $\mathcal{V}_P$

Require: CTL entry $[P^\star, \mathbb{E}(G^\star)]$ of ICert^R
1: randomly select $k \in [1, n)$
2: $t := (k)^{-1} \bmod n$
3: $G' := t \cdot P^\star$
4: generate certificate $\mathsf{ICert}_A^R[P^\star, \mathbb{E}(G')]$
5: $e' := \mathrm{Hash}(\mathsf{ICert}_A^R)$
6: $d' := e' \cdot k \bmod n$
7: $Q' := e \cdot P^\star$
8: **return** $(d', Q'), \mathsf{ICert}_A^R$

Impossible v1 Attack against Implicit Verifier $\mathcal{V}_Q$. Assuming that the verifier stores and compares the final public keys for subsequent use, we refer to this verifier as $\mathcal{V}_Q$. It reconstructs the final public key Q_0 before comparing it with its CTL entry, as shown in Fig. 3(b). The deficient $\mathcal{V}_Q$ ignores matching the domain parameters $\mathbb{E}(G_0)$ and $\mathbb{E}(G^\star)$, the same as the vulnerable $\mathcal{V}_P$. To induce the verifier to trigger the vulnerability, the attacker should make the final public key Q' identical to the target one $Q^\star$ in $\mathcal{V}_Q$'s CTL entry $[Q^\star, \mathbb{E}(G^\star)]$. By executing Algorithm 1 with the CTL entry, the attacker can obtain its forged key pair $(d', Q^\star)$ on $\mathbb{E}(G')$ where $G' := (d')^{-1} \cdot Q^\star$. However, the difficulty occurs in the following stage, when the attacker must calculate the reconstruction value P' before generating its forged certificate $\mathsf{ICert}_A^R[P', \mathbb{E}(G')]$, satisfying $Q' := \mathrm{Hash}(\mathsf{ICert}_A^R) \cdot P' = Q^\star$.

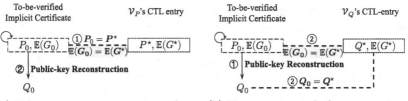

(a) $\mathcal{V}_P$ compares reconstruction values.   (b) $\mathcal{V}_Q$ reconstructs before comparison.

Fig. 3. CTL matching methods of implicit verifiers.

We define the problem of obtaining a suitable public key reconstruction value P' from a given public key $Q^\star$ as a *From-Q-to-P* (Q2P) problem, which will be proved to be hard to solve.

- If the attacker chooses a value of P', it cannot guarantee that the hash value satisfies the equation above, which is equivalent to an ECDLP problem.
- If the attacker observes a digest of the certificate, it can calculate a P but not the preimage of the hash value due to the collision resistance.

Rigorous proofs can be found in Appendix 1. Thus, the attacker cannot construct its forged impCert, and the vulnerable verifier $\mathcal{V}_Q$ with Curveball+ v1 flaw is *secure*.

4.3   Discussions

Implicit certificates can evade Curveball+ v1 attacks if the deficient implicit verifier compares the final public key value. This conclusion differs from the traditional Curveball attack described in Sect. 3 due to the unique public-key reconstruction of the impCert. Next, we discuss the two types of implicit verifiers $\mathcal{V}_Q$ and $\mathcal{V}_P$ described above.

Applicability of Two Implicit Verifiers. Since Windows Crypto API of certificate validation and other open-source implementations do not support impCerts, the discussion is based on the existing CTL comparison methods.

$\mathcal{V}_P$ matches the certificate content by comparing the EC point and its domain parameters, similar to MS Windows. After the successful matching, the verifier accepts the received top impCert, and follows the public-key reconstruction without any involvement of the CTL entry. The matching method described in Fig. 3(a) is similar to that in expCerts, and works for both *full-size* and *limited-size* CTL entry designs.

$\mathcal{V}_Q$ ensures a trusted final public key, which does not exist in the certificate content. The verifier first reconstructs the final public key of the top impCert of the chain, then matches the CTL entries, as shown in Fig. 3(b). It is only suitable for *limited-size* CTL entry design.

5 Curveball+ v1 Hybrid Attacks

This section covers the *hybrid verifiers* that support general hybrid chains where implicit certificates coexist with explicit ones.

Hybrid certificate signings are feasible in principle for two reasons: ① It is common that an expCert is the *superior* to an impCert. Such as SCMS, the vehicles' pseudonym certificates are usually implicit, but their issuers hold non-pseudonym explicit ones. ② It is suitable that an expCert is the *inferior* to an impCert. The expCert can be "a signed message" with the impCert. We present and analyze the Curveball+ v1 attacks against hybrid verifiers in general cases where the explicit and implicit certificates can be issued from one another.

5.1 Attack Overview

Curveball+ v1 hybrid attacks extend the Curveball+ v1 attacks described above to arbitrary types of target, forged, and user certificates $\{\mathsf{Cert}^R, \mathsf{Cert}^R_A, \mathsf{Cert}_{U'}\}$. The attacker's choice depends on whether the verifier supports the corresponding chain validation. A successful Curveball+ v1 hybrid attack occurs if the vulnerable verifier accepts Cert^R_A, uses the public key $Q_{U'}$ with the domain parameter $\mathbb{E}(G')$, and finally accepts any malicious message signed by $d_{U'}$.

Table 1. Four possible solutions for CTL entry of hybrid verifiers.

CTL entry	Verifier	Characteristics of the verifier
$[P^\star, \mathbb{E}(G^\star), \mathrm{Tag}]$	$\mathcal{V}_{T,P}$	store and match P with the Certificate type
$[Q^\star, \mathbb{E}(G^\star), \mathrm{Tag}]$	$\mathcal{V}_{T,Q}$	store and match Q with the Certificate type
$[P^\star, \mathbb{E}(G^\star)]$	$\mathcal{V}_{N,P}$	store and match P without the certificate type
$[Q^\star, \mathbb{E}(G^\star)]$	$\mathcal{V}_{N,Q}$	Store and match Q without the certificate type

Four possible hybrid solutions for CTL entry are described in Table 1. The first two verifiers $\mathcal{V}_{T,*}$ contain a *tag* to indicate the certificate type. The attacker's forged certificate will have the same type as the target, which is already described in Sects. 3 and 4, except for the arbitrary user certificate type. The remaining two, $\mathcal{V}_{N,*}$, mainly focus on the cross-type attacks where hybrid verifiers with Curveball vulnerability does not have the *tag* in their CTL entries. Note that the user certificate type is unrelated to the deficient CTL comparison, so we will detail specific key generations and forged certificates of cross-type Curveball+ attacks against verifiers $\mathcal{V}_{N,*}$.

5.2   Attack Details

First, we consider the vulnerable verifier $\mathcal{V}_{N,P}$. Attackers can launch both cross-type Curveball+ v1 attacks successfully.

- After selecting the target expCert $\mathsf{ECert}^{\mathrm{R}}[P^\star, \mathbb{E}(G^\star); \sigma]$, the attacker runs Algorithm 3 to obtain its generator $G' := k^{-1} \cdot P^\star$ and private key $d' := \mathsf{Hash}(\mathsf{ICert}_A^{\mathrm{R}}) \cdot k \bmod n$. The forged root impCert $\mathsf{ICert}_A^{\mathrm{R}}[P', \mathbb{E}(G')]$ is already constructed during this algorithm.
- After selecting the target impCert $\mathsf{ICert}^{\mathrm{R}}[P^\star, \mathbb{E}(G^\star)]$, the attacker runs Algorithm 1 with the given $P^\star$ to obtain its random private key d' and generator $G' := (d')^{-1} \cdot P^\star$. The public key of the forged certificate satisfies $Q' = P^\star$. Therefore, the attacker's forged self-signed expCert is $\mathsf{ECert}_A^{\mathrm{R}}[Q', \mathbb{E}(G'); \sigma']$, where the signature σ' is generated by the forged domain parameter $\mathbb{E}(G')$.

Next, we consider the vulnerable verifier $\mathcal{V}_{N,Q}$. In this case, the attacker can launch a Curveball+ v1 cross-type attack against a target implicit certificate.

- After selecting the target impCert $\mathsf{ICert}^{\mathrm{R}}[P^\star, \mathbb{E}(G^\star)]$, the attacker first calculates the target's final public key $Q^\star := \mathsf{Hash}(\mathsf{ICert}^{\mathrm{R}}) \cdot P^\star$ and runs Algorithm 1 with the input $Q^\star$ to fetch its private key d' and generator $G' := (d')^{-1} \cdot Q^\star$. The public key of the forged expCert is $Q' = Q^\star$.
- After selecting the target expCert $\mathsf{ECert}^{\mathrm{R}}[P^\star, \mathbb{E}(G^\star); \sigma]$, the attacker runs Algorithm 1 then it needs to calculate P' to generate the forged impCert $\mathsf{ICert}_A[P', \mathbb{E}(G')]$ such that $Q' := \mathsf{Hash}(\mathsf{ICert}_A^{\mathrm{R}}) \cdot P' = Q^\star$. This is the same as the complex *Q2P* problem, so the attacker cannot continue this attack.

5.3   Discussions

Summary of Curveball+ v1 Hybrid Attacks. Table 2 shows whether Curveball+ v1 attacks are successful when facing different hybrid verifiers with deficient CTL entry matching. Line $\mathrm{ATK}_{E,E}$ indicates the conclusion in Sect. 3, whereas Line $\mathrm{ATK}_{I,I}$ denotes that in Sect. 4. The table shows that the weak comparison in matching CTL entries significantly impacts $\mathcal{V}_{N,P}$, i.e., the attacker can launch attacks with arbitrary modes; $\mathcal{V}_{T,Q}$ is unaffected, and only $\mathrm{ATK}_{E,E}$ is viable.

Applicability of Hybrid Verifiers. The unmatching of the certificate types is possible for hybrid verifiers since MS Windows does not check the self-signed features and signatures. The *full-size* CTL entry format contains the whole certificate, which belongs to the verifier $V_{T,P}$. If the verifier does not match the certificate type, it will become $V_{N,P}$. In contrast, the *limited-size* CTL entry format can be adapted to any of the four hybrid verifiers.

Security of Hybrid Verifiers. It is clear that all four verifiers have no additional flaws if they do not have the Curveball vulnerability. On the surface, $V_{N,P}$ sounds irrational: the untrusted certificate may be matched to a trusted certificate of another type improperly due to the same EC point value. But in reality, it is *secure* if it does not have any Curveball flaws. Security proofs in Appendix 2 indicate the truth: a third-party attacker cannot convert the target certificate into another type that the verifier can mistakenly accept.

Table 2. Result of Curveball+ v1 hybrid attacks against vulnerable verifiers.

v1 Attack Mode	Certificate		Hybrid Verifier			
	Target Cert	Forged Cert	$V_{N,P}$	$V_{N,Q}$	$V_{T,P}$	$V_{T,Q}$
$\text{ATK}_{E,E}$	ECert	ECert	✓	✓	✓	✓
$\text{ATK}_{E,I}$	ECert	ICert	✓	✗	✗	✗
$\text{ATK}_{I,E}$	ICert	ECert	✓	✓	✗	✗
$\text{ATK}_{I,I}$	ICert	ICert	✓	✗	✓	✗

The last four columns show whether the attacker can complete the Curveball+ v1 attack using a specific attack method under a specific hybrid verifier. "✓" indicates a successful attack, while "✗" represents not.

6   Curveball+ v2 Attacks

This section discusses *Curveball+ version 2* attacks, which target implicit verifiers or hybrid verifiers. The attack exploits a flaw where the verifier does not match the public-key parameters of an implicit certificate with those in its superior. This flaw is exclusive to validating implicit certificates, irrelevant to the CKM matching method, and independent of the original Curveball vulnerability, but the two versions of attacks both neglect to align ECC domain parameters during certificate validations.

6.1   Attack Overview

Similar to a v1 attack, the v2 attack aims at forging a key pair with the same key value but different domain parameters. With a target root certificate Cert^R containing $\mathbb{E}(G^*)$, the main difference between the two attacks is that the v2 attacker directly uses the forged key pair (d', Q') with $\mathbb{E}(G')$ for signing an impCert $\mathsf{ICert}_{U'}$, without generating its forged certificate Cert_A. The issuer of the user impCert $\mathsf{ICert}_{U'}$ should be the same as the subject of the target certificate Cert^R, and the output chain is $\{\mathsf{ICert}_{U'}, \mathsf{Cert}^R\}$, which holds $G' \neq G^\star$. However, the vulnerable verifier omits the generator comparisons when reconstructing the public key of impCerts, thus directly using G' and successfully accepting the output signature and the "fake" certificate chain.

6.2   Attack Details

Unlike version 1, the version 2 attacker aims to make its (final) public-key value the same as that of the target certificate, either for vulnerable $\mathcal{V}_{*,Q}$ or $\mathcal{V}_{*,P}$, as described in Fig. 4. In detail, it can obtain its final private key d' and the domain parameters $\mathbb{E}(G')$ by executing Algorithm 1 with the input $[Q^\star, \mathbb{E}(G^\star)]$.

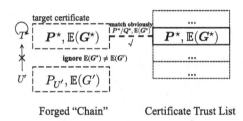

Fig. 4. Overview of a Curveball+ v2 attack targeting both $\mathcal{V}_{*,P}$ and $\mathcal{V}_{*,Q}$.

Table 3 shows the result of the Curveball+ v2 attacks targeting the hybrid verifiers. Whether the verifier is $\mathcal{V}_{*,Q}$ or $\mathcal{V}_{*,P}$ does not affect the key generation of the Curveball+ v2 attacker. Thus, all cells in the table will become "✓".

Table 3. Result of Curveball+ v2 attacks against vulnerable hybrid verifiers.

v2 Attack Mode	Target Certificate	Hybrid Verifier			
		$\mathcal{V}_{N,P}$	$\mathcal{V}_{N,Q}$	$\mathcal{V}_{T,P}$	$\mathcal{V}_{T,Q}$
$\mathrm{ATK}_{E,*}$	ECert	✓	✓	✓	✓
$\mathrm{ATK}_{I,*}$	ICert	✓	✓	✓	✓

6.3   Discussions

Now we discuss the possible vulnerability in the public-key reconstruction procedure that can lead to Curveball+ v2 Attacks.

Usage of Generators. First, v2 attacks only exist in validating impCerts. Figure 5 illustrates the different usage of generators in three-tier chains. In the implicit case, only G_2 of the end-entity is directly used for future actions, and equivalent generators indicate G_2's confidence; while in explicit cases, they are directly used for certificate signature verifications without equalities. Implicit/hybrid verifiers vulnerable in public-key reconstruction cannot establish the connection between G_2 and dependable $G_0 := G^*$.

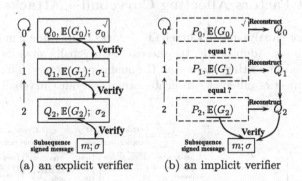

Fig. 5. Different generators' usage between verifiers with a three-tier chain.

SEC4 Standard. However, the standard does not emphasize the matching of generators between an impCert and its CA. While the standard specifies that the reconstructed user's public key should be defined over the same elliptic curve as CA's public key (the third subheading of Appendix B of [9]), "the same curve" only pertains to the EC parameters (p, a, b) but not the generator G. The Curveball+ v2 attack shows that the ECC domain parameters sextuple (p, a, b, G, n, h) of the two certificates should ultimately be compared.

```
static int internal_verify(X509_STORE_CTX *ctx) {
    ...
    while (n >= 0) { // n: current chain's length
        EVP_PKEY *pkey = X509_get0_pubkey(xi); // xi: issuer's certificate
        X509_verify(xs, pkey);  // xs: subject's certificate
        ... // update n, xi, xs
    }
    return 1;
}
```

Fig. 6. The critical code for validating an X.509 certificate chain in OpenSSL 1.1.1l.

OpenSSL Interfaces. Furthermore, we find that domain parameter comparisons in public-key reconstruction can be easily overlooked. OpenSSL 1.1.1l provides a `while` loop in Fig. 6 where the verifier extracts the public key with its domain parameters of a certificate from top to bottom into an `EVP_PKEY` object. Extending it to an implicit case, the verifier will replace `X509_verify` with the public-key reconstruction procedure. However, the point addition function `EC_POINT_add`, the last step of the public-key reconstruction, does not match the domain parameters of the two input `EC_POINT` objects. Therefore, developers must be mindful of the generator comparisons, which are not emphasized in the SEC4 standard, to prevent Curveball+ v2 attacks.

7 Format Factors Affecting Curveball+ Attacks

Previous sections analyzed two Curveball+ attacks by discussing implicit/hybrid verifier procedures. Additionally, the success of Curveball+ attacks requires certificate formats supporting custom ECC domain parameters. This section will discuss the impact of different certificate formats on our Curveball+ attacks.

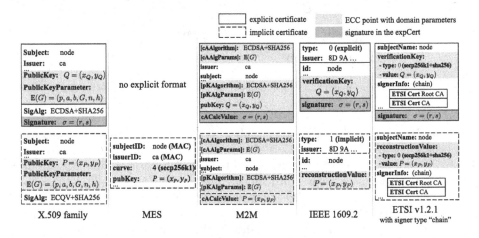

Fig. 7. Key characteristics of the five certificate formats into a simplified form.

Five certificate formats supporting implicit type are identified with various features: X.509 family [9], MES [9], M2M [11], IEEE 1609.2 [14], and ETSI v1.2 [10]. Figure 7 illustrates the intuitive differences among the total five certificate formats. Next, we sort these characteristics that are present in at least one certificate type, which may affect our Curveball+ attacks.

7.1 Basic Assumption

The basic assumption of the two versions of Curveball+ attacks is that the certificate format supports customized ECC domain parameters.

Limited Domain Parameters. MES, IEEE 1609.2, and ETSI have this restriction. They offer an enumerated number for predefined curves. MES supports all curves described in SEC2 [5], but the other two formats only contain "secp256k1". All predefined curves described in SEC2 are sextuple, containing generators. Therefore, a Curveball+ attacker cannot generate its forged/user certificate in these formats with custom domain parameters. The M2M format, based on X.509 certificate format, does not detail the public-key parameters [11]. It can be considered to support custom domain parameters.

7.2 Features Mitigating Attacks

Three other features may mitigate the success of Curveball+ attacks.

Support Implicit Certificates Only. MES has the feature. If the verifier only accepts this format, the attacker can only consider $ATK_{I,I}$.

Restrict Implicit Certificates Level. IEEE 1609.2 format has this restriction [14] due to the IoV application, where only end-entity pseudonym certificates will be implicit. The restriction also avoids the existence of a root impCert, so all Curveball+ attacks will be degraded to $ATK_{E,E}$.

Represent the Issuer by the Digest. IEEE 1609.2 and ETSI adopt the last 32-bit digest of the superior certificate as the inferior's issuer (where root certificates mark the issuer with its hash algorithm). The digest can be used directly for the *limited-size* CTL entry: [Hash(Cert)], an identical digest indicating the integrity of the certificate, including domain parameters. If the CTL entry is designed accordingly, the attacker cannot generate its forged certificate containing its custom domain parameters with the same identical digest, thus all Curveball+ v1 attacks on vulnerable CTL matching will be fruitless.

7.3 Features Magnifying Attacks

The following feature may allow for a successful Curveball+ v2 attack even if the implicit/hybrid verifier has no Curveball vulnerabilities.

Allow Optional Public-Key Parameters. Both X.509 and M2M formats allow for parameters omission, but with different methods of obtaining them. The X.509-compliant [9] allows for retrieving from superior CA certificates (until a self-signed certificate), while the M2M format has no restrictions. It is possible to extract an M2M certificate's public key parameters from its lower-level certificate's cAAlgParams field. Section 6 in the IETF draft [11] sets the rule for omitting algorithm fields. It specifies that cAAlgorithm can only be omitted when pKAlgorithm of a superior certificate *fully* specifies the algorithm and its domain parameters. The description allows for the situation above if the CA certificate contains `pKAlgorithm` field but omits `pKAlgParams` field, since the `xxAlgorithm` field and the `xxAlgParams` field are optional independently.

This method can expose the M2M certificate verifier to a severe Curveball+ v2 attack without Curveball vulnerability. Targeting an M2M root impCert with no public key parameters, the attacker can launch a Curveball+ v2 attack using a user impCert $\mathsf{ICert}_{U'}$ with a different custom generator. The verifier complying with the IETF draft will ultimately extract the custom domain parameters and apply them to further validation directly.

In principle, this design of M2M is problematic. However, the vulnerability has limited impact due to two factors: ① M2M is only a draft that has not been updated since March 2015 [11], and ② there is no widely-used open-source M2M implementation, including certificate validation. We have emailed the original author and are still waiting for a response.

7.4 Features Affecting Attackers' Calculation

The other two features do not affect the success of the attack, but they influence the calculation of the Curveball+ attacker.

Calculate the Digests Uniquely. IEEE 1609.2 has this specialty. It replaces the digests $\mathrm{Hash}(\mathsf{ICert}_U)$ and $\mathrm{Hash}(m)$ with $\mathrm{Hash}(\mathrm{Hash}(\mathsf{ICert}_U)\|\mathrm{Hash}(\mathsf{ICert}_{CA}))$ and $\mathrm{Hash}(\mathrm{Hash}(m)\|\mathrm{Hash}(\mathsf{ICert}_U))$, respectively. This means that the signer's certificate participates in the computation of the digest.

Contain CA Certificates Inside the Body. ETSI format has this feature, which puts the complete chain into the user certificate as the `signerInfo` field.

The attacker needs to customize its Curveball+ attack to accommodate these features. It uses $\mathrm{Hash}(\mathsf{ICert}^R)$ on Curveball+ v2 attacks and $\mathrm{Hash}(\mathsf{ICert}_A^R)$ on v1 attacks for the consistent digests in ECQV public-key reconstruction.

7.5 Summary

The results generalized by each certificate format are shown in Table 4. MES, IEEE 1609.2, and ETSI v1.2 do not lead to Curveball+ attacks because they do not support customized curve parameters. Verifiers with X.509-family and M2M format may have Curveball vulnerabilities, and they need to be careful with domain parameter comparisons. Additionally, M2M has a defect that the attacker may launch a successful Curveball+ v2 attack against an invulnerable verifier.

8   Related Work

Research of Certificate Validation. Several studies such as Frankencerts [8] generated mutant certificates automatically to test for defects in libraries and browsers. These tests revealed many flaws in field checking of validating a certificate. In addition, research [13] focused on API usability and documentation. Their testing libraries cover multiple platforms, devices, and program languages, but none currently support implicit certificates.

ECQV's Analysis. SEC4's appendix [9] discusses commentaries on implicit certificates, including the inability to sign implicit cross-certificates and the potential use of Wagner's tree algorithm to solve the implicit chain's combined equation. Daniel et al. [6] found that the implicit user certificate cannot be the signing message when combining the ECQV algorithm with ECDSA. These studies did not involve validations of domain parameters of implicit certificates.

Table 4. Result of Curveball+ attack for different formats.

Features of Certificate Formats	Certificate Formats				
	X.509	MES	M2M	1609.2	ETSI
Limited domain parameters		×		×	×
Support implicit certificates only		−			
Restrict implicit certificates level				−	
Represent the issuer by the digest				×^{d}	×^{d}
Allow optional public-key parameters	O		+		
Calculate the digests uniquely				O	
Contain CA certificates inside the body					O
Curveball+ Attack Result	✓	×	✓	×	×

"+", "×" or "−" mean that the certificate format supports features that can *magnify*, *fix* or *mitigate* the Curveball attacks. "^{d}" indicates storing the certificate digest in CTL entries. "✓" or "×" denote that the weak verifier supporting this format is *vulnerable* or *secure* with Curveball+ attacks.

Studies Using Similar Analysis Thought. Nikos et al. [17] described a cross-protocol attack in TLS 1.2 based on the Wagner and Scheiner attack [29] in SSL 3.0. Similarly, this attack assumes support for custom domain parameters and is analyzed as a simulation. However, the cross-protocol attack is probabilistic and depends on the vulnerable protocol; whereas our Curveball+ attacks are conditional with vulnerable verifiers.

9 Conclusion

This paper proposes two versions of possible Curveball+ attacks against ECQV implicit certificates based on the origin Curveball attack against X.509 ECC certificates. Version 1 is for implicit and hybrid verifiers with a similar vulnerability to Windows in matching CTL entries. However, it is secure if the deficient verifiers compare the final public keys rather than the reconstruction value. For hybrid verifiers, not comparing certificate types is not a flaw, but additional Curveball vulnerabilities enable easy launch of v1 attacks. Version 2 is for verifiers that easily ignore matching domain parameters during the public-key reconstructions of implicit certificates. Both v1/v2 attacks have the same consequences as the original Curveball attack, as they focus on all possible domain parameter comparisons during the implicit certificate validation process. We simulated all successful Curveball+ attacks presented in this paper[3]. In addition, MES, IEEE 1609.2, and ETSI avoid the possibility of attacks by limiting domain parameters, but the improper M2M design leads to v2 attacks even the verifiers without Curveball vulnerability. The latest RFC 8902 [18] catalyzes the development of implicit certificates. However, several existing drafts or standards for implicit certificate formats need improvements to be more developer-friendly in validating implicit certificates. We hope that the standard-setter of implicit certificates will provide clear procedures and designs, so that software developers will understand the design principle of implicit certificate crypto suites better and avoid some of the possible implementation traps in the future.

Appendix 1   Proofs of the Q2P Problem

The format $[m, P]$ represents the certificate $\mathsf{ICert}[P, \mathbb{E}(G)]$ in the security model, where m represents the other information of ICert except the EC Point P, renamed as the message. The rigorous definition of $Q2P$ is described as follows.

Definition 1. *Given an Elliptic Curve* $\mathbb{E}$, *a hash function* Hash *and an EC Point* Q, $Q2P$ *problem asks for a message* m *and another EC Point* P *such that* $Q = \mathrm{Hash}(m, P) \cdot P$.

In the random oracle model, we define the game for an adversary $\mathcal{A}$ to solve $Q2P$ problem as $\mathrm{Game}_{\mathcal{A}}^{Q2P}\left(\lambda, \mathbb{E}\right)$[4] with a hash oracle $\mathcal{O}_{\mathcal{A}}^{\mathrm{Hash}}$. Note that the attacker in reality limits the (x, y)-coordinates of G' in the output m (Sect. 4), more complex than Definition 1 with arbitrary m.

Lemma 1. *In the random oracle model, the EC-Schnorr family of signature schemes in* $\mathbb{E}(G)$ *is secure if the ECDLP problem in* $\mathbb{E}(G)$ *is intractable.*

The variant of the *Schnorr* signature for a message m with the private key b can be expressed as $\sigma := (R, s)$ where the EC Point $R := k \cdot G$ with random secret k, and the integer $s := b + k \cdot \mathrm{Hash}(m, R)$. To verify the signature, one checks that $s \cdot G = \mathrm{Hash}(m, R) \cdot R + B$ with the public key B.

Pointcheval and Stern [22] have proved Lemma 1 by constructing a reduction from ECDLP to the variant EC-Schnorr Signatures with the "forking lemma".

Theorem 1. *In the random oracle model,* $Q2P$ *problem in* $\mathbb{E}$ *is difficult if the Schnorr Signature Scheme in* $\mathbb{E}(G)$ *is secure.*

---

[3] See https://github.com/tyj956413282/curveball-plus.git for source code.

[4] λ represents the bit-number of $\#\mathbb{E}$ (the number of all EC points in $\mathbb{E}$).

Proof. We just reveal the following experience: assuming that there exists a successful adversary $\mathcal{A}$ solving the *Q2P* problem, construct a polynomial algorithm $\mathcal{B}$ that uses $\mathcal{A}$ as a subroutine to forgery the EC-Schnorr signature with nonnegligible probability. The game $\text{Game}_{\mathcal{B}}^{\text{Schnorr}}$ runs as follows:

1. After receiving the public key B, randomly select an integer $s \in [1, n)$ as a part of the output signature and calculate the final public key $Q := s \cdot G - B$;
2. To obtain the message and another part of the signature, run $\text{Game}_{\mathcal{A}}^{\text{Q2P}} (\lambda, \mathbb{E})$ with $\mathcal{O}_{\mathcal{B}}^{\text{Hash}}$;
3. If $\mathcal{A}$ wins with output (m', P'), construct and output the message with the forged signature $\left(m', \sigma' := (P', s)\right)$; otherwise, terminate $\bot$.

The following two factors allow $\mathcal{B}$ to pass the game, which proves the correctness.

1. **New message:** m' is suitable since $\mathcal{B}$ did not make any signature query.
2. **Signature verification:** the verification with signature σ' will be passed due to $\text{Hash}(m', P') \cdot P' + B = Q + B = (s \cdot G - B) + B = s \cdot G$.

If $\mathcal{A}$ runs in polynomial time and succeeds with nonnegligible probability, so will $\mathcal{B}$. But by hypothesis, no such $\mathcal{B}$ can make a forged variant EC-Schnorr signature in $\mathbb{E}(G)$. Therefore, no adversary $\mathcal{A}$ exists in the random oracle model, and the proof of this theorem is complete.

Combing Lemma 1 and Theorem 1, we can get that the Q2P problem is based on the ECDLP problem.

Appendix 2   Rationality of the Hybrid Verifier $\mathcal{V}_{N,P}$

The *rationality* of a hybrid verifier $\mathcal{V}_{N,P}$ is that any certificate holder, except a self-signed holder, cannot change the certificate type so that the verifier will accept it. That is, transforming an explicit certificate into implicit (*E2I*), and transforming an implicit certificate to explicit (*I2E*). The rationality of $\mathcal{V}_{N,P}$ is based on the ECDLP assumption with two additional oracles: an ECDSA signature oracle $\mathcal{O}^{\text{Sign}}$ and an ECQV certificate oracle $\mathcal{O}^{\text{ECQV}}$. Both ECDSA and ECQV algorithm are also based on the ECDLP assumption [7,15], thus our ECDLP attacker have the ability to ask $\mathcal{O}^{\text{Sign}}$ and $\mathcal{O}^{\text{ECQV}}$. To simplify our proofs, we use the explicit certificate as an example.

Transform Explicit Certificates. Assume that a trusted certificate chain $\{\text{ECert}_1, \text{ECert}_0^{\text{R}}\}$ is stored in the verifier $\mathcal{V}_{N,P}$. We define $\text{Game}_{\mathcal{A},\mathcal{V}_{N,P}}^{E2I}(\text{ECert}, n)$ as follows: After receiving a certificate chain $\{\text{ECert}_1[Q_1, \mathbb{E}(G_1); \sigma_0], \text{ECert}_0^{\text{R}}[Q_0,$ $\mathbb{E}(G_0); \sigma]\}$ with a private key d_1 where $Q_1 = d_1 \cdot G_1$, output a forged nonroot implicit certificate with a private key $(d', \text{ICert}_{\mathcal{A}}[P', \mathbb{E}(G_1)])$ so that the final public key satisfies $Q' := \text{Hash}(\text{ICert}_{\mathcal{A}}) \cdot P' + Q_0 = d' \cdot G_1$ and $P' = Q_1$.

Theorem 2. *In the random oracle model, I2E does not exist in normal $\mathcal{V}_{N,Q}$ if the ECDLP problem is hard to solve.*

Proof. We design $\text{Game}_{\mathcal{B}}^{\text{ECDLP}}(n, \mathbb{E}(G))$ using $\text{Game}_{\mathcal{A}, \mathcal{V}_{N,P}}^{E2I}(\text{ECert}, n)$ as follows:

1. After receiving the public key B, randomly select $d_1 \in [1, n)$ and generate the two certificates $\text{ECert}_0^R[B, \mathbb{E}(G); \sigma]$, $\text{ECert}_1[Q_1, \mathbb{E}(G); \sigma_0]$ where σ and σ_0 are obtained by asking the signature oracle $\mathcal{O}_{\mathcal{B}}^{\text{Sign}}$ and $Q_1 := d_1 \cdot G$. Send $(\{\text{ECert}_1, \text{ECert}_0^R\}, d_1)$ to $\mathcal{A}$.
2. Judge $\mathcal{A}$'s answer when $\mathcal{A}$ outputs as $(d', \text{ICert}_{\mathcal{A}})$.
3. If $\mathcal{A}$ wins, calculate $d_0 = d' - \text{Hash}(\text{ICert}_{\mathcal{A}}) \cdot d_1$, and output $b := d_0$.

We state that $B = b \cdot G$ for correctness, under the premise of $Q_1 = P'$ in $\mathcal{V}_{N,P}$. We have $B = Q' - \text{Hash}(\text{ICert}_{\mathcal{A}}) \cdot P' = (\text{Hash}(\text{ICert}_{\mathcal{A}}) \cdot d_1 + b) \cdot G - \text{Hash}(\text{ICert}_1) \cdot P' = b \cdot G$. If $\mathcal{A}$ successfully constructs the eligible nonroot implicit certificate, $\mathcal{B}$ is also successful in solving the ECDLP problem, proving the theorem.

Transform Implicit Certificates. Assume that a trusted certificate chain $\{\text{ICert}_1[P_1, \mathbb{E}(G)], \text{ECert}_0^R[B, \mathbb{E}(G); \sigma]\}$ is stored in the verifier $\mathcal{V}_{N,P}$. We define $\text{Game}_{\mathcal{A}, \mathcal{V}_{N,P}}^{I2E}(\text{ICert}, n)$ as follows: After receiving $\{\text{ICert}_1, \text{ECert}_0^R\}$ and (d_1, k') where $Q_1 := \text{Hash}(\text{ICert}_1) \cdot P_1 + Q_0 = d_1 \cdot G$, ($k'$ is defined in the ECQV procedure for ICert_1), output a forged nonroot certificate with a private key $(d', \text{ECert}_{\mathcal{A}}[Q', \mathbb{E}(G); \sigma_0])$ so that $Q' := d' \cdot G = P_1$.

Theorem 3. *In the random oracle model, I2E does not exist in normal $\mathcal{V}_{N,P}$ if the ECDLP in $\mathbb{E}(G)$ is hard to solve.*

Proof. We design $\text{Game}_{\mathcal{B}}^{\text{ECDLP}}(n, \mathbb{E}(G))$ using $\text{Game}_{\mathcal{A}, \mathcal{V}_{N,P}}^{I2E}(\text{ECert}, n)$ as follows:

1. After receiving the public key B, generate $\text{ECert}_0^R[B, \mathbb{E}(G); \sigma]$ asking an ECDSA signature oracle $\mathcal{O}_{\mathcal{B}}^{\text{Sign}}$ for σ.
2. Call ECQV procedure to generate $\text{ICert}_1[R, \mathbb{E}(G)]$ whose CA is ECert_0^R, with a median k_1 and the private key d_1. Noted that the public and private key reconstruction values are (R, s) by a query of Schnorr signature Oracle $\mathcal{O}_{\mathcal{B}}^{\text{Sign}}$ where m is defined in Appendix 1.
3. Send $(\{\text{ICert}_1, \text{ECert}_0^R\}, d_1)$ to $\mathcal{A}$.
4. Judge $\mathcal{A}$'s answer when $\mathcal{A}$ outputs as $(d', \text{ECert}_{\mathcal{A}})$.
5. If $\mathcal{A}$ wins, calculate ECert_0^R's private key $d_0 := d_1 - \text{Hash}(\text{ICert}_1) \cdot d'$, and output $b := d_0$.

We state that $B = b \cdot G$ for correctness, under the premise of $P_1 = Q'$ in $\mathcal{V}_{N,P}$. We have $B = Q_1 - \text{Hash}(\text{ICert}_1) \cdot P_1 = (\text{Hash}(\text{ICert}_1) \cdot d' + b) \cdot G - \text{Hash}(\text{ICert}_1) \cdot P_1 = b \cdot G$ If $\mathcal{A}$ successfully constructs the eligible nonroot implicit certificate, $\mathcal{B}$ is also successful in solving the ECDLP problem with the same probability.

References

1. CertVerifyCertificateChainPolicy function (wincrypt.h) (2021). https://docs.micro
   soft.com/en-us/windows/win32/api/wincrypt/nf-wincrypt-certverifycertificatech
   ainpolicy
2. Certificate key matcher (unknown). https://www.sslshopper.com/certificate-key-
   matcher.html
3. Administration, C.E.: SM2 elliptic curve public key algorithms (2010)
4. BlackBerry: Certicom device certification authority for zigbee smart energy
   (nd). https://blackberry.certicom.com/en/products/managed-certificate-service/
   smart-energy-device-certificate-service
5. Brown, D.R.: SEC 2: Recommended elliptic curve domain parameters. In: Standars
   for Efficient Cryptography (2010)
6. Brown, D.R., Campagna, M.J., Vanstone, S.A.: Security of ECQV-certified ECDSA
   against passive adversaries. Cryptology ePrint Archive (2009)
7. Brown, D.R.L., Gallant, R., Vanstone, S.A.: Provably secure implicit certificate
   schemes. In: Syverson, P. (ed.) FC 2001. LNCS, vol. 2339, pp. 156–165. Springer,
   Heidelberg (2002). https://doi.org/10.1007/3-540-46088-8_15
8. Brubaker, C., Jana, S., Ray, B., Khurshid, S., Shmatikov, V.: Using frankencerts
   for automated adversarial testing of certificate validation in SSL/TLS implementations. In: 2014 IEEE Symposium on Security and Privacy, pp. 114–129. IEEE
   (2014)
9. Campagna, M.: SEC4: Elliptic curve Qu-Vanstone implicit certificates, version 1.0.
   Tech. rep., Standards for Efficient Cryptography (2013)
10. ETSI, T.: ETSI TS 103 097 v1.1.1-intelligent transport systems (ITS); security;
    security header and certificate formats. Standard, TC ITS (2013)
11. Ford, W., Poeluev, Y.: The machine-to-machine (M2M) public key certificate for-
    mat. Internet-Draft draft-ford-m2mcertificate-00, IETF Secretariat (2015)
12. Forum, N.: Signature record type definition, technical specification, v2.0 (2014)
13. Georgiev, M., Iyengar, S., Jana, S., Anubhai, R., Boneh, D., Shmatikov, V.: The
    most dangerous code in the world: validating SSL certificates in non-browser soft-
    ware. In: Proceedings of the 2012 ACM Conference on Computer and Communi-
    cations Security, pp. 38–49 (2012)
14. IEEE 1609 Working Group and others: IEEE standard for wireless access in vehic-
    ular environments-security services for applications and management messages.
    IEEE STD 1609(2) (2016)
15. Johnson, D., Menezes, A., Vanstone, S.: The elliptic curve digital signature algo-
    rithm (ECDSA). Int. J. Inf. Secur. 1(1), 36–63 (2001)
16. Labs, M.: What CVE-2020-0601 teaches us about Microsoft's TLS certificate
    verification process (2020). https://www.mcafee.com/blogs/other-blogs/mcafee-
    labs/what-cve-2020-0601-teaches-us-about-microsofts-tls-certificate-verification-
    process/
17. Mavrogiannopoulos, N., Vercauteren, F., Velichkov, V., Preneel, B.: A cross-
    protocol attack on the TLS protocol. In: Proceedings of the 2012 ACM Conference
    on Computer and Communications Security, pp. 62–72 (2012)
18. Msahli, Cam-Winget, W.: Internet X.509 public key infrastructure certificate. Tech.
    rep., RFC 8902 (2020)
19. National Security Agency: Patch critical cryptographic vulnerability in Microsoft
    windows clients and servers (2020). https://media.defense.gov/2020/Jan/14/
    2002234275/-1/-1/0/CSA-WINDOWS-10-CRYPT-LIB-20190114.PDF

20. Paganini, P.: Two PoC exploits for CVE-2020-0601 nsacrypto flaw released (2020). https://securityaffairs.co/wordpress/96486/uncategorized/cve-2020-0601-nsacrypto-exploits.html

21. Poeluev, Y., Ford, W.: Transport layer security (TLS) and datagram transport layer security (DTLS) authentication using m2m certificate. IETF Secretariat (2015)

22. Pointcheval, D., Stern, J.: Security proofs for signature schemes. In: Maurer, U. (ed.) EUROCRYPT 1996. LNCS, vol. 1070, pp. 387–398. Springer, Heidelberg (1996). https://doi.org/10.1007/3-540-68339-9_33

23. Polk, T., Housley, R., Bassham, L.: Algorithms and identifiers for the internet X.509 public key infrastructure certificate and certificate revocation list (CRL) profile. Tech. rep., RFC 3279 (2002)

24. Pollicino, F., Stabili, D., Ferretti, L., Marchetti, M.: An experimental analysis of ECQV implicit certificates performance in VANETs. In: 2020 IEEE 92nd Vehicular Technology Conference (VTC2020-Fall), pp. 1–6. IEEE (2020)

25. Qi'an Xin Codesafe: Detailed analysis of CVE-2020-0601 vulnerability (in Chinese) (2020). https://blog.csdn.net/smellycat000/article/details/104057852

26. Romailer, Y.: CVE-2020-0601: The Chainoffools/Curveball attack explained with POC (2020). https://research.kudelskisecurity.com/2020/01/15/cve-2020-0601-the-chainoffools-attack-explained-with-poc/

27. Schnorr, C.P.: Efficient identification and signatures for smart cards. In: Brassard, G. (ed.) CRYPTO 1989. LNCS, vol. 435, pp. 239–252. Springer, New York (1990). https://doi.org/10.1007/0-387-34805-0_22

28. Simpson, J.: A technical analysis of Curveball (cve-2020-0601) (2020). https://www.trendmicro.com/en_us/research/20/b/an-in-depth-technical-analysis-of-curveball-cve-2020-0601.html

29. Wagner, D., Schneier, B., et al.: Analysis of the SSL 3.0 protocol. In: The Second USENIX Workshop on Electronic Commerce Proceedings, vol. 1, pp. 29–40 (1996)

30. Whyte, W., Weimerskirch, A., Kumar, V., Hehn, T.: A security credential management system for V2V communications. In: 2013 IEEE Vehicular Networking Conference, pp. 1–8. IEEE (2013)

Malware Classification Using Open Set Recognition and HTTP Protocol Requests

Piotr Białczak[1,2]($\boxtimes$) (ID) and Wojciech Mazurczyk[2] (ID)

[1] CERT Polska/NASK - National Research Institute,
Kolska 12, 01-045 Warsaw, Poland
`piotr.bialczak@cert.pl`
[2] Institute of Computer Science, Warsaw University of Technology,
Nowowiejska 15/19, 00-665 Warsaw, Poland
`wojciech.mazurczyk@pw.edu.pl`

Abstract. Malware is a serious threat to the modern Internet, as it is used to, e.g., sending spam or stealing bank login credentials. Typically, to communicate with the attacker, it utilizes popular network protocols such as the HyperText Transfer Protocol (HTTP). The network traffic characteristics related to this protocol can be used to detect malware and identify its family. The latter is a standard multi-class classification problem for which machine learning algorithms are utilized. However, existing methods cannot identify a real-world situation of encountering a new malware family, which was not known during their training phase. To address this issue, an Open Set Recognition (OSR) approach can be used, capable of a multi-class classification and identification of unknown class occurrence. In this paper, we apply OSR to the malware classification using HTTP requests and compare it with the existing solutions. In more detail, we analyze the classification performance of three OSR and two standard algorithms and their computation time. Additionally, we utilize two request representations: one based on *Hfinger* tool and the other relying on trigrams. The obtained experimental results allowed to select an optimal set of algorithms and HTTP request representations suitable for OSR scenarios.

Keywords: Open Set Recognition · Malware analysis · HTTP protocol

1 Introduction

Behavior analysis gives better insights into malicious software (malware) operations, assists in identifying its characteristic features, and eventually helps in its detection. Such a study typically includes, for example, investigating operating system library calls, changes in the filesystem, and specifics of network traffic. Malware generates the latter to download instructions from Command and Control (C&C) servers, execute attacks, exfiltrate collected data, etc. To communicate, various popular network protocols are utilized, including the HyperText

G. Tsudik et al. (Eds.): ESORICS 2023, LNCS 14345, pp. 235–254, 2024.
https://doi.org/10.1007/978-3-031-51476-0_12

Transfer Protocol (HTTP), which version 1.1 was originally defined in RFC 2616 [12]. HTTP works in a client-server architecture, where the client sends requests for available resources on the server. The data exchanged in version 1.1 of this protocol has a human-readable text representation.

The specifics of HTTP protocol can be used to detect malware, for example, by searching for some distinguishing features indicating maliciousness of network traffic (cf. Białczak and Mazurczyk [4]). Searching for such features and creating detection rules based on them may not be time-efficient and scalable to many malware families. In this case, a possible solution is to use machine learning methods to exploit the dependencies in the data that human operators are unable to discover. These methods are applied for detection and classification tasks.

In standard machine learning-based approaches to malware classification using the HTTP protocol (e.g., [11,28,32,36,37]) class prediction process involves only data samples of *known classes* (malware families), that is, those present in the data set during model training. However, in a real-world scenario, data samples of previously unseen classes can be present, for example, a new, unknown malware family. Standard machine learning algorithms, when encountering *unknown classes*, i.e., those whose data samples were not present during the model training phase, will incorrectly assign a label from those learned during training. To address such a limitation, *Open Set Recognition (OSR)* approach has been introduced (cf. Geng et al. [13]). It combines multi-class classification with the recognition of unknown classes.

In this paper, we apply the OSR approach to malware classification using the HTTP protocol. In particular, we experimentally evaluate three OSR algorithms, i.e., Weibull calibrated Support Vector Machines (W-SVM, Scheirer et al. [41]), Open-Set Support Vector Machines (OSSVM, Júnior et al. [24]), and Extreme Value Machine (EVM, Rudd et al. [39]). The chosen algorithms are also compared to two standard machine learning approaches, i.e., Support Vector Machines and Random Forest, extended with a mechanism for rejecting prediction when its probability is too low. Our analysis focuses on the specifics of HTTP protocol requests sent by clients because server responses are not always correct or sometimes unavailable. Such a situation can occur, for example, when the criminals' infrastructure has been taken over by security researchers, resulting in a change in the returned responses or turning off a server. Additionally, the study uses version 1.1 of the HTTP protocol, as it is still used by applications (including malware) and can be translated to newer versions of the protocol (cf. [6,44]). None of the analyzed machine learning algorithms can directly ingest HTTP requests data, so we use two types of their representation. One is based on the *Hfinger* tool proposed by Białczak and Mazurczyk in [5], which represents the request's URL, headers and their values, and request body. The second is a trigram representation based on n-gram analysis – a classic natural language processing method (cf. D. Jurafsky et al. [21]). It creates a model of the frequency of occurrence of all n-character strings in a document or set of documents. In the case of a trigram, these are 3-character strings. This creates a vector of numbers that is, unlike the original textual form, directly processed by machine learning algorithms.

Considering the above, the main contributions of this paper are: *(i)* a proposal of a novel approach for applying Open Set Recognition scenario to malware classification utilizing HTTP requests; *(ii)* an analysis of selected Open Set Recognition algorithms regarding classification performance and computation time compared to traditional machine learning techniques; *(iii)* a comparison of classification performance of HTTP requests representations based on the *Hfinger* tool and trigrams; *(iv)* a selection of an optimal set of tested algorithms and request representations for malware classification in an Open Set Recognition scenario.

To the authors' knowledge, this is the first work to utilize the OSR approach to malware classification using HTTP requests.

2   Related Work and Background

In this section, we present the OSR background, then the current state of the art of malware detection and classification using the HTTP protocol, and finally, we focus on presenting the application of the OSR scenario to malware classification and network attacks.

2.1   Open Set Recognition Fundamentals

The open set recognition problem is presented in Fig. 1. Part of the data samples of the four-class data set presented in panel (a) was used to train two classifiers. The first classifier, SVC (Support Vector Classification), is based on the support vector machine algorithm and is a standard closed set classifier provided by the Scikit-learn package [34]. The second classifier is an OSR algorithm, EVM. Panels (b) and (c) present the decision boundaries of the SVC and EVM classifiers, respectively. The boundaries determine which points in the input data space are assigned to a particular class. The decision boundaries of the SVC classifier are unlimited and cover the entire data space. For this reason, data points of unknown classes symbolized by a cross and an asterisk will be classified as one of the classes known during the classifier's training, even though they are at a considerable distance from the training points. The decision boundaries of the EVM classifier presented in panel (c) are limited. The data points in the blank area do not belong to any known classes. Thus, data points marked with a cross and an asterisk will be classified as belonging to an unknown class.

2.2   Malware Detection and Classification Using HTTP Protocol

The standard malware detection task has already been analyzed: e.g., in [11,14,43]). While determining the maliciousness of network traffic is valuable information, it still does not provide the situational awareness that is available when determining what family has been detected. The same is true for the use of information available in transmitted data - only some methods use data from all elements of an HTTP message: header values, their location in the message,

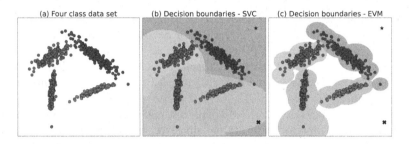

Fig. 1. An example of Open Set Recognition problem: (a) a four-class data set; (b) decision boundaries of a standard, closed set SVC algorithm based classifier; (c) decision boundaries of an OSR classifier based on EVM algorithm.

control information (e.g., request method or response code), or transmitted data (e.g., [28,30,46]). The lack of analysis of this information can potentially reduce the discriminatory capabilities of the created classifiers.

In contrast, approaches such as [2,11] or [35] require both HTTP requests and responses. Unfortunately, server responses are not always available for analysis or may not be reliable, due to criminals' infrastructure being disabled or taken over by security researchers. Finally, for some systems, it is stated that they are capable of network traffic detection of unknown malware families. Those solutions that rely on some discriminative feature or anomaly detection (e.g., [14, 40]) can indeed perform correct detection, but they are not specialized enough to report that it is a completely new family. Also, systems that perform multi-class detection (e.g., [3,31]) do not have mechanisms to report that the analyzed class is unknown. Potentially the closest to solving the OSR problem are systems that use clustering, such as: [25,35,47], or [29]. With clustering, these systems can discover unknown malware families. Unfortunately, in the situation of creating a new cluster separate from others, it is necessary to determine whether it is a completely new family or a new cluster of an already-known one.

None of the solutions discussed above meets the requirements of the open set recognition scenario, i.e., they do not perform multi-class detection and do not detect unknown classes. For this reason and because of the above mentioned problems, we propose a multi-class detection system that would use different elements of HTTP requests, while operating according to the OSR scenario.

2.3   OSR Scenario in Malware Classification and Network Attacks

Since, to the authors' knowledge, this is the first OSR classification system using the HTTP protocol requests, below we review state-of-the-art solutions on similar tasks, namely applying the OSR scenario to problems of detecting unknown network attacks by intrusion detection systems (IDS) or to detect malware based on their file related data.

To begin with IDS systems, Henrydoss et al. in [17] proposed a method using Extreme Value Machine (EVM). Then, S. Cruz et al. in [9] presented the use of

Weibull distribution calibrated Support Vector Machines (W-SVM). Also, Zhang et al. in [48] proposed an IDS system based on a convolutional neural network (CNN) and clustering.

Another approach was proposed by Souza et al. [42], where they adopted a set of single-class Energy-based Flow Classifiers to create a multi-class system.

The open set recognition scenario is also used to classify malware binary files. Hassen and Chan [16] presented a binary file classification model based on a convolutional neural network and function call graphs. Jia and Chan used similar artifacts in [20] where the system applies a self-supervised pre-training representation learning. In contrast, Guo et al. in [15] presented a system that utilizes a generative adversarial network.

In this paper, the proposed approach of malware families classification using the HTTP protocol differs from other OSR solutions presented above. Network intrusion detection systems focus on detecting unknown attacks, not just those caused by malware, mainly based on information extracted from network flows and the data transmitted in them, abstracting from specific protocols. In contrast, the approach presented in this work focuses strictly on the problem of classifying malware only by using data available in HTTP protocol requests. Obviously, other existing systems that use binary files or artifacts associated with them utilize different types of input data.

3   Overview of the Classification Procedure

The following section presents an overview of the classification procedure, including the analysis protocol and used machine learning algorithms.

3.1   Analysis Protocol

The purpose of the analysis is to compare the classification performance of different machine learning algorithms in the OSR scenario, while selecting the optimal hyperparameters for each algorithm. Standard testing protocols were developed for the closed set problem and cannot fully address the OSR problem. To solve this issue, Geng et al. proposed in [13] to use the standard testing protocol of dividing a data set into training, validation and testing parts, yet extend it by including unknown classes during the validation and testing phases.

However, the selection of hyperparameters is based on the validation part of the data set, which is selected once along with the training and testing parts. This can lead to a bias of the classification efficiency estimator. Thus, the analysis protocol proposed by Geng et al. was extended by introducing a modified holdout validation into the procedure of selecting hyperparameters.

The analysis protocol used in this work is presented in algorithm 1. The loop divides the data set into training and testing parts. It is executed 5 times, and each time a set of unknown classes is drawn from all classes with a size depending on the openness O_P parameter (cf. Equation 3). The remaining classes are treated as known classes and divided into training and test parts in an 80:20

ratio while maintaining the sample ratio of the classes. The training part of the data set is passed to the procedure for selecting the algorithm's hyperparameters. The selected hyperparameters are used to create a model using all the training data.' The testing part of the data set, consisting of known classes, is merged with unknown classes selected at the beginning of the loop, and classification evaluation is carried out on such a data set. Two measures are used: F1 and the Matthews Correlation Coefficient, which are discussed in Sect. 3.2.

Algorithm 1. Analysis protocol algorithm

Require: *data set, openness, classes, classification_measure*
Ensure: *classification effectiveness*
  unknown class number ← openness × ‖classes‖
  classification estimation ← 0
  for $i = 0$ to 5 **do**
    unknown classes ← sample(unknown class number)
    known classes ← classes − unknown classes
    training, test ← data set[known classes]
    test ← test + data set[unknown classes]
    best hyperparameters ← hyperparameter_selection(training, classification_measure)
    model_training(training, best hyperparameters)
    classification ← classification(test)
    classification   estimation   ←   classification   estimation   +
    classification_measure(classification)
  end for
  classification effectiveness ← classification estimation/5

The hyperparameter selection procedure uses as input the training part data of the main loop and the defined classification performance measure. Selection is achieved using *HalvingGridSearchCV* provided by the Scikit-learn package and a modified holdout validation, serving as a cross-validation for this method. The modified holdout validation simulates the occurrence of unknown classes by dividing the set of known classes (which are the training part of the outer loop) into five equal parts. For each of the five subsets, the classes that belong to such a subset are considered unknown. At the same time, the remaining part is divided into a training and test part in the ratio of 80:20, maintaining the numerical proportions of samples in the classes. The unknown classes obtained at the beginning of this inner loop are added to the inner test part. The protocol presented above is used to evaluate algorithms for different levels of data set openness. When the openness equals zero, the analysis protocol changes only in the hyperparameter selection procedure: the *HalvingGridSearchCV* method utilizes standard stratified 5-fold cross-validation as the cross-validation mechanism.

3.2   Classification Performance Measures

As already mentioned, the comparative analysis of the performance of the tested algorithms uses two measures: the F1 and the Matthews Correlation Coefficient (MCC).

The F1 measure examines classification efficiency and is the harmonic mean of precision and recall. Due to the multi-class nature of the data set, in the analysis, the *macro* version of the F1 measure is used. It is the arithmetic average of the F1 measures for each class. Since only the *macro* version of the F1 measure is utilized in this study, in the following sections, we will refer to it as F1.

The Matthews Correlation Coefficient is defined in Eq. 1.

$$MCC = \frac{c \times s - \sum_k^K p_k \times t_k}{\sqrt{(s^2 - \sum_k^K p_k^2) \times (s^2 - \sum_k^K t_k^2)}} \tag{1}$$

where for the confusion matrix C for classes K:

- $t_k = \sum_i^K C_{ik}$ is the number of times when class k truly occurred,
- $p_k = \sum_i^K C_{ki}$ is the number of times when class k was predicted,
- $c = \sum_k^K C_{kk}$ is the number of samples correctly predicted,
- $s = \sum_i^K \sum_j^K C_{ij}$ is the total number of samples.

An additional OSR concept is *Openness*, which defines the ratio of the number of classes known during the algorithm's training phase to the number of known and unknown classes present during the testing phase. Geng et al. [13] defined it as *Openness** with Eq. 2.

$$O^* = 1 - \sqrt{\frac{2 \times C_T}{C_T + C_E}} \tag{2}$$

where C_T is the number of classes available during the training phase, while C_E is the number of classes available in the test phase. In the analysis, it was assumed that $C_E = C_T + U$, where U is the number of unknown classes, available only during the test phase.

Due to the classification procedure and its class shuffling, an additional openness factor O_P is defined as a percentage of the number of unknown classes U divided by the number of all classes available in the data set C (Eq. 3).

$$O_P = \frac{U}{C} \times 100[\%] \tag{3}$$

3.3   Machine Learning Algorithms Used in the Analysis

During the experimental evaluation, three OSR algorithms were used: W-SVM, OSSVM, and EVM.

Weibull calibrated Support Vector Machines is an algorithm presented by Scheirer et al. in [41]. The authors utilized the Compact Abating Probability model, in which a testing sample's probability of inclusion to a known class decreases with its distance from training samples. The source code of the algorithm was obtained from [18]. The code has been adapted to the API of the Scikit-learn package, and some code bugs, which prevented execution, have been patched according to issue #2 posted on the official code repository [18].

Júnior et al. in [24] presented a modified version of the Support Vector Machines algorithm: Open-Set Support Vector Machines. According to the authors, unlike the classic SVM algorithm, OSSVM allows bounding Positively Labeled Open Space for the binary classification scenario. As a result, if OSSVM is used in a One-vs-Rest strategy in a multi-class classification scenario, it will also bound Known Labeled Open Space (a space unsupported by the training samples, in which the test sample would be labeled as belonging to one of the known classes). The source code at [23] has been used for analysis.

Extreme Value Machine is an algorithm proposed by Rudd et al. in [39]. The authors utilize Extreme Value Theory and the concept of margin distributions to create a radial inclusion function, that models the probability of sample inclusion. The original source code can be found at [38], however in the analysis, its updated version has been used from [22]. This version was adapted to the Scikit-learn package's API, and code bugs encountered during data processing were patched.

The W-SVM and EVM algorithms were chosen because of their use in previous security systems (W-SVM in Cruz et al. [9], EVM in Henrydoss et al. [17]), numerous references in the literature, and the availability of their source code. OSSVM, on the other hand, is a relatively new algorithm (published in 2021), but also based on the Support Vector Machines algorithm like W-SVM, thus it was also included for comparison purposes.

Additionally, two standard algorithms were added to the analysis as a baseline: Support Vector Machines (further abbreviated as MCR-SVM) and Random Forest (further abbreviated as MCR-RF). Both algorithms are considered good candidates for classification by the Scikit-learn package's guide [10]. The algorithms are used in a multi-class classification mode with the prediction of classification probability. This provides a mechanism for the rejection of the classification. When the probability (confidence) of classification for a given sample is lower than a defined threshold, the classification is rejected, and the sample is considered as belonging to the unknown class. However, as stated by Boult et al. [7], for most algorithms, classification confidence increases when moving away from decision boundaries. Therefore, a sample of an unknown class distant from the decision boundaries will be labeled as one of the known classes with high confidence. Neither of the two algorithms solves the OSR problem due to the lack of a bound in the positively labeled open space, and thus the open space risk remains unbounded [7]. Rejection threshold δ_R is defined as $\delta_R = 0.5 \times O^*$, where O^* is the openness defined by Eq. 2. Such a rejection threshold definition can be found in the literature (e.g., [41]) and is used as a hyperparameter in OSR algorithms: as δ_R in W-SVM and δ in EVM.

3.4 HTTP Requests' Dataset and Representation

The analysis was performed using a dataset from the authors' previous work [5]. The malware part consists of network traffic generated in CERT Polska's malware sandbox analysis laboratory and Malware Capture Facility Project [26]. The final malware dataset consists of 121 popular malware families, comprising

401,544 HTTP requests. The dataset with the network traffic of popular benign applications (browsers, office applications, etc.) contains 248,180 requests and is treated as one class.

The analyzed dataset is not balanced. The number of samples for classes ranges from 20 to 248,180 with an arithmetic mean of 5325.61 and a median of 160.5. To reduce the impact of the difference in the number of samples between classes, we decided to balance the class counts by using undersampling. A maximum limit of 200 samples was set, which is 10 times the size of the smallest class. The undersampling is performed using the *RandomUnderSampler* method of the *Imbalanced learn* package [27].

In this study, we use two representations of HTTP requests, one based on the *Hfinger* tool and the other on requests' trigrams. The representation based on the *Hfinger* provides all the information the tool analyzes, presented as floating-point numbers. Two more features extend it than are available in the default operation mode of the tool. The features are as follows: URL length, number of directories, average URL's directory length, an extension of the requested file, length of the URL's variable part, number of variables in the URL, average URL's value length, the request method, version of the protocol, order of headers, popular headers and their values, presence of non-ASCII characters, payload entropy represented as an integer, payload length represented as a float. The second type of HTTP request representation is based on trigram analysis. It has been repeatedly confirmed that the use of n-grams as a way of representing data when detecting attacks or malware is an effective solution (cf. [19, 45]). The analysis uses trigrams as a compromise between increasing the dimensionality of the data set and efficiency in correctly representing the transformed data. Studies by other authors (e.g., A. Oza et al. [33]) indicate a significant increase in detection efficiency using at least trigrams.

4   Results

This section presents the classification performance results of the five analyzed algorithms for two HTTP request representations based on *Hfinger* and trigrams. Classification performance is measured using F1 and MCC as discussed in Subsect. 3.2. Additionally, the running times of the analysis steps for each algorithm were measured: hyperparameters selection, classifier training, and classification evaluation (testing). The running-time results are presented below as a sum of the average time for each phase. It will serve as an additional measure when comparing the algorithms. Since hyperparameter selection is achieved by optimizing a single performance measure due to the usage of the *HalvingGridSearchCV* scheme, the results are presented for both analyzed measures, but in two separate scenarios: maximizing the F1 and maximizing the MCC.

The analysis focused on malware on the Windows operating system, despite the popularity of other platforms, including Android. According to the AV-Test portal [1], most malware is still created for this system. However, the approach presented here can be adapted to other platforms, too.

4.1   Analysis' Technical Overview

The algorithms' classification efficiency was tested for five openness O_P values: 0%, 10%, 25%, 50%, 75%. The values correspond to O^* openness values, respectively: 0.00%, 2.64%, 7.35%, 18.58%, 36.96%.

The hyperparameters selection phase used a pipeline model. Due to the use of two different types, two similar data processing models were used. Before forwarding data samples to data pipelines, feature encoding was performed. The text features generated by *Hfinger* were encoded using *BinaryEncoder* or *HashingEncoder* functions from *Category Encoders* [8]. The trigrams were based on the raw data from HTTP requests and encoded with Scikit-learn's *HashingVectorizer* followed by Scikit-learn's *TfidfTransformer*, and selecting k best features according to scikit-learn's *SelectKBest*. The k parameter is considered as a hyperparameter with values of: 500, 750, 1000, 1500.

Algorithm performance experiments were performed on two machines. Experiments on all five algorithms using the *Hfinger* representation were performed on a machine controlled by the Kubuntu 18.04.1 operating system, equipped with an AMD Ryzen 5 1600 processor and 16 GB of RAM. There were 10 computational threads available, but only two algorithms used it by default: EVM and MCR-RF. The analysis comparing *Hfinger's* and trigram representations was performed on a machine controlled by the Debian 11 operating system and equipped with 20 virtual processors clocked at 2992 MHz and 64 GB of RAM.

Applications and libraries used in the analysis include: Python 3.8.12, scikit-learn 1.0, imbalanced-learn 0.8.1, category-encoders 2.3.0, and Hfinger 0.2.0.

4.2   Algorithm Comparison Using *Hfinger* representation

The classification efficiency of the algorithms with hyperparameter selection with respect to F1 is presented in Fig. 2.

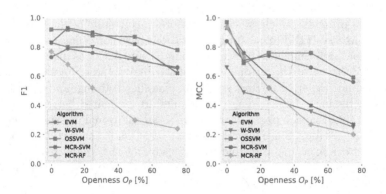

Fig. 2. The classification efficiency of the algorithms with hyperparameters selection regarding F1 using *Hfinger* representation.

As presented in Fig. 2 for the closed set scenario, all algorithms achieve good classification results in terms of both F1 and MCC measures. OSSVM achieved the highest level of F1 - 0.92. The algorithms also achieved good levels of the MCC measure - the best was again OSSVM (0.97). An increase in openness causes decreases in the classification performance of the algorithms. The largest was observed for the MCR-RF algorithm: for F1 and MCC measures by 0.53 (69%) and 0.74 (79%), respectively. The drop in MCC between the $O_P = 0\%$ and $O_P = 75\%$ levels was greater than for F1 for algorithms other than MCR-RF. Despite these declines, classification efficiency for O_P lower than 75% remains acceptable for algorithms other than MCR-RF.

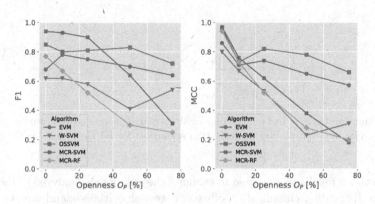

Fig. 3. The classification efficiency of the algorithms with hyperparameters selection regarding MCC using *Hfinger* representation.

Figure 3 shows the classification efficiency of algorithms with hyperparameter selection with respect to MCC. A decrease in classification efficiency is visible as the openness of the data set increases. Still, the decrease is more disrupted than it was in the previously presented hyperparameter selection scenario. The MCR-SVM algorithm achieved the best classification levels for $O_P = 0\%$: 0.94 for F1 and 0.97 for MCC. The lowest level of F1: 0.25, was achieved using the MCR-RF algorithm for $O_P = 75\%$, and the lowest level of MCC was achieved using the MCR-SVM algorithm: 0.18, for the same level of openness.

The running times of the algorithms analyzed are presented in Fig. 4. For the scenario of hyperparameter optimization for F1, it is noticeable that running times decrease for all algorithms as the level of openness increases. This is due to the decrease in the number of classes in the test data as the openness increases. For $O_P = 0\%$ the highest value was achieved by the OSSVM algorithm, and the lowest for EVM: 48 times shorter. In the case of $O_P = 75\%$, the longest running time was achieved by OSSVM, the shortest MCR-SVM - 12 times shorter. When analyzing running times for a scenario of hyperparameter optimization for MCC, visible differences in values are achieved by W-SVM compared to the previous scenario of hyperparameter optimization, as well as a somewhat different value distribution for OSSVM. The reason was the selection of significantly different values for one of the hyperparameters γ, as both algorithms are based on the SVM algorithm. However, for $O_P = 0\%$ still, OSSVM was the slowest, and the fastest was EVM, faster by 49 times. For $O_P = 75\%$ the slowest was also OSSVM, which was about 10 times slower than the fastest EVM.

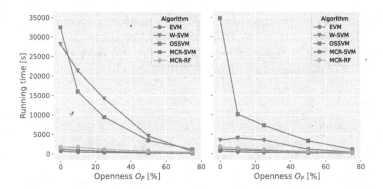

Fig. 4. Running times of five analyzed algorithms and *Hfinger's* request representation, including two hyperparameter optimization scenarios: for F1 (left) and MCC (right).

The above results can be used to evaluate the algorithms analyzed in the OSR scenario. Regarding classification efficiency, two algorithms stand out: OSSVM and MCR-SVM. Both achieve good results in the closed set scenario, better than the other algorithms, both in terms of the F1 measure and MCC. However, OSSVM classification results for higher openness levels do not decrease to such an extent as for MCR-SVM. The OSSVM algorithm achieves the best classification levels among OSR algorithms for all levels of openness, but the running time takes up to 49 times more than for EVM. Although W-SVM achieves good classification levels considering F1 when selecting hyperparameters for this measure, it achieves worse results than other OSR algorithms in the rest of the scenarios. When comparing analysis running times, EVM is better, being from 3 to 47 times faster. MCR-RF achieves good classification levels only for $O_P = 0\%$, for other openness values, the classification is worse than MCR-SVM, EVM, and OSSVM.

Given the characteristics of the three OSR algorithms studied above, a reasonable choice for malware classification in an open set scenario is the EVM algorithm, which has satisfactory classification levels and short running times. Of all algorithms tested, MCR-SVM is a good choice, providing good classification levels and, in terms of F1, better than EVM for openness levels up to 25%, although lower than MCC levels for openness levels from 25%. If it became possible to reduce the running time of the OSSVM significantly, it would probably be the best choice of all the algorithms tested.

The above recommendation about algorithm selection depends on the openness level of the analyzed data set. In real life scenarios this level is not known without prior analysis. The Open Set Recognition scenario provides a framework for detection of unknown malware families, however currently it does not answer the question how to calculate or estimate the openness level. One approach for this issue could be to introduce an additional analysis step for openness estimation. It could combine an OSR algorithm such as OSSVM or EVM and a non-OSR algorithm such as MCR-SVM, both providing prediction on a sample of network traffic, supervised by a human analyst to confirm the number of unknown malware families. Despite additional problems introduced with such an estimation scheme (e.g. False Positives or Negatives caused by human detection) it could provide a way to select the best algorithm for the monitored network. The problem of openness estimation should be further analyzed as a future work.

4.3 Comparison of Different HTTP Request Representations

In this section, two representations of HTTP requests are compared: the representation created by *Hfinger* and the trigram representation. The objective is to evaluate the usefulness of *Hfinger* for classifying malware versus the alternative method of representing requests. The comparison was performed using two machine learning algorithms selected in the previous section: EVM and MCR-SVM.

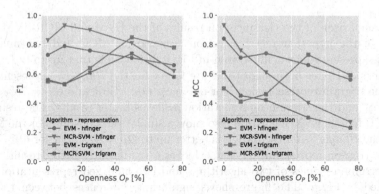

Fig. 5. Classification results of two analyzed algorithms for *Hfinger's* and trigram HTTP request representations (hyperparameter selection for F1).

A comparison of the classification results of the EVM and MCR-SVM algorithms in the hyperparameter selection scenario for F1 and two analyzed request representations is illustrated in Fig. 5. The figure shows that for F1 up to $O_P = 25\%$ *Hfinger's* representation reaches higher values than the trigram representation. The situation changes for openness at 50%. There is an increase in the values of F1 of both algorithms when using the trigram representation. Still, only EVM reaches values 16% higher for both cases $O_P = 50\%$ and $O_P = 75\%$ than when using *Hfinger's* representation. For the EVM algorithm, MCC values up to $O_P = 25\%$ are higher for *Hfinger's* representation. However, with openness increase for $O_P = 50\%$ and $O_P = 75\%$, the trigram representation performs better by 10% and 5%, respectively. In contrast, the MCR-SVM algorithm using *Hfinger's* representation for all levels of openness achieved higher MCC measure values than the trigram representation.

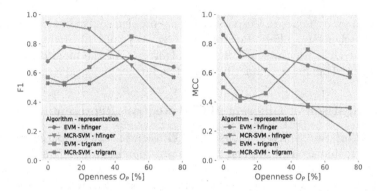

Fig. 6. Classification results of two analyzed algorithms for *Hfinger's* and trigram HTTP request representations (hyperparameter selection for MCC).

A comparison of the classification results of the EVM and MCR-SVM algorithms in the hyperparameter selection scenario for MCC and two analyzed request representations is illustrated in Fig. 6. It is visible that up to $O_P = 25\%$ the values of F1 for both algorithms are larger for the *Hfinger's* representation than the trigram representation. For openness $O_P = 50\%$ and $O_P = 75\%$ there is a swap, and the trigram representation achieves better results. The results of the MCC for the EVM algorithm also show a similar relationship. For the MCR-SVM, the *Hfinger's* representation is better up to $O_P = 50\%$, but for $O_P = 75\%$ it is the trigram representation that achieves a significantly better result.

The running times of two algorithms and two analyzed representations are presented in Fig. 7. The figure shows significant differences between the two representations' running times for both hyperparameter optimization scenarios. Also, for both cases, a decrease in the running time is seen with an increase in openness. When considering hyperparameter selection for F1, the longest running time for $O_P = 0\%$ is achieved by MCR-SVM and trigram representation, and the shortest by EVM and *Hfinger's* representation, taking 39 times more running time. The longest running time for $O_P = 75\%$ is achieved by EVM and trigram representation, and the shortest by MCR-SVM and *Hfinger's* representation, making a 26-fold difference.

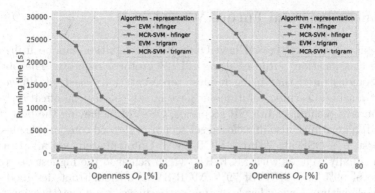

Fig. 7. Running times of two algorithms and two analyzed representations, including two hyperparameter optimization scenarios: for F1 (left) and MCC (right).

When considering hyperparameter selection for MCC, the longest running time for $O_P = 0\%$ is achieved by MCR-SVM and trigram representation, and the shortest by EVM and *Hfinger's* representation, making a 42-fold difference. The longest running time for $O_P = 75\%$ is achieved by MCR-SVM and the trigram representation, and the shortest by EVM and *Hfinger's* representation, making a 27-fold difference.

The comparison presented above shows that for openness levels up to 25%, *Hfinger's* representation achieves better classification levels than the trigram representation. Furthermore, of the two algorithms examined in this section, MCR-SVM performs better. However, for an openness greater than or equal to $O_P = 50\%$, the situation is reversed. The F1 and MCC measures increase for the EVM algorithm using the trigram representation, and it ultimately performs better than using *Hfinger's* representation, and also better than MCR-SVM regardless of the representation used by the latter.

In order to exclude particular data set selection as a cause of the reverse in classification levels between *Hfinger* and trigram representations, additional analyses for the latter were performed. Due to high computational and time demands of the trigram representation, only two different random generator seeds for data selection were chosen, and whole analysis was performed again for them using EVM algorithm. The results showed similar trend of increasing the classification metrics as the openness increases, what rules out a strong impact of data selection. With that in mind, the original results can indicate that the request features selected in *Hfinger* are less robust than those selected by trigram analysis. It can be explained by the feature selection schemes. In *Hfinger*, the features are static and selected before the analysis, whereas for trigrams, they are selected dynamically during analysis training phase. This comes for the price of high computational demand and long analysis times.

5 Conclusions and Future Work

In this paper, we investigated how Open Set Recognition can be utilized for malware classification purposes using HTTP protocol requests. The obtained results demonstrated that using request representation based on *Hfinger* and open set machine learning solutions achieve mostly better classification results than standard techniques in OSR scenarios. OSSVM, achieving the best results from OSR algorithms, also in a closed set scenario, showed comparable outcomes to the best, non-OSR algorithm – MCR-SVM. Unfortunately, not all algorithms perform equally well, as with MCR-RF, which achieved the highest decrease in F1 value of 69% and MCC of 79%. MCR-SVM, although not designed as an open set algorithm, for low levels of openness achieves good classification results relative to OSR algorithms. Considering the running time, the EVM algorithm, despite achieving worse classification results than OSSVM or partially MCR-SVM, can be seen as a reasonable choice due to its relatively fast performance. The longest time was achieved by W-SVM and OSSVM algorithms – in total, the analysis running time took up to 49 times longer.

A comparison of the HTTP request representation of *Hfinger* and the trigram representation showed that for openness up to 25%, it is *Hfinger* representation that performs much better. However, for the openness of 50%, there is a change, and the trigram representation is superior. Unfortunately, the use of this representation causes a significant increase in running times. For example, for EVM, they increased up to 39 times, and for MCR-SVM, up to 27 times.

The final recommendation for creating a malware classification system based on HTTP requests and in OSR scenarios is to use EVM and MCR-SVM algorithms based on the representation of *Hfinger*. It will be possible to see the classification results relatively fast and adapt the system to the analyzed data set. However, of the two, only the EVM algorithm is an OSR algorithm, providing open set risk bounding. Some of the elements of the conducted analysis can still be improved. The number of machine learning algorithms analyzed, as well as the number of openness levels, can be extended. Also, other request representations can be used. For example, converting requests into bitmaps and processing them as images in specialized neural networks. In the above analysis, such solutions were omitted. Classic, feature-based algorithms seemed to the authors as faster in implementation and deployment, thus promising faster verification of the research approach.

Some issues can be seen in the research protocol. It was designed with a focus on minimizing the estimation bias of classification while reducing the number of classification operations. The chosen scheme of nested hyperparameter selection or repetition of data set partitioning can be performed more times, or replaced by an adapted nested cross-validation scheme in the main estimation loop.

Finally, a rather important issue of the true openness level of real-world data. In laboratory conditions, this level was defined and completely controlled. In real-world conditions, the openness of the analyzed malware data sets is unknown. This issue should be further analyzed.

A   Hyperparameters' Values Searched During Optimization

The below hyperparameters' values were searched during model optimization phase using HalvingGridSearchCV function, provided by the Scikit-learn package and a modified holdout validation. The whole selection procedure is discussed in details in Sect. 3.1.

1. W-SVM
    (a) C: 10^{-3} - 10^3,
    (b) $gamma$: 10^{-3} - 10^3
    (c) $\delta_\tau = 0.001$ (a constant value as suggested by the authors of the algorithm),
    (d) $\delta_R = 0.5 \times O^*$.
2. EVM
    (a) τ: 25, 50, 75, 100, 150, 200, 300, 400, 500, 600, 700, 800, 900, 1000, 1500, 2000,
    (b) δ: $0.5 \times O^*$
    (c) k: 3, 4, 5, 6,
    (d) ζ: 0.1, 0.2, 0.3, 0.4, 0.5, 0.6, 0.7.
3. OSSVM
    (a) $lambda$: 0,0, 0,1, 0,2, ..., 0,9
    (b) C: 10^{-3} - 10^3,
    (c) $gamma$: 10^{-3} - 10^3
4. Multiclass SVM algorithm with rejection threshold
    (a) C: 10^{-3} - 10^3,
    (b) $gamma$: 10^{-3} - 10^3
5. Multi-class Random Forest algorithm with rejection threshold
    (a) number of trees in the forest: 100, 200, 300, 500, 750, 1000, 1500, 2000,
    (b) split quality criteria: gini, entropy,
    (c) maximum number of features when looking for the best split: auto, None, log2, 0.4, 0.5, 0.6.

References

1. AV-TEST: Malware statistics & trends report. https://www.av-test.org/en/statistics/malware/. Accessed 23 May 2023
2. Bai, H., Liu, G., Liu, W., Quan, Y., Huang, S.: N-gram, semantic-based neural network for mobile malware network traffic detection, 1–17 (2021)
3. Bekerman, D., Shapira, B., Rokach, L., Bar, A.: Unknown malware detection using network traffic classification. In: 2015 IEEE Conference on Communications and Network Security (CNS), pp. 134–142. IEEE
4. Białczak, P., Mazurczyk, W.: Characterizing anomalies in malware-generated HTTP traffic. Secur. Commun. Netw. **2020**, 1–26 (2020)
5. Białczak, P., Mazurczyk, W.: Hfinger: malware HTTP request fingerprinting. Entropy **23**(5), 507 (2021)

6. Bishop, M.: HTTP/3. RFC 9114 (2022). https://doi.org/10.17487/RFC9114, https://www.rfc-editor.org/info/rfc9114

7. Boult, T.E., Cruz, S., Dhamija, A., Gunther, M., Henrydoss, J., Scheirer, W.: Learning and the unknown: Surveying steps toward open world recognition. In: Proceedings of the AAAI Conference on Artificial Intelligence, vol. 33, no. 01, pp. 9801–9807 (2019)

8. contributors, C.E.: Category encoders. https://contrib.scikit-learn.org/category_encoders/. Accessed 23 May 2023

9. Cruz, S., Coleman, C., Rudd, E.M., Boult, T.E.: Open Set Intrusion Recognition for Fine-Grained Attack Categorization. arXiv:1703.02244 [cs] (Mar 2017)

10. scikit-learn documentation: Choosing the right estimator. https://scikit-learn.org/stable/tutorial/machine_learning_map/index.html. Accessed 23 May 2023

11. Eslahi, M., Abidin, W.Z., Naseri, M.V.: Correlation-based HTTP botnet detection using network communication histogram analysis. In: 2017 IEEE Conference on Application, Information and Network Security (AINS), pp. 7–12. IEEE (2017)

12. Fielding, R., et al.: RFC 2616: Hypertext Transfer Protocol - HTTP/1.1 (1999)

13. Geng, C., Huang, S.J., Chen, S.: Recent advances in open set recognition: a survey. IEEE Trans. Pattern Anal. Mach. Intell. 43(10), 3614–3631 (2021)

14. Grill, M., Rehak, M.: Malware detection using HTTP user-agent discrepancy identification. In: 2014 IEEE International Workshop on Information Forensics and Security (WIFS), pp. 221–226. IEEE (2014)

15. Guo, J., Guo, S., Ma, S., Sun, Y., Xu, Y.: Conservative novelty synthesizing network for malware recognition in an open-set scenario. IEEE Trans. Neural Netw. Learn. Syst. 34(2), 662–676 (2021)

16. Hassen, M., Chan, P.K.: Learning a neural-network-based representation for open set recognition. In: Proceedings of the 2020 SIAM International Conference on Data Mining, pp. 154–162. SIAM (2020)

17. Henrydoss, J., Cruz, S., Rudd, E.M., Gunther, M., Boult, T.E.: Incremental Open Set Intrusion Recognition Using Extreme Value Machine. In: 16th IEEE International Conference on Machine Learning and Applications, pp. 1089–1093. IEEE, Cancun (Dec 2017)

18. Jain, L.P.: libsvm-openset - original source code. https://github.com/ljain2/libsvm-openset. Accessed 23 May 2023

19. Jain, S., Meena, Y.K.: Byte level n-gram analysis for malware detection. In: Venugopal, K.R., Patnaik, L.M. (eds.) Computer Networks and Intelligent Computing, pp. 51–59. Springer, Berlin Heidelberg, Berlin, Heidelberg (2011)

20. Jia, J., Chan, P.K.: Representation learning with function call graph transformations for malware open set recognition. In: 2022 International Joint Conference on Neural Networks (IJCNN), pp. 1–8 (2022)

21. Jurafsky, D., Martin, J.: Speech and Language Processing, 2nd edn. Pearson, Upper Saddle River (2008)

22. Júnior, P.R.M.: Extreme value machine - updated source code. https://github.com/pedrormjunior/ExtremeValueMachine. Accessed 23 May 2023

23. Júnior, P.R.M.: Open-set support vector machines - original source code. https://github.com/pedrormjunior/ossvm. Accessed 23 May 2023

24. Júnior, P.R.M., Boult, T.E., Wainer, J., Rocha, A.: Open-set support vector machines. IEEE Trans. Syst. Man Cybern. Syst. 52, 1–14 (2021)

25. Kheir, Nizar, Blanc, Gregory, Debar, Hervé, Garcia-Alfaro, Joaquin, Yang, Dingqi: Automated classification of C&C connections through malware URL clustering. In: Federrath, Hannes, Gollmann, Dieter (eds.) SEC 2015. IAICT, vol. 455, pp. 252–266. Springer, Cham (2015). https://doi.org/10.1007/978-3-319-18467-8_17

26. Laboratory, S.R.: Malware capture facility project. https://www.stratosphereips. org/datasets-malware. Accessed 23 May 2023

27. Lemaître, G., Nogueira, F., Aridas, C.K.: Imbalanced-learn: a python toolbox to tackle the curse of imbalanced datasets in machine learning. J. Mach. Learn. Res. **18**(17), 1–5 (2017)

28. Li, K., Chen, R., Gu, L., Liu, C., Yin, J.: A method based on statistical characteristics for detection malware requests in network traffic. In: 2018 IEEE Third International Conference on Data Science in Cyberspace (DSC), pp. 527–532. IEEE (2018)

29. Li, Zhiqiang, Sun, Lichao, Yan, Qiben, Srisa-an, Witawas, Chen, Zhenxiang: DroidClassifier: efficient adaptive mining of application-layer header for classifying android malware. In: Deng, Robert, Weng, Jian, Ren, Kui, Yegneswaran, Vinod (eds.) SecureComm 2016. LNICST, vol. 198, pp. 597–616. Springer, Cham (2017). https://doi.org/10.1007/978-3-319-59608-2_33

30. Liu, Z., Li, S., Zhang, Y., Yun, X., Cheng, Z.: Efficient malware originated traffic classification by using generative adversarial networks. In: 2020 IEEE Symposium on Computers and Communications (ISCC), pp. 1–7. IEEE (2020)

31. Marín, Gonzalo, Caasas, Pedro, Capdehourat, Germán: DeepMAL - deep learning models for malware traffic detection and classification. In: Data Science – Analytics and Applications, pp. 105–112. Springer, Wiesbaden (2021). https://doi.org/10. 1007/978-3-658-32182-6_16

32. Mizuno, S., Hatada, M., Mori, T., Goto, S.: BotDetector: a robust and scalable approach toward detecting malware-infected devices. In: 2017 IEEE International Conference on Communications (ICC), pp. 1–7. IEEE (2017)

33. Oza, A., Ross, K., Low, R.M., Stamp, M.: HTTP attack detection using n-gram analysis. Comput. Secur. **45**, 242–254 (2014)

34. Pedregosa, F., et al.: Scikit-learn: machine learning in Python. J. Mach. Learn. Res. **12**, 2825–2830 (2011)

35. Perdisci, R., Ariu, D., Giacinto, G.: Scalable fine-grained behavioral clustering of HTTP-based malware. Comput. Netw. **57**(2), 487–500 (2013)

36. Qi, Biao, Shi, Zhixin, Wang, Yan, Wang, Jizhi, Wang, Qiwen, Jiang, Jianguo: BotTokenizer: exploring network tokens of HTTP-based botnet using malicious network traces. In: Chen, Xiaofeng, Lin, Dongdai, Yung, Moti (eds.) Inscrypt 2017. LNCS, vol. 10726, pp. 383–403. Springer, Cham (2018). https://doi.org/10.1007/ 978-3-319-75160-3_23

37. Resende, P.A.A., Drummond, A.C.: HTTP and contact-based features for botnet detection. Secur. Priv. **1**(5), e41 (2018)

38. Rudd, E.M., Jain, L.P., Scheirer, W.J., Boult, T.E.: Extreme value machine - original source code. https://github.com/EMRResearch/ExtremeValueMachine. Accessed 23 May 2023

39. Rudd, E.M., Jain, L.P., Scheirer, W.J., Boult, T.E.: The extreme value machine. IEEE Trans. Pattern Anal. Mach. Intell. **40**(3), 762–768 (2018)

40. Sakib, M.N., Huang, C.T.: Using anomaly detection based techniques to detect HTTP-based botnet C&C traffic. In: 2016 IEEE International Conference on Communications (ICC), pp. 1–6. IEEE (2016)

41. Scheirer, W.J., Jain, L.P., Boult, T.E.: Probability models for open set recognition. IEEE Trans. Pattern Anal. Mach. Intell. **36**(11), 2317–2324 (2014)

42. Souza, M.M.C., Pontes, C., Gondim, J., Garcia, L.P.F., DaSilva, L., Marotta, M.A.: A novel open set energy-based flow classifier for network intrusion detection (2022)

43. Taheri, S., Salem, M., Yuan, J.S.: Leveraging image representation of network traffic data and transfer learning in botnet detection. Big Data Cogn. Comput. **2**(4), 37 (2018)
44. Thomson, M., Benfield, C.: HTTP/2. RFC 9113 (2022). https://doi.org/10.17487/RFC9113, https://www.rfc-editor.org/info/rfc9113
45. Wang, K., Cretu, G., Stolfo, S.J.: Anomalous payload-based worm detection and signature generation. In: Proceedings of the 8th International Conference on Recent Advances in Intrusion Detection, pp. 227–246. RAID 2005 (2005)
46. Xie, J., Li, S., Yun, X., Zhang, Y., Chang, P.: HSTF-model: an HTTP-based trojan detection model via the hierarchical spatio-temporal features of traffics. Comput. Secur. **96**, 101923 (2020)
47. Zarras, A., Papadogiannakis, A., Gawlik, R., Holz, T.: Automated generation of models for fast and precise detection of HTTP-based malware. In: 2014 Twelfth Annual International Conference on Privacy, Security and Trust, pp. 249–256. IEEE (2014)
48. Zhang, Z., Zhang, Y., Guo, D., Song, M.: A scalable network intrusion detection system towards detecting, discovering, and learning unknown attacks. Int. J. Mach. Learn. Cybern. **12**(6), 1649–1665 (2021)

Static Semantics Reconstruction
for Enhancing JavaScript-WebAssembly
Multilingual Malware Detection

Yifan Xia, Ping He, Xuhong Zhang$^{(\boxtimes)}$, Peiyu Liu, Shouling Ji,
and Wenhai Wang$^{(\boxtimes)}$

Zhejiang University, Zhejiang University NGICS Platform, Hangzhou, China
{yfxia,gnip,zhangxuhong,liupeiyu,sji,zdzzlab}@zju.edu.cn

Abstract. The emergence of WebAssembly allows attackers to hide
the malicious functionalities of JavaScript malware in cross-language
interoperations, termed JavaScript-WebAssembly multilingual malware
(JWMM). However, existing anti-virus solutions based on static program
analysis are still limited to monolingual code. As a result, their detection effectiveness decreases significantly against JWMM. The detection
of JWMM is challenging due to the complex interoperations and semantic diversity between JavaScript and WebAssembly. To bridge this gap,
we present JWBinder, the first technique aimed at enhancing the static
detection of JWMM. JWBinder performs a language-specific data-flow
analysis to capture the cross-language interoperations and then characterizes the functionalities of JWMM through a unified high-level structure called Inter-language Program Dependency Graph. The extensive
evaluation on one of the most representative real-world anti-virus platforms, VirusTotal, shows that JWBinder effectively enhances anti-virus
systems from various vendors and increases the overall successful detection rate against JWMM from 49.1% to 86.2%. Additionally, we assess
the side effects and runtime overhead of JWBinder, corroborating its
practical viability in real-world applications.

Keywords: Malware and Unwanted Software · Software Security ·
Web Security

1 Introduction

JavaScript is a highly prevalent scripting language known for its significant role
in web application development [3]. In recent years, it has also extended its
influence beyond the browser with the support of NodeJS [19]. The ubiquity
of JavaScript naturally makes it a target for attackers, giving rise to a variety
of attack vectors, such as CryptoJacking [31], Drive-by-download attacks [34]
and JavaScript Skimmers [2]. Additionally, attackers have now started exploiting Open Source Software (OSS) by injecting malicious JavaScript third-party
packages into public registries like NPM [1].

© The Author(s), under exclusive license to Springer Nature Switzerland AG 2024
G. Tsudik et al. (Eds.): ESORICS 2023, LNCS 14345, pp. 255–276, 2024.
https://doi.org/10.1007/978-3-031-51476-0_13

To counter these threats, current anti-virus solutions employ sophisticated program analysis techniques for malicious JavaScript detection [6, 7, 20, 25, 26, 28–30, 36, 41–43]. Such approaches can be partitioned into two categories: static and dynamic approaches. Static approaches extract code features of varying granularities (e.g., Abstraction Syntax Tree (AST) [26] and Program Dependence Graph (PDG) [28]) from JavaScript without executing it. These features are then used for machine learning techniques [26, 28, 36] or program similarity analysis [41, 43] to differentiate benign and malicious code. On the other hand, dynamic approaches detect abnormal JavaScript behavior (e.g., sensitive API calls) by running it in a honey client or sandbox [6, 20]. Each approach has its own strengths and weaknesses. However, dynamic approaches are often burdened with considerable runtime overhead and struggle to detect malicious behaviors only manifesting under specific configurations. Thus, static approaches often form the preferred choice for anti-virus solutions due to their scalability and efficiency, consequently making them a prime target for attackers [27, 37, 40].

Despite the considerable ability of static approaches to detect malware, existing defense methods tend to assume that programs in the JavaScript ecosystem (e.g., Web and NodeJS) are composed purely of JavaScript. However, this assumption may no longer be held with the introduction of WebAssembly [22] in 2015. WebAssembly is an emerging binary code language that complements JavaScript. Initially designed for computation-intensive tasks, WebAssembly can be called upon by JavaScript programs through foreign language interfaces, which also provides new opportunities for attackers to create JavaScript-WebAssembly Multilingual Malware (JWMM) [24, 37]. Specifically, attackers can conceal malicious behaviors within the interoperations between JavaScript and WebAssembly. Consequently, prior works that statically extract program features solely from JavaScript [25, 26, 28–30, 36, 41–43] could hardly identify these concealed malicious behaviors. Even the existing works [38] that consider malicious WebAssembly struggle to mitigate this threat because the malicious behaviors of JWMM are concealed behind the cross-language interoperations, which are unlikely to be identified with detectors focusing on a single language.

The effectiveness of JWMM against static approaches raises legitimate concerns. However, the detection of JWMM presents two major challenges:

C1: *Interoperation Complexity.* A fundamental step in characterizing JWMM involves understanding how JavaScript interacts with WebAssembly units in JWMM. This is far from a trivial task due to the complexity stemming from the intricate mechanisms upon which the interoperations of JavaScript and WebAssembly depend. For example, there are various interfaces to initialize a WebAssembly instance in JavaScript. Additionally, both languages can import and invoke functions from each other in adherence to the language standard [16]. Without recognizing these interoperations, it is difficult to unify the semantics of different language units in JWMM.

C2: *Semantics Diversity.* Existing works capture various patterns and features in sole language for distinguishing monolingual malware [25, 29, 38, 43]. However, JavaScript and WebAssembly have disparate language semantics. Therefore, the characterization of the JWMM's functionalities necessitates the consideration of both JavaScript and WebAssembly semantics. Furthermore, even if we consider the semantics of both JavaScript and WebAssembly, the definition of malicious patterns/features in multilingual programs remains an open issue.

In this paper, we present JWBinder, the first technique that characterizes the functionalities of JavaScript-WebAssembly multilingual programs to enhance the static detection of JWMM. To tackle C1, JWBinder presents a language-specific data-flow analysis to capture the interoperations between JavaScript and WebAssembly. Specifically, for the target JWMM, JWBinder constructs and traverses the PDG of its JavaScript unit. Then, by tracing the data dependencies flowing into and out of the foreign language interfaces, JWBinder can identify the concealed WebAssembly units in JWMM and detect how JavaScript and WebAssembly interact with each other. For example, the instantiation of WebAssembly which passes JavaScript external functions to WebAssembly instances, or the invocation point of a WebAssembly internal function in the JavaScript unit.

The solution of C2 relies on the crucial observation that, while WebAssembly's semantics differs significantly from JavaScript, it shares some unified features derived from JavaScript, such as similar control-flow instructions and basic data instructions [23]. Furthermore, WebAssembly can only invoke privileged system functions by importing them from JavaScript rather than through customized implementation. These homogeneous features allow us to design a uniform abstract representation that characterizes the functionalities of JavaScript-WebAssembly multilingual programs at a high level.

Based on the above insight, we propose a novel technique called *Static Semantics Reconstruction* (SSR). Leveraging the homogeneous features between JavaScript and WebAssembly, we first design a set of abstraction rules which encapsulate the semantics of WebAssembly at a high level. Following our abstraction rules, SSR generates a JavaScript-like abstract representation of the JWMM's WebAssembly units. Then, SSR integrates the abstract representations of WebAssembly units into JavaScript PDG to construct a uniform structure termed Inter-language PDG (IPDG), which characterizes the semantics within and across the JavaScript and WebAssembly units. Rather than designing ad-hoc heuristics to enumerate the malicious patterns of JWMM using the IPDG, SSR's final phase involves translating the IPDG and reconstructing a pure JavaScript program, which serves to elucidate the functionalities of the initial JWMM. The rationale is that since the IPDG is originally constructed following JavaScript abstract syntax, it can be naturally translated back to JavaScript by node traversing. Anti-virus solutions can further examine this reconstructed pure JavaScript program to determine the malignancy of the original JWMM.

The reconstruction of pure JavaScript programs offers two primary benefits. Firstly, it transforms the challenge of identifying multilingual malware into the more straightforward task of detecting monolingual malware. This allows the reuse of detection patterns/features designed for monolingual malware, thereby effectively addressing the semantic diversity problem. Secondly, with JWBinder acting as a preliminary process, existing anti-virus solutions that concentrate solely on JavaScript can be employed directly to detect JWMM without any modifications, enhancing this approach's practicality for real-world applications.

To validate our design, we build a JWMM dataset based on 44,369 real-world JavaScript malware and evaluate JWBinder using this dataset. We have the following results. First, the approach is effective in enhancing the detection capabilities of well-known commercial Anti-Virus Systems (AV-Systems): With the application of JWBinder, the overall successful detection rate of VirusTotal [21] increases from 49.1% to 86.2%. Meanwhile, the number of AV-Systems successfully detecting malicious samples has increased from 4.1 to 8.3 on average. Second, JWBinder introduces nearly no side effects to benign programs: Processing a benign JavaScript-WebAssembly multilingual programs dataset and uploading them to VirusTotal, the results show minimal differences (0.5% false positive rate) compared to the original benign cases. This demonstrates that JWBinder does not induce suspicious behaviors which influence the detection of benign multilingual programs. Third, we investigate the generalization ability of JWBinder on AV-Systems from different vendors. The results show that more than 10 different AV-Systems significantly benefit from JWBinder. In particular, AV-Systems from different vendors may favor particular variants of JWBinder. Lastly, we find that our tool only requires, on average, 25.6 s to process a single JWMM program (with an average size of 282 KB), which is acceptable in comparison to previous JavaScript program analysis works [29,32]. Collectively, these results indicate that JWBinder is a practical tool for the enhancement of real-world anti-virus solutions.

In summary, this paper offers the following contributions:

- We propose the first program analysis technique designed to counter JWMM, which solutes the challenge of interoperation complexity and semantics diversity for analyzing JWMM.
- We implement the prototype of JWBinder, with a data-flow analysis framework for capturing cross-language interoperations in JWMM and a novel method termed static semantic reconstruction to characterize the unified functionalities of JWMM.
- We conduct a comprehensive evaluation demonstrating that our approach effectively enhances state-of-the-art anti-virus solutions and provides an analysis of their internal mechanisms.

To foster further research, we will release our experiment data and implementation at [14]. We believe that JWBinder provides valuable insights to detect JavaScript-WebAssembly multilingual malware.

2   Background and Motivation

2.1   WebAssembly

WebAssembly [22], a low-level binary instruction format, has become a fundamental web standard due to its secure and efficient characteristics. It facilitates web development by enhancing the performance of applications and enabling seamless integration with JavaScript.

The WebAssembly binary includes multiple sections. Most notably, its code section holds the functional components, while the memory and data section manages linear memory for runtime behavior. The instructions of WebAssembly work at a low level to comprise simple operations such as arithmetic, control flow, and memory access. Some of the instructions share similar semantics to high-level languages (e.g., loop, branch, variable declaration/usage instructions), while others have special functionality corresponding to specific features (e.g., memory instructions, bit-level numeric instructions) of WebAssembly.

WebAssembly does not have a standard library, which means it can not directly access system APIs. To perform such functionalities, WebAssembly must import external functions from its host language (e.g., JavaScript). To achieve this, JavaScript uses foreign language interfaces (FFI) [16] to modularize and instantiate (that is, fulfill the imports of) WebAssembly modules and call exported WebAssembly functions.

2.2 JavaScript-WebAssembly Multilingual Malware

We define JavaScript-WebAssembly Multilingual Malware (JWMM) as a family of malware which hides malicious behaviors across the interoperations between JavaScript and WebAssembly. To evade the detection of anti-virus solutions, known JWMM often abuses WebAssembly binary for hiding sensitive instructions and data, and changing the control flow of JavaScript [24,37].

Alan et al. [37] developed Wobfuscator to generate JWMM automatically and demonstrated its efficacy against academic machine-learning-based classifiers. In this paper, we extend this investigation by testing JWMM's evasion abilities against a leading anti-virus platform, VirusTotal. We found that over half of the JWMM samples successfully evaded VirusTotal's detection, more details will be discussed in Sect. 4.

2.3 A Motivating Example

Figure 1 depicts a motivating example to illustrate how JWMM evades the detection of existing anti-virus solutions for JavaScript malware.

Figure 1.a shows a real-world pure JavaScript malware successfully detected by McAfee-GW-Edition [15]. To conduct the attack, it iteratively executes the **document.write** function (lines 7–9) to insert pre-defined malicious payloads (lines 2–5) into HTML. Figure 1.b and Fig. 1.c present the JavaScript part and WebAssembly part (in human-readable format) of the JWMM which perform equivalent malicious functionalities to Fig. 1.a.

Next, we explain how this JWMM evades detection by abusing the interoperations between JavaScript and WebAssembly. In Fig. 1.b, the JavaScript part of JWMM only needs to instantiate a WebAssembly instance by calling the FFI sequence (lines 2–6), and then invokes the internal function **foo** exported from

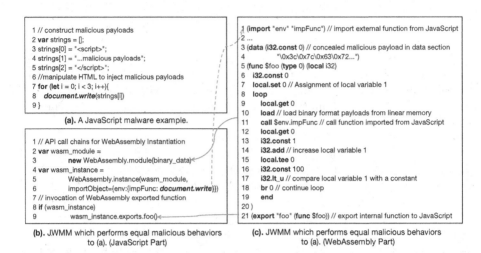

Fig. 1. An example of JWMM (b and c) and its equivalent JavaScript malware (a) (Color figure online)

the WebAssembly part (the blue solid line). In other words, it conceals the malicious functionalities in the WebAssembly. While in Fig. 1.c, the WebAssembly part imports the **document.write** from JavaScript (the red dashed line) and iteratively executes the function in a loop (lines 8–19) with transformed binary-format malicious payloads stored in its data section (lines 3–4).

Existing anti-virus solutions designed for pure JavaScript are not effective in detecting such JWMM. Also, merely analyzing the WebAssembly binary additionally could hardly reveal cross-language malicious functionalities if we are not aware of the exact imported function from JavaScript (i.e. **document.write**).

This example not only illustrates how JWMM evades the detection of monolingual anti-virus solutions, thereby emphasizing the necessity for a cross-language, comprehensive analysis, but also motivates our insights to reconstruct JWMM to a monolingual format, as depicted in Fig. 1.a. By doing so, we can expose its malicious functionalities for monolingual anti-virus solutions to identify.

3   JWBinder

This section describes our technique approach. We start with an overview (Sect. 3.1) of JWBinder and then elaborate two critical phases: language-specific data-flow analysis (Sect. 3.2) and static semantic reconstruction (Sect. 3.3).

3.1   Approach Overview

Figure 2 gives the overview of JWBinder. The input of JWBinder is the JavaScript-WebAssembly multilingual program under detection. With the input, JWBinder works in two phases. In Phase 1, JWBinder first abstracts the

JavaScript unit of the multilingual program to construct the JavaScript PDG. We adopt the definition of PDG followed Fass et al. [29], which integrates the control-flow and data-flow dependencies into the Abstract Syntax Tree of the JavaScript unit. Next, JWBinder traverses the PDG to perform a bi-directional data-flow analysis which captures the interoperation between JavaScript and WebAssembly.

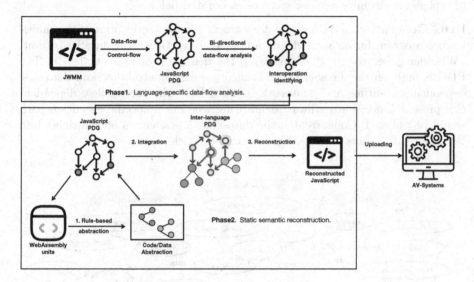

Fig. 2. An overview of JWBinder

After Phase 1, the functionalities of WebAssembly are still invisible on the JavaScript PDG. Thus, JWBinder starts its Phase 2 to construct a language-agnostic structure for characterizing the functionalities of multilingual programs. In Phase 2, JWBinder first extracts the WebAssembly units in the multilingual program based on the identified interoperations in Phase 1. For every individual WebAssembly unit, JWBinder abstracts its code and data sections following a set of abstraction rules, which concentrate on the homogeneous semantics between JavaScript and WebAssembly. The abstractions of WebAssembly units are then integrated into the JavaScript PDG to construct a uniform language-agnostic structure termed Inter-language Program Dependency Graph (IPDG). Finally, JWBinder reconstructs a pure JavaScript program based on the IPDG, transforming the problem of detecting multilingual malware back into monolingual malware. As a result, JWBinder outputs pure JavaScript programs that statically characterize the original multilingual program's functionalities, making these outputs ready for detection by monolingual anti-virus solutions (e.g., AV-Systems).

3.2   Phase 1: Language-Specific Data-Flow Analysis

At a high level, a JavaScript-WebAssembly multilingual program comprises a JavaScript program that interacts with WebAssembly through specific interfaces, with the WebAssembly units concealed in the JavaScript unit. To characterize the functionalities of the multilingual program, JWBinder should be able to recognize how JavaScript interacts with WebAssembly units. To this goal, the first phase works in two major steps as elaborated below.

PDG Generation. JWBinder first abstracts the JavaScript unit of the multilingual program for an in-depth data-flow analysis. Given the JavaScript unit, JWBinder generates its PDG following the definition of Fass et al. [29]. The PDG is built on the JavaScript AST, incorporating control-flow and data-flow dependencies during AST traversal. In the PDG, The control-flow dependencies present a decision pathway, delineating whether a specific execution path would be pursued. Concurrently, the data-flow dependencies offer insights into the interrelationships among different variables within the program.

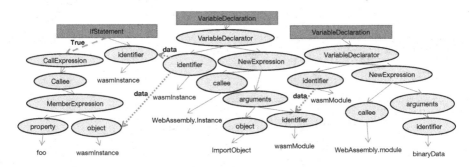

Fig. 3. Example PDG of Fig. 1.b (some nodes are simplified for clarity) (Color figure online)

For instance, Fig. 3 is the PDG of the JavaScript program shown in Fig. 1.b. The control dependency labeled as "True" (red dashed line) suggests that the program path will be pursued only when the preceding condition holds true. Meanwhile, the data dependencies (green dot lines) present the definition and usage relationships of different variables (e.g., wasmInstance and wasmModule). Both these dependencies are valuable for identifying the interoperation between JavaScript and WebAssembly.

Interoperation Identification. Once the JavaScript PDG is constructed, JWBinder conducts a bi-directional data-flow analysis to capture the interoperation between JavaScript and WebAssembly. The multilingual interoperation patterns normally contain the modularization/instantiation of WebAssembly and the invocation of WebAssembly properties. The former process enables JavaScript to pass external properties into WebAssembly, while the latter makes

JavaScript invoke the internal properties of WebAssembly. For example, in Fig. 1.b, the JWMM compiles a WebAssembly module (*wasmModule* in lines 2–3), employs the module to instantiate a WebAssembly instance (*wasmInstance* in lines 4–6) with external function *document.write()*, and finally calls an internal function from the WebAssembly instance (*wasmInstance.foo()* in line 9).

To capture the above interoperation patterns, JWBinder traverses the PDG to identify the key APIs and properties (listed in Fig. 4 within the Appendix) for WebAssembly modularization or instantiation. Upon encountering one of these key APIs, JWBinder marks the relevant PDG nodes as interoperation positions and discerns the external properties passed into WebAssembly through the APIs. Then JWBinder undertakes a forward data-flow analysis to trace the locations where JavaScript invokes internal properties of the WebAssembly instances. Meanwhile, a backward data-flow analysis is also conducted to trace the concealed binary format WebAssembly for further abstractions in Phase 2. We detail the algorithm in Algorithm 1 within the Appendix. Ultimately, JWBinder generates a JavaScript PDG where the cross-language interoperations are distinctly marked, providing a clear depiction of the intricate connections between JavaScript and WebAssembly.

3.3   Phase 2: Static Semantic Reconstruction

JWBinder performs the static semantic reconstruction (SSR) to characterize the functionalities of JWMM after the interoperations between JavaScript and WebAssembly have been identified. The key insight behind SSR is the integration of JavaScript and WebAssembly semantics into a uniform representation based on their homogeneous features. In particular, Phase 2 works in three steps as elaborated below.

Rule-Based Abstraction. A joint analysis for multilingual programs requires a uniform representation that merges both JavaScript and WebAssembly semantics. Since the main module of JWMM is the JavaScript unit, JWBinder integrates the semantics of WebAssembly units into the JavaScript PDG generated in Phase 1 for multilingual analysis. However, this is a non-trivial process due to the disparate semantics of JavaScript and WebAssembly. Most importantly, JavaScript is a dynamically typed language, while WebAssembly is a statically typed language, which has diverse data types. The disparity makes it difficult to unify the cross-language semantics within JWMM.

JWBinder addresses this challenge by introducing a set of abstraction rules, which extracts high-level semantics from WebAssembly to unify different language units. The critical insight of our abstraction rules is that they focus on homogeneous features between JavaScript and WebAssembly, such as similar data-related operations (e.g., variable declaration and usage) and logic-related instructions (e.g., loop structures and condition statements). Based on this, JWBinder is able to translate the semantics of WebAssembly to JavaScript-like AST nodes and bridge the semantic gap between JavaScript and WebAssembly.

In general, the abstraction rules fall into two categories: code abstraction and data abstraction, targeting code and data sections mentioned in Sect. 2. We now introduce different categories of abstract rules.

The **code** abstraction rules aim to characterize the functionalities of internal functions defined in WebAssembly's code section. For example, in Fig. 1.b, the definition of the function *foo* (line 9) lies in WebAssembly's code section. SSR reveals its functionality by abstracting the corresponding WebAssembly instructions (lines 5–20 in Fig. 1.c). WebAssembly code instructions execute on a stack machine, in that instructions manipulate values on an implicit operand stack, consuming (popping) argument values and producing or returning (pushing) result values [23]. To abstract these instructions, we should first capture the data relationships between stack values. Therefore, we model WebAssembly instructions based on their effects on the stack, following the simulation of [38]. According to the stack state, we design specific rules for different code instructions to extract their high-level semantics and abstract them to JavaScript ES6 [13] syntax units. We choose ES6 syntax abstractions because it helps to characterize WebAssembly instructions within JavaScript syntax, which strengthens the homogeneity between these two languages.

Table 1. Abstraction rules

Instruction	Stack Operation	Abstractions	Equivalent JavaScript
get_local v	push(v)		
i32.const c	push(c)	VariableDeclaration -> [id -> C_n , init -> c, kind -> const]	const C_n = c;
set_local v	pop() -> e	AssignStatement -> [id -> v , init -> e]	v = e ;
i32.mul	pop() -> e_1, pop() -> e_2, push(e_1 * e_2)	VariableDeclaration -> [id -> V_n , kind -> let, init -> BinaryExpression -> [left -> e_1, right -> e_2, op: *]]	let V_n = e_1 * e_2;
i32.popcnt	pop() -> e, push(popcnt())	VariableDeclaration -> [id -> V_n , kind -> let, init -> CallExpression -> [callee -> popcnt, arguments -> [e]]	let V_n = popcnt(e);
loop/block g		LabelStatement -> [body -> ForStatement -> [init, test->true, update, body -> [...]] , label -> g]	g: for(;true;){...};
if I	pop() -> e	IfStatement -> [test -> e, body-> [...], alternate -> [...]]	if (e) {...};
br g		BreakStatement -> [label -> g] (in block context) ; ContinueStatement -> [label -> g] (in loop context)	break g ; (in block context) continue g ; (in loop context))
call f	paraNum(f) -> n, for(i=0;i<n;i++) pop -> e_i	CallExpression -> [callee - > f, arguments -> [e_1, e_2, ... , e_n]]	f(e_1,e_2,...,e_n);
call_indirect	pop() -> e, paraNum(f) -> n, for(i=0;i<n;i++) pop -> e_i	CallExpression -> [callee - > f_e, arguments -> [e_1, e_2, ... , e_n]]	f_e(e_1,e_2,...,e_n);
data (type) "payloads"		VariableDeclaration -> [id -> memory , kind -> var, init -> BinaryExpression -> [left -> e_1, right -> e_2, op: *]]	var memory = "payloads";

Table 1 shows a subset of the abstraction rules. Due to the space limit, we present the full version on our website [14] and only list abstraction rules for the key data-flow and control-flow instructions. For instructions that do not assign variables or manipulate control flows, such as "local_get" which only fetches an existing local variable and pushes it onto the stack, we models their stack operation without generating abstractions.

Data-Flow Instruction. WebAssembly functions operate their variables following the "def-use" chain like high-level programming languages. We abstract such data-flow instructions as the foundation to characterize the semantics of WebAssembly's code section. Specifically, we abstract instructions that manipulate local/global variables to "AssignStatement" syntax units. As shown in row 4, Table 1, *"set_local v"* consumes a stack value e and assigns e to local variable v. The abstraction of *"set_local v"* indicates this instruction has equivalent functionality compared to JavaScript code *"v = e"*. Instructions that push new values to the stack are abstracted to "VariableDeclaration" syntax units: *"i32.const c"* declares a new constant and pushes it onto the stack. Its abstraction is equivalent to *"const C_n = c;"*, where *"C_n"* is a randomly generated name for evading name conflicts. Similarly, the instruction *"i32.mul"* and *"i32.popcnt"* are abstracted to new variable declarations. In particular, operators that are unsupported by JavaScript are simulated to user-defined functions (e.g., *popcnt* in row 5). The rest of Table 1 shows code abstraction rules for WebAssembly control flow instructions.

Control-Flow Instruction. WebAssembly supports control flow instructions, which are similar to high-level languages such as JavaScript. These instructions are significant for constructing a uniform representation. As shown in Table 1, the instructions *"loop"* and *"block"* are both abstracted to labeled "ForStatement" syntax units in Table 1. However, they construct different contexts where the *"br"* instruction is abstracted to different syntax units (i.e., Break and Continue), resulting in diverse control flow structures. *"if I"* is abstracted to "IfStatement", which is a homogeneous structure in JavaScript. In particular, the *"call"* and *"call_indirect"* instructions are non-deterministic because they can either call WebAssembly internal functions or call external functions imported from JavaScript. We determine the exact function referring to the interoperations identified in Phase 1.

We now describe our **data** abstraction rules. The data abstraction rules characterize suspicious values hidden in the WebAssembly linear memory. For example, in Fig. 1.c, the malicious payload is stored in the linear memory and loaded when the function *foo* executes. WebAssembly linear memory is related to two key sections: the memory section and the data section, where the former configures the linear memory and the latter initializes it. Besides static initialization, the linear memory can also be manipulated at runtime through specific instructions such as *store*. However, capturing the exact memory through simulation is unaffordable because precise simulation of all the memory manipulation consumes high overhead. Thus, we limit the scope of data abstraction to the initialization of linear memory. To be specific, we analyze all of the segments in WebAssembly data sections and abstract them to "VariableDeclaration" syntax units as shown in the last row of Table 1, which means every individual data segment is declared as a unique global variable.

Finally, both the code and data abstractions are presented as JavaScript-like AST nodes, facilitating seamless integration into the JavaScript PDG.

IPDG Integration and JavaScript Reconstruction. Once JWBinder finishes abstracting identified WebAssembly units. The next step is to integrate the WebAssembly abstractions into the JavaScript PDG so that we can obtain an inter-language PDG. The integration takes two kinds of inputs: interoperation positions identified in Phase 1 and the abstraction results generated in Phase 2. Specifically, JWBinder replaces the PDG nodes identified as invocation positions of WebAssembly functions with their code abstraction, thereby unveiling the previously hidden semantics. Concurrently, JWBinder integrates the data abstraction of WebAssembly units into their instantiation positions, signifying the initialization of their linear memories.

At present, the IPDG is directly reconstructed into a pure JavaScript program using Escodegen [8], making it compatible with existing monolingual anti-virus systems. Escodegen, which is a well-tested tool widely adopted in previous work [27,37,39], can generate JavaScript programs from abstract representations following ES6 standards. Nevertheless, we believe that the IPDG structure could potentially serve as a foundation for developing advanced multilingual analysis techniques. We aim to explore this avenue in our future work.

4 Evaluation

Using our JWBinder implementation in Sect. 3, the evaluation of our approach is guided by four research questions below:

RQ1: How effective is JWBinder when deployed with real-world anti-virus solutions?

RQ2: Does JWBinder introduces any side effects to the benign JavaScript-WebAssembly multilingual programs?

RQ3: What is the generalization ability of JWBinder on different commercial anti-virus solutions?

RQ4: How efficient is JWBinder in terms of its runtime overhead.

4.1 Experiment Setup and Preliminary Study

We first describe our experiment settings and conduct a preliminary study to illustrate the weakness of existing works against JWMM.

1) JWMM Dataset. To evaluate the effectiveness and efficiency of JWBinder, a multilingual malware dataset is required. However, to our best knowledge, such a dataset is not available. Meanwhile, it may not be feasible to curate the ground truth for large complex real-world programs. Thus, we take inspiration from prior works [33,37] to construct a JWMM dataset (JWBench) deriving from real-world JavaScript malware. Below, we detail our dataset construction:

– Step-1: **Initial malware selection and filtering**. The initial malware dataset consists of 44369 samples, with 39,450 samples from the Hynek Petrak JavaScript malware collection [11], 3562 samples from VirusTotal [21], and 1357 samples from the GeeksOnSecurity [10]. To ensure the semantic validity of the malware samples, We use Esprima [9], a popular standard-compliant JavaScript parser, to vet the initial samples. Additionally, we filter the samples which rely on cc_on statements to perform malicious behaviors. Cc_on statement is a special mechanism that only works in IE browser [18], which generates executable comments. Thus the detection of such samples is beyond our research scope. The final JavaScript malware dataset consists of 21191 JavaScript samples, termed $JWBench_o$. We believe it is of more validity for reasonable evaluation.

– Step-2: **JWMM generation**. We employed the technique proposed by Alan et al. in [37] to convert real-world JavaScript malware to JWMM for evasion detection. We implement Wobfuscator and apply it to malicious samples from step 1, following the original experiment configuration in [37]. As a result, the final JWBench contains 21191 JWMM samples.

2) Baseline Anti-virus Solutions.

To perform a large-scale, representative experiment, we leverage VirusTotal as our baseline anti-virus solution. VirusTotal is an online platform housing 74 real-world commercial AV-Systems, including renowned ones like McAfee [15], Microsoft [17], and BitDefender [5], which makes it the chief target for comprehensive evaluations. Currently, there are 59 AV-Systems providing detection services for malicious JavaScript. When provided a JavaScript program as input, VirusTotal generates a detection report containing binary results (malicious or benign) from these AV-Systems.

We employed two overall metrics to assess the performance of the AV-Systems on VirusTotal:

Successful Detection Rate. A sample is considered successfully detected if no less than a certain threshold number of AV-Systems on VirusTotal accurately identify it as malicious. We set this threshold at two to avoid false positives detection referring to [44]. The Successful Detection Rate (**SDR**) signifies the ratio of successfully detected samples to the overall samples.

Average Detected Engines. From a defensive perspective, it is desirable for as many AV-Systems as possible to successfully detect a malicious sample. To this end, we introduce the metric Average Detected Engines (**ADE**) as another metric to evaluate the capability of AV-Systems on VirusTotal in handling JWMM. The ADE represents the mean number of AV-Systems that successfully detect each malicious sample.

3) Performance of Existing Anti-virus Solutions. At a high level, JWMM consists of JavaScript and WebAssembly units. However, existing anti-virus solutions might address JWMM from a monolingual perspective without completely considering the interoperations between JavaScript and WebAssembly.

This oversight substantially undermines the detection capability of these anti-virus solutions when dealing with JWMM.

Table 2. The detection result of VirusTotal on different datasets

	$JWBench_o$	JWBench
Successful Detection Rate	99.9%	47.6%
Average Detected Engines	22.4	3.3

In Table 2, we list the comparison of VirusTotal's detection results on Different Datasets. As seen in Table 2, on $JWBench_o$, the SDR and ADE of VirusTotal is 99.9% and 22.4, showcasing its effectiveness against pure JavaScript malware. However, these metrics drop to 47.6% and 3.3 on JWBench, meaning that more than half of the JWMM samples can elude detection by VirusTotal. This result underscores the real-world security threats posed by JWMM.

We further investigate whether anti-virus solutions that target the malicious WebAssembly can detect JWMM effectively. Specifically, we first utilize JWBinder's data-flow analysis component to extract 10,000 WebAssembly binaries from JWBench. Subsequently, we employ MinerRay [38], a proven static detector for malicious WebAssembly (e.g., CryptoMiners), to scrutinize these extracted binaries. However, MinerRay fails to detect any suspicious activities in all the samples. This result underscores the notion that even specialized anti-virus solutions, despite their deep semantic understanding of WebAssembly, struggle to detect JWMM. This is predominantly because their focus remains limited to heuristic monolingual features.

4.2   Effectiveness of JWBinder (RQ1)

The effectiveness of the JWBinder is evaluated through a comparison of the AV-Systems' performance on the original JWMM input programs against their performance after JWBinder has been applied. For this evaluation, we randomly select 10,000 samples from the JWBench and measure the system's performance using the metrics outlined in 4.1. The primary objectives of JWBinder are to enhance SDR and the ADE of VirusTotal against the selected JWMM samples.

Table 3 shows the successful detection rate and average detected engines of VirusTotal with/without the application of JWBinder. The first column gives the detection results of VirusTotal without JWBinder, which serves as a baseline. The rest of the column shows the results after applying JWBinder with different levels of abstraction in semantic reconstruction.

$JWBinder_c$ refers for JWBinder which merely applies code abstraction in SSR and $JWBinder_d$ refers for JWBinder which merely applies data abstraction in SSR. The fourth column, $JWBinder_a$, corresponds to the complete version of JWBinder which combines the results of individual $JWBinder_c$ and $JWBinder_d$. The values in brackets indicate the difference from the baseline. For example, the second column indicates that JWBinder$_c$ can successfully detect 16.1% more malicious samples compared to the baseline, while failing to detect 0.5% of the samples that the baseline can originally detect.

Table 3. The detection result of VirusTotal on 10k JWMM processed by JWBinder

	Baseline	JWBinder$_c$	JWBinder$_d$	**JWBinder$_a$**
SDR	49.1%	64.7% ($^{+16.1\%}_{-0.5\%}$)	81.0% ($^{+33.5\%}_{-1.6\%}$)	**86.2%**($^{+37.1\%}_{-0.0\%}$)
ADE	4.1	5.0	7.5	**8.3**

Table 3 illustrates that all variants of JWBinder substantially improve the performance of AV-Systems on VirusTotal in terms of both SDR and ADE. Specially, JWBinder$_c$ and JWBinder$_d$ achieve 15.6%/31.9% increment for SDR and are successful in having each malicious sample detected by 0.9/3.4 additional engines, respectively. Moreover, the complete JWBinder$_a$ attains an SDR of 86.2% and an ADE of 8.3.

Of all the malicious samples, either JWBinder$_c$ or JWBinder$_d$ successfully identifies 59.5% of them. There are also 5.2% and 21.5% unique samples detectable exclusively by JWBinder$_c$ and JWBinder$_d$, respectively. This outcome serves as an ablation study, demonstrating that different SSR levels contribute to the detection of various samples.

The SSR applied by JWBinder could disrupt detection results if it provides AV-Systems with information that may not favor their detection capabilities. For instance, signature-based detection does not respond significantly to code-level information. We attribute the slight decrease in SDR for JWBinder$_c$ (-0.5%) and JWBinder$_d$ (-1.6%) to this factor. However, by merging the results from both individual SSR applications, JWBinder can enhance detection without any negative impact (i.e., 0% decrement).

4.3   Side Effects (RQ2)

While JWBinder has demonstrated significant improvements in JWMM detection, it is essential to evaluate its potential side effects. Specifically, we need to ensure that JWBinder enhances the effectiveness of AV-Systems on VirusTotal without introducing suspicious behaviors to the benign samples under detection.

A false positive detection occurs when the benign program is wrongly identified as malware by more than one engine. For RQ2, we evaluate the number of false positive results of VirusTotal when runs on benign samples processed by JWBinder. Following the experiment settings in Sect. 4.1, we generate a benign JavaScript-WebAssembly multilingual programs dataset from JS150k [4], which contains 150000 JavaScript source files. Due to the scaling issues, we randomly select 1000 of them which VirusTotal deems benign and manually confirm the detection results. To evaluate whether JWBinder introduces side effects on the samples it processes, we compare the AV-Systems' false positive detections on the original benign input programs when applying JWBinder.

Our experimental results reveal a relatively low false positive rate introduced by JWBinder. Of the 1000 benign samples, JWBinder$_c$ and JWBinder$_d$ only cause 4 and 1 false positive detections, respectively. As a result, the JWBinder$_a$ registers a false positive rate of only 0.5%. Given this relatively low false positive rate compared to the considerable enhancements in JWMM detection, we conclude that JWBinder introduces minimal side effects when processing JavaScript-WebAssembly multilingual programs.

4.4 Generalization Ability of JWBinder (RQ3)

In this research question, we evaluate the generalization ability of JWBinder across different commercial AV-Systems on VirusTotal. Furthermore, we aim to deduce the internal mechanisms used in these AV-Systems based on the distribution of results by comparing their benefits from different variants of JWBinder.

Table 4 shows the detection results of different commercial AV-Systems. Due to the limitation of length, we only list 5 representative AV-Systems on VirusTotal (the complete table is deferred to Table 5 in the Appendix). The results show that different levels of SSR benefit certain detectors more rather than others. For example, JWBinder$_c$ and JWBinder$_d$ both help Google and Cyren achieve 20%+ SDR increment, from which we can deduce that these two AV-Systems are likely to classify malicious JavaScript according to either code-level features and data-level features. As a result, JWBinder$_a$ has increased the SDR of Google and Cyren from 31.1%/29.4% to 61.3%/55.9%.

Table 4. The successful detection rate of individual AV-System on JWMM processed by JWBinder, highest SDR in **BOLD**

AV-System	Baseline	JWBinder$_c$	JWBinder$_d$	JWBinder$_a$
Google	31.1%	53.3%	59.4%	**61.3%**
Cyren	29.4%	50.5%	53.4%	**55.9%**
McAfee-GW-Edition	0%	47.5%	2.4%	**47.7%**
BitDefender	14.2%	19.7%	39.5%	**39.7%**
Microsoft	19.3%	16.0%	35.0%	**45.7%**

Some AV-Systems favor particular features more than others. For example, with JWBinder$_c$ revealing the code-level features of JWMM, McAfee-GW-Edition's SDR has increased from 0% to 47.5%. However, the increment is merely 2.4% with JWBinder$_d$, which shows that McAfee-GW-Edition is relatively insensitive to data-level features. In Table 4, the majority of AV-Systems (4 of 5) gain significantly from JWBinder$_d$, which corresponds to previous research [35] that signature-based matching is wide-adopted in AV-Systems.

4.5 Efficiency of JWBinder (RQ4)

Lastly, we evaluate the run-time performance of JWBinder. Since JWBinder runs the analysis of each JWMM on a single core, the reported runtime corresponds to a single CPU. There are two most time-consuming steps of JWBinder: the data-flow analysis on the JavaScript side and the SSR process which parses and abstracts the WebAssembly binary. Usually, a JWMM file has a much more complex AST than a traditional JavaScript file, making it time-consuming to be analyzed either dynamically or statically. Alan et al. [37] shows that the execution time JWMM may increase at most 2079.21% with 363.52% larger size compared to traditional JavaScript programs. On average, JWBinder needs 10.0 s for data-flow analysis to capture the interoperations between JavaScript and WebAssembly. Besides, it needs on average 15.6 s for SSR. Specially, the corresponding median times are 0.7 s and 6.7 s, while the maximum amounts of time are 207.5 s and 202.2 s, predominantly when JWBinder processes exceptionally large JWMM files (>1 Mb), with the details provided in Fig. 5 within the Appendix. This result is competitive compared to previous works for large-scale malicious JavaScript detection [29,32].

In particular, we could complete the data-flow analysis for 87.8% of our JWMM set in less than 10 s and SSR for 83.5% of them in less than 20 s. This efficiency enables JWBinder to effectively augment existing AV-Systems for detecting JWMM from the wild.

5 Limitation

Our current implementation of JWBinder effectively enhances the performance of existing anti-virus solutions. However, it also has a few limitations:

- **Threat of Run-time Code/Data Generation**. JWBinder aims to enhance existing anti-virus solutions during the static analysis phase. Therefore, it is insensitive to run-time behaviors. For example, attackers can dynamically construct malicious payloads in WebAssembly to evade our static data abstractions or generate code at runtime which is beyond the scope of our reconstructed JavaScript. However, none of the existing static approaches can effectively solve this problem, which can only rely on hybrid approaches.
- **Obfuscation**. Existing JavaScript obfuscation techniques may break the semantics required for taint analysis. Currently, JWBinder is not equipped with a de-obfuscation component. However, this threat can be mitigated with on-the-shelf de-obfuscation tools such as [7,12].

6 Conclusion

In this paper, we propose JWBinder, the first technique for enhancing the detection of JavaScript-WebAssembly multilingual malware (JWMM). JWBinder captures the interoperations between JavaScript and WebAssembly and then reconstructs a statically equal JavaScript program, which characterizes the hidden malicious behaviors of JWMM through a novel uniform structure called Inter-language Program Dependency Graph. Our evaluation shows the reconstruction process can effectively enhance real-world AV-Systems. We also show to what extent can JWBinder benefit Anti-Virus Systems from different vendors. Finally, we evaluate the efficiency of JWBinder and prove it can be scalable to large JWMM in the real world.

Acknowledgements. This work was partly supported by NSFC under No. U1936215 and the Fundamental Research Funds for the Central Universities (Zhejiang University NGICS Platform). We sincerely appreciate the anonymous reviewers for their insightful comments.

A   Appendix

This appendix contains some supplementary material.

In particular, Fig. 4 lists a series of JavaScript WebAssembly interfaces for cross-language interoperations, which we leverage in the data-flow analysis.

Figure 5 presents JWBinder run-time performance depending on the JWMM size.

Algorithm 1 details the process for identifying the cross-language interoperations on PDG.

Finally, Table 5 shows extensive detection results of different AV-Systems. We list the top 15 AV-Systems due to the space limit.

Function/Property Name	Description
WebAssembly.compile()	
WebAssembly.compileStreaming()	The modularization of WebAssmebly binaries. Return a module for Instantiation.
WebAssembly.Module	
WebAssembly.instantiate()	The Instantiation of WebAssmebly module.
WebAssembly.instantiateStreaming()	Return a instance which can call WebAssembly functions.
WebAssembly.Instance	
Instance.exports	Export WebAssembly internal properties to JavaScript.

Fig. 4. WebAssembly modularization/instantiation functions and properties

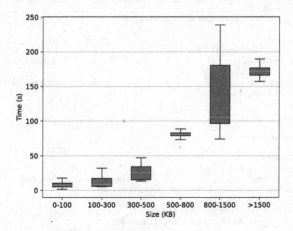

Fig. 5. Run-time performance of JWBinder depending on the JWMM size

Table 5. The successful detection rate of every individual AV-System on JWMM processed by JWBinder, highest SDR in **BOLD**

AV-System	Baseline	JWBinder$_c$	JWBinder$_d$	JWBinder$_a$
Google	31.1%	53.3%	59.4%	**61.3%**
Cyren	29.4%	50.5%	53.4%	**55.9%**
McAfee-GW-Edition	0%	47.5%	2.4%	**47.7%**
Microsoft	19.3%	16.0%	35.0%	**45.7%**
Rising	27.5%	2.6%	44.5%	**45.3%**
Arcabit	14.2%	20.0%	39.8%	**39.9%**
MicroWorld-eScan	14.2%	20.0%	39.8%	**40.0%**
FireEye	14.2%	19.9%	39.5%	**39.8%**
ALYac	13.8%	19.6%	38.9%	**39.4%**
GData	14.2%	19.0%	38.3%	**39.3%**
Emsisoft	14.0%	18.0%	36.9%	**38.6%**
BitDefender	14.2%	19.7%	39.5%	**39.7%**
VIPRE	14.1%	19.5%	39.1%	**39.5%**
MAX	14.2%	19.9%	39.6%	**39.8%**
Ikarus	2.07%	13.7%	23.6%	**24.0%**

Algorithm 1. Algorithm for identifying cross-language interoperations

---

Input: The Original PDG **P**
Output: The New PDG with Interoperation Marking **P'**
P' ⟵ **P**;
Function TraversePDG(**P'**):
    foreach $child \in getChildren($**P'**$)$ **do**
        $TraversePDG(child)$;   ▷ Iteratively traversing the PDG
        if $hasKeyAPI($**P'**$)$ **then**
            $BackwardAnalysis($**P'**$)$;   ▷ Start bi-directional data-flow analysis
            $ForwardAnalysis($**P'**$)$;
        end
    end
End Function;
Function BackwardAnalysis($node$):
    $Worklist \longleftarrow []$;
    $Worklist.push(node)$;
    while $Worklist \neq NULL$ **do**
        $CurNode = Worklist.pop()$ ▷ Backward tracing data-flow dependent parents
        foreach $parent \in getDataParent($**P'**$, CurNode)$ **do**
            $Worklist.push(parent)$
            if $isImportProperty(parent)$ **then**
                P' ⟵ $markInteroperation($**P'**$, parent)$
                ▷ Mark interoperations when encountering imported items
            end
        end
    end
End Function;
Function ForwardAnalysis($node$):
    $Worklist \longleftarrow []$;
    $Worklist.push(node)$;
    while $Worklist \neq NULL$ **do**
        $CurNode = Worklist.pop()$ ▷ Forward tracing data-flow dependent children
        foreach $child \in getDataChildren($**P'**$, CurNode)$ **do**
            $Worklist.push(child)$
            if $isExportProperty(child)$ **then**
                P' ⟵ $markInteroperation($**P'**$, child)$
                ▷ Mark interoperations when encountering exported items
            end
        end
    end
End Function;

References

1. Npm (2021). https://www.npmjs.com/
2. The year in web threats: web skimmers take advantage of cloud hosting and more (2021). https://unit42.paloaltonetworks.com/web-threats-trends-web-skimmers/
3. Github top programming languages (2022). https://octoverse.github.com/2022/top-programming-languages
4. 150k Javascript dataset (2023). https://www.sri.inf.ethz.ch/js150
5. Bitdefender (2023). https://www.bitdefender.com/
6. Box.js, a sandbox to analyze malicious Javascript (2023). https://github.com/CapacitorSet/box-js
7. De4js, Javascript deobfuscator and unpacker (2023). https://lelinhtinh.github.io/de4js/
8. Escodegen (2023). https://github.com/estools/escodegen
9. Esprima (2023). https://esprima.org/
10. Geeks on security malicious Javascript dataset (2023). https://github.com/geeksonsecurity/js-malicious-dataset

11. Petrak, H.: Javascript malware collection (2023). https://github.com/HynekPetrak/javascript-malware-collection
12. Javascript deobfuscator (2023). https://deobfuscate.io/
13. Javascript es6 standard (2023). https://www.w3schools.com/js/js_es6.asp
14. Jwbinder source code and data (2023). https://github.com/JWBinderRepository/JWBinder
15. Mcafee (2023). https://www.mcafee.com/
16. Mdn web docs (2023). https://developer.mozilla.org/en-US/docs/WebAssembly/JavaScript_interface
17. Microsoft defender antivirus (2023). https://www.microsoft.com/
18. Microsoft, internet explorer (2023). https://www.microsoft.com/download/internet-explorer
19. Nodejs (2023). https://nodejs.org/
20. Sandbox for semi-automatic Javascript malware analysis (2023). https://github.com/HynekPetrak/malware-jail
21. Virustotal (2023). https://www.virustotal.com/
22. Webassembly (2023). https://webassembly.org/
23. Webassembly core specification (2023). https://www.w3.org/TR/2022/WD-wasm-core-2-20220419/syntax/instructions.html
24. Webassembly is abused by ecriminals to hide malware (2023). https://www.crowdstrike.com/blog/ecriminals-increasingly-use-webassembly-to-hide-malware/
25. Yara (2023). https://virustotal.github.io/yara/
26. Curtsinger, C., Livshits, B., Zorn, B.G., Seifert, C.: ZOZZLE: fast and precise in-browser Javascript malware detection. In: 20th USENIX Security Symposium (USENIX Security 11) (2011)
27. Fass, A., Backes, M., Stock, B.: Hidenoseek: camouflaging malicious Javascript in benign asts. In: Proceedings of the 2019 ACM SIGSAC Conference on Computer and Communications Security, pp. 1899–1913 (2019)
28. Fass, A., Backes, M., Stock, B.: Jstap: a static pre-filter for malicious Javascript detection, pp. 257–269 (2019)
29. Fass, A., Somé, D.F., Backes, M., Stock, B.: Doublex: statically detecting vulnerable data flows in browser extensions at scale. In: Proceedings of the 2021 ACM SIGSAC Conference on Computer and Communications Security, p. 1789–1804 (2021)
30. Kolbitsch, C., Livshits, B., Zorn, B.G., Seifert, C.: Rozzle: de-cloaking internet malware. In: 2012 IEEE Symposium on Security and Privacy (SP), pp. 443–457 (2012)
31. Konoth, R.K., et al.: Minesweeper: an in-depth look into drive-by cryptocurrency mining and its defense. In: Proceedings of the 2018 ACM SIGSAC Conference on Computer and Communications Security, pp. 1714–1730 (2018)
32. Li, S., Kang, M., Hou, J., Cao, Y.: Mining node.js vulnerabilities via object dependence graph and query. In: 31st USENIX Security Symposium (USENIX Security 22), pp. 143–160 (2022)
33. Li, W., Ming, J., Luo, X., Cai, H.: {PolyCruise}: A {Cross-Language} dynamic information flow analysis. In: 31st USENIX Security Symposium (USENIX Security 22), pp. 2513–2530 (2022)
34. Provos, N., McNamee, D., Mavrommatis, P., Wang, K., Modadugu, N.: The ghost in the browser: analysis of web-based malware. In: First Workshop on Hot Topics in Understanding Botnets (HotBots 07) (2007)

35. Quarta, D., Salvioni, F., Continella, A., Zanero, S.: Toward systematically exploring antivirus engines. In: Detection of Intrusions and Malware, and Vulnerability Assessment: 15th International Conference, pp. 393–403 (2018)
36. Rieck, K., Krueger, T., Dewald, A.: Cujo: efficient detection and prevention of drive-by-download attacks. In: ACSAC '10: Proceedings of the 26th Annual Computer Security Applications Conference, pp. 31–39 (2010)
37. Romano, A., Lehmann, D., Pradel, M., Wang, W.: Wobfuscator: obfuscating Javascript malware via opportunistic translation to webassembly. In: 2022 IEEE Symposium on Security and Privacy (SP), pp. 1574–1589 (2022)
38. Romano, A., Zheng, Y., Wang, W.: Minerray: Semantics-aware analysis for ever-evolving cryptojacking detection. In: Proceedings of the 35th IEEE/ACM International Conference on Automated Software Engineering, pp. 1129–1140 (2020)
39. Shen, S., Zhu, X., Dong, Y., Guo, Q., Zhen, Y., Li, G.: Incorporating domain knowledge through task augmentation for front-end Javascript code generation. In: Proceedings of the 30th ACM Joint European Software Engineering Conference and Symposium on the Foundations of Software Engineering, pp. 1533–1543 (2022)
40. Srndic, N., Laskov, P.: Practical evasion of a learning-based classifier: a case study. In: 2014 IEEE Symposium on Security and Privacy, pp. 197–211 (2014)
41. Wang, J., Xue, Y., Liu, Y., Tan, T.H.: JSDC: a hybrid approach for Javascript malware detection and classification. In: ASIACCS 2015 - Proceedings of the 10th ACM Symposium on Information, Computer and Communications Security, pp. 109–120 (2015)
42. Xiao, F., et al.: Abusing hidden properties to attack the node.js ecosystem. In: 30th USENIX Security Symposium (USENIX Security 21), pp. 2951–2968 (2021)
43. Xue, Y., Wang, J., Liu, Y., Xiao, H., Sun, J., Chandramohan, M.: Detection and classification of malicious Javascript via attack behavior modelling. In: Proceedings of the 2015 International Symposium on Software Testing and Analysis, pp. 48–59 (2015)
44. Zhu, S., et al.: Measuring and modeling the label dynamics of online anti-malware engines. In: 29st USENIX Security Symposium (USENIX Security 20), pp. 2361–2378 (2020)

A New Model for Testing IPv6 Fragment Handling

Edoardo Di Paolo[ID], Enrico Bassetti[✉][ID], and Angelo Spognardi[ID]

Dipartimento Informatica, Sapienza University of Rome,
Viale Regina Elena 295, Rome, Italy
{dipaolo,bassetti,spognardi}@di.uniroma1.it

Abstract. Since the origins of the Internet, various vulnerabilities exploiting the IP fragmentation process have plagued IPv4 protocol, many leading to a wide range of attacks. IPv6 modified the handling of fragmentations and introduced a specific extension header, not solving the related problems, as proved by extensive literature. One of the primary sources of problems has been the overlapping fragments, which result in unexpected or malicious packets when reassembled. To overcome the problem related to fragmentation, the authors of RFC 5722 decided that IPv6 hosts MUST silently drop overlapping fragments.

Since then, several studies have proposed methodologies to check if IPv6 hosts accept overlapping fragments and are still vulnerable to related attacks. However, some of the above methodologies have not been proven complete or need to be more accurate. In this paper we propose a novel model to check IPv6 fragmentation handling specifically suited for the reassembling strategies of modern operating systems. Previous models, indeed, considered OS reassembly policy as byte-based. However, nowadays, reassembly policies are fragment-based, making previous models inadequate. Our model leverages the commutative property of the checksum, simplifying the whole assessing process. Starting with this new model, we were able to better evaluate the RFC-5722 and RFC-9099 compliance of modern operating systems against fragmentation handling. Our results suggest that IPv6 fragmentation can still be considered a threat and that more effort is needed to solve related security issues.

Keywords: Network security · IPv6 · Fragmentation · Modification Attack

1 Introduction

Internet standards allow the use of fragmentation when a router has to transmit an IP packet larger than the next link's *Maximum Transmission Unit* (MTU), i.e., the maximum number of bytes that the link can transmit in a single IP packet. The fragmentation process consists of dividing the packet into smaller units, called fragments, so that the resulting pieces can pass through a link with a smaller MTU than the original packet size.

© The Author(s), under exclusive license to Springer Nature Switzerland AG 2024
G. Tsudik et al. (Eds.): ESORICS 2023, LNCS 14345, pp. 277–294, 2024.
https://doi.org/10.1007/978-3-031-51476-0_14

Initial IPv4 specifications, RFC 791 [19], describes a reassembly algorithm that allows new fragments to overwrite any overlapped portions of previously-received fragments [22]. Unfortunately, this algorithm enabled bypassing filtering solutions and resulted in the operating system adopting different policies to reassemble fragments [18]. Over the years, various vulnerabilities that exploit the fragmentation process have been discovered, mainly using overlapping fragments, exposing the Internet to several types of attacks: *Denial of Service* (DoS), *Traffic Modification, Traffic Interception, Intrusion Detection Systems* (IDS)/*Intrusion Prevention Systems* (IPS) *evasion, Firewall evasion* [7,24].

IPv6 brought about significant changes to handling fragmentation compared to its predecessor, IPv4. It introduced a specific extension header and aimed to address the shortcomings of IPv4 fragmentation. RFC 5722 [15] tackles the fragmentation problem by explicitly forbidding overlapping fragments. However, despite these efforts, extensive literature and previous studies have demonstrated that IPv6 fragmentation still poses security risks. In particular, it has been shown that many operating systems are not entirely RFC 5722 compliant, accepting some sequences of IPv6 overlapping fragments, being exposed to several forms of detection evasion [2] and traffic hijacking [7].

Numerous studies have been conducted to assess the vulnerability of IPv6 hosts to overlapping fragments and related attacks. However, some of the existing methodologies have not been proven to be complete or accurate enough. Some others, like the Shankar and Paxson model, were proposed in the past, but they are obsolete due to recent changes in the reassembly strategies, as we will demonstrate in this work. Therefore, we propose a novel model specifically designed to evaluate the handling of IPv6 fragmentation, taking into account the reassembling strategies employed by modern operating systems.

To prove the usefulness of our model, we thoughtfully tested it over widely used operating systems. We also compared the results achieved using the Shankar and Paxson model over the same targets. As shown later, our model was able to capture the non-compliance of all operating systems that we tested, whereas the Shankar and Paxson model indicates full compliance on IPv6 fragmentation.

Additionally, to demonstrate that IPv6 fragmentation has still to be considered a real threat, we implemented a *Traffic Modification* attack. The attack requires the ability to predict the IP identification number (IP-id): IP-id prediction has been considered quite critical since a long time ago, and some successful attempts are present in literature [10,23,27–29]. In the attack, we take advantage of the partial or non-existing compliance of RFC 5722 to alter the legitimate traffic between two hosts, again exploiting the use of overlapping fragments [2].

Thus, we show that vulnerabilities inherent to IPv6 fragmentation persist. Despite numerous recommendations, attacks on IPv6 fragmentation remain feasible, necessitating more effort to eliminate all flaws in implementations.

The paper is structured as follows: the next section provides a brief background on IP fragmentation and past work on the topic. Section 3 introduces two well-known models for testing IPv6 fragmentation issues, and discusses their limitations. Section 4 reports our experiments performed to evaluate the

RFC 5722 compliance of modern operating systems. Section 5 reports our findings on RFC 9099 compliance. Section 6 report our experiment results for the Traffic Modification attacks. Finally, Sect. 7 summarizes the contributions of our work and provides some further comments to help fix the IPv6 fragmentation flaws.

2   Background and Related Works

In this section, we briefly introduce some details about IP fragmentation that provide the background for the experimental section. Then, we report a quick survey about the main contribution related to IP fragmentation vulnerabilities, focusing on IPv6.

2.1   IP Fragmentation in Internet

An essential property of an Internet link is the number of bytes it can transmit in a single IP packet, namely the *Maximum Transmission Unit* (MTU). The MTU may differ between different networking technologies. IPv4 requires every link to support a minimum MTU of 576 bytes, as recommended by RFC 791 [19], while IPv6 requires every link to support an MTU of 1280 bytes or greater (RFC 2460 [5]). When an endpoint has to transmit an IP packet greater than the next link MTU, IP calls for fragmentation, which is the process of separating a packet into units (fragments) smaller than the link MTU. The receiving host performs fragment reassembly to pass the complete (re-assembled) IP packet up to its protocol stack.

The fragmentation process is handled differently in IPv4 and IPv6. In IPv4, an IP packet can be fragmented by the source node or intermediate routers along the path between the source and the destination. However, intermediate routers may avoid fragmenting IPv4 packets by dropping the packet and forcing the Path MTU by the source host. In IPv6, only *end-to-end fragmentation* is supported; intermediate routers cannot create fragments. To discover the best MTU size, both IPv4 and IPv6 leverage on the *Path MTU Discovery*, provided by *Internet Control Message Protocol* version 4 (ICMP) or 6 (ICMPv6).

In order to reassemble all the fragments related to the same packet, IP protocol uses some information present in the header, namely: the *identification* field (shared among all the fragments of the same packet), the *fragment offset* (that specifies which is the starting fragment position in the original packet) and the *More Fragments* flag, set to 1 for all fragments except for the last one. IPv4 and IPv6 differ mainly on the identification field length (16-bit long in the former, 32-bit in the latter), and that IPv6 uses a specific extension header to hold the above information.

While not predominant, statistics show that IP fragmentation is still used in the Internet and, notably, for security protocols like IKE [13] or DNSSEC [1], that typically rely on large UDP packets for cryptographic material exchange [7].

2.2 Related Works

IP Fragmentation has been exploited to make many different types of attacks, as anticipated by Mogul and Kantarjiev back in 1987 [12]. Most of them allow realizing denial of services [14] or IDS/firewall evasion [24] or operating system fingerprinting [2]. Besides those based on IP fragmentation, many other attacks rely on the possibility of predicting the IP identification field of the victim [29]. For this reason, there has been a flurry of works focusing on the feasibility of predicting IP-id field [4,16,20,21]. While most studies about IP fragmentation are related to IPv4, only a few specifically focus on IPv6. As it will be further explored in Sect. 3, IPv6, among the other vulnerabilities [25] mitigations, has been revised to specifically fix the IP fragmentation issues, firstly with RFCs 3128 [17], 5722 [15], 6946 [8] and, later, with an updated version of the IPv6 specification, namely RFC 8200 [6]. Moreover, RFC 9099 [26] discusses extension headers with a special focus on fragments stating that, if not handled properly, they could lead to bypassing stateless filtering.

In [14], the authors exploit the IP fragmentation to prevent legitimate IKE handshakes from completing. The main idea is to flood one of the endpoints with fragments to consume all the memory resources dedicated to the fragment buffers, realizing a fragment cache overflow. The overflow prevents legitimate hosts from completing the IKE handshake because the reassembling becomes impossible. Another type of attack has been described in RFC 4963 [11], consisting of a fragment misassociation. The idea is that the attacker can poison the fragment cache of a host, sending some spoofed fragments so that when the fragments of the victim reach the poisoned host, they will be misassociated and, consequently, maliciously altered.

The most influential work for our research has been done by Gilad and Herzberg [7]. They present a DoS attack inspired by a traffic injection technique based on IP fragmentation, proposed by Zalewski[1] and appeared in the seclist mailing list in 2003. The idea is to inject the second fragment of TCP connections since the IP-id was highly predictable. Following this intuition, the authors in [7] propose performing a DoS attack against a communicating host, targeting the NAT-ing host behind which the destination endpoint resides. This type of attack allows the authors to realize a very effective DoS attack, causing more than 94% of packet loss without leveraging any fragment cache overflow.

Another pivotal work that inspired this paper has been done by Atlasis [2]. In his paper, the author performs an exhaustive battery of tests to verify the effective behavior of several operating systems when overlapping IP fragments are present. In particular, the experiments verified the different reassembly strategies and how those can be exploited to perform various evasion attacks. The methodology used in Atlasis' paper for understanding the different reassembly policies is the driving factor for realizing our Traffic Modification attack, as detailed in Sect. 6. Moreover, Atlasis in [3] shows how high-end commercial IDPS devices could be evaded by the use of IPv6 extension headers.

---

[1] Michal Zalewski, *A new TCP/IP blind data injection technique?*, https://seclists. org/bugtraq/2003/Dec/161.

3   IP Fragmentation Handling in the Wild

In this section, we evaluate RFC 5722 compliance of different operating systems. We introduce two established methodologies adopted in the literature to evaluate the IP fragmentation reassembly strategies that we discovered to be obsolete. Then, we propose a new methodology, based on the presented ones, and we discuss the results we obtained by testing widely used operating system.

3.1   Shankar and Paxson Model

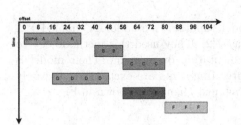
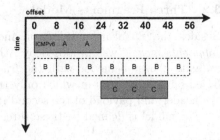

Fig. 1. Shankar and Paxson model.   **Fig. 2.** Three Fragments Model

The first methodology we consider is the one we call *Shankar and Paxson model* [24]. In their paper, the authors introduce a model consisting of six fragments of different lengths and offsets, as shown in Fig. 1, creating a diversified combination of fragment overlap and overwrite. In the figure, each fragment is represented by a block labeled with a character (e.g., 'A', 'B', 'C'), and the payload of each fragment is a sequence of bytes encoding the corresponding character. The vertical axis marked as "time" represents the temporal succession of the transmitted fragments. For example, the first fragment in Fig. 1 has offset 0 in the final (reassembled) payload, a length of 32 bytes, and contains the ICMPv6 header plus 24 'A's.

For each two adjacent fragments, X and Y, the Shankar and Paxson model guarantees that there is [24]:

- At least one fragment (X) wholly overlapped by a subsequent fragment (Y) with identical offset and length;
- At least one fragment (X) partially overlapped by a subsequent fragment (Y) with an offset greater than fragment X;
- At least one fragment (X) partially overlapped by a subsequent fragment (Y) with an offset smaller than fragment X.

By using six fragments, five different fragment reassembled sequences were found [18]: *BSD*, that favors an original fragment with an offset smaller or equal to a subsequent fragment; *BSD-right*, that favors a subsequent fragment when the original fragment has an offset smaller or equal to the subsequent one; *Linux*, that favors an original fragment with an offset that is smaller than a subsequent fragment; *First*, that favors the original fragment with a given offset; *Last*, that favors the subsequent fragment with a given offset.

In our experiments we discovered that modern operating systems don't use parts of a fragment: they assemble fragments by using or discarding them entirely, as discussed in Sect. 4.1. Due to this new behavior, the Shankar and Paxson model is no more suitable for IPv6 fragment overlapping tests as the reassembly phase may never finish in some occasion (more on this in Sect. 4.1).

3.2   Three Fragments Model

Besides the Shankar and Paxson model, another methodology named *"3-fragments model"* was proposed by Atlasis [2]. They used this methodology to evaluate a host behavior with the fragmentation overlapping. Their model is based on several tests in which only three fragments are exchanged, and only the header and payload of the second fragment change, as shown in Fig. 2.

The model is defined by these three fragments:

- The first fragment has always offset 0, and *More Fragments* flag (*M-flag* from now on) set to 1. It consists of an ICMPv6 Echo Request (8 bytes) with 16 bytes of payload for a total length of 24 bytes;
- The second fragment has variable length and offset, and within the different tests, it also varies in the value of the *M-flag*;
- The third fragment has always offset 24, *M-flag* always set to 0, and a length of 24 bytes, carrying part of the payload.

The model comprises 11 different combinations of length and offsets for the second fragment while varying the value of the *M-flag* for the second fragment and reversing the sending order of the three fragments (from 1 to 3 and from 3 to 1). This shuffling leads to a total of 44 tests.

While this test was successfully used to investigate the IP fragmentation reassembly [2], the model is now obsolete because it assumes that IPv6 endpoints may reassemble the packet using a fragment partially. As discussed in Sect. 4.1, modern operating systems assemble fragments by using or discarding them entirely.

4   A New Model for Testing IPv6 Fragment Handling

This section proposes a new model to check RFC 5722 compliance on IPv6 fragmentation. We discuss how operating systems handle IPv6 fragments nowadays, and then we present our proposal for a model for testing overlapping fragments based on the Shankar and Paxson model. Finally, we discuss the results obtained from the different experiments performed.

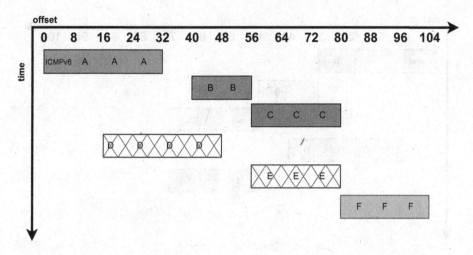

Fig. 3. Overlapping fragments discarded by operating systems may create hole and prevent a correct reassembly. In this example, the operating system decided to discard "D" and "E" fragments due to its reassembly policy, leaving a hole between "A" and "B".

4.1 Overlapping Fragments Today

Previously proposed models for testing overlapping fragments proved to be obsolete in our experiments. We noted that all operating systems in Table 1 discard entire overlapping fragments. Which fragment is discarded depends on the operating system policy, which may include the arrival time or offset position. Figure 3 shows an example of this problem with the Shankar and Paxson model when the operating system drops overlapping fragments that arrived late. Since fragments "D" and "E" overlap with "A", "B" and "C", they are discarded by the operating systems, thus producing a "hole" between fragments "A" and "B".

The gap between "A" and "B" (caused by dropping "D") does not allow the machine to reassemble the packet correctly and reply to the "ICMPv6 Echo Request", since it is missing information between offsets 32 and 40. The machine waits for a predetermined time (`ip6frag_time`, which in some systems is set to 30 s by default) and then deletes the fragments received up to that time from memory. Thus, these machines seem compliant with the RFC 5722, as there is no way to know externally whether the packet has been discarded because of the gap or because they dropped the packet and all fragments (which is the action required by the RFC).

4.2 A New Model for Testing IPv6 Fragment Handling

Our approach is based on the well-known Shankar and Paxson model, which provides a comprehensive framework for analyzing the reassembly process of fragmented packets. However, we modify the original model by reducing all fragment offsets by one, resulting in an offset reduction of 8 bytes. Also, although

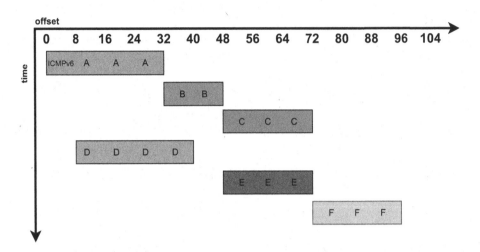

Fig. 4. The new model we are proposing. It is based on the Shankar and Paxson model but it has different offsets to better fit current reassembly policies.

we display the model using the same time sequence as the Shankar and Paxson model, our model is meant to be tested by shuffling the sequence. In other words, multiple tests should be done, and the fragments should have different arrival times on each test but the same offsets and content. The model is shown in Fig. 4.

The primary motivation behind the offset mutation is to have some combinations where the packet reassembly is done by using or discarding entire fragments, as modern operating systems do. Previous models could not expose issues in the fragmentation handling due to the problem discussed in Sect. 4.1.

It is important to note that the ICMPv6 header is excluded from this overlap. We excluded the "next header" in the payload as no operating systems allow overwriting it in any combination of fragments.

A significant contribution of our modified model lies in identifying two combinations of fragments, AAABBCCCFFF and AAABBEEEFFF, that do not create any holes during reassembly. These fragment combinations are particularly interesting, as they present scenarios where fragments can be reassembled even when partial overlapping fragments are dropped.

To avoid issues with different checksums created by different ways of reassembling fragments, we also re-defined the payload of the fragments as shown in Table 3 and presented in Sect. 4.4. By doing so, we have that any combination of fragments in our model has the same checksum (Fig. 5).

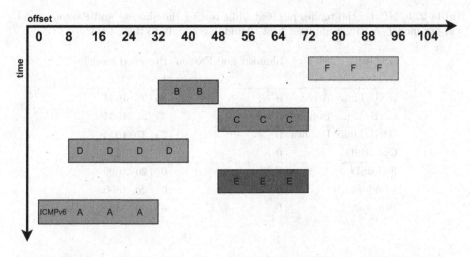

Fig. 5. One of the permutation is when the first fragment is the latest one to arrive. This particular arrangement might result in a different reassembled packet.

Table 1. Operating systems, versions tested and Vagrant box version.

Operating System	Kernel Version	Vagrant box version
GNU/Linux Arch	6.3.2-arch1-1	3.23.0522
GNU/Linux Debian 11	5.10.0-22-amd64	11.20230501.1
GNU/Linux Ubuntu 23.04	6.2.0-20-generic	20230524.0.0
OpenBSD	6.9 GENERIC.MP#473	4.2.16
FreeBSD	13.1-RELEASE	4.2.16
Microsoft Windows 10	10.0.19041.2965	2202.0.2305
Microsoft Windows 11	10.0.22621.1702	2202.0.2305

4.3   Model Validation and Results

We performed a series of experiments to assess the usefulness of our model and to catch anomalies in the reassembly procedure in operating systems. For some tests, we also compared our model with Shankar and Paxson, demonstrating that our model is able to capture the non-compliance where the Shankar and Paxson model suggests that the operating system is RFC 5722-compliant. We also tested all possible permutations of the arrival time of the fragments (720 permutations). Although some may be superfluous due to previous tests, we checked the complete set of permutations to create a dataset for further analysis. Overall, the total number of tests in our dataset is 2226^2 for each operating system listed in Table 1.

---

[2] The complete list of tests can be found in the GitHub repository.

Table 2. ICMPv6 Echo replies received while testing the Shankar and Paxson model and our model. A RFC-compliant host should never reply to these tests.

OS/Test	Shankar and Paxson	Proposed model		
		1	2	3
GNU/Linux Arch	0	35	37	1634
GNU/Linux Debian	0	35	37	1634
GNU/Linux Ubuntu	0	35	37	1634
OpenBSD	0	0	24	373
FreeBSD	0	0	20	1609
Windows 10	0	0	20	1800
Windows 11	0	0	20	1800

All tests were performed in a small laboratory created by Vagrant by Hashicorp, an open-source software that helps and simplifies the management of reproducible virtual machine environments. The lab network contains one attacker, a Debian 11 virtual machine with our fuzzer, and one victim, which rotated between all operating systems listed in Table 1. The victim and the attacker are directly connected, as in a LAN, to avoid side effects by other network elements. We performed tests multiple times to reduce the number of errors due to some transient situation in the victim.

We can summarize the tests in:

1. Single ICMPv6 packet fragmented using multiple permutations of fragments;
2. Single ICMPv6 packet fragmented using multiple permutations, but fragments are sent multiple times;
3. Multiple ICMPv6 packets fragmented using multiple permutations.

In the first test, a single packet is fragmented and sent to the victim for each different permutation in our model. In the second test, the same occurs, but all frames are sent again (in the same order) 4 more times, to simulate a network retransmission or a malicious act by the attacker. In the third test, for each different permutation, five different ICMPv6 packets are created and sent. Note that, while both the second and the third tests are sending five packets, in the second test all fragments have the same fragment ID (as they belong to the same packet), while in the third test fragments are grouped by the fragment ID, which is different for each packet.

Table 2 shows a summary of the results we obtained by running the proposed model in the virtual environment. These results not only demonstrate that all listed operating systems are violating the RFC 5722 by replying to overlapping fragments, but also that the way they handle overlapping fragments (the "reassembly policy") may pose some risk, as in the case when different reassembly policies are used between an IDS/IPS/firewall and the victim. Different reassembly policies may result in a different reassembled packet: an attacker can exploit this difference to provide a different packet to the IDS/IPS/firewall

Table 3. New payload definition. This payload exploits the checksum's commutative property to avoid re-assembly errors. The "odd" version is also used in tests with one packet, whereas both "odd" and "even" are used in tests with multiple packets.

Shankar and Paxson	Odd/single packet	Even
A	11223344	44113322
B	11332244	44331122
C	22113344	44332211
D	22331144	11224433
E	33112244	11334422
F	33221144	22114433

than the one reassembled by the victim, bypassing the IDS/IPS/firewall protection.

We performed the same set of tests using the Shankar and Paxson model. As shown in Table 2, the Shankar and Paxson model ended with no replies for all tests, which may indicate RFC 5722 compliance. However, we know that ICMPv6 Echo Replies are missing not because of discarding overlapping fragment (RFC requirement), but due to missing payload pieces in the reassembly created by the new policy of fragment reassembly (as explained in Sect. 4.1).

4.4 On IPv6 Checksum and Overlapping Fragments

IPv6 header does not contain a checksum [6], shifting the duty of checking the integrity of the transmission to the upper layers. The choice was made to speed up the packet forwarding: IPv6 intermediate devices, like routers, do not check the integrity of the datagram (except for security systems like IDS). Upper layers protocols, like ICMPv6, UDP, and TCP, may require a checksum, which is computed and verified by the transmission endpoints.

When the checksum is required (e.g., ICMPv6), the first fragment contains the checksum of the entire packet inside the upper layer header. Overlapping fragments might create a situation where the final checksum of the packet is incorrect since hosts can have different reassembly policies [2]. This, in turn, might cause the victim to discard the packet and not reply to our ICMPv6 ping tests, invalidating the results presented until now.

To rule out that packets are dropped because of the checksum mismatch, we re-defined the payload of the fragments as shown in Table 3. This new definition exploits the commutative property of the checksum: by definition, the checksum contains the sum of 2 bytes pair of the entire IPv6 packet [9]. Given that the sum has the commutative property, any combination of fragments in our model has the same checksum.

4.5   Denial of Service Due to RFC 5722 Compliance

The RFC 5722 requires dropping packets with overlapping fragments. This rule creates a vulnerable surface for a Denial-of-Service attack by a malicious third host, the "attacker". For the attacker to exploit the vulnerability, the transmission between two parties should use fragments, and the attacker should be able to predict the IP-id field and spoof the source IP address.

The attack strategy involves the attacker sending a spoofed fragment to the target host (the transmission receiver) before it can reassemble all the fragments received from the victim (the transmission source). By using the same source address as the victim and the same IP-id value, the attacker creates an overlap during the fragment reassembly phase, causing the entire packet to be discarded and preventing the victim from receiving a reply.

This Denial-of-Service vulnerability exposed by the RFC is exploitable only in certain conditions. Also, it is the desired effect as fragment handling exposes higher security issues. So, in our opinion, it does not present a real threat due to the practical difficulties of satisfying prerequisites and the low gain of such attacks.

5   RFC 9099 Compliance

This section presents the study on RFC 9099 [26] compliance, which mainly focuses on IPv6 Extension Headers. We briefly introduce the requirements stated in RFC 9099 [26]. Then, we describe the experiments we performed to verify the compliance of operating systems.

5.1   IPv6 Fragment Headers and RFC 9099

IPv6 extension headers are additional data structures that can be included in the IPv6 packet header to provide extra functionality or options beyond what is defined in the IPv6 protocol. These headers are placed between the IPv6 header and the upper-layer protocol data, allowing for features such as fragmentation, authentication, encryption, routing, and mobility.

IPv6 uses a specific extension header named "Fragment Header" to handle a fragmented packet where the packet is too big for the Maximum Transfer Unit of underlying links [6]. While not strictly required, RFC 9099 [26] suggest that security devices in the middle of the transmission (such as firewall, IDS, IPS) and the destination endpoint should drop first fragments that do not contain the entire IPv6 header chain (which include the transport-layer header). The reason for this requirement is to avoid issues when dealing with stateless filtering [6].

Some IPv6 extension headers can be expressed multiple times in a single datagram; others do not. Also, these headers are linked together in a chain, and the RFC 8200 [6] suggests an order for headers to optimize the computation and avoid processing issues. RFC 9099 strongly recommends that the correct order and the maximum number of repetitions of extension headers are enforced

Table 4. First experiment for RFC 9099 compliance. No response is expected: the first fragment should be dropped because it does not contain all the extension headers.

#	Type	Offset	More Fragment	Payload
1	ICMPv6 Echo Request	0	1	/
2	Fragment	1	1	AAAAAAAA
3	IPv6 Fragment & Dest. Options	2	0	BBBBBBBB

Table 5. Second experiment for RFC 9099 compliance. No response is expected: the first fragment should be dropped because it does not contain the full IPv6 headers chain.

#	Type	Offset	More Fragment	Payload
1	IPv6 Fragment	0	1	/
2	ICMPv6 Echo Request	0	1	/
3	IPv6 Fragment	1	0	BBBBBBBB

in endpoints and in any security device in the path. Non-conforming packets should be dropped [26].

In the context of fragmented IPv6 packets, a malicious actor may try to send additional headers in different fragments, or they might try to overwrite the upper layer header in the payload from the first fragment using a subsequent overlapping fragment. In both cases, the packet must be discarded.

5.2   Fragment Headers Experiments and Results

We designed our experiments around the two requirements from RFC 9099: the first experiment checks the requirement of having all extension headers in the first fragment, and the second experiment is on overlapping the upper layer header using an overlapping fragment.

In the first experiment (Table 4), we send a packet divided into three fragments: the first contains the ICMPv6 Header and no payload, the second contains the payload, and the last contains a Destination Options header. These fragments are not overlapping, but no response is expected as the first fragment does not contain the complete IPv6 headers chain [26].

In the second experiment (Table 5), we send a packet divided into three fragments: the first contains no headers and no payload, the second contains the ICMPv6 Echo Request header (offset for this fragment is zero, as the first fragment), and the last contains a payload. The first and the second fragments do not overlap because the first fragment is empty. Nevertheless, no response is expected as the first fragment does not contain the complete IPv6 headers chain [26].

We tested a subset of the operating system in Table 1, namely Debian 11, FreeBSD, and OpenBSD.

In the first experiment, we received an ICMPv6 Echo Reply from all the operating systems, even if the first fragment did not have the destination options header. The correct response was to discard the first fragment or the entire packet.

In the second experiment, all operating systems recognized the malformed packet; however, only FreeBSD and OpenBSD silently dropped the received packet. Debian, instead, the victim responds to the attacker with an ICMPv6 packet with code 3, which stands for "IPv6 First Fragment has incomplete IPv6 Header Chain".

The results of the first experiment show that the systems tested, at present, are not compliant with RFC 9099 since they are not dropping the first fragments or packets when extension headers are spread through fragments. Also, since test 1 contains the "Destination Options" extension header after the Fragment Header (while the RFC 8200 recommends the opposite), those systems are not dropping non-conforming packets, while RFC 9099 suggests discarding them.

Moreover, it is possible to recognize an operating system using the fragmented packet as described in Table 5 (second experiment): the different behavior between operating systems could lead an attacker to perform fingerprinting against victims. While RFCs 9099 and 5722 do not specify whether a host should silently discard these packets, we believe a silent discard is the safest option, and an RFC should mandate it.

6   Modification Attacks with Overlapping Fragments

This type of attack has been firstly performed, in a different context, by Gilad et al. [7]: the attacker aims to modify the content of the communication between the victim and a legitimate host, namely host X. We leverage the RFC 5722 non-compliance: since the victim accepts overlapping fragments, the attacker can change with another fragment the bytes sent by the host X.

In the Modification Attack, the attacker must send one or more fragments and ensure that when these fragments are reassembled with the legitimate ones, the result is a correct packet (not malformed) and that the final packet payload is the desired one. For this reason, to perform a successful modification attack, the attacker has to calculate the correct checksum to avoid the discard of a packet because of a checksum mismatch (Sect. 4.4).

We demonstrate that the modification attack is possible by altering the content of a syslog UDP transmission from host X to the victim.

6.1   Implementation of Modification Attack with Scapy

We present the implementation of the Modification Attack in a specific scenario where both host X and the victim are running the rsyslog, an open-source software for managing logs and forwarding log messages between machines. The host X is configured to send syslog messages via UDP to the victim.

This attack requires the malicious actor to know (or guess) the IP identification field value, the payload of the IPv6 packet (in this case, the log message) host X sends to the victim, and requires spoofing the host X address. The IP ID requirement can be easily satisfied: guessing the IP identification value has already been demonstrated in literature by Salutari et al. [23]. The packet payload, instead, should be predictable (for example, a TLS Client-Hello) or known in advance. Spoofing is still a problem, especially in local area networks [23].

We will alter the log line regarding a successful SSH authentication in this case. In particular, we will try to alter the fragment containing the attacker's IP address. The original line is `Jun 1 20:47:08 git sshd[88459]: Accepted publickey for git from 10.10.10.100 port 49240 ssh2: ED25519 SHA256:vNTXCU7b6C6mqvcaH7j1/uRC5unllTpG5kCtd01xxoc`

The host X sends the log line in three fragments:

1. the first fragment with the UDP header, the syslog severity and facility code, and the first 51 bytes of the message:
   `<43> Jun 1 20:47:08 git sshd[88459]: Accepted publickey ;`
2. the second fragment with 56 bytes of the message:
   `for git from 10.10.10.100 port 49240 ssh2: ED25519 SHA25;`
3. the third fragment with the rest of the log line:
   `6:vNTXCU7b6C6mqvcaH7j1/uRC5unllTpG5kCtd01xxoc;`

To successfully perform the attack, the malicious actor should send a spoofed second fragment with a different payload before or after the second fragment from the host X to the victim (depending on the reassembly policy used by the victim). When the victim re-assembles the final packet, the new payload for the second fragment will be used.

However, a different payload will likely result in a different checksum: the victim will drop the packet as corrupted. To work around this problem, the attacker exploits the commutative property of the sum in the checksum by shuffling the payload. The shuffle should swap groups of two bytes as the checksum is calculated by a series of 16-bit sums.

Another technique for keeping the same checksum is to calculate the difference between the correct checksum and the checksum of the new final packet and then add this difference to the spoofed fragment payload. Thanks to the commutative property of the sum, the result will be the original checksum.

6.2 Modification Attacks Results Discussion

In our test environment, we used two GNU/Linux Debian machines (the same version listed in Table 1). We tested this attack by sending the following payload in a spoofed second fragment to the victim just before the original second fragment: `0 0. Efromr 9225HAgi.12: 110fo55po10D240rt19t 0. 4sh S s.` This string is a permutation of the payload of the original second fragment, so the final payload (after the reassembly) will remain the same as the original one.

Jun 1 20:47:08 git sshd[88459]: Accepted publickey 0 0. Efromr 9225HAgI.12: 110fo55po10D240rt19t 0. 4sh S s6:vNTXCU7b6C
bmqvcaH7j1/uRCSunIl7pG5kCtd01xxoc

Fig. 6. The string in the log file. The log line contains the attacker's modified payload.

Since the RFC 5722 states that datagrams with overlapping fragments must be silently discarded, we should not expect any log in the victim machine. However, as the victim is not RFC 5722 compliant, we found the modified payload in the log file, as shown in Fig. 6.

These attacks can be prevented mainly by implementing RFC 5722 recommendations of dropping the entire packets in the presence of overlapping fragments. IPSec may provide additional protections.

7 Conclusions

In conclusion, this work addresses the ongoing issues associated with packet fragmentation in IPv6, explicitly focusing on the issue of overlapping fragments. Despite the requirement listed by different RFCs for hosts to drop overlapping fragments silently, our work indicates that the problem persists. Also, changes in the fragment reassembly policies by operating systems from byte-based to fragment-based made current models for testing IPv6 fragmentation issues (such as the Shankar and Paxson model) obsolete.

To address these issues, the authors propose a novel model that exploits the fragment-based strategy in modern operating systems when handling IPv6 fragmentation. By leveraging the commutative property of the checksum, the authors simplify the assessment process and propose a more accurate evaluation methodology.

Using this new model, the authors evaluate the compliance of modern operating systems with RFC-5722 and RFC-9099, which pertain to fragmentation handling in IPv6. The evaluation was performed both using ICMPv6 Echo Request/Reply, and by performing a real attack named "Modification Attack", where a fragmented transmission was altered.

The results of the evaluation reveal that IPv6 fragmentation remains a significant threat, and further efforts are required to address the related security issues. These findings underscore the need for ongoing research and development to enhance the security measures and mechanisms associated with IPv6 fragmentation.

Taking the necessary countermeasures to deal with fragmentation attacks and secure IPv6 would still be appropriate since adopting IPv6 is an irreversible and ever-growing process, especially with new technologies based on the Internet of Things.

We released the dataset and all scripts developed to run our experiments in a public GitHub repository at https://github.com/netsecuritylab/ipv6-fragmentation.

Acknowledgments. This work was partially supported by project 'Prebunking: predicting and mitigating coordinated inauthentic behaviors in social media' project, funded by Sapienza University of Rome; by the Italian Ministry of Defense PNRM project "UNAVOX", by project SERICS (PE00000014) under the MUR National Recovery and Resilience Plan funded by the European Union – NextGenerationEU.

References

1. Arends, R.: DNS security introduction and requirements. IETF RFC 4033 (2005)
2. Atlasis, A.: Attacking IPv6 implementation using fragmentation. In: Black Hat Europe Conference (2012)
3. Atlasis, A., Rey, E.: Evasion of high-end IPS devices in the age of IPv6. https:// blackhat.com/docs/us-14/materials/us-14-Atlasis-Evasion-Of-HighEnd-IPS- Devices-In-The-Age-Of-IPv6-WP.pdf
4. Bethencourt, J., Franklin, J., Vernon, M.: Mapping internet sensors with probe response attacks. In: Proceedings of the 14th Conference on USENIX Security Symposium, SSYM 2005, vol, 14, p. 13. USENIX Association, USA (2005)
5. Deering, S.E., Hinden, R.M.: Internet Protocol, version 6 (IPv6) specification. IETF RFC 2460 (1998)
6. Deering, S.E., Hinden, R.M.: Internet Protocol, version 6 (IPv6) specification. IETF RFC 8200 (2017)
7. Gilad, Y., Herzberg, A.: Fragmentation considered vulnerable. ACM Trans. Inf. Syst. Secur. **15**(4), 1–31 (2013). https://doi.org/10.1145/2445566.2445568
8. Gont, F.: Processing of IPv6 "Atomic" Fragments. IETF RFC 6946 (2013)
9. Gupta, M., Conta, A.: Internet Control Message Protocol (ICMPv6) for the Internet Protocol Version 6 (IPv6) Specification. RFC 4443 (2006). https://doi.org/10. 17487/RFC4443, https://www.rfc-editor.org/info/rfc4443
10. Göhring, M., Shulman, H., Waidner, M.: Path MTU discovery considered harmful. In: 2018 IEEE 38th International Conference on Distributed Computing Systems (ICDCS), pp. 866–874 (2018). https://doi.org/10.1109/ICDCS.2018.00088
11. Heffner, J., Mathis, M., Chandler, B.: IPv4 reassembly errors at high data rates. IETF RFC 4963 (2007)
12. Kantarjiev, C.A., Mogul, J.C.: Fragmentation considered harmful. In: Proceedings of the ACM Workshop on Frontiers in Computer Communications Technology, SIGCOMM 1987, pp. 390–401. Association for Computing Machinery, New York (1987). https://doi.org/10.1145/55482.55524
13. Kaufman, C., Hoffman, P.: Internet Key Exchange Protocol Version 2 (IKEv2). IETF RFC 5996 (2010)
14. Kaufman, C., Perlman, R., Sommerfeld, B.: Dos protection for UDP-based protocols. In: Proceedings of the 10th ACM Conference on Computer and Communication Security - CCS 2003 (2003). https://doi.org/10.1145/948109.948113
15. Krishnan, S.: Handling of overlapping IPv6 fragments. IETF RFC 5722 (2009)
16. Li, Z., Goyal, A., Chen, Y., Paxson, V.: Automating analysis of large-scale botnet probing events. In: Proceedings of the 4th International Symposium on Information, Computer, and Communications Security, ASIACCS 2009, pp. 11–22. Association for Computing Machinery, New York (2009). https://doi.org/10.1145/ 1533057.1533063
17. Miller, I.: Protection Against a Variant of the Tiny Fragment Attack (RFC 1858). IETF RFC 3128 (2001)

18. Novak, J.: Target-Based Fragmentation Reassembly. Sourcefire, Columbia (2005)
19. Postel, J.: Internet Protocol. IETF RFC 791 (1981)
20. Qian, Z., Mao, Z.M.: Off-path TCP sequence number inference attack - how firewall middleboxes reduce security. In: 2012 IEEE Symposium on Security and Privacy (2012). https://doi.org/10.1109/sp.2012.29
21. Qian, Z., Mao, Z.M., Xie, Y.: Collaborative TCP sequence number inference attack. In: Proceedings of the 2012 ACM conference on Computer and communications security - CCS 2012 (2012). https://doi.org/10.1145/2382196.2382258
22. Reed, D., Traina, P.S., Ziemba, P.: Security Considerations for IP Fragment Filtering. IETF RFC 1858 (1995)
23. Salutari, F., Cicalese, D., Rossi, D.J.: A closer look at IP-ID behavior in the wild. In: Beverly, R., Smaragdakis, G., Feldmann, A. (eds.) PAM 2018. LNCS, vol. 10771, pp. 243–254. Springer, Cham (2018). https://doi.org/10.1007/978-3-319-76481-8_18
24. Shankar, U., Paxson, V.: Active mapping: resisting NIDS evasion without altering traffic. In: Proceedings 19th International Conference on Data Engineering (Cat. No.03CH37405) (2003). https://doi.org/10.1109/secpri.2003.1199327
25. Ullrich, J., Krombholz, K., Hobel, H., Dabrowski, A., Weippl, E.: IPv6 security: attacks and countermeasures in a nutshell. In: 8th {USENIX} Workshop on Offensive Technologies ({WOOT} 14) (2014)
26. Vyncke, E., Chittimaneni, K., Kaeo, M., Rey, E.: Operational Security Considerations for IPv6 Networks. RFC 9099 (2021). https://doi.org/10.17487/RFC9099. https://www.rfc-editor.org/info/rfc9099
27. Zalewski, M.: Strange attractors and TCP/IP sequence number analysis (2001). http://lcamtuf.coredump.cx/newtcp/
28. Zalewski, M.: A new TCP/IP blind data injection technique? (2003). https://seclists.org/bugtraq/2003/Dec/161
29. Zalewski, M.: Silence on the Wire: A Field Guide to Passive Reconnaissance and Indirect Attacks. No Starch Press, San Francisco (2005)

Privacy

Trajectory Hiding and Sharing for Supply Chains with Differential Privacy

Tianyu Li(✉)[iD], Li Xu[iD], Zekeriya Erkin[iD], and Reginald L. Lagendijk[iD]

Cyber Security Group, Delft University of Technology, Delft, The Netherlands
{tianyu.li,l.xu-11,z.erkin,r.l.lagendijk}@tudelft.nl

Abstract. With the fast development of e-commerce, there is a higher demand for timely delivery. Logistic companies want to send receivers a more accurate arrival prediction to improve customer satisfaction and lower customer retention costs. One approach is to share (near) real-time location data with recipients, but this also introduces privacy and security issues such as malicious tracking and theft. In this paper, we propose a privacy-preserving real-time location sharing system including (1) a differential privacy based location publishing method and (2) location sharing protocols for both centralized and decentralized platforms. Different from existing location perturbation solutions which only consider privacy in theory, our location publishing method is based on a real map and different privacy levels for recipients. Our analyses and proofs show that the proposed location publishing method provides better privacy protection than existing works under real maps against possible attacks. We also provide a detailed analysis of the choice of the privacy parameter and their impact on the suggested noisy location outputs. The experimental results demonstrate that our proposed method is feasible for both centralized and decentralized systems and can provide more precise arrival prediction than using time slots in current delivery systems.

Keywords: Privacy-preserving · Differential privacy · Location privacy · Applied cryptography · Blockchain

1 Introduction

Today, e-commerce is playing an important role in people's daily lives. According to *Statista*, in 2020, more than two billion people made orders online, with over $4.2 trillion in transactions. In e-retail, customers care about when they can receive the products, which raises the demand for logistics. Logistic companies, such as *DHL*, *UPS*, aim to minimize the delivery time while keeping packages safe [4]. Meanwhile, logistic companies provide a time slot for delivery. Unfortunately, these time slots usually span multiple hours, which reduces customer satisfaction on many levels [1]. On some occasions, the delivery time is updated to a new date and time due to transportation problems, causing frustrations and discomfort from customers. The mismatch between the predicted and actual arrival time

G. Tsudik et al. (Eds.): ESORICS 2023, LNCS 14345, pp. 297–317, 2024.
https://doi.org/10.1007/978-3-031-51476-0_15

causes problems for both customers and companies. Customers need to wait longer for the package. For companies, every delay adds to the cost of customer retention rate, customer acquisition cost, and customer lifetime value [3].

One possible solution is to provide a more precise delivery prediction, e.g. by offering real-time location data to help calculate the exact delivery time. According to *Hublock*, real-time location sharing systems are important and needed in logistics to improve the transparency of logistics. As a result, companies can improve customer satisfaction and lower the cost of retaining or acquiring customers [13]. Besides, the system is useful for disputes and knowing the reason for delays, and unburdening the customer service department [13]. It is already possible to see the use of real-time tracking, e.g., *DHL* offers a live tracking service for selected shipments [6]. Unfortunately, sharing accurate locations introduces security and privacy issues. According to [11,27], the accurate location of trucks can be used for malicious tracking and theft. Imagine that a customer buys a very cheap product, locates the truck carrying that product, and steals other valuable packages in the same truck, resulting in economic damage [11,27].

Given that we want to improve customer satisfaction by providing a realistic time of arrival and, at the same time, preventing potential theft, it is necessary to provide technical solutions that achieve both goals. There are existing approaches using generalization [15], adding dummy data [16], applying suppression [32], or using differential privacy [33] for publishing data with anonymity or privacy concerns. The first three methods are not suitable for real-time location sharing since they require the background knowledge of attackers and the whole trajectory as input, which are not available in real-time tracking since the entire trajectory is unknown when the truck is moving, and the adversary can carry out different attacks (e.g. malicious tracking or theft) based on background knowledge, such as the road map of the city. In contrast, differential privacy [7,8] adds noise to the actual data and provides privacy guarantees, which is a strong candidate. Although there are existing approaches to publish location data with differential privacy [2,33,35,36], there is no work considering both real-time location publishing and continuous trajectory privacy on a real map.

When the adversary holds real road maps, it is challenging to hide the trajectory of a truck. Even though the noise is added to real trajectory points, the published trajectory points are possibly up and down to the actual route, which can be de-noised using a filter or analysis. Meanwhile, it is important to add proper noise considering the road density. It is sufficient to add slight noise to anonymize the road for a truck moving with high road density, such as in the city centre. However, with the same noise, the actual trajectory is distinguishable if the truck moves in an area with low road density, such as the countryside.

In this paper, we consider a network of logistic companies sharing location data with their customers using a location sharing platform. For different privacy-preservation needs and settings, protocols for centralized and decentralized platforms are needed. On the one hand, large enterprises can build their own centralized solutions. On the other hand, decentralized solutions are needed for small and medium-sized enterprises (SMEs), which occupy more than 90% of business in Europe [5]. SMEs often share similar needs but lack the technical resources to build or digitize their own supply chains. A platform shared by SMEs is desired to achieve the same functionality [34]. Blockchain is a candidate for the decentralized solution since it is traceable, immutable and transparent [25].

For trajectory hiding and secure location sharing, we focus on cities for package delivery and omit motorways. Location data of the Truck is reported based on regular intervals using the location sharing platform. The Sender and Receiver of a package in the Truck can access that information, which is used for estimating the time of arrival or any other optimization purposes. Note that using only the location perturbation algorithm cannot guarantee that the location is shared in a privacy-preserving manner on the platform. In order to provide protection, only the owner of a package and the corresponding delivery company should know the location information. We achieve this goal with cryptographic tools. Our proposal is effective regardless of the structure of the platform, which can be centralized or distributed, e.g. utilizing blockchain technology.

In summary, our contributions are as follows:

- We present a privacy-preserving location sharing system for logistics, including a location perturbation algorithm together with location sharing protocols, for tracking packages in (near) real-time to provide more precise arrival prediction than time slots. To the best of our knowledge, this is the first paper that considers real road maps and attacks for location perturbation.
- To prevent potential theft, we use differential privacy and geo-indistinguishability with different privacy levels for corresponding receivers. Our concrete privacy analysis and proof indicate the proposed approach provides better trajectory privacy preservation under real road maps and possible attacks than existing works. The detailed experiments show how privacy parameters are selected and how the utility remains in terms of arrival prediction. Also, the run-time is in the order of nanoseconds, which is feasible for real-time data sharing.
- To protect customers' privacy and the commercial interest of logistic companies, our proposed protocols provide anonymity, unlinkability and auditability in centralized and decentralized settings. Our experiments and analysis indicate that the proposed platform is privacy-preserving and has less storage cost than previous works. For feasibility, an Ethereum platform can process ~ 450 trucks due to the underlying blockchain technology, which is sufficient for average-sized cities even though the use of blockchain is not optimized.

Remark 1. The selection of platforms (blockchain) is not our focus since companies can build their own centralized or decentralized solutions according to their needs with our proposed protocols.

2   Preliminaries

Differential Privacy. Differential privacy (DP) was raised by Dwork [7,8] to protect individual privacy and better use the dataset. In Eq. 1, for neighbouring datasets, the probability of whether the output belongs to O differs less than e^ϵ with a small error factor δ, which hides the existence of any individual.

Definition 1 ((ϵ, δ)-differential privacy). *An algorithm $\mathcal{A}$ satisfies (ϵ, δ)-differential privacy iff for neighbouring datasets D, D' which only differ in one record, and with any range $O \subseteq range(\mathcal{A})$:*

$$\Pr[\mathcal{A}(D) \in O] \leq e^\epsilon \Pr[\mathcal{A}(D') \in O] + \delta . \tag{1}$$

The Gaussian mechanism is a widely used mechanism to achieve (ϵ, δ)-differential privacy [10], which adds noise as $\mathcal{N}(\mu, \sigma)$ with $\mu = 0$, $\sigma^2 = 2\ln(1.25/\delta) \cdot (\Delta_2)^2/(\epsilon^2)$. δ is the small error, such as 10^{-5}. Δ_2 is the l_2 sensitivity.

Geo-Indistinguishability. Based on the definition of differential privacy, Andrés et al. [2] define geo-indistinguishability to allow to provide location based services (LBS) considering privacy within a radius r. In general, a mechanism $\mathcal{A}$ satisfies ϵ-geo-indistinguishability iff for any radius $r > 0$, the user enjoys ϵr-privacy within r, and the privacy level is proportional to r.

Definition 2 (geo-indistinguishability). *An algorithm $\mathcal{A}$ satisfies ϵ-geo-indistinguishability iff for any two different points x, x':*

$$d_\mathcal{P}(\mathcal{A}(x), \mathcal{A}(x')) \leq \epsilon \cdot d(x, x') . \tag{2}$$

$d(\cdot, \cdot)$ denotes the Euclidean distance. For two different points x, x' s.t. $d(x, x') \leq r$, the distance $d_\mathcal{P}(\mathcal{A}(x), \mathcal{A}(x'))$ of corresponding distributions should be at most l, and $\epsilon = l/r$. Andrés et al. [2] present the Planar Laplace Mechanism which satisfies ϵ-geo-indistinguishability. Assume u is the smallest distance unit, δ_θ is the precision of the machine for angle θ, and r_{max} is the range within which the mechanism satisfies ϵ-geo-indistinguishability. If $q = u/r_{max}\delta_\theta$, we have ϵ from:

$$\epsilon' + \frac{1}{u} \ln \frac{q + 2e^{\epsilon'u}}{q - 2e^{\epsilon'u}} \leq \epsilon , \tag{3}$$

where ϵ' is the privacy parameter for $C_{\epsilon'}^{-1}(p)$. The noise is added to angle θ and distance r in Cartesian coordinates. $C_{\epsilon'}(r)$ shows the probability of any random point between 0 and r. If p is uniformly selected from $[0, 1)$, we can get $r = C_{\epsilon'}^{-1}(p) = -\frac{1}{\epsilon'}\left(W_{-1}\left(\frac{p-1}{e} + 1\right)\right)$ where W_{-1} is the Lambert W function.

3 Security Requirements

Objectives. The objective is a secure and privacy-preserving location sharing system for a number of trucks. On the one hand, the published location should have privacy preservation and good utility for arrival prediction. On the other hand, location data should be published using a privacy-preserving platform. The platform only shares the location with Sender and Receiver, while no other information is leaked. More precisely, other parties in the platform cannot access the location of certain packages or link that package to a sender or a truck.

Set-up and Assumptions. There are three roles in the platform: **Truck** collects GPS data and shares it on the platform every n minutes. n is based on the number of Trucks simultaneously in the platform (considering system capacity) and how sparse the trajectory should be (considering privacy preservation). Only Trucks can publish information on the platform. **Sender** and **Receiver** access data from the platform, and each (Sender$_i$, Receiver$_i$) pair shares the same package information for package i. It is assumed that different companies share the same platform to provide location-based services to customers. Each company has several trucks but does not know the information of others. Moreover, we assume the distance to the destination is correlated to the delivery time. Other variables may also influence the estimate, including the characteristics of the road network and the current traffic levels. These are not considered here.

Adversary Model. In package delivery, we assume Trucks always send the correct location data, which is automatically collected from sensors and shared on the platform. Malicious drivers who can turn off the sensors are not considered. Internal adversaries (Senders and Receivers) can only access information from the platform. They try to misuse the available shared data from the platform to carry out malicious actions such as theft or malicious tracking. External adversaries try to steal the location data from the platform without access. Meanwhile, we assume the adversary has background knowledge of the truck, such as the road map of the city. However, we do not consider a powerful adversary with additional capacities, including surveillance cameras or drones. Such adversaries are hard to protect against even if no location information is shared.

Attack Model. There are possible attacks on the location perturbation process and the sharing platform. For location perturbation, adversaries try to re-identify the actual location of trucks by de-noising the published location data (such as using filters). With the identified location, adversaries can find the truck and carry out theft or malicious tracking. For the sharing platform, (1) adversaries try to find the linkage between customers and packages for malicious commercial analysis, such as finding target customers for certain logistic companies. (2) Adversaries try to get information about other packages. If adversaries know the location of all packages, they can find the target truck with target packages.

4   Related Work

Location Privacy with DP. We consider DP-based location perturbation to provide privacy guarantees while publishing trajectory data in real-time. Dwork et al. [9] introduce the idea of event-level DP for DP under continual observation, but it is not robust when events are coming continuously. The actual location can be obtained by averaging the published location if the user stays in a certain area for a long time. Kellaris et al. [21] proposed ω-event DP to protect the event sequence occurring within ω successive timestamps by applying Laplace noise and budget allocation method. Fang et al. [12] gave the idea of δ-neighbourhood instead of the standard one. δ is a threshold for the generalized location point to guarantee that it is close to the actual location. Also, Xiao et al. [35] proposed δ-location set based differential privacy to account for the temporal correlations and protect the accurate location at every timestamp. The temporal correlation is modelled through a Markov chain, and they hide the actual location in the δ-location set in which location pairs are indistinguishable. However, a reliable transition matrix is difficult to be constructed in a real scenario [19]. Xiong et al. [36] applied differential privacy to cluster and select location points, but the whole trajectory is known before the perturbation. Andrés et al. [2] gave the definition of geo-indistinguishability to allow location based services (LBS) to provide a service considering the privacy of individuals within a radius r. Also, the planar Laplace mechanism is proposed, which satisfies ϵ-geo-indistinguishability.

Although many different works consider location privacy, there are no works showing whether they can protect a real trajectory in a real use case with a real map under a possible attack. For example, suppose the trajectory of a truck is published and the adversary hold the background knowledge (e.g. the city map). In that case, the adversary may infer the actual location of the truck if there is only one road which the truck can pass around the published location.

Decentralized Supply Chains. Among decentralized solutions, blockchain is potentially a disruptive technology for supply chains since it is traceable, immutable, and transparent [25], with which the participants can trace the transaction. Maouchi et al. [22] proposed DECOUPLES, a decentralized, unlinkable, and privacy-preserving traceability system for supply chains. In their design, the PASTA protocol is proposed based on the stealth address to anonymize the receiver of a transaction. Each product has a unique product ID (pID). The receiver uses pID to generate a pair of tracking keys and sends the public key to the sender. The sender uses the public key to calculate a one-time stealth address as the receiver address, so only the receiver who owns the private key can track the package. However, they only consider two parties, while three parties (Sender, Truck, Receiver) are more common in real supply chains. This results in unnecessary one-time stealth addresses and more storage costs in real use.

Sahai et al. [26] proposed a privacy-preserving supply chain traceability system based on a protocol using zero-knowledge proofs and cryptographic accumulators. The proposed system provides unlinkability and untraceability, but only two parties are considered. Sezer et al. [29] designed a traceable, auditable, and privacy-preserving framework for supply chains using smart contracts. However, package information is not encrypted, which leads to possible leakage.

5   Location Perturbation

5.1   Privacy Parameter Selection

In geo-indistinguishability, the privacy parameter ϵ controls how much noise is added to the location data. If the same amount of noise is added all the time, it is not large enough when the truck is far away from the destination and not small enough when close to the receiver, which influences the utility. The correct amount of noise should be added depending on the location of the truck. In the city centre, there are many routes within a small radius r, and it is possible

---

Algorithm 1: Location Perturbation

Input: Current location x, destination location f, previous angle $\theta_0 = 0$
Output: Sanitized version z of input x
1: Get ϵ using Equation 6.
2: Get ϵ' using Equation 3.
3: $\theta \leftarrow AngleSelection(\theta_0)$, then set $\theta_0 \leftarrow \theta$.
4: Uniformly select $p \in [0, 1)$ and set $r \leftarrow C_{\epsilon'}^{-1}(p)$.
5: $z \leftarrow x+ < r\cos(\theta), r\sin(\theta) >$.
6: **return** z.

---

to hide the real route with less noise. However, when the truck is located far away from the city centre, there are fewer alternative routes (consider a rural area with fewer roads around). To hide the real route, the radius r needs to be increased to include additional routes. Notice that we apply the distance to the city centre as the second factor for privacy parameter selection in this paper. Other factors, such as city density or road density, can also be used. We exclude motorways between cities since it is practically not possible to hide the location of a truck when there is only one road available.

With geo-indistinguishability where $l = \epsilon \cdot r$ (l is the privacy level, ϵ is the privacy parameter, and r is the radius). We can formulate l as:

$$l(x, f_i) = \begin{cases} l_s, & \text{if } d(x, f_i) \text{ is large} \\ l_m, & \text{if } d(x, f_i) \text{ is medium} \\ l_l, & \text{if } d(x, f_i) \text{ is small}, \end{cases} \tag{4}$$

where $d(x, f_i)$ is the distance between the location of truck x and receiver f_i. A smaller privacy level (stronger privacy guarantee) is applied when the truck is far from the city centre, and l is larger to provide more precise arrival predictions when the truck is close to the receiver. The function is only applied when the delivery is scheduled for the next user i. Otherwise, l is set as l_s.

Similarly, r is based on the distance $d_i(x, c)$ between the truck (x) and the city centre (c). r should be smaller when the distance is shorter, so we have:

$$r(x, c) = \begin{cases} r_s, & \text{if } d_i(x, c) \text{ is small} \\ r_m, & \text{if } d_i(x, c) \text{ is medium} \\ r_l, & \text{if } d_i(x, c) \text{ is large} \end{cases} \tag{5}$$

$$\epsilon_i(x, f_i, c) = l(x, f_i)/r(x, c). \tag{6}$$

Here, the values of different parameters are chosen based on use cases. Different distance d and different privacy parameters ϵ should be defined based on the scenario. The selection of parameters is further discussed in Sect. 8.

5.2 Angle Selection

In geo-indistinguishability, only the privacy of single location points is considered without real road maps, as shown in Fig. 11. The adversary can infer the actual

Fig. 1. An example output by PL_ϵ on a real map. Blue: actual trajectory, red: published, green: filtered. (Color figure online)

Fig. 2. An example output after the Angle Selection is applied. Blue: actual trajectory. Red: published. (Color figure online)

trajectory even if every location point is protected. With a median filter and real maps, the adversary can achieve a trajectory close to the actual one (as shown in Fig. 1). Although there are differences between the actual and published trajectories, adversaries can identify the correct road using a real map.

In this paper, we consider the connection between different location points by applying similar angles. Instead of uniformly selecting the new angle θ, we apply the Gaussian mechanism [10] to add noise to the previous θ_0, and

$$\theta = \theta_0 + \mathcal{N}(\mu = 0, \sigma = \sqrt{2\ln(1.25/\delta)} \cdot \Delta_2/\epsilon_a). \tag{7}$$

We use ϵ_a as the privacy budget for the angle selection mechanism to distinguish it from the ϵ for geo-indistinguishability. With Eq. 7, we calculate the new angle θ and round it into the range $[0, 2\pi)$ (as Algorithm 2 in Appendix). The process mitigates the filtering attack by misleading the adversary to a wrong trajectory. We further analyze privacy protection in Sects. 7 and 8.

Here the angle θ of round k_i is the input for round k_{i+1}. We need the composition theorem to calculate the privacy parameter ϵ_a with k rounds. In general, for k mechanisms M_i that all provide (ϵ, δ)-DP, the sequence of $M_i(x)$ provides $(k\epsilon_i, k\delta_i)$-DP [23]. By contrast, with the Gaussian noise, the scale is only $O(\sqrt{k})$.

Theorem 1. *For real-valued queries with sensitivity $\Delta > 0$, the mechanism that adds Gaussian noise with variance $(8k\ln(e + (\epsilon/\delta))\Delta_2^2/\epsilon^2)$ satisfies (ϵ, δ)-DP under k-fold adaptive composition for any $\epsilon > 0$ and $\delta \in (0, 1]$ [20].*

In Theorem 1, the variance for k-fold Gaussian mechanism is $(8\ln(e + (\epsilon/\delta)) \cdot k \cdot \Delta_2^2/\epsilon^2)$ while for Gaussian mechanism is $(2\ln(1.25/\delta) \cdot \Delta_2^2/\epsilon^2)$. If we set the global privacy parameter as ϵ_0, the privacy parameter for each round is at the scale of $(\epsilon_0/\sqrt{k})$. In inverse, if each round is ϵ_a-DP, the angle selection algorithm provides $(\sqrt{k}\epsilon_a, \delta')$-DP where k is the number of rounds. The small error δ' is not further explored here, and we refer interested readers to [20].

6   Decentralized Location Sharing System

Initialization. With assumptions in Sect. 3, each Truck has an account (address). Companies register valid addresses at shared certificate owners (CO). The system only accepts data from valid addresses and can track data accordingly.

Hiding Confidential Information. We encrypt the location data to provide confidentiality. A truck can transport several packages with the same location. Equation 6 implies only three possible location outputs. We apply AES-CBC to encrypt the logistic data. Then, we use the public key k_{Aa} for Elliptic Curve Integrated Encryption Scheme (ECIES) [30] to encrypt the symmetric keys. ECIES is based on Diffie-Hellman, with data and recipients' public keys as inputs.

Our Protocols. In PASTA [22] as in Sect. 4, for any specific package, Alice and Bob need two tracking keys to track the same data. Our design overcomes this shortcoming by sharing the same tracking key among them. Protocol 1 establishes a shared key based on the international standard ISO/IEC 11770-2-6 [18]. After the shared key is derived, a (Truck, Sender, Receiver) triplet shares the same (p_{id}, TK_{pid}, K_b) and return the same keys $(K_{Ab} = K_{Bb} = K_b, TK_{pidA} = TK_{pidB} = TK_{pid})$ in Protocol 2. With Protocol 3, Truck generates a random r and broadcasts the (R, P) pair. Sender and Receiver calculate the stealth address P' and find the match. The same record is shared with Receiver and Sender. In theory, we save half storage than PASTA [22].

$$
\begin{array}{ll}
\text{Alice (Sender)} & \text{Bob (Receiver)} \\
\xleftarrow{\quad N_B \quad} & \\
\xrightarrow{\{N_A, N_B, ID_B, F_{AB1}, F_{AB2}\}_{K_{AB}}} & \\
\xleftarrow{\{N_B, N_A, F_{BA1}, F_{BA2}\}_{K_{AB}}} & \\
k_{Aa} \leftarrow f(F_{AB1}, F_{BA1}) & k_{Ba} \leftarrow f(F_{AB1}, F_{BA1}) \\
k_{Ab} \leftarrow f(F_{AB2}, F_{BA2}) & k_{Bb} \leftarrow f(F_{AB2}, F_{BA2})
\end{array}
$$

Protocol 1. Key establishment mechanism. ID_i is the identity of i. N_A is a nonce. F_{AB}, F_{BA} are keying materials. f is the key derivation function. K_{AB} is the long-term key shared by Alice and Bob.

$$
\begin{array}{ll}
\text{Charlie (Truck)} \quad \text{Alice (or Bob)} \\
ID_A, ID_B, p_{id} \\
\xrightarrow{\text{Request } TK_{p_{id}A} \text{ and } TK_{p_{id}B}} \\
\qquad TK_{p_{id}A} \leftarrow H_s(p_{id}k_{Aa})G \\
\qquad K_{Ab} \leftarrow k_{Ab}G \\
\xleftarrow{TK_{p_{id}A}, K_{Ab}} \\
\text{if } (TK_{p_{id}A} \overset{?}{=} TK_{p_{id}B} \\
\text{and } K_{Ab} \overset{?}{=} K_{Bb}): \\
\qquad \text{Protocol 3}
\end{array}
$$

$$
\begin{array}{ll}
\text{Charlie (Truck)} \quad \text{Alice (or Bob)} \\
r \in_R Z_p, R \leftarrow rG \\
P \leftarrow H_s(rTK_{p_{id}})G \\
\qquad + K_b \\
\xrightarrow{\text{Broadcast } (R, P)} \\
\qquad \text{Check each } (R, P) \\
\qquad tk_{p_{id}} \leftarrow H_s(p_{id}k_{Aa}) \\
\qquad P' \leftarrow H_s(tk_{p_{id}}R)G \\
\qquad + K_{Ab} \\
\qquad P' \overset{?}{=} P
\end{array}
$$

Protocol 2. Matching function to check whether Alice and Bob return the same keys. TK is the tracking key, p_{id} is package id, H_s is a hashing function.

Protocol 3. Three-party stealth address protocol. TK and K_b are public shared keys. P is the stealth address. r is the random nonce.

Extensions. The proposed protocols can be used for centralized platforms or blockchain-based platforms. For centralized platforms, with Protocols 1, 2, the

Fig. 3. Another example output by PL_ϵ. Blue: actual, red: published, green: filtered. (Color figure online)

Fig. 4. Another example output with angle selection. Blue: actual, red: published, green: filtered. (Color figure online)

encrypted location information can be shared. For blockchain platforms, the certificate owner (CO) uses *register transaction* to control the validity of trucks. Trucks use *publish transaction* to publish real-time location data. With the contract, we can validate and trace the source of a transaction. For a *register transaction*, we verify the sender is a valid CO and the value is valid. For a *publish transaction*, the contract checks the validity of the sender and the data.

7   Analysis

7.1   Security and Privacy Analysis

Location Perturbation. Section 2 includes different trajectory publishing mechanisms, but most only consider differential privacy in theory, and all the approaches do not consider a real map. There are existing works [17] showing that a differentially private mechanism still suffers from attacks in real use cases. In this paper, with assumptions in Sect. 3, we consider privacy under real maps, showing that our proposed approach provides better privacy protection.

Figures 1, 2, 3 and 4 show example outputs from PL_ϵ and the proposed method for two different trajectories. In Figs. 1 and 3, the filtered trajectory is close to the actual, and it is predictable on which road the truck is moving. Although the trajectory is in a large city, Paris, it is hard to hide from the actual. The basic idea of our proposed angle selection approach is to mislead the adversary to a wrong trajectory that is close to the actual one but not the same one. If the noise trends in the same direction (e.g. south) as the actual trajectory, the adversary can identify the wrong road. In Fig. 4, when the published trajectory is south to the real one, it is more probable for the adversary to infer the wrong road. Moreover, we conclude Lemma 1, indicating that the proposed angle selection mechanism achieves stronger privacy guarantees than randomly selecting angles.

Lemma 1. *The angle selection mechanism can provide stronger privacy protection than randomized angle selection, considering trajectory hiding in real maps under attacks (such as median filters).*

Proof. Figure 5 shows an example trajectory with three location points $La_0(x_0, y_0)$, $La_1(x_1, y_1)$, $La_2(x_2, y_2)$. Similarly, outputs with angle selection are

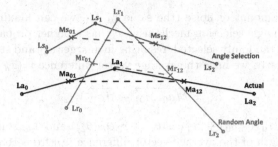

Fig. 5. An example trajectory with three location points.

Ls_0, Ls_1, Ls_2, and with random angles are Lr_0, Lr_1, Lr_2. Ma_{01}, Ms_{01}, Mr_{01} are the midpoint for the first two location points (such as La_0 and La_1). We can compare privacy protection levels between different approaches using two metrics when a median filter is applied: (1) **distance difference**. Compare the distance between the published location points (midpoints), for example, the distance between Ma_{01} and Ms_{01} to the distance between Ma_{01} and Mr_{01}. (2) **length of average vector differences**. Compare the distance of average vector difference from $Ma_{01}Ma_{12}$ to $Ms_{01}Ms_{12}$ and from $Ma_{01}Ma_{12}$ to $Mr_{01}Mr_{12}$. The average vector difference shows the distance difference among the published trajectories (as the dotted lines) since the lines can intersect in the middle. Here the average vector difference from $Ma_{01}Ma_{12}$ to $Ms_{01}Ms_{12}$ is $\frac{1}{2}(\overrightarrow{Ma_{01}Ms_{01}} + \overrightarrow{Ma_{12}Ms_{12}})$.

Assume an adversary $\mathcal{A}$ knows the perturbation is generated from the Laplace distribution. With the published location (Lp_i) and the distance $d_i \geq 0$, the probability that $\mathcal{A}$ can identify the original location (La_i) can be calculated. The probability of the guess distance $d \geq 0$ equal the published distance d_i is:

$$\frac{p(d = d_i)}{\int_0^\infty p(d)} = \frac{\frac{1}{b}\exp(-\frac{d_i}{b})}{\int_0^\infty \frac{1}{b}\exp(-\frac{d}{b})} = \frac{1}{b}\exp(-\frac{d_i}{b}) \tag{8}$$

where b is the scale and $|d|, |d_i| \geq 0$. Equation 8 shows that a smaller distance d_i means a higher probability of guessing the actual perturbation distance. The adversary can draw a circle with a radius equal to the distance to infer the actual location with a real road map. A circle with a larger radius can cover more roads, so it is harder to locate the actual location and privacy is better protected.

In Algorithm 1, the perturbation for $La_0(x_0, y_0)$ is $(r\cos(\theta), r\sin(\theta))$, $\theta \in [0, 2\pi)$. The output is $L_0(x_0 + r_0\cos(\theta_0), y_0 + r_0\sin(\theta_0))$. Similarly, we have La_1 and L_1. If the midpoint for L_0L_1 is M_{01}, we have Ma_{01} and $M_{01}(x_{01}, y_{01})$. For distance difference, we have the distance d_{01} between Ma_{01} and M_{01} that

$$\begin{aligned} 4 \cdot d_{01}^2 &= (x_{01} - (x_0 + x_1))^2 + (y_{01} - (y_0 + y_1))^2 \\ &= (r_0\cos(\theta_0) + r_1\cos(\theta_1))^2 + (r_0\sin(\theta_0) + r_1\sin(\theta_1))^2 \\ &= r_0^2 + r_1^2 + 2r_0r_1\cos(\theta_0 - \theta_1). \end{aligned} \tag{9}$$

With the same amount of noise (the same r_0, r_1), we can maximize d_{01} when $\theta_0 = \theta_1$. By the angle selection mechanism, θ_0 has a higher probability of being closer to θ_1 than randomly selected, resulting in a larger d_{01} and stronger privacy guarantee. Similarly, we have the average vector difference $v_d(x_d, y_d)$ as:

$$2v_d = \overrightarrow{Ma_{01}M_{01}} + \overrightarrow{Ma_{12}M_{12}} \qquad (10)$$

We have $4x_d = (r_0 \cos(\theta_0) + 2r_1 \cos(\theta_1) + r_2 \cos(\theta_2))$ and $4y_d$ similarly. We can calculate the length of the average vector difference $|v_d|$ from $16|v_d|^2$ as:

$$(r_0 \cos(\theta_0) + 2r_1 \cos(\theta_1) + r_2 \cos(\theta_2))^2 + (r_0 \sin(\theta_0) + 2r_1 \sin(\theta_1) + r_2 \sin(\theta_2))^2$$
$$= r_0^2 + 4r_1^2 + r_2^2 + 4r_0r_1 \cos(\theta_0 - \theta_1) + 4r_1r_2 \cos(\theta_1 - \theta_2) + 2r_0r_2 \cos(\theta_0 - \theta_2).$$
$$(11)$$

To maximize $|v_d|$, we have $\theta_0 = \theta_1 = \theta_2$. The angle selection mechanism lets every output θ_i similar to the previous angle θ_{i-1}, which results in a larger $|v_d|$.

The proposed system achieves larger distance and vector differences under filter attacks with the same amount of added noise. With Eq. 8, the angle selection mechanism provides stronger privacy guarantees than random selection.

The angle selection mechanism satisfies $(\sqrt{k}\epsilon_a, \delta')$-DP for k rounds, which means that angles are hidden among the range of $[0, 2\pi)$ with privacy budget $\sqrt{k}\epsilon_a$. In Sect. 2, we assume location points are published every n minutes. Considering half-day delivery with six hours and $n = 5$, there are $k = 72$ rounds and $\sqrt{k} \approx 8.5$. With a total desired privacy budget ϵ_{all}, $\epsilon_a = \epsilon_{all}/\sqrt{k}$ is for each round. The noise is added to angles, so the output is probably beyond the range $[-\pi, \pi)$. This can lead to a random output angle with a small $\epsilon_a (< 1)$. To achieve higher utility, we select a larger ϵ_a to output an angle with higher probability in the range of $[-\pi, \pi)$. With a larger ϵ_a, the adversary may infer that the perturbed angle is related to the previous angle. Differential privacy (DP) has the strong assumption that the adversary knows all other records in the dataset, but the adversary never knows any output angle in our scenario. It is secure to select a larger ϵ_a, such as $\epsilon_a = 5$. Section 8 shows how we select ϵ_a. From the definition of DP, the angle selection results in a larger privacy parameter than selecting uniformly, but Lemma 1 illustrates it can provide stronger privacy guarantees against real adversaries with possible attacks. It is not sufficient to only consider privacy guarantees based on the definition of DP. Instead, a stronger adversary with background knowledge should be considered since this is non-negligible in real cases. Other DP-based works [12, 21, 35] also consider location privacy similarly with analysis only in theory or lines instead of a real map.

The privacy parameter selection function provides different privacy guarantees based on distances under real maps. In a real use case, receivers only need a more precise location when the truck is close. If the receiver is far away from the city, there can be privacy leakage, and it is easy to identify the road of the truck (since there might be only one route within a small radius). Meanwhile, the delivery prediction error can be larger than hours when the package is far from the receiver, but when the truck is within k km, the error should be minimized (to minutes). With the privacy parameter selection function, we can better protect the real location of trucks and provide a more precise arrival time prediction when the truck is away or close to the receiver.

Table 1. Computational and storage analysis. N_T, N_L, N_P: number of trucks, encrypted location data, destined product information. k_{SE}: key size (bits) for AES-CBC. $e, a, (p, r)$: size (bits) of encrypted data, address, stealth address.

Protocol	Operation	Truck	Receiver/Sender	On-Chain Storage
Protocol 1	Key Derivation	–	$\mathcal{O}(N_P)$	–
Protocol 2	Tracking Key Derivation	–	$\mathcal{O}(N_P)$	–
Protocol 3	Compute Stealth Address	$\mathcal{O}(N_P)$	–	–
Confidential	Decryption	$\mathcal{O}(eN_P)$	–	–
Data Sharing	Encryption	–	$\mathcal{O}(eN_P)$	–
Smart Contract	Register	$\mathcal{O}(N_T)$	–	aN_T
Operation	Publish	$\mathcal{O}(N_L + N_P)$	–	$N_L e + N_P(k_{SE} + (p, r))$

Location Sharing System. Our encryption algorithm relies on the security of AES-CBC and ECIES encryption functions. For Protocol 1, the international standard ISO/IEC 11770 [18] guarantees Alice and Bob can securely exchange key materials. The key derivation function PBKDF2 [24] guarantees only the holders of key materials can generate the key k. The security and privacy of protocol 2 are based on the assumption that SHA-3 is a cryptographically secure hash function. If a probabilistic polynomial time (PPT) adversary $\mathcal{A}$ obtains the private tracking key $tk_{p_{idA}} = H_s(p_{id}k_{Aa})$, $\mathcal{A}$ can not derive k_{Aa} or identity of the owner since the hash function is one-way. The security and privacy of protocol 3 rely on ECDLP [14]: given two points $P, Q \in E(\mathbb{F}_p)$ where $Q \in< P >$, finding a k such that $Q = kP$ is computationally infeasible. Meanwhile, protocol 3 holds the property of anonymity and unlinkability (with proof in Appendix A.1).

Lemma 2. *(Anonymity and unlinkability) A PPT adversary $\mathcal{A}$ can not derive the receiver of a stealth address or distinguish the receiver of two different stealth addresses in Protocol 3.*

Remark 2. If an adversary aims to access 100 trajectories from multiple days and trucks, he needs to send or receive 100 packages. Also, the 100 trajectories will not follow the same routes since the receivers are not the same.

7.2 Performance Analysis

We analyze our protocols with a blockchain-based platform to show the feasibility and performance since blockchain is a potentially disruptive technology for supply chains [25]. We summarize the computation complexity and on-chain storage in Table 1, showing that the computation complexity is linear with the number of trucks or packages. Meanwhile, the proposed encryption method has a lower storage cost than DECOUPLES [22] (with proof in Appendix A.2).

The protocols can also be used for centralized platforms where the complexity is only determined by Protocols 1, 2, which is less, but a trusted and reliable centre is needed to avoid possible hardware failure or information leakage [31].

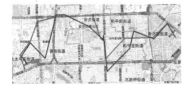

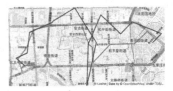

Fig. 6. Example output with $\epsilon = 0.01$.   **Fig. 7.** Example output with $\epsilon = 0.005$.

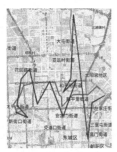

Fig. 8. Example output   **Fig. 9.** Example out-   **Fig. 10.** Relation between the out-
with $\epsilon = 0.0025$.   put with $\epsilon = 0.001$.   put probability and ϵ when the angle
                                                             noise n_i is 0.125π, 0.25π and 0.5π.

8   Experimental Evaluation

8.1   Location Perturbation

This subsection includes the selection of privacy parameters (ϵ, ϵ_a), and evaluation (run time and distance difference). We use Python for implementation, with Mac OS 11, 2 GHz Quad-Core Intel Core i5 CPU, 16 GB RAM.

Dataset. The GPS trajectory dataset (collected by GeoLife) [37] is used for evaluations. Trajectories are collected by different GPS loggers and GPS phones from 182 users, including 17,621 trajectories covering 1,292,951 kilometres. We have evaluated our algorithms using different trajectories and we use each trajectory to simulate one stop of the truck based on the map of Beijing.

Distance Metric. We use the Haversine formula as the error function to calculate the distance difference between two location points. If φ and λ are latitudes and longitudes, and r is the radius of the Earth, we have $d((\varphi_1, \lambda_1), (\varphi_2, \lambda_2))$ as (Eq. 12):

$$d = 2r \arcsin \sqrt{\sin^2\left(\frac{\varphi_2 - \varphi_1}{2}\right) + \cos\varphi_1 \cdot \cos\varphi_2 \cdot \sin^2\left(\frac{\lambda_2 - \lambda_1}{2}\right)}. \qquad (12)$$

ϵ *(for ϵ-geo-indistinguishability)* is selected by Eq. 6. We can define which distance is large, medium, or small based on city sizes. For example, inner, central, and outer rings in cities define the distance to the centre. For the first run of the algorithm, we need to scale the privacy level l with the output results using different r. Table 2 shows the relation between r and the real distance difference, so we can calculate l by multiplying the average distance and ϵ. When $l \approx 3.2$, the distance difference is approximately the same as r. We set $l_m = 3, l_s = 1$ (to better preserve location privacy by lowering ϵ) and $l_l = 5$. Considering the density of roads in a city, we can set r to contain at least n (such as 5) different roads with different distances between the truck and city centre. Here we set $r_m = 1000(m)$, $r_s = 400$, $r_l = 2000$ using the real road map of Beijing. Figures 6, 7, 8 and 9 support that the proposed parameters work well in the real map with different (l, r) pairs. For example, with $l = 3, r = 400$, we have $\epsilon = 0.0075$, whose output is similar to Figs. 6 and 7. If $l = 1, r = 1000$, we have $\epsilon = 0.001$ as shown in Fig. 9 with much larger noise. After defining parameters l and r for the first time, the value of ϵ can be calculated in real uses.

ϵ_a *(for angle selection)* can be selected based on the probability of outputting an angle ranging in $(\theta_0 - n_i, \theta_0 + n_i)$ where $n_i \in [-\pi, \pi)$ is the output noise of the Gaussian mechanism. We can draw the output probability in Fig. 10 using:

$$p(n_i) = \int_{-n_i}^{n_i} \frac{1}{\sigma\sqrt{2\pi}} e^{-\frac{x^2}{2\sigma^2}} dx \Big/ \int_{-\pi}^{\pi} \frac{1}{\sigma\sqrt{2\pi}} e^{-\frac{x^2}{2\sigma^2}} dx \qquad (13)$$

where $\sigma = \sqrt{2\ln(1.25/\delta)} \cdot \Delta_2/\epsilon_a$ and Δ_2 is the l_2-sensitivity. With different n_i, the same ϵ_a results in a similar probability when $\epsilon_a > 4$, so we can choose the desired ϵ_a (such as 5) and control the probability (such as 0.7).

Distance Difference. Based on Eq. 12, we evaluate the average distance (the distance between the actual location and the published one) and the average distance error (the error for the calculation of the distance between the current location to the destination) in Table 2. All experiments are performed 100 times based on the dataset while the average is used. A smaller ϵ has a larger error, meaning that the distance or the error is smaller when the truck is closer to the receiver (small l) and the city centre (small r).

Run Time. The run time is around 10^{-8} seconds ($< 1 \mu s$). The proposed algorithm can be applied to smart devices to sanitize location data in real-time.

Utility Analysis. Figures 6, 7, 8 and 9 and Table 2 illustrates the relation between ϵ and the distance error. With a small $\epsilon = 0.0005$, the average distance error is around 4.18 km. If the truck speed is at 50 km/h, considering the distance error is the straight-line distance (without considering road maps), the actual arrival time prediction error is around 5 to 10 min. However, for the adversary, Table 2 shows that the distance difference is 6.43 km. Even if they know that the truck is within 6.43 km of the published location, they need to check the circle area with a radius of $r_0 = 6.43$ km to find the truck. With our proposed angle selection mechanism, the adversary needs to check the roads in $\pi r_0^2 = 129.9$ km^2 to find the truck, which is infeasible in practice. In Fig. 9 with $\epsilon = 0.001$, the published location is several streets away from the original location. The adversary cannot locate the truck even if they hold the road map. Similarly, with a large $\epsilon = 0.01$, the difference or error is only around 200 m, which infers that the prediction error is within one minute. Figure 6 shows that the published trajectory is close to the actual, but the angle selection method can mislead the adversary to the south of the real trajectory. Moreover, a large ϵ is only set when the truck is close to the receiver in the city centre.

Table 2. Average distance and average distance error in meters with different ϵ.

$\epsilon = l/r$	Avg. distance	Avg. error	$\epsilon = l/r$	Avg. distance	Avg. error
0.0001	31661.92	27017.11	0.0005	6435.09	4180.74
0.001	3231.63	1963.17	0.003	1076.24	619.72
0.005	656.07	371.39	0.006	532.53	309.11
0.007	453.70	265.82	0.008	401.11	232.70
0.01	319.22	184.90	0.05	63.55	37.16

8.2 Location Sharing System

We implement and evaluate our protocols with Ethereum to test the feasibility of our protocols. In real cases, enterprises can choose their own solutions based on the proposed protocols. We use *Rust* for implementation and *JavaScript VM* to deploy the smart contract. ChaChaRng is the pseudo-random number generator. SHA-3 is the hash function. Curve25519 is the elliptic curve. AES-CBC is with a 128-bit key. All tests are with Win 10 Pro, 32GB RAM, and Intel Core i7-10700.

We evaluate the run time for our protocols (where S/R is Sender/Receiver): (1) key derivation (S/R: 0.506 s), (2) generate TK_{pid} (S/R: 0.438 ms), (3) generate stealth address P (Truck: 0.850 ms), and (4) generate user-computed stealth address P' (S/R: 0.440 ms). The key derivation limits the performance. The off-chain encryption includes (i) AES-CBC to encrypt the data and (ii) ECIES to encrypt the symmetric keys. The run time for ECIES (0.295 ms) is much longer than AES (172 ns) with $N_L = 20, N_P = 100$, which limits the performance. With 30 items and stealth addresses (512-bit), the average gas cost for our encryption method is 2.398×10^6, which is less than DECOUPLES [22] (2.864×10^6).

The scalability relies on the proof of work consensus model. For every second, Ethereum can process around 15 transactions [28], so our platform can publish location data from 15 trucks. Assume the location data is sent every five minutes. The platform can support $15 \times 60 \times 5 = 450$ trucks, which is practical for SMEs.

9   Conclusions

We propose a real-time privacy-preserving location sharing system considering real maps and possible filtering attacks. We improve the state-of-the-art in two folds. Firstly, our proposed location publishing mechanism is feasible in real applications. Based on our exclusive security and privacy argumentation and proof, the proposed angle selection algorithm can better protect the privacy of trajectories than existing works. The experiments show the location publishing method is fast and practical for real-time data processing, which only needs nanoseconds. Secondly, our proposed location sharing protocols can protect privacy-sensitive data using cryptographic constructions under centralized and decentralized settings. Our security analysis proves that the system is privacy-preserving. With Ethereum, our proposal has lower storage costs compared to the previous work [22]. It is feasible and can handle $\sim$450 trucks, a reasonable amount for an average city. Companies can build their own solutions using our protocols to improve.

A   Deferred Proofs and Figures

A.1   Proof for Lemma 2

Lemma 2.*(Anonymity and unlinkability) A PPT adversary $\mathcal{A}$ can not derive the receiver of a stealth address or distinguish the receiver of two different stealth addresses in Protocol 3.*

Proof. Assume that a PPT adversary $\mathcal{A}$ holds a stealth address (P, R) and p_{id} and a list of tuples $(TK_{i,p_{id}}, K_{b_i})$, $\mathcal{A}$ needs to compute $P' = H_s(rTK_{i,p_{id}})G + K_{b_i})$ such that $P' = P$. To find such a P', $\mathcal{A}$ need to compute $P - K_{b_i} = H_s(rTK_{i,p_{id}})G$. Because of the one-wayness of ECDLP, it is computationally infeasible to compute the $H_s(rTK_{i,p_{id}})$. And since $\mathcal{A}$ does not know the secret value r, he can not contrust $P' = H_s(rTK_{i,p_{id}})G + K_{b_i})$ himself. Therefore, it is infeasible for $\mathcal{A}$ to derive the receiver of (P, R).

Similarly, assume that $\mathcal{A}$ gets two stealth addresses (P_1, R_1) and (P_2, R_2), $\mathcal{A}$ needs to distinguish the following two scenarios: (1) two stealth addresses belong to the same receiver, and (2) two stealth addresses belong to two different receivers. For scenario (1), $\mathcal{A}$ computes $P_1 - P_2$ as:

$$P_1 - P_2 = H_s(rTK_{p_{id1}})G + K_b - (H_s(rTK_{p_{id2}}) + K_b)$$
$$= (H_s(rTK_{p_{id1}}) - H_s(rTK_{p_{id2}}))G \tag{14}$$
$$= xG \text{ for some unknown x.}$$

Since the adversary $\mathcal{A}$ does not hold p_{id1}, p_{id2} and r, $(H_s(rTK_{p_{id1}}) - H_s(rTK_{p_{id2}}))$ is a secret value x for him. For scenario (2), $\mathcal{A}$ computes $P_1 - P_2$ as:

$$P_1 - P_2 = H_s(r_1TK_{p_{id1}})G + K_{b_1} - (H_s(r_2TK_{p_{id2}}) + K_{b_2})$$
$$= (H_s(r_1TK_{p_{id1}}) - H_s(r_2TK_{p_{id2}}) + K_{b_1} - K_{b_2})G \tag{15}$$
$$= yG \quad \text{for any unknown y.}$$

The adversary $\mathcal{A}$ does not hold p_{id1}, p_{id2}, r_1, r_2, so $(H_s(r_1 T K_{p_{id1}}) - H_s(r_2 T K_{p_{id2}}) + K_{b_1} - K_{b_2})G$ is a secret for $\mathcal{A}$.

In both scenarios, the adversary $\mathcal{A}$ can not derive the secret value. Given two different stealth addresses, it is computationally infeasible for $\mathcal{A}$ to distinguish.

A.2   Proof of Lower Storage Cost

Lemma 3. *The proposed encryption method has lower storage costs than DECOUPLES [22].*

Proof. The space cost for only using ECIES is $S_{ECIES} = N_P(e + (p,r))$. To compare the space cost of the encryption algorithm S and S_{ECIES}, we compute $S - S_{ECIES}$ as follows:

$$\begin{aligned} S - S_{ECIES} &= N_L e + N_P(k_{SE} + (p,r)) - N_P(e + (p,r)) \\ &= (N_L - N_P)e + N_P(k_{SE} - e) \end{aligned} \tag{16}$$

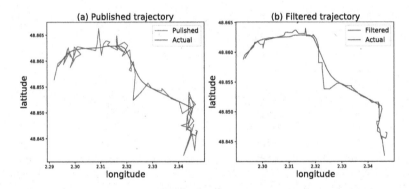

Fig. 11. An example output by PL_ϵ, and the filtered output of the sanitized trajectory. The blue line shows the actual trajectory, the red line shows the published trajectory by PL_ϵ, and the green line shows the filtered trajectory. (Color figure online)

Algorithm 2: AngleSelection

Input: Previous angle θ_0, privacy parameter ϵ_a
Output: Output perturbed angle θ
  1: Calculate the new angle θ using Equation 7.
  2: Round θ into the range $[0, 2\pi)$
  3: **return** θ

Since many products share the same location, we have $N_L < N_P < 0$. If $e > k_{SE}$, we get $S - S_{ECIES} < 0$ (the size of the encrypted data is larger than the size of the symmetric key). Our encryption method requires less storage than ECIES.

References

1. Agatz, N.A.H., Campbell, A.M., Fleischmann, M., Savelsbergh, M.W.P.: Time slot management in attended home delivery. Transp. Sci. **45**(3), 435–449 (2011). https://doi.org/10.1287/trsc.1100.0346
2. Andrés, M.E., Bordenabe, N.E., Chatzikokolakis, K., Palamidessi, C.: Geo-indistinguishability: differential privacy for location-based systems. In: Sadeghi, A., Gligor, V.D., Yung, M. (eds.) ACM CCS 2013, pp. 901–914. ACM (2013). https://doi.org/10.1145/2508859.2516735
3. Auditshipment: The true cost of package delivery delays (2021). https://www.auditshipment.com/blog/the-true-cost-of-package-delivery-delays/. Accessed 7 Nov 2021
4. Branch, A.E.: Global Supply Chain Management and International Logistics. Routledge, Abingdon (2008)
5. Brunswicker, S., Van de Vrande, V.: Exploring open innovation in small and medium-sized enterprises. New Front. Open Innov. **1**, 135–156 (2014)
6. DHL: Parcel delivery in real time (2021). https://www.dhl.de/en/privatkunden/pakete-empfangen/sendungen-verfolgen/live-tracking.html. Accessed 07 Jan 2022
7. Dwork, C.: Differential privacy. In: Bugliesi, M., Preneel, B., Sassone, V., Wegener, I. (eds.) ICALP 2006. LNCS, vol. 4052, pp. 1–12. Springer, Heidelberg (2006). https://doi.org/10.1007/11787006_1
8. Dwork, C., McSherry, F., Nissim, K., Smith, A.: Calibrating noise to sensitivity in private data analysis. In: Halevi, S., Rabin, T. (eds.) TCC 2006. LNCS, vol. 3876, pp. 265–284. Springer, Heidelberg (2006). https://doi.org/10.1007/11681878_14
9. Dwork, C., Naor, M., Pitassi, T., Rothblum, G.N.: Differential privacy under continual observation. In: Schulman, L.J. (ed.) STOC 2010, pp. 715–724. ACM (2010). https://doi.org/10.1145/1806689.1806787
10. Dwork, C., Roth, A.: The algorithmic foundations of differential privacy. Found. Trends Theor. Comput. Sci. **9**(3–4), 211–407 (2014). https://doi.org/10.1561/0400000042
11. Van den Engel, A., Prummel, E.: Organised theft of commercial vehicles and their loads in the European union. European Parliament. Directorate General Internal Policies of the Union. Policy Department Structural and Cohesion Policies. Transport and Tourism, Brussels (2007)
12. Fang, C., Chang, E.: Differential privacy with δ-neighbourhood for spatial and dynamic datasets. In: Moriai, S., Jaeger, T., Sakurai, K. (eds.) ASIA CCS 2014, pp. 159–170. ACM (2014). https://doi.org/10.1145/2590296.2590320
13. Grmiling, M.: How real time tracking can improve logistics (2021). https://www.hublock.io/how-real-time-tracking-can-improve-logistics/. Accessed 17 Nov 2021
14. Hankerson, D., Menezes, A.J., Vanstone, S.: Guide to Elliptic Curve Cryptography. Springer, Heidelberg (2006). https://doi.org/10.1007/b97644
15. Harnsamut, N., Natwichai, J., Riyana, S.: Privacy preservation for trajectory data publishing by look-up table generalization. In: Wang, J., Cong, G., Chen, J., Qi, J. (eds.) ADC 2018. LNCS, vol. 10837, pp. 15–27. Springer, Cham (2018). https://doi.org/10.1007/978-3-319-92013-9_2

16. Hayashida, S., Amagata, D., Hara, T., Xie, X.: Dummy generation based on user-movement estimation for location privacy protection. IEEE Access **6**, 22958–22969 (2018). https://doi.org/10.1109/ACCESS.2018.2829898

17. Hitaj, B., Ateniese, G., Pérez-Cruz, F.: Deep models under the GAN: information leakage from collaborative deep learning. In: Thuraisingham, B., Evans, D., Malkin, T., Xu, D. (eds.) ACM CCS 2017, pp. 603–618. ACM (2017). https://doi.org/10.1145/3133956.3134012

18. ISO: ISO/IEC 11770-2:2008, Information technology – Security techniques – Key Management – Part 2: Mechanisms using Symmetric Techniques (2009)

19. Jiang, H., Li, J., Zhao, P., Zeng, F., Xiao, Z., Iyengar, A.: Location privacy-preserving mechanisms in location-based services: a comprehensive survey. ACM Comput. Surv. **54**(1), 4:1–4:36 (2022). https://doi.org/10.1145/3423165

20. Kairouz, P., Oh, S., Viswanath, P.: The composition theorem for differential privacy. In: Bach, F.R., Blei, D.M. (eds.) ICML 2015. JMLR Workshop and Conference Proceedings, vol. 37, pp. 1376–1385. JMLR.org (2015). http://proceedings.mlr.press/v37/kairouz15.html

21. Kellaris, G., Papadopoulos, S., Xiao, X., Papadias, D.: Differentially private event sequences over infinite streams. Proc. VLDB Endow. **7**(12), 1155–1166 (2014). https://doi.org/10.14778/2732977.2732989

22. Maouchi, M.E., Ersoy, O., Erkin, Z.: DECOUPLES: a decentralized, unlinkable and privacy-preserving traceability system for the supply chain. In: Hung, C., Papadopoulos, G.A. (eds.) SAC 2019, pp. 364–373. ACM (2019). https://doi.org/10.1145/3297280.3297318

23. McSherry, F.: Privacy integrated queries: an extensible platform for privacy-preserving data analysis. In: Çetintemel, U., Zdonik, S.B., Kossmann, D., Tatbul, N. (eds.) SIGMOD 2009, pp. 19–30. ACM (2009). https://doi.org/10.1145/1559845.1559850

24. Moriarty, K.M., Kaliski, B., Rusch, A.: PKCS #5: password-based cryptography specification version 2.1. RFC **8018**, 1–40 (2017). https://doi.org/10.17487/RFC8018

25. Saberi, S., Kouhizadeh, M., Sarkis, J., Shen, L.: Blockchain technology and its relationships to sustainable supply chain management. Int. J. Prod. Res. **57**(7), 2117–2135 (2019). https://doi.org/10.1080/00207543.2018.1533261

26. Sahai, S., Singh, N., Dayama, P.: Enabling privacy and traceability in supply chains using blockchain and zero knowledge proofs. In: Blockchain 2020, pp. 134–143. IEEE (2020). https://doi.org/10.1109/Blockchain50366.2020.00024

27. Savona, E.U.: Organised property crime in the EU. European Parliament. Directorate General for Internal Policies. Policy Department for Citizens' Rights and Constitutional Affairs (2020)

28. Seres, I.A., Nagy, D.A., Buckland, C., Burcsi, P.: Mixeth: efficient, trustless coin mixing service for ethereum. Cryptology ePrint Archive, Report 2019/341 (2019)

29. Sezer, B.B., Topal, S., Nuriyev, U.: An auditability, transparent, and privacy-preserving for supply chain traceability based on blockchain. CoRR abs/2103.10519 (2021). https://arxiv.org/abs/2103.10519

30. Shoup, V.: A proposal for an ISO standard for public key encryption. IACR Cryptol. ePrint Arch, p. 112 (2001). http://eprint.iacr.org/2001/112

31. Singh, A., Click, K., Parizi, R.M., Zhang, Q., Dehghantanha, A., Choo, K.R.: Sidechain technologies in blockchain networks: an examination and state-of-the-art review. J. Netw. Comput. Appl. **149** (2020). https://doi.org/10.1016/j.jnca.2019.102471

32. Terrovitis, M., Poulis, G., Mamoulis, N., Skiadopoulos, S.: Local suppression and splitting techniques for privacy preserving publication of trajectories. IEEE Trans. Knowl. Data Eng. **29**(7), 1466–1479 (2017). https://doi.org/10.1109/TKDE.2017. 2675420

33. Wang, H., Xu, Z.: CTS-DP: publishing correlated time-series data via differential privacy. Knowl. Based Syst. **122**, 167–179 (2017). https://doi.org/10.1016/j. knosys.2017.02.004

34. Wong, L., Leong, L., Hew, J., Tan, G.W., Ooi, K.: Time to seize the digital evolution: adoption of blockchain in operations and supply chain management among malaysian smes. Int. J. Inf. Manag. **52**, 101997 (2020). https://doi.org/10.1016/j. ijinfomgt.2019.08.005

35. Xiao, Y., Xiong, L.: Protecting locations with differential privacy under temporal correlations. In: Ray, I., Li, N., Kruegel, C. (eds.) ACM CCS 2015, pp. 1298–1309. ACM (2015). https://doi.org/10.1145/2810103.2813640

36. Xiong, P., Zhu, T., Pan, L., Niu, W., Li, G.: Privacy preserving in location data release: a differential privacy approach. In: Pham, D.-N., Park, S.-B. (eds.) PRICAI 2014. LNCS (LNAI), vol. 8862, pp. 183–195. Springer, Cham (2014). https://doi. org/10.1007/978-3-319-13560-1_15

37. Zheng, Y., Zhang, L., Xie, X., Ma, W.: Mining interesting locations and travel sequences from GPS trajectories. In: Quemada, J., León, G., Maarek, Y.S., Nejdl, W. (eds.) WWW 2009, pp. 791–800. ACM (2009). https://doi.org/10.1145/ 1526709.1526816

A User-Centric Approach to API Delegations

Enforcing Privacy Policies on OAuth Delegations

Shirin Kalantari[✉], Pieter Philippaerts[✉], Yana Dimova, Danny Hughes,
Wouter Joosen, and Bart De Decker

imec-DistriNet, KU Leuven, Leuven, Belgium
{shirin.kalantari,pieter.philippaerts,yana.dimova,
danny.hughes,wouter.joosen,bart.decker}@kuleuven.be

Abstract. OAuth is the most commonly used access delegation protocol. It enables the connection of different APIs to build increasingly sophisticated applications that enhance and amplify our abilities. Increasingly, OAuth is used in applications where a significant amount of personal data is exposed about users. Despite this privacy risk, in most OAuth flows that a user encounters, there is a lack of fine-grained control over the amount of data that is shared on behalf of users. To mitigate these privacy issues we design and implement utAPIa, a middleware which enforces privacy policies on OAuth delegations. utAPIa allows users to modify API responses that are made on their behalf by filtering unrelated attributes and protecting their sensitive information. To enforce privacy policies, utAPIa uses OAuth's standardized Rich Authorization Requests (RAR) extension, requiring no modifications to the existing OAuth protocol. We evaluate utAPIa in a proof-of-concept implementation and show the feasibility of our design, which incurs a reasonable performance overhead.

Keywords: API security · OAuth · Privacy

1 Introduction

Application Programming Interfaces (APIs) define a structured interface between two systems for information exchange. APIs are used everywhere, including web applications, mobile applications, service-to-service communication, microservices, and smart home appliances. Increasingly, APIs expose a plethora of personal and private information about users. API service providers must carefully manage which services get access to an API and what data is shared with these services.

Unfortunately, API misuse has become the number one attack vector for Internet-connected applications according to Gartner [34]. This is highlighted by a number of high-profile data breaches [22,27,30,31,39], where APIs were

© The Author(s), under exclusive license to Springer Nature Switzerland AG 2024
G. Tsudik et al. (Eds.): ESORICS 2023, LNCS 14345, pp. 318–337, 2024.
https://doi.org/10.1007/978-3-031-51476-0_16

abused to compromise the privacy of users. With the advent of micro-service architectures, APIs become increasingly interconnected and are used for a wide range of activities such as smart-home and business automation. As a result, securing APIs from unauthorized access has become exceedingly challenging.

The OAuth 2.0 protocol has emerged as a de facto standard solution for secure API delegation which allows a third-party client application to access an API on behalf of a user. In OAuth, the privileges of an access token are primarily determined by its *scope*, a list of permissions that defines the set of parameters that may be shared with an application. However, the traditional approach of using scopes to minimize the privileges of a token has become increasingly inadequate as the use cases for APIs have expanded. This is because scopes typically define the actions that a third party can perform on the user's behalf, but rarely limit the data returned by these actions or enforce necessary data transformation rules for ensuring data confidentiality. Moreover, scopes are not defined and managed by users. Recent work on applications that use Google APIs shows that in most delegation flows users must either approve all requested scopes or not use that third-party client at all, without having any control over the set of requested scopes [5]. Additionally, several previous works have highlighted that users are often insufficiently informed about how scopes are used [5,35,42].

Users' lack of control over information exchange via API delegation raises significant concerns as users have to choose between their privacy and using the functionalities provided by a third-party client application. Driven by these factors, research has shown that users are becoming wary of their lack of control over API delegations and express their desire for having more fine-grained sharing rules for certain attributes in an API [5]. This lack of control can also create friction with privacy and data protection legislation which imposes restrictions on processing and sharing of personal data. In Europe for example, the General Data Protection Regulation's (GDPR) principle of *data minimization* (art. 5.1 (c)) requires controllers to only process data which is necessary to provide the service requested by the data subject. According to this principle, only the minimal amount of information should be shared when a user is provided with an SSO option. Additionally, the principle of *integrity and confidentiality* (art. 5.1 (f)) mandates that companies use appropriate technical measures to preserve the confidentiality of data. An appropriate authentication mechanism such as SSO in combination with encryption can be used to strengthen the position for compliance of applications with this legislation.

In this paper, we work toward improving user data privacy in API delegation scenarios by presenting the design and implementation of **utAPIa**, a middleware for enforcing privacy policies in OAuth flows. Specifically, **utAPIa** enables users to select and control the attributes that will be shared on their behalf in an API delegation, as well as the duration of the delegation. In achieving this goal, **utAPIa** needs to determine and express the policies that have to be enforced in a certain delegation flow, and enforce those policies on subsequent API requests without jeopardizing security and usability.

The contributions of the paper are as follows:

1. *The OAuth restriction policy.* We present the first policy language for fine-grained privacy controls on OAuth delegations. The policy enables users to define sanitization rules on API responses made on their behalf. These rules act as a privacy policy to remove unrelated attributes from an API response or modify attributes that need to be protected before being disclosed. In addition, an expiration time and access rate limitation can be set for delegations.
2. *The* **utAPIa** *enforcement middleware.* We implement an enforcement module, *Access Response Governance (ARG)*, which is implemented as a standalone application that can be installed as a proxy on the API provider's side to enforce the privacy policies on API responses using the standardized Rich Authorization Requests (RAR) [33] protocol.
3. *Proof-of-concept implementation and evaluation.* We instantiate **utAPIa** for protecting a typical API implementation, showcasing its flexibility. The results of our evaluation show that the enforcement of privacy policies in **utAPIa** incur a tolerable performance overhead. Our proof-of-concept implementation is available at https://github.com/DistriNet/utAPIa.

To our knowledge this paper presents the first generic solution for addressing privacy issues in OAuth by providing more fine-grained privacy controls to the users rather than the existing all-or-nothing consent approach. The remainder of this paper is structured as follows: Sect. 2 introduces some background on OAuth and reviews previous works to derive the desired privacy controls. In Sect. 3, we describe the design goals and our attacker model. In Sect. 4, we specify the privacy policy that **utAPIa** uses. Section 5 describes the components in **utAPIa** and discusses the performance results in Sect. 6. In Sect. 7, we present the take-away messages and findings of our research and potential future work. We discuss the related work in Sect. 8 and conclude the paper in Sect. 9.

2   Background

This paper focuses on protecting APIs that expose personal data and rely on the user for authorizing access requests. In this section, we provide some background information on OAuth, a widely adopted API authorization framework, and its recently standardized extension, Rich Authorization Requests (RAR). Furthermore, we identify the desired privacy controls within API delegation by reviewing the relevant literature and discuss the threat model for our solution.

2.1   OAuth 2.0

With its comprehensive specifications and robust security mechanisms, OAuth[1] is well-suited for securing a wide range of applications such as social media

---

[1] In this paper, the focus is solely on OAuth 2.0, and not on the older and substantially different OAuth 1.0 protocol. Therefore, whenever the term *OAuth* is used, it refers to version 2.0 of the protocol.

platforms, healthcare systems, e-commerce websites, mobile applications, and financial-grade APIs (FAPI). The OAuth specification [14] identifies four major grant types, also known as *flows*, for the protocol: authorization code, client credentials, resource owner password credentials, and implicit. It's important to note that the latter two are scheduled for deprecation due to security concerns. In its most common flow, the authorization code grant, an Authorization Server (AS) issues access tokens to third-party applications (referred to as the 'clients') to access protected resources hosted by the resource server on behalf of a user. The privileges of an issued token are determined by its *scope*, a set of permission parameters that limit the client's access to the user's data. The client can request one or more scopes in the authorization request. Although the user has the option to deny consent according to the OAuth specification, in practice most authorization servers do not allow the user to deselect scopes once they have been requested [5,15]. An access token is usually short-lived to limit the risks of leakage. The AS can set the token's expiration as determined by the `expires_in` parameter that holds the lifetime of the token in seconds. For example, the value '3600' denotes that the access token will expire one hour after its creation. Refresh tokens, which are typically issued alongside access tokens, allow the client to obtain new access tokens from the AS without requiring user involvement. While refresh tokens can also have an expiration date, their lifetime is typically much longer compared to access tokens.

2.2   Rich Authorization Requests

Rich Authorization Requests (RAR) is an OAuth 2.0 extension that enables applications to specify fine-grained authorization details in requests. It introduces a new parameter, `authorization_details`, in the authorization request that stores a JSON-encoded object (hereinafter referred to as *the RAR object*) containing fine-grained authorization requirements. The access tokens generated by an authorization flow that uses RAR are bound to the `authorization_details` parameters. When a client makes a request with such an access token, the resource server can retrieve the original RAR object either directly from within the access token, or by contacting the authorization server via token introspection. The resource server will subsequently enforce a policy according to the specification in the RAR object. The semantics of fields in the RAR object are implementation-specific to a given API or set of APIs and their evaluation happens outside of the scope of the OAuth standards.

2.3   Privacy Controls in API Delegation

We derived a set of transformation policies that must be enforced on API delegation, by surveying the relevant literature [5,16,25,35,44,46]. These works include *user studies on API ecosystems* such as Google APIs [5], Facebook APIs [16,44], and Android APIs [46]. In addition to user studies, we survey papers that focus on the privacy implications of OAuth delegations in third-party applications that are explicitly granted access to the user's personal data, rather than evaluating privacy implications that arise as a result of leaks to unauthorized parties

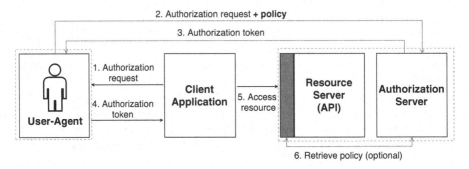

Fig. 1. Interactions and trust boundaries (dashed boxes) between entities involved in an API delegation in **utAPIa**. (Color figure online)

as in [1] and [32]. The studies have been performed in the context of single-sign-on applications [35], Facebook apps [16,17,23] and Android apps [25]. We identify two privacy controls for API delegations that empower users to utilize third-party client applications while protecting their privacy: (1) *attribute-level control*, where users can specify which part of the API responses they would like to remove [5,25,44], or replace [25] from API calls made on their behalf, and (2) *access expiration and reapproval*, which requires delegations to expire after a certain time period (e.g., after one year) [5,35].

2.4   Threat Model

Figure 1 provides a simplified overview of the OAuth authorization flow and our trust assumptions regarding the involved entities. Our key insight is that the client application should not be considered trustworthy. It may actively try to gain excessive access to user data that is not required for the functionalities it provides. Furthermore, the client may have malicious intent, such as selling the user data as an asset or sharing it with third-party trackers. The API provider is considered to be trustworthy. As such, we assume it runs the software components introduced by our solution and does not deviate from the relevant protocols. This assumption is also in line with the legal obligations of API providers under privacy regulations such as GDPR in the EU which oblige them use appropriate technical measures to protect the users' privacy. We also assume that the authorization server is properly implemented, as per OAuth specifications, and we assume it to be a trusted entity w.r.t. managing the authorization process and access tokens. For example, the authorization server has no incentive to drop the RAR object from an authorization request or omit it from introspection responses. Finally, it is our assumption that users are trusted in taking steps to protect their privacy. They are also assumed to have an understanding of the functionalities that a client application provides to them and the context in which they use it. They use this information to limit the delegation scope without intentionally trying to break the application by manipulating the attributes that are necessary for its correct functioning.

3 Design Approach

This section gives a high-level overview of the design of **utAPIa**, a privacy-enhancing solution that leverages existing OAuth-based standards and enables API providers to implement user-specified data and access minimization.

Compatibility with Existing OAuth Ecosystem: OAuth is a widely adopted API authorization protocol that has been the focus of extensive security research, with formally proven strong security guarantees [19]. However, real-world implementation errors can compromise the security and privacy of user data [37,38]. Previous studies have also conducted application-specific validation of OAuth, such as SSO, highlighting the security and privacy implications of insecure implementations [28,32,41]. Given its extensive deployment in various applications and use cases, we cannot assume that the OAuth protocol can be easily changed without potentially causing compatibility issues and introducing new vulnerabilities. Therefore, any security or privacy solution built on top of OAuth should be designed in a modular manner and should not conflict with existing standards.

To avoid these challenges, **utAPIa** leverages standardized OAuth extensions to ensure broad compatibility with existing clients and authorization servers. During the OAuth authorization process, **utAPIa** utilizes user input to generate an accompanying policy for the delegation, and incorporates it within the RAR object. The resource server can retrieve the RAR object from the access token (either directly, or via token introspection), apply the policy, and send only the sanitized data to the client application. The policy guarantees that all attributes, except those specifically chosen by the user to be shared, are replaced with predefined values (e.g., empty strings). This policy-centric design allows **utAPIa** to transmit only sanitized data to client applications without requiring modifications to the client application or APIs provided by the resource server.

Design Overview: Figure 1 provides a simplified overview of the OAuth authorization flow with **utAPIa**'s extensions marked in green. The process involves the following steps: (1) The client application initiates an authorization request to the user's user agent (e.g., a web browser), requesting access to the resource server. (2) The user agent forwards the request to the authorization server, attaching a user-specified policy that outlines data sharing preferences. (3) Upon authorization, the authorization server issues a token to the user agent (typically an access token or an authorization code). (4) The token is then forwarded to the client application. If it is an access token, the client application can directly utilize it to access the resource server. This is called the implicit flow. However, if the more secure authorization code flow is used, the client application must communicate with the authorization server to exchange the authorization code for an access token first. (5) **utAPIa** provides a proxy between the client application and the resource server (deployed on the resource server side), depicted as the green rectangle in Fig. 1. It intercepts requests and sanitizes response data according to the associated policy. (6) In cases where the policy is not directly embedded in the access token, the **utAPIa** proxy contacts the authorization server to retrieve the policy. The design of **utAPIa** empowers users with more fine-grained options for controlling and sharing their data, while ensuring compatibility with existing systems.

4   Privacy Policies in utAPIa

Policies in **utAPIa** serve as a mechanism for specifying the desired behavior and restrictions related to privacy controls, notably attribute-level control and access timeout (cf. Sect. 2.3). The policy captures the privacy preferences of users during a delegation, which are then sent to the authorization server via the RAR object. This object is a customizable data structure that is represented as a JSON string. This section describes the JSON structure, as used in **utAPIa**, to embed a policy as part of the RAR object and achieve the desired privacy controls. Listing 1 is an example of a policy to enable the two privacy controls: (1) attribute-level control on API responses through sanitization (cf. Sect. 4.1), and (2) access timeout for setting an expiration time for OAuth delegations and access rate limitations (cf. Sect. 4.2).

```
authorization_details = {
    "type": "utapia",
    "attribute_control":[
        {"endpoint":"/userinfo",
         "patch":{
            ["op":"replace", "path":"/email","value":"rand@example.com"],
            ["op":"replace","path":"/family_name","value":"Bar"],
            ["op":"replace","path":"/given_name","value":"Foo"]}},
        {"endpoint":"/people/{sub}",
         "patch":{
            ["op":"remove","path":"/dob"],
            ["op":"replace","path":"/gender","value":"x"],
            ["op":"remove","path":"/residence"]}}],
    "access_timeout":"1683208488",
    "rate_limitation": ("3", "perHour"),
    "min_delay": ("15", "min")
}
```

Listing 1. Example RAR object that carries the privacy policy for the delegation.

4.1   Attribute-Level Control

JSON has become widely adopted for data exchange in APIs due to its ease of storage, interchange, and data querying capabilities. In the context of this work, we leverage the JSON patch specification [8] for attribute-level control of JSON API responses. The JSON patch specification defines a set of operations, known as patch operations, to modify a JSON document. These operations are executed in order as a single, atomic transaction. Thus if any operation fails to complete, the changes are rolled back leaving no trace of partial modification behind. A single patch operation has three main elements: (1) *"op"* specifies the type of operation to be performed, *"remove"*, and *"replace"* are the only operations we use for attribute-level control; (2) *"path"*, which is a JSON pointer, identifies the part of the JSON document to operate on; and (3) *"value"* represents the new value when using the *"replace"* operation. To illustrate with an example, Listing 1 uses the `attribute_control` value to outline the operations that have to be performed to sanitize an API response. The initial state of the API response and the result of applying the policy are displayed in Listing 2.

```
/userinfo:{                                    /userinfo:{
  "picture":"https://lh3...",                    "picture":"https://lh3...",
  "id":"134029583920495829956",                  "id":"134029583920495829956",
  "email":"john.doe@gmail.com",                   "email":"rand@example.com",
  "family_name":"John",                           "family_name":"Bar",
  "given_name":"Doe"}                             "given_name":"Foo"}
/people/{id}:{                                  /people/{id}:{
  "dob":"10/02/2001"                             "gender":"x",
  "gender":"m",                                  "occupations":
  "occupations":                                   "CEO at Awesome Org"}
    "CEO at Awesome Org",
  "residence":"Great Islands"}
```

Listing 2. The initial (left) and sanitized API response (right) after enforcing attribute-level controls specified in Listing 1.

4.2   Access Timeout and Rate Limitation

Access timeout offers users the capability to define an expiration time for delegations. The duration of the delegation is determined by the `access_timeout` attribute in the policy example presented in Listing 1. Unlike traditional access revocation techniques that require some kind of user intervention, such as accessing the API provider dashboard to review and revoke access, access timeout enforces the expiration automatically and eliminates the need for additional user interaction. This additional layer of privacy control empowers users and applications by explicitly governing the duration of the delegation at the moment of authorization. While the concept of access timeout may appear straightforward and intuitive, its practical implementation is frequently absent. As a result, the duration of the delegation relies on the default configuration established by the authorization server. For instance, Google employs tokens that can be refreshed indefinitely, as long as they are utilized at least once every six months [26]. Without access timeout, clients can potentially track user data over time, regardless of the user's actual frequency of using client services. It should be noted that access timeout serves a distinct purpose from access token expiration, which refers to the validity period of individual access tokens. Expired tokens can often be renewed using token refresh mechanisms, allowing the client to obtain new valid tokens, potentially indefinitely. Access timeout establishes a maximum duration for OAuth delegations. Figure 2 illustrates this distinction. Once this specified timeframe elapses, access to the protected resource is terminated, irrespective of token expiration.

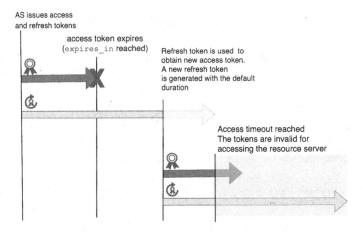

Fig. 2. Access timeout versus token expiration: Refresh tokens usually enable the acquisition of new tokens after token expiration, while access timeout sets an overall duration for OAuth delegations.

Rate limitation offers users the capability to restrict the frequency of calls a client can make on a specific API. The frequency of the API calls is determined by the `rate_limit` attribute in the policy example presented in Listing 1. The value is a tuple consisting of a number and a time-interval. Alternatively, users can specify a minimal delay between two successive calls using the `min_delay` attribute. The value is a tuple consisting of a number and a time-unit. This control becomes especially useful when continuous access to an API poses additional privacy risks for users. For instance, the absence of rate limitation when accessing a smartwatch API that exposes a user's location could potentially result in extensive user tracking.

5   Middleware Support

In this section we describe how **utAPIa** utilizes techniques discussed in the previous sections to address issues related to attribute-control and access expiration. Importantly, **utAPIa** enforces user policies without requiring modifications to the client application or AS (assuming that AS supports the RAR standard).

This makes **utAPIa** a practical and efficient option for privacy-conscious users and ASes as it enforces minimal changes to their existing infrastructure.

The overview of **utAPIa**'s architecture is shown in Fig. 3. It consists of two main modules: Authorization Request Enrichment (ARE) and Access Response Governance (ARG). The goal of ARE is to enrich the ongoing OAuth authorization request with fine-grained controls for the attributes in the API response and the duration of access. The ARG is responsible for enforcing these controls on all the subsequent access responses. Together, these two components ensure that the client access is restricted according to the user's policy without requiring any cooperation from the client itself. We organize the following discussion around the life-cycle of an API delegation, comprising the following stages: (1) Authorizing a client to access an API (Sect. 5.1); (2) Handling client access requests (Sect. 5.2).

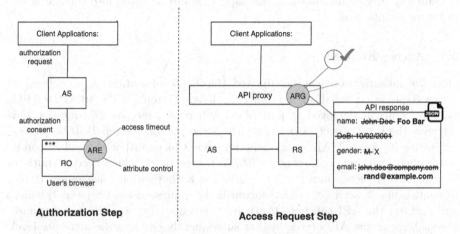

Authorization Step   **Access Request Step**

Fig. 3. An overview of the components in the **utAPIa** middleware. The blue circles represent the components of **utAPIa**: the ARE modifies the ongoing authorization requests to attach privacy policies and the ARG enforces the policy at request time. (Color figure online)

5.1   Authorization Initiation

The ARE module is responsible for including the user policies in the OAuth authorization requests. It needs to ensure that the controls in the policy are valid and consistent with the API responses that are generated as a result of the delegation. For instance, the policy in the RAR object should align with the available attributes in an API response, and the access timeout must be set to a future timestamp. To obtain this information, ARE relies on the information in the API documentation, which specifies the type and attributes of an API response. OpenAPI [43] is an example of a commonly used specification for documenting APIs.

Figure 4(left) depicts the modifications to the authorization initiation flow by the ARE. When a client application requests access to an API on the RS, it sends an authorization request to the AS. The user (i.e., the resource owner) has to consent to the privileges in the request (step 1). In this step the ARE can add the desired privacy policy as part of the RAR object in the request URL (step 2) and forward the request as before to the user for authorization confirmation (step 3). The user gives their consent (step 4) and the AS, which is RAR-enabled per standard OAuth specifications, authorizes the request and initiates a token generation flow with the client application according to the OAuth flow. It should be noted that the token generation response also includes the RAR object [33]. Consequently, the user's privacy settings can potentially get disclosed to the client. While the RAR object used by **utAPIa** does not contain any private information, this aspect should be taken into consideration in future adaptations.

5.2 Access Request

Once the authorization flow is completed, the client-application can start making access requests on behalf of the user (Fig. 4(right), step 1). The **utAPIa** ARG module, which is deployed as part of an API proxy, receives this request and retrieves the RAR object associated with the access token (step 2). If the access expiration has passed, ARG considers the request as unauthorized and responds to the client, without contacting the RS. At this point, the client needs to initiate a fresh OAuth flow, prompting the user for authorization once more. If the delegation is still active, the ARG forwards the request to the RS (step 3) which will perform the API call per OAuth requirements (step 4). The raw response is sent back to the ARG (step 5) that subsequently enforces the attribute-level policy on it (step 6) and sends the sanitized response to the client (step 7).

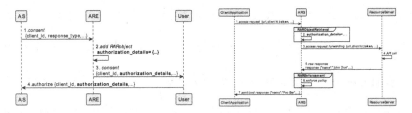

Fig. 4. The sequence diagrams of adding (left) and enforcing (right) policies to API delegations.

6   Implementation and Evaluation

We implemented a Proof-of-Concept (PoC) version of **utAPIa** to protect a baseline API. To indicate whether certain attributes in API responses can be manipulated, we extended the API description file which used OpenAPI version 3.0.1 [43]. We added two additional Boolean properties, `editable` and `removable`, to the Schema Object which is used to describe the API response objects. The ARE is implemented as a Chrome extension that intercepts and modifies OAuth authorization requests to access our API. The ARG is implemented as an API proxy. Both the API server and the proxy are implemented in Python using the `aiohttp` library[2]. The proxy logic is implemented in approximately 40 lines of code highlighting its simplicity and ease of maintenance. Our AS is implemented using Authlete[3], a cloud-based OAuth implementation provider with FAPI and OpenID certification [4,36]. By utilizing a standard third-party implementation for our AS, we ensure that the core OAuth functionalities remain untouched and unaltered, thus satisfying one of our design goals for **utAPIa**. We deployed our PoC on our institution cloud infrastructure on VM instances running Ubuntu-22.04 with 4 vCPUs and 4 GB of RAM memory per VM. The browser extension was tested on Chrome version 112 without any noticeable impact on user experience.

6.1   Policy Enforcement Overhead

The ARG module is responsible for enforcing user controls on API responses. In our PoC, for retrieving the RAR object, the proxy first looks in its cache, which is implemented using SQLite, to check whether there is a previously-stored RAR object associated with this access token. If the RAR object is not in the cache, the proxy contacts the AS to retrieve it from the token introspection response and stores the result in its cache for subsequent use. The two controls that the proxy enforces are access timeout and attribute control. The access timeout is implemented by simply comparing the current timestamp with the value stored in the `access_timeout` attribute in the RAR object which induces an insignificant overhead of integer comparison. To enforce attribute-level control, the proxy applies the operations specified in the `patch` attribute, using the JSON Patch library[4].

To examine how enforcing attribute-level control impacts the latency and throughput of our PoC, we measured the latency overhead as the computation time of additional operations executed by the proxy[5]. Figure 5 depicts the influence of policy coverage, i.e., the proportion of attributes modified by the policy,

---

[2] https://docs.aiohttp.org/.

[3] https://www.authlete.com/. We are grateful to the Authlete team for generously providing us with an academic license for utilizing their APIs.

[4] https://pypi.org/project/jsonpatch/.

[5] We also measured the latency as the relative increase in the request serving. The impact was not perceptible however, due to the minimal computational overhead.

on the latency. The attribute-level control policy in this case used randomly selected operations (`remove` or `replace`) and attribute paths. As the evaluation result shows, even in the worst-case scenario where the policy modifies all 32 attributes in the API response, the latency remains below 0.7 ms. Additionally, we assessed the latency of individual operations by modifying all attributes for varying API response sizes. Both operations appear to have a linear impact on the latency, with the `remove` operation being more lightweight than `replace`. This is unsurprising since replacing involves both removal of the old value and insertion of the new value.

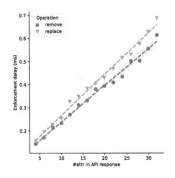

(a) The policy utilized one operation to change all the response attributes.

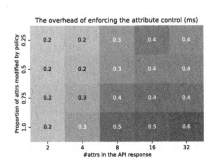

(b) The operations in the policy are randomly selected.

Fig. 5. Enforcement delay according to the attribute control operations (left) and the correlation between the proportion of attributes modified by the policy and the total number of attributes present in the response (right).

To evaluate throughput, we measured the number of concurrent requests that can be handled in the baseline implementation and the extension using **utAPIa**. As shown by the red line in Fig. 6, the throughput saturates for the baseline at 20,000 requests per second and at 12,000 requests per second when using **utAPIa**, indicating a 40% decrease in throughput.

7   Discussion and Future Work

utAPIa empowers users to exert greater control over access delegations by introducing important privacy controls such as setting expiration time for delegations and implementing enhanced controls to sanitize API responses. In achieving this, **utAPIa** leverages the unmodified OAuth protocol and an existing standardized OAuth extension. Its modifications on the API provider's side are modular, requiring no significant changes to their existing components. Our evaluation results show the feasibility of **utAPIa** in achieving its goals. While our PoC

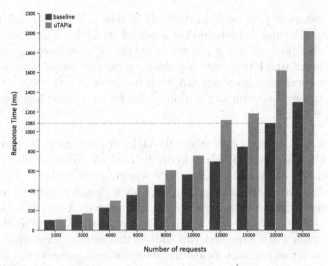

Fig. 6. The throughput of resource server in baseline implementation and when using **utAPIa**. (Color figure online)

implementation of **utAPIa** incurs a 40% decrease in throughput, it compensates with its ability to provide fine-grained controls for adjusting the delegation's scope. It also worth mentioning that the evaluation results of our PoC set a conservative upper bound on the overhead of **utAPIa** for API providers, as our implementation is not optimized for performance. There are several ways in which performance can be improved, for example by using a more performance-oriented language for implementing the ARG instead of Python.

Scrutinized Policy Validation: Allowing users to modify attributes in API responses introduces inherent security and privacy risks. Users might attempt to alter some values with malicious intent, or might lack the knowledge and control over their data to apply the appropriate privacy settings. For instance, consider an API that exposes a user's email address in a single-sign-on application: if users can replace the value with any chosen email address, they can exploit it for impersonation or spamming attacks on other users. Even without any malicious intent, to achieve a meaningful privacy enhancement, users would need to select a different email address per sign-in attempt. Therefore, when modifying attributes (i.e., using `replace` operation) the semantics of permitted replacement values needs to be governed by the API providers. Controlling and validating the replacement values help the API providers maintain the security of the system and can also lead to better privacy protection for users. For example, practical examples of concealing email addresses including Apple Hide My Email [3] and Firefox Relay [20], where random email addresses are generated and linked to a user's actual inbox. This approach not only ensures that users cannot misuse others' email addresses, thus ensuring security, but also guarantees the use of a fresh email address for each service the user attempts to sign into, which enhances privacy. Such validation rules are usually attribute- and application-specific and fall outside the scope of **utAPIa**, which is designed as a generic solution for enhancing privacy in OAuth. Future research can leverage the capabilities of **utAPIa** to develop more comprehensive privacy solutions in specific application domains where OAuth is used to exchange personal information, such as in single-sign-on applications [5, 35, 42], and smart home automation platforms [6, 9, 10, 29].

Users in Control of Privacy Choices: **utAPIa** enables users to exercise more control over the delegated API accesses on their behalf. However, it is well-known that more privacy controls can quickly overwhelm users [2, 25, 46]. Furthermore, users might not know the correct privilege-level that a client requires at the moment of authorization when policies are introduced. A too-restrictive policy can hinder the functionalities of the client or even completely break it, resulting in user frustration. Future research can address this issue by leveraging automatic permission configuration, such as using machine learning approaches for deriving the app requirements [40]. These methods can be utilized to automatically mine the required permissions of a client, thereby liberating users from making all the privacy choices from scratch.

Other Benefits of **utAPIa***:* In addition to the discussed privacy gains for the users, **utAPIa** can bring some additional benefits for stakeholders involved in an OAuth delegation. For example, access timeouts free API providers from the complexities associated with non-expiring delegations such as backward compatibility and potential security risks associated with keeping outdated APIs available to existing clients. Additionally, utilizing **utAPIa** can help API providers in complying with privacy and data protection regulations.

8 Related Work

Single-Sign-On Applications: Security and privacy of OAuth has been extensively studied in the context of SSO applications [12, 13, 18, 21, 28, 32, 35, 41, 42, 45, 47]. Several studies have focused on removing the privacy implications of SSO concerning the Identity Providers that can link user logins across different websites [13, 18, 24]. These studies use a different threat model and are orthogonal to the issue that **utAPIa** aims to address. Privacy issues that rise from the mistakes in OAuth implementation in SSO is also out of scope [28, 32, 41]. Nearly 89% of the participants in the study by Balash et al. [5] expressed their willingness to make specific parts of their Google profile inaccessible to third-party apps regardless of the requested privileges. Similar to [46], this results highlights the need for more fine-grained permission control, such as those **utAPIa** offers, rather than the existing all-or-nothing approval in SSO and Android applications. Moreover, the study by Morkonda et al. [35] performed a large-scale analysis of SSO on web and revealed that websites (the *third-party clients* in SSO) very often exhibit a malicious behavior when using SSO: they revealed a discrepancy in the amount of information that a website requests via different SSO options, with one option being more privacy-intrusive. Additionally, they discovered that the first SSO option is the most privacy-intrusive SSO position in majority of the websites, suggesting the utilization of dark patterns [7,11]. Their findings confirm the need for adaptive controls that are adjustable according to the user's preferences, such as those provided by **utAPIa**. Dimova et al. [15], recently performed a large-scale analysis of SSO login on the web. One of the experiments in their study consisted of visiting login pages of websites and trying to login via OAuth while adjusting the scope parameter to only the email address of the user. Their results indicate that only 11% of examined websites show signs of breakage or failed login. These findings suggest that the impact on functionality of tools which adjust OAuth scopes such as **utAPIa** is minimal and highlights the need for more granular privacy controls for users.

Android Applications: Participants in the study by Wijesekera et al. [46] expressed their desire to block nearly 30% of access requests made by the Android apps they were using. The main factor for blocking these requests were the participants understanding of the app's functionality and their personal privacy concerns. Hornyack et al. [25] designed and developed AppFence, an extension to the Android operating system for more fine-grained privacy controls. Similar to attribute-level controls in **utAPIa**, AppFence substitutes the data that a user wants to hide from an app with *shadow data*. The evaluation of AppFence for hiding 12 categories of sensitive data resulted in 44% of tested applications becoming less functional or broken. This finding is very relevant for **utAPIa**, as it shows that aligning the correct privacy control with an app's functionality can be challenging. Thus, there needs to be a choice between utilizing the functionalities of an app and maintaining the user's privacy goals.

9   Conclusion

The lack of granular control over data sharing in OAuth flows can give rise to serious privacy concerns for users. Previous studies have highlighted the need for increased control on delegated API accesses. In this work, we aimed to address these issues using **utAPIa** which offers attribute-level control and access timeouts for OAuth delegations with minimal deployment efforts. Our solution easily integrates with existing OAuth deployments, as it does not modify the OAuth protocol itself and leverages OAuth's standardized Rich Authorization Requests extension. On the resource provider's side, **utAPIa** functions as a proxy, seamlessly integrating with the API's software components. To the best of our knowledge, this paper represents the first proposal of a generic solution that addresses privacy issues in OAuth, using only existing and standardized OAuth extensions. We believe that the techniques introduced in **utAPIa** can serve as a foundation for developing new enhanced privacy-protecting tools, particularly in areas where OAuth is employed to authorize the exchange of personal information.

References

1. Acar, G., Englehardt, S., Narayanan, A.: No boundaries: data exfiltration by third parties embedded on web pages. Proc. Priv. Enhancing Technol. **2020**, 220–238 (2020)
2. Acar, Y., Backes, M., Bugiel, S., Fahl, S., McDaniel, P., Smith, M.: SoK: lessons learned from android security research for appified software platforms. In: 2016 IEEE Symposium on Security and Privacy (SP), pp. 433–451 (2016). https://doi.org/10.1109/SP.2016.33
3. Apple Support: What is Hide My Email?, November 2022. https://support.apple.com/en-us/HT210425. Accessed 21 Aug 2023
4. Authlete: Authlete 2.3 has been certified for the first FAPI 2.0 certifications (2023). https://www.authlete.com/news/20230509_fapi2-certifications/. Accessed 21 Aug 2023
5. Balash, D.G., Wu, X., Grant, M., Reyes, I., Aviv, A.J.: Security and privacy perceptions of third-party application access for google accounts. In: 31st USENIX Security Symposium, USENIX Security 2022, , Boston, MA, pp. 3397–3414. USENIX Association, August 2022. https://www.usenix.org/conference/usenixsecurity22/presentation/balash
6. Bastys, I., Piessens, F., Sabelfeld, A.: Tracking information flow via delayed output - addressing privacy in IoT and emailing apps. In: Nordic Conference on Secure IT Systems (2018)
7. Bösch, C., Erb, B., Kargl, F., Kopp, H., Pfattheicher, S.: Tales from the dark side: privacy dark strategies and privacy dark patterns. Proc. Priv. Enhancing Technol. **2016**, 237–254 (2016)
8. Bryan, P.C., Nottingham, M.: JavaScript Object Notation (JSON) Patch. RFC 6902, April 2013. https://doi.org/10.17487/RFC6902. https://www.rfc-editor.org/info/rfc6902
9. Chen, Y., Alhanahnah, M., Sabelfeld, A., Chatterjee, R., Fernandes, E.: Practical data access minimization in Trigger-Action platforms. In: 31st USENIX Security Symposium, USENIX Security 2022, Boston, MA, pp. 2929–2945. USENIX Association, August 2022. https://www.usenix.org/conference/usenixsecurity22/presentation/chen-yunang-practical
10. Chiang, Y.-H., Hsiao, H.-C., Yu, C.-M., Kim, T.H.-J.: On the privacy risks of compromised Trigger-Action platforms. In: Chen, L., Li, N., Liang, K., Schneider, S. (eds.) ESORICS 2020. LNCS, vol. 12309, pp. 251–271. Springer, Cham (2020). https://doi.org/10.1007/978-3-030-59013-0_13
11. Conti, G., Sobiesk, E.: Malicious interface design: exploiting the user. In: Proceedings of the 19th International Conference on World Wide Web, WWW 2010, pp. 271–280. Association for Computing Machinery, New York, NY, USA (2010). https://doi.org/10.1145/1772690.1772719
12. Dey, A., Weis, S.: PseudoID: enhancing privacy in federated login. In: Hot Topics in Privacy Enhancing Technologies, pp. 95–107 (2010). http://www.pseudoid.net
13. Dey, A., Weis, S.: PseudoID: enhancing privacy in federated login. In: Hot Topics in Privacy Enhancing Technologies, pp. 95–107 (2010). http://www.pseudoid.net
14. Dick Hardt (Editor): The OAuth 2.0 Authorization Framework. RFC 6749 (2012). https://doi.org/10.17487/RFC6749. https://www.rfc-editor.org/info/rfc6749
15. Dimova, Y., van Goethem, T., Joosen, W.: Everybody's looking for something: a large-scale evaluation on the privacy of OAuth authentication on the web. In: Proceedings on Privacy Enhancing Technologies, pp. 452–467 (2023). https://doi.org/10.56553/popets-2023-0119

16. Farooqi, S., Musa, M.B., Shafiq, Z., Zaffar, F.: CanaryTrap: detecting data misuse by third-party apps on online social networks. Proc. Priv. Enhancing Technol. **2020**, 336–354 (2020)

17. Felt, A.P., Evans, D.E.: Privacy protection for social networking platforms. In: Web 2.0 Security and Privacy 2008, W2SP 2008 (2008)

18. Fett, D., Küsters, R., Schmitz, G.: SPRESSO: a secure, privacy-respecting single sign-on system for the web. In: Proceedings of the 22nd ACM SIGSAC Conference on Computer and Communications Security, CCS 2015, pp. 1358–1369. Association for Computing Machinery, New York, NY, USA (2015). https://doi.org/10.1145/2810103.2813726

19. Fett, D., Küsters, R., Schmitz, G.: A comprehensive formal security analysis of OAuth 2.0. In: Proceedings of the 2016 ACM SIGSAC Conference on Computer and Communications Security, CCS 2016. Association for Computing Machinery (2016)

20. Firefox: Firefox Relay (2023). https://relay.firefox.com/. Accessed 21 Aug 2023

21. Ghasemisharif, M., Ramesh, A., Checkoway, S., Kanich, C., Polakis, J.: O single {Sign-Off}, where art thou? An empirical analysis of single {Sign-On} account hijacking and session management on the web. In: 27th USENIX Security Symposium, USENIX Security 2018, pp. 1475–1492 (2018)

22. Greenberg, A.: An absurdly basic bug let anyone grab all of Parler's data, January 2021. https://www.wired.com/story/parler-hack-data-public-posts-images-video/. Accessed 21 Feb 2023

23. Guha, S., Tang, K., Francis, P.: NOYB: privacy in online social networks. In: Proceedings of the First Workshop on Online Social Networks, WOSN 2008, pp. 49–54. Association for Computing Machinery, New York, NY, USA (2008). https://doi.org/10.1145/1397735.1397747

24. Hammann, S., Sasse, R., Basin, D.: Privacy-preserving openID connect. In: Proceedings of the 15th ACM Asia Conference on Computer and Communications Security, ASIA CCS 2020, pp. 277–289. Association for Computing Machinery, New York, NY, USA (2020). https://doi.org/10.1145/3320269.3384724

25. Hornyack, P., Han, S., Jung, J., Schechter, S., Wetherall, D.: These aren't the droids you're looking for: retrofitting android to protect data from imperious applications. In: Proceedings of the 18th ACM Conference on Computer and Communications Security, CCS 2011, pp. 639–652. Association for Computing Machinery, New York, NY, USA (2011). https://doi.org/10.1145/2046707.2046780

26. Google Identity: Using OAuth 2.0 to access Google APIs. https://developers.google.com/identity/protocols/oauth2#expiration. Accessed 21 Aug 2023

27. Isaak, J., Hanna, M.J.: User data privacy: Facebook, Cambridge Analytica, and privacy protection. Computer **51**(8), 56–59 (2018). https://doi.org/10.1109/MC.2018.3191268

28. Jannett, L., Mladenov, V., Mainka, C., Schwenk, J.: DISTINCT: identity theft using in-browser communications in dual-window single sign-on. In: Proceedings of the 2022 ACM SIGSAC Conference on Computer and Communications Security, CCS 2022, pp. 1553–1567. Association for Computing Machinery, New York, NY, USA (2022). https://doi.org/10.1145/3548606.3560692

29. Kalantari, S., Hughes, D., De Decker, B.: Listing the ingredients for IFTTT recipes. In: 2022 IEEE International Conference on Trust, Security and Privacy in Computing and Communications (TrustCom), pp. 1376–1383 (2022). https://doi.org/10.1109/TrustCom56396.2022.00194

30. Krebs, B.: USPS site exposed data on 60 million users, November 2018. https://krebsonsecurity.com/2018/11/usps-site-exposed-data-on-60-million-users/. Accessed 21 Aug 2023

31. Malwarebytes Labs: Second colossal Linkedin 'breach' in 3 months, almost all users affected, June 2021. https://www.malwarebytes.com/blog/news/2021/06/second-colossal-linkedin-breach-in-3-months-almost-all-users-affected. Accessed 21 Aug 2023

32. Li, W., Mitchell, C.J., Chen, T.: OAuthGuard: protecting user security and privacy with OAuth 2.0 and OpenID connect. In: Proceedings of the 5th ACM Workshop on Security Standardisation Research Workshop, SSR 2019, pp. 35–44. Association for Computing Machinery, New York, NY, USA (2019). https://doi.org/10.1145/3338500.3360331

33. Lodderstedt, T., Richer, J., Campbell, B.: OAuth 2.0 Rich Authorization Requests. RFC 9396, May 2023. https://doi.org/10.17487/RFC9396. https://www.rfc-editor.org/info/rfc9396

34. O'Neill, M., Zumerle, D., D'Hoinne, J.: API Security: What You Need to Do to Protect Your APIs, August 2019. https://www.gartner.com/en/documents/3956746

35. Morkonda, S.G., Chiasson, S., van Oorschot, P.C.: Empirical analysis and privacy implications in OAuth-based single sign-on systems. In: Proceedings of the 20th Workshop on Workshop on Privacy in the Electronic Society, WPES 2021, pp. 195–208. Association for Computing Machinery, New York, NY, USA (2021)

36. OpenID: OpenID Certification (2023). https://openid.net/certification/. Accessed 21 Aug 2023

37. Philippaerts, P., Preuveneers, D., Joosen, W.: OAuch: exploring security compliance in the OAuth 2.0 ecosystem. In: Proceedings of the 25th International Symposium on Research in Attacks, Intrusions and Defenses, RAID 2022, pp. 460–481. Association for Computing Machinery, New York, NY, USA (2022). https://doi.org/10.1145/3545948.3545955

38. Philippaerts, P., Preuveneers, D., Joosen, W.: Revisiting OAuth 2.0 compliance: a two-year follow-up study. In: 2023 IEEE European Symposium on Security and Privacy Workshops (EuroS&PW), pp. 521–525. IEEE (2023). https://doi.org/10.1109/EuroSPW59978.2023.00064

39. Singh, B.: API security: exposed API endpoint leaks over 11 million telco customers' data, October 2022. https://checkmarx.com/blog/api-security-exposed-api-endpoint-leaks-over-11-million-telco-customers-data/. Accessed 21 Aug 2023

40. Smullen, D., Feng, Y., Zhang, S., Sadeh, N.: The best of both worlds: mitigating trade-offs between accuracy and user burden in capturing mobile app privacy preferences. Proc. Priv. Enhancing Technol. **2020**, 195–215 (2020). https://doi.org/10.2478/popets-2020-0011

41. Sun, S.T., Beznosov, K.: The devil is in the (implementation) details: an empirical analysis of OAuth SSO systems. In: Proceedings of the 2012 ACM Conference on Computer and Communications Security, CCS 2012, pp. 378–390. Association for Computing Machinery, New York, NY, USA (2012). https://doi.org/10.1145/2382196.2382238

42. Sun, S.T., Pospisil, E., Muslukhov, I., Dindar, N., Hawkey, K., Beznosov, K.: What makes users refuse web single sign-on? An empirical investigation of OpenID. In: Proceedings of the Seventh Symposium on Usable Privacy and Security, SOUPS 2011. Association for Computing Machinery (2011). https://doi.org/10.1145/2078827.2078833

43. Swagger: OpenAPI specification (2021). https://swagger.io/specification/v3. Accessed 21 Aug 2023

44. Wang, N., Xu, H., Grossklags, J.: Third-party apps on Facebook: privacy and the illusion of control. In: Proceedings of the 5th ACM Symposium on Computer Human Interaction for Management of Information Technology, CHIMIT 2011, Association for Computing Machinery, New York, NY, USA (2011). https://doi.org/10.1145/2076444.2076448

45. Westers, M., Wich, T., Jannett, L., Mladenov, V., Mainka, C., Mayer, A.: SSO-monitor: fully-automatic large-scale landscape, security, and privacy analyses of single sign-on in the wild. arXiv preprint arXiv:2302.01024 (2023)

46. Wijesekera, P., Baokar, A., Hosseini, A., Egelman, S., Wagner, D., Beznosov, K.: Android permissions remystified: a field study on contextual integrity. In: 24th USENIX Security Symposium, USENIX Security 2015, pp. 499–514. USENIX Association, Washington, D.C., August 2015. https://www.usenix.org/conference/usenixsecurity15/technical-sessions/presentation/wijesekera

47. Zhou, Y., Evans, D.: {SSOScan}: automated testing of web applications for single {Sign-On} vulnerabilities. In: 23rd USENIX Security Symposium, USENIX Security 2014, pp. 495–510 (2014)

Traffic Analysis by Adversaries with Partial Visibility

Iness Ben Guirat[1]([envelope]) [ID], Claudia Diaz[1] [ID], Karim Eldefrawy[2] [ID], and Hadas Zeilberger[3] [ID]

[1] COSIC, KU Leuven, Leuven, Belgium
{ibenguir,cdiaz}@esat.kuleuven.be
[2] SRI, Menlo Park, USA
karim.eldafrawi@sri.com
[3] YALE, New Haven, USA
hadas.zeilberger@yale.com

Abstract. Mixnets are a fundamental privacy enhancing technology in the context of anonymous communication that have been extensively studied in terms of a Global passive Adversary (GPA). However a more realistic adversary that captures only a portion of the network have not yet been studied. We call these adversaries "Adversaries with Partial Visibility (APV)" In this paper we provide a framework that models the mixnet-based system and captures different types of Adversaries with Partial Visibility. Each adversary is modeled based on their goals, prior knowledge, and capabilities. We then use this model to perform traffic analysis using the Metropolis-Hastings algorithm in conjunction with a Bayesian inference engine. To the best of our knowledge this is the first time such an adversary is explicitly defined and studied, despite this adversary model being championed as more realistic than global passive adversaries in prior work. We highlight that our framework is flexible and able to encompass a broad range of different adversaries. Naturally, our model also captures the classical global passive adversary (GPA) as a special case.

Keywords: Mixnet · Local Adversary · Partial Visibility · Metropolis-Hastings

1 Introduction

The notion of a mixnet was first invented by Chaum [2]. Mixnets were designed specifically to resist an adversary with a global view who can observe all inputs and outputs in the network. Resisting such adversaries is achieved via the mixing strategy where each mix does not output messages immediately upon receiving them. Instead, a mix stores messages for some amount of time before sending them to either another mix or to a recipient. This technique hides correlations between the inputs and outputs which therefore makes mixnets resilient against a Global Passive Adversary (GPA). Currently, there is a large literature that exists that utilizes simulations and empirical evaluation in order to quantify anonymity under such a powerful adversary for generic mixnets [1,13].

G. Tsudik et al. (Eds.): ESORICS 2023, LNCS 14345, pp. 338–358, 2024.
https://doi.org/10.1007/978-3-031-51476-0_17

However, adversaries with such full visibility are of questionable practical utility, since in practice even very powerful adversaries may have blind spots in their network coverage [16]. The literature currently lacks methods to model and analyze anonymity properties with respect to an adversary who has partial visibility of the network, such an adversary (such as Iran or Russia surveillance operations) that can only control mixes within their jurisdiction. One challenge in evaluating anonymity under such an adversary is that their advantages in inferring information about messages in a network vary greatly depending on which portions of the network they have visibility over. Deriving, analytically, the probability of an event when considering such an adversary requires conditional probabilities based on the different assumptions of the portions of the network that they can or cannot see. Even a simple network results in an explosion in complexity from the derivation of such probabilities.

To address this problem, we first provide a general and flexible matrix-based mixnet model that captures different mixnet configurations, then we model adversaries based on their goals, priors, and capabilities. By performing this, we retrieve two sets of data: an *Observation* $\mathcal{O}$ and a *Hidden State* $\mathcal{HS}$. The $\mathcal{O}$ is the part of the trace the adversary has visibility over and the $\mathcal{HS}$ is the part of the trace the adversary lacks visibility over. Finally, we use this modeling to perform mixnet traffic analysis under an *APV*. The main strength of this framework is that it is able to capture a broad range of adversaries. We develop and implement a Bayesian inference engine which takes an *APV* and a network configuration as input. The inference engine then uses the Metropolis Hastings to estimate the distribution over possible traces.

In summary, our main contributions are as follows:

- A matrix-based mixnet model that is able to capture different mixnet configuration such as different topologies and mixing strategies.
- A model for an *Adversary with Partial Visibility (APV)* that can be captured by the matrix-based mixnet model. This model can be used in conjunction with Bayesian inference techniques to perform traffic analysis attacks. To the best of our knowledge such a general adversary model has not been studied in mixnets before.
- A traffic analysis framework that uses the Metropolis-Hastings algorithm to evaluate anonymity under different *APV*s.

2 Motivation and Related Work

In this section we present our motivation and related work. First, we discuss Adversaries with Partial Visibility in the context of mixnets. Second, we discuss our decision to choose the Metropolis-Hastings algorithm for traffic analysis.

Adversaries with Partial Visibility: Since Chaum's seminal work on untraceable email [2], there has been considerable research exploring and understanding the design space of mixnets [5,12,14,18]. However, most of this literature assumes a very strong notion of the adversary, called a *Global Passive*

Adversary (GPA), which observes the entire network. In [16], Syverson argues that a GPA is unrealistic and does not reflect the real anonymity of a system. Starting from adversary models that are not reasonable in practice has contributed to the lack of wide-spread adoption of anonymous communication systems. Syverson argues that in security analysis, most adversaries are subject to some constraints on their capabilities such as having a partial view of a network [16]. An adversary's ability to execute a successful attack is dependent on the adversary's available resources and their effectiveness. In other words, the measure of an adversary's ability to succeed must include the resources it will take them to learn enough information to link relations.

In [8], Gallagher et al. have argued for the need for new adversary ontologies that could better model real-world adversaries by outlining the limitations of the adversaries that are commonly used in academic literature, such as Global Passive Adversary. A GPA is unrealistic in real world scenarios where the mixnet system spans multiple administrative domains (e.g., different autonomous systems) in several countries. In fact, considering such an unnecessarily strong adversary may hinder exploring and curtail the development of mixnet designs that can scale better and provide adequate and meaningful privacy in the real world [13].

Traffic Analysis in Mixnets: Multiple variants of traffic analysis attacks in mixnets do exist in the literature [3,10,11,15]. However the focus has been on the edges of mixnets where messages are sent and received and therefore the adversary does traffic analysis on the patterns of these messages in order to correlate for example a sender to a receiver. These attacks do not capture an adversary that is also able to corrupt or monitor a portion of the network in order to de-anonymize the sender and receiver. Traffic analysis by an Adversary with Partial Visibility (APV) over the network is a hard task as it requires consideration of prior knowledge of the adversary as well as the different assumptions for the parts of the network that the adversary does not have visibility over. In [6], the authors argue that at the heart of traffic analysis lies an inference problem. Therefore applying Bayesian techniques provides a sound framework on which to build attacks and algorithms to estimate different quantities. Their main contribution is introducing the application of Bayesian inference to traffic analysis. The Metropolis-Hastings algorithm is a well known method for obtaining a sequence of random samples where direct sampling is difficult [9]. In order to estimate a function of the mapping between input and output messages of the network, they build an inference engine that samples from the distribution of network states that a set of given observations allow. However, this model only models global passive adversaries [6].

One of the key contributions of our work is to extend this bayesian-based framework in conjuction with Metropolis Hastings in order to analyse Adversaries with Partial Visibility. This encompasses a much wider set of adversaries than the Global Passive Adversary considered in prior work [6,17].

3   Adversary Model

In this paper we provide a method that solves the problem of traffic analysis under an Adversary with Partial Visibility (APV). In a nutshell the problem is presented as follows: The adversary APV has a prior knowledge about the mixnet-based system. An APV observes the network over some time interval t and produces an observation $\mathcal{O}$. Given the prior knowledge on the system model as well as the observation $\mathcal{O}$, the adversary tries to infer the probability of certain events that happened either partially or entirely outside of her visibility during the time t. We call the parts of the network trace that the adversary does not have visibility over a Hidden State $\mathcal{HS}$. Table 1 provides a handy reference for all the notations used in this paper.

One of our objectives for solving this problem is to make the adversary model as general as possible in order to accommodate different types of adversaries. We therefore start by modeling the three major aspects of any adversary: (i) Goal, (ii) Prior and (iii) Capability:

Goal: The adversary chooses a goal. For example an adversary's goal can be to infer the probability of a sender s_i communicating with receiver r_j ($Pr[s_i \rightarrow r_j]$), or correlating a specific input i_i to an output o_j ($Pr[i_i \rightarrow o_j]$). Note that in the first example, the adversary needs to track all messages from s_i to r_j, however in the second example the adversary is only interested in correlating i_i with o_j.

Prior: Depending on the system model, different adversaries can have different sets of prior knowledge. One could imagine a system that have different paths lengths for each message or different constraints on users in choosing the route (for example users in certain geographical locations are more likely to route their messages through nodes in adjacent areas). We use $\mathcal{C}$ for the system constraints. This type of information is encoded in the prior knowledge of the adversary.
To be more formal we assume that an abstract system consists of an Observations $\mathcal{O}$ and a Hidden State $\mathcal{HS}$. We therefore assign a joint probability given the constraints $\mathcal{C}$, $Pr[\mathcal{HS}, \mathcal{O} \mid \mathcal{C}]$. We further elaborate how to incorporate the joint probability in our framework in Sect. 5.

Capability: In order to achieve its goals, the adversary does traffic analysis by making use of its *Compromising* and/or *Monitoring* capabilities. Monitoring the network means that the adversary is monitoring the connections between different physical entities of the network either throughout some portion of the network or throughout the entire network in the case of a GPA. A physical entity in the network can be either a mix μ or a user u. We call this an *inter-entity connection*. An ISP is one example of an adversary that can see inter-entity connections and use this data for traffic analysis. The adversary is also able to *compromise*. Compromising a mix means this adversary has the capability of seeing inside a mix. One real world example of an adversary that can see inner-mix maappings is one that can add mixes to a volunteer-based network [7].

4   A Matrix-Based Model of a Mix Network

In this section, we describe our model for a matrix-based mix network. As explained in the previous section, the *APV* is trying to estimate the probability distribution of the Hidden State $\mathcal{HS}$ given their Observation $\mathcal{O}$ and the prior knowledge about the system constraints $\mathcal{C}$. We therefore need to provide a model for the mixnet system that encompasses the adversary's constraints $\mathcal{C}$ and partitions the message trace (defined next) into an Observation $\mathcal{O}$ and Hidden State $\mathcal{HS}$.

4.1   Trace Graph: A Graph Derived from the Message Trace

A trace, which is the full set of messages traversing the network during a time t, is represented by $\mathcal{HS}$ and $\mathcal{O}$. We now describe how to derive a graph $(\mathcal{V}, \mathcal{E})$ from a trace, where $\mathcal{V}$ is the set of vertices in the graph and $\mathcal{E}$ is the set of edges. The purpose of this graph is to split each message path into segments so that we can differentiate between the parts of each path that an adversary can see and the parts that they cannot see. We start by defining a *path*, and then show how to model each path as a graph.

Definition 1 (Path). *A **path**, $P = (s_i, \mu_1, .., \mu_n, r_j) = \{e_1, ..e_{n+2}\}$, is an ordered set of entities, users and mixes, that describes the path of the message from the sender s_i to the receiver r_j (n: length of the message path).*

If P_i is the ith path, then as it goes through mix μ_j, we will denote its input vertex in this mix as $v_{i,I}(\mu_j)$ and its output vertex as $v_{i,O}(\mu_j)$. We will denote the vertex associated with the path's sender as $(v_i(s))$ and the vertex associated with the path's receiver as $(v_i(r))$.

Definition 2 (Path Graph). *Let $P_i = (s, \mu_1, .., \mu_n, r)$ be a path. A path graph is a set of vertices $\mathcal{V}$ and a set of edges $\mathcal{E}$. A vertex represents (i) the sender of the message $(v_i(s))$ of the corresponding path, (ii) the input/output of the message to/from the different mixes, $v_{i,I}(\mu_j)$, $v_{i,O}(\mu_j)$ and (iii) the recipient of the message $(v_i(r))$. An edge is the connections between two vertices of the network, which can be between two entities (either a mix or a user) or between an input vertices and an output vertices of each mix.*

Note that a vertices in the network is not just a physical point of entry of the message. It is rather a representation of time in the graph. For example if a message m arrives to mix μ at $t_1 = 1$ and a message m_2 arrives to μ at time $t_2 = 2$, we assign different vertices in the mix to the different messages. Figure 1b shows a simple example of modeling a portion of the path and its relationship to the mix by vertices and edges.

Definition 3 (Trace). *Let M be a set of messages sent through the mixnet. For message $m \in M$, let P_m be the path of m. A **trace** $\mathcal{TR} = \{P_m : m \in M\}$ is the set of paths of all messages sent through the network during time interval t, in other words, a trace is the full set of paths that occur in a network during a time interval t.*

Definition 4 (Trace Graph). *Let M be the set of messages sent across the network during time interval t and let $\mathcal{TR} = \{P_m : m \in M\}$ be a trace of a network in that time interval. Let G_P be the Path graph of path P. The Trace Graph, $G_{TR} = \{G_P : P \in \mathcal{TR}\}$ is the set of Path Graphs associated with paths in $\mathcal{TR}$.*

We model the *Trace Graph* as a set of adjacency matrices.

Definition 5 (Adjacency Matrix). *Let $G = (\mathcal{V}, \mathcal{E})$ be a graph, where $\mathcal{V}$ is the set of vertices and $\mathcal{E}$ is the set of edges. Then an adjacency matrix Mx is a matrix with $|\mathcal{V}|$ columns and $|\mathcal{V}|$ rows, where row i and column i are both labeled by vertex $v_i \in \mathcal{V}$, for $i \in [1, |\mathcal{V}|]$. Element (i,j) of Mx is 1 if the edge $(v_i, v_j) \in \mathcal{E}$ and 0 otherwise.*

Each adjacency matrix will be associated with a subgraph of the Trace Graph, G_{TR}. We identify two types of subgraphs in the Trace Graph. The first type is an inner-mix subgraph, defined by the vertices and edges associated with each mix. We call the adjacency matrix of this subgraph an *inner-mix matrix*. This matrix represents the relationship of the input messages to a mix to the output messages of the same mix.

Definition 6 (Inner-mix matrix). *Let TG be a trace graph, let μ be a mix, and let $\mathcal{V}_I$ be the incoming vertices of messages associated with μ and $\mathcal{V}_O$ be the outgoing vertices of messages associated with μ, as described in Definition 2. For each message going through μ, there is an edge (v, w) between a vertex in $v \in \mathcal{V}_I$ and a vertex $w \in \mathcal{V}_O$, as defined by the path of that message. Let $\mathcal{E}_\mu$ be the set of such edges. Then an inner-mix matrix is the adjacency matrix of the graph $(\mathcal{V}_I \cup \mathcal{V}_O, \mathcal{E}_\mu)$.*

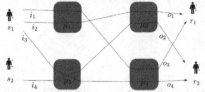
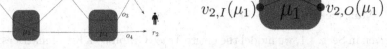

(a) An example of a network trace   (b) Mix μ_1 modeled by vertices and edges.

Fig. 1. An example of network trace $\mathcal{TR}$ and the representation of mix μ_1 by vertices and edges.

We also model *inter-entity connections* as a set of adjacency matrices. An inter-entity matrix is a matrix that represents the connections between entities that have messages going between them.

Definition 7 (Inter-entity matrix). *Let V_O be the set of outgoing vertices of a subset of the network entities that are able to send messages to subset of entities with vertices V_I. Let $\mathcal{E}_{I,O}$ be the collection of all edges that connect the vertices of V_O with the vertices V_I. Then an inter-entity matrix is the adjacency matrix of the graph $(V_O \cup V_I, \mathcal{E}_{I,O})$.*

The number of inter-entity matrices in our model vary depending on the network configuration. For example, if we have a free-route network where each mix can send a message to any mix in the network then we can have one inter-entity matrix. However, if the system's topology is stratified then mixes are arranged in a fixed number of layers and can only communicate with mixes in the subsequent layer. In this case we have an inter-entity matrix that connects every two layers (eg $\mathcal{E}_O$ is associated with layer i and $\mathcal{E}_I$ is associated with layer $i+1$).

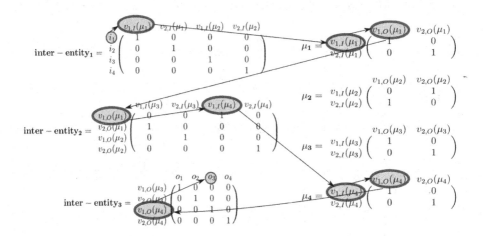

Fig. 2. Modeling the trace in Fig. 1a by matrices

4.2   Matrices in Two Sets

As given in Sect. 4.1, we model the entire Trace Graph by a list of matrices. There exists two types of matrices (i) inner-mix matrices that represent the "inside" of the mix and (ii) the inter-entities matrices that represent the connections between two sets of entities (either a mix or a user). The motivation behind this modeling is two-fold:

– Using this model we are able to trace any message by simply tracing the elements with value 1 that connect the edges in the different matrices. Figure 2 shows the matrices that are the representation of the trace depicted in Fig. 1a. We can see in the Fig. 2 how by simply following the connected edges in the matrices we are able to correlate the input i_1 to the output o_3.

– Accommodating the the adversary in our model. The set of matrices represents the full trace of the network, so in order to include the adversary in this model, we need to split the matrices into two sets: matrices that are part of the observation $\mathcal{O}$ and matrices that are part of the Hidden State $\mathcal{HS}$. For example if an adversary APV is only corrupting a mix μ_1, we put the corresponding matrix in the observation and the rest of the matrices in the hidden state. For the inter-entity matrices however, depending on which portions of the network the adversary monitors, the same matrix has to be split to $\mathcal{O}$ and $\mathcal{HS}$. For example if APV controls the connections between μ_1 and μ_3 the *inter-entity$_2$* in Fig. 2 is split in two as shown in Fig. 3.

$$\mathcal{O} = \begin{array}{c} \\ v_{1,O}(\mu_1) \\ v_{2,O}(\mu_1) \end{array} \overset{\begin{array}{cc} v_{1,I}(\mu_3) & v_{2,I}(\mu_3) \end{array}}{\begin{pmatrix} 0 & 0 \\ 1 & 0 \end{pmatrix}} \quad \mathcal{HS} = \begin{array}{c} \\ v_{1,O}(\mu_2) \\ v_{2,O}(\mu_2) \end{array} \overset{\begin{array}{cc} v_{1,I}(\mu_4) & v_{2,I}(\mu_4) \end{array}}{\begin{pmatrix} 0 & 0 \\ 0 & 1 \end{pmatrix}}$$

Fig. 3. Inter-entity matrix split into $\mathcal{O}$ and $\mathcal{HS}$

We call the *Ground Truth* the trace of messages that actually happens in reality, i.e. the trace that the adversary wants to learn information about. The adversary can see some part of the Ground Truth in its Observation $\mathcal{O}$ and proceeds to conduct the traffic analysis by traversing through the space of the different possible traces in the Hidden State $\mathcal{HS}$.

5 Traffic Analysis of Mixnets

The goal of the APV, having an observation $\mathcal{O}$ and a prior knowledge about the network $\mathcal{C}$, is to estimate the probability distribution over the possible hidden states in order to achieve its goal, for example linking senders to receivers or input messages to output messages. In other words, the APV tries to estimate the target distribution $Pr[\mathcal{HS} \mid \mathcal{O}, \mathcal{C}]$ using the Metropolis-Hastings method.

5.1 Markov Chain Monte Carlo (MCMC)

The Metropolis-Hastings method works by sampling states by conducting a random walk across a state space. In our context, a state is the Hidden State, $\mathcal{HS}$, of the trace. The Metropolis-Hastings algorithm requires that we define a transition function that allows us to propose a new Hidden State ($\mathcal{HS}_p$) for every Hidden State ($\mathcal{HS}_c$) that we encounter in our random walk. Next we compute the following ratio, α_{next_move} in order to decide whether or not to accept the $\mathcal{HS}_p$.

$$\alpha_{next\_move} = \frac{Pr[\mathcal{HS}_c|\mathcal{O}, \mathcal{C}] * Q(\mathcal{HS}_p|\mathcal{HS}_c)}{Pr[\mathcal{HS}_p \mid \mathcal{O}, \mathcal{C}] * Q[\mathcal{HS}_c|\mathcal{HS}_p]} \tag{1}$$

Note that Q is the transition function that provides the probability of moving from a current state $\mathcal{HS}_c$ to a proposed state $\mathcal{HS}_p$. Further details on how to compute Q are provided in Algorithm 1. We recall from Sect. 4 that in the set of matrices $\mathcal{MX}$ associated with a trace $\mathcal{TR}$, a matrix in $\mathcal{MX}$ is either an *inter-entities matrix* or an *inner-mix matrix*. Recall also that we divide this set of matrices into two sets; an Observation $\mathcal{O}$ and a Hidden State $\mathcal{HS}$.

The transition function we use to move from current Hidden State $\mathcal{HS}_c$ to a proposed Hidden State, $\mathcal{HS}_p$ works as follows. We start by choosing a matrix $Mx \in \mathcal{HS}$ at random, and then choosing two columns (which corresponds to vertices in the network) in Mx at random to swap. For inner-mix matrices, this corresponds to the following: let $\mathcal{M}_t$ be a set of messages in a mix with *inner-mix mapping* $F_{\mu_j} : \mathcal{M}_I \to \mathcal{M}_O$ during time t. Let $v_{1,I}, v_{2,I}(\mu_j) \in \mathcal{M}_I$, and let $v_{1,O}, v_{2,O}(\mu_j) \in \mathcal{M}_O$ such that $F_{\mu_j}(v_{1,I}) = v_{1,O}, F_{\mu_j}(v_{2,I}) = v_{2,O}$. Then swapping two columns in Mx assigns to M_t a new *inner-mix mapping* F'_μ, where $F'_\mu(v_{1,I}(\mu_j)) = v_{2,O}(\mu_j)$ and $F'_\mu(v_{2,I}(\mu_j)) = v_{1,O}(\mu_j)$ and $F'_\mu(x) = F_\mu(x)$ for all x such that $x \notin \{v_{1,I}, v_{2,I}\}$.

For inter-entity connections, the transition function corresponds to the following: Let $\mathcal{ET}_O$ and $\mathcal{ET}_I$ be two sets of entities and let $\mathcal{M}_t$ be a set of messages that are sent from entities in $\mathcal{ET}_O$ to entities in $\mathcal{ET}_I$ during time t. Let $F_e : \mathcal{ET}_O \to \mathcal{ET}_I$ be the inter-entity connection. Let $\mathcal{V}_O$ be the vertices associated with outgoing packets from $\mathcal{ET}_O$ and let $\mathcal{V}_I$ be the vertices associated with the incoming packets of $\mathcal{ET}_I$. Let $v_{1,O}, v_{2,O} \in \mathcal{V}_O$, and let $v_{1,I}, v_{2,I} \in \mathcal{V}_I$ such that $F_e(v_{1,O}) = v_{1,I}$ and $F_e(v_{2,O}) = v_{2,I}$. Then swapping two columns in Mx assigns to $\mathcal{M}_t$ a new *inter-entity connection* F'_e, where $F'_e(v_{1,O}) = v_{2,I}$, $F'_e(v_{2,O}) = v_{1,I}$ and $F'_e(x) = F_e(x)$ for all x such that $x \notin \{v_{1,O}, v_{2,O}\}$.

5.2   Computing the Probability of a State Based on Priors

Depending on the system, the adversary may have prior knowledge on the system, which will be accounted for in the estimation of the target target probability. We model the system by a list of constraints $\mathcal{C}$. Any system can have a variety of constraints, such as paths lengths [17], or user constraints in choosing nodes based on geo-locations, or having a biased distribution for routing (as in the example of Nym [7]).

To consider user constraints, the adversary, having a proposed trace $\mathcal{TR}$, computes $Pr[\mathcal{TR} \mid \mathcal{C}]$ which is the probability of the trace given its prior knowledge on the system model $\mathcal{C}$. As described in Sect. 4.2, a trace $\mathcal{TR}$ is composed of an Observation $\mathcal{O}$ and $\mathcal{HS}$, therefore:

$$Pr[\mathcal{TR} \mid \mathcal{C}] = Pr[\mathcal{HS}, \mathcal{O} \mid \mathcal{C}] \tag{2}$$

We note however that the adversary is trying to estimate $Pr[\mathcal{HS} \mid \mathcal{O}, \mathcal{C}]$ (Eq. 1). We therefore apply Bayes rule:

$$Pr[\mathcal{HS} \mid \mathcal{O}, \mathcal{C}] = \frac{Pr[\mathcal{HS}, \mathcal{O} \mid \mathcal{C}]}{Pr[\mathcal{O} \mid \mathcal{C}]} \tag{3}$$

Thus, we can rewrite $ratio_{next\_move}$ as follows:

$$
\begin{aligned}
\alpha_{next\_move} &= \frac{Pr[\mathcal{HS}_c \mid \mathcal{O}, \mathcal{C}] * Q(\mathcal{HS}_p \mid \mathcal{HS}_c)}{Pr[\mathcal{HS}_p \mid \mathcal{O}, \mathcal{C}] * Q[\mathcal{HS}_c \mid \mathcal{HS}_p]} \\
&= \frac{Pr[\mathcal{HS}_c, \mathcal{O} \mid \mathcal{C}]/Pr[\mathcal{O} \mid \mathcal{C}] * Q(\mathcal{HS}_p \mid \mathcal{HS}_c)}{Pr[\mathcal{HS}_p, \mathcal{O} \mid \mathcal{C}]/Pr[\mathcal{O} \mid \mathcal{C}] * Q[\mathcal{HS}_c \mid \mathcal{HS}_p]} \\
&= \frac{Pr[\mathcal{HS}_c, \mathcal{O} \mid \mathcal{C}] * Q(\mathcal{HS}_p \mid \mathcal{HS}_c)}{Pr[\mathcal{HS}_p, \mathcal{O} \mid \mathcal{C}] * Q[\mathcal{HS}_c \mid \mathcal{HS}_p]} \\
&= \frac{Pr[\mathcal{TR}_c \mid \mathcal{C}] * Q(\mathcal{TR}_p \mid \mathcal{TR}_c)}{Pr[\mathcal{TR}_p \mid \mathcal{C}] * Q[\mathcal{TR}_c \mid \mathcal{TR}_p]}
\end{aligned}
\tag{4}
$$

Computing the α_{next_move} is therefore reduced to computing the probabilities of the different traces $\mathcal{TR}$ given the constraints $\mathcal{C}$. Assuming paths selection is independent (we further elaborate on this point in Sect. 6). Because a trace is a set of message paths, the adversary computes:

$$
Pr[\mathcal{TR}|\mathcal{C}] = \prod_{P \in Tr} Pr[P|\mathcal{C}]
\tag{5}
$$

Based on this derivation, we execute the Metropolis-Hastings algorithm by generating a sequence of different samples (traces) starting from a random trace.

5.3   Metropolis-Hastings Algorithm

We now put everything together to present the concrete algorithm used to gain the target distribution. We describe the algorithm here, and its pseudo-code is included in Algorithm 1.

$Q(\mathcal{TR}_p|\mathcal{TR}_c)$ is the transition function, that is the probability of moving from one state $\mathcal{TR}_c$ to another state $\mathcal{TR}_p$. In our model, this translates to choosing a matrix of $Mx \in \mathcal{MX}$ and two of its columns (c_1, c_2) to permute which yields $\mathcal{TR}_p$. Therefore the transition function is symmetric and equal to $\frac{1}{|\mathcal{MX}|*|\mathcal{V}|*|\mathcal{V}|-1}$, where $|\mathcal{V}|$ is the number of columns in Mx_c. As noted in [4], the values of $Q(\mathcal{TR}_p|\mathcal{TR}_c)$ are not key to the correctness of the sampling, however different transition functions, may speed the convergence to a the stationary distribution.

6   System Model

In this section, we showcase modeling a small example of a mixnet-based system of 9 mixes in order to perform traffic analysis. We choose a stratified topology where the 9 mixes are arranged in 3 layers as shown in Appendix A.1. Each mix is assigned a layer, and messages are sent from layer l_i to layer l_{i+1}. In our experiments, we use a *threshold mix* [2] that buffers messages in the queue until the threshold parameter T is reached. At that point the mix permutes the T messages, and then outputs all messages in a random order. Finally all

---

Algorithm 1: Metropolis-Hastings Algorithm

Result: Computing $Pr[s_i \to r_j]$
Input: $\mathcal{TR} \leftarrow \{\mathcal{O}, \mathcal{HS}\}$, **APV, burn in,** n_{MH}
Initialize:
$s_i \leftarrow pick\_sender$;
$r_j \leftarrow pick\_receiver$;
$reality \leftarrow \text{check}(s_i \to r_j)$;
$P_t \leftarrow \text{compute}(Pr[TR_c])$;
$I \leftarrow 0$;
$n_{samples} \leftarrow 0$;
while $n_{samples} \leq n_{MH}$ **do**
  $MX_c \leftarrow pick\_matrice(HS_c)$;
  $MX_p \leftarrow permute(MX_c)$;
  $HS_p \leftarrow \mathcal{MX}_p = \mathcal{MX} \setminus \{Mx_c\} \cup \{Mx_p\}$;
  $TR_p \leftarrow \mathcal{O}, HS_p$;
  $violations \leftarrow check\_constraints(TR_p)$;
  if *Not violations* **then**
    $P_{t+1} \leftarrow \text{compute}(Pr[TR_p])$;
    $\alpha \leftarrow min\left[1, \frac{P_{t+1}}{P_t}\right]$;
    $r \leftarrow \mathcal{U}(0,1)$;
    if $\alpha \geq r$ **then**
      $accept(TR_p)$;
      $n_{samples} + +$;
      if $check(s_i \to r_j)$ **then**
        | $I + +$;
end
$Pr[s_i \to r_j] = \frac{I}{n_{samples}}$;
return: $\{Pr[s_i \to r_j], reality\}$

---

messages are source-routed. We emphasize that our model is not limited to this type or size of network. We argue that the matrix-based model is able to accommodate any type of mixes and/or network. However, depending on the type of the network, Eq. 5 should be adapted accordingly. Next we show how to compute the probability of a trace in a network of certain constraints $\mathcal{C}$.

6.1 Probability of a Trace

Recall from Eq. 5, that a trace $\mathcal{TR}$ is a collection of all its paths and therefore the probability of a specific trace is the product of the probabilities of different paths.

$$Pr[\mathcal{TR}|\mathcal{C}] = \prod_{P_i \in \mathcal{TR}} Pr[P_i] \qquad (6)$$

In addition, as explained in Sect. 4, a message path P_i is an ordered set of entities that describe the path of the message from a sender s_i to a receiver r_i. The routing of the message through the different mixes, as well as choosing a receiver for each message is probabilistic. Let's denote $Pr[\mu]$ the probability of the mix μ being chosen in the path P_i and $Pr[r_i]$ the probability of the receiver r_i is part of P_i, meaning sender s_i chose receiver r_i to send a message to. The probability of the path P_i is then:

$$Pr[P_i|\mathcal{C}] = \left[\prod_{\mu \in P_i} Pr[\mu])\right] Pr[r_i] \tag{7}$$

The above equation holds because we consider source routing, meaning that each user chooses the path of each message among the set of mixes and receivers. We leave other types of routing outside the scope of this work. Putting Eq. 6 and Eq. 7 together, the probability of a trace is therefore:

$$Pr[\mathcal{TR}|\mathcal{C}] = \prod_{P_i \in \mathcal{TR}} (\prod_{\mu \in P} Pr[\mu])Pr[r_i] \tag{8}$$

Considering our stratified topology system model of l layers and $N(l_i)$ mixes in each layer l_i, we now proceed to compute the probability of each path. We abuse notation slightly and also consider μ_{j,l_i} as the event that the sender s_i chooses mix $\mu_{j,i}$ as the jth mix in layer l_i, as well as r_i as the event the sender s_i in path i chooses the receiver r_i as the receiver. We first consider that each sender knows all the public parameters of the network such as all the mixes in the network as well as the number of mixes in each layer. The sender then chooses each mix as well as the receiver of each message uniformly.

$$Pr[P_i] = \left[\prod_{i=1}^{l} Pr[\mu_{j,l_i}]\right] Pr[r_i]$$
$$= \left[\prod_{i=1}^{l} \frac{1}{N(l_i)}\right] Pr[r_i] \tag{9}$$

We show how we compute the probability of a trace of a network having other requirements in Appendix A.1.

7   Empirical Evaluation

In this section we first explain how we assess the effectiveness of our model and then show the results of inferring probabilities of trace-related events under two adversaries of different capabilities.

7.1   Determining the Accuracy of Our Model

Our framework is effective if it reaches the target distribution. To evaluate the effectiveness of our model of an APV we need to assess the closeness of the samples given by our model to a target distribution based on the ground truth across many rounds of messages in a mixnet.

Recall from Sect. 5, that we first start by generating the ground truth trace $\mathcal{TR}_{GT}$ and the adversary specifies the trace related event that they want to infer probability of. We refer to the success or failure of this event in the ground truth as a *goal* and we model it as a predicate function $P : \{\mathcal{TR}_{GT}\} \rightarrow \{0, 1\}$, which takes the ground truth trace $\mathcal{TR}_{GT}$ as input and outputs 1 if the occurrence happens in $\mathcal{TR}_{GT}$ and 0 otherwise. For example, if the goal of the adversary is to infer the probability of sender s_1 sending a message to receiver r_1 during its window of observation, then we associate to this goal a predicate P, where $P(TR) = 1$ if s_1 did send a message to r_1 in the trace TR and 0 otherwise.

Then we translate this ground truth trace into a set of matrices. Depending on what portions of the network the adversary observes, we divide this set of matrices into two sets: Hidden State $\mathcal{HS}$ and $\mathcal{O}$. In order to avoid starting from a high probability state, we do a randomized uniformly chosen number of permutations on the different matrices that are part of $\mathcal{HS}$ and finally we give these two sets of matrices to the adversary as well as the list of constraints.

The adversary then execute the Metropolis-Hastings algorithm on the trace. At the end of one run of the Metropolis-Hastings algorithm, the adversary assign a probability p_{tr} to the event of interest. We refer to the probability, p_{tr}, as a goal and the output of $P(\mathcal{TR}_{GT})$ as an occurrence. We call an occurrence positive when $P(\mathcal{TR}_G) = 1$ and we call an occurrence negative when $P(\mathcal{TR}_G) = 0$.

In order to assess the accuracy of our model we need to generalize beyond a single trace. To do this, we run the Metropolis Hastings algorithm on N_{tr} number of traces for the same adversary each time using a different ground truth trace. After each run of the algorithm, we record the probability p_{tr_i} that the adversary assigns a given event to its goal, and we record the occurrence $P(TR_{GT})$. Once we have our full data set $(p_{tr_i}, occurrences)$ tuples, we compare the average inferred probability to the confidence score on the occurrences. We use the Wilson score interval [20], as it has been shown to be the most accurate [19] of binomial confidence intervals. The Wilson Score takes number of successes and number of failures as inputs, and outputs the probability of success along with the 95% confidence interval. We consider our model to be effective if the sampled probability lies within the confidence interval. Therefore, the average ability of the adversary to correctly infer the probability of the specified event across many different events can be taken into account.

7.2 Capability: Compromising

We start by analysing an adversary who has compromising capability. The goal of this adversary is to infer *whether at-least one of the messages of a sender s_i arrived to a receiver r_j*. This adversary tries to link the receiver to senders that route a message through one of the compromised mixes. Therefore we choose an adversary who is compromising one entry mix and one exit mix. We evaluate this adversary for up to 500 observations.

We can see in Fig. 4a that when there are only a few observations, the confidence interval is high, however we show that our model eventually converges into the the target distribution where the confidence interval is within tight bounds as the model is guessing with 95% confidence the correct probability. Note however that we are showing the average sampled probability of the different events. The probability of each trace related event may differ per different observation. In Fig. 4b we show the histogram of the number of experiments per bin. The idea behind this binning is to analyse beyond the average probability inferred by the adversary for the different observations. After collecting all the sampled probabilities where each probability corresponds to one trace, we store them in different bins depending on their values. Each bin corresponds to an interval of probabilities and contains the number of times the adversary inferred that probability.

We can see that for this adversary, the bin that corresponds to a probability between $[0, 0.1]$ contains the largest number of items, meaning that for most observations the adversary guessed between $[0, 0.1]$ due to lack of information. The second largest bin is the one that corresponds to the events having a probability between $[0.9, 1]$. Those events are likely to be the messages that went through both the compromised mixes (and so the APV had more information), and finally around 25% of the total events the adversary infers a probability between 0.2 and 0.7. This would intuitively match to the case where messages went through a single compromised mix that the APV could watch, but not both.

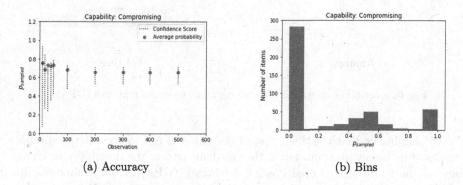

(a) Accuracy   (b) Bins

Fig. 4. Capability of APV_1: Compromising 2 mixes

7.3   Capability: Monitoring

Similar to the previous experiment, the goal of this adversary is to infer *whether at-least one of the messages of a sender* s_i *arrived to a receiver* r_j. The adversary is monitoring the inter-entity matrices, and so the adversary is what is usually called a Global Passive Adversary in mixnet literature. The adversary in this case is not compromising the mixes, and therefore all permutations of inner-mix mapping are possible.

We can see in Fig. 5a that the adversary captured by our model is able to infer probabilities correctly with enough number of observations. As opposed to the APV, the GPA can connect s_i to a receiver r_i with a higher confidence. Figure 5b shows the histogram of the different probabilities estimated by this adversary. We can see that unlike the previous adversary, the number of items inside the different bins is more balanced between probabilities, meaning that this adversary does not sample states with a very high probability compared to other states with low probability. This confirms our understanding with the modeled GPA. In the first adversary we can see that there are traces with high probabilities (a less balanced histogram) that correspond to messages being routed via at least one compromised node. We note however that the average probability inferred about the different events is similar in this scenario even though that the first adversary is more realistic as it compromises only 2 mixes as opposed to the second adversary that monitors all mixes in the network.

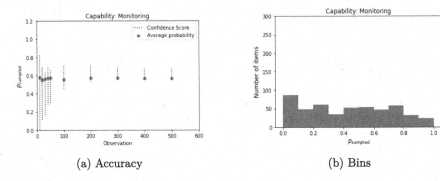

(a) Accuracy   (b) Bins

Fig. 5. Capability of APV_2: Monitoring all inter-entity matrices (GPA)

We emphasize that the main goal of the paper is not to present the specific results of de-anonymization, but rather to demonstrate the possibility of going beyond the traditional Global Passive Adversary (GPA) model in mixnets. In addition, we show that our model is also able to capture this GPA as a special case.

However, this flexible framework comes with one main drawbacks which is the Metropolis Hastings algorithm is computationally expensive, requiring a large number of state samples to be drawn in order to reach from the target distribution. Additionally, if the adversary is relatively weak, it may be more efficient to rely on the adversary's prior knowledge and analytically infer trace-related events. Nevertheless, for adversaries with a reasonable level of visibility into the network, we consider the computational cost of the algorithm to be acceptable, especially given the lack of alternative methods for studying such adversaries.

7.4   Performance Evaluation

Our Metropolis-Hastings sampler is composed by 2363 LOC of Python and run on an Intel(R) Core(TM) i9-9920X with 3.50GHz CPU and 132 GB RAM. As explained in 5.1, in order to compute α_{next_move} we need to compute the probability of every state. Depending on the adversary's knowledge, the network size and the number of messages per observation, the computation time might increase. For our simulated scenarios, it took about 6 for the full analysis. While this may seem expensive, our implementation is not optimised for size, memory usage or running time and we argue that more optimized implementations will outperform it.

8   Conclusion

To the best of our knowledge, this is the first work considering a model of an adversary whose capabilities can be modeled by the partial view of the network. In this paper we present and analyze traffic analysis by Adversaries with Partial Visibility (APV), who have a visibility over some portion of the network. We put forth a mathematical model of a mix network and use this model with the conjunction of Metropolis-Hastings to build a Bayesian inference engine that models how an adversary infer probabilities about trace-specific events. Finally, we analyzed the effectiveness of our model under different simulated adversaries.

The critiques made of previous work on mixnets by Syverson [16] are to a large extent correct, as even powerful nation-state adversaries may have only partial visibility. However, this does not mean that mixnets cannot be analyzed in terms of such adversaries, as our work shows. Our work would allow the more realistic practical engineering of privacy-enhancing technologies, especially as real-world mixnets like Nym are deployed in countries with partial adversaries such as Iran [7].

Nonetheless, the work is limited. While we studied compromised mixes, we assumed the mixnet adversaries that were compromised were honestly following the protocol. Thus, an aspect that needs to be studied is actively malicious mixes as well as users. More importantly further work should systematically study different adversaries, each having different visibility over multiples mix networks with different parameters and design decisions.

Acknowledgement. We thank the anonymous reviewers for their comments and insightful feedback. This research is partially supported by the Research Council KU Leuven under the grant C24/18/049, by CyberSecurity Research Flanders with reference number VR20192203, and by DARPA FA8750-19-C-0502. Any opinions, findings and conclusions or recommendations expressed in this material are those of the authors and do not necessarily reflect the views of any of the funding agencies.

A   System Model: Topology

A.1   Topology

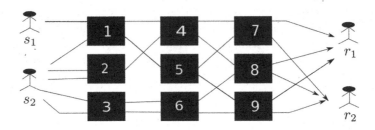

Fig. 6. Mixnet-based system Model

B   Probability of a Trace: Mixes Are Not Chosen Uniformly

Depending in the systems requirements, mixes can be chosen according to a certain weights assigned to them. We now consider the case of mixes not chosen uniformly, but according to an assigned weight. Mix weights can reflect geographic approximation, bandwidth, trust etc. Let's denote by $w(\mu_{j,l_i})$ the probability of the mix μ_{j,l_i} being chosen among the set of mixes in layer l_i. The probability of each path becomes (Fig. 6):

$$Pr[P_i] = \left[\prod_{i=1}^{l} w(\mu_{j_i,i})\right] Pr[r_i] \tag{10}$$

We can also model the case when each sender s_i only knows a subset of the mixes in each layer l_j ($\mathcal{S}(s_i, l_j)$).

$$Pr[P_i|\mathcal{S}(s_i, l_j)] = \left[\prod_{j=1}^{l} Pr[\mu_{j,l_j}|\mathcal{S}(s_i, l_j))]\right] Pr[r_i] \tag{11}$$

To compute $\texttt{Pr}[\mu_{j_i,i}|\mathcal{S}(s_i, l_j)]$, we need to divide the weight of mix $\mu_{j_i,i}$ by the sum of the weights of the all the mixes in layer l_i *that sender s_i knows*.

$$Pr[\mu_{j,l_j}|\mathcal{S}(s_i, l_j)] = \frac{w(\mu_{j_i,i})}{w(\mathcal{S}(s_i, l_i))} \tag{12}$$

Therefore:

$$Pr[P_i|\mathcal{S}(s_i, l_j)] = \left[\prod_{j=1}^{l} \frac{w(\mu_{j_i,i})}{w(\mathcal{S}(s_i, l_i))}\right] Pr[r_i] \tag{13}$$

Recipient Probability. The recipient probability $Pr[r_i]$ captures any prior knowledge of the adversary about the relationship between a specific sender and a specific receiver, for example if the adversary has a prior knowledge about *friendship* graphs of certain senders (i.e. sender s_1 is twice as likely to send a message to receiver r_1 than to a receiver r_2).

C   Constraints in Sampling

Depending on the network configuration as well as the adversary capabilities, some samples states are not possible therefore are thrown away in the Metropolis Hastings algorithm. In order for our model to be accurate we incorporate two categories of these impossible states:

Ghost Messages: In prior work using the Metropolis-Hasting algorithm [4], the authors acknowledge that one of the limitation of their model is assuming that the adversary starts observing the network when the all mixes are empty. We argue however that this is not realistic. Instead the adversary starts observing the network when there are already messages inside the mixes and those message contribute in *hiding* an item of interest. We model this scenario by *ghost messages*. Not to be confused with dummy or cover traffic, ghost messages gm are an output message whose inputs are outside the observation of the adversary and therefore are not items of interests but they do play a role in hiding an item of interest. We therefore add vertices to the subgraph associated with the matrix.

Routing: When an adversary is monitoring or compromising a mix, not only do the have knowledge about the input and output messages of that mix but also the destination and source mixes of those messages. We model this by a list of rules. Any sampled state that is the result of a violations of these rules will be thrown away.

D Table of Notation

Table 1. Summary of notation

Notation	Interpretation
Adversary	
$\mathcal{A}$	Adversary
APV	Adversary with Partial Visibility
$\mathcal{O}$	Observation
$\mathcal{HS}$	Hidden State
$\mathcal{C}$	Constraints
Messages	
μ	mix
M_t	Set of messages that are inside μ during t
$\mathcal{M}_I$	Incoming messages to a mix
$\mathcal{M}_O$	Outgoing messages of mix
Matrices	
P_m	Path of the message m
$\mathcal{V}$	Set of Vertices in a path
$\mathcal{E}$	Set of edges in a path
$\mathcal{V}_I$	Set of mix input vertices
$\mathcal{V}_O$	Set of mix output edges
$\mathcal{E}_\mu$	Set of edges in the subgraph associated with the inner-mix mappings of mix μ
$\mathcal{E}_{I,O}$	Set of edges in subgraph associated with inter-entity connections between $\mathcal{ET}_O$ and $\mathcal{ET}_I$
$v_{i,I}(\mu_j)$	ith input edge of jth mix
$v_{i,O}(\mu_j))$	ith output edge of jth mix
$\mathcal{GM}$	Set of ghost messages
Metropolis-Hastings	
$\mathcal{TR}$	Trace
$\mathcal{TR}_p$	Proposed Trace
$\mathcal{TR}_c$	Current Trace
$\mathcal{TR}_G$	Trace of the Ground Truth
Q	Transitioning function

References

1. Ben Guirat, I., Gosain, D., Diaz, C.: MiXiM: mixnet design decisions and empirical evaluation. In: Proceedings of the 20th Workshop on Workshop on Privacy in the Electronic Society, pp. 33–37 (2021)
2. Chaum, D.: Untraceable electronic mail, return addresses, and digital pseudonyms. Commun. ACM **24**(2), 84–88 (1981). https://doi.org/10.1145/358549.358563, http://doi.acm.org/10.1145/358549.358563
3. Danezis, G.: Statistical disclosure attacks. In: Gritzalis, D., De Capitani di Vimercati, S., Samarati, P., Katsikas, S. (eds.) SEC 2003. ITIFIP, vol. 122, pp. 421–426. Springer, Boston, MA (2003). https://doi.org/10.1007/978-0-387-35691-4_40
4. Danezis, G.: The traffic analysis of continuous-time mixes. In: Martin, D., Serjantov, A. (eds.) PET 2004. LNCS, vol. 3424, pp. 35–50. Springer, Heidelberg (2005). https://doi.org/10.1007/11423409_3
5. Danezis, G., Dingledine, R., Mathewson, N.: Mixminion: design of a type III anonymous remailer protocol. In: Symposium on Security and Privacy, pp. 2–15. IEEE (2003)
6. Danezis, G., Troncoso, C.: Vida: how to use Bayesian inference to de-anonymize persistent communications. In: Goldberg, I., Atallah, M.J. (eds.) PETS 2009. LNCS, vol. 5672, pp. 56–72. Springer, Heidelberg (2009). https://doi.org/10.1007/978-3-642-03168-7_4
7. Diaz, C., Halpin, H., Kiayias, A.: The NYM network (2021). https://nymtech.net/nym-whitepaper.pdf
8. Gallagher, K., Barradas, D., Santos, N.: Rethinking realistic adversaries for anonymous communication systems. In: Free and Open Communications on the Internet, FOCI'23, pp. 81–87 (2023). https://petsymposium.org/foci/2023/foci-2023-0015.pdf
9. Hastings, W.K.: Monte Carlo Sampling Methods Using Markov Chains and Their Applications. Oxford University Press, Oxford (1970)
10. Kesdogan, D., Mölle, D., Richter, S., Rossmanith, P.: Breaking anonymity by learning a unique minimum hitting set. In: Frid, A., Morozov, A., Rybalchenko, A., Wagner, K.W. (eds.) CSR 2009. LNCS, vol. 5675, pp. 299–309. Springer, Heidelberg (2009). https://doi.org/10.1007/978-3-642-03351-3_28
11. Kesdogan, D., Pimenidis, L.: The hitting set attack on anonymity protocols. In: Fridrich, J. (ed.) IH 2004. LNCS, vol. 3200, pp. 326–339. Springer, Heidelberg (2004). https://doi.org/10.1007/978-3-540-30114-1_23
12. Kwon, A., Lu, D., Devadas, S.: {XRD}: scalable messaging system with cryptographic privacy. In: 17th {USENIX} Symposium on Networked Systems Design and Implementation ({NSDI} 20), pp. 759–776 (2020)
13. Piotrowska, A.M.: Studying the anonymity trilemma with a discrete-event mix network simulator. In: Proceedings of the 20th Workshop on Workshop on Privacy in the Electronic Society, pp. 39–44 (2021)
14. Piotrowska, A.M., Hayes, J., Elahi, T., Meiser, S., Danezis, G.: The Loopix anonymity system. In: 26th {USENIX} Security Symposium ({USENIX} Security 17), pp. 1199–1216 (2017)
15. Raymond, J.-F.: Traffic analysis: protocols, attacks, design issues, and open problems. In: Federrath, H. (ed.) Designing Privacy Enhancing Technologies. LNCS, vol. 2009, pp. 10–29. Springer, Heidelberg (2001). https://doi.org/10.1007/3-540-44702-4_2

16. Syverson, P.: Why I'm not an Entropist. In: Christianson, B., Malcolm, J.A., Matyáš, V., Roe, M. (eds.) Security Protocols 2009. LNCS, vol. 7028, pp. 213–230. Springer, Heidelberg (2013). https://doi.org/10.1007/978-3-642-36213-2_25

17. Troncoso, C., Danezis, G.: The Bayesian traffic analysis of mix networks. In: Proceedings of the 16th ACM Conference on Computer and Communications Security, pp. 369–379. CCS '09, Association for Computing Machinery, New York, NY, USA (2009). https://doi.org/10.1145/1653662.1653707

18. Van Den Hooff, J., Lazar, D., Zaharia, M., Zeldovich, N.: Vuvuzela: scalable private messaging resistant to traffic analysis. In: Proceedings of the 25th Symposium on Operating Systems Principles, pp. 137–152 (2015)

19. Wallis, S.: Binomial confidence intervals and contingency tests: mathematical fundamentals and the evaluation of alternative methods. J. Quant. Linguist. **20**(3), 178–208 (2013)

20. Wilson, E.B.: Probable inference, the law of succession, and statistical inference. J. Am. Stat. Assoc. **22**(158), 209–212 (1927)

Learning Markov Chain Models from Sequential Data Under Local Differential Privacy

Efehan Guner and M. Emre Gursoy[✉]

Department of Computer Engineering, Koç University, Istanbul, Turkey
{efehanguner21,emregursoy}@ku.edu.tr

Abstract. Markov chain models are frequently used in the analysis and modeling of sequential data such as location traces, time series, natural language, and speech. However, considering that many data sources are privacy-sensitive, it is imperative to design privacy-preserving methods for learning Markov models. In this paper, we propose PRIMA for learning discrete-time Markov chain models under local differential privacy (LDP), a state-of-the-art privacy standard. In PRIMA, each user locally encodes and perturbs their sequential record on their own device using LDP protocols. For this purpose, we adapt two bitvector-based LDP protocols (RAPPOR and OUE); and furthermore, we develop a novel extension of the GRR protocol called AdaGRR. We also propose to utilize custom privacy budget allocation strategies for perturbation, which enable uneven splitting of the privacy budget to better preserve utility in cases with uneven sequence lengths. On the server-side, PRIMA uses a novel algorithm for estimating Markov probabilities from perturbed data. We experimentally evaluate PRIMA using three real-world datasets, four utility metrics, and under various combinations of privacy budget and budget allocation strategies. Results show that PRIMA enables learning Markov chains under LDP with high utility and low error compared to Markov chains learned without privacy constraints.

Keywords: Privacy · local differential privacy · sequential data · Markov chain models

1 Introduction

Sequential data arises naturally in a wide variety of contexts such as web browsing, location traces, time series, and natural language. A popular method for the analysis and modeling of sequential data is Markov chains [10]. Markov chains are stochastic models that describe a sequence of possible events, where each event depends on one or more preceding events. Markov chain models have been successfully applied to sequential data such as location traces [3,12,16,23], natural language and speech recognition [11,22], as well as others [18,19]. In recent years, Markov chain models have especially been commonly used by the trajectory synthesis literature, considering that several systems internally rely on

© The Author(s), under exclusive license to Springer Nature Switzerland AG 2024
G. Tsudik et al. (Eds.): ESORICS 2023, LNCS 14345, pp. 359–379, 2024.
https://doi.org/10.1007/978-3-031-51476-0_18

Markov chains, e.g., DPT [17], DP-Star [15], AdaTrace [16], PrivTrace [23], and so forth [14,24].

On the other hand, sequential data used in learning a Markov chain model is oftentimes recorded and stored on users' devices, such as GPS locations, text messages and web browsing histories on users' smartphones. Furthermore, this data is privacy-sensitive and its privacy must be protected. Therefore, it is imperative to design privacy-preserving methods for learning Markov chain models.

In this paper, we propose PRIMA for learning discrete-time Markov chain models under local differential privacy (LDP), a state-of-the-art privacy standard which has received significant attention from the academia and industry [4,6,7, 13,31]. In PRIMA, each user locally encodes and perturbs their sequential record on their own device, using adapted versions of bitvector-based LDP protocols. This perturbation satisfies *sequence- ε-LDP* such that the user's whole sequence is protected. To achieve LDP, we adapt and utilize two existing LDP protocols (RAPPOR and OUE) in PRIMA; in addition, we propose a novel extension of the GRR protocol called AdaGRR. As opposed to the original GRR protocol, our proposed AdaGRR protocol enables a bitvector-based implementation (which is consistent with RAPPOR and OUE) and can handle empty bitvectors which may arise in PRIMA.

In addition, PRIMA contains two more novel design components: (i) budget allocation strategies for uneven splitting of the ε privacy budget, and (ii) a novel algorithm for server-side estimation of Markov transition probabilities. For the prior, considering that some users' sequences may be shorter and allocating uniform budget to each item may lead to wasted budgets in such cases, we propose decaying budget allocation strategies. Different budget allocation strategies are also experimentally shown to be preferable for maximizing different utility metrics. For the latter, a specialized algorithm is proposed in PRIMA for estimating Markov transition probabilities from LDP protocol outputs.

We experimentally evaluate PRIMA using three real-world datasets, four utility metrics, four budget allocation strategies, and ε between 0.5 and 5. Our utility metrics are designed to compare the LDP Markov chain model against the noise-free, non-private Markov chain model which would have been learned without privacy constraints. Overall, results show that PRIMA enables learning Markov chains with high utility and low error compared to their non-private counterparts. Furthermore, we observe that: (i) OUE and RAPPOR protocols perform similarly in terms of utility, (ii) AdaGRR has worse utility than OUE and RAPPOR for small ε but its utility converges to OUE and RAPPOR as ε is increased, (iii) despite its worse utility, AdaGRR is roughly twice as fast as RAPPOR and OUE, (iv) different budget allocation strategies may be preferred to maximize utility in terms of specific metrics, but the Step strategy performs well across the board for most utility metrics and ε values.

In summary, our main contributions are the following:

- We propose a new LDP protocol called AdaGRR, which is an extension of the GRR protocol. It can also be used in contexts outside of PRIMA and/or Markov chains.

- We design and develop PRIMA for learning Markov chains while satisfying sequence-level ε-LDP. A novel algorithm is proposed for server-side estimation of Markov transition probabilities from LDP protocol outputs.
- We propose budget allocation strategies for uneven splitting of the privacy budget and thereby improving the utility of Markov chain models.
- We perform extensive experimental evaluation of PRIMA using three datasets, four utility metrics, varying privacy budgets and budget allocation strategies.

2 Preliminaries

2.1 Problem Setting and Notation

Consider a user population $\mathcal{P} = \{u_1, u_2, ..., u_{|\mathcal{P}|}\}$ and the finite domain of items $\mathcal{D} = \{I_1, I_2, ..., I_{|\mathcal{D}|}\}$. For each user $u \in \mathcal{P}$, the user's data is a sequence denoted by S_u. Formally, S_u is an ordered sequence of items $S_u = I_i \rightarrow I_j \rightarrow I_k \rightarrow ...$, such that $\forall I \in S_u$, it holds that: $I \in \mathcal{D}$. It is possible for an item to occur multiple times and/or consecutively in S_u. This formalism of sequential data is versatile and its semantic meaning can vary between applications. For example, in the context of web browsing, each item I corresponds to one webpage, S_u stores which pages u visited (ordered by time), and $\mathcal{D}$ corresponds to the set of reachable pages on the website. In the context of location traces, each item I corresponds to a location (can be discretized using grids or map-matching to roads) and S_u stores the user's time-ordered location trace.

In the rest of the paper, the following notations are used: For a sequence S_u, $|S_u|$ denotes its length and $S_u[i]$ denotes the i'th element in the sequence, e.g., $S_u[1]$ is the first element of S_u. Same notations are used for 1-dimensional arrays (vectors). For 2-dimensional arrays (matrices), say matrix M, we denote by $M[i]$ the i'th row of the matrix and by $M[i][j]$ the element at row i, column j.

2.2 Local Differential Privacy (LDP)

Each user's sequence S_u is kept locally on the user's device. The data collector (server) would like to learn a Markov chain model from users' sequences, but users are unwilling to share their sequences with the data collector due to privacy concerns. In this scenario, *Local Differential Privacy (LDP)* enables privacy-preserving learning of a Markov chain. In LDP, each user's sequence is encoded and perturbed on their local devices in a way that satisfies LDP. Afterwards, the perturbed outputs are shared with the data collector. Since only perturbed outputs are observed by the data collector and not the true data, LDP can be used in scenarios where users do not trust the data collector. Due to its desirable trust assumption and provable privacy, LDP has also been used in consumer-facing applications of companies such as Apple, Google and Microsoft [4,6,7].

When users' data is a sequence rather than a single item, LDP can be defined at two granularities: *item-level* or *sequence-level*. Sequence-level LDP aims to protect the user's entire sequence rather than a single item; thus, it is stronger than item-level LDP. Therefore, we adopt the sequence-level LDP definition which is formalized below.

Definition 1 (Sequence-level ε-LDP). *Let S_u, S'_u be two sequences such that $\forall I \in S_u$ and $\forall I' \in S'_u$, it holds that: $I \in \mathcal{D}$ and $I' \in \mathcal{D}$, where $\mathcal{D}$ denotes the domain. A randomized algorithm Ψ satisfies sequence-level ε-local differential privacy (ε-LDP), if and only if:*

$$\forall y \in Range(\Psi) : \quad \frac{Pr[\Psi(S_u) = y]}{Pr[\Psi(S'_u) = y]} \leq e^\varepsilon \tag{1}$$

where $\varepsilon > 0$ is the privacy parameter and $Range(\Psi)$ denotes the set of all possible outputs of Ψ.

ε-LDP ensures that given the perturbed output y, it is not possible for the data collector to distinguish whether the original true value was S_u or S'_u beyond the probability ratio controlled by e^ε. Here, ε is the privacy parameter (also known as the *privacy budget*). Lower ε yields stronger privacy.

2.3   LDP Protocols

Several LDP protocols were developed in the literature for minimizing utility loss or communication cost under varying conditions. In PRIMA, we adapt and use three LDP protocols: RAPPOR, OUE, and AdaGRR (adapted version of GRR). Following convention, we introduce the protocols assuming each user's true value v_u is one item. We allow either $v_u \in \mathcal{D}$ or v_u is empty (i.e., $v_u = \emptyset$).

RAPPOR was originally developed by Google and implemented in Chrome [7]. Although the original version of RAPPOR uses Bloom filters to encode strings, variants of RAPPOR were deployed in later works for data encoded in a one-hot (unary) bitvector [13,26], which is used in PRIMA and explained below.

User u initializes bitvector B_u with length $|\mathcal{D}|$. The user sets $B_u[v_u] = 1$, and for all remaining positions $j \neq v_u$, $B_u[j] = 0$. Then, the perturbation step of RAPPOR takes as input B_u and outputs a perturbed bitvector B'_u. Perturbation algorithm Ψ_{RAP} considers each bit in B_u one-by-one, and either keeps or flips it with probability:

$$\forall_{i \in [1,|\mathcal{D}|]} : \quad Pr[B'_u[i] = 1] = \begin{cases} \frac{e^{\varepsilon/2}}{e^{\varepsilon/2}+1} & \text{if } B_u[i] = 1 \\ \frac{1}{e^{\varepsilon/2}+1} & \text{if } B_u[i] = 0 \end{cases} \tag{2}$$

The user sends B'_u to the server.

The server receives perturbed bitvectors B'_u from all users $u \in \mathcal{P}$. To perform estimation for value v, $Sup(v)$ is computed as the total number of received bitvectors that satisfy: $B'_u[v] = 1$. Then, the estimate $\bar{C}(v)$ is computed as:

$$\bar{C}(v) = \frac{Sup(v) + |\mathcal{P}| \cdot (\rho - 1)}{2\rho - 1} \tag{3}$$

where ρ is the bit keeping probability: $\rho = \frac{e^{\varepsilon/2}}{e^{\varepsilon/2}+1}$.

Optimized Unary Encoding (OUE) was originally proposed in [26]. OUE also uses one-hot bitvector encoding; however, it differs from RAPPOR in its asymmetric treatment of 0 and 1 bits. In OUE, if the original bit is 1, it is kept or flipped with equal probability $\frac{1}{2}$. If the original bit is 0, it is kept with high probability $\frac{e^\varepsilon}{e^\varepsilon+1}$ and flipped with low probability $\frac{1}{e^\varepsilon+1}$.

Similar to RAPPOR, user u initializes bitvector B_u with length $|\mathcal{D}|$, sets $B_u[v_u] = 1$, and for all remaining positions $j \neq v_u$, $B_u[j] = 0$. Then, the perturbation algorithm Ψ_{OUE} takes as input B_u and outputs perturbed bitvector B'_u such that:

$$\forall_{i \in [1,|\mathcal{D}|]}: \quad \Pr[B'_u[i] = 1] = \begin{cases} \frac{1}{2} & \text{if } B_u[i] = 1 \\ \frac{1}{e^\varepsilon+1} & \text{if } B_u[i] = 0 \end{cases} \tag{4}$$

The user sends B'_u to the server.

The server receives perturbed bitvectors B'_u from all users $u \in \mathcal{P}$. To perform estimation for value v, $Sup(v)$ is computed as the total number of received bitvectors that satisfy: $B'_u[v] = 1$. Then, the estimate $\bar{C}(v)$ is computed as:

$$\bar{C}(v) = \frac{2 \cdot \left((e^\varepsilon + 1) \cdot Sup(v) - |\mathcal{P}|\right)}{e^\varepsilon - 1} \tag{5}$$

Adapted GRR (AdaGRR): Generalized Randomized Response (GRR) is a generalization of the randomized response survey technique [4,26,27]. However, the original version of GRR is not suitable for PRIMA due to two reasons: (i) it does not use bitvector-based encoding, (ii) even if it is modified to use bitvector-based encoding, it cannot handle empty bitvectors (all 0 s) which may arise in PRIMA. Hence, we develop a novel adaptation of GRR, which we call AdaGRR.

Let v_u be u's true item, and let $q = \frac{e^\varepsilon}{e^{2\varepsilon}+(|\mathcal{D}|-1)(e^\varepsilon-1)}$ and $p = \frac{q(e^\varepsilon-1)}{1-q}$ be AdaGRR protocol parameters. AdaGRR outputs perturbed bitvector $B'_u \in \{0,1\}^{|\mathcal{D}|}$ which is computed as follows:

$$B'_u = \begin{cases} \{0\}^{|\mathcal{D}|} & \text{with probability } q \\ \Psi_{\text{AGRR}}(v_u) & \text{with probability } p(1-q) \\ \Psi_{\text{RAND}}(v_u) & \text{with probability } (1-p)(1-q) \end{cases} \tag{6}$$

$\Psi_{\text{RAND}}(v_u)$ generates a random one-hot bitvector B'_u such that $B'_u[v_u] \neq 1$. That is, B'_u will contain exactly one 1 bit, but this 1 bit must be at an index other than v_u. $\Psi_{\text{AGRR}}(v_u)$ behaves as follows: If $v_u \in \mathcal{D}$, then B'_u is initialized full of 0 s, and then $B'_u[v_u] = 1$ is enforced. Otherwise, i.e., $v_u = \emptyset$, then B'_u is full of 0 s. The user sends B'_u to the server.

The server receives perturbed bitvectors B'_u from all users $u \in \mathcal{P}$. To perform estimation for value v, $Sup(v)$ is computed as the total number of received bitvectors that satisfy: $B'_u[v] = 1$. Furthermore, $Sup(\emptyset)$ is computed as the total number of received bitvectors B'_u which consist only of 0 bits. Then, the server estimates $\bar{C}(\emptyset)$ as:

$$\bar{C}(\emptyset) = \frac{Sup(\emptyset) - q|\mathcal{P}|}{p(1-q)} \tag{7}$$

Finally, the server uses $\bar{C}(\emptyset)$ to compute the estimate $\bar{C}(v)$ for value v:

$$\bar{C}(v) = \frac{(1-q)(1-p)|\mathcal{P}| - \frac{\bar{C}(\emptyset)}{|\mathcal{D}|} - Sup(v)(|\mathcal{D}|-1)}{(1-q)(1-p|\mathcal{D}|)} \tag{8}$$

ID	Items in Sequence
S_1	$I_1 \rightarrow I_2$
S_2	$I_2 \rightarrow I_3 \rightarrow I_1$
S_3	$I_1 \rightarrow I_1 \rightarrow I_2 \rightarrow I_4$
S_4	I_3
S_5	$I_4 \rightarrow I_3 \rightarrow I_2$
S_6	$I_3 \rightarrow I_3 \rightarrow I_3$

Fig. 1. Sample data and Markov chain model

Since AdaGRR is a novel protocol proposed in this paper, in Appendix A we provide proofs that AdaGRR's user-side perturbation (Eq. 6) satisfies LDP and AdaGRR's estimations are unbiased (Eqs. 7 and 8).

2.4   Markov Chain Model

A Markov chain is a stochastic model that describes a sequence of possible events, where each event depends on one or more preceding events. It is frequently used in the analysis and modeling of sequential data such as location traces, time series, natural language, speech, and others [3,11,12,15,16,18,22,23]. A Markov chain is said to be of k'th order if each event in a sequence depends on the k events preceding it, rather than all preceding events. For example, if each event depends only on one preceding event, then the order of the Markov chain is 1.

A Markov chain consists of two components: a set of states and a set of transition probabilities which represent the probabilities of moving from one state to another. In this paper, the set of states corresponds to items (or combinations of items) from $\mathcal{D}$. Then, the Markov property can be formalized as follows.

Definition 2 (Markov property).   *Given a set of discrete states* $\mathcal{D}$, *a sequence* $S = I_1 \rightarrow I_2 \rightarrow \dots \rightarrow I_n$ *follows a k'th order Markov process if for all* $I \in \mathcal{D}$ *and* $k \leq i \leq n-1$:

$$Pr\big[S[i+1]\big|S[i]...S[1]\big] = Pr\big[S[i+1]\big|S[i]...S[i-k+1]\big] \tag{9}$$

where $Pr\big[S[i+1]\big|S[i]...S[i-k+1]\big]$ *is called the transition probability from* $S[i-k+1]...S[i]$ *to* $S[i+1]$.

In order to build a Markov chain model, transition probabilities need to be learned from users' data. Let z denote a subsequence and zx denote a subsequence in which z is immediately followed by x. The transition probability $Pr[I_j|z]$ is defined as:

Algorithm 1: Overview of PRIMA

Input : $\mathcal{P}$, ε, $\mathcal{D}$, k, max length ϑ
Output: Markov chain $\mathcal{M}'$

/* **Server-side setup phase**   */
1 $\langle \varepsilon_1, \varepsilon_2, ..., \varepsilon_\vartheta \rangle \leftarrow$ BUDGET_ALLOCATE(ε, ϑ)
2 Server sends $\langle \varepsilon_1, \varepsilon_2, ..., \varepsilon_\vartheta \rangle$ to all users $u \in \mathcal{P}$
3 $responses \leftarrow \{\}$
/* **Each user computes noisy LDP response (bitmatrix M'_u) and sends
   response to server**   */
4 **foreach** $u \in \mathcal{P}$ **do**
5   Let S_u denote u's sequence; $|S_u| \leq \vartheta$
6     $M'_u \leftarrow$ ENCODE_PERTURB$(S_u, \mathcal{D}, \langle \varepsilon_1, \varepsilon_2, ..., \varepsilon_\vartheta \rangle)$
7   User sends M'_u to server
8   Server adds M'_u to $responses$
/* **Server learns Markov Chain**   */
9 $\mathcal{M}' \leftarrow$ LEARN_MC$(\mathcal{D}, k, responses, \langle \varepsilon_1, \varepsilon_2, ..., \varepsilon_\vartheta \rangle)$
10 **return** $\mathcal{M}'$

$$\Pr[I_j|z] = \frac{\sum\limits_{u \in \mathcal{P}} \varphi_u(zI_j)}{\sum\limits_{u \in \mathcal{P}} \sum\limits_{x \in \mathcal{D}} \varphi_u(zx)} \tag{10}$$

where $\varphi_u(zx)$ is a function that counts the number of occurrences of zx in user u's sequence S_u. A k'th order Markov chain contains transition probabilities $\Pr[I_j|z]$ for all $I_j \in \mathcal{D}$ and all subsequences z with length $|z| = k$. An example first order Markov chain ($k = 1$) is given in Fig. 1. Since $\mathcal{D} = \{I_1, I_2, I_3, I_4\}$, there exist four states. The transition probabilities between states are computed according to the application of Eq. 10 to the sequences given in the figure.

2.5 Problem Statement

The server would like to learn a k'th order Markov chain from users' sequences. If users' sequences could be collected without privacy concerns, it would be possible to learn the Markov chain by computing $\varphi_u(zx)$ for all combinations of z and x and thereby learning the transition probabilities via Eq. 10. Let $\mathcal{M}$ denote this noise-free, gold-standard Markov chain model. However, when sequence-level ε-LDP needs to be satisfied, it is not possible to collect users' sequences in plaintext and learn $\mathcal{M}$. Instead, a *noisy* Markov chain model will be constructed (say $\mathcal{M}'$) using LDP. From a utility perspective, it is desired to minimize the difference (error) between $\mathcal{M}$ and $\mathcal{M}'$, which we denote by: $Err(\mathcal{M}, \mathcal{M}')$. Then, the problem that we study in this paper is to propose a solution such that the server learns a Markov chain model $\mathcal{M}'$ while satisfying sequence-level ε-LDP for each user $u \in \mathcal{P}$ and the model has small $Err(\mathcal{M}, \mathcal{M}')$. In Sect. 4, we will use multiple Err metrics to quantify the difference between $\mathcal{M}$ and $\mathcal{M}'$.

3 Proposed Solution: PRIMA

3.1 Overview of PRIMA

We propose PRIMA for solving the problem stated in Sect. 2.5. An overview of PRIMA is given in Algorithm 1. The inputs are the user population $\mathcal{P}$, privacy budget ε, domain $\mathcal{D}$, and a maximum length parameter ϑ. The ϑ parameter is used to enforce a maximum length limit on users' sequences. On line 1, Algorithm 1 uses the BUDGET_ALLOCATE function which divides the total ε budget into ϑ pieces, collectively denoted by $\langle \varepsilon_1, \varepsilon_2, ..., \varepsilon_\vartheta \rangle$. Details of the BUDGET_ALLOCATE function are given in Sect. 3.2. The server shares $\langle \varepsilon_1, \varepsilon_2, ..., \varepsilon_\vartheta \rangle$ with $\mathcal{P}$ and initializes an empty collection called *responses*, which will store the noisy LDP responses collected from users. Then, between lines 4–8, each $u \in \mathcal{P}$ encodes and perturbs his/her sequence S_u into a bitmatrix, and sends the resulting bitmatrix M'_u to the server. Details of user-side encoding and perturbation are given in Sect. 3.3. Finally, having collected and stored users' perturbed matrices inside *responses*, the server uses $\mathcal{D}$, k and *responses* to learn the Markov chain on line 9. Details of Markov chain learning are given in Sect. 3.4.

3.2 Budget Allocation

The budget allocation step takes as input the total ε budget and divides it into ϑ pieces denoted by $\langle \varepsilon_1, \varepsilon_2, ..., \varepsilon_\vartheta \rangle$ such that: $\varepsilon_1 + \varepsilon_2 + ... + \varepsilon_\vartheta = \varepsilon$. Considering that S_u consists of up to ϑ items, budget allocation facilitates the assignment of ε_i to the perturbation of the i'th item of S_u. This summation ensures that the overall perturbation of the whole S_u satisfies sequence-level ε-LDP.

A straightforward way to divide ε into ϑ pieces is to do it evenly: $\varepsilon_1 = \varepsilon_2 = ... = \varepsilon_\vartheta = \frac{\varepsilon}{\vartheta}$, which we call *Uniform Allocation*. While this allocation strategy is legitimate, it does not provide much flexibility, and it is not always the best strategy utility-wise due to two main reasons. First, ϑ is an upper limit on sequence lengths, but some users' sequences may be much shorter than ϑ. In that case, budget allocated to perturb non-existing items will not be utilized effectively, causing redundant utility loss. Instead, by allocating higher budget to early items (e.g., ε_1, ε_2) and lower budget to later items (e.g., $\varepsilon_{\vartheta-1}$, ε_ϑ), we can decrease the amount of budget wasted. Second, certain budget allocations may be preferred to maximize certain utility metrics. For example, if the goal is to have a highly accurate initial state distribution for the Markov chain model, then higher budget can be allocated to the first items while lower budget can be allocated for the rest. In contrast, a more balanced budget allocation may be preferred if the goal is to preserve overall transition probabilities.

The different budget allocation strategies we consider in PRIMA are as follows:

1. **Uniform:** Budgets are allocated equally, i.e.: $\varepsilon_i = \frac{\varepsilon}{\vartheta}$ for all $i \in [1, \vartheta]$.
2. **Linear Decay:** Each subsequent budget is reduced linearly by a decay rate denoted by d. That is: $\varepsilon_i = \varepsilon_{i-1} - d$. The first budget ε_1 is chosen to satisfy $\sum_{i=1}^{\vartheta} \varepsilon_i = \varepsilon$.

3. **Exponential Decay:** Each subsequent budget is reduced compared to the previous budget; however, as opposed to linear decay, the decay occurs using the probability mass function of a discrete Exponential distribution: $\varepsilon_i = (1-\gamma)^i \gamma \varepsilon$. Here, γ is the parameter that controls the decay rate.
4. **Step:** This strategy reduces the budget in several steps. Initially, ε_1 is highest. The next budgets $\varepsilon_2, ..., \varepsilon_\alpha$ are equal to ε_1. Then, $\varepsilon_{\alpha+1}$ is equal to $\varepsilon_\alpha - \beta$, i.e., after α equal budgets, a reduction of β is applied. Then, the next budgets $\varepsilon_{\alpha+2}, ..., \varepsilon_{2\alpha}$ are equal to $\varepsilon_{\alpha+1}$. Then, $\varepsilon_{2\alpha+1}$ is equal to $\varepsilon_{2\alpha} - \beta$, and so forth. In general, every α steps, a reduction of β is enforced.

Algorithm 2: User-side encoding and perturbation

> **Input** : S_u, $\mathcal{D}$, $\langle \varepsilon_1, \varepsilon_2, ..., \varepsilon_\vartheta \rangle$
> **Output:** Noisy LDP response M'_u

1   Initialize $\vartheta \times |\mathcal{D}|$ bitmatrix M'_u
2   **foreach** $i \in [1, \vartheta]$ **do**
3   **if** $i \le |S_u|$ **then**
4       $v_u \leftarrow S_u[i]$
5   **else**
6       $v_u \leftarrow \emptyset$
7     $M'_u[i] \leftarrow \text{PERTURB}(v_u, \varepsilon_i, \mathcal{D})$ // use AdaGRR, RAPPOR or OUE
8   **return** M'_u

A visual comparison of the different budget allocation strategies is given in Fig. 2. In this figure, we use $d = 0.12$ for Linear Decay, $\gamma = 0.2$ for Exponential Decay, and $\alpha = 2$ and $\beta = 0.2$ for the Step strategy. The total ε is $\varepsilon = 6$, which is divided into 10 pieces: $\varepsilon_1, \varepsilon_2, ..., \varepsilon_{10}$. It can be observed that the budget is equally distributed in case of the Uniform allocation, whereas in the remaining budget allocation strategies, ε_i starts high and decreases as i is increased. The shape of the decrease is linear in case of Linear allocation and non-linear in case of Exponential and Step allocations.

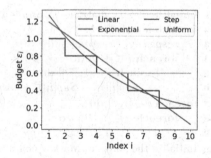

Fig. 2. Comparison of budget allocation strategies ($\varepsilon = 6$, $\vartheta = 10$).

3.3 User-Side Encoding and Perturbation

The algorithm for encoding and perturbing users' data (denoted by ENCODE_PERTURB in Algorithm 1) is given in Algorithm 2. First, it initializes the bitmatrix M'_u with ϑ rows and $|\mathcal{D}|$ columns. Then, for each i between 1 and ϑ, user's sequence $S_u[i]$ is fed into an LDP protocol (AdaGRR, RAPPOR or OUE) with budget ε_i. That is, $S_u[1]$ is perturbed with budget ε_1, $S_u[2]$ is perturbed with budget ε_2, and so forth. The result of each perturbation is a bitvector, as explained in Sect. 2.3. On line 7, the resulting bitvector is assigned to the i'th row of M'_u. Finally, after ϑ perturbations, the user reports M'_u to the server. In Appendix B, we prove that this process achieves sequence-level ε-LDP.

3.4   Learning Markov Chain Model

The algorithm for learning the Markov chain model on the server side is given in Algorithm 3. The inputs of the algorithm are domain $\mathcal{D}$, Markov order k, noisy LDP responses (bitmatrices) received from users, and budgets $\varepsilon_1, ..., \varepsilon_\vartheta$. First, between lines 2–6, Algorithm 3 performs index-by-index summation of users' bitmatrices to compute the support (Sup) of each value $v_j \in \mathcal{D}$ at each index $i \in [1, \vartheta]$. After Sup values are computed, between lines 7–9, each $Sup[i][j]$ is given as input to the ESTIMATE function, together with the budget of the corresponding index ε_i and domain $\mathcal{D}$. Depending on which LDP protocol was used on the user side (AdaGRR, RAPPOR or OUE), the ESTIMATE function calls the appropriate estimator from Sect. 2.3 and the result is stored in $T[i][j]$. Here,

---

Algorithm 3: Learn Markov Chain

Input   : $\mathcal{D}, k, responses, \langle \varepsilon_1, \varepsilon_2, ..., \varepsilon_\vartheta \rangle$
Output: Markov Chain $\mathcal{M}'$

1 Initialize $\vartheta \times |\mathcal{D}|$ matrices T, Sup both full of 0s
2 **foreach** $u \in [1, \mathcal{P}]$ **do**
3      $response \leftarrow responses[u]$
4   **foreach** $i \in [1, \vartheta]$ **do**
5   **foreach** $j \in [1, |\mathcal{D}|]$ **do**
6              $Sup[i][j] \leftarrow Sup[i][j] + response[i][j]$
7 **foreach** $i \in [1, \vartheta]$ **do**
8   **foreach** $j \in [1, |\mathcal{D}|]$ **do**
9          $T[i][j] \leftarrow$ ESTIMATE$(Sup[i][j], \varepsilon_i, \mathcal{D})$ // AdaGRR, RAPPOR or OUE
10 Initialize the states of Markov chain model $\mathcal{M}'$
11 $seqs \leftarrow$ Generate all possible item sequences of length k // $|\mathcal{D}|^k$ sequences
12 **foreach** $z \in seqs$ **do**
13   Initialize array $probs$ with length $|\mathcal{D}|$ full of 0s
14      $denominator \leftarrow$ CALC_PROB(T, z)
15   **foreach** $j \in [1, |\mathcal{D}|]$ **do**
16          $app\_z \leftarrow$ Append I_j to z // I_j is j'th item in $\mathcal{D}$
17          $probs[j] \leftarrow$ CALC_PROB$(T, app\_z)/denominator$
18   **if** $probs[j] < 0$ **then**
19              $probs[j] \leftarrow 0$
20      $probs \leftarrow probs/$SUM$(probs)$
21   Assign $probs$ as the transition probabilities of state z in $\mathcal{M}'$
22 **return** $\mathcal{M}'$

T is a matrix for storing the estimated counts for all i, j. Then, on line 10, Algorithm 3 initializes the states of the Markov chain model $\mathcal{M}'$, as determined by $\mathcal{D}$ and k. On line 11, all possible item sequences of length k are generated and stored in a list called *seqs*. These sequences represent z of $\Pr[I_j|z]$ in Eq. 10. Afterwards, the loop between lines 12–21 is executed to compute the transition probabilities $\Pr[I_j|z]$. Transition probabilities are all initialized as 0 (line 13). Then, the denominator of Eq. 10 is computed (line 14) with the help of CALC_PROB function. For each transition probability to item I_j (loop lines 15–19), I_j is appended to z to obtain zI_j, and then the equivalent of Eq. 10 is computed on line 17. Although transition probabilities must be non-negative by definition in a noise-free Markov chain model, due to LDP noise, the transition probability found on line 17 may be negative. Lines 18–19 eliminate the possibility of negative transition probabilities. Finally, line 20 ensures that outgoing transition probabilities from any state will sum to 1, and line 21 assigns the transition probabilities of state z in the Markov chain model $\mathcal{M}'$.

The CALC_PROB function is given in Algorithm 4. When a subsequence *seq* occurs in a user's sequence S_u, it can occur starting at any one index or more, e.g., starting at index $S_u[1]$ and/or index $S_u[2]$ and/or $S_u[3]$, etc. CALC_PROB uses this intuition to traverse T by starting from index 1 and going up to index $|T|-|seq|+1$ (the last possible starting index, considering the length of *seq* itself). For each index i, the occurrence probability of the whole sequence starting at index i is computed by iterating through each item in the sequence (lines 4–6). The probabilities are added to variable p_sum for all i (line 7). Finally, p_sum is returned (line 8).

Algorithm 4: CALC_PROB

Input : T, *seq*
Output: Probability sum p_sum

1 $p\_sum \leftarrow 0$
2 **foreach** $i \in \left[1,\ |T| - |seq| + 1\right]$ **do**
3      $p \leftarrow 1$
4   **foreach** $j \in [1, |seq|]$ **do**
5          $x \leftarrow seq[j]$
6          $p \leftarrow p \times \dfrac{T[i+j][x]}{\sum_{y=1}^{|\mathcal{D}|} T[i+j][y]}$
7      $p\_sum \leftarrow p\_sum + p$
8 **return** p_sum

---

4   Experimental Evaluation

4.1   Experiment Setup and Datasets

We implemented PRIMA in Python, including all protocols and budget allocation strategies. In this section, we report the experimental evaluation of PRIMA using three datasets, four utility metrics and various ε budgets. The three datasets used in our experiments are *MSNBC*, *Rockyou* and *Taxi*.

MSNBC contains sequences of users' URL page visits from the msnbc.com website[1]. Pages are recorded at the granularity of page category (news, tech, weather, sports, etc.). There are a total of $|\mathcal{P}| = 989{,}818$ users (one sequence per user) and $|\mathcal{D}| = 17$ possible page categories.

Rockyou contains users' leaked passwords[2] as part of the Rockyou data breach. We treat each password as a sequence of characters. To limit the size of $\mathcal{D}$, we removed non-alphabetic and non-numeric characters from passwords, and ensured all passwords are lowercase. Consequently, we have $|\mathcal{D}| = 36$. There are a total of $|\mathcal{P}| = 14{,}338{,}607$ passwords in the dataset.

Taxi contains location traces of taxis driving in the city of Porto [20]. Taxis' GPS locations were recorded in (latitude, longitude) format. Since the GPS coordinates are continuous, we discretized them as follows. First, via histogram analysis we found that more than 90% of the locations are within latitudes -8.58 to -8.68 and longitudes 41.14 to 41.18. Very few location points fall outside these ranges, which we eliminated in order to focus on the dense areas. Then, we implemented a 4×5 grid (total $|\mathcal{D}| = 20$ cells) and replaced each GPS location by the ID of the grid cell it fell into. Thus, each location trace was converted into a sequence of cell IDs. After this transformation, we had a total of $|\mathcal{P}| = 1{,}656{,}048$ sequences.

4.2   Utility Metrics

Let $\mathcal{M}$ denote the noise-free, gold-standard Markov chain model learned from users' sequences without any privacy guarantees. Let $\mathcal{M}'$ denote the Markov chain model learned via PRIMA while satisfying sequence-level ε-LDP. To preserve utility, it is desired that $\mathcal{M}'$ closely resembles $\mathcal{M}$. In order to measure this resemblance (or error), we use the following four utility metrics.

Initial Distribution Error (IDE): The initial distribution π_0 of a Markov chain is the probability distribution of that Markov chain at time 0, i.e., for each state i, the probability that the Markov chain starts out in state i. We compute the initial distributions of $\mathcal{M}$ and $\mathcal{M}'$, i.e.: $\pi_0(\mathcal{M})$ and $\pi_0(\mathcal{M}')$. Then, IDE is their average difference in l_1 norm:

$$\text{IDE} = \frac{||\pi_0(\mathcal{M}') - \pi_0(\mathcal{M})||}{\text{number of states in } \mathcal{M}} \tag{11}$$

Transition Probability Error (TPE): Transition probabilities constitute a key component of a Markov chain model. Let $\mathcal{M}[i][j]$ denote the transition probability from state i to j according to $\mathcal{M}$. TPE is defined as the average error across all transition probabilities in the Markov chain:

[1] UCI Machine Learning Repository: MSNBC.com Anonymous Web Data Set. http://archive.ics.uci.edu/ml/datasets/msnbc.com+anonymous+web+data.

[2] https://www.kaggle.com/datasets/wjburns/common-password-list-rockyoutxt.

$$\text{TPE} = \frac{\sum_i \sum_j |\mathcal{M}'[i][j] - \mathcal{M}[i][j]|}{\text{number of transition probabilities}} \tag{12}$$

First Passage Probability Error (FPPE): Given Markov chain $\mathcal{M}$, an integer n, and two states i and j, the first passage probability is the probability of starting from i, using random walk, first passage through j to be in exactly n steps. Let $f_p(\mathcal{M}, i, j, n)$ denote a function that calculates this first passage probability. (In our experiments, we used $n = 2$.) FPPE is defined to measure the error in first passage probabilities:

$$\text{FPPE} = \frac{\sum_i \sum_j |f_p(\mathcal{M}', i, j, n) - f_p(\mathcal{M}, i, j, n)|}{(\text{number of states})^2} \tag{13}$$

Synthetic Dataset Error (SDE): Considering the widespread applications of Markov models to synthetic data generation in DP and LDP [2,15,17,23], we generate synthetic sequential datasets using our Markov chain models. When generating each sequence, we sample its first item by following the initial distribution π_0 of the Markov chain, and for the remaining items, we perform a random walk using the transition probabilities. Following this process, let D_{syn} denote the synthetic dataset generated using $\mathcal{M}$ and let D'_{syn} denote the synthetic dataset generated using $\mathcal{M}'$. We then perform frequency estimation for each item $I \in \mathcal{D}$ in D_{syn} and D'_{syn}. Let $\mathcal{F}$ and $\mathcal{F}'$ denote the results of these

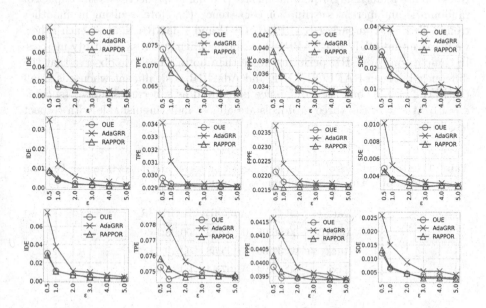

Fig. 3. Utility impacts of different LDP protocols (RAPPOR, OUE, AdaGRR) under varying ε. Uniform budget allocation strategy was used. First row is with MSNBC dataset, second row is Rockyou dataset, third row is Taxi dataset.

two frequency estimations. SDE is defined as the average difference between $\mathcal{F}$ and $\mathcal{F}'$ in l_1 norm:

$$\mathrm{SDE} = \frac{||\mathcal{F} - \mathcal{F}'||}{|\mathcal{D}|} \tag{14}$$

The above metrics are closely related to potential applications of Markov chains in different contexts. For example, in the context of location traces, IDE can indicate the accuracy of modeling trip starting locations, TPE can be used to measure the error in Markov mobility modeling, and SDE can be representative of the potential utility loss in using synthetic datasets generated via Markov chains in place of real data.

4.3   Impacts of LDP Protocols

In Fig. 3, we report experiments comparing three different LDP protocols (RAP-POR, OUE, AdaGRR) under varying datasets and ε between 0.5 and 5. In these experiments, Uniform budget allocation strategy was used. First, we observe that in general, error values decrease as ε increases. This is an intuitive outcome considering the LDP definition – as ε increases, privacy is more relaxed, therefore less noise exists in the Markov chain models. Despite the general decreasing trend in errors as ε is increased, there are a few zig-zags due to the randomized nature of LDP. We note that zig-zags are fewer and the trends are smoother on the Rockyou dataset compared to MSNBC and Taxi. The reason is because Rockyou has a much larger population size $|\mathcal{P}|$. Large $|\mathcal{P}|$ decreases the impact of randomness and increases estimation consistency, therefore resulting in smoother trends. Second, comparing RAPPOR, OUE and AdaGRR against each other, we observe that OUE and RAPPOR perform similarly across all utility metrics. In comparison, AdaGRR performs worse than both. Third, we observe that the difference between RAPPOR, OUE and AdaGRR is significant when ε is small (such as $\varepsilon = 0.5$), but their difference is reduced as ε becomes higher (such as $\varepsilon = 5$). At $\varepsilon = 5$, the three protocols are almost indistinguishable with respect to all utility metrics.

Table 1. Execution times of PRIMA for different protocols and datasets ($\varepsilon = 1$, Uniform budget allocation). Times are in hh:mm:ss format.

Dataset	OUE	AdaGRR	RAPPOR
MSNBC	00:06:08	00:02:32	00:06:14
Rockyou	02:37:56	01:05:58	02:29:34
Taxi	00:13:04	00:07:44	00:13:42

In Table 1, we report the overall execution times of PRIMA for different protocols (OUE, RAPPOR, AdaGRR). As expected, larger datasets such as Rockyou yield higher execution times. RAPPOR and OUE have similar execution times, and their time difference is small. This is because RAPPOR and OUE both work with a similar bitvector-based encoding and bit-by-bit iteration strategy, but they differ in the bit keeping and flipping probabilities. In contrast, AdaGRR is much faster than RAPPOR and OUE. On all three datasets, the execution times of AdaGRR are roughly half of RAPPOR and OUE, indicating an important speed benefit. The reason behind this speed benefit is that AdaGRR does not require bit-by-bit iteration through a bitvector, which saves $\mathcal{O}(|\mathcal{D}|)$ time cost. Combining the results in Fig. 3 and Table 1, we arrive at the following trade-off: RAPPOR and OUE provide higher utility compared to AdaGRR in low ε regimes, but this utility improvement comes at the cost of higher execution time. In high ε regimes, the utility of all three protocols are similar. Yet, AdaGRR is generally faster than RAPPOR and OUE, which is expected to hold for all ε since their execution times are not impacted by ε.

4.4   Impacts of Budget Allocation Strategies

In Fig. 4, we report experiments comparing four budget allocation strategies (Linear, Exponential, Uniform, Step) under varying ε. In these experiments, the OUE protocol was used due to its high utility. Results with only MSNBC and Rockyou datasets are reported in Fig. 4 due to the space constraint; we remark that the results with the Taxi dataset are similar. For most utility metrics, we observe that the Step strategy performs best in low ε regimes. This is best exemplified using the IDE, TPE and SDE metrics. However, by $\varepsilon = 3$, Exponential and Linear strategies catch up, because in low ε regimes, the impact of its allocation is more pronounced since the budget is small to begin with.

Recall that the IDE metric is concerned with the initial distribution π_0 of a Markov chain model. This metric is primarily impacted by the estimation accuracy of the first items in users' sequences. Thus, the budget allocated to

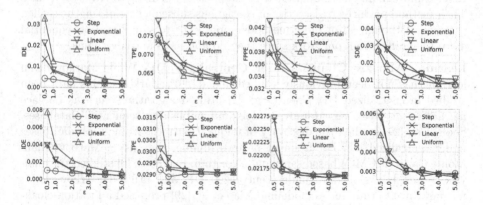

Fig. 4. Utility impacts of different budget allocation strategies (Linear, Exponential, Uniform, Step) under varying ε. OUE protocol was used. First row is with MSNBC dataset, second row is Rockyou dataset.

the first items (e.g., ε_1) is a key factor for IDE. Step, Linear and Exponential strategies allocate higher budgets to first few items, whereas Uniform allocates equal budget to all items. Consequently, we observe from Fig. 4 that the Uniform strategy performs worst in terms of IDE. Similar to the above, the differences between different strategies are more pronounced in low ε regimes (e.g., $\varepsilon = 0.5$) compared to high ε regimes (e.g., when $\varepsilon = 5$, Uniform is still worse than others in terms of IDE, but their difference is less).

Finally, in many utility metrics other than IDE, Linear strategy performs worst when $\varepsilon = 0.5$. However, for $\varepsilon \geq 1$, it starts performing similarly or better than the Exponential strategy. As $\varepsilon \geq 4$, results of all budget allocation strategies start converging. In general, the Step strategy performs well across the board for most utility metrics and ε values.

5   Related Work

Applications of LDP to Sequential Data. In recent years, LDP has emerged as an accepted privacy standard and received significant attention from the industry and academia [4,6,7,31]. While LDP has been applied to various kinds of data, related to our work are its applications to sequential data. Xiong et al. [30] worked on sequential sensor data and proposed a randomized requantization scheme that satisfies LDP. Wang et al. [25] proposed PrivTrie for frequent term discovery from text, utilizing a trie data structure to store counts of character sequences which are obtained using randomized response. In [28], Wang et al. studied a similar problem (heavy hitter identification) and proposed the PEM method which utilizes LDP protocols such as GRR and OLH. Ye et al. [32] studied the application of LDP to time series data. To preserve temporal order, they proposed an extended threshold-based mechanism. Errounda et al. [8] designed a sliding window-based approach for releasing collective location statistics under LDP. Cunningham et al. [5] studied the application of LDP to trajectory data. Their method perturbs trajectories in contiguous subsequences of length n called n-grams. Although all of these methods apply LDP to some form of sequential data, they differ from our work since they do not learn Markov chains.

Learning Markov Chains Under Centralized DP. While Markov chain learning has not been previously studied under LDP, Markov chains have been studied in centralized DP. Chen et al. [2] utilized algorithms such as Laplace mechanism for learning Markov models and publishing sequential databases. Shen et al. [21] studied the discovery of frequent patterns from graph databases under centralized DP. For frequent pattern mining, they use a Markov Chain Monte Carlo (MCMC) based sampling algorithm. Fan et al. [9] studied the analysis of web browsing data under centralized DP, and utilized Markov chains for multivariate time series modeling. Xiao et al. [29] proposed a location cloaking system called LocLok, which uses Markov chain modeling to make inferences regarding users' true locations. Chen et al. [1] proposed word differential privacy, which is an extension of DP. They proposed mechanisms to satisfy this definition when collecting data from symbolic systems, and utilized Markov chains for sequence generation. In addition, Markov chain models were commonly used in the literature for DP trajectory (location trace) synthesis. Several tools developed for this purpose rely on Markov chain models, including DPT [17], DP-Star [15], AdaTrace [16], PrivTrace [23], and others [14,24]. The key difference between PRIMA and the works surveyed in this paragraph is that PRIMA satisfies LDP, whereas the works surveyed in this paragraph satisfy centralized DP.

6   Conclusion

In this paper, we proposed PRIMA for learning Markov chain models from sequential data under LDP. In PRIMA, users encode and perturb their sequences on their local devices using LDP protocols to satisfy sequence-level ε-LDP. Three LDP protocols are used for perturbation: RAPPOR, OUE and AdaGRR, where AdaGRR is a novel extension of the GRR protocol. Budget allocation strategies are proposed for uneven splitting of the privacy budget, which improve the utility of Markov chains. Finally, a server-side estimation algorithm is developed for learning Markov transition probabilities from perturbed LDP outputs. We experimentally evaluate PRIMA using multiple datasets and utility metrics. Results show that Markov chain models learned using PRIMA have low error.

In future work, we are planning to apply PRIMA to the problem of trajectory synthesis under LDP, and evaluate its performance using utility metrics tailored for this task. We will also work on improving the scalability and efficiency aspects of PRIMA, especially for high-order Markov chains with large $\mathcal{D}$.

Acknowledgements. We gratefully acknowledge the support by The Scientific and Technological Research Council of Turkiye (TUBITAK) under project number 121E303.

A   AdaGRR Proofs

Theorem 1. *AdaGRR's user-side perturbation satisfies ε-LDP.*

Proof. Let Ψ denote the user-side perturbation process of AdaGRR, let v_u and v'_u denote two possible values of the user, and let B' denote the perturbed bitvector produced by AdaGRR. We need to show that:

$$\forall B' : \frac{\Pr[\Psi(v_u) = B']}{\Pr[\Psi(v'_u) = B']} \leq e^\varepsilon \tag{15}$$

Let P_{max} denote the maximum probability that the numerator can take and P_{min} denote the minimum probability that the denominator can take. That is:

$$P_{max} = \max(\Pr[\Psi(v_u) = B']) \quad \text{and} \quad P_{min} = \min(\Pr[\Psi(v'_u) = B']) \tag{16}$$

Then, in order to show that ε-LDP is satisfied, it is sufficient to prove that $\frac{P_{max}}{P_{min}} \leq e^\varepsilon$. There are two distinct cases for B' according to the definition of

AdaGRR: (i) B' is all 0s or (ii) B' is a one-hot encoded bitvector (contains a single 1 bit). Below, we prove that $\frac{P_{max}}{P_{min}} \leq e^\varepsilon$ holds for both cases.

Case 1: B' is all 0s.

In this case, for P_{max} to be maximized, v_u should be equal to: $v_u = \emptyset$. For P_{min} to be minimized, v'_u should be a value from $\mathcal{D}$, i.e., $v_u \in \mathcal{D}$. According to these selections of v_u and v'_u and according to the user-side perturbation of AdaGRR, we compute:

$$\frac{P_{max}}{P_{min}} = \frac{(1-q)p+q}{q} = \frac{q(e^\varepsilon - 1) + q}{q} = \frac{qe^\varepsilon - q + q}{q} = e^\varepsilon \tag{17}$$

Case 2: B' is a one-hot bitvector.

There are three distinct possibilities for B' to be obtained: (i) with probability $(1-q)p$ the original index of v_u is preserved, i.e., $B'[v_u] = 1$, (ii) with probability $\frac{(1-q)(1-p)}{|\mathcal{D}|}$ the user's true value was $v_u = \emptyset$, (iii) with probability $\frac{(1-q)(1-p)}{|\mathcal{D}|-1}$ the user's true value was $v_u \in \mathcal{D}$ but $B'[v_u] \neq 1$, i.e., a different index became 1. Among these three possibilities, taking into account the values of p and q, we observe that:

$$P_{max} = (1-q)p \quad \text{and} \quad P_{min} = \frac{(1-q)(1-p)}{|\mathcal{D}|-1} \tag{18}$$

By plugging in $p = \frac{q(e^\varepsilon-1)}{1-q}$ and $q = \frac{e^\varepsilon}{e^{2\varepsilon}+(|\mathcal{D}|-1)(e^\varepsilon-1)}$, we obtain:

$$\frac{P_{max}}{P_{min}} = \frac{p(|\mathcal{D}|-1)}{1-p} = \frac{q(e^\varepsilon-1)(|\mathcal{D}|-1)}{1-e^\varepsilon q} = \frac{\frac{e^\varepsilon(e^\varepsilon-1)(|\mathcal{D}|-1)}{(e^\varepsilon-1)(|\mathcal{D}|-1)+e^{2\varepsilon}}}{\frac{(e^\varepsilon-1)(|\mathcal{D}|-1)}{(e^\varepsilon-1)(|\mathcal{D}|-1)+e^{2\varepsilon}}} = e^\varepsilon \tag{19}$$

Theorem 2. *AdaGRR's server-side estimation of $\bar{C}(\emptyset)$ is unbiased.*

Proof. Let $C(\emptyset)$ denote the true number of users in the population for whom $v_u = \emptyset$. We need to show that $\mathbb{E}[\bar{C}(\emptyset)] = C(\emptyset)$.

$$\mathbb{E}[\bar{C}(\emptyset)] = \mathbb{E}\left[\frac{Sup(\emptyset) - q|\mathcal{P}|}{p(1-q)}\right] = \frac{\mathbb{E}[Sup(\emptyset)] - q|\mathcal{P}|}{p(1-q)} \tag{20}$$

Based on the user-side perturbation process of AdaGRR, we have:

$$\mathbb{E}[Sup(\emptyset)] = C(\emptyset)(q + p(1-q)) + (|\mathcal{P}| - C(\emptyset))q \tag{21}$$

Plugging Eq. 21 into Eq. 20, we get:

$$\mathbb{E}[\bar{C}(\emptyset)] = \frac{C(\emptyset)(q+p-pq) + q|\mathcal{P}| - qC(\emptyset) - q|\mathcal{P}|}{p(1-q)} \tag{22}$$

$$= \frac{C(\emptyset)(p-pq)}{p(1-q)} = \frac{C(\emptyset)p(1-q)}{p(1-q)} = C(\emptyset) \tag{23}$$

Theorem 3. *For $v \in \mathcal{D}$, AdaGRR's server-side estimation of $\bar{C}(v)$ is unbiased.*

Proof. Let $C(v)$ denote the true number of users in the population for whom $v_u = v$. We need to show that $\mathbb{E}[\bar{C}(v)] = C(v)$. We compute:

$$\mathbb{E}[\bar{C}(v)] = \mathbb{E}\left[\frac{(1-q)(1-p)|\mathcal{P}| - \frac{\bar{C}(\emptyset)}{|\mathcal{D}|} - Sup(v)(|\mathcal{D}|-1)}{(1-q)(1-p|\mathcal{D}|)}\right] \quad (24)$$

$$= \frac{(1-p)|\mathcal{P}|}{1-p|\mathcal{D}|} - \frac{C(\emptyset)}{(1-q)(1-p|\mathcal{D}|)|\mathcal{D}|} - \frac{\mathbb{E}[Sup(v)](|\mathcal{D}|-1)}{(1-q)(1-p|\mathcal{D}|)} \quad (25)$$

This is because $\mathbb{E}[\bar{C}(\emptyset)] = C(\emptyset)$ by Theorem 2. Then, based on the user-side perturbation process of AdaGRR, we have:

$$\mathbb{E}[Sup(v)] = C(v)(1-q)p + \frac{C(\emptyset)(1-q)(1-p)}{|\mathcal{D}|} + \frac{(|\mathcal{P}| - C(\emptyset) - C(v))(1-q)(1-p)}{|\mathcal{D}|-1} \quad (26)$$

Plugging Eq. 26 in place of $\mathbb{E}[Sup(v)]$ in Eq. 25 and continuing with arithmetic operations, we reach:

$$\mathbb{E}[\bar{C}(v)] = \frac{C(v)(1-q)(1-p) - (|\mathcal{D}|-1)C(v)(1-q)p}{(1-q)(1-p|\mathcal{D}|)} \quad (27)$$

$$= \frac{C(v)(1-p-p|\mathcal{D}|+p)}{1-p|\mathcal{D}|} = C(v) \quad (28)$$

B Proof of Sequence-Level ε-LDP

Theorem 4. *If $\varepsilon_1 + \varepsilon_2 + \ldots + \varepsilon_\vartheta \leq \varepsilon$, then Algorithm 2 satisfies sequence-level ε-LDP.*

Proof. Let $\mathcal{A}$ denote Algorithm 2. From the definition of sequence-level ε-LDP, we need to prove:

$$\frac{\Pr[\mathcal{A}(S_u) = M'_u]}{\Pr[\mathcal{A}(S^*_u) = M'_u]} \leq e^\varepsilon \quad (29)$$

For all $i \in [1, \vartheta]$, $M'_u[i]$ is constructed using an LDP protocol, which satisfies ε_i-LDP. Formally, denoting by Ψ the LDP protocol, we know that:

$$\forall i \in [1, \vartheta]: \quad \frac{\Pr[\Psi(S_u[i]) = M'_u[i]]}{\Pr[\Psi(S^*_u[i]) = M'_u[i]]} \leq e^{\varepsilon_i} \quad (30)$$

Then, since Algorithm 2 considers the rows of M_u one by one and the perturbation of each row is independent from the other rows, we can write:

$$\frac{\Pr[\mathcal{A}(S_u) = M'_u]}{\Pr[\mathcal{A}(S^*_u) = M'_u]} = \prod_{i=1}^{\vartheta} \frac{\Pr[\Psi(S_u[i]) = M'_u[i]]}{\Pr[\Psi(S^*_u[i]) = M'_u[i]]} \quad (31)$$

$$\leq \prod_{i=1}^{\vartheta} e^{\varepsilon_i} = e^{\sum_{i=1}^{\vartheta} \varepsilon_i} = e^\varepsilon \quad (32)$$

References

1. Chen, B., Leahy, K., Jones, A., Hale, M.: Differential privacy for symbolic systems with application to Markov chains. Automatica **152**, 110908 (2023)
2. Chen, R., Acs, G., Castelluccia, C.: Differentially private sequential data publication via variable-length n-grams. In: Proceedings of the 2012 ACM SIGSAC Conference on Computer and Communications Security, pp. 638–649. ACM (2012)
3. Cheng, Y., Qiao, Y., Yang, J.: An improved Markov method for prediction of user mobility. In: 2016 12th International Conference on Network and Service Management (CNSM), pp. 394–399. IEEE (2016)
4. Cormode, G., Jha, S., Kulkarni, T., Li, N., Srivastava, D., Wang, T.: Privacy at scale: local differential privacy in practice. In: Proceedings of the 2018 International Conference on Management of Data, pp. 1655–1658. ACM (2018)
5. Cunningham, T., Cormode, G., Ferhatosmanoglu, H., Srivastava, D.: Real-world trajectory sharing with local differential privacy. Proc. VLDB Endow. **14**(11), 2283–2295 (2021)
6. Ding, B., Kulkarni, J., Yekhanin, S.: Collecting telemetry data privately. In: Advances in Neural Information Processing Systems, pp. 3571–3580 (2017)
7. Erlingsson, Ú., Pihur, V., Korolova, A.: Rappor: randomized aggregatable privacy-preserving ordinal response. In: Proceedings of the 2014 ACM SIGSAC Conference on Computer and Communications Security, pp. 1054–1067. ACM (2014)
8. Errounda, F.Z., Liu, Y.: Collective location statistics release with local differential privacy. Futur. Gener. Comput. Syst. **124**, 174–186 (2021)
9. Fan, L., Bonomi, L., Xiong, L., Sunderam, V.: Monitoring web browsing behavior with differential privacy. In: Proceedings of the 23rd International Conference on World Wide Web. WWW '14, pp. 177–188. Association for Computing Machinery (2014)
10. Gagniuc, P.: Markov Chains: from Theory to Implementation and Experimentation (2017)
11. Gales, M., Young, S., et al.: The application of hidden Markov models in speech recognition. Found. Trends Sig. Process. **1**(3), 195–304 (2008)
12. Gambs, S., Killijian, M.O., del Prado Cortez, M.N.: Next place prediction using mobility Markov chains. In: Proceedings of the First Workshop on Measurement, Privacy, and Mobility, pp. 1–6 (2012)
13. Gursoy, M.E., Liu, L., Chow, K.H., Truex, S., Wei, W.: An adversarial approach to protocol analysis and selection in local differential privacy. IEEE Trans. Inf. Forensics Secur. **17**, 1785–1799 (2022)
14. Gursoy, M.E., Rajasekar, V., Liu, L.: Utility-optimized synthesis of differentially private location traces. In: 2020 Second IEEE International Conference on Trust, Privacy and Security in Intelligent Systems and Applications (TPS-ISA), pp. 30–39. IEEE (2020)
15. Gursoy, M.E., Liu, L., Truex, S., Yu, L.: Differentially private and utility preserving publication of trajectory data. IEEE Trans. Mob. Comput. **18**(10), 2315–2329 (2018)
16. Gursoy, M.E., Liu, L., Truex, S., Yu, L., Wei, W.: Utility-aware synthesis of differentially private and attack-resilient location traces. In: Proceedings of the 2018 ACM SIGSAC Conference on Computer and Communications Security, pp. 196–211 (2018)
17. He, X., Cormode, G., Machanavajjhala, A., Procopiuc, C., Srivastava, D.: DPT: differentially private trajectory synthesis using hierarchical reference systems. Proc. VLDB Endow. **8**(11), 1154–1165 (2015)

18. Meyn, S.P., Tweedie, R.L.: Markov Chains and Stochastic Stability. Springer, Heidelberg (2012). https://doi.org/10.1007/978-1-4471-3267-7
19. Mor, B., Garhwal, S., Loura, A.: A systematic review of hidden Markov models and their applications. Arch. Comput. Methods Eng. **28** (2020)
20. Moreira-Matias, L., Gama, J., Ferreira, M., Mendes-Moreira, J., Damas, L.: Predicting taxi-passenger demand using streaming data. IEEE Trans. Intell. Transp. Syst. **14**(3), 1393–1402 (2013)
21. Shen, E., Yu, T.: Mining frequent graph patterns with differential privacy. KDD '13, pp. 545–553. Association for Computing Machinery (2013)
22. Tokuda, K., Nankaku, Y., Toda, T., Zen, H., Yamagishi, J., Oura, K.: Speech synthesis based on hidden Markov models. Proc. IEEE **101**(5), 1234–1252 (2013)
23. Wang, H., et al.: Privtrace: differentially private trajectory synthesis by adaptive Markov model. In: USENIX Security Symposium (2023)
24. Wang, N., Kankanhalli, M.S.: Protecting sensitive place visits in privacy-preserving trajectory publishing. Comput. Secur. **97**, 101949 (2020)
25. Wang, N., et al.: Privtrie: effective frequent term discovery under local differential privacy. In: 2018 IEEE 34th International Conference on Data Engineering (ICDE), pp. 821–832. IEEE (2018)
26. Wang, T., Blocki, J., Li, N., Jha, S.: Locally differentially private protocols for frequency estimation. In: Proceedings of the 26th USENIX Security Symposium, pp. 729–745 (2017)
27. Wang, T., Li, N., Jha, S.: Locally differentially private frequent itemset mining. In: IEEE Symposium on Security and Privacy (SP). IEEE (2018)
28. Wang, T., Li, N., Jha, S.: Locally differentially private heavy hitter identification. IEEE Trans. Depend. Secure Comput. **18**(2), 982–993 (2019)
29. Xiao, Y., Xiong, L., Zhang, S., Cao, Y.: Loclok: location cloaking with differential privacy via hidden Markov model. Proc. VLDB Endow. **10**(12), 1901–1904 (2017)
30. Xiong, S., Sarwate, A.D., Mandayam, N.B.: Randomized requantization with local differential privacy. In: 2016 IEEE International Conference on Acoustics, Speech and Signal Processing (ICASSP), pp. 2189–2193 (2016)
31. Yang, M., Lyu, L., Zhao, J., Zhu, T., Lam, K.Y.: Local differential privacy and its applications: a comprehensive survey. arXiv preprint arXiv:2008.03686 (2020)
32. Ye, Q., Hu, H., Li, N., Meng, X., Zheng, H., Yan, H.: Beyond value perturbation: local differential privacy in the temporal setting. In: IEEE INFOCOM 2021 - IEEE Conference on Computer Communications, pp. 1–10 (2021)

Achilles' Heels: Vulnerable Record Identification in Synthetic Data Publishing

Matthieu Meeus, Florent Guepin, Ana-Maria Creţu,
and Yves-Alexandre de Montjoye$^{(\boxtimes)}$

Department of Computing and Data Science Institute,
Imperial College London, London, UK
{m.meeus22,florent.guepin20,a.cretu,deMontjoye}@imperial.ac.uk

Abstract. Synthetic data is seen as the most promising solution to share individual-level data while preserving privacy. Shadow modeling-based Membership Inference Attacks (MIAs) have become the standard approach to evaluate the privacy risk of synthetic data. While very effective, they require a large number of datasets to be created and models trained to evaluate the risk posed by a single record. The privacy risk of a dataset is thus currently evaluated by running MIAs on a handful of records selected using ad-hoc methods. We here propose what is, to the best of our knowledge, the first principled vulnerable record identification technique for synthetic data publishing, leveraging the distance to a record's closest neighbors. We show our method to strongly outperform previous ad-hoc methods across datasets and generators. We also show evidence of our method to be robust to the choice of MIA and to specific choice of parameters. Finally, we show it to accurately identify vulnerable records when synthetic data generators are made differentially private. The choice of vulnerable records is as important as more accurate MIAs when evaluating the privacy of synthetic data releases, including from a legal perspective. We here propose a simple yet highly effective method to do so. We hope our method will enable practitioners to better estimate the risk posed by synthetic data publishing and researchers to fairly compare ever improving MIAs on synthetic data.

Keywords: Synthetic Data · Privacy · Membership inference attacks

1 Introduction

There is increased demand from businesses, governments, and researchers to make data widely available to support research and innovation [16], including the development of Artificial Intelligence (AI) models. Data, however, most often relates directly or indirectly to individuals, raising privacy concerns.

Synthetic data is seen as a promising solution to share individual-level data while preserving privacy [6]. Synthetic data is generated by sampling new data

---

M. Meeus and F. Guepin—These authors contributed equally to this work.

© The Author(s), under exclusive license to Springer Nature Switzerland AG 2024
G. Tsudik et al. (Eds.): ESORICS 2023, LNCS 14345, pp. 380–399, 2024.
https://doi.org/10.1007/978-3-031-51476-0_19

values from a statistical model whose parameters are computed from the original, private data. A large range of techniques have been proposed to generate synthetic data [28,38,42]. Synthetic data, if truly privacy-preserving, can be shared and used freely as it no longer falls under the scope of data protection legislation such as the European Union's General Data Protection Regulation (EU GDPR) or California's CCPA. Consequently, synthetic data has garnered significant interest from statistical offices [4], health care agencies [27] and the financial sector [16].

Ensuring that synthetic data preserves privacy is, however, difficult. On the one hand, while the statistical model aggregates the original data, it is well known that aggregation alone is not sufficient to preserve privacy [10,30]. On the other hand, ensuring that synthetic data generation models achieve formal privacy guarantees is difficult and comes at a cost in utility [3,35].

Membership Inference Attacks (MIA) are a key tool to evaluate the privacy guarantees offered by synthetic data generation models, differentially private or not, in practice [20]. If successful, an MIA is able to infer that a particular record was part of the original data used to train the synthetic data generation model. Increasingly advanced MIAs have been proposed against synthetic data [20,35]. They are run on a per-record basis, instantiating an attacker that aims to distinguish between two worlds: (1) a world in which the synthetic dataset released was generated from a model fitted on data *including* the target record and (2) the alternative world in which the model was fitted on data *excluding* the target record. MIAs on synthetic data have already successfully disproved the believe that aggregation alone is sufficient to preserve privacy as well as detected issues with differentially private synthetic data generation models [35].

Fully evaluating the privacy risk of a dataset using MIAs is however out-of-reach. Indeed state-of-the-art MIAs rely on shadow models which require training a large number, often in the order of thousands, of synthetic data generators to learn the optimal decision boundary for each record. Running a state-of-the-art MIA on a record takes in our experiments, depending on the generator and the dataset, approximately 1.5 to 6 h on dedicated computation facilities. Even for the (relatively) small datasets of 1,000 records we consider, fully estimating the privacy risk of a dataset, would take up to 250 days of compute.

Current evaluation of the privacy risk posed by synthetic data, and of their privacy-utility trade-off, is thus currently the result of ever more advanced MIAs evaluated on only a handful of records selected using ad-hoc methods. Stadler et al. [35] evaluate their attack on ten records, half random and half hand-picked outliers selected based on a rare attribute value, while Houssiau et al. [20] evaluate their attack on one record selected based on the lowest log-likelihood.

Such ad-hoc approaches to selecting vulnerable records could strongly underestimate the privacy risks of a synthetic data release, missing highly vulnerable records or wrongly concluding that most records are not at risk.

Contribution. We here propose what is, to the best of our knowledge, the first vulnerable record identification strategy for synthetic data.

We formalize the problem and propose a principled and simple metric to identify vulnerable records in the original, private dataset: the mean distance to its closest neighbors. While simple, we show our method to outperform previous ad-hoc approaches by 7.2% points (p.p.) on average on two datasets and two generators. Both when comparing the performance of ever improving attack methodologies as well as to estimate the potential privacy risk in real world synthetic data publishing, this is a significant difference.

We then extensively evaluate our method. First, we evaluate its applicability across different MIA approaches. We develop a fundamentally different MIA approach and show the risk estimated using our vulnerable record identification method to be consistently and significantly higher compared to prior methods. More specifically, in contrast with Houssiau et al. [20], who train a meta-classifier to infer the membership of a record based on hand-engineered aggregate statistics computed on the synthetic dataset, we develop an attack that trains a meta-classifier directly on the synthetic dataset viewed as *a set of records*. After performing the same extensive empirical evaluation, we find that the performance of our attack increases also significantly when computed on records identified by our method, by 5.2 p.p. on average across datasets and generators. Next, we evaluate the sensitivity of our results on both the number of neighbors included in our metric as well as the distance metric. In both cases, we find that the results do not change significantly and confirm that our chosen metric is justified. Finally, we evaluate our metric on a differentially private synthetic data generator for varying values of the privacy budget ϵ. We confirm that MIAs fail when the privacy budget is decreased to $\epsilon = 1$, and find that our metric consistently identifies more vulnerable records for larger values of ϵ.

With this principled method, we hope to eliminate the need to rely on ad-hoc record selection and potentially underestimate the privacy risk in synthetic data publishing. A formal vulnerable record identification method would enable (1) researchers to fairly compare future state-of-the-art attacks and (2) practitioners to, in line with EU legislations, evaluate the privacy protection of synthetic data on the worst-case scenario.

2   Background

2.1   Synthetic Data Generation

We consider an entity (e.g., a company) that wants to give a third-party access to a private dataset for analysis. A dataset is a multiset of records $D = \{x_1, \ldots, x_n\}$, where each record relates to a unique individual. In the case of narrow datasets, multiple individuals can however have the same record. We assume the dataset to be sensitive, containing information such as healthcare records or financial transactions. We assume each record to consist of F attributes $x_i = (x_{i,1}, \ldots, x_{i,F}) \in \mathcal{V}_1 \times \ldots \times \mathcal{V}_F$, where $\mathcal{V}_j$ denotes the space of values that can be taken by the j-th attribute. We denote by $\mathcal{V} = \mathcal{V}_1 \times \ldots \times \mathcal{V}_F$ the universe of possible records, and assume the dataset to be sampled i.i.d. from a distribution $\mathcal{D}$ over $\mathcal{V}$.

An increasingly popular approach to release data while mitigating the privacy risk is to instead generate and publish a synthetic dataset [13]. Synthetic data is generated from a statistical model trained to have similar statistical properties to the real data.

We refer to the statistical model as the *synthetic data generator*. Formally, this is a randomized function $\Phi : \mathcal{V}^n \to \mathcal{V}^m$ mapping a private dataset D to a synthetic dataset $D^s = \Phi(D)$ of m records. The synthetic data generator can take the form of a probabilistic model such as a Bayesian Network [42] or a Generative Adversarial Network (GAN) such as CTGAN [39].

2.2   Differential Privacy

Differential Privacy (DP) [12] is a formal privacy guarantee. Originally developed to protect the release of aggregate statistics, it has since been extended to machine learning models and recently to synthetic data generators.

DP relies on a notion of *neighboring* datasets. Two datasets $D, D' \sim \mathcal{D}$ are neighboring, if they differ by only one record. Intuitively, a DP randomized function Φ ensures that one attacker cannot infer the difference between $\Phi(D)$ and $\Phi(D')$ bounded by a certain probability, effectively providing formal guarantees against privacy risks and, in particular, membership inference attacks.

Formally, the definition of differential privacy is the following:

Definition 1 (ϵ-Differential Privacy). *A randomised function Φ is said to be ϵ-Differentially Private (ϵ-DP) if for every pair of neighboring datasets D, D', and for all subsets of outputs $S \in Range(\Phi)$, the following inequality holds:* $\mathbb{P}[\Phi(D) \in S] \leq e^\epsilon \mathbb{P}[\Phi(D') \in S]$.

The parameter ϵ is referred to as the privacy budget. It quantifies the privacy leakage of a data release, with smaller ϵ providing more protection. Achieving DP with small to reasonable values of ϵ can however require significant noise to be added to a machine learning model, decreasing its utility. Efficiently achieving DP guarantees for ML models, including synthetic data generation models, is an active area of research. In this paper, we used the DP generator PrivBayes from the work of Zhang et al. [42]. We refer the reader to Sect. 5.3 for details.

2.3   Membership Inference Attacks

Threat Model. Membership Inference Attacks (MIAs) aim to infer whether a target record x_T is part of the original dataset D used to generate a synthetic dataset D^s, i.e., whether $x_T \in D$. The traditional attacker in MIAs is assumed to have access to the published synthetic dataset, D^s, as well as to an auxiliary dataset, D_{aux}, with the same underlying distribution as D: $D_{aux} \sim \mathcal{D}$. Additionally, the attacker is assumed to have access to the target record x_T and to know the generative model type and its hyperparameters, but not to have access to the model [20,35].

Privacy Game. MIAs are instantiated as a privacy game. The game consists of a challenger and an attacker and is instantiated on a target record x_T. The challenger samples datasets D of $n-1$ records from $\mathcal{D}$, such that all records are different from x_T. With equal probability, the challenger adds x_T to D or a random, different record $x_R \sim \mathcal{D}$, with $x_R \neq x_T$, to D. The challenger then trains a generator Φ_T on D and uses it to generate a synthetic dataset D^s. The challenger shares D^s with an attacker whose goal is to infer whether or not $x_T \in D$. If the attacker correctly infers, they win the game. The privacy risk is estimated by playing the game multiple times and reporting the average.

Shadow Modeling. State-of-the-art MIAs against synthetic data generators rely on the shadow modeling technique [20,34,35]. With this technique, the attacker leverages their access to the auxiliary dataset as well as the knowledge of the model, to train multiple instances of Φ_T (called Φ_{shadow}) and evaluate the impact of the presence or absence of a target record on the resulting model. An attacker aiming to perform an MIA will proceed as follows. They will first create (e.g. by sampling) multiple datasets D_{shadow} from D_{aux}, such that $|D_{shadow}| = |D| - 1$. Note that we ensure $x_T \notin D_{aux}$. The attacker then adds x_T to half of the D_{shadow} and a random record x_R, distinct from x_T, to the other half. Using the completed D_{shadow} (now $|D_{shadow}| = |D|$) and the knowledge of model Φ_T, the attacker will now train multiple shadow generators Φ_{shadow}. The attacker will then use the Φ_{shadow} to produce synthetic datasets D^s_{shadow}, each labeled with either IN if $x_T \in D_{shadow}$ or OUT otherwise. Using the labeled dataset, the attacker can now train a meta-classifier $\mathcal{M}_{meta}$ to distinguish between cases where the target record was and was not part of the training dataset. More specifically, $\mathcal{M}_{meta}$ would be trained using D^s_{shadow} and the constructed binary label IN or OUT. At inference time, the attacker would then query the $\mathcal{M}_{meta}$ on the released D^s for records of interest, and return its prediction.

3   Related Works

Membership Inference Attacks (MIAs) were first developed by Homer et al. [19] to study whether the contribution of an individual to a Genome-Wide Associated Study can be inferred from released genomic aggregates. Their attack was based on a statistical test aiming to distinguish between aggregates that include the individual and aggregates computed on individuals randomly drawn from a reference population. Sankararaman et al. [33] extended the analysis soon after and showed the risk of membership inference to increase with the number of aggregates released m, but decrease with the number of individuals n in the dataset. MIAs have since been widely used to evaluate the privacy risk in aggregate data releases such as location [30] or survey data [5].

MIAs Against Machine Learning (ML) Models. Shokri et al. [34] proposed the first MIA against ML models. Their attack relies on a black-box access to the model and the shadow modeling technique (see Sect. 2.3 in the context of synthetic data generators). MIAs against ML models have since been extensively studied in subsequent works [23,26,32,36,41], both from a privacy perspective but also to better understand what a model learns. These works have, for instance, shown the risk to be higher in overfitted models [41] and smaller datasets [34], and to be mitigated by differentially private training, albeit at a cost in utility [21,23].

Disparate Vulnerability of Records. Previous work on MIA against ML models has shown that not all records are equally vulnerable to MIAs. The measured risk has e.g. been shown to vary with the label [34] and to be higher for outlier records [7,24] and members of subpopulations [8]. Feldman proposed a theoretical model demonstrating that models may, in fact, need to memorise rare or atypical examples in order to perform optimally when trained on long-tailed distributions such as those found in modern datasets [14,15]. Carlini et al. [7] showed this effect to be relative, as removing the most vulnerable records increases the vulnerability of remaining ones. Importantly for this work, Long et al. [24] argued that attacks should be considered a risk even when they only perform well on specific records. Long et al. proposed an approach to select vulnerable records prior to running the attack so as to increase its efficiency and precision. While their work [24] shows that records further away from their neighbors are more vulnerable, it only considers ML classification models.

MIAs Against Synthetic Tabular Data. MIAs have been extended to synthetic tabular data, the focus of our work. From a methodological standpoint, they fall broadly into two classes. The first class of methods directly compares synthetic data records to the original, private records, searching for exact or near-matches [11,17,25,40]. The second class of methods instantiates the shadow modeling technique in the black-box setting, assuming the adversary has knowledge of the algorithm used to generate synthetic data and to an auxiliary dataset. Stadler et al. [35] trained a meta-classifier on aggregate statistics computed on the synthetic shadow datasets, specifically the mean and standard deviation of the attributes, correlation matrices and histograms. Houssiau et al. [20] extended this work using k-way marginal statistics computed over subsets of the attribute values of the targeted record. They also extended the threat model from the standard black-box setting, which assumes knowledge of the generative model used, to the no-box setting that lacks this assumption. In this paper, we focus exclusively on shadow modeling-based attacks which are the state of the art.

4   Identifying Vulnerable Records

We here propose and validate a simple, yet effective, approach to identify vulnerable records in synthetic data publishing. Our approach is motivated by findings of previous works in the ML literature that records further away from their neighbors present a higher risk compared to randomly selected records. To identify such records, we compute a distance metric $d(x_i, x_j)$ between every pair of records in the dataset $(x_i, x_j) \in D \times D$, with $i \neq j$[1]. Then, for every record $x_i \in D$, we define its *vulnerability score* $V_k(x_i)$ as the average distance to its closest k neighbors in the dataset.

---

[1] Note that since the dataset D can contain repeated records (i.e., two or more individuals sharing the same attributes), the closest record to x_i can be a duplicate $x_j = x_i, j \neq i$ such that the distance between them is zero: $d(x_i, x_j) = 0$.

Definition 2 (Vulnerability Score). *Given a dataset D, a record $x_i \in D$, and a distance metric d, the vulnerability score of the record is defined as $V_k(x_i) = \frac{1}{k}\sum_{j=1}^{k} d(x_i, x_{i_j})$, where $x_{i_1}, \ldots, x_{i_{|D|-1}}$ is the re-ordering of the other records according to their increasing distance to x_i, i.e., $d(x_i, x_{i_1}) \leq \cdots \leq d(x_i, x_{i_{|D|-1}})$, with $i_j \neq i$ for every $j = 1, \ldots, |D| - 1$.*

Finally, we rank the records in D decreasingly by their vulnerability score $V_k(x_{r_1}) \geq \cdots \geq V_k(x_{r_{|D|}})$ and return the top-R records as the most vulnerable records. In the unlikely event that the last record(s) included in the top-R and the first one(s) not included have the exact same value for the vulnerability score, then a random subset is chosen.

Our distance metric d carefully distinguishes between categorical and continuous attributes. Recall that the dataset consists of F attributes. When the space of values that can be taken by an attribute is discrete, e.g., the gender of an individual $\mathcal{V}_f = \{\text{female}, \text{male}\}$, we refer to the attribute as *categorical*, while when the space of values is continuous, e.g., the income of an individual, we refer to the attribute as *continuous*. Denote by $\mathcal{F}_{\text{cont}}$ and $\mathcal{F}_{\text{cat}}$ the subsets of continuous and categorical attributes, with $\mathcal{F}_{\text{cont}} \cup \mathcal{F}_{\text{cat}} = \{1, \ldots, F\}$ and $\mathcal{F}_{\text{cont}} \cap \mathcal{F}_{\text{cat}} = \emptyset$. We preprocess each record $x_i = (x_{i,1}, \ldots, x_{i,F}) \in D$ as follows:

1. We convert every categorical attribute $x_{i,f}$, with $f \in \mathcal{F}_{\text{cat}}$ and $|\mathcal{V}_f|$ possible values $v_1, \ldots, v_{|\mathcal{V}_f|}$ to a one-hot encoded vector:

$$h(x_{i,f}) := (\mathbb{1}(x_{i,f} = v_1), \ldots, \mathbb{1}(x_{i,f} = v_{|\mathcal{V}_f|})), \tag{1}$$

i.e., a binary vector having 1 in the q-th position if and only if the attribute value is equal to v_q. Here, $\mathbb{1}$ denotes the indicator function. We then concatenate the one-hot encoded categorical attributes into a single vector:

$$h(x_i) := (h(x_{i,f}))_{f \in \mathcal{F}_{\text{cat}}} \tag{2}$$

2. We normalise every continuous attribute $x_{i,f}$, with $f \in \mathcal{F}_{\text{cont}}$ to range between 0 and 1, using min-max scaling:

$$n(x_{i,f}) := \frac{x_{i,f} - m_f(D)}{M_f(D) - m_f(D)}, \tag{3}$$

that is, we scale the values using the minimum $m_f(D) := \min_{j=1,\ldots,|D|}(x_{j,f})$ and maximum $M_f(D) := \max_{j=1,\ldots,|D|}(x_{j,f})$ values of the attribute estimated from the dataset D. We then concatenate the normalised continuous attributes into a single vector:

$$c(x_i) := (n(x_{i,f}))_{f \in \mathcal{F}_{\text{cont}}} \tag{4}$$

Using this notation, we define our distance metric between two records x_i and x_j as follows:

$$d(x_i, x_j) := 1 - \underbrace{\frac{|\mathcal{F}_{\text{cat}}|}{F} \frac{h(x_i) \cdot h(x_j)}{||h(x_i)||_2 * ||h(x_j)||_2}}_{\substack{\text{cosine similarity between} \\ \text{categorical attributes}}} - \underbrace{\frac{|\mathcal{F}_{\text{cont}}|}{F} \frac{c(x_i) \cdot c(x_j)}{||c(x_i)||_2 * ||c(x_j)||_2}}_{\substack{\text{cosine similarity between} \\ \text{continuous attributes}}}, \quad (5)$$

where $\cdot$ denotes the dot product between two vectors, $*$ denotes scalar multiplication, and $||a||_2 := \sqrt{\sum_{l=1}^{L} a_l^2}$ is the Euclidean norm of a vector $a \in \mathbb{R}^L$.

The resulting distance is a generalisation of the cosine distance across attribute types. It ranges between 0 and 1, with larger values indicating records to be less similar. The distance is equal to 0 if and only if the records are identical.

5   Experimental Setup

5.1   State-of-the-Art MIA Against Synthetic Tabular Data

Houssiau et al. [20] developed an MIA that instantiates the shadow modeling technique (see Sect. 2.3 for details) by training a random forest classifier on a subset of k-way marginal statistics that select the targeted record. The authors evaluated this approach on only one outlier record and found it to outperform other methods. Throughout our experiments, we found the attack to consistently outperform alternative methods and thus confirm it to be the state-of-the-art attack against synthetic tabular data. We refer to it as the *query-based attack*.

Given a target record x_T and a synthetic dataset D^s sampled from a generator fitted on a dataset D, this attack computes *counting queries* Q^A to determine how many records in the synthetic dataset match a subset $A \subset \{1, \dots, F\}$ of attribute values of target record x_T. We denote by a_i the i-th attribute for every $x \in D^s$ in the following: $Q^A(x_T) = \text{COUNT WHERE } \bigwedge_{i \in A}(a_i = x_{T,i})$. Counting queries are equal to k-way marginal statistics computed on the attribute values of the target record, multiplied by the dataset size $|D^s|$.

Our intuition behind this attack is twofold. First, when these statistics are preserved between the original and synthetic datasets, the answers are larger by 1, on average, when $x_T \in D$ compared to when $x_T \notin D$, since the queries select the target record. Second, the impact of the target record on the synthetic dataset is likely to be local, i.e., more records matching a subset of its attribute values are likely to be generated when $x_T \in D$, leading to statistically different answers to the same queries depending on the membership of x_T.

Like Houssiau et al. [20], we randomly sample a predetermined number N of attribute subsets A and feed the answers to the associated Q^A, computed on the synthetic shadow dataset, to a random forest meta-classifier. For computational efficiency reasons, we here use a C-based implementation of the query computation [9] instead of the authors' Python-based implementation [20].

We further extend the method to also account for continuous columns by considering the less-than-or-equal-to $\leq$ operator on top of the equal operator $=$ that was previously considered exclusively. For each categorical attribute we then use $=$, while using the $\leq$ for each continuous attribute.

5.2   Baselines for Identifying Vulnerable Records

We compare our approach against three baselines to identify vulnerable records:

Random: randomly sample target records from the entire population.

Rare Value (Groundhog) [35] sample a target record that either has a rare value for a categorical attribute or a value for a continuous attribute that is larger than the 95th percentile of the respective attribute.

Log-likelihood (TAPAS) [20]: sample target records having the lowest log-likelihood, assuming attribute values are independently drawn from their respective empirical distributions. Note that this approach is defined by the authors only for categorical attributes $f \in \mathcal{F}_{\text{cat}}$: for each record x_i, they compute the frequency of the value $x_{i,f}$ in the entire dataset, resulting in $p_{i,f}$. The likelihood of a record is defined by the product of $p_{j,f}$ across all attributes. We here extend this approach to also account for continuous attributes $f \in \mathcal{F}_{\text{cont}}$ by discretising them according to percentiles.

To evaluate the different methods to select vulnerable records, we run the query-based MIA described in Sect. 5.1 on the ten records identified by each of the three methods as well as our own approach.

5.3   Synthetic Data Generation Models

We evaluate our results against three generative models using the implementation available in the `reprosyn` repository [1].

SynthPop first estimates the joint distribution of the original, private data to then generate synthetic records. This joint distribution consists of a series of conditional probabilities which are fitted using classification and regression trees. With a first attribute randomly selected, the distribution of each other attribute is sequentially estimated based on both observed variables and previously generated synthetic columns. Initially proposed as an R package [28], the reprosyn repository uses a re-implementation in Python [18].

Table 1. Different parameters used throughout experiments

	$|D_{aux}|$	$|D_{test}|$	n_{shadow}	n_{test}
Adult	10000	5000	4000	200
UK Census	50000	25000	4000	200

BayNet uses Bayesian Networks to model the causal relationships between attributes in a given dataset. Specifically, the attributes are represented as a Directed Acyclic Graph, where each node is associated with an attribute and the directed edges model the conditional independence between the corresponding attributes. The corresponding conditional distribution of probabilities

$\mathbb{P}[X|Parents(X)]$ is estimated on the data using a GreedyBayes algorithm (for more details we refer to Zhang et al. [42]). Synthetic records can then be sampled from the product of the computed conditionals, i.e. the joint distribution.

PrivBayes is a differentially private version of the BayNet algorithm described above. Here, a first Bayesian Network is trained under an ϵ_1-DP algorithm. The conditional probabilities are then computed using an ϵ_2-DP technique, leading to a final $\epsilon = (\epsilon_1 + \epsilon_2)$-DP mechanism. From this approximate distribution, we can generate synthetic records without any additional cost of privacy budget. Note that for $\epsilon \to \infty$ PrivBayes becomes equivalent to BayNet. Again, we refer the reader to Zhang et al. [42] for a more in-depth description.

5.4   Datasets

We evaluate our method against two publicly available datasets.

UK Census [29] is the 2011 Census Microdata Teaching File published by the UK Office for National Statistics. It contains an anonymised fraction of the 2011 Census from England and Wales File (1%), consisting of 569741 records with 17 categorical columns.

Adult [31] contains an anonymized set of records from the 1994 US Census database. It consists of 48842 records of 15 columns. 9 of those columns are categorical, and 6 are continuous.

5.5   Parameters of the Attack

Table 1 shows the parameters we use for the attack. We use a given dataset Ω (e.g. Adult) to select our most at-risk records as the target records. We then partition Ω randomly into D_{test} and D_{aux}. D_{aux} is the auxiliary knowledge made available to the attacker, while D_{test} is used to sample n_{test} datasets used to compute the attack performance. n_{shadow} represents the number of shadow datasets used, sampled from the auxiliary knowledge D_{aux}. We considered, in all experiments, the size of the release synthetic dataset (D^s) to be equal to the size of the private dataset D, $|D| = |D^s| = 1000$. To create the shadow datasets, while ensuring that D_{aux} does not contain the target record, we randomly sample $|D|-1$ records in D_{aux}. Then we add the target record x_T in half of the datasets, and in the other half, we used another record randomly sampled from D_{aux}.

We run the query-based attack using $N = 100000$ queries randomly sampled from all possible count queries (2^F in total) and a random forest meta-classifier with 100 trees, each with a maximum depth of 10.

In order to measure the attack performance, we compute the Area Under the receiver operating characteristic Curve (AUC) for the binary classification of membership on n_{test} datasets.

Lastly, in line with the auditing scenario, we use $k = 5$ neighbors in the private dataset Ω to select the most vulnerable records using our vulnerability score V_k.

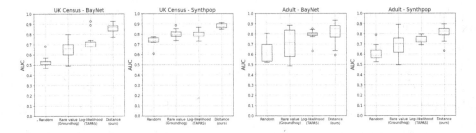

Fig. 1. AUC of MIAs across record identification techniques for the query-based attack, for datasets UK Census and Adult and synthetic data generators BayNet and Synthpop.

Table 2. Mean and standard deviation for AUC for the query-based attack method

Method	UK census		Adult	
	Synthpop	BayNet	Synthpop	BayNet
Random	0.732 ± 0.046	0.535 ± 0.055	0.613 ± 0.084	0.618 ± 0.120
Rare value (Groundhog)	0.802 ± 0.044	0.644 ± 0.086	0.699 ± 0.113	0.704 ± 0.140
Log-likelihood (TAPAS)	0.790 ± 0.041	0.731 ± 0.090	0.742 ± 0.033	0.787 ± 0.057
Distance (ours)	**0.879 ± 0.021**	**0.858 ± 0.040**	**0.804 ± 0.072**	**0.810 ± 0.110**

6   Results

6.1   Performance of Vulnerable Record Identification Methods

We evaluate the effectiveness of vulnerable record identification methods across the two datasets UK Census and Adult, and two synthetic data generators Synthpop and BayNet. For each dataset, each of the four record identification methods selects 10 target records. We then perform the MIA, as a privacy game, on each of these records and report its AUC.

Figure 1 show that our vulnerable record identification method consistently outperforms both the random baseline and the two ad-hoc techniques previously used in the literature. The median risk of records identified by our method is indeed consistently higher than all other methods, up to 18.6 p.p. higher on the UK Census dataset using BayNet. On average, the AUC of the records we identified are 7.2 p.p. higher than the AUC of the records selected by other methods (Table 2). Importantly, our method also consistently manages to identify records that are more or equivalently at-risk compared to other methods.

6.2   Applicability of the Method to New Attacks

MIAs against synthetic data is an active area of research with a competition [2] now being organised to develop better, more accurate, MIAs. To evaluate the effectiveness of our vulnerable record identification, we developed a new attack which we aimed to be as different as possible to the existing state of the art. We call this new attack *target attention*.

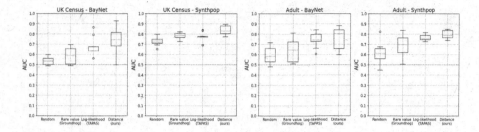

Fig. 2. AUC of MIAs across record identification techniques for the target attention attack, for datasets UK Census and Adult and synthetic data generators BayNet and Synthpop.

In contrast with the state-of-the-art method, which first computes features from a synthetic dataset to then use these as input for a meta-classifier, our new attack takes as input (a part of) the synthetic dataset to directly predict membership. As such, the model would be able to extract directly from the synthetic dataset the information that is most useful for the MIA. To our knowledge, it is the first method that is record-focused and allows for trainable feature extraction. For more information about the new method, we refer the reader to Appendix A. We then follow the same methodology as above to evaluate the effectiveness of the four vulnerable record identification methods when using the target attention approach.

Figure 2 shows that, again, our vulnerable record identification method strongly outperforms both the random baseline and the two ad-hoc techniques previously used in the literature. The mean risk of records identified by our method is again consistently higher than all other methods, up to 10.89 p.p. higher on UK Census using BayNet. Across datasets and generators, the records we identify are 5.2 p.p. more at risk than the records selected by other methods (Appendix A).

6.3 Robustness Analysis for k

Throughout the paper, we use $k = 5$, meaning that our vulnerability score $V_k(x_i)$ is computed using the 5 closest records to the record of interest. We here evaluate the impact of a specific choice of k for the record identification and associated results. More specifically, we compute the mean distance for each record using values of k ranging from 1 to 50 and report the mean AUC for the ten records selected by the method on the Adult dataset using Synthpop.

Figure 3(a) shows our method to be robust to specific choices of k. The mean AUC of the top ten records varies indeed only slightly for different values of k. Looking at the top 10 records selected for different values of k, we find that only a handful of records are distinct, suggesting our method to not be too sensitive to specific values of k.

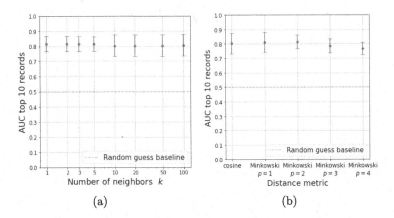

Fig. 3. Mean and standard deviation of the AUC of MIAs for 10 records selected by the vulnerability score for varying (a) number of neighbors considered and (b) distance metrics considered. Results on Adult, Synthpop for the query-based attack.

6.4 Robustness Analysis for the Cosine Distance

We here rely on a generalized form of cosine distance across attribute types. We now evaluate the susceptibility of our results to different choices of distance metrics. We do this using several versions of the Minkowski distance between two vectors $a, b \in \mathbb{R}^L$. For a given value $p \in \mathbb{N}^*$, the Minkowski distance is defined as $d^p_{\text{Minkowski}}(a, b) = \sqrt[p]{\sum_{l=1}^{L} |a_l - b_l|^p}$. Similarly to Eq. 5, we generalise this distance metric for two records $x_i, x_j \in D$ to:

$$d(x_i, x_j) := \frac{|\mathcal{F}_{\text{cat}}|}{F} d^p_{\text{Minkowski}}(h(x_i), h(x_j)) + \frac{|\mathcal{F}_{\text{cont}}|}{F} d^p_{\text{Minkowski}}(c(x_i), c(x_j)). \quad (6)$$

Notably, the Minkowski distance with $p = 2$ closely relates to the cosine distance. As before, we compute the mean distance for each record using Minkowski distances with p ranging from 1 to 4 and report the mean AUC for the ten records selected by the method on the Adult dataset using Synthpop.

Figure 3(b) shows the attack performance to, again, be robust to different choices of distance metric. In particular, mean AUC is not significantly different for the cosine distance and $p \in \{1, 2\}$, while slightly decreasing for higher p values. Cosine being the standard distance metric in the literature, we prefer to use it.

6.5 Vulnerable Records and Differentially Private Generators

An active line of research aims at developing differentially private (DP) synthetic data generators. As discussed above however, developing models that achieve DP with meaningful theoretical ϵ while maintaining high utility across tasks remains a challenge. MIAs are thus an important tool to understand the privacy protection offered by DP models for various values of ϵ.

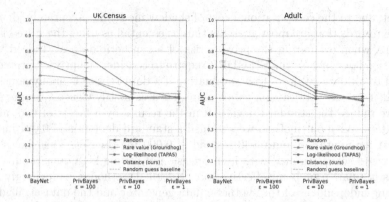

Fig. 4. Mean and standard deviation of the AUC of the MIAs for varying values of ϵ in DP-based generator PrivBayes. Results on UK Census (left) and Adult (right) for the query-based attack and for the 10 points for each record identification method.

We here evaluate the performance of our vulnerable record identification approach when DP generators are used. Specifically, we report the mean and standard deviation AUC for the 10 records identified as being at risk by our approach and by the three baselines for varying values of ϵ using PrivBayes [42].

Figure 4 shows that our approach outperforms both the random baseline and the two ad-hoc techniques previously used in the literature. As expected though, the AUC drops when ϵ decreases. The attack still performs quite well for $\epsilon = 100$ and manages to identify at-risk records for $\epsilon = 10$. Importantly, the general utility of synthetic data generated by PrivBayes for low value of ϵ is being debated.

7   Discussion

Our results show that our simple distance-based method is able to consistently identify vulnerable records, and more effectively so than previously proposed ad-hoc methods. We believe this to be due to limitations of previous work. Indeed *Rare value (Groundhog)* only considers the value of one specific attribute to determine whether a record is at risk while *Log-likelihood (TAPAS)* assumes independence across all attributes to compute a record's likelihood, an assumption that is typically not met in real-world datasets. In contrast, our distance-based metric considers the neighborhood of the record, therefore encompassing all attributes without making any assumptions on the underlying distribution.

Across datasets and generators, we find that records identified by our method are on average 7.2 p.p. more vulnerable than previous work when using the state-of-the-art MIA. In practice, we believe this to be highly significant. Researchers and practitioners who wish to evaluate new attack methods and the privacy risk of synthetic data publishing are indeed unable to evaluate all records in the dataset, due to the computational cost of shadow modeling. Accurately identifying the records that are most at risk is thus as essential as using the state-of-the-art MIA when evaluating the privacy risk of a synthetic dataset. Indeed, data protection laws such as the EU GDPR require to consider the privacy protection offered to all data subjects when evaluating if a data release is anonymous.

When we use only categorical columns, such as in UK Census, results show that we reduce the standard deviation in the results by a factor of two, across generators. With our method we obtained a standard deviation of 0.021 instead of 0.041 for Synthpop and 0.040 instead of 0.090 for BayNet. This shows that our method selects records with high precision of having high vulnerability.

Lastly, apart from being effective, our principled method is compellingly easy. By being independent of the synthetic data generator and the dataset, it allows for pragmatic and efficient cross-generator and dataset comparison.

Future Work. We here distinguished between categorical features and continuous attributes. Future research could explore if considering ordinal as a subset of the categorical features could lead to a better record selection. Similarly, we here focused on the difference in metrics between the cosine similarity and the Minkowski metrics of order $p \in \{1, 2, 3, 4\}$. We leave for future work to see if other distances, such as Minkowski of higher order, the Chebyshev distance or Hamming distance, could lead to a better record selection.

Additionally, one could study whether removing the most vulnerable records is an effective defense against attacks. Prior work on MIAs against ML models suggests that, when vulnerable records are removed, other records then become more vulnerable [7]. We leave for future work whether this holds true for MIAs against synthetic data.

Finally, we presented results on three widely used synthetic data generators. Future work should evaluate whether more specific metrics could be beneficial for other generators such as GANs.

8   Conclusion

Due to computational costs, the identification of vulnerable records is as essential as the actual MIA methodology when evaluating the privacy risks of synthetic data, including with respect to data protection regulations such as the EU GDPR. We here propose and extensively evaluate a simple yet effective method to select vulnerable records in synthetic data publishing, which we show to strongly outperform previous ad-hoc approaches.

Acknowledgements. We acknowledge computational resources and support provided by the Imperial College Research Computing Service (http://doi.org/10.14469/hpc/2232).

A   Appendix: Target Attention

Inspired by developments in natural language processing [37], the target attention model computes record-level embeddings. Through a modified attention mechanism, these embedding are able to interact with the embedding of the target record, which in turn leads to a dataset-level embedding that is used as input for a binary classifier. The detailed steps are laid out below.

We start by preprocessing the synthetic dataset used as input D^s. First, we compute the one-hot-encoded values for all categorical attributes and apply this consistently to all the synthetic records and the target record. The continuous attributes remain untouched. Second, we compute all the unique records in the dataset and their multiplicity. Third, we compute the distance following equation (1) between all unique synthetic records and the target record. Finally, we rank all unique synthetic record by increasing distance to the target record and, optionally, only keep the *top* X closest records, where X is a parameter.

The final pre-processed synthetic dataset $D^{s,p} \in \mathbb{R}^{X \times F'}$ is a matrix containing the top X unique records, their multiplicity and the distance, ranked by the latter, where F' denotes the number of features after one-hot-encoding of the categorical attributes added by 2 to account for the multiplicity and the distance. For consistency, the target record x_t is processed in the same way, with one-hot-encoded categorical attributes, multiplicity 1 and distance 0, resulting in the pre-processed target record $x_{t,p} \in \mathbb{R}^{F'}$.

Figure 5 illustrates our target attention model, which we describe in Algorithm 1. The model takes as input the pre-processed synthetic dataset $D^{s,p}$. First, a multilayer perceptron (MLP) is used to compute embeddings of both the pre-processed records as well as the target record. Second, after computing a query vector for the target record and keys and values for the records, an attention score is computed for each record. After applying a *softmax* function across all attention scores, all record values are summed weighted by the respective attention score to eventually lead to the dataset-level embedding which is used as input for a final MLP as binary classifier. The output of the entire network is a single float, which after applying a *sigmoid* function σ results in a probability of membership. This model is then trained with all synthetic shadow datasets using a binary cross-entropy loss function with the known binary value for membership.

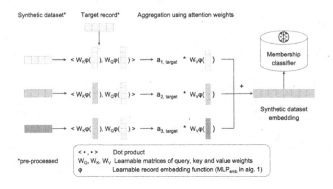

Fig. 5. Illustration of our target attention architecture.

Algorithm 1. Forward propagation for target-attention

1: **Inputs:**

    1. $D^{s,p} \in \mathbb{R}^{X \times F'}$ the preprocessed synthetic dataset with its unique records, their multiplicity and distance to the target record.

    2. The pre-processed target record values $x_{t,p} \in \mathbb{R}^{F'}$.

    3. Learnable MLP for the embedding $\mathbf{MLP}_{emb}$ with F' input features and F_{emb} output features, weight matrices $\mathbf{W}_q, \mathbf{W}_k,$ and $\mathbf{W}_v \in \mathbb{R}^{F_{emb} \times F_{att}}$ to compute the target query and record keys and values with attention size F_{att}, and MLP for the prediction $\mathbf{MLP}_{pred}$ with F_{att} input features and 1 output feature

2: **Output:**

    $h_{pred} \in \mathbb{R}$, which leads to the predicted probability for binary membership after applying a sigmoid transformation $\sigma(h_{pred})$

3: // Compute the embeddings of all records and the target record

4: $D_{emb} \leftarrow \mathbf{MLP}_{emb}[D^{s,p}]$ with $D_{emb} \in \mathbb{R}^{X \times F_{emb}}$

5: $x_{t,emb} \leftarrow \mathbf{MLP}_{emb}[x_{t,p}]$ with $x_{t,emb} \in \mathbb{R}^{1 \times F_{emb}}$

6: // Compute the target query, and the keys and values for each record

7: $q_t \leftarrow \mathbf{W}_q x_{t,emb}$ with $q_t \in \mathbb{R}^{1 \times F_{att}}$

8: $K \leftarrow \mathbf{W}_k D_{emb}$ with $K \in \mathbb{R}^{X \times F_{att}}$

9: $V \leftarrow \mathbf{W}_v D_{emb}$ with $V \in \mathbb{R}^{X \times F_{att}}$

10: // Compute the target attention scores for each record

11: $a_j \leftarrow <q_t, v_j>$ for $j = 1..X$ to get $a \in \mathbb{R}^{1 \times X}$

12: $a_j \leftarrow \exp a_j / (\sum_{j=1}^{X} \exp a_j)$ for $j = 1..X$

13: $D_{att} \leftarrow aV$ with $D_{att} \in \mathbb{R}^{1 \times F_{att}}$ // Sum values weighted by target attention

14: $\mathbf{h}_{pred} \leftarrow \sigma(\mathbf{MLP}_{pred}[D_{att}])$ // Compute the final membership score.

Table 3. Mean and standard deviation for AUC for the Target Attention method

Method	UK census		Adult	
	Synthpop	BayNet	Synthpop	BayNet
Random	0.727 ± 0.038	0.535 ± 0.035	0.609 ± 0.112	0.594 ± 0.083
Rare value (Groundhog)	0.783 ± 0.030	0.587 ± 0.079	0.691 ± 0.103	0.638 ± 0.104
Log-likelihood (TAPAS)	0.770 ± 0.046	0.674 ± 0.085	0.765 ± 0.027	0.745 ± 0.068
Distance (ours)	$\mathbf{0.838 \pm 0.041}$	$\mathbf{0.737 \pm 0.118}$	$\mathbf{0.797 \pm 0.038}$	$\mathbf{0.763 \pm 0.103}$

Throughout the experiments, we used $F_{emb} = 20$, $F_{att} = 15$ and $|top\ X| = 100$. Both MLP_{emb} and MLP_{pred} consist of one hidden layer with 20 and 10 nodes respectively, and use ReLU as activation and a dropout ratio of 0.15. The network is trained for 500 epochs, using the Adamax optimizer [22] with a learning rate of $10e - 3$ and batch size of 20. 10% of the training data is used as validation data and the model that achieves the lowest validation loss is selected. Results in Table 3 display the details of results compiled in Fig. 2.

References

1. Alan Turing Institute: Resprosyn (2022). https://github.com/alan-turing-institute/reprosyn
2. Allard, T.: Snake challenge (2023). https://www.codabench.org/competitions/879/
3. Annamalai, M.S.M.S., Gadotti, A., Rocher, L.: A linear reconstruction approach for attribute inference attacks against synthetic data. arXiv preprint arXiv:2301.10053 (2023)
4. Bates, A., Spakulová, I., Dove, I., Mealor, A.: ONS methodology working paper series number 16-synthetic data pilot. https://www.ons.gov.uk/methodology/methodologicalpublications/generalmethodology/onsworkingpaperseries/onsmethodologyworkingpaperseriesnumber16syntheticdatapilot (2019), accessed on 02/06/2023
5. Bauer, L.A., Bindschaedler, V.: Towards realistic membership inferences: the case of survey data. In: Annual Computer Security Applications Conference, pp. 116–128 (2020)
6. Bellovin, S.M., Dutta, P.K., Reitinger, N.: Privacy and synthetic datasets. Stan. Tech. L. Rev. **22**, 1 (2019)
7. Carlini, N., Jagielski, M., Zhang, C., Papernot, N., Terzis, A., Tramer, F.: The privacy onion effect: memorization is relative. In: Advances in Neural Information Processing Systems, vol. 35, pp. 13263–13276 (2022)
8. Chang, H., Shokri, R.: On the privacy risks of algorithmic fairness. In: 2021 IEEE European Symposium on Security and Privacy (EuroS&P), pp. 292–303. IEEE (2021)
9. Cretu, A.M., Houssiau, F., Cully, A., de Montjoye, Y.A.: Querysnout: automating the discovery of attribute inference attacks against query-based systems. In: Proceedings of the 2022 ACM SIGSAC Conference on Computer and Communications Security, pp. 623–637 (2022)
10. Dinur, I., Nissim, K.: Revealing information while preserving privacy. In: Proceedings of the twenty-second ACM SIGMOD-SIGACT-SIGART Symposium on Principles of Database Systems, pp. 202–210 (2003)
11. Domingo-Ferrer, J., Ricci, S., Soria-Comas, J.: Disclosure risk assessment via record linkage by a maximum-knowledge attacker. In: 2015 13th Annual Conference on Privacy, Security and Trust (PST), pp. 28–35. IEEE (2015)
12. Dwork, C.: Differential privacy. In: Bugliesi, M., Preneel, B., Sassone, V., Wegener, I. (eds.) ICALP 2006, Part II. LNCS, vol. 4052, pp. 1–12. Springer, Heidelberg (2006). https://doi.org/10.1007/11787006_1
13. Edge, D., et al.: Design of a privacy-preserving data platform for collaboration against human trafficking. arXiv preprint arXiv:2005.05688 (2020)

14. Feldman, V.: Does learning require memorization? A short tale about a long tail. In: Proceedings of the 52nd Annual ACM SIGACT Symposium on Theory of Computing, pp. 954–959 (2020)

15. Feldman, V., Zhang, C.: What neural networks memorize and why: discovering the long tail via influence estimation. In: Advances in Neural Information Processing Systems, vol. 33, pp. 2881–2891 (2020)

16. Financial Conduct Authority: Synthetic data to support financial services innovation (2022). https://www.fca.org.uk/publication/call-for-input/synthetic-data-to-support-financial-services-innovation.pdf. Accessed 02 June 2023

17. Giomi, M., Boenisch, F., Wehmeyer, C., Tasnádi, B.: A unified framework for quantifying privacy risk in synthetic data. arXiv preprint arXiv:2211.10459 (2022)

18. Hazy: Synthpop (2019). https://github.com/hazy/synthpop

19. Homer, N., et al.: Resolving individuals contributing trace amounts of DNA to highly complex mixtures using high-density SNP genotyping microarrays. PLoS Genet. 4(8), e1000167 (2008)

20. Houssiau, F., et al.: Tapas: a toolbox for adversarial privacy auditing of synthetic data. In: NeurIPS 2022 Workshop on Synthetic Data for Empowering ML Research (2022)

21. Jayaraman, B., Evans, D.: Evaluating differentially private machine learning in practice. In: USENIX Security Symposium (2019)

22. Kingma, D.P., Ba, J.: Adam: a method for stochastic optimization. arXiv preprint arXiv:1412.6980 (2014)

23. Leino, K., Fredrikson, M.: Stolen memories: leveraging model memorization for calibrated white-box membership inference. In: 29th USENIX Security Symposium (USENIX Security 20), pp. 1605–1622 (2020)

24. Long, Y., et al.: A pragmatic approach to membership inferences on machine learning models. In: 2020 IEEE European Symposium on Security and Privacy (EuroS&P), pp. 521–534. IEEE (2020)

25. Lu, P.H., Wang, P.C., Yu, C.M.: Empirical evaluation on synthetic data generation with generative adversarial network. In: Proceedings of the 9th International Conference on Web Intelligence, Mining and Semantics, pp. 1–6 (2019)

26. Nasr, M., Shokri, R., Houmansadr, A.: Comprehensive privacy analysis of deep learning: passive and active white-box inference attacks against centralized and federated learning. In: 2019 IEEE Symposium on Security and Privacy (SP), pp. 739–753. IEEE (2019)

27. NHS England: A&e synthetic data (2020). https://data.england.nhs.uk/dataset/a-e-synthetic-data. Accessed 02 June 2023

28. Nowok, B., Raab, G.M., Dibben, C.: synthpop: Bespoke creation of synthetic data in R. J. Stat. Softw. 74, 1–26 (2016)

29. Office for National Statistics: Census microdata teaching files (2011). https://www.ons.gov.uk/census/2011census/2011censusdata/censusmicrodata/microdatateachingfile

30. Pyrgelis, A., Troncoso, C., De Cristofaro, E.: Knock knock, who's there? Membership inference on aggregate location data. arXiv preprint arXiv:1708.06145 (2017)

31. Ronny, K., Barry, B.: UCI machine learning repository: adult data set (1996). https://archive.ics.uci.edu/ml/datasets/Adult

32. Salem, A., Zhang, Y., Humbert, M., Berrang, P., Fritz, M., Backes, M.: Ml-leaks: model and data independent membership inference attacks and defenses on machine learning models. arXiv preprint arXiv:1806.01246 (2018)

33. Sankararaman, S., Obozinski, G., Jordan, M.I., Halperin, E.: Genomic privacy and limits of individual detection in a pool. Nat. Genet. 41(9), 965–967 (2009)

34. Shokri, R., Stronati, M., Song, C., Shmatikov, V.: Membership inference attacks against machine learning models. In: 2017 IEEE Symposium on Security and Privacy (SP), pp. 3–18. IEEE (2017)
35. Stadler, T., Oprisanu, B., Troncoso, C.: Synthetic data-anonymisation groundhog day. In: 31st USENIX Security Symposium (USENIX Security 22), pp. 1451–1468 (2022)
36. Truex, S., Liu, L., Gursoy, M.E., Yu, L., Wei, W.: Demystifying membership inference attacks in machine learning as a service. IEEE Trans. Serv. Comput. **14**(6), 2073–2089 (2019)
37. Vaswani, A., et al.: Attention is all you need. In: Advances in Neural Information Processing Systems, vol. 30 (2017)
38. Xu, L., Skoularidou, M., Cuesta-Infante, A., Veeramachaneni, K.: Modeling tabular data using conditional GAN. In: Advances in Neural Information Processing Systems, vol. 32 (2019)
39. Xu, L., Skoularidou, M., Cuesta-Infante, A., Veeramachaneni, K.: Modeling tabular data using conditional GAN. In: Wallach, H., Larochelle, H., Beygelzimer, A., d'Alché-Buc, F., Fox, E., Garnett, R. (eds.) Advances in Neural Information Processing Systems, vol. 32. Curran Associates, Inc. (2019). https://proceedings.neurips.cc/paper_files/paper/2019/file/254ed7d2de3b23ab10936522dd547b78-Paper.pdf
40. Yale, A., Dash, S., Dutta, R., Guyon, I., Pavao, A., Bennett, K.P.: Assessing privacy and quality of synthetic health data. In: Proceedings of the Conference on Artificial Intelligence for Data Discovery and Reuse, pp. 1–4 (2019)
41. Yeom, S., Giacomelli, I., Fredrikson, M., Jha, S.: Privacy risk in machine learning: analyzing the connection to overfitting. In: 2018 IEEE 31st Computer Security Foundations Symposium (CSF), pp. 268–282. IEEE (2018)
42. Zhang, J., Cormode, G., Procopiuc, C.M., Srivastava, D., Xiao, X.: Privbayes: private data release via Bayesian networks. ACM Trans. Database Syst. **42**(4) (2017). https://doi.org/10.1145/3134428

Enforcing the GDPR

François Hublet[✉][iD], David Basin[iD], and Srđan Krstić[✉][iD]

Institute of Information Security, Department of Computer Science, ETH Zürich,
Zurich, Switzerland
{francois.hublet,basin,srdan.krstic}@inf.ethz.ch

Abstract. Violations of data protection laws such as the General Data
Protection Regulation (GDPR) are ubiquitous. Currently, building IT
support to implement such laws is difficult and the alternatives such
as manual controls augmented by auditing are limited and scale poorly.
This calls for new automated enforcement techniques that can build on,
and enforce, a formalization of the law.

In this paper, we present the first enforceable specification of a core
set of GDPR provisions, centered on data-subject rights, and describe an
architecture that automatically enforces this specification in web applications. We evaluate our architecture by implementing three case studies
and show that our approach incurs only modest development and runtime overhead, while covering the most relevant privacy-related aspects
of GDPR that can be enforced at runtime.

Keywords: Data protection · Runtime enforcement · Temporal logic

1 Introduction

As of May 2023, nearly € 3b in fines [13] have been imposed on organizations
violating the EU's General Data Protection Regulation (GDPR). Despite these
fines, GDPR violations are still ubiquitous [10,32]. In a world where data processing permeates most aspects of life, it is unlikely that ex-post auditing and
fines can achieve compliance at scale. Hence, an ex-ante, automated approach
to privacy is needed.

Runtime verification (RV) [5] provides a framework for monitoring and enforcing complex properties of computer systems at runtime. In RV, system actions
are represented as time-stamped events. System execution then constitutes a
trace of events that is checked for compliance with a specification, i.e., a trace
property describing the system's desired executions. In particular, online RV
tools can check compliance in real-time, with violations being either reported
(in the case of *runtime monitoring* [23]) or prevented (in the case of *runtime
enforcement* [39]).

The challenge of using RV techniques for automated enforcement of privacy
laws is threefold. First, legal provisions must be *faithfully translated* into a formal
specification: relevant actions by both software systems and individuals must be
encoded as events, and legal provisions turned into a formal specification. Second, the resulting specification must be *enforceable* by an automatic process, also

G. Tsudik et al. (Eds.): ESORICS 2023, LNCS 14345, pp. 400–422, 2024.
https://doi.org/10.1007/978-3-031-51476-0_20

called an enforcer (Sect. 2.1): one must identify which actions can be suppressed or caused to prevent violations, and then check that all potential violations of the specification can be prevented by such suppression or causation. Third and finally, applications must be *instrumented* so that they emit appropriate events and can suppress or cause relevant actions. In particular, a core requirement of privacy laws is for applications to track information flows in order to faithfully determine where and how personal data is used. Dynamic information-flow control mechanisms can be used to deduce data ownership during execution (Sect. 2.2).

In this paper, we propose the first comprehensive approach to privacy enforcement that addresses all of the above challenges for a core set of GDPR provisions. Specifically, we leverage an RV approach that uses a logical specification language supporting first-order quantification and (metric) temporal operators, providing both a high degree of expressiveness and real-time enforcement support [24]. The provided expressiveness is crucial for a faithful formalization of GDPR provisions.

We first formalize a core set of GDPR provisions as an enforceable specification (Sect. 3). Our specification builds on previous work [2] on formalizing and *monitoring* the GDPR using Metric First-Order Temporal Logic (MFOTL) [8]. We show here how GDPR provisions can be *enforced* rather than just monitored. Specifically, we extend the previous work to cover a larger fragment of GDPR provisions, and then use the theory of MFOTL enforcement [24] to show the enforceability of our specification. We cover purpose and consent-based data usage, as well as the rights to access, rectify, erase, restrict, and object to data processing.

We then build an architecture that enforces this specification in web applications (Sect. 4). Our architecture consists of three components: data subjects' *browsers*, the *WebTTC+ execution environment* where data controllers deploy their applications, and a *privacy platform* to which data subjects delegate the enforcement of their privacy preferences. WebTTC+ is an extension of the recently introduced WebTTC environment (TTC stands for Taint, Track, and Control) for enforcing information-flow policies using taint tracking [25]. WebTTC+ ensures that the applications' behavior complies with privacy laws by interacting with an enforcer deployed at the privacy platform. WebTTC+ reports relevant events to the enforcer, which in turn responds with remedial actions (i.e., sets of events to cause or suppress) that WebTTC+ must execute to ensure compliance. Additionally, the data subjects can directly interact with the privacy platform to manage their consent and exercise their rights. The platform sends events representing data subject queries (e.g., requests for data access or erasure) to the enforcer.

We evaluate our architecture by implementing three web applications: a microblogging app, a conference management system, and a health record manager. We show that our architecture effectively enforces core GDPR provisions while preserving the application's functionality and introducing only a modest overhead (Sect. 5). In summary, we make the following contributions:

- We propose the first enforceable specification for core GDPR provisions.
- We develop an architecture for enforcing this specification in web applications and show how to instrument relevant actions to obtain appropriate events.
- We evaluate a prototype implementation of our architecture on three case studies. Our approach incurs only modest development and runtime overhead, while covering all relevant GDPR provisions that can be enforced at runtime.

We show that this is the first approach that comprehensively enforces core GDPR provisions (Sect. 6). The companion repository [26] contains all artifacts.

2 Background

We introduce Metric First-Order Temporal Logic (MFOTL), runtime enforcement, and the WebTTC environment that instruments applications for enforcement.

2.1 Runtime Enforcement with Metric First-Order Temporal Logic

Given a specification describing intended system execution, runtime enforcement [39] is the process whereby the system execution is observed by an *enforcer* that detects attempted violations and reacts to *prevent* them. In this paper, we use MFOTL [8] as the specification language and the EnfPoly tool [24] as the enforcer.

Let $\Sigma = (\mathbb{D}, \mathbb{E}, a)$ be a first-order signature, containing an infinite set $\mathbb{D}$ of constant symbols, a finite set of *event names* $\mathbb{E}$, and an arity function $a : \mathbb{E} \to \mathbb{N}$. An *event* is a pair $e(d_1, \ldots, d_{a(e)}) \in \mathbb{E} \times \mathbb{D}^{a(e)}$ of an event name e with arity $a(e)$, and $a(e)$ parameters. Events represent system actions *observable* by the enforcer. Some observable events can be suppressed or caused by the enforcer, while others can only be observed. Hence, $\mathbb{E}$ can be partitioned into sets of suppressable (Sup), causable (Cau), and only-observable (Obs) event names. Given a signature Σ, a *trace* is a sequence of pairs $\sigma = ((\tau_i, D_i))_i$, where the $\tau_i \in \mathbb{N}$ are nondecreasing timestamps and $D_i \in \mathbb{DB}$ is a finite set of events. The empty trace is denoted by ε, the set of traces by $\mathbb{T}$, and a *(trace) property* is any set $P \subseteq \mathbb{T}$. For two traces σ, σ' with σ finite, $\sigma \cdot \sigma'$ is their concatenation, and $|\sigma'|$ is the length of σ'.

Let $\mathbb{I}$ be the set of intervals over $\mathbb{N}$ and let $\mathbb{V}$ be for a countable set of variables. MFOTL formulae over a signature Σ are defined by the grammar

$$\varphi ::= r(t_1, \ldots, t_{a(r)}) \mid \neg\varphi \mid \varphi \vee \varphi \mid \exists x.\ \varphi \mid \bullet_I \varphi \mid \bigcirc_I \varphi \mid \varphi\, \mathsf{S}_I\, \varphi \mid \varphi\, \mathsf{U}_I\, \varphi,$$

where $x \in \mathbb{V}$, $t_1, \ldots, t_{a(r)} \in \mathbb{V} \cup \mathbb{D}$, $r \in \mathbb{E}$, and $I \in \mathbb{I}$. We derive Boolean $\top := p \vee \neg p$, $\bot := \neg\top$, $\varphi \wedge \psi := \neg(\neg\varphi \vee \neg\psi)$, $\varphi \Rightarrow \psi := \neg\varphi \vee \psi$, and temporal operators "once" ($\blacklozenge_I \varphi := \top\, \mathsf{S}_I\, \varphi$) and "always" ($\square_I \varphi := \neg(\top\, \mathsf{U}_I\, \neg\varphi)$). We also define a shorthand for the "inclusive since" operator as $\varphi\, \hat{\mathsf{S}}_I\, \psi := \varphi\, \mathsf{S}_I\, (\varphi \wedge \psi)$. Temporal operators with no interval explicitly given have the interval $[0, \infty)$ instead. Predicates are formulae of the form $r(t_1, \ldots, t_{a(r)})$. A formula that contains no future temporal operators is called a *past-only* formula. We use $\mathsf{fv}(\varphi)$ for the set of φ's free variables.

A *valuation* is any function $v : \mathbb{V} \cup \mathbb{D} \to \mathbb{D}$ such that $v(d) = d$ for all $d \in \mathbb{D}$. We write $v[x \mapsto d]$ for the function equal to v, except for $v(x) = d$. Given a trace $\sigma = ((\tau_i, D_i))_i$, a timepoint $1 \le i \le |\sigma|$, a valuation v, and a formula φ, the satisfaction relation $\models$ is defined in Fig. 1. We write $v \models_\sigma \varphi$ for $v, 1 \models_\sigma \varphi$ and $\{\sigma \mid \exists v.\ v \models_\sigma \varphi\}$ for the trace property P_φ defined by the formula φ. We focus on closed MFOTL formulae, which are formulae φ where $\mathsf{fv}(\varphi) = \emptyset$.

$$
\begin{array}{ll}
v, i \models_\sigma \neg\varphi & \text{iff } v, i \not\models_\sigma \varphi \\
v, i \models_\sigma \exists x.\ \varphi & \text{iff } v[x \mapsto d], i \models_\sigma \varphi \text{ for } d \in \mathbb{D} \\
v, i \models_\sigma \bullet_I \varphi & \text{iff } i > 1 \text{ and } v, i-1 \models_\sigma \varphi \text{ and } \tau_i - \tau_{i-1} \in I \\
v, i \models_\sigma \bigcirc_I \varphi & \text{iff } i+1 \le |\sigma| \text{ and } v, i+1 \models_\sigma \varphi, \text{ and } \tau_{i+1} - \tau_i \in I \\
v, i \models_\sigma \varphi\,\mathsf{S}_I\,\psi & \text{iff } v, j \models_\sigma \psi \text{ for some } j \le i,\ \tau_i - \tau_j \in I, \text{ and } v, k \models_\sigma \varphi \text{ for all } k \in (j, i] \\
v, i \models_\sigma \varphi\,\mathsf{U}_I\,\psi & \text{iff } v, j \models_\sigma \psi \text{ for some } |\sigma| \ge j \ge i,\ \tau_j - \tau_i \in I \text{ and } v, k \models_\sigma \varphi \text{ for all } k \in [i, j)
\end{array}
$$

$$
\begin{array}{ll}
v, i \models_\sigma r(t_1, \ldots, t_n) & \text{iff } r(v(t_1), \ldots, v(t_n)) \in D_i \\
v, i \models_\sigma \varphi \vee \psi & \text{iff } v, i \models_\sigma \varphi \text{ or } v, i \models_\sigma \psi \\
& \mid v, i \models_\varepsilon \varphi
\end{array}
$$

Fig. 1. MFOTL semantics

Trace properties may be defined in terms of infinite traces, whereas enforcers can only observe a finite (prefix of a) trace. Intuitively, a trace must be checked 'prefix-wise', i.e., by evaluating its prefixes in increasing order. A trace complies with a property iff an enforcer for this property accepts all of its prefixes.

An enforceable property must contain the empty trace, i.e., the system must initially comply with the property. Additionally, for any extension $\sigma \cdot (\tau, D)$ of a (non-violating) prefix σ, the enforcer must have enough information to *decide* on its compliance with the property. In MFOTL, this means that the formula should not depend on future information in the trace; for example, it can be a past-only formula. Furthermore, there must exist finite sets D^- and D^+ of suppressable and causable events respectively that the enforcer can respectively suppress and cause to ensure satisfaction of the property at the new time point, i.e., $\sigma \cdot (\tau, D \setminus D^- \cup D^+)$ satisfies the property. In general, the problem of checking whether an MFOTL formula defines an enforceable property is undecidable [24]. Instead, we can consider a syntactic fragment, called *guarded* MFOTL (GMFOTL) [24], where each formula is guaranteed to define an enforceable property:

$$
\psi ::= \bot \mid s(t_1, \ldots, t_n) \mid \neg c(t_1, \ldots, t_n) \mid \psi \wedge \varphi \mid \psi \vee \psi \mid \exists x.\ \psi.
$$

Here, $s \in \mathsf{Sup}, c \in \mathsf{Cau}$, and φ is any MFOTL formula. When $\mathsf{Sup} \cap \mathsf{Cau} = \emptyset$, GMFOTL is expressively complete [24], i.e., any MFOTL formula that defines an enforceable property can be rewritten to an equivalent GMFOTL formula:

Theorem 1. *Let φ be a past-only closed MFOTL formula φ and $\mathsf{Sup} \cap \mathsf{Cau} = \emptyset$. Then $P_{\Box\varphi}$ is enforceable iff there exists a GMFOTL formula ψ with $\Box\varphi \equiv \Box\neg\psi$.*

EnfPoly [24] is an implementation of an MFOTL enforcer. It takes an GMFOTL formula and a trace, which it incrementally processes. At each processing step it reports sets of events to be suppressed or caused to satisfy the formula.

2.2   The WebTTC Execution Environment

WebTTC is an execution environment for web applications that can enforce information-flow policies specified as MFOTL formulae [25]. Such formulae are expressed over *information-flow traces* whose events capture inputs, outputs, and the influence of inputs on outputs. For example, the policy "Alice's inputs must not influence outputs to any user for marketing purposes" is formalized in WebTTC as

$$\Box\,[\forall o, ds.\ \mathtt{Out}(ds, \mathrm{Marketing}, o) \Rightarrow \neg(\exists i.\ \mathtt{Itf}(i, o) \wedge (\blacklozenge\mathtt{In}(\mathrm{Alice}, i)))]\,.$$

Here, $\mathtt{Out}(u, \mathrm{Marketing}, o)$ means "the output with identifier o is performed to user ds for marketing purposes", $\mathtt{In}(\mathrm{Alice}, i)$ means "Alice inputs the input with identifier i", and $\mathtt{Itf}(i, o)$ means "the input with identifier i *interferes* with the output with identifier o." The $\mathtt{Itf}$ event captures (non-)interference between inputs and outputs as in the information-flow control (IFC) literature [22].

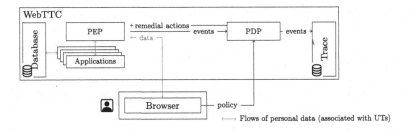

Fig. 2. WebTTC architecture

To enforce such information-flow policies, WebTTC follows a dynamic approach that uses a policy enforcement point (PEP) that supervises application execution together with a policy decision point (PDP) implemented by EnfPoly (see Fig. 2). Applications written in a Python-like programming language with an IFC semantics [25] (provided by WebTTC) are deployed inside WebTTC where they interact with a database. All inputs and outputs are observable by the PDP, which can suppress outputs to ensure compliance with a user-specified information-flow policy. User inputs to applications are processed in three steps:

TAINT: The PEP tags a new input from a user u with a fresh input identifier, called a *unique taint* (UT), and sends an event $\mathtt{In}(u, ut)$ to the PDP, which stores it in the trace. The input and its UT are forwarded to the application.

TRACK: The semantics of the WebTTC-provided programming language propagates UTs during execution. Each data item in memory or in the database is always tagged with the UTs of all inputs that interfered with its current value.

CONTROL: WebTTC requires that every application output be labeled with a purpose. When an application attempts to output to a user u for some purpose

p, the PEP generates a fresh output identifier o as well as events $\texttt{Out}(u, p, o)$ and $\texttt{Itf}(ut, o)$ for each UT ut tagging the output value. It then sends these events to the PDP, which instructs the PEP to suppress the output if it would cause a policy violation. If the output is not suppressed, the trace is updated. To summarize, WebTTC uses the following first-order signature Σ_{TTC}:

Event	Description	Type
$\texttt{In}(u, ut)$	Data subject ds inputs a value with UT ut	
$\texttt{Out}(u, p, ut)$	Value with UT ut is output to data subject ds for purpose p	⑤
$\texttt{Itf}(ut, o)$	Input with UT ut interferes with output o	

⑤ = Suppressable; unmarked events are only-observable

3 Formalizing GDPR Provisions

We now review the core GDPR provisions (Sect. 3.1), present a first-order signature (Sect. 3.2), and an MFOTL formula formalizing these core GDPR provisions (Sect. 3.3). Finally, we show that the formula is enforceable (Sect. 3.4).

3.1 Core GDPR Provisions

We focus on the provisions laid out in Chaps. 2 and 3 of the GDPR, which define the *principles* of data processing and the *rights* of the data subject (DS):

- **Purpose and consent-based usage** [Art. 5(1)(b), 6(1), 7(1,3), 9(1,2)]. The processing of personal data is lawful only if the DS has consented to processing *for one or more specific purposes*, unless the data controller can claim a specific legal ground. The DS can revoke consent at any time. Specific legal grounds are applicable in the case of sensitive data (*special data categories*, Art. 9).
- **Right to access** and **right to data portability** [Art. 15(1), 20(1)]. A DS has the right to access any personal data relating to them. They have the right to obtain a copy of this data in a machine-readable format.
- **Right to rectification** [Art. 5(1)(d), Art. 16]. A DS has the right to rectify any inaccurate personal data relating to them.
- **Right to erasure ("right to be forgotten")** [Art. 17(1,2)]. A DS has the right to obtain the erasure of any personal data relating to them. Other controllers with whom the data has been shared shall be notified about it.
- **Right to restriction of processing** [Art. 18(1)]. A DS has the right to restrict the processing of any personal data relating to them.
- **Right to object** [Art. 21(1)]. A DS has the right to object to the processing of data relating to them based on specific legal grounds.

For simplicity, we focus on the case where the DS interacts with applications, each managed by a single data controller. We then formalize the above provisions for each individual application, rather than for each data controller.

3.2   First-Order Signature for Core GDPR Concepts

We encode key GDPR concepts as a first-order signature representing observable system actions. The signature (Table 1a) consists of two sets of events. The first set represents actions triggered by a DS: consent (DSConsent) and revocation (DSRevoke) thereof; requests for accessing (DSAccess), deleting (DSErase), rectifying (DSRectify), or restricting the use of data (DSRestrict); repealing restrictions (DSRepeal); and objections to processing (DSObject). Each event in this set has a name prefixed with DS. The second set represents actions triggered by the application: collection (Collect), usage (Use), and sharing of data (ShareWith); granting access to (GrantAccess), erasure (Erase), and rectification of data (Rectify); notifications of data deletion to third-party controllers (NotifyErase); and claims of legal grounds to process data (LegalGround). All predicates refer to single data items by their unique taints (UTs). The Collect (resp. LegalGrounds) event has a Boolean parameter sp that is true if and only if the data collection (resp. the claim of legal grounds) involves (resp. applies to) 'special' data. We call sp the *special-data flag* of the data or claim.

DS-triggered actions are not controlled by the enforcer, and hence the corresponding events are only-observable. The collection of data, sharing, and claims for legal grounds, which are not constrained by any core GDPR provision, are also only-observable. In contrast, the usage of data (Use) is subject to restrictions and must therefore be suppressable (⊖). Finally, GrantAccess, Erase, Rectify and NotifyErase events, which a DS must be able to request, must be causable (⊙).

3.3   MFOTL Formula Formalizing Core GDPR Provisions

The core GDPR provisions are formalized by the formula Φ given in Table 1b, which is a past-only formula of the form $\Box\neg(\varphi_{\text{Purp}} \vee \cdots \vee \varphi_{\text{Obj}})$ with seven subformulae that describe the *violations* of the provisions in Sect. 3.1.

Provisions Restricting Data Usage. The formulae $\varphi_{\text{Purp}}, \varphi_{\text{Restr}}$, and φ_{Obj} respectively capture violations of purpose-based usage, the right to restrict processing, and the right to object. Purpose-based usage is violated when the following hold:

1. The data with UT ut is used for purpose prp, which is exactly $\text{Use}(prp, ut)$;
2. The data with UT ut was collected from the DS ds with the special-data flag sp, which is $\blacklozenge\text{Collect}(ds, ut, sp)$;
3. (a) Neither the DS ds has given consent to process data with UT ut for purpose prp and has not revoked that consent since then, which is exactly $\neg\text{DSRevoke}(ds, prp, ut) \mathbin{\hat{\text{S}}} \text{DSConsent}(ds, prp, ut)$,
   (b) nor has the application claimed a legal ground grd to use data with UT ut with the special-data flag sp, i.e., $\exists grd. \blacklozenge\text{LegalGround}(grd, ut, sp)$.

The corresponding formula φ_{Purp} is shown in Table 1b. The formula φ_{Restr} is similar, but does not allow claims of legal grounds. The formula φ_{Obj} formalizes the right to object. This right is violated when all of the following hold:

Table 1. MFOTL formalization of core GDPR provisions

(a) MFOTL signature

Predicate	Description	Type
	The data subject ds:	
DSConsent(ds, prp, ut)	gives consent to use data with UT ut for purpose prp	
DSRevoke(ds, prp, ut)	revokes consent given to use data with UT ut for purpose prp	
DSAccess(ds, ut)	requests access to data with UT ut	
DSErase(ds, ut)	requests erasure of data with UT ut	
DSRectify(ds, ut, val)	requests rectification of data with UT ut to new value val	
DSRestrict(ds, ut)	requests restriction of data with UT ut	
DSRepeal(ds, ut)	repeals restriction of data usage for data with UT ut	
DSObject(ds, ut)	objects to usage of data with UT ut by application	
	The application:	
Collect(ds, ut, sp)	collects data with UT ut of data subject ds^*.	
Use(prp, ut)	uses data with UT ut for purpose prp	Ⓢ
ShareWith(ctr, ut)	shares data with UT ut with third-party controller ctr	
GrantAccess(ds, ut)	gives data subject access to data with UT ut	Ⓒ
Erase(ut)	erases data with UT ut	Ⓒ
Rectify(ut, val)	rectifies data with UT ut to new value val	Ⓒ
NotifyErase(ctr, ut)	notifies controller ctr about erasure of data with UT ut	Ⓒ
LegalGround(grd, ut, sp)	claims legal ground grd for using data with UT ut^*	

Ⓒ = Causable; Ⓢ = Suppressable; unmarked events are only-observable

$^*sp$ is a *special-data* Boolean flag that is true iff the data belongs to a special category

(b) MFOTL formula

Description	Formula
Overall formula	$\Phi = \Box\neg\,(\varphi_{\text{Purp}} \vee \varphi_{\text{Acc}} \vee \varphi_{\text{Rect}} \vee \varphi_{\text{Er}} \vee \varphi_{\text{Restr}} \vee \varphi_{\text{Obj}})$
Purpose-based usage	$\varphi_{\text{Purp}} = \exists prp, ut, ds, sp.\ \text{Use}(prp, ut) \wedge \blacklozenge\text{Collect}(ds, ut, sp)$
	$\wedge\neg\left(\left(\neg\text{DSRevoke}(ds, prp, ut)\,\hat{\text{S}}\,\text{DSConsent}(ds, prp, ut)\right)\right.$
	$\left.\vee\,(\exists grd.\ \blacklozenge\text{LegalGround}(grd, ut, sp))\right)$
Right to access	$\varphi_{\text{Acc}} = \exists ds, ut, sp.\ \left(\neg\text{GrantAccess}(ds, ut)\,\hat{\text{S}}_I\,\text{DSAccess}(ds, ut)\right)$
	$\wedge\blacklozenge\text{Collect}(ds, ut, sp) \wedge \neg\text{GrantAccess}(ds, ut)$
	$\underline{or}\ \exists ds, ut, sp.\ \text{DSAccess}(ds, ut)$
	$\wedge\blacklozenge\text{Collect}(ds, ut) \wedge \neg\text{GrantAccess}(ds, ut)$
Right to rectification	$\varphi_{\text{Rect}} = \exists ds, ut, val, sp.\ \left(\neg\text{Rectify}(ds, ut, val)\,\hat{\text{S}}_I\,\text{DSRectify}(ds, ut, val)\right)$
	$\wedge\blacklozenge\text{Collect}(ds, ut, sp) \wedge \neg\text{Rectify}(ds, ut, val)$
	$\underline{or}\ \exists ds, ut, sp.\ \text{Rectify}(ds, ut, val)$
	$\wedge\blacklozenge\text{Collect}(ds, ut, sp) \wedge \neg\text{Rectify}(ds, ut, val)$
Right to erasure (1)	$\varphi_{\text{Er1}} = \exists ds, ut, sp.\ \left(\neg\text{Erase}(ut)\,\hat{\text{S}}_I\,\text{DSErase}(ds, ut)\right)$
	$\wedge\blacklozenge\text{Collect}(ds, ut, sp) \wedge \neg\text{Erase}(ut)$
	$\underline{or}\ \exists ds, ut, sp.\ \text{DSErase}(ds, ut)$
	$\wedge\blacklozenge\text{Collect}(ds, ut, sp) \wedge \neg\text{Erase}(ut)$
Right to erasure (2)	$\varphi_{\text{Er2}} = \exists ctr, ut.\ \text{Erase}(ut)$
	$\wedge\ \blacklozenge\text{ShareWith}(ctr, ut) \wedge \neg\text{NotifyErase}(ctr, ut)$
Right to restriction	$\varphi_{\text{Restr}} = \exists prp, ut, ds, sp.\ \text{Use}(prp, ut) \wedge \blacklozenge\text{Collect}(ds, ut, sp)$
	$\wedge\left(\neg\text{DSRepeal}(ds, ut)\,\hat{\text{S}}\,\text{DSRestrict}(ds, ut)\right)$
Right to object	$\varphi_{\text{Obj}} = \exists prp, ut, ds, sp.\ \text{Use}(prp, ut) \wedge \blacklozenge\text{Collect}(ds, ut, sp)$
	$\wedge\blacklozenge\,(\text{DSObject}(ds, ut) \wedge \blacklozenge\,(\exists grd.\ \text{LegalGround}(grd, ut, sp)))$

I denotes any interval $[i \text{ days}, \infty)$ with $i \leq 30$.

1. The data with UT ut is used for purpose prp;
2. The data with UT ut was collected from the DS ds;
3. At some time in the past:
   (a) the application has claimed legal ground grd to use data with UT ut,
   (b) and meanwhile, the DS ds has objected to the use of data with UT ut.

We formalize 3. as $\blacklozenge(\texttt{DSObject}(ds, ut) \land \blacklozenge(\exists grd, sp.\ \texttt{LegalGround}(grd, ut, sp)))$.

Provisions Regulating DS Requests. The formulae φ_{Acc}, φ_{Rect} φ_{Er1}, and φ_{Er2} respectively capture the rights to access, rectification, and (two types of) erasure. Formulae φ_{Acc}, φ_{Rect}, and φ_{Er1} share a similar structure, which requires that the application performs some action in a timely manner when the DS requests it (a so-called *response pattern* [17]). We describe erasure in detail.

According to Art. 12(3) GDPR, erasure must be performed "*without undue delay and in any event within one month of receipt of the request.*" To ensure compliance with this provision, it suffices that an appropriate Erase event is caused within 30 days after any DSErase event. Both the 'zealous' approach causing Erase immediately after DSErase and the 'lazy' approach causing it $i \le 30$ days after DSErase are acceptable. These translate into the GMFOTL formulae:

$$\varphi_{\text{Er1,zealous}} = \Box\neg\,(\exists ds, ut.\ \neg\texttt{Erase}(ut) \land \texttt{DSErase}(ds, ut))$$

$$\varphi_{\text{Er1,lazy},i} = \Box\neg\left(\exists ds, ut.\ \neg\texttt{Erase}(ut)\,\hat{\mathsf{S}}_{[i,\infty)}\,\texttt{DSErase}(ds, ut)\right) \qquad \forall i \le 30.$$

The phrase "*without undue delay*" from Art. 12(3) suggests that the 'zealous' variant is closer to the spirit of the law. As this aspect remains open to interpretation, we show both in Table 1b. The cases of φ_{Rect} and φ_{Acc} are similar.

According to Art. 17(2), erasure of any data item should be accompanied by notifying all controllers with whom this data item was shared. This is formalized by the formula φ_{Er2} in Table 1b. It is violated when some data with UT ut has been shared with a controller at some point in the past ($\blacklozenge\texttt{ShareWith}(pro, ut)$), this data is erased ($\texttt{Erase}(ut)$), and no notification has been issued ($\neg\texttt{NotifyErase}(pro, ut)$).

3.4 Enforceability

To use EnfPoly, we must show that formula Φ defines an enforceable property P_Φ.

Lemma 1. $\Psi = \varphi_{\text{Purp}} \lor \varphi_{\text{Acc}} \lor \varphi_{\text{Rect}} \lor \varphi_{\text{Er}} \lor \varphi_{\text{Restr}} \lor \varphi_{\text{Obj}}$ *is in GMFOTL.*

Proof. Each disjunct is a GMFOTL formula. The subformulae φ_{Purp}, φ_{Restr}, and φ_{Obj} are all of the form $\exists x_1 \ldots x_k.\ \texttt{Uses}(\ldots) \land \psi$ with ψ past-only, which is a GMFOTL formula since Uses is suppressable. The subformulae φ_{Acc}, φ_{Rect}, φ_{Er1}, and φ_{Er2} are all of the form $\exists x_1 \ldots x_k.\ \neg\mathsf{X}(\ldots) \land \psi$ or $\exists x_1 \ldots x_k.\ \psi \land \neg\mathsf{X}(\ldots)$ where ψ is past-only and X is a causable event (GrantAccess, Rectify, Erase, or NotifyErase), and are therefore also GMFOTL formulae. Hence formula Ψ, being a disjunction of GMFOTL formulae, is itself a GMFOTL formula.

Since $\Phi = \Box\neg\Psi$ a closed past-only formula, we use Theorem 1 to obtain:

Lemma 2. *P_Φ is enforceable.*

Since Φ is also monitorable [8], we use EnfPoly to enforce it. EnfPoly's algorithm guarantees compliance with the negated disjunction by preventing violations of each disjunct. Violations of φ_{Purp}, φ_{Restr}, and φ_{Obj} are prevented by suppressing Use events (i.e., preventing usage), while violations of φ_{Acc}, φ_{Rect}, φ_{Er1}, and φ_{Er2} are prevented by causing `GrantAccess`, `Rectify`, `Erase`, and `NotifyErase`.

4   Enforcement Architecture

Figure 3 depicts our enforcement architecture. A DS interacts with applications through their *web browser*, equipped with a browser extension. The extension helps the DS view purposes and set their consent preferences, and sends the corresponding consent events to the PDP. It also allows the DS to declare some inputs as containing special data or personal data of another DS. Finally, the DS can access the platform's privacy dashboard to see how their data has been used.

A controller deploys their applications in the *WebTTC+ execution environment*, which extends WebTTC with support for deletion, rectification, DS access, and notification of other controllers. As in WebTTC, applications' inputs and outputs are controlled by a PEP, which reports critical operations to the PDP and can suppress or cause actions at the PDP's request. However, unlike in WebTTC, the PDP is no longer located inside of WebTTC+, but deployed on a *privacy platform*.

The privacy platform consists of three components: a PDP (as in WebTTC) instantiated with the policy formalized by the MFOTL formula Φ (Sect. 3.3); a trace (as in WebTTC) storing events of the current application execution; and a *privacy dashboard* [9,35,36] used by the DS to query and review events related to their data and exercise their rights. The dashboard can read events from the trace and emit new ones (the DS events in Table 1a) on behalf of the DS.

We now explain how the actions corresponding to the events in Sect. 3.2 are instrumented. We first consider purpose-based usage, the right to restriction, and the right to object, which are enforced through the suppression of Use (Sect. 4.1). Next, we discuss erasure and rectification, whose enforcement requires causation (Sect. 4.2). Finally, we consider the right to access (Sect. 4.3).

4.1   Purpose and Consent-Based Usage, Restriction, and Objection

Data collection and consent are captured by the events `Collect` and `DSConsent`, which are only-observable. The browser extension plays a key role in the data and consent collection process. Recall that it allows the DS to set their privacy preferences (i.e., which data can be processed for which purposes), to declare if some data belongs to a special category, and to declare *whose* personal data they input. An example of the latter is when a physician enters patient data

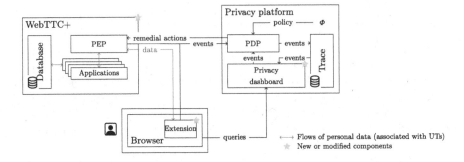

Fig. 3. GDPR enforcement architecture

into a software system; the physician would use the extension to declare the patient's identity. Formally, the extension keeps three maps M_{prp}, M_{owners}, and M_{spec} each associating pairs (url, arg) of an URL and argument name to a set of purposes, a set of data subjects, and a special-data flag, respectively. A value sent as argument arg to URL url is considered to belong to $M_{\mathsf{owners}}[(url, arg)]$ data subjects, to contain special data if $M_{\mathsf{spec}}[(url, arg)]$, and can be used for $M_{\mathsf{prp}}[(url, arg)]$ purposes.

Data collection consists of three steps. First, a DS attempts to make a request to an application's URL; the extension retrieves the data DS's preferences and immediately logs the relevant consent events to the PDP. Then, the extension modifies the request to add fresh UTs for each input. Finally, the application receives the request and logs `Collect` events for each input. More formally:

1. The DS ds queries the URL url deployed on a WebTTC+ server with arguments a_i and values v_i, for $1 \le i \le k$. The extension intercepts the request and tags the new inputs with fresh UTs $(ut_i)_{1 \le i \le k}$. It then sends `DSConsent`(ds, prp, ut_i) to the PDP for all $1 \le i \le k$ and $prp \in M_{\mathsf{prp}}[(url, a_i)]$.
2. The extension sends to the application the original request together with the UTs ut_i, the owners $M_{\mathsf{owners}}[(url, a_i)]$, and the special-data flags $M_{\mathsf{spec}}[(url, a_i)]$.
3. Finally, after it receives the new inputs and their UTs, WebTTC+ logs an event `Collect`(ds', app, ut_i, sp_i) for each $1 \le i \le k$, $ds' \in M_{\mathsf{owners}}[(url, a_i)]$, and $sp_i = M_{\mathsf{spec}}[(url, a_i)]$, and waits for the PDP to acknowledge the logging of all events. Only then can the collected data be processed.

Data usage is captured by `Use`. Purpose-based usage, the right to restriction, and the right to object are all enforced through the suppression of `Use` events.

WebTTC+ emits `Use`(prp, ut) whenever WebTTC would emit `Out`(ds, prp, o) and `Itf`(ut, o) simultaneously. Thus, `Use`(prp, ut) holds whenever the application performs an output for the purpose prp whose value is influenced by input ut. Any `Use` event can be suppressed by suppressing the corresponding output. Being based on non-interference, our definition captures not only the usage of the original DS inputs, but also the usage of any data *derived from DS inputs*.

Extending the notion of personal data to data derived from user inputs is in line with the GDPR. Namely, the GDPR defines personal data as "*any information relating to an identified or identifiable natural person*" [Art. 4(1)], a definition that generally encompasses both raw and derived data.

At first glance, controlling data usage only at outputs may appear to depart from the GDPR's definition of processing as "*any operation or set of operations which is performed on personal data or on sets of personal data*" [Art. 4(2)]. However, we claim that this approach does not restrict the violations that we can prevent. First, *purpose* is best understood as an attribute of *business processes* [7] that rely on interactions between computer systems and human agents. Such interactions necessarily involve outputs. Moreover, according to the GDPR, data must be "*limited to what is necessary in relation to the purposes for which they are processed*" ('data minimization', Art. 5(1)(c)). The principle of data minimization is unmonitorable [2], and therefore not amenable to runtime enforcement. Now, data which has no influence on outputs can hardly be considered 'necessary' in relation to the purposes of the business process, since interaction with humans is what business processes are designed for. Hence, any violation of purpose-based usage that cannot be captured by observing outputs is also a violation of data minimization, and thus cannot be prevented using runtime enforcement.

Legal grounds can be claimed by WebTTC+ applications through a special instruction `claim_legal_ground`(grd, sp, x). This claims a legal ground grd to use the data contained in a term x with special-data flag sp. When the instruction is executed by an application *app*, WebTTC+ logs a `LegalGround`(grd, ut, sp) event for each UT *ut* associated with the value that x evaluates to. Note that the system cannot check that these claims are *legally valid*, as such a check cannot be automated. It therefore only logs the events, which can be objected to later on.

DS requests can be sent by the DS for each of their inputs collected by the applications by interacting with the privacy dashboard. These requests are captured by `DSRevoke`, `DSRestrict`, `DSRepeal`, and `DSObject` events sent to the PDP by the privacy dashboard. In addition to using the extension, users can provide consent manually (i.e., emit `DSConsent` events) through the dashboard.

4.2   Erasure and Rectification

Erasure and rectification can be requested by users through the privacy dashboard, which emits `DSErase` and `DSRectify` events on their behalf.

WebTTC+ extends WebTTC's with two functions `erase`(ut) and `rectify`(ut, v) that can be caused by the PDP to erase (resp. rectify) data stored in the database. Additionally, WebTTC+ allows applications to declare *handler functions* that can be used to restore a consistent application state in the event of erasure. Assuming a relational database, `erasure`(ut) is implemented as follows:

1. Identify all tables, rows, and fields tagged with ut;

2. Perform erasure by deleting the identified table content or rows or setting the identified fields to a default value;
3. For each erased table, row, or field, call the handling function, if it exists;
4. Emit $\texttt{Erase}(ut)$.

The case of rectification is slightly more complex. Namely, rectification should behave differently for raw data and derived data. For raw data, the old input value can be immediately replaced with the new input value. Derived data can only be set to a default, after which the application can provide a way for it to be re-computed using the new input value. The algorithm for $\texttt{rectify}(ut, v)$ is as follows:

1. Identify all tables, rows, and fields tagged with ut;
2. Erase the content of any identified tables or rows;
3. For any identified field, if it contains raw data, replace its value by v, otherwise, set it to a default value;
4. For each identified table, row, or field, call the handling function, if it exists;
5. Emit $\texttt{Rectify}(ut, v)$.

To distinguish raw data from derived data, we extend TTC's memory model with *integrity tags*. Instead of pairs $\langle v, \alpha \rangle$ of a value v and a set of UTs α, our memory model relies on triples $\langle v, \alpha, \beta \rangle$, where β is either Derived or Raw(ut), where ut is a UT. Whenever a data item in memory is equal to $\langle v, \alpha, \mathsf{Raw}(ut) \rangle$, its value v must be equal to the original value of the input with UT ut. When it is equal to $\langle v, \alpha, \mathsf{Derived} \rangle$, its value may not be equal to the value of any input.

After erasure, the formula φ_{Er2} triggers notification of all controllers with whom the erased data has been previously shared. WebTTC+ triggers an event $\texttt{ShareWith}(pro, ut)$ on each output influenced by ut whose recipient is a third-party controller, rather than a DS. The causable event $\texttt{NotifyErase}$ is instrumented by exposing a function $\texttt{notify}(ut, ctr)$ that can be triggered by the PDP. This function notifies the third-party controller ctr about the erasure of ut.

4.3 Access to Data

The DS requests access to data through the privacy dashboard, which emits $\texttt{DSAccess}$ events. On receiving a $\texttt{DSAccess}$ event, the PDP instructs the PEP to cause a corresponding $\texttt{GrantAccess}$ event. The PEP then calls a function $\texttt{access}(ds, ut)$ exposed by WebTTC+, which has the following behavior:

1. Identify all tables, rows, and fields tagged with ut;
2. Copy all identified tables, rows, and fields into a specific $\texttt{access}$ table.
3. Provide the DS with a link to an interface that supports browsing, and downloading, a machine-readable dump of the data (for data portability).
4. Emit $\texttt{GrantAccess}(ds, ut)$.
5. In the interface, use the standard WebTTC+ mechanism to show ds *only the data that can be shown without violating other data subjects' consent.*

Step 5 resolves the tension arising between the right to access and other rights when several users' inputs are aggregated. When some data d has been produced by combining inputs from users A and B, granting A access to d may violate purpose-based usage from B's viewpoint, hamper B's capacity to erase or rectify d, and interfere with B's right to restrict the processing of d (see [29] for a discussion of the GDPR's ambiguity in matters of shared data ownership). We take a conservative approach that prioritizes consent-based usage over access, subjecting the extracted data to the same enforcement procedures as application outputs.

5   Evaluation

We now evaluate a prototype implementation of our enforcement architecture with regard to its development and runtime overhead and its coverage of GDPR provisions. Our prototype includes the WebTTC+ environment, the privacy platform, and a Firefox extension. Overall it has 5.5k lines of code (LoC) in Python with 2.7k LoC reused from the WebTTC environment from previous work [25]. The WebTTC+ environment and the privacy dashboard use the Flask web framework and SQLite databases. The PDP is based on EnfPoly [24], with additional Python code ensuring synchronization with a QuestDB time-series database storing the log. Appendix B shows screen captures of the privacy dashboard, the browser extension, and one of the deployed case study applications. Our evaluation aims to answer the following research questions:

RQ1: Can realistic web applications be developed in WebTTC+? If yes, how do the additional privacy requirements impact the size of their code base?

RQ2: How much runtime overhead does WebTTC+ incur compared to a baseline application without support for automated privacy enforcement?

RQ3: What share of the GDPR's provisions does our implementation effectively enforce? What aspects are not covered?

To answer the above questions, we port the following applications:

- **Minitwit+**, a clone of the microblogging **Minitwit** application [46];
- **Conf**, a conference management system [49]; and
- **HIPAA**, a health record management system [49].

These applications have been previously used to evaluate the performance of various IFC frameworks [25,30,34,46,49]. We use the variants of these applications presented in Hublet et al. [25] where every output is labeled with a purpose in {Service, Analytics, Marketing}, and compare our WebTTC+ implementation to a baseline implementation in Python/Flask with the same database backend.

RQ1: Development Effort. We have implemented all three applications in our framework, preserving their original functionality. Most of the code from the baseline implementation has been reused with only minor changes. This makes porting Flask applications to WebTTC+ straightforward. Privacy-specific code (e.g., the handling functions) accounts for less than 10% of all application code in the WebTTC+ implementations. We show examples of such code in **Minitwit⁺** in Appendix A. Table 2 shows the number of LoC for each case study.

Table 2. Lines of code of the WebTTC+ and the baseline implementations

Application	WebTTC+			Python/Flask	
	Functionality	Privacy	Template	Functionality	Template
Minitwit⁺	140	16	100	121	119
Conf	312	47	502	284	508
HIPAA	142	25	852	136	846

RQ2: Performance Overhead. We compare the runtime performance of WebTTC+ with a Python/Flask baseline implementation. Since our baseline does not enforce privacy, this yields an upper bound on the overhead of GDPR enforcement for web apps. We measure the latency of the following representative workloads:

- In **Minitwit⁺**, we show 30 TIMELINE messages and post a NEW MESSAGE;
- In **Conf**, we show ALL PAPERS and ONE PAPER, and SUBMIT a paper;
- In **HIPAA**, we show ONE PATIENT and ALL PATIENTS.

The ALL PAPERS and ALL PATIENTS workloads constitute stress tests [49] used to measure the runtime behavior of applications in the presence of large outputs. In real production scenarios, showing all entities stored in a system is generally avoided and pagination is used to improve runtime performance.

For each workload, we measure the time spent on (1) registering CONSENT at the PDP, (2) waiting for the PDP's VERDICTs, and (3) COMPUTATION within WebTTC+. Additionally, we measure the latency of revoking consent (REVOKE), erasing an input (ERASE) or rectifying it (RECTIFY), and opening the privacy DASHBOARD. We perform the measurements on a high-end laptop (Intel Core i5-1135G7, 32 GB RAM) over $N = 100$ repetitions, while varying the number u of users and the number n of entities (messages for **Minitwit⁺**, papers for **Conf**, and patients for **HIPAA**) in the database. The results are shown in Fig. 4.

For all workloads displaying a constant number of entities (i.e., TIMELINE, NEW MESSAGE, ONE PAPER, SUBMIT, ONE PATIENT, REVOKE, ERASE, and REC-TIFY), our architecture incurs an overhead of at most one order of magnitude with respect to the Flask/Python baseline. Executing applications in WebTTC+ (i.e., COMPUTATION) adds at most 10 ms of extra latency with respect to the baseline. The PDP is the main performance bottleneck: WebTTC+ spends 70%–90% of its running time waiting for PDP verdicts, whose latency grows logarithmi-cally. The total latency however remains below 75 ms, allowing for the seamless usage of the applications. For the stress-test workloads showing a number of enti-ties linear in n (ALL PAPERS and ALL PATIENTS), runtime performance remains within one order of magnitude of Flask/Python, with logarithmic growth. Comparable runtime performance was obtained in previous studies using the same applications [25,49].

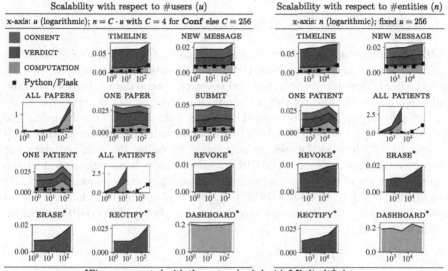

Scalability with respect to #users (u)

x-axis: u (logarithmic); $n = C \cdot u$ with $C = 4$ for **Conf** else $C = 256$

Scalability with respect to #entities (n)

x-axis: n (logarithmic); fixed $u = 256$

*Figures computed with the system loaded with **Minitwit**[+] data

Fig. 4. Workload latency (y-axis: seconds per request, avg. over $N = 100$ requests)

RQ3: GDPR Coverage. Beyond articles 5(1)(b,d), 6(1), 7(1,3), 9(1,2), 13(1), 15(1), 20(1), 16, 17(1,2), 18(1), and 21(1), our implementation provides at least a technical starting point for enforcing the following provisions:

- **Lawfulness** [Art. 5(1)(a)];
- **Transparency** [Art 12(1,3)]. Any DS-requested information shall be provided in transparent form, without undue delay and within at most one month;
- **Right to information** [Art. 13(1), 15(1)]. A DS has a right to be informed when their personal data is collected and processed;
- **Privacy by design** [Art. 25(1)]. Appropriate technical measures shall be implemented to provide privacy by design;
- **Record of processing activities** [Art. 30(1)]. Data controllers shall keep a record of all processing activities conducted under their responsibility.

Together, articles 5(1)(a, b, d), 6–7, 9, 12–13, 15–18, 21, 25, and 30 appear in 66% of the violations reported on www.enforcementtracker.com (May 2023). While this only provides a rough estimate of the (maximal) coverage that can be expected from our approach, it also clearly underlines the potential of runtime enforcement techniques. The following non-covered provisions are cited in at least 5% of the cases: Art. 32 (security of processing, 22%); Art. 5(1)(c) (data minimization, 10%), and Art. 5(1)(f) (storage limitation, 9%). Security is a concern orthogonal to ours, whereas data minimization and storage limitation are generally not monitorable [2].

6 Related Work

GDPR Formalization. Our formalization of a core of GDPR is closest to Arfelt et al.'s work on monitoring the GDPR [2]. We extend their formalization by introducing UTs as input identifiers and covering special data categories and the right to erasure. We also fix two inaccuracies that we report in Appendix C.

Robaldo et al. have formalized a large part of the GDPR using reified Input/Output logic [37,38] and validated their formalization with legal experts [6]. Their work focuses on accurately encoding the law, but does not support enforcement. Smaller GDPR fragments have been represented in formalisms with some support for automated reasoning, such as deontic logic [1,31], LegalRuleML [33], OCL [44], OWL2 [11], and Prolog [16]. In a different line of research, several policy languages were designed explicitly with GDPR provisions in mind [3,20,41,47,48].

Language-based

	Consent	Purpose	Legal grounds	Special data	Right to... access	rectification	erasure	restriction	object	Derived data	Implementation
This work	✓	✓	✓	✓	✓	✓	✓	✓	✓	✓	✓
Ferrara & Spoto [18]	✓	✓									✓
Ferreira et al. [19]	✓	✓								✓	✓
Hublet et al. [25]	✓	✓								✓	✓
Karami et al. [28]	✓	✓					✓				
Tokas et al. [43]	✓	✓	✓					✓			
Wang et al. [47,48]	✓	✓								✓	✓

Data-store-based

	Consent	Purpose	Legal grounds	Special data	Right to... access	rectification	erasure	restriction	object	Derived data	Implementation
Barati et al. [4]	*	✓									✓
Chhetri et al. [12]	*	✓									✓
Dauden et al. [14]	*	✓			*	*	*	*	*		✓
Davari & Bertino [15]	*	✓									✓
Gjermundrød et al. [21]	*	✓					*				✓
Schwarzkopf et al. [40]	✓	✓			✓	✓		✓	✓		
Truong et al. [45]	*				*	*	*	*			✓

* Provision is covered, but data leaving the data store is not protected.

Fig. 5. GDPR compliance by design: coverage of the provisions in Sect. 3.1

GDPR Compliance by Design. Many approaches enforce a specific GDPR provision in software systems. To the best of our knowledge, none of these relies on a logical formalization of the GDPR. Figure 5 shows existing approaches based on their GDPR coverage: *consent*-based usage, *purpose*-based usage, *legal grounds*, *special data* categories; coverage of the *rights to access, rectification, erasure, restriction,* and *objection*; protection of *derived data*; and availability of an *implementation*.

Existing work can be classified into language-based approaches [42], which include TTC [25], and data-store-based approaches [27]. In language-based approaches, a programming language is instrumented to ensure privacy compliance either statically [18,19,43,46,47] or at runtime [19,25,28]. Language-based approaches can typically protect derived data, but they have not been widely applied so far beyond consent-based usage. In data-store-based approaches, personal data is stored in protected database containers (*data stores*) that controllers query through an API. Access-control mechanisms ensure data is only accessed with user consent. Within data stores, most GDPR rights can be exercised seamlessly [14,45]. Data processing, however, happens mainly outside of the data stores; as a result, data that leaves the database – and in particular, derived data – is no longer protected. The only work discussing the protection of derived data with such an approach [40] provides just a high-level roadmap without a concrete implementation.

7 Conclusion

We have presented the first enforceable specification of core GDPR provisions that comes together with an enforcement architecture for web applications. To the best of our knowledge, this work is the first to enforce a core set of GDPR provisions and protect derived data by tracking information flows.

We envision three main directions for future work. First, our coverage of legal provisions can be extended beyond the current fragment by relying on a more comprehensive but still enforceable formalization of the GDPR, which we plan to develop. Second, we will further investigate the performance of our enforcement mechanism under very large data volumes and number of users and study optimizations that may ease its deployment in real-world settings. Finally, we plan to extend our architecture by incorporating complementary techniques that allow for the coverage of those aspects of the GDPR (e.g., data and storage minimization) not readily amenable to monitoring techniques.

Acknowledgments. Arduin Brandts contributed to a preliminary version of the enforcement signature presented in Sect. 3.2. Jonas Degelo contributed to the development of the PDP prototype. Ahmed Bouhoula provided feedback on a earlier draft of the paper. François Hublet is supported by the Swiss National Science Foundation grant "Model-driven Security & Privacy" (204796).

A Privacy Code in Minitwit

In **Minitwit$^+$**, the additional code can be summarized as follows:

– In functions displaying user messages, we use a function filter_check to select only those messages for which the DS have given consent for purpose `Service`.

```
def filter_check(messages):
    messages2 = []
    checks = check_all('Service', messages)
    for i in range(0, len(messages)):
        if checks[i]:
            messages2.append(messages[i])
    return messages2
```

The function **check_all** is provided by WebTTC+. It takes a purpose p and a list of pairs of values and sets of UTs $[\langle v_1, \alpha_1 \rangle, \ldots, \langle v_k, \alpha_k \rangle]$, and returns a list of Booleans $[b_1, \ldots, b_k]$ such that each b_i is true iff v_i can be used with purpose p. To obtain the b_i, WebTTC+ communicates with the PDP [25].

– We define handlers to support the deletion and rectification of messages and friendship relationships. Deleting the text of the message or the ID of the friend should trigger the deletion of the entire message or relation, while messages whose text has been rectified should be marked as [edited]:

```
@handle_field_deletion('message', 'text')
def handle_message_text_deletion(i):
    sql("DELETE FROM message WHERE id = ?0", [i])
    return None


@handle_field_rectification('message', 'text')
def handle_message_text_rectification(i, new_text):
    row = sql("""SELECT author_id, text, pub_date
            FROM message WHERE id = ?0""", [i])[0]
    sql("""INSERT INTO message (author_id, text, pub_date)
            VALUES (?0, ?1, ?2)""",
        [row[0], new_text + " [edited]", row[2]])
    sql("DELETE FROM message WHERE id = ?0", [i])
    return None
```

The correctors **handle_field_deletion** and **handle_field_rectification**, provided by WebTTC+, allow programmers to define handlers.

B   User Interface

(See Fig. 6)

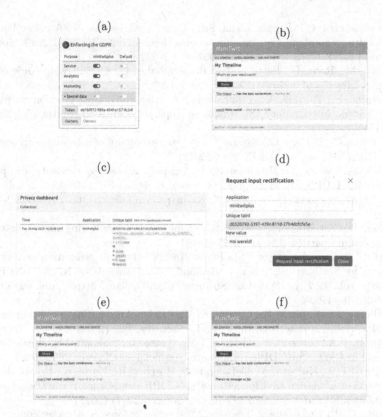

Fig. 6. (a) The browser extension (b) The Minitwit⁺ application (c) The dashboard entry corresponding to the "Hello world" in b (d) Requesting rectification of "Hello world" (e) After performing rectification (f) After revoking consent for "Hello world"

C   Inaccuracies in Arfelt et al. [2]

1. Arfelt et al.'s specification lacks $\blacklozenge\texttt{Collect}(ds, ut, sp)$ conjuncts, allowing consent given by *any user* to justify data usage.
2. In the right to object, the condition "there has been an objection since legal grounds have been claimed" is $\exists \ldots \neg (\neg\texttt{DSObject}(\ldots) \text{ S } \texttt{LegalGround}(\ldots))$, allowing applications to reclaim the same legal grounds to override objections.

References

1. Amantea, I.A., Robaldo, L., Sulis, E., Boella, G., Governatori, G.: Semi-automated checking for regulatory compliance in e-health. In: EDOCW 2021. IEEE (2021)
2. Arfelt, E., Basin, D., Debois, S.: Monitoring the GDPR. In: Sako, K., Schneider, S., Ryan, P.Y.A. (eds.) ESORICS 2019. LNCS, vol. 11735, pp. 681–699. Springer, Cham (2019). https://doi.org/10.1007/978-3-030-29959-0_33

3. Baramashetru, C.P., Tapia Tarifa, S.L., Owe, O., Gruschka, N.: A policy language to capture compliance of data protection requirements. In: IFM 2022. Springer, Cham (2022). https://doi.org/10.1007/978-3-031-07727-2_16

4. Barati, M., Rana, O., Petri, I., Theodorakopoulos, G.: GDPR compliance verification in Internet of Things. IEEE Access 8 (2020)

5. Bartocci, E., Falcone, Y., Francalanza, A., Reger, G.: Introduction to runtime verification. Introductory and Advanced Topics, Lectures on Runtime Verification (2018)

6. Bartolini, C., Lenzini, G., Santos, C.: A legal validation of a formal representation of GDPR articles. In: JURIX 2018 (2018)

7. Basin, D., Debois, S., Hildebrandt, T.: On purpose and by necessity: compliance under the GDPR. In: Meiklejohn, S., Sako, K. (eds.) FC 2018. LNCS, vol. 10957, pp. 20–37. Springer, Heidelberg (2018). https://doi.org/10.1007/978-3-662-58387-6_2

8. Basin, D., Klaedtke, F., Müller, S., Zălinescu, E.: Monitoring metric first-order temporal properties. JACM **62**(2) (2015)

9. Bier, C., Kühne, K., Beyerer, J.: PrivacyInsight: the next generation privacy dashboard. In: Schiffner, S., Serna, J., Ikonomou, D., Rannenberg, K. (eds.) APF 2016. LNCS, vol. 9857, pp. 135–152. Springer, Cham (2016). https://doi.org/10.1007/978-3-319-44760-5_9

10. Bollinger, D., Kubicek, K., Cotrini, C., Basin, D.: Automating cookie consent and GDPR violation detection. In: USENIX Security 2022 (2022)

11. Bonatti, P.A., Ioffredo, L., Petrova, I.M., Sauro, L., Siahaan, I.R.: Real-time reasoning in OWL2 for GDPR compliance. Artificial Intelligence 289 (2020)

12. Chhetri, T.R., Kurteva, A., DeLong, R.J., Hilscher, R., Korte, K., Fensel, A.: Data protection by design tool for automated GDPR compliance verification based on semantically modeled informed consent. Sensors **22**(7) (2022)

13. CMS: GDPR Enforcement Tracker (2023). www.enforcementtracker.com

14. Daudén-Esmel, C., Castellà-Roca, J., Viejo, A., Domingo-Ferrer, J.: Lightweight blockchain-based platform for GDPR-compliant personal data management. In: CSP 2021 (2021)

15. Davari, M., Bertino, E.: Access control model extensions to support data privacy protection based on GDPR. In: BigData 2019. IEEE (2019)

16. de Montety, C., Antignac, T., Slim, C.: GDPR modelling for log-based compliance checking. In: Meng, W., Cofta, P., Jensen, C.D., Grandison, T. (eds.) IFIPTM 2019. IAICT, vol. 563, pp. 1–18. Springer, Cham (2019). https://doi.org/10.1007/978-3-030-33716-2_1

17. Dwyer, M.B., Avrunin, G.S., Corbett, J.C.: Property specification patterns for finite-state verification. In: FMSP 1998 (1998)

18. Ferrara, P., Spoto, F.: Static analysis for GDPR compliance. In: ITASEC (2018)

19. Ferreira, M., Brito, T., Santos, J.F., Santos, N.: RuleKeeper: GDPR-aware personal data compliance for web frameworks. In: S&P 2023. IEEE (2022)

20. Gerl, A., Bennani, N., Kosch, H., Brunie, L.: LPL, towards a GDPR-compliant privacy language: formal definition and usage. Transactions on Large-Scale Data- and Knowledge-Centered Systems XXXVII (2018)

21. Gjermundrød, H., Dionysiou, I., Costa, K.: privacyTracker: a privacy-by-design GDPR-compliant framework with verifiable data traceability controls. In: Casteleyn, S., Dolog, P., Pautasso, C. (eds.) ICWE 2016. LNCS, vol. 9881, pp. 3–15. Springer, Cham (2016). https://doi.org/10.1007/978-3-319-46963-8_1

22. Goguen, J.A., Meseguer, J.: Security policies and security models. In: S&P 1982. IEEE (1982)

23. Havelund, K., Rosu, G. (eds.): Runtime Verification, ENTCS, vol. 55. Elsevier (2001)
24. Hublet, F., Basin, D., Krstić, S.: Real-time policy enforcement with metric first-order temporal logic. In: ESORICS 2022. vol. II. Springer, Cham (2022). https://doi.org/10.1007/978-3-031-17146-8_11
25. Hublet, F., Basin, D., Krstić, S.: User-controlled Privacy: Taint, Track, and Control. In: Proceedings of Privacy Enforcing Technologies (PoPETS) (2024), to appear
26. Hublet, F., Basin, D., Krstić, S.: Companion repository for "Enforcing the GDPR" (2023). https://gitlab.ethz.ch/fhublet/enforcing-the-gdpr
27. Janssen, H., Cobbe, J., Norval, C., Singh, J.: Decentralized data processing: personal data stores and the GDPR. International Data Privacy Law 10(4) (2020)
28. Karami, F., Basin, D., Johnsen, E.B.: DPL: a language for GDPR enforcement. In: CSF 2022. IEEE (2022)
29. Kutyłowski, M., Lauks-Dutka, A., Yung, M.: GDPR-challenges for reconciling legal rules with technical reality. In: ESORICS 2020, vol. I. Springer (2020)
30. Lehmann, N., et al.: STORM: refinement types for secure web applications. In: OSDI 2021 (2021)
31. Libal, T.: Towards automated GDPR compliance checking. In: Heintz, F., Milano, M., O'Sullivan, B. (eds.) TAILOR 2020. LNCS (LNAI), vol. 12641, pp. 3–19. Springer, Cham (2021). https://doi.org/10.1007/978-3-030-73959-1_1
32. Nguyen, T.T., Backes, M., Marnau, N., Stock, B.: Share first, ask later (or never?)-studying violations of GDPR's explicit consent in android apps. In: USENIX Security (2021)
33. Palmirani, M., Governatori, G.: Modelling legal knowledge for GDPR Compliance Checking. In: JURIX 2018 (2018)
34. Polikarpova, N., Stefan, D., Yang, J., Itzhaky, S., Hance, T., Solar-Lezama, A.: Liquid information flow control. PACMPL 4(ICFP) (2020)
35. Puhlmann, N., Wiesmaier, A., Heinemann, A.: Privacy dashboards for citizens and GDPR services for small data holders: a literature review. arXiv (2023)
36. Raschke, P., Küpper, A., Drozd, O., Kirrane, S.: Designing a GDPR-compliant and usable privacy dashboard. IFIP 2017 (2018)
37. Robaldo, L., Bartolini, C., Palmirani, M., Rossi, A., Martoni, M., Lenzini, G.: Formalizing GDPR provisions in reified I/O logic: the DAPRECO knowledge base. JLLI 29 (2020)
38. Robaldo, L., Sun, X.: Reified input/output logic: combining input/output logic and reification to represent norms coming from existing legislation. J. Log. Comput. 27(8) (2017)
39. Schneider, F.B.: Enforceable security policies. TISSEC 3(1) (2000)
40. Schwarzkopf, M., Kohler, E., Frans Kaashoek, M., Morris, R.: Position: GDPR compliance by construction. In: Gadepally, V., Mattson, T., Stonebraker, M., Wang, F., Luo, G., Laing, Y., Dubovitskaya, A. (eds.) DMAH/Poly -2019. LNCS, vol. 11721, pp. 39–53. Springer, Cham (2019). https://doi.org/10.1007/978-3-030-33752-0_3
41. Tokas, S., Owe, O.: A formal framework for consent management. In: Gotsman, A., Sokolova, A. (eds.) FORTE 2020. LNCS, vol. 12136, pp. 169–186. Springer, Cham (2020). https://doi.org/10.1007/978-3-030-50086-3_10
42. Tokas, S., Owe, O., Ramezanifarkhani, T.: Language-based mechanisms for privacy-by-design. Privacy and Identity Management, Data for Better Living (2020)
43. Tokas, S., Owe, O., Ramezanifarkhani, T.: Static checking of GDPR-related privacy compliance for object-oriented distributed systems. JLAMP 125 (2022)

44. Torre, D., Soltana, G., Sabetzadeh, M., Briand, L.C., Auffinger, Y., Goes, P.: Using models to enable compliance checking against the GDPR: an experience report. In: MODELS 2019. IEEE (2019)
45. Truong, N.B., Sun, K., Lee, G.M., Guo, Y.: GDPR-compliant personal data management: A blockchain-based solution. TIFS 15 (2019)
46. Wang, F., Ko, R., Mickens, J.: Riverbed: Enforcing user-defined privacy constraints in distributed web services. In: NSDI 2019 (2019)
47. Wang, L., et al.: PrivGuard. Privacy regulation compliance made easier. In: USENIX Security 2022 (2022)
48. Wang, L., Near, J.P., Somani, N., Gao, P., Low, A., Dao, D., Song, D.: Data capsule: a new paradigm for automatic compliance with data privacy regulations. In: Gadepally, V., Mattson, T., Stonebraker, M., Wang, F., Luo, G., Laing, Y., Dubovitskaya, A. (eds.) DMAH/Poly -2019. LNCS, vol. 11721, pp. 3–23. Springer, Cham (2019). https://doi.org/10.1007/978-3-030-33752-0_1
49. Yang, J., Hance, T., Austin, T.H., Solar-Lezama, A., Flanagan, C., Chong, S.: Precise, dynamic information flow for database-backed applications. In: Krintz, C., Berger, E. (eds.) PLDI 2016 (2016)

Remote

Identity-Based Matchmaking Encryption with Enhanced Privacy – A Generic Construction with Practical Instantiations

Xavier Boyen[1] and Qinyi Li[2]([✉])

[1] QUT, Brisbane, Australia
[2] Griffith University, Brisbane, Australia
qinyi.li71@gmail.com

Abstract. Identity-based matchmaking encryption (IB-ME), proposed by Ateniese et al. (Crypto 2019), is a type of matchmaking encryption (ME). In IB-ME, the sender can specify a target identity rcv during encryption, and the receiver can set a target identity snd during decryption. The ciphertext can be decrypted if snd matches the sender's identity σ, and rcv matches the receiver's identity ρ. The basic security notion of IB-ME is privacy, whose original definition ensures that σ, rcv, and the message remain hidden as long as rcv $\neq \rho$, regardless the relation between snd and σ. Francati et al. (IndoCrypt 2021) argue that the original privacy notion is unsatisfactory as it does not match the intuitive privacy guarantee of matching encryption. They revise the original privacy notion with an *enhanced privacy* notion to characterise meaningful privacy under the condition snd $\neq \sigma$ and construct an IB-ME system with the enhanced security in the plain model, albeit under a q-type pairing-based assumption. Chen et al. (AsiaCrypt 2022) leave how to construct IB-ME systems with enhanced privacy as an open problem. In this paper, we solve the problem by a generic construction of IB-ME with enhanced privacy. Instantiating our construction gives practical IB-ME systems with enhanced privacy from various standard assumptions.

Keywords: Identity-based · Matchmaking encryption · Enhanced privacy · Quantum resistance · Standard assumptions

1 Introduction

Matchmaking encryption (ME), proposed by Ateniese et al. [3], is a type of expressive encryption that allows both the sender and receiver to specify access policies so that the messages get decrypted when the policies are satisfied. Identity-based matchmaking encryption (IB-ME) is a special form of ME that supports equality policies over strings. While admitting less expressive access control policies, IB-ME, as showed by Ateniese at al. [3], is already powerful and allows interesting privacy-preserving applications, e.g., a fully anonymous bulletin board over the Tor network.

In an IB-ME system, the trusted authority issues identity-associated encryption and decryption keys. Each encryptor obtains an encryption key ek_σ on

G. Tsudik et al. (Eds.): ESORICS 2023, LNCS 14345, pp. 425–445, 2024.
https://doi.org/10.1007/978-3-031-51476-0_21

its identity σ. To encrypt a message m, the encryptor specifies the receiver's identity rcv and creates the ciphertext as ct $\leftarrow$ Enc(ek$_\sigma$, rcv, m). The decryptor whose identity is ρ obtains a decryption key dk$_\rho$ from the authority. To decrypt ct, the decryptor sets an identity snd, and runs the decryption algorithm Dec(dk$_\rho$, snd, ct). The decryption returns the message m if the matching conditions $\rho =$ rcv and snd $= \sigma$ are satisfied. The security of IB-ME, addressed by a series of works [3,7,13], requires authenticity and privacy. Authenticity ensures that no one can create a valid ciphertext on an identity σ without knowing the encryption key ek$_\sigma$. Ciphertext privacy ensures that under a non-matching condition, the ciphertext ct does not reveal the underlying message *and* the identities σ and rcv.

While the authenticity definition is natural, the privacy definition is subtle. The original IB-ME privacy definition ensures that the message and the sender's identity σ remain hidden as long as the receiver's identity ρ does not match with rcv, the identity specified during encryption, regardless of the relations between snd and σ. In other words, the sender's identity σ plays no role in privacy. The original privacy definition, therefore, as argued by Francati et al. [13], does not meet the intuitive privacy guarantee of matchmaking encryption – "(the ciphertext cannot be decrypted if the) sender's attributes do not satisfy the policies held by the receiver" [3].

The generic construction of IB-ME proposed by Wang et al. [23] gives an example. In the construction, a message is encrypted using a 2-level hierarchical identity-based encryption (HIBE) with the augmented identity rcv|σ. The receiver's private decryption key sk$_\rho$ is for the higher level identity ρ. The ciphertext can be decrypted by first delegating sk$_\rho$ to a level-2 identity key sk$_{\rho|\text{snd}}$ with snd chosen on the fly. Decryption works under the matching conditions, i.e., ρ|snd = rcv|σ. However, most HIBE systems allow using the private key of an identity to directly decrypt the ciphertext under any extended identities, e.g., sk$_\rho$ can decrypt ciphertexts under identity ρ|$\star$, often faster than delegation. So, the receiver does not have to match the sender's identity σ for decryption. We note this is the case with lattice-based instantiation of the generic construction suggested by Wang et al. [23].

To characterise meaningful privacy for IB-ME under the mismatch condition snd $\neq \sigma$ (even when $\rho =$ rcv) with snd chosen on the fly by any decryptor, Francati et al. [13] revise the original privacy notion with an *enhanced privacy* notion. The enhanced privacy notion ensures that the identities σ and rcv, and the underlying message from the ciphertext remain hidden, as long as one of the non-matching conditions $\sigma \neq$ snd and $\rho \neq$ rcv is satisfied. The model allows the adversary to get a decryption key for the identity ρ that equals rcv). Meanwhile, in IB-ME, any user, including the adversary, can generate strings snd, trying to match with the sender's identity σ. The enhanced privacy notion then requires that σ is from an (adversarially chosen) distribution with sufficient min-entropy, so a simple guessing attack does not work.

All known IB-ME systems do not meet the enhanced privacy notion except the one proposed by Francati et al. [13], which is based on Gentry's anonymous identity-based encryption system [14] secure in the plain model under the q-ABDHE assumption, a q-type assumption from pairings. Chen et al. [7] give an IB-ME system from the standard SXDH assumption without the enhanced privacy and leave the following open problem:

> "*How can we construct IB-ME systems that satisfy the enhanced privacy under standard assumptions?*" —Chen at al. (AsiaCrypt 2022)

1.1 Our Results

We solve the problem with a generic construction of IB-ME. Our construction uses several well-studied cryptographic primitives, including an anonymous IBE system [6], an identity-based signature system [17], an average-case randomness extractor [9], and a reusable computational extractor [8].

Table 1. Comparison among IB-ME systems

IB-ME Systems	Enhanced Privacy	Assumption	ROM	Quantum Resistant
Ours + DLP'14 [11] + Cert-Falcon [12]	✔	NTRU	✔	✔
Ours + ABB'10–IBE [1] + ABB'10–IBS [1]	✔	LWE	✔	✔
Ours + BW'06 [6] + PS'06 [21]	✔	DLin+CDH	✗	✗
FGRV'21 [13]	✔	q-ABDHE	✗	✗
CLWW'22 [7]	✗	SXDH	✗	✗
AFNA'19 [3]	✗	BDH	✔	✗
WWLZ'22 [23]	✗	LWE	✔ or ✗	✔

Instantiating the primitives with existing efficient constructions from standard assumptions in the plain model leads to several concrete IB-ME systems to solve the open problem left by Chen et al. [7].

Moreover, in the random oracle model (ROM), the aforementioned primitives have practical constructions, giving practical IB-ME systems in the ROM. For example, using the practical anonymous IBE system by Ducas et al. [11] with IBS system derived from the Falcon signature [12], the certification-based approach (Scheme 1, [17]), and simple random-oracle-based (reusable) randomness extractors, we obtain the first piratical IB-ME system with enhanced privacy and quantum resistance from the NTRU assumption. Table 1 compares our instantiated IB-ME systems and the existing IB-ME systems. We discuss the instantiations of our generic IB-ME system in Sect. 5.

2 Preliminaries

Let $x \leftarrow X$ denote drawing a sample x from the distribution X. We let $x \leftarrow U(\mathcal{X})$ denote by drawing a sample x uniformly at random from a finite set $\mathcal{X}$.

Let $\mathcal{D}$ be a countable domain. The statistical distance between $X \in \mathcal{D}$ and $Y \in \mathcal{D}$ is $SD(X, Y) := \frac{1}{2} \sum_{v \in \mathcal{D}} |\Pr[X = v] - \Pr[Y = v]|$. The min-entropy of a random variable $X \in \mathcal{X}$ is $\mathrm{H}_\infty(X) := -\log(\max_x(\Pr[X = x]))$. The average min-entropy of a random variable $X \in \mathcal{X}$ given a random variable $Y \in \mathcal{Y}$ is $\tilde{\mathrm{H}}_\infty(X|Y) := -\log(\mathbb{E}_{y \leftarrow Y}[2^{-\mathrm{H}_\infty(X|Y=y)}])$. We need the following useful lemma.

Lemma 1 ([9] Lemma 2.2). *Let X, Y and Z be random variables where Z has at most 2^λ positive-probability values. Then $\tilde{\mathrm{H}}_\infty(X|Y, Z) \geq \tilde{\mathrm{H}}_\infty(X|Y)$, and in particular, $\tilde{\mathrm{H}}_\infty(X|Z) \geq \mathrm{H}_\infty(X) - \lambda$.*

We abbreviate "probabilistic polynomial time" as "p.p.t". We denote by $\mathsf{negl}(n)$ some negligible function in n, i.e., it decreases faster than the inverse of any polynomial function. We use collision-resistant hash functions defined as follows.

Definition 1. *Let λ be the security parameter, $\mathcal{X}$, $\mathcal{Y}$ be two sets. A hash function $H : \mathcal{X} \rightarrow \mathcal{Y}$ is collision-resistant if for all p.p.t adversary $\mathcal{A}$, $\mathsf{Adv}^{\mathsf{coll}}_{H,\mathcal{A}}(\lambda) := \Pr[\mathcal{A}(\lambda, H) \rightarrow x_1, x_2 \in \mathcal{X} : x_1 \neq x_2 \land H(x_1) = H(x_2)]$ is negligible in λ.*

2.1 Randomness Extractors

We use information-theoretical average-case randomness extractors [9] and computational reusable randomness extractors [8].

Definition 2 (Average-Case Randomness Extractor). *A p.p.t commutable function $\mathsf{Ext} : \{0,1\}^v \times \{0,1\}^\ell \rightarrow \{0,1\}^d$ is an average-case (ℓ, k, d, ϵ)-randomness extractor if for all random variables (X, Y) with $X \in \{0,1\}^\ell$, $\tilde{\mathrm{H}}_\infty(X|Y) \geq k$,*

$$SD((K, \mathsf{Ext}(K, X), Y), (K, U(\{0,1\}^d), Y)) \leq \epsilon$$

where $K \leftarrow U(\{0,1\}^v)$.

Definition 3 (Computational Reusable Extractor). *Let λ be the security parameter. A p.p.t algorithm $\mathsf{ReExt} : \mathcal{X} \times \mathcal{K} \rightarrow \mathcal{Y}$ is a (k, m)-reusable extractor for $m = \mathsf{poly}(\lambda)$ if for all efficiently samplable random variables $\Sigma \in \mathcal{K}$ and Aux such that $\tilde{\mathrm{H}}_\infty(\Sigma|\mathsf{Aux}) \geq k$, the advantage $\mathsf{Adv}^{\mathsf{ReExt}}_{\mathcal{A}}(\lambda)$, defined as*

$$\left| \Pr[\mathcal{A}(\lambda, \mathsf{Aux}, \{(x_i, \mathsf{ReExt}(x_i, \sigma))\}_{i \in [m]}) = 1] - \Pr[\mathcal{A}(\lambda, \mathsf{Aux}, \{(x_i, y_i)\}_{i \in [m]}) = 1] \right|$$

is negligible in λ for all p.p.t adversaries $\mathcal{A}$, where $\sigma \leftarrow \Sigma$, $x_i \leftarrow U(\mathcal{X})$ and $y_i \leftarrow U(\mathcal{Y})$ are sampled independently.

2.2 Identity-Based Matchmaking Encryption

Let λ be the security parameter. An IB-ME system with identity space $\mathcal{I}$, message space $\mathcal{M}$, and ciphertext space $\mathcal{C}$ consist of five p.p.t algorithms. $\mathsf{Setup}(1^\lambda)$ returns a master public key pub and a master private key msk. We assume pub is an implicit input to other algorithms. Given $\sigma \in \mathcal{I}$, SKGen(msk, σ) returns an encryption key ek_σ. RKGen(msk, ρ) returns a decryption key dk_ρ for $\rho \in \mathcal{I}$. Given rcv $\in \mathcal{I}$ and m $\in \mathcal{M}$, Enc(ek_σ, rcv, m) returns a ciphertext ct. Dec(dk_ρ, snd, ct) returns a message in $\mathcal{M}$ or a special symber $\perp$.

The correctness of an IB-ME system requires that if the algorithms are followed correctly, and the matching condition (i.e., $\sigma = $ snd $\wedge \rho = $ rcv) is satisfied, the decryption algorithm will recover the message from the ciphertext w.h.p. We follow Francati et al. [13] to define the *enhanced* privacy and authenticity.

Definition 4 (Correctness of IB-ME). *An IB-ME system* (Setup, SKGen, RKGen, Enc, Dec) *is correct if for all* λ, (pub, msk) $\leftarrow$ Setup(1^λ), σ, ρ, rcv, snd $\in \mathcal{I}$, *and* m $\in \mathcal{M}$ *with* $\sigma = $ snd $\wedge \rho = $ rcv:

$$\Pr\left[\mathsf{Dec}(dk_\rho, snd, ct) = m\right] \geq 1 - \mathsf{negl}(\lambda)$$

where $ek_\sigma \leftarrow$ SKGen(msk, σ), $dk_\rho \leftarrow$ RKGen(msk, ρ), *and* ct $\leftarrow$ Enc(ek_σ, rcv, m).

Definition 5 (Enhanced IB-ME Privacy). *Let* λ *be the security parameter. We say that an IB-ME system* Π *has privacy if for all* k-*admissible p.p.t adversary* $\mathcal{A} = (\mathcal{A}_1, \mathcal{A}_2)$:

$$\mathsf{Adv}^{\mathsf{priv}^+}_{\Pi,\mathcal{A}}(\lambda) := \left| \Pr\left[\mathsf{Exp}^{\mathsf{priv}^+-0}_{\Pi,\mathcal{A}}(\lambda) = 1\right] - \Pr\left[\mathsf{Exp}^{\mathsf{priv}^+-1}_{\Pi,\mathcal{A}}(\lambda) = 1\right]\right| \leq \mathsf{negl}(\lambda)$$

where the security experiments $\mathsf{Exp}^{\mathsf{priv}^+-b}_{\Pi,\mathcal{A}}(\lambda)$ *for* $b \in \{0,1\}$ *are defined in 1 and the probability is over the randomness of the algorithms. An adversary* $\mathcal{A} = (\mathcal{A}_1, \mathcal{A}_2)$ *is* k-*admissible if* $\forall \rho \in L_2$, *it satisfies the following invariant:*

$$(\rho \neq rcv_0^* \wedge \rho \neq rcv_1^*) \vee (\mathrm{H}_\infty(\mathcal{ID}_0) \wedge \mathrm{H}_\infty(\mathcal{ID}_1) \geq k)$$
$$\vee (\rho \neq rcv_0^* \wedge \mathrm{H}_\infty(\mathcal{ID}_1) \geq k) \vee (\mathrm{H}_\infty(\mathcal{ID}_0) \geq k \wedge \rho \neq rcv_1^*)$$

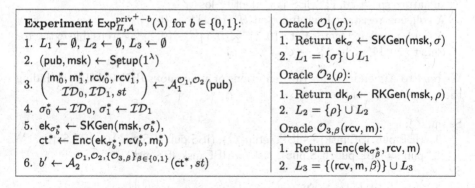

Fig. 1. IB-ME Enhanced Privacy Experiments

Definition 6 (IB-ME Authenticity). *Let λ be the security parameter. Consider the security experiment $\mathsf{Exp}^{\mathsf{auth}}_{\Pi,\mathcal{A}}(\lambda) = 1$ defined in Fig. 2. We say that an IB-ME system Π has authenticity if for all p.p.t adversary $\mathcal{A}$:*

$$\mathsf{Adv}^{\mathsf{auth}}_{\Pi,\mathcal{A}}(\lambda) := \Pr\left[\mathsf{Exp}^{\mathsf{auth}}_{\Pi,\mathcal{A}}(\lambda) = 1\right] \le \mathsf{negl}(\lambda)$$

where the probability is over the randomness of $\mathcal{A}$ and the IB-ME system.

Experiment $\mathsf{Exp}^{\mathsf{auth}}_{\Pi,\mathcal{A}}(\lambda)$:	Oracle $\mathcal{O}_1(\sigma)$:
1. $L_1 \leftarrow \emptyset,\ L_2 \leftarrow \emptyset,\ L_3 \leftarrow \emptyset$	1. Return $\mathsf{ek}_\sigma \leftarrow \mathsf{SKGen}(\mathsf{msk}, \rho)$
2. $(\mathsf{pub}, \mathsf{msk}) \leftarrow \mathsf{Setup}(1^\lambda)$	2. $L_1 = \{\sigma\} \cup L_1$
3. $(\mathsf{ct}^*, \rho^*, \mathsf{snd}^*) \leftarrow \mathcal{A}_1^{\mathcal{O}_1, \mathcal{O}_2, \mathcal{O}_3}(\mathsf{pub})$	Oracle $\mathcal{O}_2(\rho)$:
4. $\mathsf{dk}_{\rho^*} \leftarrow \mathsf{RKGen}(\mathsf{msk}, \rho^*)$	1. $\mathsf{dk}_\rho \leftarrow \mathsf{RKGen}(\mathsf{msk}, \rho)$
5. $\mathsf{m}^* \leftarrow \mathsf{Dec}(\mathsf{dk}_{\rho^*}, \mathsf{snd}^*, \mathsf{ct}^*)$	2. $L_2 = \{\rho\} \cup L_2$
6. If $\forall \sigma \in L_1 : (\sigma \neq \mathsf{snd}^*) \wedge (\mathsf{m}^* \neq \bot)$	Oracle $\mathcal{O}_3(\sigma, \mathsf{rcv}, \mathsf{m})$:
and $(\rho^*, \mathsf{rcv}^*, \mathsf{m}^*) \notin L_3$, return 1;	1. $\mathsf{ct} \leftarrow \mathsf{Enc}(\mathsf{ek}_\sigma, \mathsf{rcv}, \mathsf{m})$
Otherwise, return 0	2. $L_3 = \{(\sigma, \mathsf{rcv}, \mathsf{m})\} \cup L_3$

Fig. 2. IB-ME Authenticity Experiment

3   Construction

Let $\lambda \in \mathbb{N}$ be the security parameter. All parameters are functions of λ. Our construction uses the following components:

- An IBE system IBE with identity space $\mathcal{I} = \{0,1\}^\ell$, message space $\mathcal{M}_{\mathsf{ibe}}$, and ciphertext space $\mathcal{C}_{\mathsf{ibe}}$; An IBS system IBS with identity space $\mathcal{I} = \{0,1\}^\ell$ and signature space $\{0,1\}^d$. IBS is η-identity lossy.
- A collision-resistant hash function $H : \{0,1\}^* \to \{0,1\}^t$.
- A randomness extractor $\mathsf{Ext} : \{0,1\}^v \times \{0,1\}^\ell \to \{0,1\}^d$; A reusable extractor $\mathsf{ReExt} : \{0,1\}^s \times \{0,1\}^\ell \to \mathcal{C}_{\mathsf{ibe}}$.

We refer to Appendix A for the definitions of anonymous IBE and IBS, including their correctness and security.

$\mathsf{Setup}(1^\lambda)$:
    1. $(\mathsf{IBE.pub}, \mathsf{IBE.msk}) \leftarrow \mathsf{IBE.Setup}(1^\lambda)$, $(\mathsf{IBS.pub}, \mathsf{IBS.msk}) \leftarrow \mathsf{IBS.Setup}(1^\lambda)$
    2. $\mathsf{pub} := (\mathsf{IBE.pub}, \mathsf{IBS.pub})$, $\mathsf{msk} := (\mathsf{IBE.msk}, \mathsf{IBS.msk})$
$\mathsf{SKGen}(\mathsf{msk}, \sigma)$:
    1. $\mathsf{sk}_\sigma \leftarrow \mathsf{IBS.Extract}(\mathsf{IBS.msk}, \sigma)$, $\mathsf{ek}_\sigma := (\mathsf{sk}_\sigma, \sigma)$
$\mathsf{RKGen}(\mathsf{msk}, \rho)$:
    1. $\mathsf{sk}_\rho \leftarrow \mathsf{IBE.Extract}(\mathsf{IBE.msk}, \rho)$, $\mathsf{dk}_\rho := (\mathsf{sk}_\rho, \rho)$

$\mathsf{Enc}(\mathsf{ek}_\sigma, \mathsf{rcv}, \sigma, \mathsf{m})$:

1. $r \leftarrow U(\{0,1\}^\ell)$, $K_1 \leftarrow U(\{0,1\}^s)$, $K_2 \leftarrow U(\{0,1\}^v)$
2. $\kappa_1 \leftarrow \mathsf{ReExt}(K_1, \sigma)$, $\kappa_2 \leftarrow \mathsf{Ext}(K_2, r)$
3. $\tilde{c} \leftarrow \mathsf{IBE}.\mathsf{Enc}(\mathsf{rcv}, (\mathsf{m}||r))$, $c \leftarrow \tilde{c} \oplus \kappa_1$
4. $\tilde{s} \leftarrow \mathsf{IBS}.\mathsf{Sign}(\mathsf{sk}_\sigma, H(c||r||K_1||K_2))$, $s \leftarrow \tilde{s} \oplus \kappa_2$
5. Return $\mathsf{ct} := (c, s, K_1, K_2)$

$\mathsf{Dec}(\mathsf{dk}_\rho, \mathsf{snd}, \mathsf{ct})$:

1. Parse ct into (c, s, K_1, K_2), return $\perp$ if ct doesn't parse
2. $\kappa_1' \leftarrow \mathsf{ReExt}(K_1, \mathsf{snd})$, $\mathsf{m}'||r' \leftarrow \mathsf{IBE}.\mathsf{Dec}(\mathsf{dk}_\rho, c \oplus \kappa_1')$
3. Return m' if $1 \leftarrow \mathsf{IBS}.\mathsf{Ver}(\mathsf{snd}, H(c||r'||K_1||K_2), s \oplus \mathsf{Ext}(K_2, r'))$;
   Otherwise, return $\perp$

Correctness. We show that under the matching condition, i.e., $\sigma = \mathsf{snd} \wedge \rho = \mathsf{rcv}$, the original message will be recovered, i.e., $\mathsf{m}' = \mathsf{m}$. The condition $\sigma = \mathsf{snd}$ ensures $\kappa_1 = \mathsf{ReExt}(K_1, \sigma) = \mathsf{ReExt}(K_1, \mathsf{snd}) = \kappa_1'$. Under the condition $\rho = \mathsf{rcv}$ and the correctness of the IBE system IBE, with all but negligible probability, step 2 of the decryption algorithm $\mathsf{Dec}(\mathsf{dk}_\rho, \mathsf{snd}, \mathsf{ct})$ gives

$$\mathsf{m}'||r' = \mathsf{IBE}.\mathsf{Dec}(\mathsf{dk}_\rho, c \oplus \kappa_1')) = \mathsf{IBE}.\mathsf{Dec}(\mathsf{dk}_\rho, c \oplus \kappa_1))$$
$$= \mathsf{IBE}.\mathsf{Dec}(\mathsf{dk}_\rho, \tilde{c}) = \mathsf{m}||r$$

Moreover, under the condition $\sigma = \mathsf{snd}$ and the correctness of the IBS system IBS, step 3 of the decryption algorithm returns

$$\mathsf{IBS}.\mathsf{Ver}(\mathsf{snd}, H(c||r'||K_1||K_2), s \oplus \mathsf{Ext}(K_2, r'))$$
$$= \mathsf{IBS}.\mathsf{Ver}(\sigma, H(c||r||K_1||K_2), s \oplus \mathsf{Ext}(K_2, r))$$
$$= \mathsf{IBS}.\mathsf{Ver}(\sigma, H(c||r||K_1||K_2), \mathsf{IBS}.\mathsf{Sign}(\mathsf{sk}_\sigma, H(c||r||K_1||K_2))) = 1$$

with all but negligible probability. Hence, the decryption algorithm finally outputs the encrypted message m with all but negligible probability.

4   Security of the IB-ME System

The enhanced privacy (5) and authenticity (Definition 6) of the proposed generic construction can be stated by the following theorems. We refer to Appendix A for the security notions of anonymous IBE and IBS.

Theorem 1. *Let λ be the security parameter. If IBE has INDr-ID-CPA security (Definition 8), IBS is η-identity lossy (Definition 11), and ReExt is a $(k', \mathsf{poly}(\lambda))$-reusable extractor (Definition 3), and Ext is a $(\ell, k, d, \mathsf{negl}(\lambda))$-strong extractor with $k \geq \ell - t$ (Definition 2), the IB-ME system Π has the enhanced privacy (Definition 5) for all p.p.t $(k' + \eta)$-admissible adversaries.*

Theorem 2. *If IBS is EUF-ID-CMA secure (Definition 10) and hash function H is collision-resistant (Definition 1), the IB-ME system Π has authenticity.*

4.1   Proof of Enhanced Privacy

Proof (Proof of Theorem 1). In order to be valid, i.e., $k' + \eta$-admissible, according to Definition 5, the adversary $\mathcal{A}$ must satisfy one of the four mismatch conditions:

$$\bar{\mathsf{M}}_1 : \forall \rho \in L_2, \rho \neq \mathsf{rcv}_0^* \wedge \rho \neq \mathsf{rcv}_1^*$$
$$\bar{\mathsf{M}}_2 : (\mathsf{H}_\infty(\mathcal{ID}_0), \mathsf{H}_\infty(\mathcal{ID}_1)) \geq k' + \eta$$
$$\bar{\mathsf{M}}_3 : \mathsf{H}_\infty(\mathcal{ID}_0) \geq k' + \eta \wedge \forall \rho \in L_2, \rho \neq \mathsf{rcv}_1^*$$
$$\bar{\mathsf{M}}_4 : \forall \rho \in L_2, \rho \neq \mathsf{rcv}_0^* \wedge \mathsf{H}_\infty(\mathcal{ID}_1) \geq k' + \eta$$

We prove Lemmas 2, 3, 4, and 5 to prove the theorem. We use sequences of hybrid experiments. Each of the hybrid experiments outputs a binary value. We denote by $\mathsf{Hyb}_i \Rightarrow \mu$ that the i-th hybrid experiment outputs a bit value μ.

Lemma 2. *Under the condition* $\bar{\mathsf{M}}_1$, *for some negligible* $\mathsf{negl}_1(\lambda)$, *we have*

$$\left| \Pr[\mathsf{Exp}_{\Pi,\mathcal{A}}^{\mathsf{priv}^+ - 0}(\lambda) = 1 | \bar{\mathsf{M}}_1] - \Pr[\mathsf{Exp}_{\Pi,\mathcal{A}}^{\mathsf{priv}^+ - 1}(\lambda) = 1 | \bar{\mathsf{M}}_1] \right| \leq 4\mathsf{Adv}_{\mathsf{IBE},\mathcal{B}}^{\mathsf{indr}}(\lambda) + \mathsf{negl}_1(\lambda)$$

Proof. We define the hybrid experiments below under the condition $\bar{\mathsf{M}}_1 : \forall \rho \in L_2, \rho \neq \mathsf{rcv}_0^* \wedge \rho \neq \mathsf{rcv}_1^*$. We assume that in all hybrid experiments, for $i = 0, 1$, $\mathcal{ID}_i$ are constant distributions, so the adversary knows σ_i^*.

Hyb_0: Identical to $\mathsf{Exp}_{\Pi,\mathcal{A}}^{\mathsf{priv}^+ - 0}(\lambda)$ defined in Definition 5. On receiving $(\mathsf{m}_0^*, \mathsf{m}_1^*, \mathsf{rcv}_0^*, \mathsf{rcv}_1^*, \mathcal{ID}_0, \mathcal{ID}_1, st)$ from the adversary $\mathcal{A}_1$, the challenge ciphertext ct^* is constructed as follows:
  1. For $i = 0, 1$, $\sigma_i^* \leftarrow \mathcal{ID}_i$, $\mathsf{ek}_{\sigma_i^*} \leftarrow \mathsf{IBS.Extract}(\mathsf{IBS.msk}, \sigma_i^*)$
  2. $r^* \leftarrow U(\{0,1\}^\ell)$, $K_1^* \leftarrow U(\{0,1\}^s)$, $K_2^* \leftarrow U(\{0,1\}^v)$
  3. $\kappa_1^* \leftarrow \mathsf{ReExt}(K_1^*, \sigma_0^*))$, $\kappa_2 \leftarrow \mathsf{Ext}(K_2^*, r^*)$
  4. $\tilde{c}^* \leftarrow \mathsf{IBE.Enc}(\mathsf{rcv}_0^*, (\mathsf{m}_0^* || r^*))$, $c^* \leftarrow \tilde{c}^* \oplus \kappa_1^*$
  5. $\tilde{s} \leftarrow \mathsf{IBS.Sign}(\mathsf{sk}_\sigma, H(c^* || r^* || K_1^* || K_2^*))$, $s^* \leftarrow \tilde{s}^* \oplus \kappa_2^*$
  6. Return $\mathsf{ct} := (c^*, s^*, K_1^*, K_2^*)$

Hyb_1: This is identical to Hyb_0 except that the component $\tilde{c}^* \leftarrow U(\mathcal{C}_{\mathsf{ibe}})$.

Hyb_2: Same as Hyb_1 except $s^* \leftarrow \mathsf{IBS.Sign}(\mathsf{sk}_{\sigma_0^*}, H(c^* || r_0^* || K_1^* || K_2^*)) \oplus w$ for a random string $w \leftarrow U(\{0,1\}^d)$.

Hyb_3: Same as Hyb_2 except that s^* is generated using IBS with σ_1^*, $\mathsf{ek}_{\sigma_1^*}$, and r_1^*, i.e., $s^* \leftarrow \mathsf{IBS.Sign}(\mathsf{sk}_{\sigma_1^*}, H(c^* || r^* || K_1^* || K_2^*)) \oplus w$.

Hyb_4: Same as Hyb_3 except $s^* \leftarrow \mathsf{IBS.Sign}(\mathsf{sk}_{\sigma_1^*}, H(c^* || r^* || K_1^* || K_2^*)) \oplus \mathsf{Ext}(K_2^*, r^*)$.

Hyb_5: Same as Hyb_4 except that κ_1^* is computed using σ_1^*, i.e., $\kappa_1^* \leftarrow \mathsf{ReExt}(K_1^*, \sigma_1^*)$.

Hyb_6: Same as Hyb_5 except $\tilde{c}^* \leftarrow \mathsf{IBE.Enc}(\mathsf{rcv}_1^*, (\mathsf{m}_1^* || r^*))$.

The difference between Hyb_0 and Hyb_1 is how $\tilde{c}$ is computed. In Hyb_0, $\tilde{c} \leftarrow \mathsf{IBE.Enc}(\mathsf{rcv}_o^*, (\mathsf{m}_0^* || r^*))$ and in Hyb_1, $\tilde{c} \leftarrow U(\mathcal{C}_{\mathsf{ibe}})$. Under the condition $\bar{\mathsf{M}}_1$, rcv_0^* is not known to the adversary. By the INDr-ID-CPA security of IBE, a routine reduction gives an algorithm $\mathcal{B}$ (see Sect. B, Appendix) such that

$$|\Pr[\mathsf{Hyb}_0 \Rightarrow 1] - \Pr[\mathsf{Hyb}_1 \Rightarrow 1]| \le 2\mathsf{Adv}^{\mathsf{indr}}_{\mathsf{IBE},\mathcal{B}}(\lambda) \tag{1}$$

Hyb_2 differs from Hyb_1 by using a random d-bit string w to replace $\mathsf{Ext}(K^*_2, r^*)$. In Hyb_1, r^* is only used to compute s^*. Note that $H(c^* \| r^* \| K^*_1 \| k^*_2) = h$ contains at most 2^t values. Hence, as per Lemma 1, $\tilde{\mathsf{H}}_\infty(r^*_0|h) \ge \mathsf{H}_\infty(r^*_0) - t = \ell - t$. Since Ext is an $(\ell, k \ge \ell - t, d, \mathsf{negl}'_1(\lambda))$-randomness extractor, $SD((K^*_2, \mathsf{Ext}(K^*_2, r^*_0), (K^*_2, w)) \le \mathsf{negl}'_1(\lambda)$, and thus,

$$|\Pr[\mathsf{Hyb}_1 \Rightarrow 1] - \Pr[\mathsf{Hyb}_2 \Rightarrow 1]| \le \mathsf{negl}'_1(\lambda) \tag{2}$$

The change from Hyb_2 and Hyb_3 does not change the distribution of s^* as it is uniformly random over $\{0,1\}^d$ due to the one-time pad w. Hence,

$$\Pr[\mathsf{Hyb}_2 \Rightarrow 1] = \Pr[\mathsf{Hyb}_3 \Rightarrow 1] \tag{3}$$

Hyb_4 differs from Hyb_3 by using $\mathsf{Ext}(K^*_2, r^*)$ instead of a random string w. Using the same argument as in the proof of Inequality 2, we have

$$|\Pr[\mathsf{Hyb}_3 \Rightarrow 1] - \Pr[\mathsf{Hyb}_4 \Rightarrow 1]| \le \mathsf{negl}''_1(\lambda) \tag{4}$$

Hyb_5 differs from Hyb_4 on computing κ^*_1 using σ^*_1. This does not change the distribution of the challenge ciphertext because κ^*_1 can only affect c^*, which, is random and independent of σ^*_0 due to the one-time pad $\tilde{c}^*$. So, we have

$$\Pr[\mathsf{Hyb}_4 \Rightarrow 1] - \Pr[\mathsf{Hyb}_5 \Rightarrow 1]| \le \mathsf{negl}'''_1(\lambda) \tag{5}$$

Hyb_6 sets $\tilde{c}^* := \mathsf{IBE}.\mathsf{Enc}(\mathsf{rcv}^*_1, (m^*_1 \| r^*))$ instead of $\tilde{c}^* \leftarrow U(\mathcal{C}_{\mathsf{ibe}})$ as in Hyb_5. Using the same proof for Inequality 1 gives

$$|\Pr[\mathsf{Hyb}_5 \Rightarrow 1] - \Pr[\mathsf{Hyb}_6 \Rightarrow 1]| \le 2\mathsf{Adv}^{\mathsf{indr}}_{\mathsf{IBE},\mathcal{C}}(\lambda) \tag{6}$$

As Hyb_6 is identical to $\mathsf{Exp}^{\mathsf{priv}^+ - 1}_{\Pi,\mathcal{A}}(\lambda)$, under the condition $\bar{\mathsf{M}}_1$, we conclude with

$$\left| \Pr[\mathsf{Exp}^{\mathsf{priv}^+ - 0}_{\Pi,\mathcal{A}}(\lambda) = 1|\bar{\mathsf{M}}_1] - \Pr[\mathsf{Exp}^{\mathsf{priv}^+ - 1}_{\Pi,\mathcal{A}}(\lambda) = 1|\bar{\mathsf{M}}_1] \right|$$
$$\le |\Pr[\mathsf{Hyb}_6 \Rightarrow 1] - \Pr[\mathsf{Hyb}_0 \Rightarrow 1]| \le 4 \cdot \mathsf{Adv}^{\mathsf{indr}}_{\mathsf{IBE},\mathcal{B}}(\lambda) + \mathsf{negl}_1(\lambda)$$

Lemma 3. *Under the condition $\bar{\mathsf{M}}_2$, for some negligible* $\mathsf{negl}(\lambda)$, *we have*

$$\left| \Pr[\mathsf{Exp}^{\mathsf{priv}^+ - 0}_{\Pi,\mathcal{A}}(\lambda) = 1|\bar{\mathsf{M}}_2] - \Pr[\mathsf{Exp}^{\mathsf{priv}^+ - 1}_{\Pi,\mathcal{A}}(\lambda) = 1|\bar{\mathsf{M}}_2] \right| \le \mathsf{Adv}^{\mathsf{ReExt}}_{\mathcal{D}}(\lambda) + \mathsf{negl}_2(\lambda)$$

Proof. We define hybrid experiments below under the condition $\bar{\mathsf{M}}_2 : (\mathsf{H}_\infty(\mathcal{ID}_0), \mathsf{H}_\infty(\mathcal{ID}_1)) \ge k' + \eta$. The adversary does not directly know σ^*_0 and σ^*_1.

Hyb_0: Identical to $\mathsf{Exp}^{\mathsf{priv}^+ - 0}_{\Pi,\mathcal{A}}(\lambda)$ (Fig. 1). On receiving $(m^*_0, m^*_1, \mathsf{rcv}^*_0, \mathsf{rcv}^*_1, \mathcal{ID}_0, \mathcal{ID}_1, st)$ from the adversary $\mathcal{A}_1$, the ciphertext ct^* is constructed as:
1. For $i = 0, 1$, $\sigma^*_i \leftarrow \mathcal{ID}_i$, $\mathsf{ek}_{\sigma^*_i} \leftarrow \mathsf{IBS}.\mathsf{Extract}(\mathsf{IBS}.\mathsf{msk}, \sigma^*_i)$
2. $r^* \leftarrow U(\{0,1\}^\ell)$, $K^*_1 \leftarrow U(\{0,1\}^s)$, $K^*_2 \leftarrow U(\{0,1\}^v)$

3. $\kappa_1^* \leftarrow \mathsf{ReExt}(K_1^*, \sigma_0^*)), \kappa_2 \leftarrow \mathsf{Ext}(K_2^*, r^*)$
4. $\tilde{c}^* \leftarrow \mathsf{IBE.Enc}(\mathsf{rcv}_0^*, (\mathsf{m}_0^*||r^*)), c^* \leftarrow \tilde{c}^* \oplus \kappa_1^*$
5. $\tilde{s} \leftarrow \mathsf{IBS.Sign}(\mathsf{sk}_\sigma, H(c^*||r^*||K_1^*||K_2^*)), s^* \leftarrow \tilde{s}^* \oplus \kappa_2^*$
6. Return $\mathsf{ct} := (c^*, s^*, K_1^*, K_2^*)$

Hyb_1: Same as Hyb_0 except that $\kappa_1^* \leftarrow U(\mathcal{C}_{\mathsf{ibe}})$ instead of $\kappa_1^* \leftarrow \mathsf{ReExt}(K_1^*, \sigma_0^*)$.

Hyb_2: Same as Hyb_1 except that $\tilde{c}^* \leftarrow \mathsf{IBE.Enc}(\mathsf{rcv}_1^*, (\mathsf{m}_1^*||r^*))$.

Hyb_3: Same as Hyb_2 except that $s^* \leftarrow \mathsf{IBS.Sign}(\mathsf{sk}_{\sigma_0^*}, H(c^*||r^*||K_1^*||K_2^*)) \oplus w$ for $w \leftarrow U(\{0,1\}^d)$.

Hyb_4: Same as Hyb_3 except that s^* is generated using $\mathsf{ek}_{\sigma_1^*}$ instead of using $\mathsf{ek}_{\sigma_0^*}$, i.e., $s^* \leftarrow \mathsf{IBS.Sign}(\mathsf{sk}_{\sigma_1^*}, H(c^*||r^*||K_1^*||K_2^*)) \oplus w$ where $w \leftarrow U(\{0,1\}^d)$.

Hyb_5: Same as Hyb_4 except $s^* \leftarrow \mathsf{IBS.Sign}(\mathsf{sk}_{\sigma_1^*}, H(c^*||r^*||K_1^*||K_2^*)) \oplus \mathsf{Ext}(K_2^*, r^*)$.

Hyb_6: Same as Hyb_5 except $\kappa_1^* = \mathsf{ReExt}(K_1^*, \sigma_1^*)$.

Hyb_1 differs from Hyb_0 by setting $\kappa_1^* \leftarrow U(\mathcal{C}_{\mathsf{ibe}})$. It is easy to see that oracle queries in Hyb_1 are responded in the same way as those in Hyb_0. As per Definition 5, the adversary $\mathcal{A}$ makes polynomial times, e.g., $Q_{\mathcal{O}_3}$, queries to $\mathcal{O}_{3,0}$. Assume the i-th query results in a response $\mathsf{ct}_i = (c_i, s_i, K_{1,i}, K_{2,i})$ where $c_i := \mathsf{IBE.Enc}(\mathsf{rcv}_i, (\mathsf{m}||r)) \oplus \mathsf{ReExt}(K_{1,i}, \sigma_0^*), s_i := \mathsf{IBS.Sign}(\mathsf{sk}_{\sigma_0^*}, H(c_i||r_i||K_{1,i}||K_{i,2})) \oplus \mathsf{Ext}(K_{2,i}, r_i)$. Note that other than $\kappa_i := \mathsf{ReExt}(K_{1,i}, \sigma_0^*)$, the maximum information the queries can give about σ_0^* is $\mathsf{sk}_{\sigma_0^*}$. Since IBS is η-identity lossy,

$$\tilde{H}_\infty(\sigma_0^*|\mathsf{sk}_{\sigma_0^*}, \{s_i\}_{i\in[Q_{\mathcal{O}_3}]}) = \tilde{H}_\infty(\sigma_0^*|\mathsf{sk}_{\sigma_0^*}) \geq H_\infty(\sigma_0^*) - \eta$$
$$= k' + \eta - \eta = k'$$

Since ReExt is an $(k', \mathsf{poly}(\lambda) \geq Q_{\mathcal{O}_3} + 1)$-reusable extractor, no p.p.t adversary can tell between the distributions of κ_1^* in Hyb_0 and Hyb_1, and for some $\mathcal{D}$,

$$|\Pr[\mathsf{Hyb}_0 \Rightarrow 1] - \Pr[\mathsf{Hyb}_1 \Rightarrow 1]| \leq \mathsf{Adv}_\mathcal{D}^{\mathsf{ReExt}}(\lambda) \tag{7}$$

The modification from Hyb_2 does not change the adversary's view, because of the one-time pad $\kappa_1^* \leftarrow U(\mathcal{C}_{\mathsf{ibe}})$, c^* is uniform over $\mathcal{C}_{\mathsf{ibe}}$, regardless of $\tilde{c}^*$. Hence

$$\Pr[\mathsf{Hyb}_1 \Rightarrow 1] = \Pr[\mathsf{Hyb}_2 \Rightarrow 1] \tag{8}$$

Hyb_3 differs from Hyb_2 by using $w \leftarrow U(\{0,1\})^d$ instead of $\mathsf{Ext}(K_2^*, r^*)$. Note that in Hyb_2, the only information about r^* for the adversary $\mathcal{A}$ is from s^* (c^* is unifromly random). Using the same argument in proving Inequality 2, we have $SD((K_2^*, \mathsf{Ext}(K_2^*, r^*), (K_2^*, w)) \leq \mathsf{negl}(\lambda)$, and thus,

$$|\Pr[\mathsf{Hyb}_2 \Rightarrow 1] - \Pr[\mathsf{Hyb}_3 \Rightarrow 1]| \leq \mathsf{negl}_2'(\lambda) \tag{9}$$

Hyb_4 differs from Hyb_3 by using $\mathsf{sk}_{\sigma_1^*}$ to compute s^*. Since s^* is uniform, so

$$\Pr[\mathsf{Hyb}_3 \Rightarrow 1] = \Pr[\mathsf{Hyb}_4 \Rightarrow 1] \tag{10}$$

Hyb_5 uses $\mathsf{Ext}(K_2^*, r^*)$ not w. Using the same argument for Inequality 9,

$$|\Pr[\mathsf{Hyb}_4 \Rightarrow 1] - \Pr[\mathsf{Hyb}_5 \Rightarrow 1]| \leq \mathsf{negl}_2''(\lambda) \tag{11}$$

The difference between Hyb_6 and Hyb_5 is similar to the difference between Hyb_1 and Hyb_0. Applying the same reasoning for Inequality 7, we have

$$\left|\Pr[\mathsf{Hyb}_5 \Rightarrow 1] - \Pr[\mathsf{Hyb}_6 \Rightarrow 1]\right| \leq \mathsf{negl}_2'''(\lambda) \tag{12}$$

Note that Hyb_6 is identical to the security experiment $\mathsf{Exp}_{\Pi,\mathcal{A}}^{\mathsf{priv}^+-1}(\lambda)$, under the condition $\bar{\mathsf{M}}_2$. Hence, $\left|\Pr[\mathsf{Exp}_{\Pi,\mathcal{A}}^{\mathsf{priv}^+-0}(\lambda) = 1|\bar{\mathsf{M}}_2] - \Pr[\mathsf{Exp}_{\Pi,\mathcal{A}}^{\mathsf{priv}^+-1}(\lambda) = 1|\bar{\mathsf{M}}_2]\right|$

$$\leq \left|\Pr[\mathsf{Hyb}_0 \Rightarrow 1] - \Pr[\mathsf{Hyb}_6 \Rightarrow 1]\right| \leq \mathsf{Adv}_{\mathcal{D}}^{\mathsf{ReExt}}(\lambda) + \mathsf{negl}_2(\lambda).$$

Lemma 4. *Under the condition $\bar{\mathsf{M}}_3$, for some negligible $\mathsf{negl}(\lambda)$, we have*

$$\left|\Pr[\mathsf{Exp}_{\Pi,\mathcal{A}}^{\mathsf{priv}^+-0}(\lambda) = 1|\bar{\mathsf{M}}_3] - \Pr[\mathsf{Exp}_{\Pi,\mathcal{A}}^{\mathsf{priv}^+-1}(\lambda) = 1|\bar{\mathsf{M}}_3]\right| \leq 2\mathsf{Adv}_{\mathsf{IBE},\mathcal{B}}^{\mathsf{indr}}(\lambda) + \mathsf{negl}_3(\lambda)$$

Proof. We define the hybrid experiments below under the condition $\bar{\mathsf{M}}_3$: $\mathsf{H}_\infty(\mathcal{ID}_0) \geq k' + \eta \land \forall \rho \in L_2, \rho \neq \mathsf{rcv}_1^*$. We assume $\mathcal{ID}_1$ is a constant distribution, so the adversary knows σ_1^*. Also, the adversary can get rcv_0^* but *not* rcv_1^*.

Hyb_0 is identical to the experiment $\mathsf{Exp}_{\Pi,\mathcal{A}}^{\mathsf{priv}^+-0}(\lambda)$, as defined in Fig. 1. In particular, upon receiving $(\mathsf{m}_0^*, \mathsf{m}_1^*, \mathsf{rcv}_0^*, \mathsf{rcv}_1^*, \mathcal{ID}_0, \mathcal{ID}_1, st)$ the adversary $\mathcal{A}_1$, the challenge ciphertext ct^* is constructed as follows:

1. For $i = 0, 1$, $\sigma_i^* \leftarrow \mathcal{ID}_i$, $\mathsf{ek}_{\sigma_i^*} \leftarrow \mathsf{IBS.Extract}(\mathsf{IBS.msk}, \sigma_i^*)$
2. $r^* \leftarrow U(\{0,1\}^\ell)$, $K_1^* \leftarrow U(\{0,1\}^s)$, $K_2^* \leftarrow U(\{0,1\}^v)$
3. $\kappa_1^* \leftarrow \mathsf{ReExt}(K_1^*, \sigma_0^*))$, $\kappa_2 \leftarrow \mathsf{Ext}(K_2^*, r^*)$
4. $\tilde{c}^* \leftarrow \mathsf{IBE.Enc}(\mathsf{rcv}_0^*, (\mathsf{m}_0^* || r^*))$, $c^* \leftarrow \tilde{c}^* \oplus \kappa_1^*$
5. $\tilde{s} \leftarrow \mathsf{IBS.Sign}(\mathsf{sk}_\sigma, H(c^* || r^* || K_1^* || K_2^*))$, $s^* \leftarrow \tilde{s} \oplus \kappa_2^*$
6. Return $\mathsf{ct} := (c^*, s^*, K_1^*, K_2^*)$

Hyb_1: Same as Hyb_0 except that $\kappa \leftarrow U(\mathcal{C}_{\mathsf{ibe}})$ instead $\mathsf{ReExt}(K_1^*, \sigma_0^*)$.

Hyb_2: Same as Hyb_1 except that $\tilde{c}^*$ is random from $\mathcal{C}_{\mathsf{ibe}}$, i.e., $\tilde{c}^* \leftarrow U(\mathcal{C}_{\mathsf{ibe}})$.

Hyb_3: Same as Hyb_2 except that the a random d-bit string w is used for computing s^*, i.e., $s^* \leftarrow \mathsf{IBS.Sign}(\mathsf{sk}_{\sigma_0^*}, H(c^* || r_0^* || K_1^* || K_2^*)) \oplus w$.

Hyb_4: Same as Hyb_3 except that s^* is generated using $\mathsf{ek}_{\sigma_1^*}$ instead of using $\mathsf{ek}_{\sigma_0^*}$, i.e., $s^* \leftarrow \mathsf{IBS.Sign}(\mathsf{sk}_{\sigma_1^*}, H(c^* || r_1^* || K_1^* || K_2^*)) \oplus w$ where $w \leftarrow U(\{0,1\}^d)$.

Hyb_5: Same as Hyb_4 except that $\mathsf{Ext}(K_2^*, r_1^*)$ is used to compute s^*, not w.

Hyb_6: Same as Hyb_5 except that κ is computed using $\kappa \leftarrow \mathsf{ReExt}(K_1^*, \sigma_1^*)$.

Hyb_7: Same as Hyb_6 except $\tilde{c}^* \leftarrow \mathsf{IBEEnc}(\mathsf{rcv}_1^*, (\mathsf{m}_1^* || r^*))$.

The difference between Hyb_1 and Hyb_0 here (under condition $\bar{\mathsf{M}}_3$) is similar to the difference between Hyb_1 and Hyb_0 under condition $\bar{\mathsf{M}}_2$. It is easy to see that the oracle queries in Hyb_1 are responded to the same as those in Hyb_0. Applying the same proof for Inequality 7, we get, for some $\mathcal{D}$

$$\left|\Pr[\mathsf{Hyb}_0 \Rightarrow 1] - \Pr[\mathsf{Hyb}_1 \Rightarrow 1]\right| \leq \mathsf{Adv}_{\mathcal{D}}^{\mathsf{ReExt}}(\lambda) \tag{13}$$

The modification from Hyb_2 does not change the adversary's view, because of the one-time pad $\kappa_1^* \leftarrow U(\mathcal{C}_{\mathsf{ibe}})$, c^* is uniform over $\mathcal{C}_{\mathsf{ibe}}$, regardless of $\tilde{c}^*$. Hence

$$\Pr[\mathsf{Hyb}_1 \Rightarrow 1] = \Pr[\mathsf{Hyb}_2 \Rightarrow 1] \qquad (14)$$

Hyb_3 uses a random d-bit string w to compute s^*, rather than $\mathsf{Ext}(K_2^*, r^*)$. Using the same proof for Inequality 9, we get

$$|\Pr[\mathsf{Hyb}_2 \Rightarrow 1] - \Pr[\mathsf{Hyb}_3 \Rightarrow 1]| \leq \mathsf{negl}_3'(\lambda) \qquad (15)$$

The changes made by Hyb_4 from Hyb_3, i.e., using $\mathsf{sk}_{\sigma_1^*}$ instead of using $\mathsf{sk}_{\sigma_0^*}$ to compute s^*, does not change the distribution of s^*, because s^* is uniformly random due the one-time pad w. Therefore,

$$\Pr[\mathsf{Hyb}_3 \Rightarrow 1] = \Pr[\mathsf{Hyb}_4 \Rightarrow 1] \qquad (16)$$

The difference between Hyb_5 and Hyb_4 is essentially the same as that between Hyb2 and Hyb3. Applying the same argument in proving Inequality 15 leads to

$$|\Pr[\mathsf{Hyb}_4 \Rightarrow 1] - \Pr[\mathsf{Hyb}_5 \Rightarrow 1]| \leq \mathsf{negl}_3''(\lambda) \qquad (17)$$

The changes in Hyb_6 do not modify the distribution of ct^* (in particular c^*). This is because the ciphertext component c^* is masked by $\tilde{c}^*$, which is uniformly random on $\mathcal{C}_{\mathsf{ibe}}$ in both hybrid experiments, even the adversary knows σ_1^*. So,

$$\Pr[\mathsf{Hyb}_5 \Rightarrow 1] = \Pr[\mathsf{Hyb}_6 \Rightarrow 1] \qquad (18)$$

Hyb_7 changes the way of computing $\tilde{c}$ by $\tilde{c}^* \leftarrow \mathsf{IBE.Enc}(\mathsf{rcv}_1^*, (\mathsf{m}_1^* \| r))$. Recall that under condition $\bar{\mathsf{M}}_3$, rcv_1^* is not known to the adversary. Under the security of IBE, a routine reduction gives

$$|\Pr[\mathsf{Hyb}_6 \Rightarrow 1] - \Pr[\mathsf{Hyb}_7 \Rightarrow 1]| \leq 2\mathsf{Adv}_{\mathsf{IBE},\mathcal{B}}^{\mathsf{indr}}(\lambda) \qquad (19)$$

for some INDr-ID-CPA adversary $\mathcal{B}$.

Hyb_7 is identical to the experiment $\mathsf{Exp}_{\Pi,\mathcal{A}}^{\mathsf{priv}^+-1}(\lambda)$, under the condition $\bar{\mathsf{M}}_3$. We conclude with $\left|\Pr[\mathsf{Exp}_{\Pi,\mathcal{A}}^{\mathsf{priv}^+-0}(\lambda) = 1 | \bar{\mathsf{M}}_3] - \Pr[\mathsf{Exp}_{\Pi,\mathcal{A}}^{\mathsf{priv}^+-1}(\lambda) = 1 | \bar{\mathsf{M}}_3]\right|$

$$\leq |\Pr[\mathsf{Hyb}_0 \Rightarrow 1] - \Pr[\mathsf{Hyb}_7 \Rightarrow 1]| \leq 2\mathsf{Adv}_{\mathsf{IBE},\mathcal{B}}^{\mathsf{indr}}(\lambda) + \mathsf{Adv}_{\mathcal{D}}^{\mathsf{ReExt}}(\lambda) + \mathsf{negl}_3(\lambda)$$

Lemma 5. *Under the condition* $\bar{\mathsf{M}}_4$, *for some negligible* $\mathsf{negl}(\lambda)$, *we have*

$$\left|\Pr[\mathsf{Exp}_{\Pi,\mathcal{A}}^{\mathsf{priv}^+-0}(\lambda) = 1 | \bar{\mathsf{M}}_3] - \Pr[\mathsf{Exp}_{\Pi,\mathcal{A}}^{\mathsf{priv}^+-1}(\lambda) = 1 | \bar{\mathsf{M}}_3]\right| \leq 2\mathsf{Adv}_{\mathsf{IBE},\mathcal{B}}^{\mathsf{indr}}(\lambda) + \mathsf{negl}_4(\lambda)$$

Proof. The proof is identical to that of Lemma 4 and thus omitted.

Combining Lemma 2, Lemma 3, Lemma 4, and Lemma 5, we have

$$\mathsf{Adv}_{\Pi,\mathcal{A}}^{\mathsf{priv}^+}(\lambda) = \left|\Pr\left[\mathsf{Exp}_{\Pi,\mathcal{A}}^{\mathsf{priv}^+-0}(\lambda) = 1\right] - \Pr\left[\mathsf{Exp}_{\Pi,\mathcal{A}}^{\mathsf{priv}^+-1}(\lambda) = 1\right]\right|$$

$$\leq \sum_{j=1}^{4} \left|\Pr[\mathsf{Exp}_{\Pi,\mathcal{A}}^{\mathsf{priv}^+-0}(\lambda) = 1 | \bar{\mathsf{M}}_i] - \Pr[\mathsf{Exp}_{\Pi,\mathcal{A}}^{\mathsf{priv}^+-1}(\lambda) = 1 | \bar{\mathsf{M}}_i]\right|$$

$$\leq 8 \cdot \mathsf{Adv}_{\Pi,\mathcal{B}}^{\mathsf{indr}}(\lambda) + 2 \cdot \mathsf{Adv}_{\mathcal{D}}^{\mathsf{ReExt}}(\lambda) + \mathsf{negl}(\lambda)$$

which is negligible under the hypotheses. This ends the proof of Theorem 1.

4.2 Proof of Authenticity

Proof (Proof of Theorem 2). Let $(\mathsf{ct}^*, \rho^*, \mathsf{snd}^*) \notin L_3$ where $\mathsf{ct}^* = (c^*, s^*, K_1^*, K_2^*)$ be the adversary $\mathcal{A}$'s output in $\mathsf{Exp}_{\Pi,\mathcal{A}}^{\mathsf{auth}}(\lambda)$ such that $\mathsf{m}^* \| r^* \leftarrow \mathsf{IBE.Dec}(\rho^*, c^*)$. Let $(\sigma_i, \mathsf{rcv}_i, \mathsf{m}_i)$ be $\mathcal{A}$'s i-th query to the oracle $\mathcal{O}_3$, and $(c_i, s_i, K_{1,i}, K_{2,i})$ be the response where $K_{1,i}, K_{2,i}$ are random; $c_i = \mathsf{IBE.Enc}(\mathsf{rcv}_i, (\mathsf{m}_i \| r_i))$, and $s_i = \mathsf{IBS.Sign}(\mathsf{sk}_{\sigma_i}, H(c_i \| r_i \| K_{i,1} \| K_{i,2})) \oplus \mathsf{Ext}(K_{i,2}, r_i)$. Let E be the event that there is i such that $(c^*, r^*, K_1^*, K_2^*) \neq (c_i, r_i, K_{1,i}, K_{2,i})$ but $H(c^* \| r^* \| K_1^* \| K_2^*) = H(c_i \| r_i \| K_{1,i} \| K_{2,i})$. It is easy to see that The probability the E happens is bounded by $\mathsf{Adv}_{H,\mathcal{B}}^{\mathsf{coll}}(\lambda)$ for some p.p.t adversary $\mathcal{B}$.

We show that if the event $\mathsf{Exp}_{\Pi,\mathcal{A}}^{\mathsf{auth}}(\lambda) = 1$ happens conditioned on $\neg E$, we can build an algorithm $\mathcal{B}'$ that breaks the EUF-ID-CMA security of IBS. The reduction between $\mathcal{B}'$ and an EUF-ID-CMA security challenger works as follows.

1. Upon receiving $\mathsf{IBS.pub}$ from the EUF-ID-CMA security challenger, $'\mathcal{B}$ generates $(\mathsf{IBE.pub}, \mathsf{IBE.msk}) \leftarrow \mathsf{IBE.Setup}(1^\lambda)$, outputs $\mathsf{pub} := (\mathsf{IBE.pub}, \mathsf{IBS.pub})$, and keeps $\mathsf{IBE.msk}$. It also initialises three lists $L_1, L_2, L_3 \leftarrow \emptyset$.
2. $\mathcal{B}'$ responds to $\mathcal{A}$'s queries as follows:
   - For an $\mathcal{O}_1$-query σ: $\mathcal{B}'$ queries the oracle $\mathsf{OExt}(\sigma)$ to get sk_σ, and forwards $\mathsf{ek}_\sigma = (\mathsf{sk}_\sigma, \sigma)$ to $\mathcal{A}$, and then sets $L_1 \leftarrow L_1 \cup \sigma$. We note that in this case, $\sigma \in L_{\mathsf{id}}$ of the IBS challenger.
   - For an $\mathcal{O}_2$-query ρ: $\mathcal{B}'$ returns $\mathsf{dk}_\rho \leftarrow \mathsf{IBE.Extract}(\mathsf{IBE.msk}, \rho)$ to $\mathcal{A}$. Then, $\mathcal{B}'$ updates the list by $L_2 \leftarrow L_2 \cup \rho$.
   - For an $\mathcal{O}_3$-query $(\sigma, \mathsf{rcv}, \mathsf{m})$: $\mathcal{B}'$ samples random r, K_1, K_2, and computes $c \leftarrow \mathsf{IBE.Enc}(\mathsf{rcv}, (\mathsf{m} \| r)) \oplus \mathsf{ReExt}(K_1, \sigma)$, $\kappa_2 \leftarrow \mathsf{Ext}(K_2, r)$. Then, $\mathcal{B}'$ makes a query $(\sigma, H(c \| r \| K_1 \| K_2))$ to the oracle OSig to receive a signature $\tilde{s}$. $\mathcal{B}'$ returns the IB-ME ciphertext $(c, s \leftarrow \tilde{s} \oplus \kappa_2, K_1, K_2)$ as the response to the $\mathcal{A}$'s query and sets $L_3 \leftarrow L_3 \cup (\sigma, \mathsf{rcv}, \mathsf{m})$. We note that the tuple $(\sigma, H(c \| r \| K_1 \| K_2), \tilde{s}) \in L_s$ of the IBS challenger.
3. Finally, the adversary outputs a tuple $(\mathsf{ct}^*, \rho^*, \mathsf{snd}^*)$. $\mathcal{B}'$ proceeds as follows:
   - Parse $\mathsf{ct}^* = (c^*, s^*, K_1^*, K_2^*)$; Abort if ct^* does not parse correctly.
   - Set $\mathsf{sk}_{\rho^*} \leftarrow \mathsf{IBE.Extract}(\mathsf{IBE.msk}, \rho)$, compute $\mathsf{m}^* \| r^* \leftarrow \mathsf{IBE.Dec}(\mathsf{sk}_{\rho^*}, c^* \oplus \mathsf{ReExt}(K_1^*, \mathsf{snd}^*))$.
   - Abort if $\mathsf{snd}^* \in L_1$ or $(\mathsf{snd}^*, \rho^*, \mathsf{m}^*) \in L_3$.
   - Output $(\mathsf{snd}^*, H(c^* \| r^* \| K_1^* \| K_2^*), s^* \oplus \mathsf{Ext}(K_2^*, r^*))$ to the challenger if $\mathsf{IBS.Ver}(\mathsf{snd}^*, H(c^* \| r^* \| K_1^* \| K_2^*), s^* \oplus \mathsf{Ext}(K_2^*, r^*)) \neq 1$.

We analyse the reduction. It is easy to see that the distribution of pub and the output distributions of the oracles $\mathcal{O}_1$, $\mathcal{O}_2$, and $\mathcal{O}_3$ simulated by $\mathcal{B}'$ are identical to those from the IB-ME authenticity security experiment. We argue that if $\mathcal{A}$'s output $(\mathsf{ct}^*, \rho^*, \mathsf{snd}^*)$ makes the experiment $\mathsf{Exp}_{\Pi,\mathcal{A}}^{\mathsf{auth}}(\lambda)$ output 1, then the output of $\mathcal{B}'$, i.e., $(\mathsf{snd}^*, H(c^* \| r^* \| K_1^* \| K_2^*), s^* \oplus \mathsf{Ext}(K_2^*, r^*))$ gives a valid forgery, making the experiment $\mathsf{Exp}_{\mathsf{IBS},\mathcal{B}'}^{\mathsf{euf}}(\lambda)$ output 1. We prove this by contrapositive.

1. If $(\mathsf{snd}^*, H(c^* \| r^* \| K_1^* \| K_2^*), s^* \oplus \mathsf{Ext}(K_2^*, r^*))$ cannot be verified by the IBS system IBS, then $(\mathsf{ct}^*, \rho^*, \mathsf{snd}^*)$ cannot be a valid ID-ME ciphertext.

2. If $snd^* \in L_{id}$, we must have $snd^* \in L_1$. Therefore, (ct^*, ρ^*, snd^*) is not a valid forgery to IB-ME authenticity.

3. Considering that the tuple $(snd^*, H(c^*||r^*||K_1^*||K_2^*), s^* \oplus Ext(K_2^*, r^*)) \in L_s$, i.e., the tuple was asked by $\mathcal{B}'$ to the signing oracle OSig where c^* was created by rcv^*. This must be caused by an $\mathcal{O}_3$-query $(\sigma^* = snd^*, rcv^* = \rho^*, m^*)$, made by $\mathcal{A}$. Under the condition $\neg E$, there is no tuple $(c, r, K_1, K_2) \neq (c^*, r^*, K_1^*, K_2^*)$. By the IB-ME construction, $c^* = IBE.Enc(rcv^*, (m^*||r^*)) \oplus ReExt(K_1^*, \sigma^*)$. Since ReExt is deterministic under the inputs K_1^* and σ^*, there is no another message $m \neq m^*$ such that $c^* = IBE.Enc(rcv^*, (m||r^*)) \oplus ReExt(K_1^*, \sigma)^1$ and $(snd^* = \sigma^*, \rho^* = snd^*, m) \notin L_3$. Hence, it must be the case that the invalid IBS forgery $(snd^*, H(c^*||r^*||K_1^*||K_2^*), s^* \oplus Ext(K_2^*, r^*))$ (as it is in L_s) links to $(ct^*, snd^* = \sigma^*, \rho^* = rcv^*)$, an invalid IB-ME forgery due to $(snd^* = \sigma^*, \rho^* = snd^*, m) \notin L_3$.

To sum up, conclude the proof by

$$Pr[Exp_{\Pi,\mathcal{A}}^{auth}(\lambda) = 1] = Pr[Exp_{\Pi,\mathcal{A}}^{auth}(\lambda) = 1|E] Pr[E] + Pr[Exp_{\Pi,\mathcal{A}}^{auth}(\lambda) = 1|\neg E] Pr[\neg E]$$
$$\leq Pr[E] + Pr[Exp_{\Pi,\mathcal{A}}^{auth}(\lambda) = 1|\neg E] \leq Adv_{H,\mathcal{B}}^{coll}(\lambda) + Adv_{IBS,\mathcal{B}'}^{euf}(\lambda).$$

5 Instatiations

5.1 Anonymous IBE Systems and IBS Systems

Our IB-ME construction requires the underlying anonymous IBE system to have INDr-ID-CPA security, which most anonymous IBE systems satisfy.

Table 2. Example anonymous IBE systems applicable to our IB-ME system

Schemes	Assumption	ROM	Quantum Resistant
BF'01–Basicident [5]	DBDH	✔	✗
BW'06 [6]	DLin	✗	✗
DLP'14 [11]	NTRU/RLWE	✔	✔
GPV'08 [15]	LWE	✔	✔
ABB10'10–Select-ID [1]	LWE	✗	✔

Table 2 summarises a list of anonymous IBE systems applicable to our generic construction. Some anonymous IBE systems, e.g., BW'06 system, are proven in a weaker selective identity model (INDr-sID-CPA). These systems are efficient and INDr-ID-CPA secure via complexity leveraging [4].

Identity-based signature is another well-studied primitive needed by our construction. One of the simple and effective ways to construct IBS systems is the certification-based approach (termed Cert below in Table 3). The

---

[1] Otherwise the ciphertext decrypts to two different messages.

certification-based approach uses a normal digital signature system. Applying the certification-based approach to practical post-quantum digital signature systems, e.g., Falcon [12] and Dilithium [10] yield efficient IBS systems comparable to the direct post-quantum IBS systems. We refer to Scheme 1, [17] for the formal descriptions of the IBS system based on the certification-based approach.

Table 3. Example IBS Systems applicable to our IB-ME system

Schemes	Assumption	ROM	Quantum Resistant
Cert+ Falcon [12]	NTRU	✔	✔
Cert+ Dilithium [10]	MLWE	✔	✔
GS'02 [16]	CDH	✔	✗
PS'06 [21]	CDH	✗	✗
ABB'10 [15]	SIS	✗	✔

Our IB-ME construction requires IBS systems to be identity lossy (Definition 11), i.e., the identity key contains less information than that of the identity if the identity is sampled uniformly at random. Without changing the IBS system construction much, identity lossiness is easy to satisfy: Assuming the identity space is large enough and a collision-resistant hash function $H : \{0,1\}^n \to \{0,1\}^m$ that compresses the inputs (note, most hash functions compress), i.e., $n > m$, we use $H(\mathsf{id})$ as the actual identity for the IBS identity key extraction and other algorithms. Since $H(\mathsf{id})$ losses information of id, the identity key $\mathsf{sk_{id}}$ has at most m bits information, and the IBS system is $(n - m)$-identity lossy. Table 3 lists IBS systems applicable to our IB-ME construction.

5.2 Randomness Extractors

Our IB-ME construction uses average-case randomness extractors and reusable computational extractors. The two types of extractors have simple and practical instantiations in the ROM. Let $F : \{0,1\}^\ell \to \{0,1\}^d$ be a random oracle. We use $\mathsf{Ext} := F(\cdot)$ equivalently as the $(\ell, k, d, \mathsf{negl}(\lambda))$-randomness extractor for us whose security is based on Lemma 2, [18].

The reusable computational extractor for our IB-ME system can be constructed as $\mathsf{ReExt}(\cdot, \sigma) := G(\cdot, F'(\sigma))$ where secret seed σ is from a distribution over $\{0,1\}^\ell$ with min-entropy k, $F' : \{0,1\}^\ell \to \{0,1\}^d$ and $G : \{0,1\}^s \times \{0,1\}^d \to \mathcal{C}_{\mathsf{ibe}}$ are independent random oracles. Each randomness extraction chooses a random value $K \leftarrow U(\{0,1\}^s)$ and outputs $(K, G(K, F'(\sigma)))$. The security of the above reusable extractor follows from Lemma 2, [22].[2] Note that we use F as a randomness extractor to extract nearly uniformly random values $F'(\sigma)$ for

---

[2] The Lemma was originally for proofs in the Quantum Random Oracle Model. It also applies to the ROM as indicated by Saito et al.

ReExt := $G(\cdot, F'(\sigma))$ so that Lemma 2, [22] applies. In practice, we can set Ext := $F(\cdot)$ and ReExt := $G(\cdot, F(\sigma))$ with secure hash functions, e.g., SHA-3.

In the plain model, the average-case randomness extractor can be obtained from *universal hash functions*. We refer to the work of Dodis et al. [9] for more details. If the plain model does not require quantum resistance, we can instantiate reusable computational extractors by Noar and Segev's DDH-based construction [20]. To ensure quantum resistance, we can use the reusable extractor on the Learning Parity with Noise (LPN) problem and the Learning With Errors (LWE) problem – Dodis et al. [8] design a reusable extractor from a leaky LPN assumption. Yu and Zhang [24] give direct proof that the hardness of the leaky LPN problem is polynomially equivalent to the standard LPN problem. Consequently, we can obtain a reusable extractor using Dodis et al.'s construction and base its security on the standard LPN problem. Similarly, we can use the leaky LWE problem by Alwen et al. [2], which was proved as hard as the standard LWE problem (for certain parameters), to build a reusable extractor. The extractor construction is essentially the same as Dodis et al.'s construction.

5.3   A Practical IB-ME Instantiation from NTRU

According to the discussion, we can use, for example, the Boneh-Frankin IBE system [5] and the Gentry-Silverberg IBS system [16] (obtained via the 2-level Gentry-Silverberg HIBE) to get a practical IB-ME system with enhanced privacy in the ROM, provided quantum resistance is not a concern. To get a practical quantum-resistant IB-ME system, we consider the anonymous IBE system by Ducas et al. [11] (referred to as DLP-IBE) and the IBS system from Falcon signature [12] using the certification-based approach.

For DLP-IBE, we consider the improved implementation by McCarthy et al. [19] that achieves 192-bit security (Parameter Set 3, Table 3, [19]). The implemented system has master public key size, private key size, and ciphertext size ≈ 2950 bytes, ≈ 2180 bytes, and ≈ 3720 bytes, respectively.

We use Falcon-1024, which achieves 256-bit security, together with the above implementation of the DLP'14 system, to provide 192-bit security (NIST security level 4). As per Table 3.3, [12], the public-key size is ≈ 1790 bytes, signature size is 1280 bytes. The size of the Falcon's signing key can be at most 3090 bytes as per Sect. 4.4.3, [12]. We summarise the parameters in Table 4, where |pub|, $|ek_\sigma|$, $|dk_\rho|$, and |ct| represent the size of the master public key, the encryption key, the decryption key, the ciphertext of the IB-ME system. Computational performance-wise, DLP-IBE has an encryption time of 0.239 ms and a decryption time of 0.057 ms, and Falcon has a signing time of 0.34 ms and a verification

Table 4. Example practical IB-ME Instantiations Based on NTRU

|pub|	$|ek_\sigma|$	$|dk_\rho|$	|ct|	Assumption
≈ 4740 bytes	≈ 5250 bytes	< 6160 bytes	≈ 6530 bytes	NTRU

time of 0.07 ms (speed depends on the hardware used in [12,19]). For our IB-ME systems in the ROM, the encryption involves an IBE encryption and an IBS signing, and the decryption involves an IBE decryption and an IBS verification. The extractors' operations are hashing operations. The overall computational performance of our IB-ME system is practical.

Appendix A   Identity-Based Encryption and Signature

An Identity-Based Encryption (IBE) system IBE with identity space $\mathcal{I}$ and message space $\mathcal{M}$ and ciphertext space $\mathcal{C}$ consists of four p.p.t algorithms. IBE.Setup(1^λ) returns a master public key pub and a master private key msk. We assume that pub is an implicit input to the other algorithms. IBE.Extract(msk, id) generates a private key $\mathsf{sk_{id}}$. IBE.Enc (id, m) returns a ciphertext ct $\in \mathcal{C}$. IBE.Dec ($\mathsf{sk_{id}}$, id, ct) returns a message m $\in \mathcal{M}$ or $\bot$. We define the correctness as follows.

Definition 7. *An IBE system* (IBE.Setup, IBE.Extract, IBE.Enc, IBE.Dec) *with identity space* $\mathcal{I}$, *message space* $\mathcal{M}$, *and ciphertext space* $\mathcal{C}$ *is correct if for all* $\lambda \in \mathbb{N}$, (pub, msk) $\leftarrow$ IBE.Setup(1^λ), id $\in \mathcal{I}$, m $\in \mathcal{M}$, *we have*

$$\Pr\left[\mathsf{IBE.Dec}(\mathsf{sk_{id}}, \mathsf{id}, \mathsf{Enc}(\mathsf{id}, \mathsf{m})) = \mathsf{m}\right] \geq 1 - \mathsf{negl}(\lambda)$$

where $\mathsf{sk_{id}} \leftarrow$ IBE.Extract(msk, id) *and* $\mathsf{negl}(\lambda)$ *is negligible in* λ, *and the probability is taken over the randomness of the algorithms.*

We recall the notions of ciphertext indistinguishability from random under adaptive chosen-identity and chosen plaintext attacks, denoted by INDr-ID-CPA which implies semantic security and recipient identity anonymity.

Definition 8 (INDr-ID-CPA Security). *Let* λ *be the security parameter. We say that an IBE system* IBE *is INDr-ID-CPA secure if for all p.p.t adversary* $\mathcal{A} = (\mathcal{A}_1, \mathcal{A}_2)$ *that makes queries to* OExt,

$$\mathsf{Adv}^{\mathsf{indr}}_{\mathsf{IBE}, \mathcal{A}}(\lambda) := \left|\Pr\left[\mathsf{Exp}^{\mathsf{indr}}_{\mathsf{IBE}, \mathcal{A}}(\lambda) = 1\right] - 1/2\right| \leq \mathsf{negl}(\lambda)$$

where the security experiment $\mathsf{Exp}^{\mathsf{indr}}_{\mathsf{IBE}, \mathcal{A}}(\lambda)$ *is defined in Fig. 3 and the probability is over the randomness of the* IBE *algorithms and the randomness of the attacker.*

An IBS system IBS with identity space $\mathcal{I}$ consists of four p.p.t algorithms. IBS.Setup(1^λ) returns a master public key pub and a master private key msk. We assume that pub is an implicit input to other algorithms. IBS.Extract(msk, id). IBS.Sign($\mathsf{sk_{id}}$, m) returns a signature s. IBS.Ver(id, m, s) returns 1 or 0. We define the correctness as follows.

Definition 9. *An IBS system* IBS = (IBS.Setup, IBS.Extract, IBS.Sign, IBS.Ver) *is correct if for all* (IBS.pub, IBS.msk) $\leftarrow$ IBS.Setup(1^λ), $\mathsf{sk_{id}} \leftarrow$ IBS.Extract (IBS.msk, id),

$$\Pr\left[\mathsf{Ver}(\mathsf{id}, \mathsf{m}, \mathsf{Sign}(\mathsf{sk_{id}}, \mathsf{m})) = 1\right] \geq 1 - \mathsf{negl}(\lambda)$$

where $\mathsf{negl}(\lambda)$ *is negligible in* λ, *and the probability is over the algorithms.*

Experiment $\mathsf{Exp}^{indr}_{IBE,\mathcal{A}}(\lambda)$:	**Experiment** $\mathsf{Exp}^{euf}_{IBS,\mathcal{A}}(\lambda)$:
1. $L_{id} \leftarrow \emptyset$	1. $L_{id} \leftarrow \emptyset$, $L_s \leftarrow \emptyset$
2. $(pub, msk) \leftarrow \mathsf{Setup}(1^\lambda)$	2. $(pub, msk) \leftarrow \mathsf{Setup}(1^\lambda)$
3. $(m*, id^*, st) \leftarrow \mathcal{A}_1^{OExt()}(pub)$	3. $(id^*, m^*, s^*) \leftarrow \mathcal{A}^{OExt(), OSig()}(pub)$
4. $b \leftarrow U(\{0,1\})$	4. If $id^* \in L_{id}$, return 0
5. $ct^*_0 \leftarrow \mathsf{IBE.Enc}(id^*, m^*b)$, $ct^*_1 \leftarrow \mathcal{C}_{ibe}$	5. If $(id^*, m^*, s^*) \in L_s$, return 0
6. $b' \leftarrow \mathcal{A}_2^{OExt()}(pub, ct^*_b, st)$	6. Return $\mathsf{Ver}(id^*, m^*, s^*)$
7. Return $(b = b') \wedge (id^* \notin L_{id})$	Oracle $\mathsf{OExt}(id)$:
Oracle $\mathsf{OExt}(id)$:	1. Return $sk_{id} \leftarrow \mathsf{Extract}(msk, id)$
1. Return $sk_{id} \leftarrow \mathsf{Extract}(msk, id)$	2. $L_{id} = \{id\} \cup L_{id}$
2. $L_{id} = \{id\} \cup L_{id}$	Oracle $\mathsf{OSig}(id, m)$:
	1. $sk_{id} \leftarrow \mathsf{Extract}(pub, msk, id)$
	2. Return $s \leftarrow \mathsf{Sign}(sk_{id}, m)$
	3. $L_s = \{id, m, s\} \cup L_s$

Fig. 3. INDr-ID-CPA and EUF-ID-CMA Security Experiments

We consider the standard unforgeability under chosen-identity and chosen-message attacks (EUF-ID-CMA). We also need a property called identity lossiness.

Definition 10. *Let λ be the security parameter. Consider the security experiment (game) defined in Fig. 3. We say an IBS system* IBS *is EUF-ID-CMA secure if for any p.p.t adversary $\mathcal{A}$ that makes polynomially many (in λ) queries the oracles* OExt() *and* OSig()*,*

$$\mathsf{Adv}^{euf}_{IBS,\mathcal{A}}(\lambda) := \Pr[\mathsf{Exp}^{euf}_{IBS,\mathcal{A}}(\lambda) = 1] \leq \mathsf{negl}(\lambda)$$

where the probability is over the randomness of $\mathcal{A}$ and the IBS system.

Definition 11. *We say that an IBS system* IBS $=$ (IBS.Setup, IBS.Extract, IBS.Sign, IBS.Ver) *with identity space $\mathcal{I}$ is η-identity lossy with respect to distribution $\mathcal{ID}$ over $\mathcal{I}$ if* $\tilde{H}_\infty(id|sk_{id}) \geq H_\infty(id) - \eta$ *for all* (IBS.pub, IBS.msk) $\leftarrow$ IBS.Setup(1^λ), $sk_{id} \leftarrow$ IBS.Extract(IBS.msk, id)*,* id $\leftarrow \mathcal{ID}$.

Appendix B   Reduction for Proving Inequality (1)

We construct the reduction algorithm $\mathcal{B}$ that uses a distinguisher that distinguishes between Hyb_0 and Hyb_1 to break the INDr-ID-CPA security of the underlying IBE system IBE. We note that the proof works under the condition $\bar{M}_1 : \forall \rho \in L_2, \rho \neq rcv^*_0 \wedge \rho \neq rcv^*_1$. $\mathcal{B}$ is interacting with an INDr-ID-CPA challenger and works as follows.

$\mathcal{B}$ initialises three empty list L_1, L_2, and L_3. On receiving a master public key IBE.pub of the IBE system IBE. $\mathcal{B}$ sets (IBS.pub, IBS.msk) $\leftarrow$ IBS.Setup(1^λ), and pub := (IBE.pub, IBS.pub), msk := IBS.msk

Then, $\mathcal{B}$ responds to the IB-ME adversary $\mathcal{A}$'s queries as follows:

1. Query $\mathcal{O}_1(\sigma)$: $\mathcal{B}$ simply runs $\mathsf{sk}_\sigma \leftarrow \mathsf{IBS.Extract}(\mathsf{IBS.msk}, \sigma)$, returns $\mathsf{ek}_\sigma = (\mathsf{sk}_\sigma, \sigma)$, and sets $L_1 = \{\sigma\} \sup L_1$.
2. Query $\mathcal{O}_2(\rho)$: $\mathcal{B}$ makes an OExt query on ρ to its IBE challenger, receives back $\mathsf{sk}_{\mathsf{id}}$ and sets $\mathsf{dk}_\rho := (\mathsf{sk}_\rho, \rho)$, and sets $L_2 = \{\sigma\} \cup L_2$.

Then, $\mathcal{A}$ announces $(\mathsf{m}_0^*, \mathsf{m}_1^*, \mathsf{rcv}_0^*, \mathsf{rcv}_1^*, \mathcal{ID}_0, \mathcal{ID}_1, st)$ and $\mathcal{B}$ creates the challenge ciphertext as follows:

1. For $i = 0, 1$, $\sigma_i^* \leftarrow \mathcal{ID}_i$, $\mathsf{ek}_{\sigma_i^*} \leftarrow \mathsf{IBS.Extract}(\mathsf{IBS.msk}, \sigma_i^*)$
2. $r^* \leftarrow U(\{0,1\}^\ell)$, $K_1^* \leftarrow U(\{0,1\}^s)$, $K_2^* \leftarrow U(\{0,1\}^v)$
3. $\kappa_1^* \leftarrow \mathsf{ReExt}(K_1^*, \sigma_0^*))$, $\kappa_2 \leftarrow \mathsf{Ext}(K_2^*, r^*)$
4. Send $(\mathsf{id}^* = \mathsf{rcv}_0^*, m^* := \mathsf{m}_0^* \| r^*, st = \emptyset)$ to the challenger, receive back ct_b^* and set $\tilde{c}^* \leftarrow \mathsf{ct}_b^*$.
5. $\tilde{s} \leftarrow \mathsf{IBS.Sign}\,(\mathsf{sk}_\sigma, H(c^* \| r^* \| K_1^* \| K_2^*))$, $s^* \leftarrow \tilde{s}^* \oplus \kappa_2^*$
6. Return $\mathsf{ct} := (c^*, s^*, K_1^*, K_2^*)$.

Then $\mathcal{A}$ makes oracle queries to $\mathcal{O}_1, \mathcal{O}_2, \mathcal{O}_{3,\beta}$. The $\mathcal{O}_1$ and $\mathcal{O}_2$ queries are answered in the same way as before. For the query $(\mathsf{rcv}, \mathsf{m})$ to $\mathcal{O}_{3,\beta}$, $\mathcal{B}$ returns $\mathsf{ct} = \mathsf{Enc}(\mathsf{ek}_{\sigma_\beta^*}, \mathsf{rcv}, \mathsf{m})$ where Enc is the encryption algorithm of the IB-ME construction. Finally, $\mathcal{B}$ outputs what $\mathcal{A}$ outputs.

We analyse the reduction. First of all, Hyb_0 and Hyb_1 have the same distribution on pub, which is correctly simulated by $\mathcal{B}$. Second, all $\mathcal{B}$ answers all queries properly. The only difference between Hyb_1 and Hyb_0 is the distribution of the value $\tilde{c}$. We can see that when the IBE challenger chose $b = 0$, i.e., the IBE challenge ciphertext ct^* is an encryption of IBE system, and $\mathcal{B}$ simulates Hyb_0. On the other hand, when the IBE challenger chose $b = 1$, ct^* is a random ciphertext, and $\mathcal{B}$ simulates Hyb_1. Let $\mathcal{B}\mathsf{Win}$ be the event that $\mathcal{B}$'s output equals to b. So,

$$\Pr[\mathcal{B}\mathsf{Win}] = \frac{1}{2} \left(\Pr[\mathcal{B}\mathsf{Win}|b = 1] + \Pr[\mathcal{B}\mathsf{Win}|b = 0] \right)$$

$$= \frac{1}{2} \left(1 - \Pr[\mathcal{A} \rightarrow 0|b = 1] + \Pr[\mathcal{A} \rightarrow 0|b = 0] \right)$$

$$= \frac{1}{2} \left(1 - \Pr[\mathsf{Hyb}_1 \Rightarrow 1] + \Pr[\mathsf{Hyb}_0 \Rightarrow 1] \right)$$

which gives $| \Pr[\mathsf{Hyb}_0 \Rightarrow 1] - \Pr[\mathsf{Hyb}_0 \Rightarrow 1] | \leq 2 \cdot \mathsf{Adv}_{\mathsf{IBE},\mathcal{A}}^{\mathsf{indr}}(\lambda)$ and ends the proof.

References

1. Agrawal, S., Boneh, D., Boyen, X.: Efficient Lattice (H)IBE in the standard model. In: Gilbert, H. (ed.) EUROCRYPT 2010. LNCS, vol. 6110, pp. 553–572. Springer, Heidelberg (2010). https://doi.org/10.1007/978-3-642-13190-5_28
2. Alwen, J., Krenn, S., Pietrzak, K., Wichs, D.: Learning with rounding, revisited. In: Canetti, R., Garay, J.A. (eds.) CRYPTO 2013. LNCS, vol. 8042, pp. 57–74. Springer, Heidelberg (2013). https://doi.org/10.1007/978-3-642-40041-4_4

3. Ateniese, G., Francati, D., Nuñez, D., Venturi, D.: Match me if you can: matchmaking encryption and its applications. J. Cryptol. **34**(3), 1–50 (2021)
4. Boneh, D., Boyen, X.: Efficient selective-ID secure identity-based encryption without random oracles. In: Cachin, C., Camenisch, J.L. (eds.) EUROCRYPT 2004. LNCS, vol. 3027, pp. 223–238. Springer, Heidelberg (2004). https://doi.org/10.1007/978-3-540-24676-3_14
5. Boneh, D., Franklin, M.: Identity-based encryption from the weil pairing. In: Kilian, J. (ed.) CRYPTO 2001. LNCS, vol. 2139, pp. 213–229. Springer, Heidelberg (2001). https://doi.org/10.1007/3-540-44647-8_13
6. Boyen, X., Waters, B.: Anonymous hierarchical identity-based encryption (without random Oracles). In: Dwork, C. (ed.) CRYPTO 2006. LNCS, vol. 4117, pp. 290–307. Springer, Heidelberg (2006). https://doi.org/10.1007/11818175_17
7. Chen, J., Li, Y., Wen, J., Weng, J.: Identity-based matchmaking encryption from standard assumptions. In: Agrawal, S., Lin, D. (eds.) ASIACRYPT 2022, pp. 394–422. Springer, Cham (2022). https://doi.org/10.1007/978-3-031-22969-5_14
8. Dodis, Y., Kalai, Y.T., Lovett, S.: On cryptography with auxiliary input. In: STOC 2009, pp. 621–630 (2009)
9. Dodis, Y., Ostrovsky, R., Reyzin, L., Smith, A.: Fuzzy extractors: how to generate strong keys from biometrics and other noisy data. SIAM J. Comput. **38**(1), 97–139 (2008)
10. Ducas, L., et al.: Crystals-dilithium: a lattice-based digital signature scheme. IACR Trans. Cryptographic Hardware Embedded Syst., pp. 238–268 (2018)
11. Ducas, L., Lyubashevsky, V., Prest, T.: Efficient identity-based encryption over NTRU lattices. In: Sarkar, P., Iwata, T. (eds.) ASIACRYPT 2014. LNCS, vol. 8874, pp. 22–41. Springer, Heidelberg (2014). https://doi.org/10.1007/978-3-662-45608-8_2
12. Fouque, P.-A., et al.: Falcon: fast-fourier lattice-based compact signatures over NTRU. Submission to the NIST's post-quantum cryptography standardization, 36(5) (2018)
13. Francati, D., Guidi, A., Russo, L., Venturi, D.: Identity-based matchmaking encryption without random oracles. In: Adhikari, A., Küsters, R., Preneel, B. (eds.) INDOCRYPT 2021. LNCS, vol. 13143, pp. 415–435. Springer, Cham (2021). https://doi.org/10.1007/978-3-030-92518-5_19
14. Gentry, C.: Practical identity-based encryption without random oracles. In: Vaudenay, S. (ed.) EUROCRYPT 2006. LNCS, vol. 4004, pp. 445–464. Springer, Heidelberg (2006). https://doi.org/10.1007/11761679_27
15. Gentry, C., Peikert, C., Vaikuntanathan, V.: Trapdoors for hard lattices and new cryptographic constructions. In: STOC 2008. ACM, pp. 197–206
16. Gentry, C., Silverberg, A.: Hierarchical ID-based cryptography. In: Zheng, Y. (ed.) ASIACRYPT 2002. LNCS, vol. 2501, pp. 548–566. Springer, Heidelberg (2002). https://doi.org/10.1007/3-540-36178-2_34
17. Kiltz, E., Neven, G.: Identity-based signatures. Identity-based cryptography **2**(31), 75 (2009)
18. Krawczyk, H.: Cryptographic extraction and key derivation: the HKDF scheme. Cryptology ePrint Archive, Paper 2010/264 (2010). https://eprint.iacr.org/
19. McCarthy, S., Smyth, N., O'Sullivan, E.: A practical implementation of identity-based encryption over NTRU lattices. In: IMACC 2017, pp. 227–246. Springer, Cham (2017)
20. Naor, M., Segev, G.: Public-key cryptosystems resilient to key leakage. In: Halevi, S. (ed.) CRYPTO 2009. LNCS, vol. 5677, pp. 18–35. Springer, Heidelberg (2009). https://doi.org/10.1007/978-3-642-03356-8_2

21. Paterson, K.G., Schuldt, J.C.N.: Efficient identity-based signatures secure in the standard model. In: Batten, L.M., Safavi-Naini, R. (eds.) ACISP 2006. LNCS, vol. 4058, pp. 207–222. Springer, Heidelberg (2006). https://doi.org/10.1007/11780656_18

22. Saito, T., Xagawa, K., Yamakawa, T.: Tightly-secure key-encapsulation mechanism in the quantum random oracle model. In: Nielsen, J.B., Rijmen, V. (eds.) EURO-CRYPT 2018. LNCS, vol. 10822, pp. 520–551. Springer, Cham (2018). https://doi.org/10.1007/978-3-319-78372-7_17

23. Wang, Y., Wang, B., Lai, Q., Zhan, Y.: Identity-based matchmaking encryption with stronger security and instantiation on lattices. Cryptology ePrint Archive, Paper 2022/1718, 2022. https://eprint.iacr.org/

24. Yu, Yu., Zhang, J.: Cryptography with auxiliary input and trapdoor from constant-noise LPN. In: Robshaw, M., Katz, J. (eds.) CRYPTO 2016. LNCS, vol. 9814, pp. 214–243. Springer, Heidelberg (2016). https://doi.org/10.1007/978-3-662-53018-4_9

Item-Oriented Personalized LDP for Discrete Distribution Estimation

Xin Li, Hong Zhu$^{(\boxtimes)}$, Zhiqiang Zhang, and Meiyi Xie

School of Computer Science and Technology, Huazhong University of Science and
Technology, Wuhan 430074, China
{lising,zhuhong,kylinzhang,xiemeiyi}@hust.edu.cn

Abstract. Discrete distribution estimation is a fundamental statistical tool, which is widely used to perform data analysis tasks in various applications involving sensitive personal information. Due to privacy concerns, individuals may not always provide their raw information, which leads to unpredictable biases in the final results of estimated distribution. Local Differential Privacy (LDP) is an advanced technique for privacy protection of discrete distribution estimation. Currently, typical LDP mechanisms provide same protection for all items in the domain, which imposes unnecessary perturbation on less sensitive items and thus degrades the utility of final results. Although, several recent works try to alleviate this problem, the utility can be further improved. In this paper, we propose a novel notion of LDP called Item-Oriented Personalized LDP (IPLDP), which independently perturbs different items with different privacy budgets to achieve personalized privacy protection. Furthermore, to satisfy IPLDP, we propose the Item-Oriented Personalized Randomized Response (IPRR) based on Mangat's RR. Theoretical analysis and experimental results demonstrate that, our method can provide fine-grained privacy protection and improve data utility simultaneously, and our scheme does at most one order of magnitude better performance than previous work.

Keywords: Discrete distribution estimation · Local differential privacy · Item-oriented personalization · Randomized response

1 Introduction

Discrete distribution estimation is widely used as a fundamental statistics tool and has achieved significant performance in various data analysis tasks, including frequent pattern mining [15], histogram publication [36], and heavy hitter identification [30]. With the deepening and expansion of application scenarios, these data analysis tasks inevitably involve more and more sensitive personal data. Due to the privacy concerns, individuals may not always be willing to truthfully provide their personal information. When dealing with such data, however, discrete distribution estimation is difficult to play its due role. For instance, a health organization plans to make statistics about personal unhealthy levels, so

G. Tsudik et al. (Eds.): ESORICS 2023, LNCS 14345, pp. 446–466, 2024.
https://doi.org/10.1007/978-3-031-51476-0_22

they issued a questionnaire survey containing three options: Serious (e.g., HIV or various cancers), Moderate (e.g., Hepatitis), and Healthy. Undoubtedly, this question is highly sensitive, especially for people who actually have one or more of specific diseases. As a result, they may not give authentic information when filling the questionnaire, and this will eventually lead to unpredictable biases in the estimation of the distribution of diseases. Therefore, under the requirement of privacy protection, how to conduct discrete distribution estimation is increasingly drawn the attention of researchers.

Differential Privacy (DP) [11,12] is an advanced and promising technique for privacy protection. Benefiting from its rigorous mathematical definition and lightweight computation demand, DP has rapidly become one of the trend in the field of privacy protection. Generally, we can categorize DP into Centralized DP (CDP) [6,9,12,19,21] and Local DP (LDP) [7,10,29]. Compared with the former, the latter does not require a trusted server, and hence it is much more appropriate for privacy protection in the tasks of the discrete distribution estimation. Based on Randomized Response (RR) [34] mechanism, LDP provides different degrees of privacy protection through the assignment of different privacy budget. Currently, typical LDP mechanisms, such as K-ary RR (KRR) [18] and RAPPOR [13], perturb all items in the domain with the same privacy budget, thus providing uniform protection strength. However, in practical scenarios, each item's sensitivity is different rather than fixed. For example, in the questionnaire mentioned above, "Serious" undoubtedly has a much higher sensitivity than "Moderate", but a relatively less population of individuals with it than that of the latter. Additionally, "Healthy" is a non-sensitive option, which naturally accounts for the largest population. Therefore, if we provide privacy protection for all items at the same level without considering their distinct sensitivity, unnecessary perturbation will be imposed on those less sensitive (and even non-sensitive) items that account for a much more population, which severely degrades the data utility of the final result.

Recently, several works proposed to improve the utility by providing different levels of protection according to various sensitivities of items. Murakami et al. introduced the Utility-Optimized LDP (ULDP) [25], which partitions personal data into sensitive and non-sensitive data and ensures privacy protection for the sensitive data only. While ULDP has better utility than KRR and RAPPOR by distinguishing sensitive data from non-sensitive data, it still protects all the sensitive data at the same level without considering the different sensitivities among them. After that, Gu et al. proposed the Input-Discriminative LDP (ID-LDP) [14], which further improved utility by providing fine-grained privacy protection for items with different privacy budgets of inputs. However, under ID-LDP, the strength of perturbation is severely restricted by the minimum privacy budget. As the minimum privacy budget decreases, the corresponding perturbations imposed on different items will approach the maximum level, which greatly weakens the improvement of utility brought by differentiating handling for each item with an independent privacy budget, thereby limiting the applicability of this method.

Therefore, the current methods of discrete distribution estimation in local privacy setting leave much room to improve the utility. In this paper, we propose a novel notion of LDP named Item-Oriented Personalized LDP (IPLDP). Unlike previous works, IPLDP independently perturbs different items with different privacy budgets to achieve personalized privacy protection and utility improvement simultaneously. Through independent perturbation, the strength of perturbation imposed on those less sensitive items will never be influenced by the sensitivity of others. To satisfy IPLDP, we propose a new mechanism called Item-Oriented Personalized RR (IPRR), and it uses the direct encoding method as in KRR to guarantee the equivalent protection for inputs and outputs simultaneously.

Our main contributions are:

1. We propose a novel LDP named IPLDP, which independently perturbs different items with different privacy budgets to achieve personalized privacy protection and utility improvement simultaneously.
2. We propose IPRR mechanism to provide equivalent protection for inputs and outputs simultaneously using the direct encoding method.
3. By calculating the $l1$ and $l2$ losses through the unbiased estimator of the gound-truth distribution under IPRR, we theoretically prove that our method has tighter upper bounds than that of existing direct encoding mechanisms.
4. We evaluate our IPRR on a synthetic and a real-world dataset with the comparison with the existing methods. The results demonstrate that our method achieves at most one order of magnitude better performance than previous work in data utility.

The remainder of this paper is organized as follows. Section 2 lists the related works. Section 3 provides an overview of several preliminary concepts. Section 4 presents the definition of IPLDP. Section 5 discusses the design of our RR mechanism and its empirical estimator. Section 6 analyzes the utility of the proposed RR method. Section 7 shows the experimental results. Finally, in Sect. 8, we draw the conclusions.

2 Related Work

Since DP was firstly proposed by Dwork [11], it has attracted much attention from researchers, and numerous variants of DP have been studied including Pufferfish privacy [19] which allows experts in different application domains to create customized privacy definitions, Concentrated DP [6] which introduced the concept of concentrated DP as a relaxation of DP, and Rényi DP [24] which proposed a new relaxation of DP based on Rényi divergence. However, all of these methods require a trusted central server. To address this issue, Duchi et al. [10] proposed LDP, which quickly became popular in a variety of application scenarios, such as frequent pattern mining [8,28,29], histogram publication [5], heavy-hitter identification [4,30], and graph applications [22,27,35]. Based on RR [34] mechanism, LDP provides different degrees of privacy protection through the assignment of privacy budget. Currently, typical RR mechanisms, such as KRR [18] and RAPPOR [13], perturb all items in the domain with the same privacy budget, thus providing uniform protection strength.

In recent years, several fine-grained privacy methods have been developed for both centralized and local settings. For example, in the centralized setting, Personalized DP [16,26] and Heterogeneous DP [3] allow users to specify their own privacy requirements for their data, and One-sided DP [20] specifies that a set of tuples is considered non-sensitive based on their values. Since these methods are centralized DP, we cannot directly apply them in the local settings. To address the non-uniformity of protection in local settings, Murakami et al. proposed ULDP [25], which partitions the value domain into sensitive and non-sensitive sub-domains. While ULDP optimizes utility by reducing perturbation on non-sensitive values, it does not fully consider the distinct privacy requirements of sensitive values. Gu et al. introduced ID-LDP [14], which protects privacy according to the distinct privacy requirements of different inputs. However, the perturbation of each value is influenced by the minimum privacy budget. As the minimum privacy budget decreases, the perturbations of different items approach the maximum, which degrades the improvement of utility.

3 Preliminaries

In this section, we formally describe our problem. Then, we describe the definitions of LDP and ID-LDP. Finally, we introduce the distribution estimation and utility evaluation methods.

3.1 Problem Statement

A data collector or a server desires to estimate the distribution of several discrete items from n users. The set of all personal items held by these users and its distribution are denoted as $\mathcal{D}$ and $\boldsymbol{p} \in \mathbb{S}^{|\mathcal{D}|}$, respectively, where $\mathbb{S}$ stands for a probability simplex and $|\cdot|$ is the cardinality of a set. For each $x \in \mathcal{D}$, we use $\boldsymbol{p}_x$ to denote its respective probability. We also have a set of random variables $X^n = \{X_1, ..., X_n\} \in \mathcal{D}$ held by n users, which are drawn i.i.d. according to $\boldsymbol{p}$. Additionally, since the items may be sensitive or non-sensitive for users, we divide $\mathcal{D}$ into two disjoint partitions: $\mathcal{D}_S$, which contains sensitive items, and $\mathcal{D}_N$, which contains non-sensitive items.

To apply LDP, each $x \in \mathcal{D}_S$ will be perturbed by users according to a corresponding privacy budget ε_x determined by the server and we denote all ε_x as a privacy budget set $\mathcal{E} = \{\varepsilon_x\}_{x \in \mathcal{D}_S}$. After perturbation, the data collector can only estimate $\boldsymbol{p}$ from users by observing $Y^n = \{Y_1, ..., Y_n\}$ which is the perturbed version of X^n through a mechanism $\boldsymbol{Q}$, and the mechanism $\boldsymbol{Q}$ maps an input item $x \in \mathcal{D}$ to an output $y \in \mathcal{D}$ with probability $\boldsymbol{Q}(y|x)$.

Our goals are: (1) to design $\boldsymbol{Q}$ that maps inputs $\forall x \in \mathcal{D}$ to outputs $\forall y \in \mathcal{D}$ according to the corresponding $\varepsilon_y \in \mathcal{E}$, and improves data utility as much as possible; (2) to estimate the distribution vector $\boldsymbol{p}$ from Y^n.

We assume that the data collector or the server is untrusted, and users never report their data directly but randomly choose an item from $\mathcal{D}$ to send, where $\mathcal{D}$ is shared by both the server and users. $\mathcal{E}$ should be also public with $\mathcal{D}$, so that users can calculate Q for perturbation, and the server can calibrate the result according to Q.

3.2   Local Differential Privacy

In LDP [10], each user perturbs its data randomly and then send the perturbed data to the server. The server can only access these perturbed results, which guarantees the privacy. In this section, we list two definitions of LDP notions, that is, the standard LDP and the ID-LDP [14].

Definition 1 (ε-LDP). *A randomized mechanism Q satisfies ε-LDP if, for any pair of inputs x, x', and any output y:*

$$e^{-\varepsilon} \leqslant \frac{Q(y|x)}{Q(y|x')} \leqslant e^{\varepsilon}, \qquad (1)$$

where $\varepsilon \in \mathbb{R}^+$ is the privacy budget that controls the level of confidence an adversary can distinguish the output from any pair of inputs. Smaller ε means that an adversary feels less confidence for distinguishing y from x or x', which naturally provides a stronger privacy protection.

Definition 2 ($\mathcal{E}$-ID-LDP). *For a given privacy budget set $\mathcal{E} = \{\varepsilon_x\}_{x \in \mathcal{D}} \in \mathbb{R}_+^{|\mathcal{D}|}$, a randomized mechanism Q satisfies $\mathcal{E}$-ID-LDP if, for any pair of inputs $x, x' \in \mathcal{D}$, and any output $y \in Range(Q)$:*

$$e^{-r(\varepsilon_x, \varepsilon_{x'})} \leqslant \frac{Q(y|x)}{Q(y|x')} \leqslant e^{r(\varepsilon_x, \varepsilon_{x'})}, \qquad (2)$$

where $r(\cdot, \cdot)$ is a system function of two privacy budgets.

Generally, we use $\mathcal{E}$-MinID-LDP in practical scenarios, where $r(\varepsilon_x, \varepsilon_{x'}) = \min(\varepsilon_x, \varepsilon_{x'})$.

3.3   Distribution Estimation Method

The empirical estimation [17] and the maximum likelihood estimation [17,31] are two types of useful methods for estimating discrete distribution in local privacy settings. We use the former method in our theoretical analysis and use both in our experiments. Here, we explain the details of the empirical estimation.

Empirical Estimation Method. The empirical estimation method calculates the emprical estimate $\hat{p}$ of p using the empirical estimate $\hat{m}$ of the distribution m, where m is the distribution of the output of the mechanism Q. Since both p and m are $|\mathcal{D}|$-dimensional vectors, Q can be viewed as a $|\mathcal{D}| \times |\mathcal{D}|$ conditional stochastic matrix. Then, the relationship between p and m can be given by $m = pQ$. Once the data collector obtains the observed estimation $\hat{m}$ of m from Y^n, the estimation of p can be solved by $\hat{m} = \hat{p}Q$. As n increases, $\hat{m}$ remains unbiased for m, and hence $\hat{p}$ converges to p as well. However, when the sample count n is small, some elements in $\hat{p}$ can be negative. To address this problem, several normalization methods [31] can be utilized to truncate and normalize the result.

3.4   Utility Evaluation Method

In this paper, the l_2 and l_1 losses is utilized for our theoretical analysis of utility. Mathematically, they are defined as $l_2(p,\hat{p}) = \sum_{x \in \mathcal{D}}(\hat{p}_x - p_x)^2$, and $l_1(p,\hat{p}) = \sum_{x \in \mathcal{D}}|\hat{p}_x - p_x|$. Both l_2 and l_1 losses evaluate the total distance between the estimate value and the ground-truth value. The shorter the distance, the better the data utility.

4   Item-Oriented Personalized LDP

In this section, we first introduce the definition of our proposed IPLDP. Then, we discuss the relationship between IPLDP and LDP. Finally, we compare IPLDP with MinID-LDP.

4.1   Privacy Definition

The standard LDP provides the same level of protection for all items using a uniform privacy budget, which can result in excessive perturbation for less sensitive items and lead to poor utility. To avoid this problem, IPLDP uses different privacy budgets for outputs of the mechanism to provide independent protection for each item. However, using the output as the protection target may not provide equal protection for the input items. Therefore, in IPLDP, we force the input and output domains to be the same $\mathcal{D}$. Formally, IPLDP is defined as follows.

Definition 3 $((\mathcal{D}_S, \mathcal{E})$-IPLDP). *For a privacy budget set $\mathcal{E} = \{\varepsilon_1, \cdots, \varepsilon_{|\mathcal{D}_S|}\}$ $\in \mathbb{R}_+^{|\mathcal{D}_S|}$, a randomized mechanism Q satisfies $(\mathcal{D}_S, \mathcal{E})$-IPLDP if and only if it satisfies following conditions:*

1. for any $x, x' \in \mathcal{D}$ and for any $x_i \in \mathcal{D}_S (i = 1, \cdots, |\mathcal{D}_S|)$,

$$e^{-\varepsilon_i} \leqslant \frac{Q(x_i|x)}{Q(x_i|x')} \leqslant e^{\varepsilon_i}, \tag{3}$$

2. *for any $x \in \mathcal{D}_N$ and for any $x' \in \mathcal{D}$,*

$$\mathbf{Q}(x|x') > 0 \text{ for } x = x' \text{ and } \mathbf{Q}(x|x') = 0 \text{ for any } x \neq x' \qquad (4)$$

Since non-sensitive items need no protection, the corresponding privacy budget can be viewed as an infinity value. However, we cannot set the privacy budget to infinity in practice. Hence, inspired by ULDP, IPLDP handles $\mathcal{D}_S$ and $\mathcal{D}_N$ separately.

According to the definition, IPLDP guarantees that the adversary's ability to distinguish any $x \in \mathcal{D}_S$ whether it is from any pair of inputs $x_1, x_2 \in \mathcal{D}$ would not exceed the range determined by the respected ε_x. That is to say, for $\forall x \in \mathcal{D}_S$, it should satisfy ε_x-LDP. For $\forall x \in \mathcal{D}_N$, It can only be perturbed to any $x \in \mathcal{D}_S$ or itself.

4.2 Relationship with LDP

We hereby assume $\mathcal{D} = \mathcal{D}_S$. Then, the obvious difference between LDP and IPLDP is the number of the privacy budgets. A special case is that, when all the privacy budgets are identical, i.e. $\varepsilon_x = \varepsilon$ for all $x \in \mathcal{D}$, then IPLDP becomes the general ε-LDP. Without loss of generality, on the one hand, if a mechanism that satisfies ε-LDP, it also satisfies $(\mathcal{D}, \mathcal{E})$-IPLDP for all $\mathcal{E}$ with $\min\{\mathcal{E}\} = \varepsilon$. On the other hand, if a mechanism satisfies $(\mathcal{D}, \mathcal{E})$-IPLDP, it also satisfies $\max\{\mathcal{E}\}$-LDP. Therefore, IPLDP can be viewed as a relaxed version of LDP. Noticeably, the relaxation does not mean that IPLDP is weaker than LDP in terms of the privacy protection, but LDP is too strong for items with different privacy needs. IPLDP has the ability to guarantee the personalized privacy for each item.

4.3 Comparison with MinID-LDP

According to the definition of notion, the main difference between IPLDP and MinID-LDP lies in the corresponding target of the privacy budget. Our IPLDP controls the distinguishability according to the output, while MinID-LDP focuses on the any pair of inputs. Both notions can be considered as a relaxed version of LDP. However, from Lemma 1 in [14], $\mathcal{E}$-MinID-LDP relaxes LDP in $\varepsilon = 2\min\{\mathcal{E}\}$ at most, which means that the degree of relaxation is much lower than IPLDP with the same $\mathcal{E}$. Therefore, as the minimum privacy budget of $\mathcal{E}$ decreases, the utility improvement under MinID-LDP is limited, and we will further experimentally verify this in Sect. 7.

5   Item-Oriented Personalized Mechanisms and Distribution Estimation

In this section, to provide personalized protection, we first propose our IPRR mechanism for the sensitive domain $\mathcal{D}_S = \mathcal{D}$. We then extend the mechanism to be compatible with the non-sensitive domain $\mathcal{D}_N$. Finally, we present the unbiased estimator of IPRR using the empirical estimation method.

5.1   Item-Oriented Personalized Randomized Response

According to our definition of IPLDP, it focuses on the indistinguishability of the mechanism's output. Then, the input and output domains should keep the same to ensure the equivalent protection for both inputs and outputs. Therefore, the only way to design the mechanism Q is to use the same direct encoding method as in KRR. To use such method, we need to calculate $|\mathcal{D}|^2$ different probabilities for the $|\mathcal{D}| \times |\mathcal{D}|$ stochastic matrix of Q. However, it is impossible to directly calculate these probabilities which make Q invertible and satisfy IPLDP constraints simultaneously. To calculate all the probabilities of Q, a possible way is to find an optimal solution of minimizing the expectation of $l_2(\hat{p}, p)$ subject to the constraints of IPLDP, i.e.

$$\min_{Q} \; \mathbb{E}_{Y^n \sim m(Q)} [l_2(\hat{p}, p)] \quad \text{s.t.} \; \ln |Q(y|x)/Q(y|x')| \leqslant \varepsilon_y, (\forall x, x', y \in \mathcal{D}). \quad (5)$$

Nevertheless, we still can not directly solve this optimization problem. Firstly, it is complicated to calculate a close-form of Q, since the objective function is likely to be non-convex and all constraints are non-linear inequalities. Secondly, even if we solve this problem numerically, the complexity of each iteration will become very large as the cardinality of the items increases, since we have to calculate an inverse matrix of Q to calculate the objective function in (5).

To address this problem, we reconsider the relationship between the privacy budget and the data utility. The privacy budget determines the indistinguishability of each item, i.e., $y \in \mathcal{D}$, by controlling the bound of $|\ln[Q(y|x)/Q(y|x')]|$ for any $x, x' \in \mathcal{D}$. Among all inputs, the contribution to the data utility comes from the honest answers (when $y = x$). Therefore, within the range controlled by the privacy budget, as long as the more honest answer can be distinguished from the dishonest ones, the more the utility can be improved. In other words, the ratio of $Q(x|x)$ (denote as q_x) and $Q(x|x')$ (denote as $\bar{q}_x$) should be as large as possible within the bound dominated by ε_x. Hence, we can reduce the computation complexity of probabilities from $|\mathcal{D}|^2$ to $2|\mathcal{D}|$ by making a tradeoff of forcing all $\bar{q}_x$ to be identical for all $x' \neq x$, and

$$q_x = e^{\varepsilon_x} \bar{q}_x, x \in \mathcal{D}. \quad (6)$$

Then, we can calculate each element p_x of p through each element m_x of m for all $x \in \mathcal{D}$ as follows:

$$m_x = p_x q_x + (1 - p_x) \bar{q}_x = p_x (e^{\varepsilon_x} - 1) \bar{q}_x + \bar{q}_x. \quad (7)$$

Next, we use the estimate $\hat{m}$ and $\hat{p}$ with (7) to calculate our objective function in (5). Since $n\hat{m}_x$ follows the binomial distribution with parameters n and m_x, its mean and variance are $\mathbb{E}(n\hat{m}_x) = nm_x$ and $\text{Var}(n\hat{m}_x) = nm_x(1 - m_x)$. We now can calculate the objective function in (5) according to (7):

$$
\mathop{\mathbb{E}}_{Y^n \sim m(Q)} [\ell_2(\hat{\boldsymbol{p}}, \boldsymbol{p})] = \sum_{x \in \mathcal{D}} \mathbb{E}\left[(\hat{\boldsymbol{p}}_x - \boldsymbol{p}_x)^2\right] = \sum_{x \in \mathcal{D}} \frac{1}{\left(e^{\varepsilon_x} - 1\right)^2 \bar{q}_x^2} \cdot \frac{m_x - m_x^2}{n}
$$

$$
= \sum_{x \in \mathcal{D}} \frac{\boldsymbol{p}_x \left(e^{\varepsilon_x} - 1\right) + 1}{n \left(e^{\varepsilon_x} - 1\right)^2 \bar{q}_x} - \sum_{x \in \mathcal{D}} \frac{\left[\boldsymbol{p}_x \left(e^{\varepsilon_x} - 1\right) + 1\right]^2}{n \left(e^{\varepsilon_x} - 1\right)^2}. \tag{8}
$$

The second term and n in (8) can be viewed as constants since they are irrelevant to $\bar{q}_x$. Therefore, by omitting these two constants, our final optimization problem can be given as

$$
\min_{\{q_x, \bar{q}_x\}_{x \in \mathcal{D}}} \sum_{x \in \mathcal{D}} \frac{\boldsymbol{p}_x \left(e^{\varepsilon_x} - 1\right) + 1}{\left(e^{\varepsilon_x} - 1\right)^2 \bar{q}_x} \quad \text{s.t.} \quad q_x + \sum_{x' \in \mathcal{D} \setminus \{x\}} \bar{q}_{x'} = 1, \forall x \in \mathcal{D}. \tag{9}
$$

Since the objective is a convex function of $\bar{q}_x$ for all $x \in \mathcal{D}$ and all the constraints are linear equations, we can efficiently calculate all the q_x and $\bar{q}_x$ for all $x \in \mathcal{D}$ via the Sherman-Morrison formula [2] at the intersection point of the hyper planes formed by the constraints in (9). After solving the linear equation groups, we can finally define our Item-Oriented Personalized RR (IPRR) mechanism as follows.

Definition 4 ($(\mathcal{D}, \mathcal{E})$-IPRR). *Let $\mathcal{D} = \{x_1, \cdots, x_{|\mathcal{D}|}\}, \mathcal{E} = \{\varepsilon_1, \cdots, \varepsilon_{|\mathcal{D}|}\} \in \mathbb{R}_+^{|\mathcal{D}|}$, Then $(\mathcal{D}, \mathcal{E})$-IPRR is a mechanism that maps $x' \in \mathcal{D}$ to $x \in \mathcal{D}$ with the probability $\boldsymbol{Q}_{\mathrm{IPRR}}(x|x')$ defined by*

$$
\boldsymbol{Q}_{\mathrm{IPRR}}(x|x') = \begin{cases} q_x & \text{if } x = x', \\ \bar{q}_x & \text{otherwise}, \end{cases} \tag{10}
$$

where $\bar{q}_x = [(e^{\varepsilon_x} - 1)(1 + \sum_{x \in \mathcal{D}_S}(e^{\varepsilon_x} - 1)^{-1})]^{-1}$ and $q_x = e^{\varepsilon_x}\bar{q}_x$.

In addition, the special case is that, when all the elements in $\mathcal{E}$ are identical, IPRR becomes KRR.

Theorem 1. *$(\mathcal{D}, \mathcal{E})$-IPRR satisfies $(\mathcal{D}, \mathcal{E})$-IPLDP.* [1]

5.2   IPRR with Non-sensitive Items

We hereby present a full version of IPRR that incorporates the non-sensitive domain $\mathcal{D}_N$. Inspired by URR in ULDP, for all $x \in \mathcal{D}_N$, privacy protection is not needed, which is equivalent to $\varepsilon_x \to \infty$. Thus, to maximize the ratio of q_x and $\bar{q}_x$, we also set $\bar{q}_x$ to zero as same as in URR. Then, we define IPRR with the non-sensitive domain as follows.

---

[1] For the proofs of all theorems, please refer to the full version in https://www.preprints.org/manuscript/202306.0289.

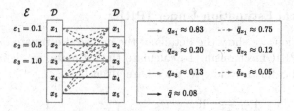

Fig. 1. Item-Oriented Personalized RR with $\mathcal{D}_S = \{x_1, x_2, x_3\}, \mathcal{D}_N = \{x_4, x_5\}$, and $\mathcal{E} = \{\varepsilon_1, \varepsilon_2, \varepsilon_3\} = \{0.1, 0.5, 1.0\}$. For instance, x_1 = HIV, x_2 = Cancer, x_3 = Hepatitis, x_4 = Flu, and x_5 = None.

Definition 5 $((\mathcal{D}_S, \mathcal{D}_N, \mathcal{E})$-IPRR). *Let $\mathcal{D}_S = \{x_1, \cdots, x_{|\mathcal{D}_S|}\}, \mathcal{E} = \{\varepsilon_1, \cdots, \varepsilon_{|\mathcal{D}_S|}\} \in \mathbb{R}_+^{|\mathcal{D}_S|}$, then $(\mathcal{D}_S, \mathcal{D}_N, \mathcal{E})$-IPRR is a mechanism that maps $x' \in \mathcal{D}$ to $x \in \mathcal{D}$ with the probability $\boldsymbol{Q}_{\mathrm{IPRR}}(x|x')$ defined by:*

$$\boldsymbol{Q}_{\mathrm{IPRR}}(x|x') = \begin{cases} q_x & \text{if } x \in \mathcal{D}_S \wedge x = x', \\ \bar{q}_x & \text{if } x \in \mathcal{D}_S \wedge x \neq x', \\ \tilde{q} & \text{if } x \in \mathcal{D}_N \wedge x = x', \\ 0 & \text{otherwise}, \end{cases} \tag{11}$$

where $\tilde{q} = 1 - \sum_{x \in \mathcal{D}_S} \bar{q}_x = (1 + \sum_{x \in \mathcal{D}_S} \frac{1}{e^{\varepsilon x} - 1})^{-1}$.

In addition, the special case is that, when all the elements in $\mathcal{E}$ are identical (denoted as ε), it is equivalent to the $(\mathcal{D}_S, \varepsilon)$-URR.

Theorem 2. *$(\mathcal{D}_S, \mathcal{D}_N, \mathcal{E})$-IPRR satisfies $(\mathcal{D}_S, \mathcal{E})$-IPLDP.*

Figure 1 depicts an example of the $(\mathcal{D}_S, \mathcal{D}_N, \mathcal{E})$-IPRR, which illustrates the perturbation of our IPRR, and also shows detailed values of all involved probabilities under $\mathcal{E} = \{0.1, 0.5, 1.0\}$. As shown in Fig. 1, as the privacy budget decreases, users with sensitive items are more honest, which is different from the perturbation style of mainstream RR mechanisms. In those mechanisms, the probability of an honest answer will decrease as the privacy budget decreases. However, data utility is hard to be improved if we follow the mainstream methods to achieve independent personalized protection. Inspired by Mangat's RR [23], data utility can be further improved through a different style of RR while guaranteeing the privacy as long as we obey the definition of LDP. Mangat's RR requires users in the sensitive group always answer honestly and uses dishonest answers from other users to contribute to the perturbation. Then, the data collector still can not distinguish one response whether it is an honest answer or not. Furthermore, in practical scenerios, the sensitivity of data is usually inversely proportional to the size of the population it pertains. As a result, indistinguishability can be guaranteed by a large proportion of dishonest responses from less sensitive or non-sensitive groups, even if individuals in the sensitive group are honest. Therefore, in our privacy scheme, we can guarantees the privacy of the clients with improvement of utility as long as both server and clients reach an agreement on this protocol.

5.3   Empirical Estimation Under IPRR

In this subsection, we show the details of the emprical estimate of p under our $(\mathcal{D}_S, \mathcal{D}_N, \mathcal{E})$-IPRR mechanism. To calculate the estimate, we define a vector r and a function $\mathcal{S}$ for convenience, which are given by

$$r_x = \begin{cases} \frac{1}{e^{\varepsilon_x}-1} & \text{if } x \in \mathcal{D}_S \\ 0 & \text{if } x \in \mathcal{D}_N \end{cases}, \text{ and } \mathcal{S}_{\cdot} = \frac{1}{\sum_{x\in\cdot} r_x + 1},$$

where r_x is the corresponding element of r to $x \in \mathcal{D}$, and "$\cdot$" can be any domains, i.e., $\mathcal{S}_{\mathcal{D}_S} = [\sum_{x\in\mathcal{D}_S} r_x + 1]^{-1}$. Then, for all $x \in \mathcal{D}_S$, we have $\bar{q}_x = \frac{1}{(e^{\varepsilon_x}-1)} \cdot \frac{1}{\sum_{i=1}^{|\mathcal{E}|}(e^{\varepsilon_i}-1)^{-1}+1} = r_x\mathcal{S}_{\mathcal{D}_S}$, and, based on (7), we can calculate m and the estimate $\hat{p}$ with each element m_x and $\hat{p}_x$ for all $x \in \mathcal{D}$ as

$$m_x = p_x\mathcal{S}_{\mathcal{D}_S} + r_x\mathcal{S}_{\mathcal{D}_S} \Rightarrow \hat{p}_x = \hat{m}_x/\mathcal{S}_{\mathcal{D}_S} - r_x. \tag{12}$$

As the sample count n increases, $\hat{m}$ remains unbiased for m, and hence $\hat{p}$ converges to p as well.

6   Utility Analysis

In this section, we first evaluate the data utility of IPRR based on the l_2 and l_1 losses of the empirical estimate $\hat{p}$. Then, for each loss, we calculate its tight upper bound independent to the unknown distribution p. Finally, we discuss the upper bound in both high and low privacy regimes.

First, we evaluate the expectation of l_2 and l_1 losses under our IPRR mechanism.

Theorem 3 *(l_2 and l_1 losses of $(\mathcal{D}_S, \mathcal{D}_N, \mathcal{E})$-IPRR). According to the Definition 5 and the empirical estimator given in (12), for all $\mathcal{E}$, the expected l_2 and l_1 losses of the $(\mathcal{D}_S, \mathcal{D}_N, \mathcal{E})$-IPRR are given by*

$$\mathbb{E}[l_2(p,\hat{p})] = \mathbb{E}\left[\sum_{x\in\mathcal{D}}(\hat{p}_x - p_x)^2\right] = \frac{1}{n}\sum_{x\in\mathcal{D}}\left[(p_x + r_x)\left(\mathcal{S}_{\mathcal{D}_S}^{-1} - (p_x + r_x)\right)\right], \tag{13}$$

and for large n,

$$\mathbb{E}[l_1(p,\hat{p})] = \mathbb{E}\left[\sum_{x\in\mathcal{D}}|\hat{p}_x - p_x|\right] \approx \sqrt{\frac{2}{n\pi}}\sum_{x\in\mathcal{D}}\sqrt{(p_x + r_x)(\mathcal{S}_{\mathcal{D}_S}^{-1} - (p_x + r_x))}, \tag{14}$$

where $a_n \approx b_n$ represents $\lim_{n\to\infty} a_n/b_n = 1$.

According to (13) and (14), we can see that the two losses share the similar structure. Hence, to conveniently discuss the property of the losses, we define a general loss L as follows.

Definition 6 (general loss of $(\mathcal{D}_S, \mathcal{D}_N, \mathcal{E})$-IPRR). *The general loss L of $(\mathcal{D}_S, \mathcal{D}_N, \mathcal{E})$-IPRR can be defined as*

$$L(\mathcal{E}; \boldsymbol{p}, \hat{\boldsymbol{p}}, \mathcal{D}) = C \sum_{x \in \mathcal{D}} g \circ f_x, \tag{15}$$

where $f_x = (\boldsymbol{p}_x + \boldsymbol{r}_x)\left(\mathcal{S}_{\mathcal{D}_S}^{-1} - (\boldsymbol{p}_x + \boldsymbol{r}_x)\right)$, g is any monotonically increasing concave function with $g(0) = 0$, and C is a non-negative constant.

With this definition, we show that, for any distribution $\boldsymbol{p}$, privacy budget set $\mathcal{E}$, $\mathcal{D}_S$, and $\mathcal{D}_N$, both $l2$ and $l1$ losses of $(\mathcal{D}_S, \mathcal{D}_N, \mathcal{E})$-IPRR are lower than that of $(\mathcal{D}_S, \min\{\mathcal{E}\})$-URR.

Through the assignment of fine-grained privacy budgets to each items in IPRR, the emprical estimator in Sect. 5.3 is a general version for mechanisms which use the direct encoding method. Due to the generality of our estimator, we can use it to calculate the empirical estimate of URR or KRR as long as all the privacy budgets are identical in $\mathcal{E}$. Therefore, based on the general empirical estimator, (13) and (14) are also applicable to these two mechanisms, even other mechanisms that use direct encoding method. To show that the losses of IPRR are lower than that of URR, we first give a lemma below.

Lemma 1. *Let $\overset{\frown}{\cdot}$ be a sorted version of any given set $\cdot$. For any two privacy budget sets $\mathcal{E}_1$ and $\mathcal{E}_2$ with same dimension k, $L(\mathcal{E}_1; \boldsymbol{p}, \hat{\boldsymbol{p}}, \mathcal{D}) \leqslant L(\mathcal{E}_2; \boldsymbol{p}, \hat{\boldsymbol{p}}, \mathcal{D})$, if $\mathcal{E}_1 \leqslant \mathcal{E}_2$, where $A \leqslant B$ stands for that, for all $a_i \in \hat{A}$ and $b_i \in \hat{B}(i = 1, \cdots k)$, we have $a_i \leqslant b_i$.*

Based on Lemma 1, for any distribution $\boldsymbol{p}$, privacy budget set $\mathcal{E}$, $\mathcal{D}_S$, and $\mathcal{D}_N$, since $\mathcal{E} \geqslant \{\min\{\mathcal{E}\}\} \in \mathbb{R}_+^{|\mathcal{E}|}$, the general loss L of $(\mathcal{D}_S, \mathcal{D}_N, \mathcal{E})$-IPRR are lower than that of $(\mathcal{D}_S, \min\{\mathcal{E}\})$-URR. Since l_2 and l_1 losses are specific versions of L when $g(x) = x$ and $g(x) = \sqrt{x}$, respectively, both two losses of IPRR also lower than that of URR in the same setting.

Next, we evaluate the worst case of the loss L. Observe that L is closely related to the original distribution $\boldsymbol{p}$. However, since $\boldsymbol{p}$ is unknown for theoretical analysis, we need to calculate a tight upper bound of the loss that does not depend on the unknown $\boldsymbol{p}$. Then, to obtain the tight upper bound, we need to find an optimal $\boldsymbol{p}$ that maximizes L. To address this issue, we convert this problem to an optimization problem subject to $\boldsymbol{p}$ being a probability simplex as

$$\max_{\boldsymbol{p}} \sum_{x \in \mathcal{D}} g \circ f_x \qquad \text{s.t. } \boldsymbol{p} \in \mathbb{S}^{|\mathcal{D}|}. \tag{16}$$

Then, the optimal solution can be given as the following lemma.

Lemma 2. *Let $\mathcal{D}^*$ be a subset of $\mathcal{D}$. For all $x \in \mathcal{D}$, if $\boldsymbol{r}_x$ satisfies*

$$\begin{cases} (|\mathcal{D}^*|\mathcal{S}_{\mathcal{D}^*})^{-1} - 1 < r_x < (|\mathcal{D}^*|\mathcal{S}_{\mathcal{D}^*})^{-1} & \text{if } x \in \mathcal{D}^*, \\ r_x \geqslant (|\mathcal{D}^*|\mathcal{S}_{\mathcal{D}^*})^{-1} & \text{otherwise,} \end{cases} \tag{17}$$

p^* is the optimal solution that maximizes the objective function in (16), which is given by

$$p_x^* = \begin{cases} (|\mathcal{D}^*|\mathcal{S}_{\mathcal{D}^*})^{-1} - r_x & \text{if } x \in \mathcal{D}^*, \\ 0 & \text{otherwise.} \end{cases} \tag{18}$$

According to Lemma 2, we can obtain the following general upper bounds of (13) and (14) as

Theorem 4 (General upper bound of l_2 and l_1 losses of IPRR). *Eq.* (13) *and* (14) *can be maximized by* p^*:

$$\mathbb{E}[l_2(p, \hat{p})] \leqslant \mathbb{E}[l_2(p^*, \hat{p})] = \frac{1}{n}\left(\frac{1}{\mathcal{S}_{\mathcal{D}}^2} - \frac{1}{|\mathcal{D}^*|\mathcal{S}_{\mathcal{D}^*}^2} - \sum_{x \in \mathcal{D} \backslash \mathcal{D}^*} r_x^2\right); \tag{19}$$

$$\mathbb{E}[l_1(p, \hat{p})] \lesssim \mathbb{E}[l_1(p^*, \hat{p})]$$

$$= \sqrt{\frac{2}{n\pi}}\left[\sum_{x \in \mathcal{D} \backslash \mathcal{D}^*}\sqrt{r_x(\mathcal{S}_{\mathcal{D}}^{-1} - r_x)} + \sqrt{\mathcal{S}_{\mathcal{D}^*}^{-1}(|\mathcal{D}^*|\mathcal{S}_{\mathcal{D}}^{-1} - \mathcal{S}_{\mathcal{D}}^{-1})}\right], \tag{20}$$

where $a_n \lesssim b_n$ *represents* $\lim_{n \to \infty} a_n/b_n \leqslant 1$.

Finally, we discuss the losses in the high and low privacy regimes based on the general upper bounds. Let $\varepsilon_{\min} = \min\{\mathcal{E}\}$ and $\varepsilon_{\max} = \max\{\mathcal{E}\}$.

Theorem 5 (l_2 and l_1 losses in high privacy regime). *When* $\varepsilon_{\max}$ *is close to 0, for all* $x \in \mathcal{D}$, *we have* $e^{\varepsilon_x} - 1 \approx \varepsilon_x$. *Then, the worst case of* l_2 *and* l_1 *losses are:*

$$\mathbb{E}[l_2(p, \hat{p})] \leqslant \mathbb{E}[l_2(p^*, \hat{p})] \approx \frac{1}{n}\sum_{x \in \mathcal{D}_S}\sum_{x' \in \mathcal{D}_S \backslash \{x\}}\frac{1}{\varepsilon_x \varepsilon_{x'}}; \tag{21}$$

$$\mathbb{E}[l_1(p, \hat{p})] \lesssim \mathbb{E}[l_1(p^*, \hat{p})] \approx \sqrt{\frac{2|\mathcal{D}_S|}{n\pi}\sum_{x \in \mathcal{D}_S}\sum_{x' \in \mathcal{D}_S \backslash \{x\}}\frac{1}{\varepsilon_x \varepsilon_{x'}}}. \tag{22}$$

According to [25], in high privacy regime, the expectation of l_2 and l_1 losses of $(\mathcal{D}_S, \varepsilon_{\min})$-URR are $\frac{|\mathcal{D}_S|(|\mathcal{D}_S|-1)}{n\varepsilon_{\min}^2}$ and $\sqrt{\frac{2}{n\pi}} \cdot \frac{|\mathcal{D}_S|\sqrt{|\mathcal{D}_S|-1}}{\varepsilon_{\min}}$, accordingly. Thus, the losses of our method is much smaller than that of URR in current setting.

Theorem 6 (l_2 and l_1 losses in low privacy regime). *When* $\varepsilon_{\min} > \ln(|\mathcal{D}_N| +1)$, *for all* $x \in \mathcal{D}$, *the worst case of* l_2 *and* l_1 *losses are:*

$$\mathbb{E}[l_2(p, \hat{p})] \leqslant \mathbb{E}[l_2(p^*, \hat{p})] = \left[\sum_{x \in \mathcal{D}_S}\frac{|\mathcal{D}_S| + e^{\varepsilon_x} - 1}{|\mathcal{D}_S|(e^{\varepsilon_x} - 1)}\right]^2\left(1 - \frac{1}{|\mathcal{D}|}\right); \tag{23}$$

$$\mathbb{E}[l_1(p, \hat{p})] \lesssim \mathbb{E}[l_1(p^*, \hat{p})] = \sqrt{\frac{2(|\mathcal{D}| - 1)}{n\pi}} \cdot \sum_{x \in \mathcal{D}_S}\frac{|\mathcal{D}_S| + e^{\varepsilon_x} - 1}{|\mathcal{D}_S|(e^{\varepsilon_x} - 1)}. \tag{24}$$

Table 1. Synthetic and Real-world Datasets

Datasets	# Users	# Items
Zipf	100000	20
Kosarak [1]	646510	100

Table 2. Parameter Settings

#	Mechanisms to Compare	ε_{min}	ε_{max}	LC	NR	SR
1	KRR,URR	0.1	1	4	0.5	0.2–1.0
2	KRR,URR	1	10	4	0.5	0.2–1.0
3	KRR,URR	0.1	10	4	0.5	0.2–1.0
4	URR	0.1	10	4	0.0–0.8 * 0.1–0.9 **	1.0
5	IDUE	0.1	10	4	0	0.1–1.0

* is used on Zipf dataset and ** is used on Kosarak dataset

According to [25], in low privacy regime, the expectation of l_2 and l_1 losses of $(\mathcal{D}_S, \varepsilon_{min})$-URR are $\frac{(|\mathcal{D}_S| + e^{\varepsilon_{min}} - 1)^2}{n(e^{\varepsilon_{min}} - 1)^2}\left(1 - \frac{1}{|\mathcal{D}|}\right)$ and $\sqrt{\frac{2(|\mathcal{D}| - 1)}{n\pi}} \cdot \frac{|\mathcal{D}_S| + e^{\varepsilon_{min}} - 1}{e^{\varepsilon_{min}} - 1}$, accordingly. Thus, the losses of our method is much smaller than that of URR in current setting.

7   Evaluation

In this section, we evaluate the performance of our IPRR based on the emprical estimation method with the Norm-sub (NS) truncation method and maximum likelihood estimation (MLE) method, and compare it with the the KRR, URR, and Input-Discriminative Unary Encoding (IDUE) [14] satisfying ID-LDP.

7.1   Experimental Setup

Datasets. We conducted experiments over two datasets, and show their details in Table 1. The first dataset, Zipf, was generated by sampling from a Zipf distribution with an exponential parameter $\alpha = 2$, followed by filtering the results using a specific threshold to control the size of the item domain and the number of users. The second dataset, Kosarak, is one of the largest real-world datasets, which contains millions of records related to the click-stream of news portals from users (e.g. see [8,32,33]). For Kosarak dataset, we randomly selected an item for every user to serve as the item they hold, and then applied the same filtering process used for the Zipf dataset.

Metrics. We use Mean Square Error (MSE) and Relative Error (RE) as the metrics of the performance, which are defined as

$$\text{MSE} = \sum_{x \in \mathcal{D}} \frac{(f_x - \hat{f}_x)^2}{n}, \quad \text{RE} = \sum_{x \in \mathcal{D}} \frac{|f_x - \hat{f}_x|}{f_x}, \tag{25}$$

where f_x (resp. $\hat{f}_x$) is the true (resp. estimated) frequency count of x. We take the sample mean of one hundred repeated experiments for analysis.

Settings. We conduct five experiments for both Zipf and Kosarak datasets, where the experiments #1~#3 compare the utility of IPRR with that of KRR and URR under various privacy level groups with different sample ratios, the experiment #4 compares IPRR with URR under different $|\mathcal{D}_N|$, and the experiment #5 compares IPRR with IDUE under different sample ratios. We use SR (sample ratio) to calculate $SR \cdot |\mathcal{D}|$ as the sample count n. In each experiment, we evaluate the utility under various privacy levels. Since the sensitivity of data shows an inverse relationship with the population size of respective individuals, we first sort the dataset based on the count of each item, and items with smaller counts are assigned to higher privacy levels. Then, we choose items with larger size as $\mathcal{D}_N$ (others as $\mathcal{D}_S$) by using NR (non-sensitive ratio), which controls the ratio of $|\mathcal{D}_N|$ over $|\mathcal{D}|$. For $\mathcal{D}_S$, we use $\varepsilon_{\min}$, $\varepsilon_{\max}$, LC (level count) to divide $\mathcal{D}_S$ into different privacy levels, where LC divides $\mathcal{D}_S$ and a range $[\varepsilon_{\min}, \varepsilon_{\max}]$ evenly to assign the privacy level, accordingly. For example, assume we have $\mathcal{D} = \{A, B, C, D, E, F\}$ with sizes 6, 5, 4, 3, 2, and 1 for each item. Under $\varepsilon_{\min} = 0.1$, $\varepsilon_{\max} = 0.3$, $LC = 3$, and $NR = 0.5$, we can obtain $\mathcal{D}_N = \{A, B, C\}$, with privacy budgets of 0.3, 0.2, and 0.1 assigned to items D, E, and F, respectively. In practical scenarios, it is unnecessary to assign a unique privacy level to every item. Thus, we set $LC = 4$ for all experiments in our settings. Additionally, in all experiments, KRR and URR satisfy $\varepsilon_{\min}$-LDP and $(\mathcal{D}_S, \mathcal{D}_S, \varepsilon_{\min})$-ULDP, respectively. Table 2 shows the details of the parameter settings for all experiments.

7.2   Experimental Results

Utility Under Various Privacy Level Groups. In Fig. 2 we illustrate the results of the experiments #1~#3. We conducted these experiments to compare the utility of our IPRR with other types of direct encoding mechanisms under various combinations of privacy budgets with fixed NR. Fristly, Fig. 2(a) and (d) show the comparison of the utility in a high privacy regime among IPRR, URR and KRR on both datasets. As we can see in the high privacy regime, our method outperforms the others by approximate one order of magnitude. As the sample count n increases, the loss decreases as well. Noticeably, in the figure, the results of KRR under both the NS and MLE methods are almost indistinguishable, while our results of the latter method are improved significantly compared with that of the former method. The reason is that the former method may truncate the empirical estimate for lacking samples. Furthermore, the high privacy regime will also escalate the degree of truncation for the emprical estimate, which naturally introduces more errors than the latter method. Secondly, the results of Fig. 2(b) and (e) present the comparison of the utility in a low privacy regime. It is clear that our method also has better performance than the others. Notably, in the current setting, the improvement of the MLE method over the NS method is less significant compared with that in the high privacy regime. We argue that a large privacy budget does not result in much truncation for the emprical estimate, so

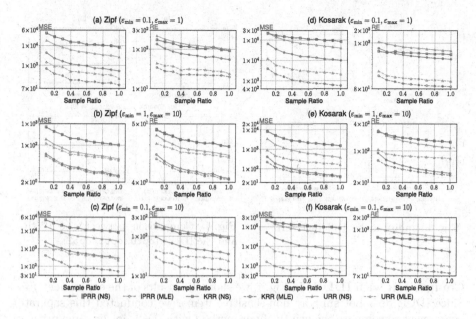

Fig. 2. Utility under Various Privacy Levels.

the results are close to each other. Finally, Fig. 2(c) and (f) give the results of the hybrid high and low privacy regimes. The results are close to Fig. 2(a) and (d), accordingly. Although the improvement is limited in this setting, it does not mean that all perturbations in our method are greatly influenced by the minimum privacy budget similar to IDUE.

Figure 3 shows the results of the experiment #4. In this experiment, we compare the utility of our IPRR with URR in the same privacy budget set to check the influence of different $|\mathcal{D}_N|$. We only compare with URR because only these two mechanisms support non-sensitive items. We restricted the maximum value of NR to 80% for the Zipf dataset since $|\mathcal{D}_S|$ will be less than $LC = 4$ if NR exceeds 0.8. As one can see, as $|\mathcal{D}_N|$ increases, our method outperforms URR, and all metrics decrease.

After all, our IPRR shows better performance than URR and KRR on the two corresponding metrics in the two datasets, which verifies our theoretical analysis. Compared with KRR, URR reduces the perturbation for non-sensitive items by coarsely dividing the domain into sensitive and non-sensitive subsets, resulting in lower variance than that of KRR under the identical sample ratio. Thus, URR has better overall performance than KRR. Our method further divides the sensitive domain into finer-grained subsets with personalized perturbation for each item, which reduces the perturbation for less sensitive items. Therefore, with the same sample ratio, our method reduces much more total variance than URR, and thus our method performs better than other mechanisms.

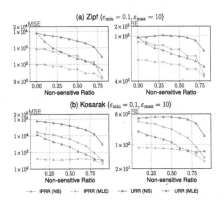

Fig. 3. Unility under Different NR.

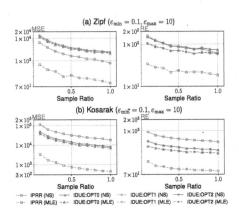

Fig. 4. Comparison between the IPRR and the IDUE (opt0, opt1, opt2).

Comparison with IDUE. In Fig. 4, we show the results of the experiment #5. Since IDUE does not support non-sensitive items, we conducted this separate experiment to compare the utility of our method with IDUE in the same privacy setting. It is clear that IPRR owns better performance than IDUE over Zipf with both NS and MLE methods, while IDUE outperforms IPRR over Kosarak with the NS method. The reason is that the unary encoding method used by IDUE has more advantages when processing an item domain with a larger size, and this may reduce the truncation for the empirical estimate. However, under the MLE method without the influence of truncation, IPRR outperforms IDUE even over Kosarak with the larger $|\mathcal{D}|$. We think that our IPRR effectively reduces unnecessary perturbation for less sensitive items than IDUE since the strength of perturbation is highly affected by the minimum privacy budget. In the current setting of our experiment, the perturbation for items with the maximum privacy budget only needs to satisfy 10-LDP in our method, while IDUE can only relax their perturbation at most 0.2-LDP according to the Lemma 1 in [14].

8   Conclusion

In this paper, we first proposed a novel notion of LDP called IPLDP for discrete distribution estimation in local privacy setting. To improve utility, IPLDP perturbs items independently for personalized protection according to the outputs with different privacy budgets. Then, to satisfy IPLDP, inspired by the phenomenon that the sensitivity of data is usually inversely proportional to the size of the population it pertains, we proposed a new mechanism named IPRR based on Mangat's RR. We prove that IPRR has tighter upper bound than that of existing direct encoding methods under both l_2 and l_1 losses of emprical estimate. Finally, we conducted related experiments on a synthetic and a real-world datasets. Both theoretical analysis and experimental results demonstrate that our scheme owns better performance than existing methods by at most one order of magnitude.

Acknowledgement. This work is jointly supported by the National Natural Science Foundation of China under Grant 61772215 and in part by the Major Science and Technology Project of Wuhan Science and Technology Bureau under Grant 2022013702025185.

A Proof of Lemma 2

Proof. To prove this lemma, we first consider a more general optimization problem as

$$F(w) = \max_{\boldsymbol{\theta}} \sum_{i=1}^{K} g[(\theta_i + c_i)(C - (\theta_i + c_i))] \quad \text{s.t. } \boldsymbol{\theta}^\top \mathbf{1} = w, \ \mathbf{0} \leqslant \boldsymbol{\theta} \leqslant \mathbf{1}w,$$

where $\boldsymbol{\theta}$ and $\boldsymbol{c}$ are vectors with k-dimension, $\boldsymbol{c}$ is a constant vector, $w \in (0, 1)$, and C is a large enough positive constant (e.g. $C \gg \boldsymbol{c}^\top \mathbf{1} + 1$).

First, we find a proper constant vectors $\boldsymbol{c}$ to obtain the optimal $\boldsymbol{\theta}$ without zero elements. Since g is any monotonically increasing concave function with $g(0) = 0$, according to Jensen inequality, we have

$$\sum_{i=1}^{K} g[(\theta_i + c_i)(C - (\theta_i + c_i))] \leqslant g\left[K \sum_{i=1}^{K} [(\theta_i + c_i)(C - (\theta_i + c_i))]\right],$$

where the equality holds iff $\theta_1 + c_1 = \cdots = \theta_K + c_K$. Hence, to satisfy the equality condition, we have

$$\sum_{i=1}^{K} (\theta_i + c_i) = w + \sum_{i=1}^{K} c_i \Rightarrow \theta_i = \frac{w + \sum_{j=1}^{K} c_j}{|k|} - c_i.$$

Then, since $0 < \theta_i < w$,

$$0 < \frac{w + \sum_{j=1}^{K} c_j}{K} - c_i < w.$$

Therefore, if all elements of $\boldsymbol{c}$ satisfy

$$\frac{w + \sum_{j=1}^{K} c_j}{K} - w < c_i < \frac{w + \sum_{j=1}^{K} c_j}{K},$$

we can ensure that the optimal $\boldsymbol{\theta}$ has no zero elements, and the maximum value is

$$
\begin{aligned}
F(w) &= g\left[K\sum_{i=1}^{K}\left[\frac{w+\sum_{j=1}^{K}c_j}{K}\left(C-\frac{w+\sum_{j=1}^{K}c_j}{K}\right)\right]\right] \\
&= g\left[K^2 \cdot \frac{w+\sum_{i=1}^{K}c_i}{K}\left(C-\frac{w+\sum_{i=1}^{K}c_i}{K}\right)\right] \\
&= g\left[\left(w+\sum_{i=1}^{K}c_i\right)\left(KC-\left(w+\sum_{i=1}^{K}c_i\right)\right)\right]
\end{aligned}
$$

Next, we consider the general case, where the optimal $\boldsymbol{\theta}$ contains zero elements. Let

$$
\tilde{F}(w) = \sum_{t=1}^{T}\tilde{F}_t(w) = \sum_{t=1}^{T} g[((1-w)\phi_t + c_t)(C - ((1-w)\phi_t + c_t))],
$$

where c_t is a constant which satisfies $c_t \geqslant \frac{w+\sum_{i=1}^{K}c_i}{K}$, and ϕ_t is a constant which satisfies $\sum_{t=1}^{T}\phi_t = 1$ and $0 < \phi_t < 1$.

Let $H(w) = F(w) + \tilde{F}(w)$. Then,

$$
\begin{aligned}
H' &= F' \cdot \left[KC - \left(w+\sum_{i=1}^{K}c_i\right) - \left(w+\sum_{i=1}^{K}c_i\right)\right] \\
&\quad + \sum_{t=1}^{T}\phi_t \tilde{F}_t' \cdot [((1-w)\phi_t + c_t) - (C - ((1-w)\phi_t + c_t))] \\
&= \frac{KC - 2\left(w+\sum_{i=1}^{K}c_i\right)}{1/F'} + \sum_{t=1}^{T}\frac{2[(1-w)\phi_t + c_t] - C}{1/\left(\phi_t \tilde{F}_t'\right)} \\
&= \sum_{t=1}^{T}\left[\frac{C - 2\frac{w+\sum_{i=1}^{K}c_i}{K}}{T/(KF')} + \frac{2[(1-w)\phi_t + c_t] - C}{1/\left(\phi_t \tilde{F}_t'\right)}\right] \\
&\geqslant \sum_{t=1}^{T}\frac{C - 2\frac{w+\sum_{i=1}^{K}c_i}{K} + 2[(1-w)\phi_t + c_t] - C}{\max\left[T/(KF'), 1/\left(\phi_t \tilde{F}_t'\right)\right]} \\
&= 2\sum_{t=1}^{T}\frac{(1-w)\phi_t + c_t - \frac{w+\sum_{i=1}^{K}c_i}{K}}{\max\left[T/(KF'), 1/\left(\phi_t \tilde{F}_t'\right)\right]} \\
&\geqslant 0,
\end{aligned}
$$

where $F' = g'\left[\left(w+\sum_{i=1}^{K}c_i\right)\left(KC - \left(w+\sum_{i=1}^{K}c_i\right)\right)\right]$, and $\tilde{F}_t' = g'[((1-w)\phi_t + c_t)(C - ((1-w)\phi_t + c_t))]$ Since $H' \geqslant 0$, $H(w)$ reaches its maximum when $w = 1$.

Finally, because any general case of the optimization problem in this lemma can be convert to the function H, the lemma holds.   □

References

1. kosarak dataset. http://fimi.uantwerpen.be/data/
2. Abstracts of Papers. Ann. Math. Stat. **20**(4), 620 – 624 (1949). https://doi.org/10.1214/aoms/1177729959
3. Alaggan, M., Gambs, S., Kermarrec, A.: Heterogeneous differential privacy. J. Priv. Confidentiality **7**(2) (2016)
4. Bassily, R., Nissim, K., Stemmer, U., Thakurta, A.G.: Practical locally private heavy hitters. In: NIPS, pp. 2288–2296 (2017)
5. Bassily, R., Smith, A.D.: Local, private, efficient protocols for succinct histograms. In: STOC, pp. 127–135. ACM (2015)
6. Bun, M., Steinke, T.: Concentrated differential privacy: simplifications, extensions, and lower bounds. In: Hirt, M., Smith, A. (eds.) TCC 2016. LNCS, vol. 9985, pp. 635–658. Springer, Heidelberg (2016). https://doi.org/10.1007/978-3-662-53641-4_24
7. Chen, R., Li, H., Qin, A.K., Kasiviswanathan, S.P., Jin, H.: Private spatial data aggregation in the local setting. In: ICDE, pp. 289–300. IEEE Computer Society (2016)
8. Chen, Z., Wang, J.: Ldp-fpminer: Fp-tree based frequent itemset mining with local differential privacy. CoRR arxiv:2209.01333 (2022)
9. Cuff, P., Yu, L.: Differential privacy as a mutual information constraint. In: CCS, pp. 43–54. ACM (2016)
10. Duchi, J.C., Jordan, M.I., Wainwright, M.J.: Local privacy and statistical minimax rates. In: FOCS, pp. 429–438. IEEE Computer Society (2013)
11. Dwork, C.: Differential privacy. In: Bugliesi, M., Preneel, B., Sassone, V., Wegener, I. (eds.) ICALP 2006. LNCS, vol. 4052, pp. 1–12. Springer, Heidelberg (2006). https://doi.org/10.1007/11787006_1
12. Dwork, C., McSherry, F., Nissim, K., Smith, A.: Calibrating noise to sensitivity in private data analysis. In: Halevi, S., Rabin, T. (eds.) TCC 2006. LNCS, vol. 3876, pp. 265–284. Springer, Heidelberg (2006). https://doi.org/10.1007/11681878_14
13. Erlingsson, Ú., Pihur, V., Korolova, A.: RAPPOR: randomized aggregatable privacy-preserving ordinal response. In: CCS, pp. 1054–1067. ACM (2014)
14. Gu, X., Li, M., Xiong, L., Cao, Y.: Providing input-discriminative protection for local differential privacy. In: ICDE, pp. 505–516. IEEE (2020)
15. Han, J., Pei, J., Yin, Y.: Mining frequent patterns without candidate generation. In: SIGMOD Conference, pp. 1–12. ACM (2000)
16. Jorgensen, Z., Yu, T., Cormode, G.: Conservative or liberal? personalized differential privacy. In: ICDE, pp. 1023–1034. IEEE Computer Society (2015)
17. Kairouz, P., Bonawitz, K.A., Ramage, D.: Discrete distribution estimation under local privacy. In: ICML. JMLR Workshop and Conference Proceedings, vol. 48, pp. 2436–2444. JMLR.org (2016)
18. Kairouz, P., Oh, S., Viswanath, P.: Extremal mechanisms for local differential privacy. In: NIPS, pp. 2879–2887 (2014)
19. Kifer, D., Machanavajjhala, A.: Pufferfish: a framework for mathematical privacy definitions. ACM Trans. Database Syst. **39**(1), 3:1–3:36 (2014)

20. Kotsogiannis, I., Doudalis, S., Haney, S., Machanavajjhala, A., Mehrotra, S.: One-sided differential privacy. In: ICDE, pp. 493–504. IEEE (2020)

21. Lin, B., Kifer, D.: Information preservation in statistical privacy and bayesian estimation of unattributed histograms. In: SIGMOD Conference, pp. 677–688. ACM (2013)

22. Lin, W., Li, B., Wang, C.: Towards private learning on decentralized graphs with local differential privacy. IEEE Trans. Inf. Forensics Secur. **17**, 2936–2946 (2022)

23. Mangat, N.S.: An improved randomized response strategy. J. Royal Stat. Soc. Ser. B (Methodol.) **56**(1), 93–95 (1994). http://www.jstor.org/stable/2346030

24. Mironov, I.: Rényi differential privacy. In: CSF, pp. 263–275. IEEE Computer Society (2017)

25. Murakami, T., Kawamoto, Y.: Utility-optimized local differential privacy mechanisms for distribution estimation. In: USENIX Security Symposium, pp. 1877–1894. USENIX Association (2019)

26. Nie, Y., Yang, W., Huang, L., Xie, X., Zhao, Z., Wang, S.: A utility-optimized framework for personalized private histogram estimation. IEEE Trans. Knowl. Data Eng. **31**(4), 655–669 (2019)

27. Qin, Z., Yu, T., Yang, Y., Khalil, I., Xiao, X., Ren, K.: Generating synthetic decentralized social graphs with local differential privacy. In: CCS, pp. 425–438. ACM (2017)

28. Wang, N., et al.: Privtrie: effective frequent term discovery under local differential privacy. In: ICDE, pp. 821–832. IEEE Computer Society (2018)

29. Wang, T., Li, N., Jha, S.: Locally differentially private frequent itemset mining. In: IEEE Symposium on Security and Privacy, pp. 127–143. IEEE Computer Society (2018)

30. Wang, T., Li, N., Jha, S.: Locally differentially private heavy hitter identification. IEEE Trans. Dependable Secur. Comput. **18**(2), 982–993 (2021)

31. Wang, T., Lopuhaä-Zwakenberg, M., Li, Z., Skoric, B., Li, N.: Locally differentially private frequency estimation with consistency. In: NDSS. The Internet Society (2020)

32. Wang, T., et al.: Improving utility and security of the shuffler-based differential privacy. Proc. VLDB Endow. **13**(13), 3545–3558 (2020)

33. Wang, Z., Zhu, Y., Wang, D., Han, Z.: Fedfpm: a unified federated analytics framework for collaborative frequent pattern mining. In: INFOCOM, pp. 61–70. IEEE (2022)

34. Warner, S.L.: Randomized response: a survey technique for eliminating evasive answer bias. J. Am. Stat. Assoc. **60**(309), 63–69 (1965)

35. Wei, C., Ji, S., Liu, C., Chen, W., Wang, T.: ASGLDP: collecting and generating decentralized attributed graphs with local differential privacy. IEEE Trans. Inf. Forensics Secur. **15**, 3239–3254 (2020)

36. Xu, J., Zhang, Z., Xiao, X., Yang, Y., Yu, G.: Differentially private histogram publication. In: ICDE, pp. 32–43. IEEE Computer Society (2012)

Intelligent Zigbee Protocol Fuzzing via Constraint-Field Dependency Inference

Mengfei Ren[1,3], Haotian Zhang[1(✉)], Xiaolei Ren[1(✉)], Jiang Ming[2(✉)], and Yu Lei[1(✉)]

[1] University of Texas at Arlington, Arlington, TX 76019, USA
`mengfei.ren@uah.edu`, {`haotian.zhang,xiaolei.ren`}`@mavs.uta.edu`, `ylei@cse.uta.edu`
[2] Tulane University, New Orleans, LA 70118, USA
`jming@tulane.edu`
[3] University of Alabama in Huntsville, Huntsville, AL 35899, USA

Abstract. Zigbee is one of the global most popular IoT standards widely deployed by millions of devices and customers. Its fast market growth also incentivizes cybercriminals. Inference-guided fuzzing has shown promising results for security vulnerability detection, which infers the relationship between input bytes and path constraints. However, deploying such a technique on Zigbee protocol implementation is not a trivial task because of the vendor-specific requirements and particular hardware configuration. In this paper, we propose *TaintBFuzz*, an intelligent Zigbee protocol fuzzing by inferring the dependency between message fields and path constraints. We then use the inference to prioritize the corresponding fields in the mutation process and generate inputs that could explore untouched branches. We implemented a prototype of TaintBFuzz and evaluated it on a mainstream Zigbee protocol implementation called Z-Stack. Compared with state-of-the-art protocol fuzzing tools, including Boofuzz, Peach, and Z-Fuzzer, TaintBFuzz outperforms them in code coverage with the assistance of constraint-field dependency inference. Notably, TaintBFuzz efficiently identifies eight distinct vulnerabilities, of which two are previously unidentified.

Keywords: Fuzzing · Taint Analysis · IoT Wireless Protocols · Zigbee

1 Introduction

Due to the new sensors and more reliable mobile connectivity, the Internet of Things (IoT) device market is projected to reach hundreds of millions of dollars by 2023 [1]. Zigbee protocol [2] is one of the dominant wireless communication protocols deployed in resource-efficient IoT devices. According to the recent

M. Ren—This research work is completed when the author takes her Ph.D. degree at University of Texas at Arlington.

G. Tsudik et al. (Eds.): ESORICS 2023, LNCS 14345, pp. 467–486, 2024.
https://doi.org/10.1007/978-3-031-51476-0_23

market report from Connectivity Standards Alliance, about four billion Zigbee devices are expected to be sold globally by 2023 [3]. This fast market growth of Zigbee also incentivizes cybercriminals. Several recent research works have revealed the security issues on Zigbee protocol [4–7]. These detected vulnerabilities could be exploited for DDoS attacks and remote malicious execution. Therefore, discovering security issues in Zigbee protocol implementations is necessary and practical.

Fuzz testing has shown promising results for finding security vulnerabilities. Many fuzzers [8–13] apply various techniques to infer the relationship between input bytes and path constraints for generating test inputs efficiently, which can explore the deeper code of the target program. Data flow analysis (e.g., dynamic taint analysis) is one of the most adopted methods for dependency inference. VUzzer [10], and GREYONE [11] utilize it to determine where and how to mutate inputs. REDQUEEN [14] aims to solve magic values and checksum in fuzzing, which colors an input seed by replacing each input byte with the largest number of random bytes possible. Angora [12] uses it to depict the pattern of input bytes related to path constraints. PATA [13] proposes a path-aware taint analysis to identify and mutate critical bytes to solve path constraints.

However, it is not a trivial task to directly deploy those fuzzers to Zigbee protocol implementations. First, they have difficulty compiling the Zigbee protocol. For example, as shown in Fig 1, Texas Instruments (TI) deploys specific compiler check in its Zigbee protocol stack Z-Stack. It prevents general compil-

```
18:  /*
19:   * Check that the correct C compiler is used.
20:   */
21:  #ifndef __ICCARM__
22:      #error "File intrinsics.h can only be used together with iccarm."
23:  #endif
24:
25:  #ifndef __ICCARM_INTRINSICS_VERSION__
26:      #error "Unknown compiler intrinsics version"
27:  #elif __ICCARM_INTRINSICS_VERSION__ != 2
28:      #error "Compiler intrinsics version does not match this file"
29:  #endif
```

Fig. 1. An example of compiler check deployed in a system library used by Z-Stack [15], a popular Zigbee protocol stack developed by Texas Instruments.

ers (e.g., GCC, Clang, and LLVM) compiling the full protocol stack, which are instead widely used by the existing fuzzing solutions [16].

Moreover, those fuzzing approaches cannot provide a proper simulated execution environment for the Zigbee protocol due to the particular hardware configuration required by the Zigbee protocol vendors. The Zigbee protocol stack is usually executed in particular system-on-chip (SoC) devices and a bare-metal program containing a single control loop for scheduling tasks and handling events [17]. Existing fuzzers with simulation platforms (e.g., QEMU) not only require a Linux kernel or an abstraction layer for execution but also support limited embedded devices which are not satisfied the Zigbee protocol vendors' device requirements [16]. The vendor-specific devices also have particular peripheral interrupts not supplied in existing simulation solutions [18]. The current simulation platform cannot, or only with significant engineering effort, provide support for all device-specific hardware configurations required by the Zigbee protocol vendors. Hence, these limitations prevent those state-of-the-art fuzzing methods from directly deploying on the Zigbee protocol implementations.

In this paper, we propose *TaintBFuzz*, an intelligent Zigbee protocol fuzzing with constraint-field dependency inference. Our solution intends to assist IoT application developers in evaluating the security threats associated with the Zigbee protocol implementation in developing their applications. We leverage static taint analysis to infer the relationship between the message field and the path constraints. The dependency inference then guides the fuzzing engine to prioritize the critical message fields for further mutation, which have higher chance to exercise unvisited branches.

The fuzzing engine of TaintBFuzz is designed based on grammar-based fuzzing with code coverage heuristics. It constructs the initial test seeds based on the message format script from scratch. To execute the Zigbee protocol stack in a simulation environment, we use an industrial embedded device development platform, IAR Embedded Workbench [19], to interact with the fuzzing engine of TaintBFuzz. The IAR is used by many Zigbee protocol vendors, such as TI, Samsung, and Toshiba, and provides a particular compiler and a software simulator. The IAR simulator also supports many vendor-specific embedded devices with pre-defined hardware interrupt/peripheral configurations. We also develop a stack driver and a proxy server to bridge the communication gap between the IAR simulator and the fuzzing engine.

We implemented a prototype of TaintBFuzz and evaluated its effectiveness in security vulnerability detection on Z-Stack [15], a mainstream Zigbee protocol stack developed by Texas Instruments. We compare TaintBFuzz with three state-of-the-art protocol fuzzing tools, Peach [20], Boofuzz [21], and Z-Fuzzer [16]. Peach and Boofuzz are conventional protocol fuzzers widely used in academia and industry. Z-Fuzzer is a recently proposed coverage-guided protocol fuzzer specialized for the Zigbee protocol implementation. Our experiment results show that TaintBFuzz outperforms those fuzzers in terms of the number of unique edges found and statements covered. TaintBFuzz has also identified eight unique vulnerabilities in Z-Stack, of which two are previously undiscovered. We have also reported the detected two crashes to the protocol vendor, which are under review when writing this paper. To summarize, we make the following contributions:

- We propose a framework to infer the relationship between the message fields and path constraints by leveraging static taint analysis, which specifically addresses the Zigbee protocol vendor-specific compiler requirement.
- We propose an intelligent mutation strategy utilizing the constraint-field dependency inference to tune the direction of fuzzing, able to prioritize which message field for mutation.
- We implement a prototype of TaintBFuzz and evaluate it on a mainstream Zigbee protocol stack, showing that it outperforms several state-of-the-art protocol fuzzers in terms of code coverage. TaintBFuzz discovers eight vulnerabilities in Z-Stack, two of which are previously unknown.

Open Source. To facilitate the reproducibility of the research results, we release TaintBFuzz's source code, which is publicly available at https://github.com/zigbeeprotocol/TaintBFuzz.

2   Related Work

In this section, we first introduce background knowledge of the Zigbee protocol. As TaintBFuzz is a protocol fuzzer based on taint inference for the Zigbee protocol, we then discuss related work in the security analysis of the Zigbee protocol and fuzz testing with the taint analysis technique.

2.1   Zigbee Protocol

The Connectivity Standard Alliance standardizes the Zigbee protocol as a resource-efficient two-way wireless communication protocol for IoT devices [23]. The protocol stack is shown in Fig 2. The alliance defines the Application Layer (APL) and the Network Layer (NWK) on top of the IEEE 802.15.4 standard, which defines the Medium Access Control Layer (MAC) and the Physical Layer (PHY). The MAC and PHY support packet transmission through the 2.4GHz radio channel. While the NWK layer administers the Zigbee network and forwards packets, the APL is in charge of application-level functionality. Zigbee Cluster Library (ZCL) is a core component in the APL, providing essential API for the manufacturers to implement the device functionalities. From the user's point of view, the ZCL is a protocol that runs at the application layer and serves as the core library for the device's functionalities. Therefore, we will use ZCL as a case study in the following subsections and remaining parts of this paper.

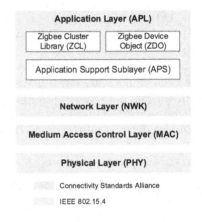

Fig. 2. Zigbee protocol stack overview [22].

2.2   Security Analysis on Zigbee

Since the Zigbee protocol was standardized in 2003, various research work has been published to analyze the security risks of the Zigbee protocol. Specifically, prior work [4–6, 24–27] focuses on the security of the Zigbee network transmission. Z3Sec [5], and Snout [24] utilize penetration testing to assess existing vulnerabilities in a Zigbee network. To analyze the security of the Zigbee protocol on specific embedded devices, IoTcube [28], and beSTORM [26] have also been developed. Akestoridis et al. [27] proposed Zigator to analyze encrypted Zigbee packets for selective jamming and spoofing attacks. Wang et al. [6] developed an automated verification tool VEREJOIN via the model checking technique to evaluate the Zigbee network rejoin procedure. Ronen et al. [4] demonstrated that a worm affecting all Zigbee-enabled lamps might damage the smart lighting in a city. Most of these solutions are black-box solutions that monitor and manipulate Zigbee network traffic to detect security issues.

One of the most well-liked vulnerability identification techniques is fuzz testing (e.g., AFL [29]), which is widely used and researched in the community. Cui et al. proposed two fuzzing approaches to detect security risks on Zigbee: FSM-Fuzzing, which is based on a finite state machine [30], and CG-Fuzzing, which is based on a genetic algorithm [31]. However, both are closed sources thus we failed to compare with state-of-the-art protocol fuzzers. The most recent approach closest to our method is Z-Fuzzer [16], which leverages the code coverage heuristic to guide the fuzzing process on a mainstream Zigbee protocol stack. However, it still has limitations in efficiently exploring the target program's deeper code by ignoring the path constraints' structure.

Compared to the prior work, our work target security issues in Zigbee protocol implementation rather than the real-time Zigbee network. Specifically, our work leverages the relationship between the message field and the path constraints via the static taint analysis technique to efficiently guide the mutation of test inputs, which could explore deeper code of the target program.

2.3 Taint Inference Based Fuzz Testing

A significant drawback of mutation-based fuzzers is efficiently generating test input satisfying complex path constraints. Many fuzzers, such as Driller [8] and QSYM [32], utilize symbolic execution to resolve the complicated branch condition constraints. However, they are not scalable to the extensive application due to the slow execution speed and path explosion issue.

In order to efficiently resolve path constraints, more lightweight solutions are proposed, which infer the relationship between input bytes and path constraints to guide seed mutation. VUzzer [10] focuses on generating test cases to pass magic value validations. It uses taint analysis to identify critical bytes mutated to satisfy the path constraints. Angora [12] locates input bytes that flow into path constraints based on byte-level taint tracking. It then mutates these bytes with a gradient descent algorithm to satisfy the path constraints. REDQUEEN [14] aims to solve magic values and checksum in fuzzing. While reserving the execution path, it colors an input seed by replacing every input byte with as many random bytes as possible. Matryoshka [33] explores nested branches for fuzzing based on both control flow and taint flow. GREYONE [11] utilizes taint analysis to locate the critical input bytes and decides how to mutate them. PATA [13] proposes a path-awareness taint analysis for fuzzing inferring taints based on control flow and value changes. TRUZZ [34] infers the relationship between input bytes and validation checks and prevents those bytes being mutated during the fuzzing.

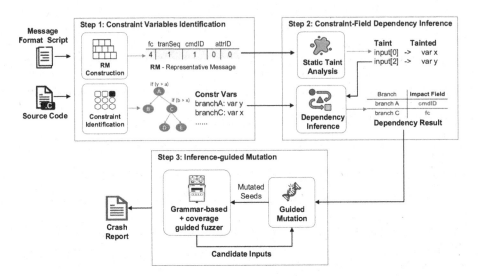

Fig. 3. Overall design of TaintBFuzz. The black arrows mean the main workflow of TaintBFuzz. The red arrows mean the intermediate results generated by the related components. (Color figure online)

Though these fuzzers have shown good performance on general applications, they are hard to directly deploy on the Zigbee protocol implementation due to the vendor-specific requirements of compiler and underlying hardware configuration [16]. Most of these fuzzers develop their approaches with general compilers such as LLVM or Clang, which are not supported by many Zigbee protocol vendors in their protocol implementations. Compared to these fuzzers, our method first pre-process the Zigbee protocol implementation with the compiler specified by the protocol vendor. The pre-processed code is then parsed and type-checked for the further taint analysis.

3   Design of TaintBFuzz

Figure 3 presents the overall design of TaintBFuzz. As the ZCL is the core library of Zigbee protocol stack to implement an IoT device's functionalities, we will deploy it to present the details of each step in the following subsections.

3.1   Constraint Variable Identification

The first challenge of TaintBFuzz design is to identify the constraint variables reasonably. A constraint variable consists of a set of program variables used in a path constraint. To address this challenge, TaintBFuzz collects program variables used in all constraints based on the AST analysis of the program. A program variable can directly or indirectly influence a constraint. Notably, a temporary

ZCL Header				ZCL Payload
Frame Control (fc)	Manufacturer Code (manu)	Transaction Sequence Number (tranSeq)	Command Identifier (cmdID)	......

Fig. 4. ZCL frame format [22].

variable saves an intermediate result that can be used in the following constraints, e.g., in the statements $temp = Function\_A(x, y); if(temp)...$, the result of a function call is saved as a temporary variable that impacts the IF condition. In addition to the regular conditional constraint statements like *IF, LOOP, and SWITCH*, TaintBFuzz also collects program variables used in every function call to address the temporary variable propagation. Accordingly, a *constraint variable* is defined as a tuple (V, t, loc), where V is a set of program variables, $t \in T$ that T is a set of pre-defined constraint types (*IF, LOOP, SWITCH, CALL*), and *loc* is a statement line number of a constraint. A path constraint can be parsed as several sub-constraints during the AST analysis; thus, we save *loc* to assemble a completed dependent fields list during the following inference phase.

Additionally, TaintBFuzz constructs a set of Representative Messages (RM) based on the given protocol message format script[1]. An RM is defined as a tuple $(F, Len, data)$, where $F = (F_1, ..., F_n)$ is a set of message fields defined in the script, $Len = (L_1, ..., L_n)$ is the length of every message field, and *data* is a real ZCL message. Each RM represents a unique type of ZCL message. The generated RMs will be used for taint analysis to identify the critical fields that impact program variables.

3.2 Constraint-Field Dependency Inference

The second challenge of TaintBFuzz is inferring the relationship between the message fields and the path constraints. A standard solution is utilizing dynamic taint analysis (DTA) to identify which input bytes are used in branch instructions. However, it could fail to compile the Zigbee protocol because of the vendor-specific compiler requirement as shown in Fig 1. To tackle this challenge, TaintBFuzz performs static taint analysis on a pre-processed source code compiled by the protocol vendor-specific compiler to distinguish the dependency between message fields and path constraints.

Algorithm 1 illustrates the primary process for the dependency inference. First, we track an external input's impact on the program execution through static taint analysis. For each RM, we taint each message value (e.g., input[0] whose value is 4 as shown in Fig. 3) and perform static taint analysis to collect the tainted variables (lines 4–6). After collecting the taint analysis result, we perform dependency inference based on the constraint variables collected from Step 1 and the taint analysis result. For each constraint variable, we first identify if its program variable exists in the tainted variables (line 10).

---

[1] An example of the message format script is presented in Appendix A.

Algorithm 1: Constraint-Field Dependency Inference

Input   : A set of representative message: $\mathcal{R}$,
         A set of constraint variables: $\mathcal{P}$,
         Preprocessed source code: $\mathcal{S}$
Output: Hashmap(constraint $\rightarrow$ fields): $Deps$

1 $tainted \leftarrow \emptyset$
2 $Deps \leftarrow \emptyset$
3 **foreach** $rm \in \mathcal{R}$ **do**
4 | $taint \leftarrow$ **taintField** (rm)
5 | $taint\_vars \leftarrow$ **taintAnalysis** $(\mathcal{S}, taint)$
6 | $tainted \leftarrow tainted \cup (taint, taint\_vars, rm.data)$
7 **end**

8 **foreach** $constraint \in \mathcal{P}$ **do**
9 | **foreach** $var \in constraint.V$ **do**
10 | | **if** **isTainted** $(var, tainted)$ **then**
11 | | | $tainted\_record \leftarrow$ **getTainted** $(var, tainted)$
12 | | | $field \leftarrow$ **searchField** $(\mathcal{R}, tainted\_record)$
13 | | | $Deps[constraint] \leftarrow Deps[constraint] \cup field$
14 | | **end**
15 | **end**
16 **end**
17 $Deps \leftarrow$ **assembleDependency** $(Deps)$

If a variable is a tainted variable, then we collect its tainted record (line 11) including the tainted label like `input[0]` in Step 2 and the message value like the array `[4,1,1,0,0]` in Step 1. Then the tainted record is used to search the corresponding message field in the set of RMs (line 12). Finally, we gather all message fields related to the program variables used in a path constraint, e.g., constraint A is impacted by the message field `cmdID` as shown in Fig. 3. The collected result is saved as a map where the key is the constraint, and the value is the message fields influencing the constraint. As a path constraint could consist of several sub-constraints, we combine all constraint-field dependencies based on the constraint's *loc* value as the final dependency inference result and pass it to the mutation engine (line 17).

3.3   Inference-Guided Mutation

The main challenge of TaintBFuzz is effectively leveraging dependency analysis results, which implicates inference-guided mutation. Our objective is to enhance the mutation process through dependency inference when a fuzzer is hard to explore more paths of a program. Remarkably, we use coverage-guided fuzzing (CGF) in our main fuzzing engine because it is low-cost and efficiently covers the majority of easy-to-cover branches. Only for hard-to-cover branches, we introduce the constraint-field dependency to augment the mutation process and generate diversified seeds. Algorithm 2 shows the primary process of coverage-guided

---

Algorithm 2: Fuzzing Process with Constraint-Field Dependency Inference

---

Input : Input seed: s, Inference result: *Infer*,
           Control flow graph: $\mathcal{G}$, Timeout: *timeout*
           Program for coverage tracking: $\mathcal{P}$,
           Program for inference tracking: $\mathcal{P}'$
Output: Detected crash: *crash*

1   $execPath \leftarrow \emptyset$
2   $crash \leftarrow \emptyset$
3   $threshold \leftarrow$ `user_predefined_value`
4 **def main**():
5   **while** *not timeout* **do**
6          $cov, execPath, crash \leftarrow$ **execCheckCoverage** $(s, \mathcal{P})$
7   **if** *noUpdate* (*cov, threshold*) **then**
8              $s \leftarrow$ **mutateWithInfer** $(s, cov, execPath)$
9   **else**
10             $s \leftarrow$ **mutate** (s)
11   **end**

12 **def mutateWithInfer** $(s, cov, execPath)$:
13      $pid \leftarrow$ len $(execPath)$
14      $uncovered \leftarrow$ **checkPath** $(cov, execPath, pid, \mathcal{G})$
15      $inferFields \leftarrow$ **getInferFields** $(uncovered, Infer)$
16   **while** $pid \geq 0$ **do**
17   **foreach** $f \in inferFields$ **do**
18              $s', mutated \leftarrow$ **mutate** (s, f)
19   **if** *mutated* **then**
20   **break**
21   **end**
22          $cov', path', crash \leftarrow$ **executeGetCovered** $(s', \mathcal{P}')$
23   **if** *hasCovered* (*uncovered, cov'*) **then**
24   **return** s'
25   **else if** *callStackChanged* (*execPath, path'*) **then**
26              $inferFields \leftarrow$ **updateFieldState** $(s, execPath, inferFields)$
27   **else if** *not mutated* **then**
28              $pid \leftarrow pid - 1$
29              $uncovered \leftarrow$ **checkPath** $(cov', execPath, pid, \mathcal{G})$
30              $inferFields \leftarrow$ **getInferFields** $(uncovered, Infer)$
31   **end**
32   **end**

---

fuzzing with constraint-field dependency inference. A *threshold* is a pre-defined value of the number of mutations since the last updated code coverage, indicating when to utilize the constraint-field dependency for mutation on a particular path to explore more uncovered branches.

Grammar Based with Coverage Guided Fuzzing. TaintBFuzz uses a grammar based fuzzer with coverage-guided feedback as its fuzzing engine. We generate the initial seed corpus based on the given protocol message script from scratch so that each seed would satisfy the sanity check of message processing. If a new edge is discovered, the seed is saved as a favored test case with higher prioritization in the following mutations. The fuzzer also monitors the protocol stack execution result and reports any detected crashes. If the code coverage has not been updated after several seed mutations (*threshold*), we utilize the inference result for mutation optimization.

Mutation with Dependency Inference. Once no more new codes are explored after the pre-defined threshold, we mutate the seed based on the constraint-field dependency of the current execution path. Assume a sample input's message fields are $[fc, manu, seqID, cmd, attrId, type, data]$ and a covered basic block sequence is $[B_1, B_2, B_4, B_6, B_7]$. In order to explore deeper of the path, TaintBFuzz backtracks the block sequence to identify the last uncovered block in the current path by examining the control flow graph and coverage feedback (lines 12–14), e.g., B_6 is the predecessor block of B_7 that contains a condition check and has an uncovered block B_8. Then TaintBFuzz searches the corresponding constraint of B_6 in the dependency inference result. For example, we find the fields $[fc$ and $cmd]$ that influence the constraint. TaintBFuzz sequentially mutates each field to generate new inputs (lines 16–20), and executes the program with the new inputs (line 21). If the block B_8 has been accessed (lines 22–23) indicating the code coverage is increased, then we return to regular coverage-guided fuzzing with the new input.

A mutation on the dependent field may change the predecessor block sequence of the previously uncovered block. For example, the predecessor block sequence of B_8 is $B_1 \rightarrow B_2 \rightarrow B_4 \rightarrow B_6$. A new value of the inferred field cmd leads to a new execution path that does not exercise B_6 any more. Then, TaintBFuzz first tries other candidate values of the field cmd and checks if the previously predecessor block sequence can be re-accessed (line 25). The worst case is that all candidate values of the field never explore the uncovered branch. In that case, TaintBFuzz restores the original value of this field and filters out this field from the inferred fields list without further mutation. Furthermore, suppose mutations on all dependent fields of a constraint fail to access the uncovered branch, i.e., the variable *mutated* is FALSE, indicating the completed mutation on the fields (line 26). In that case, TaintBFuzz then back-traces to the next uncovered block in the path to mutate with the inferred fields until all blocks in the block sequence have been traversed (lines 27–29).

4   Implementation

The purpose of TaintBFuzz is to assist Zigbee protocol vendors and IoT application manufacturers in avoiding security risks during their development phase. Thus, the Zigbee protocol message format and related IoT device configuration are assumed to be aware and configured in the format script. As Fig 3 shows, the constraint variables identifier, the constraint-field dependency inferrer, and the inference-guided mutator are the three main components of TaintBFuzz. We illustrated the details of each component as follows.

The representative message constructor is implemented using the message generator of Boofuzz [21] with a pre-defined message format script that conforms to protocol format definition [35]. The constraint variables identifier and taint analysis tool are developed based on Frama-C [36]. Frama-C is an open-source platform dedicated to source-code analysis of C software and perform static analysis based on abstract syntax tree (AST). The constraint variable collector is performed with a pre-processing file of the source code that is compiled with the IAR compiler to avoid compiler check problem. We modify Frame-C to analyze pre-processed code with the vendor-specific syntax that are not initially supported (e.g., _intrinsic, _nounwind, #Pragma rtmodel and so on) for AST analysis. We also implement a script using Ocaml to analyze AST and collects the constraint variables used in IF, LOOP, SWITCH, and CALL statements.

The constraint-field dependency inferrer implements Algorithm 1. According to the generated RMs and taint analysis result, it maps message fields to several message fields that could impact the condition decision. The inference-guided mutator implements Algorithm 2. Suppose no more new edges are explored after several mutations (a threshold). In that case, it evaluates each input seed along its execution path and collects constraint variables helpful in exploring new branches. Then it mutates the critical fields to generate new seeds to explore the deeper of the path. We currently set up the threshold as 50 based on our experiment results.

Moreover, several message fields in Zigbee are enumerated types with pre-defined values defined in the Zigbee protocol specification. The protocol checks if such a field has a particular value that requires a specific handling process. Existing protocol fuzzers mutate such a field by the following methods: (a) randomly selecting values (e.g., selecting any value between [0, 255] if the field is byte type), (b) enumerating all possible values based on the field size, (c) selecting values based on their fuzzing dictionary defined according to human heuristics. Such mutation methods lead to ineffective fuzzing performance. To tackle this problem, we customize the fuzzing dictionary of those message fields by considering their pre-defined values in the protocol specification along with several negative values to reduce the searching space.

The coverage-guided fuzzing engine is developed based on Z-Fuzzer's fuzzing engine that considers the code coverage feedback. We integrate our inference-guided mutator with its fuzzing engine. We utilize the embedded device simulator C-SPY [37] of IAR Workbench to execute the Zigbee protocol stack. We also create a proxy server to enable the connection between the fuzzing engine and the simulator, as the simulator lacks a network interface for sending test messages. According to the static analysis result, we noticed that some functions do not have any callers, which would be used depending on the IoT application vendor's device feature requirements. Thus, we also add corresponding handlers in the source code to fuzz these corner cases.

5   Evaluation

In this section, we evaluate TaintBFuzz through multiple experiments. The experiments are designed to answer the following research questions:

- **RQ1**: Can TaintBFuzz achieve better fuzzing performance compared to state-of-the-art protocol fuzzers?
- **RQ2**: How efficient is TaintBFuzz at detecting vulnerabilities compared to state-of-the-art protocol fuzzers?

We illustrate the novelty and efficiency of TaintBFuzz in comparison with three baseline protocol fuzzers, Peach [20], Boofuzz [21], and Z-Fuzzer [16]. Boofuzz is the successor of Sulley [38], an industry-standard protocol fuzzer more actively maintained than Sulley. Both are open source and have been used in existing research papers [39,40]. Z-Fuzzer is a device-agnostic fuzzing tool for Zigbee protocol implementation that leverages code coverage heuristic on grammar-based fuzzing. Boofuzz and Peach do not initially work with the Zigbee protocol. Hence, we incorporated them with our proxy server and simulation platform to send test inputs for Zigbee protocol execution.

All of our experiments were performed on a machine with eight cores (Intel® Core™ i7-6700 CPU @ 3.40GHz) and 32 GB memory running the Windows 10 Pro operating system and IAR Embedded Workbench for ARM 8.3. We use a widespread Zigbee protocol implementation Z-Stack [15] as the target program, developed by Texas Instruments with various sample project code bases, and its source code is available. From the user's point of view, the ZCL is a protocol that runs at the application layer and serves as the core library for the Zigbee protocol stack. We employ ZCL as a case study in our evaluation. We ran each fuzzer on Z-Stack over 24 h. All experiments were repeated ten times. We also set the threshold for inference-guided mutation as 50 when compared with other protocol fuzzers.

5.1   Fuzzing Performance

To answer **RQ1**, we performed a set of fuzzing experiments on each fuzzer to examine their generated test cases, statement coverage, and edge coverage. The fuzzers produce test cases with the given message format script using the user-specific or pre-defined fuzzing dictionary, for which the total number of test cases is finite. Results[2] are presented in Table 1. The results show that TaintBFuzz is more effective than state-of-the-art protocol fuzzers.

---

[2] During our evaluation, we noticed that existing research has incorrect percentage calculations on state-of-the-art fuzzers. Thus, we recalculate them and show in Table 1.

Test Case Genera-
tion. We examine the
uniqueness of the test
cases produced by all
fuzzers. TaintBFuzz can
achieve higher code cov-
erage than other fuzzers
with fewer test cases,
especially with five times

Table 1. Evaluation results of fuzzing performance of all fuzzers on Z-stack in 10 runs. We report the code coverage in average.

Fuzzer	Unique Test Cases	Statement Coverage		Edge Coverage	
		total	%	total	%
TaintBFuzz	12,493	1111	**68.88**	800	**74.42**
Z-Fuzzer	61,386	971	63.18	769	71.53
Boofuzz	16,756	912	59.33	680	63.26
Peach	18,271	850	55.30	628	58.42

fewer test cases than Z-Fuzzer, due to the reduced input space of several message fields with the customized fuzzing dictionary. In addition, to differentiate between different fuzzers on test case creation, we classify test cases according to the Zigbee protocol standard using the field *Command Identification* in the ZCL header. TaintBFuzz generated 194 distinct types of test cases in total, of which only 34 of them can be generated by other fuzzers. More than half of these distinct types are generated after mutating the dependent fields in the constraint-field dependency inference. We also measure how the different *thresh-old* values affect the test generation. The result is shown in Appendix B

Code Coverage. We measure the code coverage on all fuzzers. Peach and Boofuzz cannot directly work with Z-Stack execution, so we integrated them with our protocol simulation platform via the proxy server. As shown in Table 1, TaintBFuzz can achieve higher statement coverage and edge coverage with fewer test cases. As we reduced the searching space of several message fields with predefined values in the Zigbee protocol specification, TaintBFuzz can efficiently generate test seeds with dependency inference to explore more paths in the target program. Our primary focus is on effectively creating test cases that conform to the Zigbee protocol specification's message format and exploring more normal execution paths. As a result, we cannot fully cover the exception-handling code in the protocol implementation.

Figure 5 presents the variation of code coverage of fuzzing in all fuzzers. For better result presentation, we plot the coverage trend of the first 6000 test cases generation to show in Fig. 5. The zoomed-in graph in the lower left corner display more details about how the code coverage varies in the first 100 test cases. It shows that Boofuzz, Z-Fuzzer and TaintBFuzz quickly proliferated at an early phase. Minor changes in the header can significantly impact the code and path that is performed since the Zigbee protocol first validates a ZCL header before processing any other fields of the message. Peach slowly increased its code coverage because it randomly fuzzed a message field. The other three fuzzers started mutation from the first message field resulting in the rapid code coverage increment in the early phase.

Notably, the coverage increment of TaintBFuzz is the fastest due to the guidance from the constraint-field dependency inference. Boofuzz mutated a single field at a time based on their placement order in the format script, in which the field is reset to the initial value after mutation completes. Therefore, it can enumerate a limited number of ZCL header types. Though Z-Fuzzer leverages

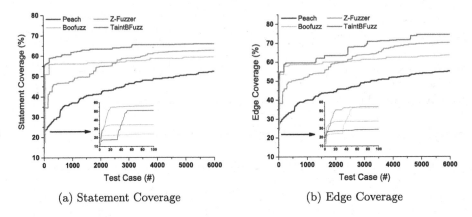

(a) Statement Coverage   (b) Edge Coverage

Fig. 5. Statement coverage and edge coverage achieved by fuzzers over 10 runs. The X-axis represents the median number of test cases. The Y-axis represents the percentage of statement coverage and edge coverage on average. We also display a zoomed-in graph in the left corner of the coverage variation in the first 100 test cases for each coverage graph.

code coverage to prioritize the favored test cases for further mutation, it is hard to consider all possible header values by only considering the coverage feedback. For example, a test case whose *Command Identifier* is 0x05 triggers a new edge and is saved as a favored test case for further mutation. In contrast, the field *Frame Control* is reset to the initial value 0x00. Z-Fuzzer continues fuzzing succeeding fields of *Command Identifier*, which does not explore any new codes. However, a path constraint requires a particular value of *Frame Control* to trigger another branch. With the guidance from the constraint-field dependency inference, TaintBFuzz efficiently generates such a test case to explore the uncovered branch.

Summary. TaintBFuzz's constraint-field dependency inference allows it to attain a greater code coverage rate than Peach, Boofuzz, and Z-Fuzzer. We observed that many ZCL functions handle the message payload value for the higher-level application object. To run more in-depth code in those functions, they could need a test case to meet specific branch conditions. The values of specific message fields, which may meet such a dependence condition, are neglected throughout the fuzzing process by Peach, Boofuzz, and Z-Fuzzer. TaintBFuzz, on the other hand, can deduce such a correlation from the constraint-field dependency inference. The inferred message fields have higher priority for the further mutation to generate test cases, which satisfy those specific requirements and covering more codes and edges.

5.2   Vulnerability Detection

We measure the number of unique vulnerabilities discovered by all fuzzers to answer **RQ2**. On each fuzzer, we performed the experiments ten times and presented the result in Table 2. The vulnerabilities are distinguished by comparing the call stack and performing manual analysis.

As shown in Table 2, TaintBFuzz can detect the known vulnerabilities and two new crashes. We cross-checked the vulnerabilities detected by all fuzzers. Though Z-Fuzzer has generated more test cases for discovering CVE-2020-27891 and CVE-2020-27892 than TaintBFuzz, only 11% of them can be manually reproduced. Instead, most test cases generated by TaintBFuzz for the detected vulnerabilities are reproducible. For CVE-2020-27892, TaintBFuzz has fewer test cases than Z-Fuzzer because we reduced the input space of several message fields in the ZCL payload by customizing the fuzzing dictionary with pre-defined values in the protocol specification. Z-Fuzzer regards these fields as a regular byte or word variable and mutates it with a more extensive fuzzing dictionary, in which many test cases instead have no impact on path exploration and bug detection.

Moreover, TaintB-Fuzz has detected two new crashes in functions *zcl_SendReadReportCfgCmd* and *zcl_SendCommand*, which are corner cases that have not been tested before in previous research. The root cause is the long list of attribute identifiers whose value is random. In practice, an IoT device

Table 2. Summary of unique vulnerabilities detected all fuzzers over ten fuzzing runs in 24 h. We present the total amount of test cases triggering the vulnerability on average.

Vulnerability	Peach	Boofuzz	Z-Fuzzer	TaintBFuzz
CVE-2020-27890	✗	✗	96	103
CVE-2020-27891	1	57	71	17
CVE-2020-27892	4	10	47	10
zclParseInReportCmd	✗	✗	2	3
zclParseInReadRspCmd	✗	✗	3	2
zclProcessInWriteCmd	2	✗	5	2
zcl_SendReadReportCfgCmd	✗	✗	✗	2
zcl_SendCommand	✗	✗	✗	2
Total	7	67	224	141

may have a few defined features (e.g., less than 20), each having a unique attribute identifier to perform the device functionalities. The protocol vendor usually customized their memory management functions rather than using functions from the standard C library, e.g., Z-Stack use *zcl_mem_alloc()* instead of *malloc()* from `libc`, due to the limited hardware resources on IoT devices. When the attribute list is too long, the protocol stack requires more memory space to process them, which results in memory corruption when allocating space using the above self-implemented memory function. We have reported these two new crashes to the protocol vendor, which are under review when writing this paper.

We also evaluate how the constraint-field dependency inference assists TaintBFuzz in detecting the vulnerabilities. The constraints and corresponding message fields are shown in Table 3. All vulnerabilities are triggered by messages with random payload values, which also satisfy the listed constraints. We noticed that all detected vulnerabilities are influenced by the message field *Command Identifier*, which is reasonable since the Zigbee protocol takes different message parser and processor based on the *Command Identifier*. Moreover, for the two newly discovered bugs, mainly the vulnerable function *zcl_SendCommand*, there is a constraint to validate the device operation based on the ZCL message type, which returns failure if not satisfied. TaintBFuzz can generate proper test cases satisfying the constraint with the constraint-field dependency inference, which guides the fuzzer to mutate the field *Frame Control*.

Summary. TaintBFuzz can efficiently discover vulnerabilities compared to state-of-the-art protocol fuzzers for known vulnerabilities and new crashes in Z-Stack. We notice that most vulnerabilities are caused by the memory allocation function developed by the Zigbee protocol vendors, which takes the place of the

Table 3. The constraints and message fields assisting TaintBFuzz to trigger the vulnerabilities, in which fc represents the field *Frame Control*, cmdID represents the field *Command Identifier*, attrID represents the field *Attribute Identifier* as shown in Fig. 4.

Vulnerability	Constraints & Fields
CVE-2020-27890	cmdID == 0x05
CVE-2020-27891	fc == 0x08 ∧ cmdID == 0x09
CVE-2020-27892	cmdID ∈ [0x12, 0x14]
zclParseInReportCmd	cmdID == 0x0A ∧ (attrID ∈ [0x7fff, 0x7ff7])
zclParseInReadRspCmd	cmdID == 0x01 ∧ attrID == 0x7ff9
zclProcessInWriteCmd	cmdID == 0x02
zcl_SendReadReportCfgCmd	cmdID == 0x08
zcl_SendCommand	cmdID == 0x08 ∧ (hdr.fc.type == 0x00)

C library's standard functions. It is difficult for resource-efficient IoT devices to support all C standard API because of the hardware and computing power limitation. Such customized system API from protocol vendors may bring more potential security risks during the IoT application development, which the developers may not be aware of before releasing their applications. The mitigation of potential security risks now depends on whether the vendors are active or not for the reported issues [41]. This situation is what inspired us to propose this approach to help IoT application developers identify possible security issues in advance during the development phase.

6   Conclusion

This paper presents TaintBFuzz, an intelligent Zigbee protocol fuzzing with constraint-field dependency inference. It first identifies the path constraint variables and generates representative messages based on the Zigbee protocol format specification. Then it leverages static taint analysis to infer which critical message field impacts the constraint variables. Finally, with the constraint-field dependency inference, TaintBFuzz precisely mutates the critical field of constraint variables to explore the uncovered statements. In terms of code coverage, TaintBFuzz outperforms several state-of-the-art protocol fuzzers on a mainstream Zigbee protocol implementation called Z-Stack developed by Texas Instruments. Particularly, TaintBFuzz can identified eight unique vulnerabilities in Z-Stack, two of them are previously unknown.

Acknowledgments. We would like to thank the anonymous paper reviewers for their insight and helpful feedback. This work was supported by the National Science Foundation (NSF) under grant CNS-2128703. Jiang Ming was also supported by Carol Lavin Bernick Faculty Grant.

Appendix A   Representative Messages Generation

To generate highly structured test cases and Representative Messages, we developed a message format script based on the ZCL specification [42]. Figure 6 presents an example of message format script that generates ZCL messages based on the format definition

```
1   s_initialize("ZCLMessage")
2   s_group("frame_control", values=<USER_GIVEN_VALUES>)
3   with s_block("manuCode", dep="frame_control", dep_values =
        <USER_GIVEN_VALUES>):
4       s_word(0, endian='<', name="manu")
5   s_static(1, name="tranSeq")
6   s_group("commandId", values=<USER_GIVEN_VALUES>)
7   with s_block("payload", dep="commandId", values =
        <USER_GIVEN_VALUES>):
8   ......
```

Fig. 6. Pseudo-code of Message Format Script.

shown in Fig 4. In the script, the message fields are defined according to their data types, such as enumerations (enum). For those enumerated fields, we created the fuzzing dictionary with candidate values defined in the specification. For the remaining fields, we concretized them with random values during the fuzzing process. In our evaluation experiments, all the fuzzers utilized the same format script for the initial seed construction, ensuring consistency in the initial test case generation across the different fuzzing tools.

Appendix B   Threshold Tuning

In this study, we propose an intelligent Zigbee protocol fuzzing *TaintB-Fuzz* by inferring the dependency between message fields and path constraints. When the fuzzer

Table 4. Summary of test cases generated by TaintB-Fuzz for different inference threshold.

	Threshold = 10	Threshold = 25	Threshold = 50
Favored Test Cases	50	49	**52**
Test Case Types	36	22	**57**
Type Difference	29	35	(base)

reaches a point where no new execution paths are being explored over a certain period of time, TaintBFuzz employs the constraint-field dependency to augment the mutation process and generate diversified seeds.

To simplify the implementation, we defined a *threshold* as the number of mutation times since the last updated code coverage to represent the timeout. Thus, we performed an empirical experiments to decide the proper value of the threshold. In our experiment, we compared three different threshold values *10, 25, 50* and found that fuzzing performs achieves better result when setting the threshold as 50.

Table 4 presents the comparison results. We categorized all generated test cases based on the field *Command Identifier*. The result indicates that there are more different test cases types when threshold setting to 50, in which 29 are not generated by threshold 10 and 35 are not generated by threshold 25, while threshold 50 can generate all types in other two sets. The diversity of generated test cases also provides the fuzzer more probability to access more codes and paths in the target program. Therefore, we use threshold 50 for the TaintBFuzz's mutation when comparing the fuzzing performance with state-of-the-art fuzzers.

References

1. Allied Market Research. IoT Device Market Expected to Reach $413.7 Billion By 2031 (2022). https://www.globenewswire.com/news-release/2022/08/08/2493893/0/en/IoT-Device-Market-Expected-to-Reach-413-7-Billion-By-2031-Allied-Market-Research.html
2. The Connectivity Standards Alliance. Zigbee: The Full-Stack Solution for All Smart Devices (2015). https://csa-iot.org/all-solutions/zigbee/
3. BusinessWire. Analysts Confirm Half a Billion Zigbee Chipsets Sold, Igniting IoT Innovation; Figures to Reach 3.8 Billion by 2023 (2018). https://www.businesswire.com/news/home/20180807005170/en/Analysts-Confirm-Half-a-Billion-Zigbee-Chipsets-Sold-Igniting-IoT-Innovation-Figures-to-Reach-3.8-Billion-by-2023
4. Ronen, E., O'Flynn, C., Shamir, A., Weingarten, A.O.: IoT goes nuclear: creating a ZigBee chain reaction. In: Proceedings of the 38th IEEE Symposium on Security and Privacy (S&P 2017), Piscataway, NY, USA, pp. 195–212. IEEE (2017)
5. Morgner, P., Mattejat, S., Benenson, Z., Müller, C., Armknecht, F.: Insecure to the touch: attacking ZigBee 3.0 via touchlink commissioning. In: Proceedings of the 10th ACM Conference on Security and Privacy in Wireless and Mobile Networks (WiSec 2017), New York, NY, USA, pp. 230–240. Association for Computing Machinery (2017)
6. Wang, J., Li, Z., Sun, M., Lui, J.C.S.: Zigbee's network rejoin procedure for IoT systems: vulnerabilities and implications. In: Proceedings of the 25th International Symposium on Research in Attacks, Intrusions and Defenses (RAID 2022), New York, NY, USA. Association for Computing Machinery (2022)
7. Common Vulnerabilities and Exposures. Zigbee CVE Records (2022). https://cve.mitre.org/cgi-bin/cvekey.cgi?keyword=zigbee
8. Stephens, N., et al.: Driller: augmenting fuzzing through selective symbolic execution. In: Proceedings of the 23rd Network and Distributed Systems Security Symposium (NDSS 2016), San Diego, CA, USA, pp. 1–16 (2016)
9. Cho, M., Kim, S., Kwon, T.: Intriguer: field-level constraint solving for hybrid fuzzing. In: Proceedings of the 26th ACM SIGSAC Conference on Computer and Communications Security (CCS 2019), New York, NY, USA, pp. 515–530. Association for Computing Machinery (2019)
10. Rawat, S., Jain, V., Kumar, A., Cojocar, L., Giuffrida, C., Bos, H.: VUzzer: application-aware evolutionary fuzzing. In: Proceedings of the 24th Network and Distributed Systems Security Symposium (NDSS 2017), San Diego, CA, USA, vol. 17, pp. 1–14. Network and Distributed Systems Security Symposium (2017)
11. Gan, S., et al.: GREYONE: data flow sensitive fuzzing. In: Proceedings of the 29th USENIX Security Symposium (USENIX Security 2020), Berkeley, CA, USA, pp. 2577–2594. USENIX Association (2020)
12. Chen, P., Chen, H.: Angora: efficient fuzzing by principled search. In: Proceedings of the 39th IEEE Symposium on Security and Privacy (S&P 2018), Piscataway, NJ, USA, pp. 711–725. IEEE (2018)
13. Liang, J., et al.: PATA: fuzzing with path aware taint analysis. In: Proceedings of the 43rd IEEE Symposium on Security and Privacy (S&P 2022), Piscataway, NJ, USA, pp. 154–170. IEEE (2022)
14. Aschermann, C., Schumilo, S., Blazytko, T., Gawlik, R., Holz, T.: REDQUEEN: fuzzing with input-to-state correspondence. In: Proceedings of the 26th Network and Distributed Systems Security Symposium (NDSS 2019), San Diego, CA, USA, vol. 19, pp. 1–15. Network and Distributed Systems Security Symposium (2019)

15. Texas Instruments. A fully compliant ZigBee 3.x solution: Z-Stack (2018). http://www.ti.com/tool/Z-STACK
16. Ren, M., Ren, X., Feng, H., Ming, J., Lei, Y.: Z-fuzzer: device-agnostic fuzzing of zigbee protocol implementation. In: Proceedings of the 14th ACM Conference on Security and Privacy in Wireless and Mobile Networks (WiSec 2021), New York, NY, USA, pp. 347–358. Association for Computing Machinery (2021)
17. Gislason, D.: Zigbee Wireless Networking, 1st edn. Newnes, London (2008)
18. Clements, A.A., et al.: HALucinator: firmware re-hosting through abstraction layer emulation. In: Proceedings of the 29th USENIX Security Symposium (USENIX Security 2020), Berkeley, CA, USA, pp. 1201–1218. USENIX Association (2020)
19. IAR System. IAR Embedded Workbench. https://www.iar.com/products/architectures/arm/iar-embedded-workbench-for-arm/
20. Peach Tech. Peach Fuzzer: Discover unknown vulnerabilities. https://www.peach.tech/
21. Pereyda, J.: Boofuzz: Network Protocol Fuzzing for Humans (2020). https://boofuzz.readthedocs.io/en/latest/
22. Zigbee Alliance. Zigbee Specification. https://zigbeealliance.org/wp-content/uploads/2019/11/docs-05-3474-21-0csg-zigbee-specification.pdf. Accessed 5 Aug 2015
23. BusinessWire. ZigBee Alliance Accelerates IoT Unification with 20 ZigBee 3.0 Platform Certifications From Eight Silicon Providers (2016). https://www.businesswire.com/news/home/20161206005020/en/ZigBee-Alliance-Accelerates-IoT-Unification-with-20-ZigBee-3.0-Platform-Certifications-From-Eight-Silicon-Providers
24. Mikulskis, J., Becker, J.K., Gvozdenovic, S., Starobinski, D.: Snout - an extensible IoT pen-testing tool. In: Poster presented at: the 26th ACM SIGSAC Conference on Computer and Communications Security (CCS 2019) (2019)
25. Morgner, P., Mattejat, S., Benenson, Z.: All your bulbs are belong to us: investigating the Current State of Security in Connected Lighting Systems. CoRR arxiv:1608.03732 (2016)
26. Beyond Security. Dynamic, Black Box Testing on the ZigBee (2021). https://beyondsecurity.com/dynamic-fuzzing-testing-zigbee.html?cn-reloaded=1
27. Akestoridis, D.G., Harishankar, M., Weber, M., Tague, P.: Zigator: analyzing the security of zigbee-enabled smart homes. In: Proceedings of the 13th ACM Conference on Security and Privacy in Wireless and Mobile Networks (WiSec 2020), New York, NY, USA, pp. 77–88. Association for Computing Machinery (2020)
28. IoTcube. Blackbox-testing zfuzz (2021). https://iotcube.net/userguide/manual/zfuzz
29. Zalewski, M.: American fuzzy lop (2015). http://lcamtuf.coredump.cx/afl
30. Cui, B., Liang, S., Chen, S., Zhao, B., Liang, X.: A novel fuzzing method for zigbee based on finite state machine. Int. J. Distrib. Sens. Netw. **10**(1), 762891 (2014)
31. Cui, B., Wang, Z., Zhao, B., Liang, X.: CG-fuzzing: a comprehensive fuzzy algorithm for zigbee. Int. J. Ad Hoc Ubiquitous Comput. **23**(3–4), 203–215 (2016)
32. Yun, I., Lee, S., Xu, M., Jang, Y., Kim, T.: *QSYM*: a practical concolic execution engine tailored for hybrid fuzzing. In: Proceedings of the 27th USENIX Security Symposium (USENIX Security 2018), Berkeley, CA, USA, pp. 745–761. USENIX Association (2018)
33. Chen, P., Liu, J., Chen, H.: Matryoshka: fuzzing deeply nested branches. In: Proceedings of the 26th ACM SIGSAC Conference on Computer and Communications Security (CCS 2019), New York, NY, USA, pp. 499–513. Association for Computing Machinery (2019)

34. Zhang, K., Xiao, X., Zhu, X., Sun, R., Xue, M., Wen, S.: Path transitions tell more: optimizing fuzzing schedules via runtime program states. In: Proceedings of the 44th International Conference on Software Engineering (ICSE 2022) (2022)
35. Boofuzz. Boofuzz Protocol Definition (2020). https://boofuzz.readthedocs.io/en/stable/user/protocol-definition.html
36. Kirchner, F., Kosmatov, N., Prevosto, V., Signoles, J., Yakobowski, B.: Frama-C: a software analysis perspective. Formal Aspects Comput. **27**(3), 573–609 (2015)
37. IAR Systems. C-SPY Debugging Guide for Amr cores (2015). https://wwwfiles.iar.com/arm/webic/doc/EWARM_DebuggingGuide.ENU.pdf
38. Devarajan, G.: Unraveling SCADA protocols: using sulley fuzzer. In: Defon 15 Hacking Conference (2007)
39. Luo, Z., Zuo, F., Shen, Y., Jiao, X., Chang, W., Jiang, Y.: ICS protocol fuzzing: coverage guided packet crack and generation. In: The 57th ACM/IEEE Design Automation Conference (DAC 2020), New York, NY, USA, pp. 1–6. ACM/IEEE (2020)
40. Yu, B., Wang, P., Yue, T., Tang, Y.: Poster: fuzzing IoT firmware via multi-stage message generation. In: Proceedings of the 21st ACM SIGSAC Conference on Computer and Communications Security (CCS 2019), CCS 2019, New York, NY, USA, pp. 2525–2527. Association for Computing Machinery (2019)
41. Alrawi, O., Lever, C., Antonakakis, M., Monrose, F.: SoK: security evaluation of home-based Iot deployments. In: Proceedings of the 40th IEEE Symposium on Security and Privacy (S&P 2019), Piscataway, NJ, USA, pp. 1362–1380. IEEE (2019)
42. Zigbee Alliance. Zigbee Cluster Library Specification. https://zigbeealliance.org/wp-content/uploads/2019/12/07-5123-06-zigbee-cluster-library-specification.pdf. Accessed 14 Jan 2016

FSmell: Recognizing Inline Function in Binary Code

Wei Lin[1,2], Qingli Guo[1(✉)], Jiawei Yin[1,2], Xiangyu Zuo[1,2], Rongqing Wang[1,2], and Xiaorui Gong[1,2]

[1] Institute of Information Engineering, Chinese Academy of Sciences, Beijing, China
`guoqingli@iie.ac.cn`
[2] School of Cyber Security, University of Chinese Academy of Sciences, Beijing, China

Abstract. Function recognition is one of the most critical tasks in binary analysis and reverse engineering. However, the recognition of inline functions still remains challenging. This is mainly due to two factors. Firstly, in binaries, there exist no expert patterns, e.g., prologue/epilogue instructions, for inline functions. Secondly, instruction reordering introduced by compiler optimization makes the address space of the instruction from the same inline function discontinuous. The address space of an inline function is often mingled with that of regular functions. This paper proposes FSmell, a graph theory based function recognition framework that specifically targets inline functions. FSmell introduces Instruction Topology Graph (ITG) to represent the data flow dependencies for instructions in a basic block. With the help of ITG, the problem of distinguishing inline instructions from caller instructions is transformed into the graph connectivity problem, which is solved by computing the minimum vertex separator. We have applied FSmell to analyze 78 binaries compiled by GCC and CLANG with 3 different optimization levels. Of the 205,890 inline functions in the 78 binaries, FSmell reports 76,777, with a precision of 67.5%, and a recall of 39.2%. With the help of FSmell, 50% of the vulnerabilities missed by other methods are detected and located.

Keywords: binary analysis · inline function · function recognition

1 Introduction

Binary analysis aims to understand the behavior of executable binaries that are obtained from a third party and whose source code is unavailable. The ability to analyze binaries makes it more difficult to hide harmful or stolen code. Therefore, binary analysis has become a critical step for many security tasks, including malware behavior understanding [1,2], vulnerability discovery and patching [3, 4], software IP protection [5], and so on.

Function recognition, which recognizes the boundaries of possible functions in a stripped binary, is the foundation of binary analysis. For example, in decompilation [6–8], accurate information of function boundary is critical in the recovery

© The Author(s), under exclusive license to Springer Nature Switzerland AG 2024
G. Tsudik et al. (Eds.): ESORICS 2023, LNCS 14345, pp. 487–506, 2024.
https://doi.org/10.1007/978-3-031-51476-0_24

of other high level constructs such as function parameters or local variables. Besides, many analysis tasks, including binary2source similarity analysis [9–11], debug information recovery [12–14], control flow integrity [15,16], binary instrumentation [17], and so on, depends on effective function recognition.

Function inlining brings great difficulties to the task of function recognition. Generally, function recognition is realized by pattern matching prologues and epilogues of functions [18–20]. Due to function inlining, the structures of the two functions are mixed together, and the control flow and data flow within the function become complicated. What makes things worse, in the source code, a function may inline multiple functions, which increases the number of variables, enlarges the body of the function, and complicates the logic of a single function.

Function inlining is widespread in binaries. 35% to 70% of binary functions inline other source code functions [21], with each inlining 2–4 source code functions on average. Unfortunately, in many binary analysis tasks, function inlining is neglected and brings obvious performance degradation. In the test conducted in [21], due to the neglect of inline functions, code search suffers a 30% performance loss, and vulnerability detection suffers a 40% performance loss. Therefore, it is of great significance to consider function inlining in binary analysis.

Compared with regular functions which are not inlined, the recognition of inline functions is confronted with more challenges. On the one hand, stripped binaries eliminate all calls and jumps to inline functions, and do not contain prologues and epilogues of them. In binary function, there is no difference between an inline function and the rest code. On the other, instruction reorder optimizations [22] during compilation make the address space of inline functions discontinuous. Just defining the boundary of a function with a start address and an end address doesn't work for inline functions. Therefore, pattern matching based techniques are not applied to inline function recognition.

In this paper we propose FSmell, a graph theory based framework that specifically targets inline function recognition. Firstly, FSmell identifies inline CFGs (i.e., candidate CFGs for inline functions) from caller CFGs (i.e., the CFGs of a caller). Candidate inline CFGs mark a blurred boundary between inline instructions (instructions that belong to inline functions) and caller instructions(instructions belong to the caller). Then, FSmell removes caller instructions from candidate CFGs. By introducing Instruction Topology Graph (ITG) to represent the data flow dependencies between instructions, FSmell transforms the problem of caller instruction identification in inline CFGs into the graph connectivity problem. Finally, through interface analysis and further filtering, the exact boundary and interface information of the inline functions are obtained. We evaluate FSmell on 78 binaries built from 13 programs. Experimental results show that FSmell is effective in the task of inline function recognition and is robust while the compiler and optimization level changes. This paper makes the following contributions:

1. This paper makes a clear definition on the task of inline function recognition, based on the discontinuity of inline functions' address space in binaries.

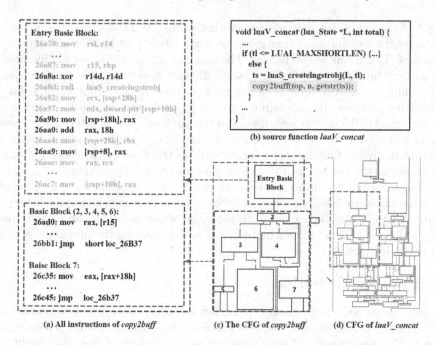

Fig. 1. The Instructions of *copy2buff* (Color figure online)

2. We propose a novel framework, FSmell, for inline function recognition. By introducing ITG, FSmell transforms the problem of caller instruction identification in candidate inline CFGs into the graph connectivity problem, and solves it using a connectivity algorithm.

3. Experimental results show that FSmell is effective in inline function recognition. On the total dataset, the precision is 67.5% and the recall is 39.2%. In addition, FSmell is proven to be able to facilitate 1-day vulnerability detection by detecting 50% vulnerabilities missed by other methods.

2   A Motivating Example

We start with a motivating example shown in Fig. 1. Function *copy2buff* is called by Function *luaV_concat* as an inline function. Compiling *luaV_concat* using GCC with -O3, *copy2buff* is inlined in the binary, and the assembly instructions are presented in Fig. 1(a). Function *copy2buff* contains 5 intervals (bold in Fig. 1(a)) which are discontinuous:

$$\{[26a8a, 26a8d], [26a9b, 26aa4], [26aa9, 26aae], [26ad0, 26bb8], [26c35, 26c4a]\}.$$

Most existing works related to function recognition are only able to recognize the boundary of regular functions, such as Function *luaV_concat* in

Fig. 1. Although a few function recognition works [23–27] declare they process inline function with special treatment, accurate interval recognition still remains unsolved. This is due to two factors. The first one is that, the code of inline functions, i.e., the black code in Fig. 1(a), is difficult to extract. We can see that, the calling site of copy2buff does not pass parameters according to the calling convention and does not contain expert-recognizable patterns such as function prologue and epilogue which manipulates the stack or frame pointer. The second factor is that, due to instruction reordering introduced by the compiler, instructions of the inline function are mingled with instructions of the caller function (as shown in the red box in Fig. 1) and it is hard to tell them apart.

The solve the first problem, we extract the CFGs of inline functions based on some elaborate heuristic rules, in order to mark a blurred boundary between inline functions and their callers. To solve the second problem, we identify the instructions of callers by constructing ITG and computing the minimum vertex separator for them.

3   Problem Definition

In existing works, the problem of function boundary recognition is defined as to recognize the start and end bytes of each function in a binary. However, due to the discontinuity of code intervals, such a definition does not apply to inline functions. In addition, different from regular function invocation, parameter passing in inline functions does not obey calling conventions. The parameters of the inline function become local variables of the caller function, participate in register allocation, and are stored in general-purpose registers or stack memory.

The recognition of inline functions includes the recognition of the boundary and interfaces. The task of inline function recognition is defined as follows:

Definition 1. The Inline Function Boundary recognition (IFBR) problem is to recognize the start and end bytes (s_i, e_i) for each interval. An inline function may include K intervals. Different intervals are discontinuous in the address space i.e., $IFB = \{(s_1, e_1), (s_2, e_2), ..., (s_k, e_k)\}$.

Definition 2. The Inline Function Interface recognition (IFIR) problem is to recognize the location of parameters and the return value for each inline function in a binary, i.e., $IFI = \{(p_1, p_2, ..., p_m), ret\}$. m is the parameter number of the inline function. ret represents the return value of the function.

Definition 3. The Inline Function recognition (IFR) problem is to output a set $\{(IFB_1, IFI_1), (IFB_2, IFI_2), ..., (IFB_n, IFI_n)\}$ for a given binary. n is the number of inline functions in the binary. IFB_i and IFI_i are the boundary and interfaces for inline function i.

4   Instruction Topology Graph

The basis of FSmell is Instruction Topology Graph(ITG). In this paper, ITG is proposed to represent the data flow dependencies among the instructions related to a basic block.

4.1   Key Components of ITG

For an instruction I, $v\_read(I)$ refers to the variables, including register variables and stack variables, that instruction I reads, and $v\_write(I)$ refers to the variables(including register variables and stack variables) that instruction I writes. $addr(I)$ denotes the address of instruction I. Let $\mathcal{M}$ denote the global memory (excluding stack memory) that is accessible to all functions, if instruction I reads $\mathcal{M}$, $read(I, \mathcal{M}) = true$, otherwise, $read(I, \mathcal{M}) = false$. If instruction I writes $\mathcal{M}$, $write(I, \mathcal{M}) = true$, otherwise, $write(I, \mathcal{M}) = false$.

Nodes. Let BB denote a basic block that contains multiple instructions in the ITG of BB, there are three kinds of nodes:

- **Instruction nodes:** $\mathbf{I} = \{I_0, I_1, ...I_n\}$. One instruction node, I_i, corresponds to one IR instruction in the basic block. According to the definition, the length of $\mathbf{I}$, n, is equal to the number of instructions in BB.
- **Previous auxiliary node:** H. Previous auxiliary node includes all or part of the instructions that are executed before BB. Instructions in H can be customized according to the task. In an ITG, there is only one previous auxiliary node.
- **Succeeded auxiliary node:** L. Succeeded auxiliary node includes all the instructions that are executed after BB. Instructions in L can be customized according to the task. In an ITG, there is only one succeeded auxiliary node.

Based on whether the instruction reads or writes $\mathcal{M}$, instructions in the ITG are classified into three categories:

- Global memory irrelevant instructions refer to the instructions that only operate on registers, stack, or immediate values, and do not read or write $\mathcal{M}$ or interact with the environment. The set that contains global memory irrelevant instructions is notated as $\mathbf{I}^{irrl}$, and $\mathbf{I}^{irrl} = \{I | read(I, \mathcal{M}) = false \ \& \ write(I, \mathcal{M}) = false\}$.
- Global memory-read instructions refer to the instructions that read but not write $\mathcal{M}$. The set of global memory read instructions is notated as $\mathbf{I}^{read}$, and $\mathbf{I}^{read} = \{I | read(I, \mathcal{M}) = true \ \& \ write(I, \mathcal{M}) = false\}$
- Global memory-write instructions refer to instructions that write $\mathcal{M}$. Function call instructions are global memory-write instructions. The set of global memory-write instructions are notated as $\mathbf{I}^{write} = \{I | write(I, \mathcal{M}) = true\}$.

Edges. If there is a data dependency between instruction I_i and instruction I_j which are executed sequentially($addr(I_i) < addr(I_j)$), then there is an edge $E_{ij} = (I_i, I_j)$ on ITG. There are 4 kinds of edges, whose attributes are:

- Variables write-after-read (*VWAR*): I_i writes a variable which will be read by I_j, which means $v\_write(I_i) \cap v\_read(I_j) \neq \emptyset$
- Global memory read-after-write (*GRAW*): $I_i \in \mathbf{I}^{read} \ \wedge \ I_j \in \mathbf{I}^{write}$.
- Global memory write-after-read (*GWAR*): $I_i \in \mathbf{I}^{write} \ \wedge \ I_j \in \mathbf{I}^{read}$.
- Global memory write-after-write (*GWAW*): $I_i \in \mathbf{I}^{write} \ \wedge \ I_j \in \mathbf{I}^{write}$.

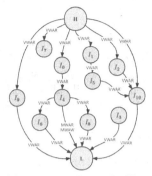

(a) The ITG of copy2buff's entry block.

```
 0 mov    r14.8, rsi.8
 1 mov    rcx.8, %var_70.8
 2 mov    edx.4, %var_88.4
 3 mov    #0.8, r14.8
 4 mov    call $luaS_createlngstrobj
 5 mov    %var_70.8, rcx.8
 6 mov    rax.8, %var_80.8
 7 mov    rbx.8, %var_70.8
 8 add    rax.8, #0x18.8, %var_90.8
 9 sub    rbp.8, (#0x10.8*rcx.8), r15.8
10 add    (rbp.8+(#0x10.8*(xdu.8(%var_88.4)-rcx.8))),\
          #0x10.8, %var_88.8
```

(b) copy2buff's entry block IR

Fig. 2. The ITG of copy2buff's entry block and its corresponding IR.

The ITG of *BB* is a 3-tuple element $G = (\mathbf{V}, \mathbf{E}, \delta)$, where

- $\mathbf{V}$ is the collection of nodes which contain **I**, *H*, and *L*.
- $\mathbf{E}$ is the collection of edges, and $\mathbf{E} \subseteq \mathbf{V} \times \mathbf{V}$.
- $\delta : \mathbf{E} \to \mathbf{A}$ is the function mapping from edges in $\mathbf{E}$ to attributes in $\mathbf{A}$ which refers the collection of edge attributes. The attributes of the edges in E can be *VWAR*, *GRAW*, *GWAR*, *GWAW*, or the combination of them.

4.2 ITG Construction

ITG is constructed on IR. We use IDA [18] to generate the assembly code of the binary and lift it to IR, which is named *microcode* [28]. Then, for each instruction I_i, we analyze its operands, obtaining $v\_read(I_i)$ and $v\_write(I_i)$, and analyze whether the instruction write $\mathcal{M}$. Moreover, if I_i is a "call" instruction, inter-procedural analysis and alias analysis are too complicated. In order avoid that, "call" instructions are assumed to write $\mathcal{M}$, and $v\_read(I_i)$ and $v\_write(I_i)$ are obtained through function signature recovery [29].

Then, we perform use-def analysis for all instructions in binary functions to obtain the definition and use information of all variables, which is used for analyzing data dependency between instruction nodes and H or L. And then we analyze the data dependency between instruction nodes in *BB* and connect them for constructing ITG. Algorithm 1 shows the algorithm for constructing ITG. The input of Algorithm 1 is a basic block *BB* and the output is *BB*'s ITG. In line 3–5, for each instruction node I_i, we analyze each variable in $v\_read(I_i)$. If one variables is defined outside *BB*, connect I_i to H. In line 6–8, we analyze the only variable in $v\_write(I_i)$. If the variable is used outside the basic block, connect I_i to L. Line 9–17 analyze the data dependencies between instruction nodes. If there are data dependencies between I_i and I_j, connect I_i and I_j and add attributes to the edge according to the data dependencies. The attributes can be *VWAR*, *GRAW*, *GWAR*, *GWAW*, or their combination.

Algorithm 1: Construct ITG for a Basic Block

Input: Basic Block BB
Output: ITG G

1 L := BB.Length - 1;
2 **for** $i := 0$ to L **do**
3   **for** v in $v\_read(I_i)$ **do**
4   **if** $v.def$ not in BB **then**
5   G.add_edge(H, I_i, attr= VWAR);

6   **for** v in $v\_write(I_i)$ **do**
7   **if** $v.use \cap B \neq \emptyset$ **then**
8   G.add_edge(I_i, L, attr = VWAR);

9   **for** $j := i+1$ to L **do**
10   **if** $v\_write(I_i) \cap v\_read(I_j) \neq \emptyset$ **then**
11   G.add_edge(I_i, I_j, attr= VWAR);
12   **if** $I_i \in \mathbf{I}^{read} \wedge I_j \in \mathbf{I}^{write}$ **then**
13   G.add_edge(I_i, I_j, attr= MRAW);
14   **if** $I_i \in \mathbf{I}^{write} \wedge I_j \in \mathbf{I}^{read}$ **then**
15   G.add_edge(I_i, I_j, attr= MWAR);
16   **if** $I_i \in \mathbf{I}^{write} \wedge I_j \in \mathbf{I}^{write}$ **then**
17   G.add_edge(I_i, I_j, attr= MWAW);

Figure 2 shows the ITG of *copy2buff*'s entry block and the corresponding IR. There are 10 instruction nodes on the graph corresponding to 10 IR instructions. I_0 (*mov* $r14.8$, $rsi.8$) is taken as an example to illustrate the data dependencies between nodes. I_0 reads register variable $r14$ and writes register variable rsi. $r14$ is defined outside the entry basic block, so H is connected to I_0 with edge attribute *VWAR*. Because rsi is one of the parameters of Function *luaS_createlngstrobj*, and will be read by I_4, so I_0 is connected to I_4 with edge attribute *VWAR*.

4.3 Topological Order and Code Semantics

In an ITG, if there is an edge between two instructions, the execution order of the two instructions cannot be changed. Otherwise, the execution order of the two instructions can be changed. For a basic block, the sequence relationship of instructions constitutes its topological order.

For one basic block, if the direction and the order of data transmission between instructions are the same, the output to the same input will not change. Therefore, as long as the topological order does not change, the code semantics will remain unchanged. For example, since there is no edge between I_2 and I_5 in Fig. 2(a), swapping their order will not affect code semantics.

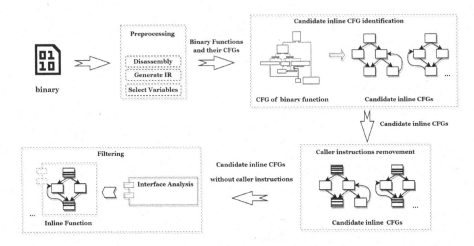

Fig. 3. Overview of FSmell

5   FSmell

To recognize inline functions from a binary function, FSmell needs to address two challenges:

- *How to identify inline CFGs?*
  An inline CFG refers to the CFG of an inline function, which is a subgraph of the caller's CFG. Inline CFGs separate the code of the inline functions from the rest of the code at the basic block level. However, inline CFGs are merged into callers' CFGs, and there is a lack of a clear boundary that can help extract inline CFGs.
- *How to remove caller instructions from the CFG of an inline function?*
  Caller instructions refer to the instructions that not belongs to the inline functions. Inline instructions refer to the instructions that belong to inline functions. Although the CFG of the inline function is correctly identified, due to instruction reordering (here we only consider intra-block reordering) optimization, caller instructions are mingled with inline instructions in the boundary basic block (can be the entry basic block and the exit basic block).

5.1   FSmell Overview

The overview of FSmell is shown in Fig. 3. FSmell proceeds in four phases: preprocessing, candidate inline CFG identification, caller instruction removement, and filtering. The two challenges above are addressed in Phase 2 and Phase 3 respectively.

- *Phase 1: Preprocessing.* In this phase, FSmell obtains the function boundaries identified by IDA. Then, FSmell performs use-def analysis [30] on the operands of the instructions in the IR. According to the analyzed results, FSmell selects variables and stores their information in a database. This information includes the storage location, the definition location, and the usage location of variables.

- *Phase 2: Candidate inline CFG identification.* This phase finds possible inline CFGs, which we call candidate inline CFGs. Candidate inline CFGs are identified by adopting a strategy of *enumerating+filtering*. This strategy is based on two heuristics: (1) An inline CFG contains a complete control structure;(2) The entry point for inline functions in the binary is single.
- *Phase 3: Caller instructions removement.* This phase removes caller instructions from the boundary basic blocks of inline CFGs. We first construct the ITGs for boundary basic blocks. Then, caller instructions are recognized and removed by computing the minimum vertex separator on the ITGs. The remaining instructions in the inline CFGs constitute the accurate boundary of inline functions.
- *Phase 4: Filtering.* We extract the interface information of candidate inline CFGs after removing caller instructions. Then, further filtering is performed to reduce the false positive rate.

5.2   Candidate Inline CFG Identification

Inline CFGs are identified from the caller's CFG based on two heuristic rules:

- *Rule 1. The control structure of an inline CFG should be complete.*
  Control-flow structuring is a process that recovers the high-level control construct (e.g., if-then-else or while loops) for a binary [31]. The input of the control flow structuring is CFG, and the output is Abstract Syntax Tree (AST) which encodes how statements and expressions are nested to produce a program. In order to preserve the integrity of code semantics, the AST of an inline function should contain complete If-statements or While-statements. We recover the AST based on the method proposed in [31] for the caller function, and then enumerate sub-trees that contain complete control structures in the AST. Finally, we recover the CFGs for the subtrees.
- *Rule 2. There is one and only one entry point for an inline CFG.*
  The inline CFG can only have one entry point, which means that, external instructions in the caller function can only reach the inline CFG through one particular entry point. By counting the number of jump targets for instructions outside the candidate inline CFG, we can judge whether this rule is obeyed.

For the CFG of a binary function, we first let it go through Rule 1 to obtain multiple subgraphs with complete control structures. Then these subgraphs are used as the input of Rule 2, and subgraphs containing multiple entries are filtered out. Finally, the remaining subgraphs construct the set of candidate inline CFGs.

5.3   Caller Instructions Removement

In the entry basic block of an inline CFG, the instruction set, the caller instruction set, and the inline instruction set is denoted as $\mathbf{E}$, $\mathbf{E}^{caller}$, and $\mathbf{E}^{inline}$ ($\mathbf{E} = \mathbf{E}^{caller} + \mathbf{E}^{inline}$). In the exit basic block the corresponding instruction sets are $\mathbf{U}$, $\mathbf{U}^{caller}$ and $\mathbf{U}^{inline}$ ($\mathbf{U} = \mathbf{U}^{caller} + \mathbf{U}^{inline}$). In the IR of the binary, the instruction set before the entry basic block is $\mathbf{H}$, and the instruction set after the exit basic block is $\mathbf{L}$. The set of instructions in the inline CFG but not in the boundary basic blocks is $\mathbf{M}$.

$\mathbf{E}^{\mathbf{inline}} + \mathbf{M} + \mathbf{U}^{\mathbf{inline}}$ form the precise boundary of the inline function. However, as mentioned at the beginning of this section, in the boundary basic blocks of an inline CFG, inline instructions are discontinuous and mingled with caller instructions. To recover the precise boundary for inline functions, caller instructions need to be removed from boundary basic blocks. Therefore, $\mathbf{E}^{caller}$ need to be removed from $\mathbf{E}$, and $\mathbf{U}^{caller}$ need to be removed from $\mathbf{U}$.

Goal Definition. To address this challenge, we first need to recognize $\mathbf{E}^{caller}$ and $\mathbf{U}^{caller}$. Take the identification of $\mathbf{E}^{caller}$ as an example, we formulate a principled assumption that there is low data coupling between the code of an inline function and the rest of the code in a binary function. Based on this assumption, we define an goal function f which computes the data coupling between ($\mathbf{H} + \mathbf{E}^{caller}$) and ($\mathbf{E}^{inline} + \mathbf{M} + \mathbf{U}$). Data coupling is the number of variables passed between them. Based on the definitions above, the problem of identifying caller instructions in the entry basic block can be formalized as the following optimization problem:

$$\operatorname*{argmin}_{\mathbf{E}^{caller}} f(\mathbf{H} + \mathbf{E}^{caller}, \mathbf{E}^{inline} + \mathbf{M} + \mathbf{U})$$
$$s.t. \ \ \mathbf{E}^{caller} + \mathbf{E}^{inline} = \mathbf{E} \tag{1}$$

Using ITG to Identify Caller Instructions. We transform the above optimization problem into the graph connectivity problem and use a connectivity algorithm to solve it. First, we construct the ITG of boundary basic blocks as described in Algorithm 1. For an entry basic block, H is constructed from instructions in $\mathbf{H}$, and L is constructed from $\mathbf{M} + \mathbf{U}$.

Then the optimization problem in Eq. 1 can be understood as dividing the graph into two subgraphs so that the data coupling between the two subgraphs is minimized. The data coupling can be represented by the node number of vertex separators on ITG. In graph theory, a vertex subset $S \subset V$ is a vertex separator for nonadjacent vertices a and b if the removal of S from the graph separates a and b into distinct connected components. So, we can divide ITG into two subgraphs by computing the minimum vertex separator. Compared with other separate results, the data coupling between the two subgraphs at this time is the smallest. $\mathbf{E}^{caller}$ lies in the subgraph containing H, and is composed by instructions except those in $\mathbf{H}$.

Algorithm 2: Identifying Caller Instructions

  Input: boundary basic block: $\mathcal{B}$
  Output: caller instruction set: **C**
1 $ITG,H,\ L=$ construct_itg($\mathcal{B}$);
2 separator_set = minimum_node_cut(ITG, H, L);
3 **for** *node in separator_set* **do**
4   **for** *succ_node in ITG.successors(node)* **do**
5   **if** *succ_node not in separator_set* **then**
6   ITG.remove_edge(node, succ_node);

7 **for** *g in weakly_connected_components(ITG)* **do**
8   **if** $\mathcal{B}$ *is entry basic block* $\wedge$ $\mathbf{H} \subset g$ **then**
9          $\mathcal{C} = g.nodes()$;
10   **if** $\mathcal{B}$ *is exit basic block* $\wedge$ $\mathbf{L} \subset g$ **then**
11        $\mathcal{C} = g.nodes()$;

The process of $\mathbf{U}^{caller}$ recognition is similar to that of $\mathbf{E}^{caller}$. Only a few differences exist. Firstly, H is constructed from $\mathbf{M} + \mathbf{E}$, and L is constructed from $\mathbf{L}$. Secondly, $\mathbf{U}^{caller}$ lies in the subgraph containing L, and is composed by instructions except those in $\mathbf{L}$.

Algorithm 2 shows how to identify caller instructions in the boundary basic block by vertex separator. The input to the algorithm is a boundary basic block $\mathcal{B}$, and the output is caller instructions $\mathcal{C}$. If $\mathcal{B}$ is an entry basic block, $\mathcal{C}$ corresponds to $\mathbf{E}^{caller}$. If $\mathcal{B}$ is an exit basic block, $\mathcal{C}$ corresponds to $\mathbf{U}^{caller}$. Line 1 construct the ITG for $\mathcal{B}$. The vertex separator for H and L in the ITG is computed in Line 2 with function *minimum_node_cut*. In lines 3–6, We judge whether the successor node of each vertex in the minimum vertex separator still belongs to the minimum vertex separator. If not, remove the edge between the vertex and its successor. Then, the ITG is divided into two subgraphs. In lines 7–11, we first get two subgraphs by computing the weakly connected components. Then, we can get caller instructions in $\mathcal{B}$ by judging whether H and L is contained in the subgraphs.

Dividing ITG leveraging minimum vertex separator does not break data dependencies between caller instructions and inline instructions. Therefore, such a graph split does not change the semantics of the program.

Example. We use the *copy2buff* shown in Fig. 2 as an example to illustrate the method for identifying caller instructions in the entry basic block. For the ITG shown in Fig. 2(a), it's minimum vertex separator is $\{I_4, I_5, I_{10}\}$, which divides instructions in the ITG into two sets: $\mathbf{E}^{caller} = \{I_0, I_1, I_2, I_4, I_5, I_7, I_9, I_{10}\}$ and $\mathbf{E}^{inline} = \{I_3, I_6, I_8\}$. The address interval of I_3 is [26a8a, 26a8d]. The address interval of I_6 is [26a9b, 26aa4] which contains two assembly instructions. The address interval of I_8 is [26aa9, 26aae]. The discontinuity in the address space of I_3, I_6, I_8 results from instruction reordering optimization introduced by the compiler. The address intervals of the boundary basic block, plus the address intervals of the non-boundary basic block form the accurate boundary of the whole inline function. In this example, the intervals of non-boundary basic blocks are [26ad0, 26bb8], [26c35, 26c4a]. Now, all intervals of the *copy2buff* inline function are recognized by us.

5.4   Filtering

Interface Analysis. After identifying the caller instructions in the candidate CFG, we can identify its accurate boundary information as described in Sect. 5.3. Then, we can perform a use-def analysis for all variables in the boundary to obtain the interface information. If a variable is not defined in the candidate inline CFGs from which caller instructions have been removed, it is considered to be a parameter of the inline function. If a variable is defined in and used outside candidate inline CFGs, and the variable is not a global variable, it is considered to be a return value.

Filters. The candidate CFGs obtained previously may not be CFGs of inline functions. In order to reduce false positives, after removing caller instructions from boundary basic blocks, the following filters are applied.

- *Long parameter list filter.* Refactoring theory states that a long parameter list is a bad code smell [32]. Therefore, we assume that inline functions will not have more than 5 parameters. That is, we think that the case where $|parameters| > 5$ does not satisfy the coupling constraints of the inline function.
- *Multiple return-value filter.* A function can only have one return value. If a candidate CFG has more than one return values, it will be filtered out.
- *Internal data constraint filter.* In order to prevent simple code snippets from being mistaken for an inline function, such as judging the value range of a certain variable, we assume that the number of local variables inside the function is greater than the number of parameters. That is, if $|Local\ variables| < |parameters|$, We consider that it does not satisfy the internal data constraints of the function and should be removed.

Finally, the remaining inline CFGs without caller instructions are considered as inline function's boundary recognized by FSmell.

6   Evaluation

Based on FSmell, We develop a plugin for IDA to recognize inline functions in binaries. The whole system run on a desktop with an Intel i7-8809G CPU employing 4 cores. The frequency of the CPU is 3.1 GHz, and the RAM is 64 GB.

The evaluation aims to answer the following questions:

- RQ1: How effective is FSmell in inline function recognition?
- RQ2: How robust is FSmell while the compiler, and optimization level change?
- RQ3: Can FSmell contribute to security tasks?

Table 1. Overall Performance of FSmell. P, R, and F refer to precision, recall, and F-score respectively.

OPT Level	GCC						CLANG					
	TP	FP	FN	P(%)	R(%)	F	TP	FP	FN	P(%)	R(%)	F
Os	3,479	1,741	3,187	66.6	52.2	0.585	12,740	7,096	21,538	64.2	37.2	0.471
O2	7,785	3,970	11,478	66.2	40.4	0.502	19,396	12,139	33,318	61.5	36.8	0.460
O3	13,836	6,363	24,321	68.5	36.3	0.474	19,541	12,262	35,271	61.4	35.7	0.451
Overall	25,100	12,074	38,986	67.5	39.2	0.496	51,677	31,497	90,127	62.1	36.4	0.459

6.1   Dataset and Evaluation Metrics

FSmell is evaluated on binaries compiled from a set of carefully selected open-source projects. These projects exert substantial influence and span diverse application domains, including but not limited to compilers, virtualization solutions, file format parsers, system services, and version control systems. To ensure that the data set comprises programs that are both substantial and representative, binaries with sizes less than 1MB are excluded. Finally, 13 programs, including binutils, findutils, and lua, are selected in the evaluation set.

The programs are compiled using GCC 11.3.0 and CLANG 14.0.0 with the -gdwarf-4 debug information format. The ground truth for boundary and interface information was extracted from the DWARF debug information using the dwarfdump [33] tool. Three different optimization levels were applied: O2, O3, and Os. In total, 78 binaries were obtained, encompassing a significant number of functions, with a total of 205,890 functions being inlined.

For a binary, FSmell outputs the boundary and interfaces of inline functions. We need to note that, considering inline functions with only a few instructions will introduce a large number of false positives. Therefore, inline functions whose byte size is smaller than 48 will be ignored.

We denote the ground truth information of inline functions as

$$D = \{(DIFB_1, DIFI_1), (DIFB_2, DIFI_2), ..., (DIFB_m, DIFI_m)\}.$$

The output of FSmell is

$$F = \{(IFB_1, IFI_1), (IFB_2, IFI_2), ..., (IFB_n, IFI_n)\}.$$

We say $(DIFB_i, DIFI_i)$ matches (IFB_j, IFI_j) if $(DIFB_i = IFB_j)$ and $(IFI_i = DIFI_j)$. If either of the two conditions is not satisfied, (IFB_i, IFI_i) does not match (IFB_j, IFI_j). In D, if there is a match for (IFB_i, IFI_i), it is a true positive. Otherwise, (IFB_i, IFI_i) is a false positive. For $(DIFB_j, DIFI_j)$, if there is not a match in F, it is a false negative.

6.2   RQ1: Performance of FSmell

FSmell recognizes the boundary and interface of inline functions from 78 binaries mentioned in Sect. 6.1. Since 2 compilers with 3 optimization levels are applied

Table 2. FSmell's Performance for GCC

Project	Os			O2			O3		
	P(%)	R(%)	F	P(%)	R(%)	F	P(%)	R(%)	F
gcc_cpp	62.5	29.0	0.396	65.4	50.9	0.573	61.9	29.7	0.401
git_http-push	67.0	57.0	0.616	66.3	36.0	0.467	66.9	36.0	0.468
git_imap-send	66.9	57.3	0.617	66.3	36.2	0.468	69.8	35.6	0.472
qemu-ga	59.8	42.3	0.496	70.9	41.2	0.521	71.7	39.5	0.509
qemu_pr-helper	68.0	40.9	0.511	63.4	57.5	0.603	63.7	31.5	0.421
systemd_networkd	67.4	53.0	0.594	64.5	31.1	0.419	69.5	30.7	0.426
lua	67.7	44.6	0.537	68.8	41.3	0.516	68.7	36.6	0.478
findutils_find	61.8	42.0	0.500	69.9	37.4	0.487	59.8	36.7	0.455
binutils_ar	65.6	55.6	0.602	67.6	47.0	0.555	68.9	42.3	0.524
binutils_nm	67.8	55.0	0.607	62.2	47.1	0.536	68.2	39.0	0.496
binutils_objcopy	66.6	53.9	0.596	60.3	46.6	0.526	67.9	37.8	0.486
binutils_objdump	64.6	46.2	0.538	72.3	41.5	0.527	69.9	33.8	0.456
binutils_readelf	72.1	46.5	0.565	69.0	44.6	0.542	61.6	41.7	0.498
overall	66.6	52.2	0.585	66.2	40.4	0.502	67.5	36.3	0.472

for compiling, there are 6 binaries for each program. The overall performance of FSmell is shown in Table 1. For all the binaries compiled by GCC, the overall TP, FP, and FN are 25,100, 12,074, and 38,986 respectively. The precision reaches 67.5% and the recall reaches 39.2%. On the binaries compiled with CLANG, the TP, FP, and FN are 51,677, 31,497, and 90,127 respectively. The precision reaches 62.1% and the recall reaches 36.4%. All the inline functions recognized by FSmell are not recognized by IDA or Ghidra.

Table 1 also shows that, FSmell has more false negatives than false positives. This is because FSmell errs on the side of caution. That is to say, under the boundary condition, FSmell is inclined to believe there is no inline function, instead of inaccurately recognizing the boundary.

The precision and recall are limited by *MACROS* and the coding style of developers. Besides inline functions, *MACROS* in source code will also be expanded when compiling. The CFGs and data dependencies of *MACROS* exhibit the same characteristics as that of inline functions. Therefore, the *MACROS* may be misrecognized as inline functions. Beyond that, function encapsulation is heavily dependent on the developer's coding style. Many code fragments have the characteristics of functions. For example, they are less coupled to the rest of the code and contain complete control structures. Since these code fragments are not written as a function they may also be misidentified as inline functions.

Taking the binary of function *luaV_concat* in Sect. 2 as an example, despite the lack of expert patterns, FSmell accurately recognizes the 5 intervals and the

Table 3. FSmell's Performance for CLANG

Project	Os			O2			O3		
	P(%)	R(%)	F	P(%)	R(%)	F	P(%)	R(%)	F
gcc_cpp	67.3	35.5	0.465	60.9	42.4	0.500	62.8	40.1	0.489
git_http-push	63.6	37.0	0.468	61.4	38.0	0.470	61.0	35.9	0.452
git_imap-send	63.1	36.0	0.459	58.4	37.2	0.454	57.7	36.1	0.444
qemu-ga	61.6	31.7	0.419	64.6	31.7	0.425	66.5	33.2	0.443
qemu_pr-helper	66.5	30.3	0.417	63.8	30.0	0.409	61.3	32.0	0.421
systemd_networkd	65.4	36.2	0.466	64.9	31.2	0.422	64.8	32.3	0.431
lua	65.8	40.2	0.499	67.9	42.4	0.522	67.4	41.5	0.514
findutils_find	61.5	35.3	0.449	58.7	37.5	0.457	57.4	36.6	0.447
binutils_ar	64.1	42.6	0.512	60.2	35.9	0.449	61.6	34.2	0.440
binutils_nm	67.9	43.1	0.527	64.9	35.6	0.460	62.4	32.5	0.428
binutils_objcopy	64.2	45.5	0.532	59.3	35.4	0.443	61.2	32.1	0.421
binutils_objdump	68.5	45.6	0.548	64.9	43.9	0.524	66.4	41.8	0.513
binutils_readelf	65.7	47.9	0.554	62.5	38.7	0.478	64.3	37.4	0.473
overall	64.2	37.2	0.471	61.5	36.8	0.460	61.4	35.7	0.451

interfaces of the inline function *copy2buff*. FSmell is proven to be able to capture the characteristics of low coupling between inline functions and remaining code, and recognize the discontinuous instruction intervals caused by instruction reordering.

6.3   RQ2: Effect of Optimization Level and Compiler

Effect of Optimization Level. Table 2 shows the detailed performance of FSmell for binaries compiled by GCC. For most binaries compiled with GCC, while the optimization level increases, the recall decreases. For example, the recall for *binutils_objcopy* at Os, O2, O3, are 53.9%, 46.6% and 37.8% respectively. The overall recall also decreases with the increase of optimization level. The F-score of GCC shows the same trend as recall, and the overall F-score of *binutils_objcopy* drops from 0.596 to 0.486 when the optimization level ranges from Os to O3. The change in precision is relatively small. For example, the precision of *binutils_objcopy* fluctuates between 60.3% and 67.9%.

The trend of precision, recall, and F-score of CLANG is similar to that of GCC. For example, Table 3 shows that, while the optimization increases, the recall of *binutils_objcopy* decreases from 45.5% to 32.1%, the F-score decreases from 0.532 to 0.421, but the fluctuation of the precision is less than 5%.

The relatively stable precision suggests that FSmell can deal with the challenges posed by higher optimizations. From the trend of recall and F-score, it can be inferred that, a higher optimization level makes inline function recognition harder. This is because, when a higher optimization level is adopted, more functions are inlined, and more complex optimization strategies are adopted. Therefore, some of the inline functions are beyond the capability of FSmell.

Effect of Compiler. Comparing the data in Table 2 and Table 3, it can be found that, in most cases, FSmell's performance for CLANG is lower than that for GCC. In the worst case(*binutils_objcopy* with O3), comparing FSmell's performance for CLANG and GCC, the precision drops by 6.7%, the recall has dropped by 5.7%, and the F-Score drops by 0.065. Compared to GCC, the inline functions in the binaries compiled by CLANG are more difficult to recognize.

Although the performance of FSmell for CLANG is not so good as that for GCC, the overall precision is over 61%, and the recall is over 35%. Performance improvement for binaries compiled by CLANG needs further research.

6.4   RQ3: Contributions to Vulnerability Detection

Binary code similarity analysis [26,27] is employed to detect security risks introduced by code-reuse. This approach is predicated on the assumption that binary functions harboring the same 1-day vulnerability are likely to exhibit similar content. The methodology entails mapping correspondences between an unidentified query binary function and target binary functions, which may be linked to a vulnerability, license, or software patch. For instance, if function A is identified as vulnerable, it suggests that a myriad of binaries may be at risk due to code reuse. To uncover 1-day vulnerabilities that may emanate from the reuse of function A, existing research typically scans for functions within the binary that exhibit a high degree of similarity to A in the source code.

However, when function A is inlined into function B, existing methodologies fail to identify an individual binary function corresponding to A. In such scenarios, FSmell isolates all plausible inlining boundaries within B. By comparing the functions in these boundaries with A, matched functions are subsequently identified, thereby enabling the successful detection of 1-day vulnerabilities.

We manually analyzed 35 CVE vulnerabilities on binutils 2.28 compiled by GCC with -O3. As shown in Table 4 in the Appendix, these 35 vulnerabilities are distributed in 20 different functions in the source code. After compiling with -O3, 8 functions with 22 vulnerabilities are inlined in the binary. Leveraging existing methods, the 8 functions that are inlined in the binary cannot be identified, leading to a failure to detect the 22 vulnerabilities introduced by these functions. FSmell is capable of accurately identifying the boundaries of 4 inline functions. By comparing these boundaries with the corresponding source code functions for similarity, we discover 11 vulnerabilities that may have been introduced by these 4 inlined functions. That is to say, on the binutils project, FSmell can help detect 50% of 1-day vulnerabilities. However, these vulnerabilities that are missed by existing methods because they do not take inline functions into account.

7   Related Work

Function Recognition with Machine Learning. Rosenblum et al. [34] first consider function recognition as a classification problem that can be solved by machine learning. After this, more and more machine learning techniques are proposed to improve the performance in function recognition [23,35–38]. However, experiments on ByteWeight [23] and XDA [37] show that they are not able to recognize inline functions.

Function Identification. Some works related to function identification take inline functions into consideration [24–27]. But they only focus on whether functions in the source code exist in binaries, and do not recognize the boundary and interfaces of these functions.

8   Conclusion

This paper proposes FSmell, a new function recognition framework that specifically targets inline functions. FSmell first marks a blurred boundary for inline functions by extracting candidate inline CFGs, and applies a graph theory based algorithm to distinguish inline instructions from caller instructions. Our experimental results show that FSmell is effective in recognizing the boundary and interface information of inline functions from binaries. Moreover, it is also proved that FSmell helps the detecting of 1-day vulnerabilities in binary files.

Acknowledgement. This research was supported in part by Key Laboratory of Network Assessment Technology (Chinese Academy of Science) and Beijing Key Laboratory of Network Security and Protection Technology.

Appendix

Table 4 presents the information of vulnerabilities associated with inline functions recognized by FSmell. "Caller Functions" refer to functions that invoke inline functions. "CVEs" denote the CVE numbers of vulnerabilities in these inline functions. The column labeled "found?" indicates whether FSmell successfully recognized the boundaries of the inline functions.

Table 4. Vulnerability distribution. Inline functions are the functions found by FSmell.

Caller Function	Inline Function	CVEs	Found?
apply_relocations	target_specific_reloc_handling	CVE-2017-6966, CVE-2017-6965	✓
disassemble_section	show_line	CVE-2017-8392	✓
disassemble_section	disassemble_bytes	CVE-2017-9756, CVE-2017-9755, CVE-2017-9751, CVE-2017-9750, CVE-2017-9749, CVE-2017-9743, CVE-2017-9742	✓
display_any_bfd	display_object_bfd	CVE-2017-9754, CVE-2017-9753, CVE-2017-9752, CVE-2017-9748, CVE-2017-9747, CVE-2017-9745, CVE-2017-9744	×
dump_dwarf_section	load_specific_debug_section	CVE-2017-8397, CVE-2017-8396	✓
parse_stab_type	parse_stab_enum_type	CVE-2017-7210	×
process_note	print_symbol_for_build_attribute	CVE-2017-9044	×
process_object	process_arch_specific	CVE-2017-9040	×

References

1. Perkins, J.H., et al.: Automatically patching errors in deployed software. In: Proceedings of the ACM SIGOPS 22nd Symposium on Operating Systems Principles, pp. 87–102 (2009)
2. Cesare, S., Xiang, Y., Zhou, W.: Control flow-based malware VariantDetection. IEEE Trans. Dependable Secure Comput. **11**(4), 307–317 (2013)
3. Gu, F., et al.: {COMRace}: detecting data race vulnerabilities in {COM} objects. In: 31st USENIX Security Symposium (USENIX Security 2022), pp. 3019–3036 (2022)
4. Xu, X., Liu, C., Feng, Q., Yin, H., Song, L., Song, D.: Neural network-based graph embedding for cross-platform binary code similarity detection. In: Proceedings of the 2017 ACM SIGSAC Conference on Computer and Communications Security, pp. 363–376 (2017)
5. Luo, L., Ming, J., Wu, D., Liu, P., Zhu, S.: Semantics-based obfuscation-resilient binary code similarity comparison with applications to software plagiarism detection. In: Proceedings of the 22nd ACM SIGSOFT International Symposium on Foundations of Software Engineering, pp. 389–400 (2014)

6. Schwartz, E.J., Lee, J., Woo, M., Brumley, D.: Native x86 decompilation using semantics-preserving structural analysis and iterative control-flow structuring (2013)
7. Gussoni, A., Di Federico, A., Fezzardi, P., Agosta, G.: A comb for decompiled C code. In: Proceedings of the 15th ACM Asia Conference on Computer and Communications Security, pp. 637–651 (2020)
8. Burk, K., Pagani, F., Kruegel, C., Vigna, G.: Decomperson: how humans decompile and what we can learn from it. In: 31st USENIX Security Symposium (USENIX Security 2022), pp. 2765–2782 (2022)
9. Zeping, Yu., Zheng, W., Wang, J., Tang, Q., Nie, S., Shi, W.: CodeCMR: cross-modal retrieval for function-level binary source code matching. In: Advances in Neural Information Processing Systems, vol. 33, pp. 3872–3883 (2020)
10. Yuan, Z., et al.: B2SFinder: detecting open-source software reuse in COTS software. In: 2019 34th IEEE/ACM International Conference on Automated Software Engineering (ASE), pp. 1038–1049. IEEE (2019)
11. Ban, G., Lili, X., Xiao, Y., Li, X., Yuan, Z., Huo, W.: B2SMatcher: fine-grained version identification of open-source software in binary files. Cybersecurity **4**(1), 1–21 (2021)
12. He, J., Ivanov, P., Tsankov, P., Raychev, V., Vechev, M.: Debin: predicting debug information in stripped binaries. In: Proceedings of the 2018 ACM SIGSAC Conference on Computer and Communications Security, pp. 1667–1680 (2018)
13. Lacomis, J., et al.: DIRE: a neural approach to decompiled identifier naming. In: 2019 34th IEEE/ACM International Conference on Automated Software Engineering (ASE), pp. 628–639. IEEE (2019)
14. Schwartz, E.J., Cohen, C.F., Duggan, M., Gennari, J., Havrilla, J.S., Hines, C.: Using logic programming to recover C++ classes and methods from compiled executables. In: Proceedings of the 2018 ACM SIGSAC Conference on Computer and Communications Security, pp. 426–441 (2018)
15. Zhang, M., Sekar, R.: Control flow and code integrity for COTS binaries: an effective defense against real-world ROP attacks. In: Proceedings of the 31st Annual Computer Security Applications Conference, pp. 91–100 (2015)
16. Abadi, M., Budiu, M., Erlingsson, U., Ligatti, J.: Control-flow integrity principles, implementations, and applications. ACM Trans. Inf. Sys. Secur. (TISSEC) **13**(1), 1–40 (2009)
17. Nethercote, N., Seward, J.: Valgrind: a framework for heavyweight dynamic binary instrumentation. ACM Sigplan Not. **42**(6), 89–100 (2007)
18. Hex Rays. Ida pro (2020). https://www.hex-rays.com/products/ida
19. Brumley, D., Jager, I., Avgerinos, T., Schwartz, E.J.: BAP: a binary analysis platform. In: Gopalakrishnan, G., Qadeer, S. (eds.) CAV 2011. LNCS, vol. 6806, pp. 463–469. Springer, Heidelberg (2011). https://doi.org/10.1007/978-3-642-22110-1_37
20. Shoshitaishvili, Y., et al.: SOK: (state of) the art of war: offensive techniques in binary analysis. In: 2016 IEEE Symposium on Security and Privacy (SP), pp. 138–157. IEEE (2016)
21. Jia, A., et al.: 1-to-1 or 1-to-n? Investigating the effect of function inlining on binary similarity analysis. ACM Trans. Softw. Eng. Methodol. (2022). Just Accepted
22. Serrano, M.: Inline expansion: *When* and *how*? In: Glaser, H., Hartel, P., Kuchen, H. (eds.) PLILP 1997. LNCS, vol. 1292, pp. 143–157. Springer, Heidelberg (1997). https://doi.org/10.1007/BFb0033842

23. Bao, T., Burket, J., Woo, M., Turner, R., Brumley, D.: {BYTEWEIGHT}: learning to recognize functions in binary code. In: 23rd USENIX Security Symposium (USENIX Security 2014), pp. 845–860 (2014)
24. Ahmed, T., Devanbu, P., Sawant, A.A.: Learning to find usages of library functions in optimized binaries. IEEE Trans. Softw. Eng. 48(10), 3862–3876 (2021)
25. Qiu, J., Su, X., Ma, P.: Using reduced execution flow graph to identify library functions in binary code. IEEE Trans. Softw. Eng. 42(2), 187–202 (2015)
26. Chandramohan, M., Xue, Y., Xu, Z., Liu, Y., Cho, C.Y., Tan, H.B.K.: BinGo: cross-architecture cross-OS binary search. In: Proceedings of the 2016 24th ACM SIGSOFT International Symposium on Foundations of Software Engineering, pp. 678–689 (2016)
27. Ding, S.H.H., Fung, B.C.M., Charland, P.: Asm2Vec: boosting static representation robustness for binary clone search against code obfuscation and compiler optimization. In: 2019 IEEE Symposium on Security and Privacy (SP), pp. 472–489. IEEE (2019)
28. Guilfanov, I.: Decompiler internals: microcode (2018)
29. Lin, Y., Gao, D.: When function signature recovery meets compiler optimization. In: 2021 IEEE Symposium on Security and Privacy (SP), pp. 36–52. IEEE (2021)
30. Beyer, D., Fararooy, A.: A simple and effective measure for complex low-level dependencies. In: 2010 IEEE 18th International Conference on Program Comprehension, pp. 80–83. IEEE (2010)
31. Yakdan, K., Eschweiler, S., Gerhards-Padilla, E., Smith, M.: No More Gotos: decompilation using pattern-independent control-flow structuring and semantic-preserving transformations. In: NDSS. Citeseer (2015)
32. Becker, P., Fowler, M., Beck, K., Brant, J., Opdyke, W., Roberts, D.: Refactoring: Improving the Design of Existing Code. Addison-Wesley Professional, New York (1999)
33. Anderson, D.: Libdwarf and dwarfdump (2011)
34. Rosenblum, N.E., Zhu, X., Miller, B.P., Hunt, K.: Learning to analyze binary computer code. In: AAAI, pp. 798–804 (2008)
35. Shin, E.C.R., Song, D., Moazzezi, R.: Recognizing functions in binaries with neural networks. In: 24th USENIX security symposium (USENIX Security 2015), pp. 611–626 (2015)
36. Wang, S., Wang, P., Wu, D.: Semantics-aware machine learning for function recognition in binary code. In: 2017 IEEE International Conference on Software Maintenance and Evolution (ICSME), pp. 388–398. IEEE (2017)
37. Pei, K., Guan, J., King, D.W., Yang, J., Jana, S.: XDA: accurate, robust disassembly with transfer learning. In: Proceedings of the 2021 Network and Distributed System Security Symposium (NDSS) (2021)
38. Yu, S., Qu, Y., Hu, X., Yin, H.: DeepDi: learning a relational graph convolutional network model on instructions for fast and accurate disassembly. In: Proceedings of the USENIX Security Symposium (2022)

LFuzz: Exploiting Locality-Enabled Techniques for File-System Fuzzing

Wenqing Liu[✉] and An-I Andy Wang

Florida State University, Tallahassee, FL 32306, USA
{liu,awang}@cs.fsu.edu

Abstract. File systems (FSes) store crucial data. However, FS bugs can lead to data loss and security vulnerabilities. FS fuzzing is an effective technique for identifying FS bugs that may be difficult to detect through traditional regression suites and human testing. FS fuzzing involves two parts: (1) File image fuzzing often involves altering bits of an FS at random storage locations; (2) File operation fuzzing typically issues random sequences of file operations to an FS image.

Since leading FS fuzzers tend to access a *small* set of files to encourage the exploration of deep code branches, the accessed FS image locations tend to be clustered and localized. Thus, altering bits at random FS locations is ineffective in triggering bugs, as these locations are often not referenced by file operations. Furthermore, the minimum FS image is insufficiently small for frequent image saves and restores due to performance and storage overhead.

In this paper, we introduce LFuzz, which exploits the locality shown in typical FS fuzzing workloads. LFuzz tracks recently accessed image locations and nearby locations to predict which locations will soon be referenced. The scheme is adaptive to migrating file access patterns. Moreover, since modified image locations are localized, LFuzz can compactly and incrementally accumulate FS image changes so that FS states can be fuzzed from intermediary images instead of top-level seed images. LFuzz further explores the use of partially updated images to simulate corrupted FSes with mixed versions of metadata.

We applied LFuzz to ext4, BTRFS, and F2FS and found 21 new bugs. Compared to JANUS, LFuzz reduced the fuzzing area by up to 8x with unique edges deviated by up to 15%.

Keywords: File-system · Locality · Fuzzing

1 Introduction

File systems (FSes) are important for holding consistent and persistent data and metadata, or FS *states* that survive reboots and crashes. FS bugs can have negative consequences, ranging from deadlocking and crashing an operating system to losing data and exposing security vulnerabilities. An adversary can lure a user to mount a crafted FS storage image via a swapped or misplaced USB device or a malware-infected USB charging port [3, 7]. An adversary can also issue a sequence of file operations that lead to vulnerabilities or the escalation of privileges [13].

© The Author(s), under exclusive license to Springer Nature Switzerland AG 2024
G. Tsudik et al. (Eds.): ESORICS 2023, LNCS 14345, pp. 507–525, 2024.
https://doi.org/10.1007/978-3-031-51476-0_25

Traditional FS bug identification methods rely on manual testing and regression test suites [1, 23]. However, human enumerations of testing cases may miss bugs triggered by complex constraints. One can also exhaustively test a small number of file operations (e.g., 3) [15], but it can miss bugs that involve many file operations.

An alternative is *fuzzing*, which uses random inputs and can identify bugs that evade regression test suites. Syzkaller [26] is a popular kernel fuzzer. Running continuously, Syzkaller has identified 2,800 + bugs in 2.5 years to upstream Linux kernels. Other kernel fuzzers (e.g., kAFL [22] and Syzkaller derivatives [28]) can also detect > 8 new bugs within days of fuzzing, indicating that fuzzing is promising for exploring difficult corner-case bugs.

FS fuzzing has unique properties since an FS accepts two streams of inputs—file operations and the stored bits that hold the content and states of an FS or an *FS image*. *FS image fuzzing* often involves altering bits at random locations of an FS image. *FS operation fuzzing* typically involves applying random sequences of file operations to an FS image. There are two challenges. First, even though the minimum sizes of FSes are small (8MB to 128MB) compared to modern storage, leading FS fuzzers tend to avoid saving and restoring FS images (states) across fuzzing iterations due to prohibitive performance and storage overheads. The avoidance methods generally involve regenerating FS images or reducing the reproducibility of bugs.

Another challenge is assuring that file operations access the fuzzed FS image areas. For example, fuzzing file X's metadata will not affect the FS code execution branch coverage if the file operations only reference file Y's metadata. One solution is to trace accessed FS image regions for a sequence of file operations, fuzz these regions, and replay the file operations. However, accessing a fuzzed bit during one operation can alter the accessed FS stored regions for subsequent file operations. For instance, if the allocation bit for the first metadata slot is fuzzed and marked as allocated, then the next file creation (e.g., file Z) will allocate the second slot. Fuzzing the first slot based on the trace is not effective, as file Z's operations will reference the second slot.

We designed, implemented, and evaluated LFuzz, an FS fuzzing framework, to address these challenges. We observed that FS fuzzers typically access a small set of files (e.g., < 100 within 240 CPU fuzzing hours) to encourage deeper state explorations, even for an FS with many files. This means that the accessed FS image locations can be clustered and localized. Thus, fuzzing recently accessed and neighboring image locations can increase the probability that the next file operations will access those locations. The locality of the FS image updates also leads to smaller and clustered modified image ranges, reducing the overhead for saving and restoring FS images in incremental deltas. Additionally, we discovered that incompletely restoring deltas emulates an FS with mixed metadata versions, which is another effective fuzzing method.

We applied LFuzz to ext4 [12], BTRFS [21], and F2FS [9] for 240 CPU hours. Compared to JANUS [30], unique edges explored by LFuzz deviated from those of JANUS by up to 15%, and FS fuzzing area was reduced by up to 8x. Furthermore, LFuzz discovered 21 new bugs.

2 Background

FS basics: Each file is associated with an *i-node*, which is a per-file data structure. The allocation of i-nodes and data *blocks* (1KB-8KB) may involve allocation *bitmaps*, in which each bit indicates whether an i-node or a data block is allocated. A *directory* maps file names to i-node numbers. A single file operation can update multiple data structures. For example, moving a file from one directory to another directory involves changes to both directories). To make such operations appear indivisible, an FS may provide a *journal* to record multiple operations in a transaction. Each FS also has a *superblock*; that provides global information about the FS type, the total number of free blocks, etc. File content is referred to as *data*, while the remaining data structures (e.g., i-nodes) are referred to as *metadata*.

Some FSes use *copy-on-write* (*COW*) mechanisms. Instead of making updates in place, COW FSes write updates to unwritten locations with a version stamp. An application program issues file operations to an FS through *system calls* (or *syscalls*, for short). A block-based FS typically accesses storage devices through a *block layer*, which translates file-level requests into block-level requests (e.g., block writes). To optimize performance, a referenced FS block can be cached in a memory *page* (1KB-8KB, typically the same as the block size) to accelerate future access to the same block.

Leading FS fuzzers: *Syzkaller* [26] creates an FS image by picking a parameter set and prefilling the FS with files and directories. For each fuzzing iteration, a random sequence of fuzzed file operations is applied. The random file operations follow FS semantics (e.g., a file write is issued only to an opened file [27]). The test directories are deleted after each iteration. The number of files being fuzzed can be limited. Within 240 CPU fuzzing hours, Syzkaller references up to four files on average within each iteration, with up to 13 file operations in a sequence. The average number of operations on the files is two.

Syzkaller generally does not save FS images (except syz-mount-image fuzzing). File operation sequences are tested one after another without resetting the kernel until a time limit or until the container VM needs to reboot. Therefore, when a bug is detected (e.g., system crashes, kernel panics, BUG() and KASAN [5] error messages, time outs), it is difficult to discern whether the bug was caused by the last file operation sequence or the cumulative FS state changes up to that point. From our experience, when the last file operation sequence is applied to the original image, only 50% of the bugs can be reproduced. Xu et al. [30] discovered that all crash-related bugs for Syzkaller are not reproducible.

AFL [32] has been used to fuzz FS images [17], which can be used to run regression tests. AFL fuzzes only nonzero metadata blocks because data blocks generally do not affect FS integrity. Therefore, AFL may skip valid metadata blocks that are zero-initialized. Moreover, for COW FSes, obsolete nonzero metadata blocks can dilute fuzzing targets because fuzzed obsolete blocks are unlikely to be referenced and contribute to identifying new execution branches.

JANUS [30], which is based on AFL, fuzzes file operations and FS images. To reduce the FS image area to be fuzzed, JANUS extracts the image regions that are initially allocated for metadata with prepopulated files and fuzzes only that fixed region. Whenever JANUS idenfties new code execution branch coverage after applying file operations, it saves a new seed image by recording the file operation sequence and the old seed image *before* the operations are applied. The new seed image can be regenerated by applying the saved file operation sequence to the old image.

JANUS also handles blocks with checksums, such as superblocks. Fuzzing a superblock likely leads to mount failures, precluding the exploration of deeper code branches beyond checksum verification. Thus, JANUS makes checksums consistent with fuzzed content, simulating corruptions before the checksums are computed.

3 Image Access Locality of FS Fuzzers

Accessed FS image locations differ based on the seed image and migrate over time. The challenge in deciding which FS image locations to fuzz lies in predicting how accessing the fuzzed bits will alter subsequent access locations. To address this issue, we examined the size of the accessed areas for a fuzzing iteration, their temporal relationship across fuzzing iterations, and their interactions with structured FS layouts.

Size of accessed FS image locations: By intercepting bio_endio() at the block layer, we traced the FS locations (in 64B subblocks or *buckets*) accessed by 200 random file operations issued by JANUS and aggregated the accessed size. The results for ext4, BTRFS, and F2FS are shown in Table 1. The total accessed size by these operations was < 0.02% of the smallest FS image. Although JANUS narrowed the fuzzing to the initial metadata regions, the accessed image size was still < 13% of the reduced region, indicating that *the chance of random file operations accessing a randomly fuzzed region was small* (<13% even when fuzzing is limited to the initial metadata). This finding also implies that *the overhead of tracking, saving, and restoring just the accessed FS image locations might be affordable*.

Table 1. Size of image locations accessed by 200 random file operations issued by JANUS.

	ext4	BTRFS	F2FS
Smallest FS image	8MB	128MB	64MB
Initial metadata size fuzzed under JANUS	111KB	41KB	90KB
Accessed image size by 200 random file operations	1.3KB	3.3KB	12KB

Temporal correlations of accessed image locations: During the image fuzzing phase of JANUS, the same file-operation sequence was repeatedly applied in iterations to the same FS image fuzzed in different ways. One hypothesis was that the image locations accessed in one fuzzing iteration would likely correlate with the next fuzzing iteration.

To test this hypothesis, we modified JANUS to trace accessed image locations from one iteration to the next iteration during the image fuzzing phase. After 6K iterations, we discovered that, for ext4, 78% of the accessed image locations for one iteration overlapped with the accessed image locations of the next iteration. Similarly, the overlapping rates for BTRFS and F2FS were 75% and 80%, respectively. Thus, *fuzzing the current accessed image locations led to a high probability that they would be accessed by the next fuzzing iteration.*

Spatial correlations of referenced image locations: Since stored FS metadata blocks are not randomly allocated (e.g., sequentially and hierarchically), we examined whether there is a block distance relationship between the updated 4KB blocks from one iteration to the next iteration. Assume that iteration one updated blocks 1 and 2 and iteration two updated blocks 3 and 4. We computed all pair-wise distances from the newly referenced blocks from the second iteration to the blocks from the first iteration: (3 - 1), (3 - 2), (4 - 1), and (4 - 2). Thus, we had 2, 1, 3, and 2. The newly accessed block had a 50% chance of being two blocks from any blocks in the first iteration and a 25% chance of being one or three blocks away from any blocks in the first iteration. We bound the distance to 50 blocks. Since an update might involve different metadata structures located in different areas (e.g., journal and i-node blocks), the distance between these areas minimally reflects how metadata blocks of the same type are allocated.

We ran modified JANUS to fuzz 64B buckets accessed from the previous iteration for two hours and measured the distance between updates in blocks (Figs. 1, 2 and 3). For ext4, the most popular update neighbor distance was 1, indicating that the blocks were sequentially allocated. In addition, when fuzzing the next iteration, the next referenced blocks were likely to be within three blocks of a block referenced within the current iteration. For BTRFS, the range was more scattered due to the use of b-trees. For F2FS, the most popular update neighbor distances are 1, -1, and 5. These results indicate that *fuzzing the neighbors of the accessed blocks for this fuzzing iteration can increase the chance that these blocks will be accessed in the next iteration*.

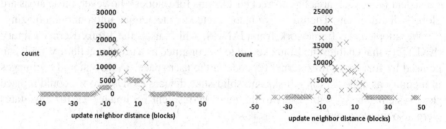

Fig. 1. Frequency of distances between updated blocks across iterations for ext4.

Fig. 2. Frequency of distances between updated blocks across iterations for BTRFS.

4   LFuzz Design

Although locality is used to optimize FSes, it is counterintuitive to apply locality to fuzzing because fuzzing thrives on the use of random inputs to increase code execution branch coverage. Based on the findings in Sect. 3, we designed and implemented LFuzz, an FS fuzzing framework that exploits spatial and temporal localities. Regarding temporal locality, LFuzz fuzzes currently accessed image locations, since the next fuzzing iteration will likely have overlapping accessed locations. Regarding spatial locality, LFuzz fuzzes neighboring blocks of currently accessed image locations, since the next fuzzing iteration will likely access surrounding locations.

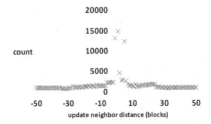

Fig. 3. Frequency of distances between updated blocks across iterations for F2FS.

LFuzz maps 4KB memory pages to FS storage blocks when they are cached in memory. LFuzz also tracks 64B memory accesses to identify the corresponding accessed 64B FS subblock regions. Accessed FS image locations are stored in a least-recently-used (LRU) list with a bounded length to adapt to locality changes. For each iteration, LFuzz fuzzes these accessed FS locations and some neighboring locations. Thus, when an FS image is saved and restored, so is the LRU list. We utilized 64B list elements (< 4KB blocks) to reduce the storage and saving/restoration overhead.

To reduce the cost of saving FS images, we also introduced the notion of deltas, which were obtained by subtracting modified image I' from image I before applying fuzzed file operations. The deltas are captured in 256B subblocks (< 4KB block) to reduce the storage and saving/restoration overhead.

In addition, we found that partially restored deltas could lead to many FS bugs. A partially restored delta creates two FS image areas, each of which is largely self-consistent (e.g., each area has correct checksums for i-nodes); however, these areas are globally inconsistent. Therefore, we incorporated this technique into our delta fuzzing.

We adopted the framework from JANUS, which used the Linux Kernel Library (LKL) [20] that enables the Linux kernel to be compiled as a user-level library. LKL can be used by fuzzers to fuzz kernel FS code in the user space. JANUS stored FS images in memory as opposed to on disks and solid-state devices (SSDs), so we could replace slow system reboots with resets to the memory-resident FS image. All fuzzing states were also memory-resident.

4.1 Fine-Grained Tracking of Accessed FS Storage Image Locations

To track fine-grained (64B) access of FS storage image locations, it is insufficient to intercept FS traffic to and from storage devices, where fined-grained accesses are aggregated into 4KB block access units. We also need to intercept fine-grained memory accesses to cached FS storage blocks to identify fine-grained storage accesses. One implication is that we need to map accessed addresses of memory-cached FS blocks to 64B FS storage locations via an M2F table (Table 2).

LFuzz instruments the block layer. As FS blocks are read into the memory, LFuzz creates the mapping of memory pages to FS storage blocks. To create a fine-grained mapping, we also need to determine which 64B area of a 4KB memory page is accessed. We injected code during the compilation stage (details in Sect. 5), which reports accessed FS memory addresses to capture this fine-grained information.

For example, if the memory address 0x7FF0041a3088 was accessed, it would be within 0x7FF0041a3000 + memory page size (0x1000 bytes); thus, based on the M2F table, FS storage image block 9217 was accessed. Since the accessed memory address belongs to the 2nd 64B area or bucket of a 4KB memory page, the 2nd bucket of the corresponding 4KB FS storage block is accessed. Once the block number and bucket number are identified, it is stored in the LRU bucket list (Table 3).

Table 2. Memory Address to FS Storage Image Block (M2F) Mapping Table.

Memory address	Image block number
0x7FF004195000	5121
0x7FF0041a3000	**9217**
...	...

Table 3. LRU List.

Image block number	Bucket number	Timestamp
9221	17	1
9217	**0**	**16**
...	...	...

4.2 Exploiting Locality for Fuzzing

Temporal locality: LFuzz exploits temporal locality by using an LRU list to track recently accessed image locations as potential targets for fuzzing. This is particularly helpful when the locality changes over time. Metadata blocks may be dynamically allocated beyond the initial metadata regions, and the LRU list can adapt to the workload and include dynamically allocated blocks for fuzzing.

In addition, the LRU list is bounded so that less frequently accessed locations will be dropped as potential fuzzing targets. COW FSes may leave obsolete blocks behind and dilute the fuzzing targets. Dropping obsolete blocks from the fuzzing targets increases the probability that fuzzed locations will be referenced in the next iteration.

Spatial locality: Accessed image locations change when metadata areas are fuzzed. For instance, when a file creation request is issued, an FS needs to assign an unused i-node to the created file. If the i-node bitmap is fuzzed to mark some i-nodes as used, then the newly allocated i-node will skip those entries. To increase the probability that fuzzed image locations will be referenced in the next fuzz iteration, LFuzz chooses neighboring and referenced locations as fuzzing targets.

Intra-block locality: Since the image fuzzing phase typically involves a few files with a limited number of operations in a testing sequence, i-nodes, directory entries, and other metadata tend to be allocated in succession. Thus, an allocation is likely to be fulfilled with nearby free space. With a 64B bucket size, we discovered that > 75% of image bucket locations accessed in this fuzz iteration were accessed in the next fuzz iteration. Thus, fuzzing the currently accessed image locations and the surrounding locations increases the probability that these locations will be referenced in the next fuzz iteration.

Inter-block locality: Since metadata blocks can be allocated in succession, neighboring blocks will likely be accessed in the next fuzzing iteration. For example, a COW FS may write a metadata block to another (potentially neighboring) metadata block. Thus, if LFuzz accessed a bucket with a particular offset within the current block, we will add buckets with the same offset from neighboring blocks as potential targets for fuzzing. For example, if in the current fuzzing iteration, ext4 accesses byte 8 of block 51, in the next iteration, LFuzz will fuzz bucket 0 containing bytes 0–63 in block 51, and its neighboring block $51 + 1 = 52$, where one is the most frequently occurred block neighboring distance.

4.3 Image Deltas

Given the locality in fuzzing workloads, LFuzz uses image deltas to reduce the FS image storage and saving/restoration overhead. Image delta D is defined as modified FS image I' subtracted from original image I_0 (before modifications). This subtraction can be expensive if only a few places are modified due to locality. Thus, LFuzz applies a COW mechanism to I_0 so that only modified image regions are copied and tracked.

Unlike leading FS fuzzers, which save images when new coverage or bugs are discovered, LFuzz saves lightweight delta images whenever an FS image is modified. Therefore, instead of replaying file operations from the top-level image, a newly fuzzed file operation only needs to be applied to the saved delta image, which has accumulated the FS state changes for all proceeding file operations.

Note that LFuzz only accumulates the differences in FS images; dynamic states, which track whether a file is open and the file pointer position, are excluded. To illustrate this point, the behavior of opening a file and writing a block to that file is different from that of opening a file, saving and restoring a delta image, and writing a block to that file. In the latter case, writing a block is expected to fail (not a bug) because the file has not been opened after an image restoration. Thus, the behavior of the restored LFuzz image deviates from the behavior of restoring an image regenerated from the seed image by applying all operations in a sequence, which also restores dynamic states.

While not saving and restoring dynamic states, deltas can accumulate modified states at a faster rate. For example, if an FS image is repeatedly fuzzed and tested with the same file operation sequence that creates random files, created files and various updates accumulate and stay from one fuzzing iteration to the next instead of being reset via regeneration from the seed image. Unlike Syzkaller, LFuzz reproduces bugs by applying the latest file operation sequence to the latest delta instead of the root image. LFuzz's bug reproducibility rate is ~ 85%.

4.4   Partially Updated Images

While developing the image delta technique, we found that partially restored deltas led to FS bugs and crashes. Further investigation revealed that partially restored deltas emulated the scenario in which two versions of FS states coexisted. Thus, segments of the FS states were self-consistent, while, globally, the FS states were inconsistent. Since we identified quite a few bugs in this way, we incorporated this fuzzing technique into delta fuzzing. Based on empirical experience, we set the probability of triggering a partial update as the current length of syscall sequence L divided by (L + 5). Since the average syscall length is ~ 30–60, the probability of triggering a partial write is ~ 90%. Initially, with shorter syscall sequences, the fuzzing coverage can grow with just delta fuzzing. As the lengthening of syscall sequences with delta fuzzing finds fewer new execution branches, the partial-write technique is more frequently triggered.

```
1   for corpus C = {image I, file ops F, LRU L from the first iteration}
2   L' = fuzzed L
3   for (iteration j < bound B) {
4     I' = apply L' to I
5     Apply F to I'
6     if (new coverage found} {
7       save(I', F, L')
8       if (B < max_bound) {
9         B *= 2;
10      }
11    }
12    L' = fuzzed L'
13  }
14 }
```

Fig. 4. LFuzz LRU-based fuzzing phase.

```
1   for corpus C = {image I, file ops F, image delta D} {
2     F' = F + file ops // append random new file ops
3     D' = applying D to I
4     for (iteration j < bound B) {
5       D' = applying F' to D
6       if (no new coverage found) {
7         move on to the next corpus (I, F', D')
8       } else {
9         save(I, F', D')
10        if (B < max_bound) {
11          B *= 2;
12        }
13        F' = F + fuzzed file ops // append random new file ops
14      }
15    }
16 }
```

Fig. 5. LFuzz delta-image-based fuzzing phase.

4.5 LFuzz Phases

LFuzz's fuzzing order has three phases: LRU-based fuzzing, syscall fuzzing (JANUS-based), and syscall fuzzing with delta. We appied a similar fuzzing order to make LFuzz and JANUS comparable. Syscall fuzzing was needed since an FS needs file operations to change FS image states. Another similarity is that the next fuzzing phase is only triggered when the current phase cannot find any new coverage.

Figure 4 presents the LRU-based fuzzing phase, in which the same syscall sequence is applied to the same image fuzzed differently. At line 1, a new corpus is loaded with initial image I, sequence of file operations F, and LRU regions L from the first fuzzing iteration. A subset of buckets L' in LRU L are fuzzed (line 2), and L' is applied to the original image I (line 4) to form fuzzed image I'. The sequence of file operations F is applied to fuzzed image I' (line 5). If new coverage is found, modified image I', sequence of file operations F, and modified LRU regions L' are saved (line 7). The number of fuzzing iterations (bound B) is decided by AFL's initial execution speed, which is the fuzzing framework JANUS is based on. In our experiment, B is initialized to 128. B can be increased is based on when new coverage is found (lines 8–9). At the end of the iteration, LRU regions L' are fuzzed for the next iteration (line 12).

Figure 5 presents the delta-based syscall fuzzing phase, in which an incrementally increased file operation sequence is applied to delta images updated after each iteration. At line 1, a new corpus is loaded with initial image I, sequence of file operations F, and saved delta image D. Sequence of file operations F is appended with randomly selected file operations to form F' (line 2). Fuzzed delta image D' is formed by applying delta region D to initial image I (line 3). The newly formed delta image D' is updated by applying the new sequence of file operations F' to itself to accumulate states for each iteration (line 5). If new coverage is not found, LFuzz moves on to the next temporary corpus (with image updated to the I + D') (line 7). If new coverage is found, initial image I, updated sequence of file operations F', and updated delta image D' (line 9) are saved, and the number of iterations is increased (lines 10–11). Finally, randomly selected file operations are appended to F' for the next iteration (line 13).

5 Implementation

We chose to build LFuzz on top of JANUS instead of Syzkaller because of the reproducibility of crash-based bugs and because JANUS' syscall generation follows FS semantics. Since JANUS is based on the LKL, which is infrequently updated, we had to port the Linux kernel from Linux 5.3 to 5.15. Furthermore, we based our tests on lkl-5.15 (LKL with Linux 5.15).

Predicting accessed locations for fuzzing: We added a stub to the bio_endio() function in block/bio.c, which was called after the bio request was finished, and the memory addresses were assigned to the bio structure. Then, we used LLVM to instrument the stub function to obtain the storage block information that had been loaded to the memory, including the storage offset, total loaded size, and memory addresses of cached FS content. In addition, load and memcpy LLVM intermediary representations were instrumented to obtain the fine-grained storage accessed locations by comparing the loaded or memcpyed source memory addresses with the memory addresses of cached

FS content. Knowing the memory address of cached FS content, the instrumentation can also filter out memory accesses that do not affect the FS image. With the fine-grained accessed locations, LFuzz maintains an LRU bucket list to exploit localities and generate candidate FS bucket locations for fuzzing. After fuzzing the FS image, LFuzz also fixed various checksums as JANUS.

Capturing deltas: To incrementally track FS image updates, instead of instrumenting the bio_endio() function, LFuzz leveraged JANUS' page-fault handler in user-faultfd to capture accesses to FS images that triggered page faults. The reason is that we only need to compare the final state of an image after delta stage file operations are applied to the image, while bio_endio() captures the intermediate state of the image during the execution of the file operations. JANUS allocated a temporary empty buffer I' with the size of an FS image. When executing a file request sequence, JANUS (LKL) triggered a page fault whenever a memory page in I' did not hold the content of the original FS image (I_0) and copied the FS image page content to the temporary buffer page. To enhance performance, I_0 was stored in memory pages instead of storage devices.

LFuzz leveraged this mechanism to track all FS image page offsets that triggered page faults. When the execution ended, LFuzz compared the modified pages in I' with the corresponding pages in I_0 and stored the differences at 256B granularity (based on our preliminary empirical results to balance storage and comparison overhead). Therefore, if only 256B of a 4KB block was modified, we only stored 256B. For fuzzing, deltas restored to various locations of an FS image.

To perform partial updates for a file request sequence $R_1 \ldots R_n$, we gathered page fault information from R_1 to a random file request $R_{i<n}$ in the sequence. Furthermore, for page faults F_1 to F_m triggered by $R_{j<m}$, we captured page fault information from F_1 to a random page fault F_j in the page fault sequence. To perform partial updates, we replayed the file request sequence up to R_j and restored storage blocks accessed with page faults up to F_m.

Line count: We added 1,193 lines to the LLVM runtime for locality fuzzing, 239 lines to the LLVM pass, 864 lines to wrap different FSes, 264 lines to AFL, 64 lines to intercept the block layer, and 72 lines to implement delta and missing write fuzzing.

6 Evaluation

Since JANUS has demonstrated more effective coverage than Syzkaller [30], we only compared LFuzz with JANUS. We fuzzed ext4 (the default FS for Linux), BTRFS (a COW FS), and F2FS (an FS for SSDs). These are the three FSes supported by JANUS' Github, in terms of providing the code to extract the fixed initial metadata regions for JANUS fuzzing. We used two Dell Precision 7820 workstations with Intel® Xeon® Gold 5218R 40 cores with 128GB of memory. The LFuzz and JANUS tests each comprised 10 processes. LFuzz used the default test seed from JANUS. LFuzz and JANUS tested the following syscalls: read(), write(), open(), seek(), getdents64(), pread64(), pwrite64(), stat(), lstat(), rename(), fsync(), fdatasync(), access(), ftruncate(), truncate(), utimes(), mkdir(), rmdir(), link(), unlink(), symlink(), readlink(), chmod(), setxattr(), fallocate(), listxattr(), and removexattr(). The figures were presented with a 90% confidence interval.

Overall overhead: Although the overhead of instrumenting all loads was high to predict locality, the overhead was incurred when a new seed image was loaded or new coverage was found. The delta state overhead mainly stemmed from comparing the deltas with the seed image, which happened during every delta fuzzing iteration. The overhead depended on the number of unique pages triggering page faults. We ran each configuration for three hours and repeated the experiments three times. The average overhead for ext4 was < 5%; for BTRFS, < 1%; and for F2FS, < 15%. F2FS has a higher overhead because F2FS has referenced more bytes (~10 times) than the other two FSes. This outcome led to a higher overhead to copy the fuzzed content to the target image.

6.1 New Bugs

We ran LFuzz and JANUS for one week and identified 35 bugs (Appendix I), 21 of which were only identified by LFuzz. JANUS reported some crashes that LFuzz did not report, but those crashes were not reproducible. We believe the main reason that JANUS did not detect bugs that LFuzz could not find was that JANUS has been used by people to fuzz the target Fses. Therefore, we assume that most of the bugs that JANUS could identify were already fixed, and LFuzz may not be able to detect all of them. LFuzz found 13 memory bugs with security implications. The bugs were reported to Red Hat and upstream maintainers. Ten of these bugs have been patched by the maintainers, and we have requested three CVEs with assigned numbers. We will request CVEs for the other bugs in the future. Note that we are not claiming that LFuzz is better than JANUS. LFuzz and JANUS are different fuzzing strategies and explore different execution branches.

To assess the effectiveness of LFuzz's locality and delta (with built-in partial updates) fuzzing methods, we tested one method at a time. When conducting LRU locality fuzzing without deltas, we found 16 bugs (3, 7, 14–20, 23, and 28–33), including two new bugs (3 and 29). When fuzzing with deltas without locality, we found only one new bug (9). At first glance, these numbers suggested that our fuzzing methods were not effective. However, with the combined use of locality and delta fuzzing, LFuzz identified 35 bugs, including 21 new bugs (1–6, 8–13, 21–22, 24–27, 29, and 34–35).

To assess the effect of partial updates, we used locality and delta fuzzing with partial updates disabled. Eight (bugs 12–13, 21–22, 24–27, 34–35) of 21 new bugs were attributed to the presence of partial updates. Partial updates were more effective for BTRFS, a COW FS, which may have strong assumptions about FS consistency and does not interact well with partially consistent FS images.

Case study: CVE-2022–1184 (bug 4): When ext4 added a directory entry, it used `inode- > i_size` to locate or allocate the next logical directory block. The `i_size` field was affected by a corrupted FS image, and ext4 did not check whether the field was in the correct range. When `inode- > i_size` was corrupted, the computed block index could point to a block in use. Thus, the in-use block could be corrupted by this error index. In addition, if the other index pointing to the block freed the block, this index pointer would have led to a use-after-free bug. KASAN identified this problem in `do_split()` [LOR22].

Since JANUS did not accumulate files during the image fuzzing phase, we also created an almost full image for JANUS to test. However, the metadata region was too large for the AFL component to fuzz. LFuzz used locality fuzzing to reduce the fuzzing area and track the reference migration patterns, and delta fuzzing accumulated files to fill the directory block to trigger this bug.

Case study: CVE-2021–44879 (bug 29): This bug occurred because the fuzzed image marked a data block as a special file (e.g., character, block, FIFO, and socket file). Right before the block was migrated due to the F2FS garbage collection, it invoked a_ops-> set_dirty_page(). However, the operation pointer was NULL for the special files, triggering a NULL pointer dereference [14].

To trigger this bug, the fuzzer needed to either modify the segment summary area (SSA) entry, pointing the migrated block's parent to a special file i-node, or fuzz the corresponding parent i-node's imode field as a special file. If the fuzzed i-node imode or SSA entries were in a state to trigger the bug, the block had to be migrated to make it happen.

JANUS fuzzed the initial metadata block regions, consuming 90KB for F2FS. During the first iteration of fuzzing, LFuzz tracked 12KB as potential fuzzing locations, which was approximately one-seventh of the size fuzzed by JANUS. Focused image fuzzing helped LFuzz detect this bug.

6.2 LFuzz Coverage

We fuzzed JANUS and LFuzz under each configuration for 240 CPU hours and compared their edge coverage, which was defined as unique edge transitions between compiled basic blocks. Specifically, we assigned each basic block a unique ID and used each unique ID pair to denote a unique edge. We defined the *unique edge deviation rate* as the total number of unique edges that were only covered by LFuzz divided by the total unique edges covered by JANUS. We ran LFuzz with and without delta (and its integrated missing write fuzzing). Based on preliminary tests, we chose the configurations that generated the best results. For the LRU fuzzing option, we tested list lengths of 512 buckets and 2K buckets, which could hold 32KB and 128KB, respectively. Each test was repeated five times and the overall edges covered by each configuration were collected. Figures 6, 7 and 8 present the edge deviation rate results for ext4, BTRFS, and F2FS. Overall, the edge coverages under various LFuzz configurations were comparable to those of JANUS. In the best cases, LFuzz explored unique edges that deviated from those of JANUS' by up to 15% for ext4, 7% for F2FS, and 3% for BTRFS with statistical significance.

We discovered that a single LFuzz configuration was unable to achieve the best coverage for all three FSes. For ext4 (Fig. 6), since the working set was smaller than 512 buckets, the edge coverage was approximately the same with a longer LRU length bound. The combination of LRU fuzzing and delta fuzzing achieved the highest coverage. For F2FS (Fig. 7), LRU fuzzing with a shorter LRU length degraded the edge coverage because the working set for F2F2 exceeded 512 buckets. Therefore, useful buckets could have been removed before the next reference. When combined with LRU, delta fuzzing increased the edge coverage. For BTRFS (Fig. 8), the variations across the configurations were within 1%. Out of curiosity, we tested delta/missing write fuzzing alone without locality fuzzing (not shown); the discovered edges were less than half of the configurations with the locality.

In general, it was difficult to attribute the cause of the coverage increase to a particular fuzz method since new coverage could be built on previously discovered and saved coverage via different fuzzing methods.

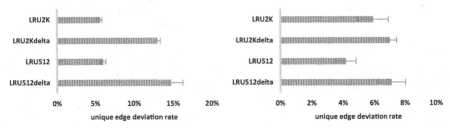

Fig. 6. Unique edges visited by LFuzz that deviated from those of JANUS' for ext4.

Fig. 7. Unique edges visited by LFuzz that deviated from those of JANUS' for F2FS.

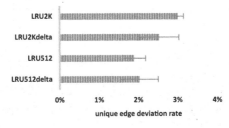

Fig. 8. Unique edges visited by LFuzz that deviated from those of JANUS' for BTRFS.

6.3 LFuzz Fuzzed Regions

Figure 9 compares the JANUS and LFuzz fuzzed region sizes during the 24th hour of the experiments, with error bars indicating the variation within one standard deviation. For ext4, LFuzz's fuzzed area was approximately one-eighth of JANUS' fuzzed area while achieving a 6% increase in the unique edge deviation rate. For BTRFS, LFuzz's fuzzed area could have been 30% smaller while achieving a 2% increase in the unique edge deviation rate. For F2FS with 2K LRU buckets, LFuzz's fuzzed area could be as large as that of JANUS, reflecting F2FS' wear leveling for its designed use on SSDs. However, with 512 buckets, LFuzz achieved a 5% increase in the unique edge deviation rate with a fuzzed area that is 34% as large as that of JANUS.

We also found that the bound on the LRU length interacted with the fuzzing results. If the bound was too large, the content held by the LRU list approached the entire working set, which contained frequently and infrequently accessed areas for fuzzing. If the bound was too small, useful content was removed before it could be soon accessed again. Based on the preliminary test results, we only systematically tested the lengths of 512 and 2K buckets to avoid the exponential explosion of the test space.

We also tried some extreme LRU length values. For example, for ext4, we tested an LRU length of 36 buckets, which could hold approximately 2KB of content. Since, for each update operation, ext4 accessed the journal last, the LRU list mostly held journal content for fuzzing, with prior content removed due to the LRU length limit. We were able to detect a journal bug at ext4_jbd2.h: ext4_inode_journal_mode() after 12 h. This bug did not appear in the first 12 h when the LRU list length was longer than 64 buckets. Our future work will examine the effects of LRU list length.

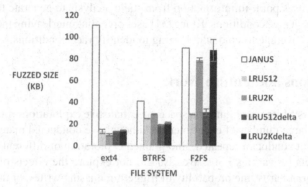

Fig. 9. Comparison of JANUS and LFuzz fuzzed region sizes under different configurations.

6.4 Fuzzing an FS Without Preknowledge of Layout

To test how easy it is to apply LFuzz to an FS without the preknowledge of the FS metadata layout (no fixing for checksums), we tested LFuzz on ntfs3. We tested LFuzz with 30 cores for three days in Linux 5.15; it found six bugs (two new) that are not fixed in the latest Linux long term (6.1.29). The first bug is kernel NULL pointer dereference in hdr_find_e, and the second bug is use-after-free in ntfs_read_hdr. We have reported these two bugs to the ntfs3 maintainer.

7   Related Work

FS fuzzers and exercisers: In addition to Syzkaller [26], AFL [17, 32], and JANUS [30] mentioned in Sect. 2, CrashMonkey [15] exhaustively tests FSes with bounded, short file operation sequences. CrashMonkey constructs FS crash states and runs FS recovery operations. It then compares the FS states to detect bugs such as incorrect file sizes and files not removed during renaming. CrashMonkey can miss bugs caused by longer file operation sequences, and LFuzz can detect memory bugs (e.g., out-of-bounds, use-after-free, protection faults, and NULL-pointer dereferencing).

Kernel fuzzers: KAFL [22] uses the Intel® processor-tracer result to guide the fuzzing to reduce overhead. HFL [6] utilizes symbolic execution to solve hard branches with complex logic. USBFuzz [19] and Periscope [24] fuzz the drivers by modifying the MMIO and DMA interfaces.

Some kernel fuzzers focus on improving the quality of syscall sequences for fuzzing. When new coverage is detected, Moonshine [18] exploits syscall read/write dependencies to filter out calls that do not contribute to the state changes of the new coverage, thereby minimizing the length of the syscall sequence for further fuzzing. DIFUZE [2] analyzes ioctl-related code to generate valid structured input for fuzz drivers.

Instead of code coverage, some fuzzers improved the feedback strategy. SyzVegas [28] changes the seed image scheduling using multi-armed-bandit algorithms. StateFuzz [33] tracks variables that lead to state changes to prioritize test cases.

Razzer [4] uses point-to information from static analysis to generate test cases that are likely to cause race conditions. Krace [31] uses potential interleaving memory access instructions as coverage to guide the fuzzing to identify race conditions.

8 Limitations and Future Work

Since LFuzz has a large configuration space, an exhaustive exploration would involve an exponentially large number of experiments. Although we conducted many preliminary tests, we did not conduct a repeated, fine-grained exploration of different LRU lengths and their effects on various FSes. We also did not explore the effects of bucket size, delta storage granularity, the probability of triggering missing writes, or the ordering of fuzzing phases. We plan to conduct such studies in the future. Since each FS interacts with LFuzz differently, we will also explore FS-specific fuzzing.

Some code execution branches are controlled by compile time configuration, which means that fuzzing itself can never reach some code regions. We plan to explore a different fuzzing framework for fuzz compiler-enabled code branches.

Furthermore, since we fuzzed small FSes, we were unable to fuzz code branches triggered by large file sizes (e.g., 500MB). In the future, we will try to solve the hard branches with the exact referenced locations.

9 Conclusion

We have designed, implemented, and evaluated LFuzz, an FS fuzzer that exploits locality-enabled fuzzing techniques. We determined that random FS image fuzzing is insufficient because many fuzzed locations are not referenced by file operations. We analyzed the locality feature of fuzzing FS workloads on FS image modifications and proposed a locality-aware fuzzing approach for kernel FSes. Locality fuzzing is adaptive to changing reference patterns, so we do not need preknowledge of FS layouts. Our locality fuzzing scheme allowed us to perform incremental accumulation of delta states and perform partial updates. When all these methods were applied, LFuzz found 21 new bugs. In addition, we discovered that LFuzz can reduce the target fuzzing region by up to 8x compared to JANUS and visit unique edges that deviate from JANUS' edges by up to 15%.

Acknowledgements. We thank anonymous reviewers for their invaluable feedback. This work is sponsored by the National Science Foundation (DGE-2146354). Opinions, findings, and conclusions or recommendations expressed in this document do not necessarily reflect the views of the NSF, Florida State University, or the U.S. government.

Appendix I: Bugs Detected by LFuzz and JANUS

FS	Bug number	Bug type	Ver	Bug location	status	JANUS	LRU + delta (+ partial updates)	delta (+ partial updates)	no parial updates	LRU
ext4	1	stack-out-of-bounds	5.18	__blk_flush_plug	Ack'd	X	O	X	O	X
	2	page fault	5.18	fs/ext4/namei.c: do_split()	Ack'd	X	O	X	O	X
	3	out-of-bounds read	4.19	ext4_search_dir()	patched	X	O	X	O	O
	4	use after free	5.18	CVE-2022–1184	patched	X	O	X	O	X
	5	slab-out-of-bounds	5.18	fs/ext4/xattr.c: ext4_xattr_set_entry()	reported	X	O	X	O	X
	6	use after free	5.18	fs/ext4/namei.c:ext4_insert_dentry()	reported	X	O	X	O	X
	7	BUG()	5.18	fs/ext4/extents_status.c:202	reported	O	O	X	O	O
	8	BUG()	5.18	fs/ext4/ext4_jbd2.h: ext4_inode_journal_mode()	reported	X	O	X	O	X
	9	BUG()	5.18	fs/ext4/extent.c: ext4_ext_determine_hole()	patched	X	O	O	O	X
	10	BUG()	6.0-rc7	fs/ext4/ext4.h: ext4_rec_len_to_disk()	reported	X	O	X	O	X
	11	BUG()	5.19	fs/ext4/extents.c: ext4_ext_insert_extent()	confirmed	X	O	X	O	X
	12	NULL pointer deref	6.0-rc7	fs/ext4/ialloc.c: ext4_read_inode_bitmap()	reported	X	O	X	X	X
	13	NULL pointer deref	6.0-rc7	ext4_free_blocks()	reported	X	O	X	X	X
BTRFS	14	array out of bound access	5.16	fs/btrfs/struct-funcs.c:btrfs_get_16()	reported	O	O	X	O	O
	15	NULL pointer deref	5.17	fs/btrfs/ctree.c:btrfs_search_slot()	reported	O	O	X	O	O
	16	gen. Protection fault	5.16	fs/btrfs/struct-funcs.c:btrfs_get_32()	patched	O	O	X	O	O
	17	gen. Protection fault	5.17	fault at fs/btrfs/tree-checker.c: check_dir_item()	reported	O	O	X	O	O
	18	gen. Protection fault	5.17	fs/btrfs/print-tree.c: btrfs_print_leaf()	reported	O	O	X	O	O
	19	gen. Protection fault	5.17	fs/btrfs/treelog.c: btrfs_check_ref_name_override()	reported	O	O	X	O	O
	20	gen. Protection fault	5.18	fs/btrfs/file-item.c: btrfs_csum_file_blocks()	reported	O	O	X	O	O
	21	gen. Protection fault	5.15.57	fs/btrfs/volumes.c: btrfs_get_io_geometry()	reported	X	O	X	X	X
	22	gen. Protection fault	5.15.57	fs/btrfs/lzo.c: lzo_decompress_bio()	reported	X	O	X	X	X
	23	BUG()	5.19	fs/btrfs/inode.c: btrfs_finish_ordered_io()	reported	O	O	X	O	O
	24	BUG()	5.18	fs/btrfs/extent_io.c: extent_io_tree_panic()	reported	X	O	X	X	X
	25	BUG()	5.15.57	fs/btrfs/extent-tree.c: update_inline_extent_backref()	reported	X	O	X	X	X
	26	BUG()	5.15.57	fs/btrfs/root-tree.c: btrfs_del_root()	reported	X	O	X	X	X
	27	BUG()	5.18	fs/btrfs/delayed-ref.c: update_existing_head_ref()	reported	X	O	X	X	X
fs	28	BUG()		fs/inode.c:611	reported	O	O	X	O	O
F2FS	29	NULL pointer deref	5.15	CVE-2021–44879	patched	X	O	X	O	O
	30	use after free	5.15	CVE-2021–45469	patched	O	O	X	O	O
	31	array-index-out-of-bounds	5.17-rc6	fs/f2fs/segment.c:3460	patched	O	O	X	O	O
	32	NULL pointer deref	5.17	f2fs/dir.c:f2fs_add_regular_entry()	patched	O	O	X	O	O
	33	use after free	5.19	fs/f2fs/segment.c: f2fs_update_meta_page()	patched	O	O	X	O	O
	34	use-after-free	5.19	fs/f2fs/recovery.c:check_index_in_prev_nodes()	patched	X	O	X	X	X
	35	slab-out-of-bounds	5.15-6.0	fs/f2fs/segment.c:reset_curseg	reported	X	O	X	X	X

References

1. Aota, N., Kono, K.: File systems are hard to test—learning from XFStests. IEICE Trans. Inf. Syst. **102**(2), 269–279 (2019)
2. Corina, J., et al.: DIFUZE: interface aware fuzzing for kernel drivers. In: Proceedings of the 2017 ACM SIGSAC Conference on Computer and Communications Security (CCS) (2017)
3. Federal Communications Commission: What is 'Juice Jacking' and Tips to Avoid It, Federal Communications Commission (2023)

4. Jeong, D.R., Kim, K., Shivakumar, B., Lee, B., Shin, I.: Razzer: finding kernel race bugs through fuzzing. In: Proceedings of the 2019 IEEE Symposium on Security and Privacy (2019)
5. Jeon, Y., Han, W., Burow, N., Payer, M.: FuZZan: efficient sanitizer metadata design for fuzzing. In: Proceedings of the 2020 USENIX Annual Technical Conference (ATC) (2020)
6. Kim, K., Jeong, D.R., Kim, C.H., Jang, Y., Shin, I., Lee. B.: HFL: hybrid fuzzing on the Linux kernel. In: Proceedings 2020 Network and Distributed System Security Symposium (2020)
7. Langner, R.: Stuxnet: dissecting a cyberwarfare weapon. In: Proceedings of the 32nd IEEE Symposium on Security and Privacy (2011)
8. Lattner, C., Adve, V.: LLVM: A compilation framework for lifelong program analysis & transformation. In: Proceedings of 2004 International Symposium on Code Generation and Optimization (CGO) (2004)
9. Lee, C., Sim, D., Hwang, J.Y., Cho, S.: F2FS: a new file system for flash storage. In: Proceedings of the 13th USENIX Conference on File and Storage Technologies (FAST) (2015)
10. https://lore.kernel.org/all/20220704142721.157985-1-lczerner@redhat.com/
11. Luk, C.K., et al.: Pin: building customized program analysis tools with dynamic instrumentation. ACM SIGPLAN Notices 40(6), 190–200 (2005)
12. Mathur, A., Cao, M., Bhattacharya, S., Dilger, A., Tomas, A., Vivier, L.: The new ext4 filesystem: current status and future plans. In: Proceedings of the Linux Symposium (2007)
13. MITRE Corporation. CVE-2009–1235 (2009)
14. https://cve.mitre.org/cgi-bin/cvename.cgi?name=CVE-2021-44879
15. Mohan, J., Martinez, A., Ponnapalli, S., Raju, P., Chidambaram, V.: CrashMonkey and ACE: systematically testing file-system crash consistency. ACM Trans. Storage 15(2), 1–34 (2019). https://doi.org/10.1145/3320275
16. Nethercote, N., Seward, J.: Valgrind: a framework for heavyweight dynamic binary instrumentation. ACM SIGPLAN Notices 42(6), 89–100 (2007)
17. Nossum, V., Casasnovas, Q.: Filesystem fuzzing with american fuzzy lop. In: Proceedings of Vault Linux Storage and Filesystems Conference (2016)
18. Pailoor, S., Aday, A., Jana, S.: MoonShine: optimizing OS fuzzer seed selection with trace distillation. In: Proceedings of the 27th USENIX Security Symposium (2018)
19. Peng, H., Payer, M.: USBFuzz: a framework for fuzzing USB drivers by device emulation. In: Proceedings of the 29th USENIX Security Symposium, USENIX Security (2020)
20. Purdila, O., Grijincu, L.A., Tapus, N.: LKL: the Linux kernel library. In: Proceedings of the 9th RoEduNet IEEE International Conference (2010)
21. Rodeh, O., Bacik, J., Mason, C.: BTRFS: the Linux B-tree filesystem. ACM Trans. Storage 9(3), 1–32 (2013)
22. Schumilo, S., Aschermann, C., Gawlik, R., Schinzel, S., Holz, T.: kAFL: hardware-assisted feedback fuzzing for OS kernels. In: Proceedings of the 26th USENIX Security Symposium (2017)
23. SGI, OSDL and Bull: Linux Test Project (2023). https://github.com/linux-test-project/ltp
24. Song, D., et al.: PeriScope: an effective probing and fuzzing framework for the hardware-OS boundary. In: Proceedings of the 26th Annual Network and Distributed System Security Symposium (NDSS) (2019)
25. syzbot: Google (2023). https://Syzkaller.appspot.com/upstream
26. Syzkaller: Google (2023). https://github.com/google/Syzkaller
27. Syzkaller: Syscall descriptions (2022). https://github.com/google/Syzkaller/blob/master/docs/syscall_descriptions.md
28. Wang, D., Zhang, Z., Zhang, H., Qian, Z., Krishnamurthy, S.V., Abu-Ghazaleh, N.: Beating kernel fuzzing odds with reinforcement learning. In: Proceedings of the 30th USENIX Security Symposium (2021)

29. Wen, C., et al.: MemLock: memory usage guided fuzzing. In: Proceedings of the 42nd International Conference on Software Engineering (2020)
30. Xu, W., Moon, H., Kashyap, S., Tseng, P.N., Kim, T.: Fuzzing file systems via two-dimensional input space exploration. In: Proceedings of the 2019 IEEE Symposium on Security and Privacy (SP) (2019)
31. Xu, M., Kashyap, S., Zhao, H., Kim, T.: Krace: Data race fuzzing for kernel file systems. In: Proceedings of the 2020 IEEE Symposium on Security and Privacy (SP) (2020)
32. Zalewski, M.: American Fuzzy Lop (2.52b) (2018). http://lcamtuf.coredump.cx/afl
33. Zhao, B., et al.: StateFuzz: system call-based state-aware linux driver fuzzing. In: Proceedings of the 31st USENIX Security Symposium (2022)

Author Index

Printed in the United States
by Baker & Taylor Publisher Services